Books to Help Children Cope
with Separation and Loss™

SERVING SPECIAL NEEDS SERIES

ACCEPT ME AS I AM
Best Books of Juvenile Nonfiction on Impairments and Disabilities
by Joan Brest Friedberg, June B. Mullins, and Adelaide Weir Sukiennik

BOOKS FOR THE GIFTED CHILD
by Barbara H. Baskin and Karen H. Harris

BOOKS FOR THE GIFTED CHILD, Volume 2
by Paula Hauser and Gail A. Nelson

HIGH/LOW HANDBOOK, Third Edition
Encouraging Literacy in the 1990s
by Ellen V. LiBretto

MORE NOTES FROM A DIFFERENT DRUMMER
A Guide to Juvenile Fiction Portraying the Disabled
by Barbara H. Baskin and Karen H. Harris

NOTES FROM A DIFFERENT DRUMMER
A Guide to Juvenile Fiction Portraying the Handicapped
by Barbara H. Baskin and Karen H. Harris

PORTRAYING PERSONS WITH DISABILITIES
An Annotated Bibliography of Fiction for Children and Teenagers, Third Edition
by Debra E. J. Robertson

PORTRAYING PERSONS WITH DISABILITIES
An Annotated Bibliography of Nonfiction for Children and Teenagers, Second Edition
by Joan Brest Friedberg, June B. Mullins, and Adelaide Weir Sukiennik

Books to Help Children Cope with Separation and Loss™

An Annotated Bibliography

FOURTH EDITION

Masha Kabakow Rudman
Kathleen Dunne Gagne
Joanne E. Bernstein

R. R. BOWKER®
A Reed Reference Publishing Company
New Providence, New Jersey

Published by R. R. Bowker
a Reed Reference Publishing Company
Copyright © 1993 by Masha Kabakow Rudman, Kathleen Dunne Gagne
and Joanne E. Bernstein
All rights reserved
Printed and bound in the United States of America
Books to Help Children Cope with Separation and Loss is a trademark of
Reed Properties Inc., used under license.

Library of Congress Cataloging-in-Publication Data
Rudman, Masha Kabakow, 1933–
   Books to help children cope with separation and loss: an annotated
bibliography/Masha Kabakow Rudman, Kathleen Dunne Gagne, and
Joanne E. Bernstein. — 4th ed.
      p.   cm.
   ISBN 0-8352-3412-6: $45.00
   1. Separation (Psychology)—Bibliography. 2. Bereavement—
Juvenile literature—Bibliography.   I. Gagne, Kathleen Dunne,
1948–   . II. Bernstein, Joanne E.   III. Title.
Z7204.S45B47 1993
[BF575.G7]
016.1559'3—dc20

                                                           93-32768
                                                              CIP

ISBN 0 - 8352 - 3412 - 6

9 780835 234122

For my sisters, Sunny Kabakow Fischer and
Sara Kabakow Mandell, whose advocacy
for women, children, and families makes a
difference in this world.
M.K.R.

For Masha Rudman and Jane Yolen,
sources of inspiration, love, and genius,
whose dedication to children and literature
has enriched us all.
K.D.G.

Contents

PART II
Reading about Separation and Loss:
An Annotated Bibliography

PART III
Selected Reading for Adults

Preface

Life is a series of losses, large and small. Loss is the complex set of reactions with which we respond to the changes and separations we meet through the years. Loss never ceases to challenge us, for with every change—even those we have elected—and, indeed, in every manifestation of growth, there are adjustments to be made.

For each of us life begins with a major loss experience as we are thrust from the warmth of our mothers' wombs. Soon thereafter, we are likely to be confronted with another loss situation, when a new sibling enters the family and we no longer occupy center stage.

And the loss cycle continues. As youngsters, we endure separation from our parents when a baby-sitter comes; we suffer loss when we go off to school, leaving the family circle for new horizons.

Among the most shocking of loss experiences are those that alter the structure and functioning of family life. Responses to the tragic separations caused by death, divorce, desertion, illness, and war are of lasting impact. Experiences that are often a response to the initial separation—living with stepparents, adjusting to foster care or adoption, and sometimes shifting for oneself—also carry with them the elements of separation and loss.

These and related topics are among the subjects treated in the books for young people annotated in this, the fourth edition of *Books to Help Children Cope with Separation and Loss*. This book, like the previous volumes, is a bibliographic guide to fiction and nonfiction books for young people, ages 3 to 16, on the themes of separation and loss. It is designed to provide adult guides—those parents, librarians, teachers, and counselors who have the opportunity to influence the lives of children—with as much information as they need to choose books suitable for the children they serve. Increasingly, these adults are aware of the burgeoning supply of books dealing with loss situations and they want to know more about them—where to find them, how they can be used to help young people handle their problems, which ones deal with the particular problems that they are interested in, and which ones are good literature. *Books to Help Children Cope with Separation and Loss,* Fourth Edition, is offered in response to this continuing need.

Following the format of the first three volumes, the book is divided into three parts. Part I contains two updated essays from the 1989 volume. Chapter 1, "Separation and Loss," discusses the significance and manifestations of separation and loss in child development, elucidating children's concepts and reactions, and summarizing recent theories and research in the field. Information and ideas on how to use children's books for therapeutic value are provided in Chapter 2, "Bibliotherapy: A Means of Helping Young People Cope with Separation and Loss." This chapter is devoted to the principles and practices of bibliotherapy, with specific reference to the use of bibliotherapy in dealing with problems of loss. It includes a definition of the term as well as a review of research findings and discussion of the limitations of bibliotherapy, a topic of continuing interest and debate in professional literature.

Part II, the major portion of the book, is an annotated bibliography of more than 740 books (including some of the highly recommended titles from the 1989 volume) for young people relating to the experiences of separation and loss. Criteria for judging the value of books on each theme within the larger categories serve to guide the adult in selection and presentation. Entries are arranged in thematic categories, such as death, divorce, serious illness, and adoption, and each entry includes a descriptive, evaluative annotation, noting the book's strengths and weaknesses both as literature and as a bibliotherapeutic medium. Users of this book are urged to read the Introduction for a detailed description of book selection criteria and notes on the arrangement of annotations.

For those who wish further guidance in the study of separation and loss and bibliotherapy, an extensive series of revised and updated bibliographies citing selected references for adults is included in Part III. The Appendix lists names and addresses of organizations providing services or literature to adult guides and children coping with problems of separation and loss. These organizations include a variety of self-help groups, as well as professional and voluntary organizations. As an aid to users, four indexes provide access to the text by author, title, subject, and interest level.

Acknowledgments

A work of this magnitude requires many resources and many helpers. Masha's and Kathy's thanks go to:

Joanne E. Bernstein, who conceived the idea of this series of volumes. Her vision and depth serve as ongoing inspiration.

The staff at the Jones Library in Amherst and the University of Massachusetts Reference Room, who have unfailingly and generously given their expertise and time.

Students and staff—Kimberly Russell, Joanna Farewell, Michael Roldan, Su Flickinger, Jodi Levine, Mike Mitchell, Han Pho, Kerri O'Malley, and Kathy Boron—who helped with computer use, reference checks, and the nitty-gritty of compilation and organization. They made the project their own and were tireless in their work.

The seventh-grade humanities class at Chestnut Middle School in Springfield, Massachusetts, who offered opinions, helped with cutting and pasting, and provided essential emotional support.

Finally, we thank our families, especially Masha's grandson Sam and Kathy's sons Tim and Jeff, for providing inspiration, encouragement, and love. We also thank our husbands for putting up with our late hours at the computer and lost weekends at the office.

Introduction

In the years since the publication of the first edition (1977) of *Books to Help Children Cope with Separation and Loss*, publishers have supplied a virtual torrent of books on loss subjects. The body of literature produced for children and young adults has included thousands of titles on such topics as war and displacement, death, divorce, stepfamilies, adoption, desertion, substance abuse, serious illness, and family alienation. A variety of criteria and considerations were applied in selecting titles for inclusion in this volume.

Criteria for Book Selection

The initial step in preparing this bibliography was an exhaustive search of such notable book review media as *School Library Journal, Publishers Weekly, Kirkus Reviews, Horn Book, Bulletin of the Center for Children's Books,* and *The New York Times Book Review* for titles of books published from 1989 to 1993 that appeared suitable for inclusion. Publishers were invited to submit appropriate titles from their most recent lists. Each "candidate" for inclusion in this bibliography was read carefully and critically examined in light of the following questions:

What is the book's scope and nature?

How accurate and up to date are the statements within the book?

What is the book's emotional impact?

How are sensitive or potentially inflammatory issues handled, if at all?

Is the book worthwhile from a literary viewpoint, satisfying readers on the verbal and emotional levels and, possibly, on the spiritual level?

Do the illustrations (if any) avoid stereotypes or distortions? How appropriate is the medium to the text?

In the works of nonfiction, how even-handed is the presentation? How well does the author avoid bias?

The more than 740 books included here were chosen because they have lasting value, are good literature, and continue to circulate widely among children. Over 50 percent of the books in this fourth volume cover the years 1989 to 1993.

In each case, primary emphasis was placed on the utilization of literary criteria. These criteria include excellence of character, worthiness of theme, beauty of style, and appropriateness of plot.

Underlying all criteria is the compilers' firm conviction that books selected for any bibliography for children should serve to connect people with all other people, reinforcing the universality of the human condition in all its aspects. Only then can there follow interaction between reader and printed word. And only if there is involvement will the world of the reader enlarge with the insight that others have shared the same problems and found a variety of solutions.

Other Considerations

As in any process of selection some exceptions were made to the accepted rule. Adult guides who select books for particular youngsters should have adequate information about those books that contain damaging misinformation or may lead to false hopes on the part of a child, as well as those that are concerned with controversial subject matter or are biased. Thus, certain recent books that enjoy considerable popularity and wide circulation have been included, even though, in the opinion of the compilers, they are not very well written or have not conformed to all criteria. In such cases, the compilers have taken care to point out pertinent strengths or weaknesses in the annotations.

Other books have been listed even though they have not been reviewed in any of the aforementioned sources. Because many loss experiences are avoided as subjects for discussion in our culture, these books either were not welcomed in the reviewing media or were dismissed as inappropriate or lacking in interest for young people. Other times, the books were not reviewed widely because they were products of small, specialized presses (for example, those dealing primarily with feminist, ethnic, or family issues). Consequently, such books are often not generally available to the public, even though they may be of considerable value in helping young people accept separation and loss. Therefore, one of the purposes of this bibliography has been to locate such books, many of which were published before the time was ripe, and to give them new light.

Interested adults may find it useful to consider some additional factors that entered into the selection process. The explosion of realistic books for children during the last decade has brought to the fore a multitude of books that deal with previously taboo topics; it is in these books that the themes of loss are confronted in terms and settings that are actually met by children today. The child who is groping toward an understanding of his or her own feelings of loss will most clearly identify with the characters in such books, and thus a major goal of bibliotherapy will have been met.

The emphasis in selection has been on books published between 1985 and 1993. A major purpose has been to sift through the current surfeit of these realistic books and to discard those that are of surface or momentary value and retain those that, because of their universality of theme and superior literary treatment, are likely to be sought after by young readers. In addition, some high-quality books by small and large publishers appearing prior to 1985 are now included.

In order to create a unified reference work and one that is manageable in terms of size, this volume has, for the most part, confined its scope to realistic works. It includes only a sampling of fantasy, history, biography, and folktales, even though separation and loss are recurring themes in many of these works. Similarly, short stories and poetry have not been included in large numbers.

In general, more books have been selected for readers aged 12 and under. This is partly because readers between the ages of 12 and 16 usually read adult fare in addition to works written primarily for young people. For the younger readers especially, works that approach loss through the symbolic world are plentiful. Many books in which animals reflect the emotions of human beings gain response from small children.

The works of certain authors are seen repeatedly in the bibliography, not because of any particular bias toward these authors but because certain writers seem to be frequently drawn to themes of loss and the challenge of change as it affects the human condition.

It will be noticed that the number of books listed within each category varies considerably. Some groups boast more than 100 books, while others contain fewer than 10. Also, the distribution of books for each age group in the several categories reflects the overabundance of books in some areas and the dearth in others. In both cases, careful selection was necessary.

It will also be noted that since the first volume, when dealing with death was a predominant theme, the focus of publishers' lists seems to have shifted. In addition to death, the topics highlighted in their catalogs today are stepparents, stepsiblings, child abuse, homelessness, desertion, and serious illnesses, such as AIDS and cancer. Also, realistic books for young people have become more specialized. Having adequately investigated the usual aspects of birth, death, and divorce many times over, authors and publishers are now attending to special needs. Thus, we have books related to specific deaths, such as the death of a friend or the death of a relative, and we have books about specific illnesses, such as leukemia and diabetes, including books written or adapted from the writings of children under ten years of age. Some books are guides for seeking professional help with family problems. Often, these specialized books have been published by small publishing houses, but increasingly the larger publishers are issuing titles designed to meet specific interests and needs in a heterogeneous society.

Another noteworthy trend is the recent publication of many nonfiction books about loss themes. These range from discussion of drugs and drug abuse to coping with death and divorce.

In addition, there is a gray area in publishing today. Some books seem to straddle the fence between fiction and nonfiction. Clearly written with the primary aim of informing and helping, these books, nonetheless, resemble fiction in format. The reader is asked to follow along with the life problems of imaginary characters. In compiling the bibliography, it was often difficult to classify such books. At times, the compilers used the classification systems that the publishers of the books used. Other times, it became more a matter of the compilers' reactions to the tone of the book. How much did the book focus on one character, thereby more closely resembling fiction? What portion of the book, regardless of the presence of a fictional character, consisted of instructions to the reader and his or her parent?

Arrangement of Annotations

The annotations are arranged in a number of categories in accordance with the loss experience that is the focus of attention. In fiction, for instance, this would be the key loss faced by the protagonist. When a book includes more than one important loss experience, the additional experiences as well as the primary loss are given in the Subject Index. Within each category, books have been alphabetically arranged by the author's surname.

Each annotation includes current bibliographic data—author, title, illustrator, publisher, publication date, number of pages, and availability in hardbound or paperback editions—and a classification of the book as fiction or nonfiction. Because prices change so rapidly, book prices are not given. Users are advised to see the latest edition of *Books in Print* for price information.

Most of the books listed are still in print. However, some out-of-print titles are still valuable and worth searching for in libraries or secondhand bookstores. These titles are noted as o.p. They may come back into print, so the reader is urged not to abandon hope. ISBN numbers for both cloth and paper editions have been listed wherever possible.

Reading levels have been omitted because readability level descriptions are but one guideline for selection and should be viewed in terms of their limitations as well as their usefulness. Such formulas as Fry's are based on word and sentence length and do not take into account a book's ideas, which may be expressed in very simple language but actually involve sophisticated concepts demanding greater life experience to enable understanding.

On the other hand, children will often read complex material on subjects that interest them and can often display remarkable ability to comprehend long words and complicated passages.

It should be noted that some books with an interest level appropriate for young children have a much wider audience because they are meant to be read aloud. By the same token, some books with a high interest level are appropriate for older children with limited reading ability and for younger children with a wide range of interests. As a further aid to adult guides, an index grouping books by interest level is included.

PART I

Using Books to Help Children Cope with Separation and Loss

1

Separation and Loss

JOANNE E. BERNSTEIN

It is incumbent on each of us to learn about separation and loss simply because, whether we will it or not, so much of life is given over to coping with these crises. The way in which we, as adult guides, handle loss is one indicator of the way in which we handle all aspects of life. If we ignore feelings of loss, it is not because we haven't handled them. We have merely falsely implied that they will take care of themselves. Rabbi Earl Grollman, a noted expert on divorce, death, and other separations has said, "Mental health is not the denial of tragedy but a frank acknowledgement of it. Better to say to child or adult, 'I could cry, too' rather than, 'There, there, you mustn't cry.'"[1] For both adults and children, there is no genuine protection from trauma.

At the same time, to help children cope with their losses adequately, adult guides need information. They need clarification of children's concepts of separation, for they differ from those of adults. Such information will yield insights into children's behavior. They also need to know about the range of possible reactions to separation so that they can determine if the youngsters are mourning appropriately or, in repressing mourning, are planting seeds that may lead to increased trouble and even continued problems in adulthood. Finally, adult guides need to determine ways to aid youngsters actively through periods of loss.

The separations mentioned within these pages are stressful for adults. Imagine how much more stressful they are for children, who live in an environment vastly different from that of their adult guides—in years, in intellectual growth, in psychological insight, and in ability to cope emotionally. For many years, youngsters are dependent on others for their practical needs. Magical thoughts and imagination are some of the means they use to explain the complex world they live in. Without the life experience with which adults develop resources for coping with crises, they are more vulnerable when loss strikes. They ask their questions with greater fear of the unknown. Why is this happening to me? Why am I different from other children? Why must I hurt this way? When will it end?

Children's Concepts of Separation

Children's ideas about temporary and permanent separation develop slowly, on a par somewhat similar to their ideas concerning time. Those who have dealt with children in any capacity recognize that until about the age of nine, youngsters do not properly estimate durations of time. Nor do they firmly grasp what being old or young truly means.

The Beginnings

The concept of temporary separation begins with awareness of alternate states of wakefulness and sleeping. Infants in cribs begin to see a pattern—they will be alone for a period and then a comforting figure will return. The next development for babies is their playful investigation of this curious phenomenon of absence and presence. Games of "peek-a-boo, I see you" are evidence of children's desire to master this concept. Other youthful experiments include the common act of throwing toys from cribs and high chairs. For as long as other family members will participate in the game, babies do not tire of it.

Next, the young investigators take on the concept of permanent separation. They have noticed that some things do *not* reappear, ever. "How amazing," they reflect, as they fiddle with the functions of trash can pedals and toilet flush systems. Actually, they ponder a phenomenon instinctively called "all-gone" by parents for generations. And when allowed safe opportunity to examine temporary and permanent separation in a context of games, youngsters pave the way toward a healthy concept of that most shocking of permanent separations, death.

A Difference of Degree

Children's concepts of death are integrally related to their ideas about all other permanent separations, for the bereavement felt in related loss situations, such as divorce, desertion, and other instances, is of the same kind suffered after the death of someone close. The difference is one of degree, not kind. To understand this, think of the way people react on losing a treasured piece of jewelry. A low feeling, perhaps resembling psychosomatic sickness, may linger for a day or two, reappearing with renewed intensity at the next appropriate time to wear the jewelry. This is bereavement. After death or divorce, somatic symptoms such as fatigue and listlessness and emotional manifestations such as depression and sadness last much longer. They are far more intense and may be somewhat more complex, but the difference remains primarily of degree, not kind. The ways in which individuals cope with all types of permanent separation are tied to their concepts of death.

Before Age Five

The person who is probably best known for research concerning children's concepts of death is Maria Nagy,[2] whose investigations involved groups of Hungarian children. Her findings reveal that children under five years of age (an approximation) usually do not see death as irreversible. Unable to separate death from life, they see life in death. They often view the dead as living in some limited state, either within the grave or in another place. The psychological reason behind such perceptions is that young children know that they themselves are alive. Viewing the entire world through egocentric glasses, they cannot imagine anything so totally unlike themselves. For this reason, very young children will defend the idea that mountains are alive. Those children under five who are able to assimilate the idea of physical death may think that to be dead is to be asleep or on a journey. At this age death is likely to be viewed as temporary, gradual, and/or reversible. We never completely overcome this immature concept of death. Adults bear remnants of this attitude when using the term "rest in peace." Perhaps this is a comforting example of retaining the concepts of a child. But at other times, bearing remnants of years gone by is not so comforting, as indicated when the bereaved become enveloped in turmoil if it rains on the grave weeks after a burial.

Ages Five through Nine

Between the approximate ages of five and nine, children begin to see death as a permanent state. In Nagy's study, children in this age group were likely to personify death, perhaps seeing it as an angel or as an old man. Children often feel that they cannot see the "death man," but that the person carried off sees him for a brief moment. In this stage, the existence of death is accepted, but it must be externalized to escape the grasp of the death carrier. The externalization of death can be readily seen in children who hide under the bed after hearing of a death. What they express is a need for protection from the rampage of death; perhaps it is contagious.

Gerald Koocher, an American investigator, has examined children's concepts of death in the United States.[3] His findings agree with those of Nagy, with one interesting twist. In the five to nine age range, none of the American children mentioned either a "death man" or "death angel." Instead, they wanted to know all they could about procedures regarding survival, death, and burial. Koocher feels that this is akin to the idea of protection. His subjects are saying, "Perhaps my knowledge will keep me safe. If not, I will go through the experience with the support of my own background and skill. It will be as painless as possible because I have prepared."

Ages Nine and Up

Finally, at age nine or thereafter, children acknowledge freely that death is permanent and universal. They now know that one cannot escape the "death man," for there is no such being. Death is a natural part of life, governed by laws. Although the concepts of children age nine and over regarding permanent separation parallel those of adults, their emotional reactions are not those of adults.

Young People's Reaction to Separation

Separation is a universal, necessary part of life. Without separation, it is impossible to develop individual personality, make choices, or mature. Still, throughout life there remains an important drive for attachment, interdependency, and contact.

A crucial task of the first two years of life is to develop strong enough bonds with a parent (or parent figure) so that separation can succeed in the toddler period and beyond. How to separate and still maintain the connection is one of the main issues for young children, indeed for the rest of our years. In going off to a baby-sitter, grandparent, or teacher, young children unconsciously ask themselves if they will be any less significant if they allow these other individuals into their circle. Do they have enough identity to carry on through this separation?

If, in their bonding, children find a way to carry a consistent internal picture and memory of the loved parent within themselves (this phenomenon is called object constancy), they will be better able to bridge the separation. At times, failure to adapt to a normal separation experience, such as going away to camp or college, really is an echo of earlier inadequate or overindulged bonding and earlier failures to separate. One of life's central struggles is to maintain an appropriate balance between attachment and self-actualization, between dependence and independence, and between connectedness and the establishment of identity. This seesaw between closeness and distance continues to challenge every human being.

In recent years, aspects of grief and mourning have become subjects for study by psychiatrists, doctors, the clergy, hospital staffs, psychologists, educators, and others. In exploring this new field, called thanatology, investigators have found that reactions to separation are fairly predictable, involving a range of emotions that are reported time and again. The following is an overview of these reactions. If children do not react in all the ways listed, do not be overly concerned. Some people do not respond in the "usual order of things." In fact a usual order of things may not truly exist. For example, some children may respond to a loss by becoming quiet or wanting to be alone; others may become silly. Some may cry a lot, others hardly or not at all. No one response is the correct one. What's more, there is no timetable for grief, after which people should be able to put the event "behind them."

What is of essence after a major loss experience is that there be *some* change in habits or response—that is, youngsters not ignore the impact of the experience but react to it in some way. The loss experience is not just an event taking place in one moment in time. It is an ongoing experience that must be grappled with for years or even a lifetime.

Shock

When first confronted with a significant separation, many people respond with a dazed feeling. "Oh, no," a young girl may wail, after a parent announces plans to remarry. "You can't do this to me!" In the days that follow, nothing has meaning; daily chores and responsibilities are barely carried out; if done at all, they are accomplished while her mind is concentrated elsewhere.

Somatic Symptoms

Acute grief is often accompanied by bodily symptoms. Common manifestations of bereavement are shallowness of breath, fatigue accompanied by inability to sleep, and lack of appetite. There are many other possibilities. Sudden physiological changes can be explained to children, so that they will realize that these changes are a normal part of life.

Denial

Childhood mourning has been described by Gilbert Kliman.[4] The first step in the mourning process is testing and accepting the reality of the loss. Until children meet the irreversibility of the separation numerous times, they will not be convinced of its finality. For example, one child instinctively runs up to the bedroom, expecting to find the father who has left the mother. Another absentmindedly sets a place at dinner, only to be reminded once again about a death or separation. A third child sets up a bargaining scheme in her head: "If I do all my homework and never argue with Mommy, maybe you'll come back." The parent doesn't return no matter what the child does, and so the bargain is eventually proven false.

Underlying both children's and adults' denial is intense wishing, also magical thinking. In our wish to control the event, our minds impose a new, more satisfying set of circumstances so things will go our way. Denial fades as the loss sets in; however, it may not disappear completely and can be accepted as such. Like many emotions surrounding our deepest experiences, denial can suddenly appear, an unexpected guest, long after the loss has ostensibly been integrated. For example, a young woman whose father died when she was an adolescent finds at her wedding, eight years later, that she is feeling dazedly incomplete. She discovers that she is absentmindedly "looking" for her father that day, for in her heart he should be there. Every necessary change following a big loss, no matter how much later in time, may be viewed as another small death.[5]

Anger, Guilt, and Depression

Separation is often followed by reactions of anger. It is a justifiable response and quite normal. Young people may rail against other family members or berate bystanders, simply because they haven't gone through the same loss. For example, one youngster deliberately picked a fight with her best friend, severing the relationship, because she could no longer bear visiting a house where there were two parents.

Sometimes anger is an attempt to do the past over, thereby changing it. Thus a child might do everything within imagination to try to get thrown out of a foster placement, repeating the abandonment trauma in hopes that this time the emotions will be mastered.

Anger may also be directed at self, in the form of guilt. "Why did I always say fresh things? Why was I always so nasty?" Youngsters, even more than adults, blame themselves for what befalls them. It may be difficult to convince them that a grandfather died because he was old, not because unpleasant things were said. Nor will youngsters easily accept the intervention of bad luck or fate in their lives, being unable to fully imagine events without a reason. And, they think, the reason *must* concern them. Thus, the truck didn't simply careen down the block, suddenly killing their dog. *They* must have done something careless. Guilt is sometimes greater in accidents. We do not feel we can control disease, but accidents may be viewed as preventable.

Youngsters often do not recognize that mean thoughts exert no influence on actual happenings. For them, a teenage uncle may have joined the army and gone far away because the child wished he would drop dead—that wish made long ago, when the uncle was teasing one ill-equipped to answer back.

In *Beyond Grief: A Guide for Recovering from the Death of a Loved One*, Carol Staudacher advises that when death or other permanent loss occurs, children may feel they are fighting forces larger than themselves. Death and loss are powerful, and they are inadequate. Additionally, some may wonder if their future has been taken away from them. "I was looking forward to interacting in a unique way with my sibling or parent. Now, I don't have anything to look forward to."[6]

For many people, anger is foisted upon God. "What did I do? Why is God doing this to me?" The cruel, unwanted twists of life are difficult to fathom; wrath against the Supreme Being is a common, normal response.

Fantasies of reunion or return to old situations are especially intense if children feel guilty about circumstances before the change. Even love can be a source of guilt, as exemplified by the parent who remarries. When the child responds to the stepparent with warmth, he or she might feel pangs of disloyalty to the absent biological parent. Sometimes, in reaction to conflict, not knowing which side to identify with, a child may withdraw or become hostile. Actually this is a response to the pain of depriving oneself of needed attachments.

Being egocentric, youngsters may see an event as the manifestation of an adult's wish to abandon. They ask themselves if they were loved. If they were, how could they be deserted in this unnatural way, they ponder. In reaction to their own emotional development, they hold onto daydreams of reunion longer than they might. At the very least, this lengthens the period of denial. If carried farther, perhaps youngsters act on their desires. In the extreme, guilt and longing may appear as suicidal tendencies.

Depression has been termed anger turned inward. Youngsters coming to terms with the finality of change often feel depressed. A lackluster dullness may seem to pervade for a while. Some children feel helpless, even hopeless, as they are drained of emotion. It is difficult for them to realize that they are not alone in their emptiness, and the depression may intensify.

Embarrassment

For many children separation is a source of embarrassment—and a difficult one at that. They know they've done nothing wrong—it's not their fault that their parents are divorced, or that their mother died. Yet they feel awkward when asked about it, or speak of it only when they must, or are humiliated every time it comes up. They wonder why this is so and react with additional guilt.

Fear

It is natural that youngsters who confront a loss experience should fear further such experiences. If one relative dies, will another? If a school year has been marked by one teacher leaving after another, can security be found in the teacher presently in the classroom? If the natural parents gave up their child for adoption, might the adoptive parents decide to do the same?

Children also respond to global events with fear. Following the Challenger tragedy in 1986, youngsters readily identified with the surviving children of the lost astronauts and expressed relief that their parents were safe.[7]

Some children react with action instead of talk. Some may pick themselves up bodily and run away from their anxieties. Others, in attempts to master the trauma, may need to play out the scenes repeatedly, trying to understand through dramatic play. Still others may respond with a crisis of lost self-esteem and identity; fearing deprivation of their love object endangers their integrity and they may fall apart.

Underlying most of these fears is the basic question, "Who will take care of me?" As loss is mastered in stages, it is a good idea to allow children to touch base with the important adults in their lives in times of need. A call from the child to the parent at work, a drop-in visit from the child to a favorite teacher from days gone by, a note in the child's lunch box—these ways to keep in touch help allay anxieties.

Curiosity and Need to Master

Children are curious about death and other loss experiences. Both those who have been directly affected and those who have not are highly interested. They do not shy away until they are taught that the sad aspects of existence, particularly death, are considered by many adults to be improper subjects for discussion and investigation.

Children's dramatic play may reflect death and other loss themes. Whenever one group of six-year-olds got together, their play seemed inevitably to get around to acting out a traumatic event in one of the youngster's lives, the imprisonment of a brother. Day after day the scenario was acted out. The role-play was an effort to come to terms with the pain of loss.

Even the youngest children play out their fears and confusions about loss. In *Why Did Daddy Die? Helping Children Cope with the Loss of a Parent,* author Linda Alderman writes, "One day before Lara had given up her high chair, she sat at lunch grasping a fork in one hand and a spoon in the other. The spoon spoke first: 'Don't worry, dear. Mommy's just going to the office. I'll be right back.'

The fork asked in a high-pitched voice, 'You won't die, Mommy?'

'No,' the spoon reassured the fork."[8]

Other youngsters have great interest in looking at and touching dead birds and animals. They may kill insects. Such play, instead of being morbid preoccupation, is also a way to master feelings of loss, in this case, the permanence and irreversibility of death.

Children need to confront their losses and that confrontation will help them toward mastery of the event. As we are aware, children often master the environment through actions and making something concrete rather than through words. We can help them by allowing them their dramatic representation for as long as it is necessary and by facilitating that play by providing materials—paints, puppets, blocks, games, dolls, and so forth. Even teenagers may need concrete ways to explore emotional events, and their card games and sports activities may serve as a way to reenact the troublesome situation. Adult guides need to reflect on reasonable bounds as well. Children need the dramatic play and concrete learning opportunities. However, if a child keeps playing out the same scenario day after day, week after week and the action does not change, or if a child has an inordinate interest in killing animals to see what happens, perhaps this child is not working out the behavior through play. A professional consultation should be considered.

Sadness

Along with the other feelings and reactions described, it is common for youngsters to feel sad after a separation—to cry and let it out. But children's sadness is often not like that of those more mature. This difference, called the "short-sadness span" by Martha Wolfenstein,[9] is often a source of consternation to the adults who observe it without understanding. When youngsters experience loss, they feel deeply unhappy for a while, but then they quickly replace their distress with industrious, joyous pursuits. The adult is often shocked at the behavior, which resembles lack of feeling.

Actually, according to Wolfenstein, the child becomes preoccupied with normal living only because the sadness is so huge that it would be overwhelming and intolerable to continue to experience it. One child in Wolfenstein's study group said the following would occur if children allowed their full feelings to surface:

> They would cry and cry. They could cry for a month and not forget it. They could cry every night when they went to bed and dream . . . and the tears roll down their eyes and they won't know it and they were thinking about it and tears just running down their eyes at night while they are dreaming.[10]

It is understandable that youngsters would hesitate to relinquish control. After all, they have spent all their years in quest for control—in toilet training, diminished outbursts, and the development of conscience. It is hard now to let go, no matter what the provocation might be.

Absent or Delayed Mourning

When children do not react at all to a significant separation, they often displace their feelings onto another event. One might be surprised to see sudden and bitter tears over a death on a television show. Mourning may be delayed if the significant adults in children's lives consciously or unconsciously indicate that loss is shameful and that mourning must be limited.

If mourning continues to be delayed, or seems absent altogether, it constitutes a danger signal for the family and others. Those who suffer in silence plant seeds for future, continued pain. It is in the expression of grief that the pain is exorcised. Without its expression, it remains—a nagging, inexplicable depression against which battle must continually be waged.

In youngsters, unexpressed grief may surface in many possible manifestations, ranging from academic failure to juvenile delinquency, from sullen withdrawal to promiscuity, from fear of being alone to unwillingness to make friends.

If, in the face of trauma, mourning remains absent or delayed throughout childhood, it can interfere with normal adult life. Those children who will not allow their emotions direct expression are in effect saying, "This event has hurt me so much I can never again let anything touch me." The authors of *Life After Loss: The Lessons of Grief* feel that youngsters who lose a parent before the completion of adolescence who have no one to help them mourn may end up as "perennial mourners," with the parent becoming a haunting absence. They cite Marilynne Robinson's novel, *Housekeeping*, in which the character states, "My mother left me waiting for her and established in me the habit of waiting and expectation which makes the present moment most significant for what it does not contain."[11] Remaining fearful of rejection and abandonment, those who cannot mourn may shy away from the fulfillment of love relationships. Coming to grips with the inevitability of loss and expressing reactions to those losses when they come enable human beings to survive them. Only then do they become fully available to risk going on with the joys of living.

Vamik Volkan and Elizabeth Zintl put it this way: "When we mourn fully, we end up knowing more about ourselves and the human condition. We gain not only greater psychological maturity but, eventually, a heightened capacity for joy. That a painful and debilitating loss could leave us richer is an unappealing concept, but true enough. Loss is a brutal gift."[12]

Helping Children Cope

One must ask why, if loss experiences are so inevitable and universal, they are ignored in almost all school curricula. Few adults living today have had formal training with which to meet whatever changes life will hold. There are several reasons.

Until recently, little was known about loss experiences. As the major and most significant loss area, death was taboo, and so research focused neither on death nor on related loss subjects. Another reason is that today's youth has been falsely called a deathless generation. Most youngsters have two parents throughout childhood. Separated from their grandparents by hundreds of miles, the deaths of older relatives can appear as remote incidents, without emotional effect. And if there should be a death within the immediate family, technical advances are such that the person rarely dies at home. Children are deliberately and specifically excluded from hospitals. In addition, today's children live in megalopolises, unable to see the natural life and death cycle of a farm.

American society has been one of great promise. In our culture, death and other separations have come to be looked on as unnatural events, perhaps even sins. In a system that can send people to the moon, why can't we master disease, old age, and the final mystery of death? We're embarrassed, but to pretend we're not, we hide those who remind us, the ill and aged, in segregated facilities, hesitating to answer questions about them.

But we cannot fool ourselves. We are not without death, and we are not without loss. According to the 1992 Statistical Abstract, 14 million-plus children under age 18 in the United States live only with a mother and 2 million live only with a father. In 1990, 1.5 million people immigrated and nearly one family in five moves yearly. News of losses of this magnitude cannot be kept from youngsters. If they do not undergo these traumas themselves, surely they hear of the losses of neighbors and schoolmates.

Honesty about Loss Experiences

Children look to adults for guidance. Those adults aid youngsters best if they are honest—honest about the fact that along with life's ecstasies go life's agonies, and honest about the nature of those agonies.

Children want to know. They want to know about divorce: Who decides whom the children stay with? Will they get a stepparent? Will it constitute disloyalty to the natural parent if they love their stepparent? They want to know about cemeteries: what they are, why we need them, and what happens there. Honest information about these and other loss situations helps youngsters to master the facts of their existence.

Children deserve honesty without euphemism or unnecessary complication. If told a dead person went to sleep, many youngsters fear going to sleep. Likewise, if parents unnecessarily make a baby-sitting separation into a trauma by sneaking out on children, fear is the result. Finally, it is unjust to make children angry or fearful of God, as often happens when youngsters are told God "took" someone in death. "What kind of God is this?" they ask. "And who will He take next?" Some religious groups, however, focus positively on the love of God, which is with people both in life and in death.

It takes years for youngsters to master concepts of permanent separation. If children are not told anything about a loss situation, they are left with only their own fantasies, which can be worse than the reality. The message becomes "This topic is too dreadful to talk about at all." To sabotage children's efforts to understand seems unfair, whether by omission or euphemism. Likewise, children deserve explanations of the confusing aspects of the media. In cartoons, animals and people may be electrocuted or thrown from cliffs, yet they get up to do battle once more, seemingly unscarred. The number of losses in newscasts also presents a dilemma—in their enormity, the tragedies depicted may become meaningless. Adult guides can play a role in keeping children's concepts of reality on course by being on hand to discuss issues as they arise.

Aware of death, divorce, and other separations, children are naturally fearful. They may ask if they will be abandoned. Honest replies are called for. Many children have been left distraught, after being boldly reassured that their parents would never die or divorce, only to have it happen. Life has no pat assurances.

Explanations to children need not be lengthy and should be couched in terms geared to their ability to understand. Children are more concerned with how events affect them than causes, but it is important to establish an atmosphere of openness early. Even bearing in mind children's needs to make everything "all better," false hopes are diminished by open discussion.

Bruce Danto, psychiatrist and head of Detroit's Suicide Prevention Center, has said about response to suicide:

> Kids are the most lied-to group of people next to the Internal Revenue Service. . . . Rather than grieving and working out the problems as a family, they are generally shunted away and almost never told the truth.[13]

Although these remarks refer to suicide, they could easily refer to other losses—divorce, adoption, and so forth—perhaps in lesser degree.

When approaching an impending or a current change, children benefit from being prepared. They should be told in advance. They need to be given an idea of how their routines and living style will be restructured with the change. Most of all, they need reassurances of family affection. Sometimes parents and other adult guides must explain the change repeatedly, cognizant that difficult emotional material may not be absorbed or may be distorted. Besides honesty, no matter how cruel, the best gift children can be given in times of stress is personal attention.

Grief Must Be Expressed

Each time children are allowed to express feelings of loss, their mastery over the irreversibility of permanent separation becomes more complete. For adult guides to enable this to happen, they must not deny youngsters' grief or protect them from hurt. It is unwise to brush over the feelings, trying to thrust the experience ever so quickly into the past. It is better to acknowledge children's feelings by reflecting them back to them, for example, "I know you are (scared, worried, angry, hurting, and so on)." When adults quickly remove a dead pet from view, they keep an experience in mastery away from children. Looking at it, perhaps touching it, will create a lasting impression of death's finality. If they go the next step and swiftly replace the pet, they announce that loved ones are quickly replaceable, almost interchangeable. Again, children are cheated of opportunities to express and master feelings. In addition, young people sense and assimilate the dismay and shame of their guides.

Youngsters need help as they go through the process of mourning. Kliman elucidates three stages.[14] In the first, testing and accepting the reality of loss, youngsters need to be allowed to have the painful experiences. Each time they look for the absent person, they are reminded.

Willingness to discuss the experience will enable youngsters to bring it out in the open. This can be achieved when adults talk about feelings they've had.

The second stage is working over and coming to terms with memories related to the loss. For example, one youngster wants to look at photographs of his beloved aunt who has moved across the country. Another wants to hear and rehear stories about the times shared with a deceased grandmother. In sharing memories with children, adults state that it is permissible to talk about loss. If they make sure to bring up some of the bad times along with the good, youngsters are prevented from developing idealized pictures of people gone by. Those times gain perspective.

The third stage, according to Kliman, involves the cultivation of substitute object relationships. For example, a child who has lost a mother begins to gravitate to a particular aunt at family functions or enjoys warm rapport with a teacher at school. Kliman's stages are but one framework for putting into words the grief experience. No matter whose framework you use or what stage or phase you're at (and you can seem to be in more than one at any time), C. S. Lewis may have expressed it as well as any psychologist, saying, "In grief nothing stays put. One keeps on emerging from a phase, but it always recurs. Round and round."[15] (C. S. Lewis, *A Grief Observed*, p. 1)

Adults often wonder if children should attend funerals. A funeral service has several functions: It is a way of saying good-bye. It is also a way of reinforcing the reality of permanent separation. At funeral services participants also share and release feelings among family, friends, and members of the community. Psychologists feel that funeral attendance is far more beneficial than protection, for fantasies are often worse than the real thing. If children experience vivid reality, subsequent fantasies of reunion will be less intense. The funeral also takes place early in the mourning process and sets the tone of sharing for subsequent stages of bereavement. The difference between deliberate exclusion and an invitation to share in family sorrow can mean the difference between children who hide grief and those who are able to talk about feelings. In sharing feelings with another person, children gain release. They also realize they are not alone in their problems.

Children of any age can safely be permitted to attend funerals of immediate family members if they want to go, and it is recommended that children age seven or more be encouraged to attend the funerals of close relatives so that they can set the stage for later sharing. Children should be given an overview of what they can expect to experience before the funeral itself—the room can be described, the likely content of the service, if and how the body will be viewed. It is further recommended that a relative or friend who is well known to each child but not one of the primary grievers be assigned to care for the child. That person's assignment is to follow the child's lead, letting him sleep at the service if that is what he must do, getting up and leaving with her if that is what she must do.

Children need to know that it is permissible to feel unhappy. They also need to know that even in their grief they can enjoy themselves—this, too, is permissible. They need to see the nature of mourning: At one moment, one family member may need comforting, while another seems unscathed and becomes the source of comfort. Then the seesaw shifts and the comforter may need to be comforted.

In seeing and being part of the mourning process, children find out one of life's truths: While part of a group, each of us is alone—sadly, inevitably, alone—separate. In keeping with this idea, it is unfair to expect children to play a role, acting out an adult's world view. Thus, if the adult's philosophy implies being courageous in the face of loss, that approach shouldn't be imposed on others. Each person must find his or her own approach and philosophy.

Adult guides can help children express emotions by allowing youngsters to follow their own bent, by allowing them to act age-appropriate (instead of parentifying them), and by maintaining as much order and consistency as possible amid disruption.

Awareness

Adult guides will be helpful if they are aware—aware of their own pain, rejection, and isolation; aware of differences between themselves and children; aware when outside help is needed; and aware of avenues for obtaining help.

Several significant differences exist between the responses of adults and children to separation. Children lack adult means for resolving crisis in every sphere—economic, emotional, and social. Youngsters cannot themselves make the decision to leave an unbearable situation, electing to change schools, move, or live with a new family. Adults are more apt to make these choices for them, choices that all too often result in the continuation of the loss cycle for children, as they move into new and unfamiliar situations, while at the same time attempting to cope with the original bereavement.

Children do not have the experiential perspective with which to evaluate, subjectively and objectively, what happens to them. As noted earlier, youngsters lack the notion of chance. What is more, the number and variety of relationships that adults build over the years is unavailable to children. For adults, these become avenues for problem resolution. Couched within the confines of a singular, insulated, nuclear family, youngsters can rarely take advantage of wider horizons.

Youngsters are also more likely to be deficient in using the language of emotion. Unable to say, "I am in pain," children are more likely to act out in puzzling ways or to develop somatic symptoms of distress. Finally, children often do not realize that help is available if pain is expressed. They imagine they must suffer in silence.

Some adult guides have found the following ideas beneficial: (1) talking about troubling behavior at a calm time, not when it is occurring; (2) helping children find the words for their pain by giving their emotions names, while at the same time trying not to intimidate, for example, a divorced woman discussing her boyfriend with her son: "You seem to pout when I go out with Tom. I could be wrong, but I wonder if you pout because you feel left out"; (3) encouraging outside adults to be involved with the loss situation as it affects the child, for example, sending condolence cards, sharing memories, visiting; and (4) setting up a time at appropriate intervals (daily, weekly, whatever) to discuss the situation. At such times family members could work toward honest discussion that neither goes out of control nor bottles up emotion.

It is the obligation of adult guides to recognize signs that bereavement presents a crisis worthy of outside intervention. Adults should consider professional help if:

a youngster has pretended absolutely nothing has happened

schoolwork takes a dramatic decline or a youngster develops a phobic fear of school

news of a death or other significant loss was kept from a youngster for a long time or if that youngster was told lies

a youngster threatens suicide

a youngster panics frequently

a youngster frequently physically assaults others

a youngster could not get along with the family member who is gone or gets along poorly with the family members who remain

suicide is a cause of death

a youngster becomes deeply involved with drugs

a youngster begins committing serious socially delinquent acts

a youngster is totally unwilling or unable to socialize with other children

any family member is depressed for a lengthy period

there is physical assault, uncontrollable anger, or incapacitating fear in the family

the family seems overwhelmed by the event/problem

Psychotherapy can be beneficial. The goals of therapy will likely include some or all of the following: finding ways to express feelings about the loss situation, clarifying fantasies and their meanings and diminishing distortions, minimizing self-destructive behavior and fears, enriching communication patterns in central relationships, and finally healing wounds and gaining a perspective for the future that is hopeful.

The choices in treatment today are varied and rich. Therapy can be either short-term, usually revolving around resolution of a crisis, or it can be long-term, aiming at clearing up deeper, long-standing problems. People can seek individual, group, or family therapy. Each mode has its own benefits, individual therapy affording the client time and a new, neutral but supportive relationship for only the client, for example. In the so-called human laboratory of a group, adults or children can learn how they interact and use what they learn to improve their outside relationships. And in family therapy, the entire system of functioning can be examined and strengthened.

As there are many choices for mode of treatment, therapists have different training. An effective therapist can be a psychiatrist, psychologist, clinical social worker, pastoral counselor, psychiatric nurse practitioner, family therapist, and so forth. Their outlooks can differ, too. Some may stress cognitive therapy, looking at present behavior patterns first, then attitude. Others may stress psychodynamics, looking at how past life events have shaped thought and behavior patterns, aiming for insight that can lead to behavioral change. Still others may look at family systems, investigating how several generations may contribute to the present balance of family roles and how those roles might change for improved functioning.

In choosing a therapist, it is important to ask what formal training the person has and what approach will be taken to the problem. What is equally important as the training or the outlook, however, is a good relationship with the therapist. It has been shown that all the methods can lead to an improvement if two factors are present: The client feels understood and the client feels the therapist cares.

In the past decade an important source of comfort has come onto the scene, supplementing psychotherapy or being sought instead. This is the self-help group, which could also be called the "shared help" group, for the thrust is one of helping oneself through an environment in which others are helped by one's presence. Frank Reissman, founder of the National Self-Help Clearinghouse, estimates that 5,000,000 Americans are presently involved in 500,000 such groups across the nation.

The self-help movement has spread for many reasons. One is the diminution of government services for social and emotional crises.

Another is the decline of the family, place of worship, and neighborhood as sources for succor and support. A third reason is the trend in mental health care in this country toward deinstitutionalization. But perhaps the most important reason is this: "Who can better help heal the wound of another, as one who has felt the same wound?"

Self-help groups may take many forms. Some are bridge groups, to which people turn in distress so they can cope with their crises on an emergency basis. When they no longer need the group's support, they leave, and others come in. Other groups, also addressing a predicament, are sought for more long-term support. Some groups offer direct services to members; others focus on research, education, information, and referral. Many of the groups function superbly because their focus is one that requires only minimal professional caretaking (such as a chronic disorder), but is helped by large doses of human concern.

The very strength of the self-help movement is testament to the disillusionment of citizens over the government's provision of human and social services. There is a concomitant fear, however, that if government officials see organizations performing admirably, often on no more than a volunteer basis, government will continue to diminish services and relieve itself of responsibility. Problems notwithstanding, self-help is a sweeping movement capturing the energies of thousands. The University of Texas–Arlington Graduate School of Social Work offers an organized curriculum in self-help, the first professional school to do so. Thus, the self-help movement serves to revitalize professionals.

What does a self-help group do for individual members? Whatever their plight—be it divorce, anorexia nervosa, bereavement, child abuse, starting a stepfamily—people can start to see themselves as sources of strength; their experiences, no matter how terrible, can provide information and emotional comfort to others. With the realization comes change in self-perception and also change in public perception. In concentrating on abilities rather than disabilities, self-help groups can provide objectivity, an exchange of ideas, fellowship, new friends, and encouragement during bleak times. The group may offer a lifeline where none existed before. By participating in discussion meetings or through reading the materials published or disseminated by the group, members may find a way to cope with stigma, maintain independence, and release feelings that have been sources of shame. The shared condition members rally around can itself help them deal with the outside world that seems to exclude them. Members can often confide to the group feelings they can't share at home. Another benefit is that by being part of a self-help chain, members save money that might have been spent for professional care.

In seeking a self-help group, potential members should examine the group carefully. Is it part of a national affiliate? If so, what has the group accomplished on a national level? Does the group publish or provide reading materials? Does the group meet the specific needs of your problem? What resources does it have for children's growth? Is it likely to continue to focus on the needs you have now? How is the group structured? Is there adequate leadership so that your needs can be met? Is there leadership training? Is the atmosphere helpful from the start? Does everyone's opinion garner respect, or is there a cliquishness? Depending on individual need, the answers to some of these questions may be important.

A list of some self-help groups that may be of interest to readers appears in the Appendix of this volume.

A Final Word

To varying extents, our sorrows do not completely go away. People who ask, "Have you gotten over your grief yet?" are asking the wrong question. Grief has no set, prescribed timing. Instead, a more realistic and self-comforting question we should ask ourselves is, "Are things better today than they were six months ago?"[16]

Young people look to adult guides for direction in forming their lives. It is from adults that they will learn their behavior patterns for the future: whether grieving is normal and permissible or whether it is forbidden and wrong and a source of discomfort. Perhaps the most important aspect of helping young people cope with loss is the willingness of adult guides to expose their own grief while at the same time encouraging children to express theirs, for the way in which adults handle trauma determines youngsters' ability to survive their own difficulties. And only if they survive, physically and mentally, can they come forth from crisis strong and ready once again to celebrate life.

Notes

1. Earl Grollman, ed., *Explaining Death to Children* (Beacon, 1967), p. ix.
2. Maria Nagy, "The Child's View of Death," in *Meaning of Death*, ed. Herman Feifel (McGraw-Hill, 1959), pp. 79–98.
3. Gerald Koocher, "Childhood, Death, and Cognitive Development," *Developmental Psychology* 9, no. 3 (1973): 369–375.
4. Gilbert Kliman, *Psychological Emergencies of Childhood* (Grune & Stratton, 1968), pp. 86–88.
5. Carol Staudacher. *Beyond Grief: A Guide for Recovering from the Death of a Loved One* (New Harbinger Publications, 1987), p. 144.
6. Ibid., p. 135.
7. Ibid., p. 146.
8. Linda Alderman. *Why Did Daddy Die? Helping Children Cope with the Loss of a Parent* (Pocket, 1989), p. 184.

9. Martha Wolfenstein and Gilbert Kliman, eds., *Children and the Death of a President* (Doubleday, 1965), pp. 239–240.
10. Ibid.
11. Vamik Volkan and Elizabeth Zintl. *Life After Loss: The Lessons of Grief* (Scribner, 1993), pp. 104–105.
12. Ibid., p. 7.
13. Harriet Sarnoff Schiff, *The Bereaved Parent* (Crown, 1977), p. 42.
14. Kliman, *Psychological Emergencies.*
15. C. S. Lewis. *A Grief Observed* (Faber, 1963), p. 1.
16. Robert Buckman. *I Don't Know What to Say: How to Help and Support Someone Who Is Dying* (Little, Brown, 1988), p. 143.

2

Bibliotherapy

A Means of Helping
Young People Cope
with Separation and Loss

Adult guides who wish to help children come to terms with loss have a good ally in books, for books have been tools for preventing and solving psychological problems for as long as both books and problems have existed. As far back as ancient Grecian times, the door of the library at Thebes bore the inscription "healing place of the soul." The idea it expressed is both very old and very new.

Definitions

The term "bibliotherapy," most simply defined, means helping with books. The Greek roots of the word are *biblion* (book) and *therapeia* (healing). Most practitioners of bibliotherapy have spoken of the communication that takes place between the reader and the material, but some have further delineated concepts of bibliotherapy. Caroline Shrodes, a pioneer in the field, states that interaction is "between the personality of the reader and imaginative literature," going on to state that it "may engage his emotions and free them for conscious and productive use."[1] Shrodes's definition would seem to restrict bibliotherapy primarily to fiction and poetry. Karl Menninger does not limit his definition of bibliotherapy to one form of reading or another but points to "designating carefully selected books on mental hygiene for therapeutic purposes."[2]

A definition from the *Dictionary of Education* states that bibliotherapy is the "use of books to influence total development, a process of interaction between the reader and literature which is used for personality assessment, adjustment, growth, clinical and mental hygiene purposes; a concept that ideas inherent in selected reading material can have a therapeutic effect upon the mental or physical ills of the reader."[3]

Webster's Third New International Dictionary also refers to selection of materials in its definition of bibliotherapy: "The use of selected reading materials as therapeutic adjuvants in medicine and psychiatry; *also*, guidance in the solution of personal problems through directed reading."[4] First published in 1961, this definition was officially accepted by the American Library Association in 1966.[5] It is important to note that the definition does not suggest that bibliotherapy offers a complete solution to any problem; rather, it is an "adjuvant" or facilitator of treatment. The definition also implies some additional professional or nonprofessional input other than the selection of reading matter.

Within the context of library services, Margaret Monroe views bibliotherapy as an extension of reference services and reading guidance. All three are sought for informational, instructional, or guidance needs. According to Monroe, reference services are primarily objective, informational, and of short duration. Reading guidance is more subjective and geared toward education. Bibliotherapy functions as a long-term service approach with a therapeutic goal. Bibliotherapy, as one arm of readers' services, is espoused by Margaret Hannigan as well, who claims a bibliotherapist brings "a refined application of [the] normal librarian's function as readers' advisor."[6]

Rhea Rubin, author of the *Bibliotherapy Sourcebook* and *Using Bibliotherapy: A Guide to Theory and Practice,* defines bibliotherapy as "a program of activity based on the interactive processes of media and the people who experience it. Print or non-print material, either imaginative or informational, is experienced and discussed with the aid of a facilitator." The goal is "either insight into normal development or changes in disturbed behavior." "Clients" are categorized in three broad groups: patients and prisoners, individuals with behavioral or emotional problems, and normal persons in times of crisis.[7]

An investigation of bibliotherapy in the *Australian School Librarian* uncovered two opposing schools of thought. One group viewed bibliotherapy as "a highly specialized process for treating specific disorders of emotional or nervous origin, to be used only by skilled practitioners." The other conceived of bibliotherapy as "a guidance tool which may be used by virtually anyone interested in books, reading, and other people's problems."[8] No wonder author Ruth Churchyard titled her article "Bibliotherapy: What's That?" Despite the continuing lack of consensus, it is important and useful to be aware of the stated definitions and their appropriateness in certain cases.

In addition, the premise of this book tends to contrast with some aspects of the stated definitions. The premise of this book is that everyone can be helped through reading. One might not necessarily be faced with a problem, one might not be in therapy, and one might not be directed to the reading material. The authors feel bibliotherapy is a process in which every literate person participates at one time or another. Bibliotherapy is seen as the self-examination and insights gained from reading, no matter what the source. The source can be fiction or nonfiction; the reading can be directed (in settings ranging from reading guidance to formal therapy), self-directed, or accidental. The reader might begin reading when actively looking for insights, or the insights might come unexpectedly. In any case, the insight is utilized to create a richer and healthier life. Salient factors must be present: The author must communicate with readers in either aesthetic form or discourse with readers; the readers must, in turn, understand and respond, hopefully with conscious awareness, leading to attitudinal and/or behavioral changes. Such changes can be brought about with the help of an outsider or can be self-induced.

Evalene P. Jackson, another early advocate of bibliotherapy, recognizes this view, distinguishing between two kinds of bibliotherapy, calling one explicit and the other implicit. The first is conducted by a trained therapist with a hospital librarian as a partner in the team. Implicit bibliotherapy is called "a resource of the culture, present under some circumstances for those who can find and make use of it. The reader's advisor may provide guidance in the implicit sense."[9] This distinction allows for the inclusion of happy accidents that help individuals and also allows guides other than medical staff to take part. Explicit bibliotherapy might be compared to bibliotherapy as a science, whereas implicit bibliotherapy might be compared to bibliotherapy as an art. The latter might also be termed bibliotherapeutic rather than therapy itself.

Thus we see that definitions of bibliotherapy vary, from the inclusion of very formalized programs administered by physicians in cooperation with librarians for the benefit of seriously disturbed patients[10] to the very informal activity that is within the grasp of every adult guide who gains familiarity with literature and respectful awareness of possible beneficial or deleterious effects of literature on young people.[11]

History and Research

One of the early advocates of bibliotherapy as a helping agent for mental patients was Benjamin Rush, who as early as 1812 recommended novels to patients.[12] John Minson Galt II seems to have been the first American to write about the benefits of literature in treating the mentally ill, starting his work in the early 1800s. His best-known work is an essay titled "On Reading, Recreation, and Amusements for the Insane," published in 1853. Galt thought of the library as a place in which remedies for emotional difficulties could be found, emphasizing medical supervision and guidance. One of the first to use the word "bibliotherapy" was Samuel McChord Crothers, in an article in the *Atlantic Monthly* in 1916.[13]

In the 1930s there was a new interest in the field, which still saw itself aligned formally with mental institutions and medical staff and which viewed books as a pharmacy for the mind. One noteworthy study of this period was done by Elizabeth Pomeroy, when an attempt to study the field from an empirical base resulted in "Bibliotherapy—A Study in Results of Hospital Library Service."[14] In the paper, 1,538 case reports were studied, a sample that is hardly matched today.

The most important figure of that period, however, is William Menninger, who in 1937 read a paper before the American Psychiatric Association on the subject. Along with his brother, Karl Menninger, he utilized his ideas at the famed Menninger Clinic. The two believed that physicians should assign readings, with the physician approving purchases and responsible for the shape and growth of the library collection. The librarian was a technical member of the team, but the doctor was in charge.

In the 1940s, additional articles and papers on the subject appeared, examining the psychological validity of the field. In one, Salomon Gagnon, a psychiatrist, stated a guiding principle that "of all the remedies to the sick man, reading is the only one he accepts naturally."[15] During the 1950s, some of the seminal thinking in the field was done by Caroline Shrodes and others who examined the state of the art, influencing the field greatly from a philosophical point of view.

In 1962, Artemisia J. Junier, then a librarian at a Veterans Administration hospital, expressed the thoughts of the times in asking how bibliotherapy could be made into a more acceptable science. The arguments over definitions of the term were already known (and continue until this day), and Junier asked that work be done toward standardization.[16] The hopeful movement toward consensus was an important theme in a history-making 1962 issue of *Library Trends* devoted to bibliotherapy.[17] The fact that an entire issue, edited by Ruth Tews, was concerned with the field was in itself impressive; the articles explored the problems of bibliotherapy without conclusion. In a historical overview, W. K. Beatty expressed the thought that standardized practices and philosophical agreement in bibliotherapy were unlikely.[18] Also significant that year was the inclusion of a "Bibliotherapy Clearinghouse" in the *Association of Hospital and Institution Libraries Quarterly.*

During the 1960s, further on-site research was reported. In 1963 a pilot bibliotherapy program began in New York under the guidance of

Margaret Hannigan and William Henderson, who were working with young drug addicts close to parole. Case studies indicated the success of bibliotherapy.[19]

Although many people have struggled to define bibliotherapy, few institutions formally structure their services to include ongoing bibliotherapeutic services. A few psychiatric hospitals in Finland have literary circles that operate in ways similar to bibliotherapy groups.[20] There are programs at St. Elizabeth's Hospital in Washington, D.C., and the Santa Clara Free Library in San Jose, California, sponsors a program. But most other programs fall into the category of the short-term experiment.

Rhea Rubin is hopeful for more societal utilization of bibliotherapy. Reflecting on current trends that would make this more likely, she points to a public interested in psychological causes for events, a populace obsessed with self-actualization, and a society in which many of those who would previously have been institutionalized (mental patients and offenders) are now released. The result, according to Rubin, is that public and private agencies are forced to provide services to meet the needs of these groups and to examine the training necessary for the provision of these services. "Bibliotherapy is one means to satisfy public interest in self-actualization. It promotes self-growth based on shared experience and discussion of literature."[21]

Rubin points to the interdisciplinary nature of bibliotherapeutic possibilities, citing recent literature in which 35 percent of the articles on this subject appeared in library journals and 65 percent were found in the journals of other fields, such as psychology, education, nursing, and occupational therapy. Rubin feels this is because bibliotherapy is usually practiced in a group setting and inherits its thrust from group psychology and adult education programs such as the Great Books program.[22]

In her articles and books about bibliotherapy, Rubin divides today's bibliotherapy into three categories: institutional, clinical, and developmental. The first takes place in institutions such as hospitals and prisons, using informational and insight-oriented literature. Clinical bibliotherapy is used with groups of clients with emotional or behavioral problems and can take place either in an institution or within the larger community. The goals can be either insight or behavioral change, and the materials are likely to be imaginative literature. The facilitator is either a librarian or a doctor, with one acting as consultant for the other in most cases. Developmental bibliotherapy is likely to include both imaginative and informational literature and is used with the average, normal populace. The goal is to promote and maintain mental health and to foster self-actualization. This is the approach most often used in public libraries and schools. Rubin makes particular note of the role schools have taken, pointing out that schools "have been obvious sites for bibliotherapy because it is compatible with the goals of contemporary education, which include fostering development of a whole, adjusted personality able to deal with today's world. Students are already in an atmosphere conducive to reading and discussion, a library is usually available, the students are gathered five days a week, and curriculums are often varied and flexible."[23]

Rubin foresees greater community use of bibliotherapy in the future, with local institutions in the vanguard. Halfway houses, addiction centers, nursing homes, and outpatient centers are some of the obvious locations. The National Council on the Aging has started a reading and discussion program aimed at fostering self-esteem and human potential, and it is offering the service to senior citizen centers and nursing homes.[24]

At present, although model training programs for bibliotherapists have been described by Rubin, Margaret Kinney, and others, few ongoing, established bibliotherapy services exist, and little formal training is available. The first course in bibliotherapy for college credit was offered in 1980, by the Villanova University Graduate School of Library Science. In that same year the New School for Social Research offered the first college course in poetry therapy. The first comprehensive program for training was begun in 1973 at St. Elizabeth's Hospital. A two-year program, it includes a minimum of 448 training hours. The end result is a certificate as a poetry therapist given by the Association for Poetry Therapy.

Currently there is no bibliotherapy certification procedure. Rubin calls for guidelines for certification as interest in this field grows. She suggests a multilevel certification system that distinguishes among the types of bibliotherapy and whether the person will be working alone or as part of a team. All of her recommendations call for background knowledge of the literature of both mental health and librarianship.[25]

Other studies of note include the following: J. Webster managed to diminish fear of the dark and fear of dogs in first graders by reading stories that demonstrated the positive side of the feared phenomena, and following up with discussion.[26] Interviews three months after the stories were completed indicated that of 35 children fearful of the dark, 21 were less fearful, and all five children afraid of dogs were less frightened. It is not known, however, if change in attitude was accompanied by changes in behavior. In another study concerning fear of the dark, William L. Mikulas and his associates conducted four experiments using a children's story and related games designed to help children overcome their fear. The materials incorporated behavior modification of fear reduction, including modeling, counterconditioning, and shaping. Overall, the story and games were found therapeutic, cost-effective, and enjoyable.[27] A third study about fear was conducted by Robert C. Newhouse. He attempted to determine the effectiveness of bibliotherapy to reduce generalized fear in 30 second-grade students. Results supported the hypothesis that fear would be reduced through bibliotherapy, but Newhouse warns that measures should be taken to ensure a good research design and maximization of the treatment over an extended period.[28]

Researchers have tried to use books to change perceptions and behavior about family situations. One example is the work of John Sheridan and his associates. In their study, 48 seventh to ninth graders from changing families (as a result of divorce, separation, death, military service, remarriage, or other causes of parental absence) were assigned to one of two treatment groups: structured group counseling or explicit bibliotherapy, or a wait-control group that received standard individual counseling. Subjects were administered the Piers-Harris Children's Self-Concept Scale pre- and post-treatment; they also completed an attitudinal survey of the help they received. Subjects in the group counseling and bibliotherapy groups rated the help they received higher than subjects in individual counseling.[29] On a smaller scale, Terry Connor and associates undertook to prepare a nine-year-old boy for family placement through the use of the creation of a life storybook. Life storybooks are designed to answer the what, where, and why questions about a child's life experiences and to allow the child to express feelings about these events.[30] Through the creation of his own book, the boy began to unravel his confusion and discard some of his negative emotions.

Researchers have also found that attitudes toward sociological and anthropological groups can be altered by reading. The effect of reading material upon second- and seventh-grade students' attitudes toward blacks has been investigated by E. P. Jackson[31] and John Litcher and David W. Johnson.[32] Attitudes toward Eskimos have been investigated in a bibliotherapeutic framework by R. H. Tauron,[33] who worked with third graders; American Indians were the group considered by F. L. Fisher, who worked with fifth graders.[34] All four investigating researchers believed that attitudinal changes could be effected toward other minorities as well. All four reported changes of significance. When minority characters were given favorable presentation, readers were likely to respond in a positive direction.[35] When minority group characters were portrayed in an unfavorable light, the attitudes of readers were negative.[36] Again, in these studies, the findings reflect paper-and-pencil tests or students' stated opinions, suggesting identification with literary characters. They do not reflect subsequent behavior.

Means of doing bibliotherapeutic work must come under discussion when evaluating the success. One study that yielded interesting results is Fisher's, mentioned above. Three groups of fifth-grade students took part, each being treated differently. One group consisted of middle-class whites; the second was lower-class blacks; the third, racially mixed, middle-class youngsters. Within each group, three different procedures took place. In one subgroup, children read stories. In the second, they read stories and participated in discussions led by the classroom teacher. In the third subgroup, there was no story reading. All subgroups took attitudinal and information tests regarding American Indians. As expected, reading the stories produced positive attitudinal changes, but when stories and discussion took place, the attitudinal changes were even more significant. Discussion also led to greater information gain on the post-test. Attitudinal change took place most frequently in the middle-class, racially mixed group; and the attitudes of blacks toward American Indians showed greater change than those of whites. Once again, it is suggested that identification with the characters yields this result.

Another study emphasizing group discussion after reading is that of D. W. Biskin and K. Hoskisson, in which a group of fourth and fifth graders who both read and talked about moral conflicts encountered by fictional characters gained considerably in moral maturity over the group that merely read the stories.[37]

Time spent in discussion was also important in a study conducted by Dorrie Prouty, in which fourth graders read story and information books about death.[38] Students were helped toward clarifying which books of those they had read meant most to them and then they met and wrote to the authors of these books. Both actions released some of their feelings and fears regarding the subject.

It is also important to investigate behavioral changes brought about by bibliotherapy. At present, few studies do this effectively. Few studies also demonstrate the permanence of attitudinal changes. One study that does give evidence of behavioral change is that of David Gerald Jarmon, in which the effectiveness of rational-emotive therapy, bibliotherapy, and attention-placebos was examined in the treatment of speech anxiety.[39] Perhaps Jarmon tells us something of great importance when indicating that although of the three treatments used, bibliotherapy was the most effective, the gains were not maintained in a follow-up investigation. Jarmon's hypothesis that this might be due to the "brief nature of the treatment" is one that must be investigated in future studies.

A survey of 50 Australian primary school teacher-librarians revealed that most felt there was a strong connection between children's level of ability and the influence of books on their intellectual development, the link being more marked for those of above-average ability. However, the majority considered that books could not influence personal behavior or moral and ethical values. Most of the respondents practiced a form of bibliotherapy that they called reader guidance.[40]

In contrast to this study, in which the above-average learner stands a better chance to benefit from books, Barbara Lenkowsky and Ronald Lenkowsky presented a case study in which they claim that there is little evidence that bibliotherapy helps the normal child to cope better, but that reading about problems and their resolutions may enable the learning-disabled adolescent to live a more fulfilling life. Unfortunately, this study does not present findings for many adolescent subjects over a long period.[41]

A word of warning is given by Lucy Warner in an article in *School Library Journal*. Recent research has "called into question whether exposure to vicarious experiences really purges intense emotions or merely stirs them up."[42] This assertion is corroborated by Anne Marrelli's dissertation, in which school anxiety was treated through reading. The children became more anxious than before.[43]

Warner reviewed 28 doctoral theses in the bibliotherapy field since 1969. All used control groups. In 10, bibliotherapy was found unsuccessful. Among the studies in which bibliotherapy was deemed successful, almost all qualified their conclusions. In four studies, short-term gains, when followed up, were not maintained. In two studies, improvement in theory did not translate into behavioral change. Four studies produced positive results only with subjects who had already acknowledged their problem and expressed desire to change. Four studies revealed other techniques to be more successful than bibliotherapy, but two of these made positive claims for it in conjunction with other techniques. Only two studies gave unqualified endorsement to bibliotherapy![44]

In the 1980s, interest and investigation in both the art and science of bibliotherapy have continued, with publications growing rapidly in number. Those who wish to practice bibliotherapy and those who wish to study its effects will continue to learn as the field advances.

Reading Can Help Children Cope

Books can help children cope with many of life's vicissitudes. Children rely on their imaginations, need symbolic ideas and images, because so much happens both within them and around them that they find hard to understand.[45] Because loss is a recurring problem throughout all stages of life, it would logically follow that loss would be a common theme in children's books and that such books would be very popular, sought after as sources of information. Books that concern moving and the advent of a new sibling are available in multitudes, but it is only in recent years that numerous books about death, divorce, and other separations have become available for children.

Reading Offers an Opportunity to Identify with Others

In psychology, people are said to identify when they behave or imagine themselves behaving as though they were actually other individuals, individuals with whom they have an emotional connection. In reading, identification takes place when the readers see themselves as aligned with characters, groups, settings, or ideas presented in the material.

Identification serves several purposes. First, readers can discover their own problems when they perceive the problems of others. Reading about the grief of others can create sudden pangs of identification, as problems that heretofore had not been consciously or completely recognized are allowed to surface. In fact, reading may actually be better than life, for it is sometimes easier to accept an unfortunate aspect of ourselves from the distance literature offers.

The fact that the reading process is a private one is an advantage to children with problems—to everyone, in fact. Most readers have had the experience of hiding a book because it is an identification they wish to keep secret. Books fit well into the human need for solitude, for reading is a private experience that allows our inner resources to grow while no one is looking. In the privacy of the home, readers may cry, pound pillows, pray, think deeply, even scream if they are so provoked. Alone, readers have time to contemplate the wonders of daily existence—the beauty of a flower, the complexity of time passing, the magnificence of the human body, the artistry of literature.

Certain subjects are kept secret by youngsters, such as being molested by a family member or being cruelly abandoned. Embarrassment caused by the problem is minimized because readers are allowed to reflect on characters and themselves within the chambers of the mind. If in reading such books as *Gillyflower,* by Ellen Howard, young people recognize that allying themselves with a sole stable adult can be the path out of an imprisoning situation, they have then found value in the literary form.

If readers wish to rehearse solutions to their dilemmas, they can do so without observation or interference. The identification process often evokes thought about solutions when readers realize that a character has coped with a situation. It is then important to examine the fictional adjustment in terms of a personal parallel, to weigh alternate proposals, and to progress toward individual solutions. At times readers then become more amenable to translating their thoughts into action and to making decisions that had formerly been repressed, set aside, postponed, or thought impossible.

In some instances, after reading about a character who has a problem, readers may want to talk about their difficulties. The literary character or the information a book provides can create the shield necessary for those unable to address such topics directly. They can then speak about the character instead of about themselves, while releasing information and revealing their feelings both to themselves and others.

Reading Helps Children Realize They Are Not Alone

According to Abraham Maslow, human beings have certain basic needs that must be met if they are to function. After physiological and safety needs, Maslow ranks the needs for belonging and love as next in importance.[46]

Reading is one way to enhance feelings of belonging. Through identification with characters and situations, readers are helped to feel less isolated. Children who are separated from a parent because of death or other reasons realize that others share their plight. This causes them to reason that they might, after all, be within the range of normality. Or, if they do conclude that they are *not* normal, it is then a relief to know that others suffer as they do. When children feel less isolated, they lose some of their embarrassment about their family situations.

The stages of mourning are readily seen, even in books for younger readers. As elucidated by Gilbert Kliman,[47] children first test and retest reality, eventually convincing themselves of the awful thing that has happened. For example, in Deborah Gould's book *Grandpa's Slide Show,* young Douglas poignantly tries to grab his grandfather's image from the screen, hoping to recapture him although he has died.

The second stage, going over the powerful memories, can be seen in Paul Fleischman's *Rear-View Mirrors.* In this book, the protagonist, Olivia, takes a symbolic bicycle ride to commune with her now-dead father, a man who had neglected her most of her life. Recounting the good and the bad puts these matters in perspective.

Kliman's third stage of mourning is the establishment of a substitute object relationship. As is the case with the previous stages, this one is portrayed in many books for youngsters. And, happily, in most books it is not portrayed in a Pollyanna, easy-does-it style, but with honesty. One such book is Joan Drescher's *My Mother's Getting Married,* in which a young girl has mixed emotions at the possibility of having a stepfather— "Everything will change," Katy says. Dinner won't be flexible anymore, and how can she possibly let Ben see her in her pajamas? In short, Katy thinks "it stinks."

Other themes of bereavement are seen in books and offer reassurance. The physical symptoms of grief are often portrayed. One example is Constance C. Greene's *Beat the Turtle Drum.* In the grief that Kate experiences after her sister Joss is killed in an accident, she remarks, "My bones feel hollow with loneliness." The short sadness span is also depicted. In Candy Dawson Boyd's *Circle of Gold,* the character Mattie Benson tries to get back into the swim of things after loss by baby-sitting, entering a writing contest, and occupying her time in various other ways.

If the reading material is sufficiently effective and succeeds in enhancing feelings of normalcy and belonging, it can, in turn, act as an agent for increasing self-esteem. As the chain continues, after self-image is bolstered, readers may show a new readiness to search for adjustment to their problems.

Reading Can Extend Horizons

Reading offers avenues to broadened interests and adventure. Books provide opportunities to be something or someone new. When readers extend their horizons and empathize with characters unlike themselves, they open themselves to several types of enrichment.

Perhaps they will grow to understand the motivations, goals, and feelings of members of another group. For example, what is it like to wait for a parent to return from prison? What are the economic, social, and emotional pressures suffered by a child such as the one in Inez Maury's *My Mother and I Are Growing Strong.* Through the eyes of a youngster whose father has been imprisoned, children may perceive, possibly for the first time, the nature of the interactions that take place between the new group and the group with which they affiliate. Through reading children may begin to see how some relationships work, economically and socially, between the children of incarcerated parents and other children. How does such a child feel and behave in school? How does he or she affect the others? Why? These are questions that can be illuminated through reading. Children who have never had to cope with a loss situation can imagine it, rehearse a solution, and remember, however vaguely, their literary experiences when a real-life situation comes about. This is particularly true of books about death and general separation, events that eventually befall all of us.

Reading about new people and situations can lead to the development of new interests. On a minimal level, the new interest can serve as a means to point children in the direction of thinking about something other than themselves. For many troubled individuals, both children and adults, this is a significant accomplishment. Once people are able to place focus away from themselves, they may become eager to gain new knowledge or hobbies. There is an added benefit: In the pursuit of information about a new area of concentration, children and adults often demonstrate increased interest in reading. For reluctant readers, material that extends horizons and contains high-interest but low-vocabulary levels can serve as an ego booster. Patricia MacLachlan's *Sarah, Plain and Tall* is such a book, written on a third-grade reading level but appealing to older readers. There can be an expansion of previous reading habits to include new forms—reference works, magazines, and so forth. Finally, there can be an increase in the difficulty of the material, which readers can effectively perceive in all its implications.

One important aim of education is establishing the ability to think critically and then using that ability to evaluate difficult, thought-provoking material and ideas. Through books, youngsters can become aware of their own value systems, considering what is important to them and examining what is important to others. They can look over those objects and goals that are treasured by each character, evaluate conflicts between value systems, and weigh solutions to the problems these conflicts present. The answers youngsters give are self-revealing. When brought to a conscious level, either in reading or in the discussion that follows, young people are offered the opportunity either to strengthen the patterns developing or to alter those patterns.

As an example of value theory in action, the book *I Never Asked You to Understand Me*, by Barthe DeClements, demonstrates conflicting life patterns. The protagonist, Didi, becomes truant during her mother's terminal illness, terrified at being left with a distant father and a great-grandmother who sees illness as something we will on ourselves. The action revolves around Didi's struggle to see her own truth and find her own ideas on how responsible each of us is for our destiny.

Reading Can Aid the Catharsis Process

The discharge of repressed emotions is a valuable aspect of a therapy program, indeed of good mental hygiene. Through involvement, readers vicariously experience the difficulties and feelings of characters, leading to catharsis. This "may provide a release of tension through symbolic gratification of socially unacceptable urges or substituting gratification of socially approved motives."[48] The purging of fear, anger, grief, and other emotions can come about in many ways. Reading is one way, as books can act as the agents that bring about tears (shed in private or shared) and evoke discussion of previously hidden feelings. Ventilation is helpful, but its benefits are usually temporary. In order for symptoms of distress to be alleviated, more is usually needed. The development of insight and an ability to work through the problems causing distress are usually components in the true resolution of difficulties.

Reading Can Lead to Insight

When tensions are partly relieved by catharsis, the emotions are freed, clearing the mind to develop insight. The ability to perceive part or most of whatever can be known of the true or underlying nature of an experience is most helpful in evaluating that experience. Without such perception or insight, it is difficult, if not impossible, to see one's motivations and those of others. Reading can help to facilitate insight: In reading about a loss experience, it is possible to relive prior loss occasions while being aware of common ground held with the literary character and material. It is indeed possible, when armed with this awareness, to come to new self-discoveries—to experience the "aha phenomenon," as it is known in psychiatric circles.

Reading provides at least one advantage over shared discussion. In reading, the discoveries, sometimes of personal shortcomings, can be faced privately without disclosure to others until readers choose to do so. Caroline Shrodes has explained: "Literature, being at once a fantasy and yet a realistic portrayal of human behavior, permits the reader, paradoxically, both an illusion of psychic distance and immediacy of experience."[49]

Nonfiction books have a special place in the process leading to insight. Books such as Eda LeShan's *When a Parent Is Very Sick* perform the same functions as adult self-help books and are valuable in solving problems. They enable children to look at themselves in relation to what is considered "normal." They can then see, with clearer vision, their strengths and weaknesses, their assets and liabilities. A clearer vision helps in the identification of motivations and in the formulation of realistic goals for the future.

Reading Can Facilitate the Sharing of Problems

Beyond insight and other processes of bibliotherapy, there is an additional desirable avenue for working through sources of difficulty: the sharing of problems. Through reading, children come to realize that the characters are imperfect, as they are. What is more, they recognize that it is permissible to be imperfect, even acceptable to admit to another (or others) that they are imperfect. Once the step of admission has been taken, the listeners are likely to reciprocate and consider their own imperfections

in discussion. The overall benefit is that other people become less idealized.

This is especially important in relation to the second stage of mourning. In families where death has occurred, there is an unfortunate tendency
for the deceased to be remembered automatically as perfect in every way.
In divorce, however, the absent parent's weaknesses are often exaggerated
and strengths overlooked by the parent who has the primary responsibility
for the children. In the children's eyes, the absent parent becomes something of a villain. The children realize that they have inherited a part of the
genetic makeup of the parent removed by death or divorce. The image of
this parent as either angel or villain is likely to result in a loss of the
child's self-esteem, for humans can never hope to match the behavior of
an angel and they do not want to be thought of as inheriting the characteristics of a villain. In contrast, open discussion based on an honest
appraisal of the absent person results in greater self-acceptance by the
child.

Bibliotherapy can give young people the language with which to communicate their pain. Often, difficulties are felt, but people of many ages
suffer in silence, not realizing help is available. A book can offer the ideas
and avenues for getting that help. For example in *Shira: A Legacy of
Courage,* by Sharon Grollman, the protagonist aids herself by keeping a
journal and writing poems. She pours the anger and other emotions arising
from her severe diabetes into her writing. In the same book, visits to therapists are discussed, which might lead youngsters toward that path.

In discussion, readers review the material. They respond to one
another about what they have read. They compare their experiences in
terms of the actions and feelings of the characters and find areas of both
agreement and disagreement. They investigate the consequences of the
characters' actions, and in doing so reflect aloud on their own. It is natural
that the sharing of problems also gives readers opportunities to find new
solutions and/or modes of action to follow. If one person talks with one
other person, at least two approaches to one problem are likely to be considered; in discussion, more than two personal approaches will undoubtedly be included, as each person gets to know the others, with their unique
backgrounds and solutions. If more than two are present, even more solutions are available for consideration. Adult guides might wish either to
group together people with the same experiences or to mix the types of
problems within a group. Either position has valid support.

When readers share their problems, they also make themselves ready
and receptive, as a preliminary step, for formal therapy if it is indicated. In
Bibliotherapy: Methods and Materials, Ruthanna Penny is quoted as suggesting steps for getting readers to share their thoughts.[50] At first, readers
read nonfictional material aloud, without dialogue. This teaches them to

speak without fear. In the second step, readers react to questions of fact. No opinions are asked for. Finally, in the third step, readers are asked about their personal convictions.

Another technique is having young people retell the story and then examine the way one of the characters behaved and felt. This often leads to instances in which youngsters tell of similar incidents in their own lives, opening up avenues for further discussion.

Doris Robinson has related bibliotherapy to an integrated curriculum for special education students, devising specific discussion topics for particular books. For example, using *The Terrible Thing That Happened at Our House,* Marge Blaine's book about the trauma of one's mother going off to join the working force, Robinson brings up this question with her class: "Can you change a bad thing? If so, how?" Thus, the limited subject of one book becomes grist for a larger mill. Robinson also informs readers that everything in her bibliotherapy program seemed to go in slow motion, with children lingering for long periods over one idea.[51] This is echoed by H. Elser, who recently began a patient library program centered around bibliotherapy with selected materials at Danvers State Hospital in Massachusetts, perhaps the only bibliotherapy program in the country funded in part by the federal government. Elser found that the attention span of her groups, be they schizophrenic, geriatric, or adolescent, was very short, and she had to develop her own resource materials of short poems and literary passages.[52]

Discussion of materials can range from the most informal, as would be the case in a popular classroom activity called a poetry cycle, to a highly structured series of steps, as might be found in some bibliotherapy groups. In a poetry cycle, children are asked to select three poems on a topic of their choice. The classroom library boasts many poetry anthologies from which to choose. When the children share their discoveries, the teacher might ask what makes a particular child interested in poems about colors, why blue is his favorite color, how blue makes him feel, and so on.

On a more formal side of the continuum is the set of recommended steps proposed by J. Bodart:

> (1) retelling of the material, highlighting feelings, characters, and situations relevant to the problem being discussed; (2) probing into what happened in the material, to facilitate a shift in feeling and relationship, making identification more easy and vivid; (3) stimulation for the group to identify similar situations in real life or from other books to lend validity to the idea that books can extend actual experience; (4) opportunity for the group to explore the consequences of certain behavior or feelings and recapitulate what happened as a result of these feelings or actions; (5) opportunity for the group to draw conclusions or generalizations as to whether specific actions in certain situa-

tions had positive or negative effects; (6) opportunity for the group to determine the desirability or effectiveness of several actions in the specific situation.[53]

These steps, Bodart feels, whether handled in a group or with an individual, can help an individual see that he or she is not alone, that there is more than one solution to a problem, and get basic understanding of others when planning one's own solution. As Nancie Atwell has said, "Books are a powerful social tool, a way of creating instant community."[54]

Successful Bibliotherapy

Bibliotherapy is not yet at a stage where it has been fully accepted and established as a means of therapy. While its tenets are informally accepted, it is akin to, but somewhat behind, poetry and art therapy in its use in formal programs. The materials of bibliotherapy are known: fiction, nonfiction information books, biographies, science books, mythology, and more. Yet exhaustive studies of the effectiveness of bibliotherapy have not been undertaken; even if they were, results would be nearly impossible to quantify. Bibliotherapists will probably have to be satisfied (at least for the time being) that bibliotherapy exists as a tool within the many spheres of therapy. As stated earlier, it is called on as an adjuvant in many types of mental hygiene programs. Bibliotherapy can help. According to Margaret Hannigan, it is therapeutic rather than therapy.[55] It would seem unwise to look toward bibliotherapy as a cure. Just as giving children books about the facts of life does not constitute adequate sex education and can actually be a way to sidestep obligation, so it is that the offering of books about dying, moving, or divorce cannot be considered adequate education or preparation for loss. Such is the case for the use of all books in the curing of social or emotional ills.

Some feel that bibliotherapy should only be undertaken by those well versed in psychodynamics, neurosis, and psychotherapy. Others, such as ourselves, feel that it can be and is safely undertaken by those with less sophisticated expertise in human nature: teachers, librarians, doctors, lawyers, parents, and others. Bibliotherapy is often undertaken by children on their own. Perhaps, since it is the case that books are indeed consulted by people of every age in search of answers to problems *without* the presence of a formal therapeutic setting, adults who find themselves in guiding positions need not and should not feel embarrassed by their inadequate backgrounds in psychology. Perhaps, instead, adult guides should try to meet other obligations. These include the obligations of knowing how and when to introduce the materials, being sufficiently familiar with the materials, and knowing each child's particular situation.

Timing

Timing is important in utilizing literature as a tool for happier living. Preparation and planning are of the essence. Books about death and other forms of loss can be included in a school or home literature collection, along with less emotion-provoking material. Doctors can leave such books in their waiting rooms, intermingled with other reading material. The principle is the same as in a public library: The materials are readily and obviously available, but the choice is left to the individual. Range in tastes is great. The larger the collection is, the more choices there are. Some practitioners of bibliotherapy believe that books should be chosen by adults and given to children. On the other hand, Patricia Cianciolo's study concluded that, while in therapy, children preferred to select their own books rather than having them offered by the therapist.[56] The suggestion of the book by its presence in a collection, rather than by its prescription, gives children the central role. The book is not forced on children with the implication "It's good for you." Instead, children are self-motivated.

While the adult keeps books on loss available, it is often a long and patient wait until children are ready to make use of the books. Often, bereaved children will ignore these books within the collection and seek out less threatening fare. At the peak of their grief, people of all ages often cannot face mirrors of their emotions. They know their problems all too well and need other relief. And when grief is ebbing, some children may guiltily wonder if that means they have stopped loving the person, which may become exacerbated if they happen to read about the loss at that time.[57] These are additional reasons for making the books available instead of prescribing them.

The possibility of intensifying difficulties or raising defenses is avoided if guessing about timing is eliminated. Tensions within readers may prevent books from influencing their attitudes or behavior. Perhaps, when identification with character is strongest, if that character reminds readers of the very weaknesses they hate in themselves, they will respond with intense venom toward the literary figure, missing, in fact, any positive resolution of the problem found in the book.

Also, the problems of readers may prevent them from seeing what really is relevant to them. Distorted reactions, differing from those adult guides had hoped for, are indeed possible. The fears, guilts, and depression of readers may actually be intensified by reading. For some mentally ill individuals, the worlds of their own creation can be magnified and given new "reality," additionally aggravating adjustment.

When children make their own selections, there is no guessing to be done. By allowing the children to choose, the adult, aware of the children's general background, diminishes possibilities of offending children or their parents on emotional, religious, moral, or other grounds.

Adult guides can facilitate self-selection by providing means to attract youngsters to such books. This might mean decorating bulletin boards to include books about loss and compiling book lists on loss topics and placing them discreetly on racks or librarians' desks. It might mean giving book talks before groups or placing on exhibit actual copies of such books.

In developing book displays and other means to attract readership, it is additionally helpful to be on the lookout for books in which loss or other problem areas are side issues. Not as likely to frighten the timorous, sometimes these books have deep impact, as characters within a literary context struggle with bereavement. Youngsters pluck out the minor themes, seeing them in relation to the more major themes and also in relation to themselves. In many ways, such books are greater mirrors of life than those that focus strongly and continually on one loss event. In actual life, the major themes probably include growing, using one's capacities, survival itself. Although change and growth are major determinants of loss and loss is a continuing theme in life, usually one trauma is not *the* theme of one's life. Thus, adult guides should keep in mind aspects of life depicted in books besides the loss events. Are all the events authentic, and not merely those that depict loss?

Obligations Concerning Discussions of the Book

The skilled adult understands a long waiting period and is ready for the moment when children begin to read books concerning their problems; the adult is equally sensitive to definite, overt, clearly stated signs that children are amenable to having such books given to them. Under such circumstances, the offering of a book by the adult guide is acceptable. After a book has been read by or with children, in most circumstances it is advisable that the adult be available for discussion. Although children and adults can gain some insight from reading alone, openness to discussion is a factor as important as the literature itself. However, just as the adult did not force the children to use the books, so the adult does not intrude with unwanted discussion.

The American Library Association volume entitled *Bibliotherapy: Methods and Materials* shows three factors present in the dynamic interactions that take place in successful bibliotherapy. These include the author's communication with the reader, the reader's ability to understand and respond to the material and the therapist's ability to perceive alterations in attitude and to bring those changes to a level of awareness in the reader.[58]

Whether the adult guide is therapist, teacher, parent, librarian, or other concerned person, certain things can be done in order to help children have the optimal growth experience after reading. An optimal experience is what the child has in mind, not the adult guide. When asked what a reader should achieve by reading *Bridge to Terabithia*, author Katherine Paterson responded, "My job is to write the best book I know how to write. Your job is to decide what you're to achieve by reading it."59 A book is truly "a cooperative venture. The writer can write a story down, but the book will never be complete until a reader . . . takes that book and brings it to his own story."60

Perhaps most important is that the adult listen. Instead of pushing forth inquiry into the reasons for choosing the book or an analysis of it, the adult can learn how to proceed by listening instead of talking.

In listening, it is useful to appreciate the differences between sympathy and empathy in order to offer maximum help. Norman Paul has made a clear distinction.

> In sympathy . . . the subject is principally absorbed in his own feelings as projected on the object's special, separate experience. In sympathy, the subject is likely to use his own feelings as standards against which to measure the object's feelings and behavior. Sympathy, then, bypasses real understanding of the other person. . . . The empathic relationship is generous; the empathizer does not use the object as a means for gratifying his own sense of importance, but is himself principally concerned with encouraging the other person to sustain and express his feelings and fantasies.61

There are no feelings that one *should* feel and no guilt when they are not felt.

Thomas Newkirk and Patricia McLure suggest ways to actively listen and support the speaker, including nodding and saying, "mm-hm." "The 'mm-hms' suggest to the speaker that the listener recognizes the turn is not over, that he or she is not impatient to take a turn. They seem to say, 'Keep going; take your time.'"62

Listening with empathy offers children maximum opportunity for expression. It allows for the development of trust. It also provides cues that attitudinal change may have taken place. When the adult listens skillfully, it is then possible to react to the individual, receiving the necessary inspiration for ways to continue. Only after listening can the adult take the threads of conversation that children have begun and develop a more accurate conception of areas and possibilities for further discussion, as well as areas of investigation to be avoided. Only after listening does the adult know which concepts might be worth expanding and/or reinforcing and which reading material might be effective in accomplishing expansion or reinforcement. The adult will also then be a better judge of other media and techniques to use, such as films and dramatic role-play.

Other Obligations of the Adult Guide

Before beginning bibliotherapy or including a particular book that may be used therapeutically in a collection, the adult guide has several additional obligations besides good timing and skillful listening. The first, which seems most obvious, is to read the book before including it in a collection or bibliotherapy program.

The adult guide will then apply many of the same criteria utilized in selecting books for this bibliography. What is the book's scope? Is it accurate, or does it contain information that should be clarified or corrected? What is its moral or religious viewpoint? Is it worthwhile as literature? These criteria are given in the Introduction.

After examining the book, it is then necessary to reflect on the intended audience, an audience that must be thoroughly understood before the adult guide can respond to the following questions: Is the book appropriate for the age, interests, and reading level of the audience? Will the book's length, format, or level of difficulty impede any possible gains? Is the book's content in keeping with the reader's general developmental life tasks, such as the teenager's need to develop independence from parents?

The adult guide's understanding of the young people using the books should include a knowledge of their reading levels and any unusual features in their backgrounds, such as physical handicaps, that require special materials. This would include the visually handicapped, who might need recordings or large-print books. Of course, those guides who know which books for young people are available in these forms and which have high interest-low vocabulary for problem readers are ahead of the game in making proper selections. While increased comprehension and improved speed may inadvertently take place during bibliotherapeutic reading, pressure for improvement is inappropriate.[63]

Beyond these questions, which pertain to all types of bibliotherapy, many areas of controversy pertain to the use of books that deal with loss, particularly with those that treat death. Many people ask: "Should books about death and other forms of loss be included among possible selections for children who have never themselves experienced loss? Shouldn't children be protected from pain as long as possible?" Children who have not experienced grief through death, divorce, or other separations can benefit from exposure to books on these themes. Although they are young and have not been bereaved themselves, in today's world it is probable that they have had contact with others—in school, around the neighborhood, or at home—who *have* had these experiences. Such children may have unspoken concerns and questions; reading books on themes of loss declares that it is acceptable to think about and discuss these matters. In addition, the inclusion of such books as possibilities for selection by anyone and everyone diminishes the mythical concept that children who have been bereaved may be abnormal. Instead, the inclusion reinforces a concept that is more true to life, that there are many styles of normal living that children experience on their way to maturity. Furthermore, the inclusion of books on themes of loss provides a framework for facing the problems, if necessary, at a future date. Children can look back on a vicarious experience and apply the material remembered to the reality that must now be faced.

Many other questions arise concerning books that deal with loss. It is incumbent on adults to include such books in a collection *only* after they have answered these questions with satisfaction.

Successful bibliotherapy is usually accomplished when guides themselves have a fairly good emotional adjustment to life. In keeping with their understanding of the difference between sympathy and empathy, such individuals are generally tolerant of other people's wishes, weaknesses, behavior patterns, and needs. When maximally effective, they usually also ask themselves questions about their own needs, ascertaining if they are genuinely motivated to help others or if they are acting from other less beneficial needs of their own. If guides respond to youngsters because of their own needs for power or because they themselves need emotional involvement with young people, the results are not likely to be successful. Success is more likely if guides care about people, can communicate that caring, and can read other people's communications, both verbal and nonverbal.

The most important question to ask is one that is asked of oneself. That is, have I come to reasonable terms with my own fears, distastes, and past experiences with loss? It is difficult to offer guidance unless one can examine one's own attitudes toward death and loss. One highly recommended way to bring about a confrontation with one's own predispositions is to arrange for small-group workshop discussions among adults who have like interests in using books to help children cope with loss. Reading some of the books proposed for a collection can provide the necessary spark for reflecting, questioning, and arguing until the adults in the group themselves come to terms with their own attitudes and values.

When adults participate in workshop discussions, a principle evolves that is crucial for the work with children that follows. That principle states that what is right for one person in one setting is not necessarily proper for another. Each person within the workshop offers unique and very individual responses to the hard-core issues that surface, and these responses must be respected. Some of the questions that might come up in a workshop include the following:

Is this book really most fit for the home and inappropriate for the school or library?

Might an adult guide using this book cause more problems than will be solved?

Might the book offend the childrens' families on religious or moral grounds? If so, what should be done?

Should a book on death and other forms of loss ever be read with a group, such as a class?

Could children who have not encountered loss be frightened by the book? Should they be protected from such insecurities?

On the contrary, should those who have encountered loss be protected from the book?

Should books on loss be graphic, as exemplified by a description of rigor mortis?

Whether adult guides reflect on these and other sticky questions alone or with the support of a workshop environment, if they can come out with confidence about the acceptability and appropriateness of their own responses, then individual growth can take place. It is this type of growth that can extend itself to help children.

Limitations of Bibliotherapy

As an art, bibliotherapy has many limitations. Many individuals are not inveterate readers. The help that those who don't approach books even occasionally might derive is, of course, minimal. Second, although many people are deeply affected by what they do read, there is little or no evidence indicating that all individuals are so swayed by reading material. Thus, possibilities for an imagined alliance with literary characters is greatly diminished.

In selecting materials for bibliotherapy, it is clear that personal tastes vary widely. In 1948, N. B. Smith conducted a study with children in which they were asked to name titles of books, stories, and poems that had influenced their lives.[64] Although two-thirds indicated alterations in attitude as a result of reading and one in ten felt that changes in behavior had taken place, with only one exception the books named by the children were totally diverse. This points up the fact that satisfaction and growth are indeed individual.

It becomes even more complex to select books when one realizes that it is a natural inclination for adult guides to inject their own tastes into what is made available. Often adult guides come from a different social class, professional role, and outlook from those of the readers they serve. As a result, a host of situations are seen from different eyes. The way in which adult guides view the world is likely to influence selection. At times, this is appropriate and desirable, for all of us tend to read material that reflects the nuances of our own lives. Reading that which we already are, we simply interpret the pages of the material with the background of our own experiences. Although we do seek out and become more involved in material related to our own personal experience, readers often ascribe values to characters that are actually not contained in the story, filling in with their own background.[65] In fact, when readers feel intensely about the material, the likelihood is greater that an inaccurate interpretation of the author's intent will occur. Thus, it is the case that we bring to reading material certain attitudes, and we utilize these to process the print. All too often the words can become what we want them to be.

It is dangerous to rely on books too much. Reading cannot solve all problems, and at times it can reinforce fears, add to defenses, and foster rationalization in place of action. Instead, it may be wiser to enjoy books merely for their own sake. Lucy Warner explains: "By expecting too much of books, bibliotherapists may paradoxically be diminishing their importance. Books can provide pleasure and emotional release, bring about insights, and foster new understandings, but they are not a bad influence if they stir up violent feelings. They do not fail if they cannot change a person's score on a psychological test or change his or her behavior. In fact, it is a credit to the human spirit that it resists such flagrant propagandizing."[66]

If attitudes and behavior are molded in part by reading material, then it can at times be beneficial for adult guides to bring varying viewpoints to readers, thus providing material that might counter and broaden already established opinions. But it is incumbent on the guides to be aware that readers may become less involved and may even shun the material that would serve to broaden them. Guides should also realize that such children are merely doing what human beings of all ages everywhere tend to do, even the guides themselves. When one adds to this that behavioral changes are not always easily seen by observers and attitudinal alterations are not easily or accurately measured by use of standard measurement techniques, it is evident that the selection and success of bibliotherapy are often matters of chance.

After problems of self-examination, book selection, timing, discussion and limitations are acknowledged and taken into account, the adult guide must meet one final obligation. That is maintaining the conviction that bibliotherapy is merely one component of a mental hygiene program. It is of utmost importance to keep a vigilant reminder of that fact, so that neither adults nor children begin to believe, even for a moment, that reading will magically solve problems or that insight gained from reading and discussion will replace the active work that is necessary to overcome personal difficulties.

Notes

1. Mildred Moody and Hilda Limper, Association of Hospital and Institutional Libraries, *Bibliotherapy: Methods and Materials* (American Library Association, 1971), p. 7.
2. Sister Miriam Schultheis, *A Guidebook for Bibliotherapy* (Psychotechnics, 1972), p. 6.
3. Carter Good, *Dictionary of Education* (McGraw-Hill, 1969), p. 58.
4. *Webster's Third New International Dictionary* (Merriam, 1966), p. 212.
5. Rhea Rubin, "Uses of Bibliotherapy in Response to the 1970s," *Library Trends* 28 (Fall 1979): 242.
6. Ibid., p. 241.
7. Ibid.
8. Ruth Churchyard, "Bibliotherapy: What's That?" *Australian School Librarian* 15 (Autumn 1978): 9.
9. Evalene P. Jackson, "Reading Guidance: A Tentative Approach to Theory," *Library Trends* 11 (October 1962): 99.
10. Ruth Tews, "Bibliotherapy," *Library Trends* 2 (October 1962): 97–105.
11. David Russell and Caroline Shrodes, "Contributions of Research in Bibliotherapy to the Language Arts Program," *The School Review* 58 (September 1950): 335–347.
12. Philip J. Weimerskirsh, "Benjamin Rush and John Minson Galt II, Pioneers of Bibliotherapy in America," *Bulletin of the Medical Library Association* 53 (October 1965): 510–513.
13. Samuel McChord Crothers, "A Literary Clinic," *Atlantic Monthly* (August 1916): 291.
14. Elizabeth Pomeroy, "Bibliotherapy—A Study in Results of Hospital Library Service," *Medical Bulletin of the Veterans Administration* 13 (April 1937): 360–364.
15. Salomon Gagnon, "Is Reading Therapy?" *Diseases of the Nervous System* 3 (July 1942).
16. Artemisia J. Junier, "Bibliotherapy: Projects and Studies with the Mentally Ill Patient," *Library Trends* 2 (October 1962): 136–146.
17. Ruth Tews, ed., *Library Trends* 2 (October 1962).
18. W. K. Beatty, "A Historical Review of Bibliotherapy," *Library Trends* 2 (October 1962): 106–117.
19. Margaret Hannigan and William Henderson, "Narcotics Addicts Take Up Reading," *The Bookmark* 22 (July 1963): 281–284.
20. Leena Sippola, "Parantavakirja" (A Healing Book), *Kirjastolenti* 71 (1978): 330–334.
21. Rubin, "Uses of Bibliotherapy," pp. 239–240.
22. Ibid., p. 242.
23. Ibid., pp. 243–245.
24. Ibid.

25. Ibid., p. 248.
26. J. Webster, "Using Books to Reduce Fears of First Grade Children," *The Reading Teacher* 14 (January 1961): 159–162.
27. William L. Mikulas and others, "Behavioral Bibliotherapy and Games for Testing Fear of the Dark," *Child and Family Behavior Therapy* 7 (Fall 1985): 1–7.
28. Robert C. Newhouse, "Generalized Fear Reduction in Second-Grade Children," *Psychology in the Schools* 24 (January 1987): 48–50.
29. John Sheridan, Stanley Baker, and Vladimir de Lissovoy, "Structured Group Counseling and Explicit Bibliotherapy as In-School Strategies for Preventing Problems in Youth of Changing Families," *School Counselor* 32 (November 1984): 134–141.
30. Terry Connor and others, "Making a Life Story Book," *Adoption and Fostering* 9 (2): 32–35; 46.
31. E. P. Jackson, "Effects of Reading upon Attitudes toward the Negro Race," *Library Quarterly* 14 (1944): 47–54.
32. John Litcher and David W. Johnson, "Changes in Attitudes toward Negroes of White Elementary School Students after Use of Multi-ethnic Readers," *Journal of Educational Psychology* 60 (April 1969): 148–152.
33. R. H. Tauron, "The Influences of Reading on the Attitudes of Third Graders toward Eskimos" (Ph.D. diss., University of Maryland, 1967).
34. F. L. Fisher, "The Influences of Reading and Discussion on the Attitudes of Fifth Graders toward American Indians" (Ph.D. diss., University of California, Berkeley, 1965).
35. Jackson, "Effects of Reading"; Litcher and Johnson, "Changes in Attitudes"; Tauron, "The Influences of Reading on the Attitudes of Third Graders"; Fisher, "The Influences of Reading and Discussion on the Attitudes of Fifth Graders."
36. Tauron, "The Influences of Reading on the Attitudes of Third Graders."
37. D. W. Biskin and K. Hoskisson, "An Experimental Test of the Effects of Structured Discussions of Moral Dilemmas Found in Children's Literature on Moral Reasoning" (paper presented at the annual meeting of the American Educational Research Association, Washington, D.C., 1975).
38. Dorrie Prouty, "Read about Death? Not Me!" *Language Arts* 53 (September 1976): 679–682.
39. David Gerald Jarmon, "Differential Effectiveness of Rational-Emotive Therapy, Bibliotherapy, and Attention-Placebo in the Treatment of Speech Anxiety" (Ph.D. diss., Southern Illinois University, 1972).
40. Churchyard, "Bibliotherapy," pp. 12–13.
41. Barbara Lenkowsky and Ronald Lenkowsky, "Bibliotherapy for the LD Adolescent," *Academic Therapy* 14 (November 1978): 179–185.
42. Lucy Warner, "The Myth of Bibliotherapy," *School Library Journal* 27 (October 1980): 108.
43. Anne Marrelli, "Bibliotherapy and School Anxiety in Young Children" (Ph.D. diss., University of Southern California, 1979).
44. Warner, "The Myth of Bibliotherapy," pp. 107–110.
45. Nina Bawden, "Through the Dark Wood." In Harrison, Barbara, and Gregory Maguire, compilers and editors. *Innocence and Experience: Essays and Conversations on Children's Literature* (Lothrop, Lee and Shepard, 1987), p. 67.

46. Abraham Maslow, "A Theory of Human Motivation," *Psychological Review* 50 (July 1943): 370–396.
47. Gilbert Kliman, *The Psychological Emergencies of Childhood* (Grune & Stratton, 1968).
48. Russell and Shrodes, "Contributions of Research in Bibliotherapy."
49. Rubin, "Uses of Bibliotherapy," p. 250.
50. Moody and Limper, *Bibliotherapy: Methods and Materials,* pp. 15–16.
51. Doris Robinson, "A Bibliotherapy Program with Special Education Students," *Top of the News* 36 (Winter 1980): 189–193.
52. H. Elser, "Bibliotherapy in Practice," *Library Trends* 30 (Spring 1982): 647–659.
53. J. Bodart, "Bibliotherapy: The Right Book for the Right Person at the Right Time— and More," *Top of the News* 36 (Winter 1980): 183. Reprinted with permission of the American Library Association; copyright © 1980 by ALA.
54. Nancie Atwell, *Side By Side: Essays on Teaching to Learn* (Heinemann, 1991), p. 58.
55. Margaret Hannigan, "Counseling and Bibliotherapy for the General Reader," in *Reading Guidance and Bibliotherapy in Public Hospital and Institution Libraries,* ed. Margaret Monroe (Madison: Library School, University of Wisconsin, 1971), pp. 45–50.
56. Patricia Cianciolo, "Children's Literature Can Affect Coping Behavior," *Personnel and Guidance Journal* 43 (May 1965): 897–903.
57. Paula Christman. "When Guilt Goes with Grief," *Catholic Digest* (February 1993), pp. 118–120.
58. Moody and Limper, *Bibliotherapy: Methods and Materials,* p. 18.
59. Atwell, *Side by Side*, p. 60.
60. Ibid.
61. Norman Paul, "Psychiatry, Its Role in the Resolution of Grief," in *Death and Bereavement,* ed. Austin Kutscher (Charles C. Thomas, 1969), p. 187. Reprinted with the permission of the publisher.
62. Thomas Newkirk with Patricia McLure. *Listening In: Children Talk About Books* (Heinemann, 1992), pp. 120–121.
63. Edward G. Haldeman and Sandra Idstein. *Bibliotherapy* (Univ. Press of America, 1979), p. 12.
64. N. B. Smith, "Personal and Social Values of Reading," *Elementary English* 25 (December 1948): 490–500.
65. A. C. Purves and R. Beach, *Literature and the Reader,* final report to the National Endowment for the Humanities (National Council of Teachers of English, 1972).
66. Warner, "The Myth of Bibliotherapy," p. 110.

PART II

Reading about Separation and Loss: An Annotated Bibliography

3

Typical Childhood Encounters with Loss

Accepting a New Sibling/Sibling Rivalry

Children who gain a new sibling also suffer a loss. They lose their established place in the family, that of only child or youngest child, or perhaps that of only boy or only girl. Especially in the former cases, they may also lose the special enjoyment of being the apple of everyone's eye. All youngsters, no matter what their position in the family, lose much of the parental attention they have heretofore taken for granted when a new sibling arrives on the scene. The anger, fears, guilt, and depression aroused are part of the mourning for what once was and now can never be again.

Even well after the birth of a new baby, sibling interaction can continue to involve feelings of loss: of parental attention, of self-esteem (especially from the perspective of the younger sibling), and of control that accompanies sibling rivalry. Books that offer solace and coping strategies are helpful. The most effective books refrain from caricaturing or stereotyping any of the characters, and from pat, unrealistic endings. They demonstrate a respect for each child's feelings and an understanding of different siblings' perspectives.

1. Adler, C. S. *The Lump in the Middle*. Clarion, 1989 (0-89919-869-4). 160 pp. Fiction.

    Interest level: Ages 9–12

Kelsey is resentful of her place in the family. She calls herself "the lump in the middle." Her older sister is perfect in their parents' eyes; her younger sister is charming and favored by everyone. Kelsey's mother does seem to treat her unfairly, but in the end Kelsey begins to understand her mother's perspective and even starts to behave in a way that makes her mother deal with her more sympathetically. The middle child's position is frequently a difficult one, and this book amply exemplifies that situation.

2. Adoff, Arnold. *Hard to Be Six*. Illus. by Cheryl Hanna. Lothrop, 1991 (0-688-09013-3). 32 pp. Picture book.

   Interest level: Ages 4–8

A six-year-old boy, growing up in a loving, extended, biracial family, finds it difficult to tolerate not being as able and competent as his ten-year-old sister. At her birthday party, he can't pin the tail on the appropriate anatomical part of the donkey. He's messier than she is. And he can't even reach the pedals on her two-wheeler or see out the window of the car when they go for a ride. She does not tease him or deliberately set out to make him unhappy, urging him to look at the things he *can* do for himself, but he suffers from his own perceived shortcomings nevertheless. Other family members try to reassure him that he is growing up, providing him with such palpable proof as his old sneakers that he has outgrown. His grandmother points out the muscle in his arm. It is only when she takes him to the cemetery and reminds him of his deceased grandfather's philosophy of taking time slowly and making it count by passing love on that he becomes a little more resigned to his place in the developmental scheme of things.

3. Anholt, Catherine. *Aren't You Lucky!* Illus. by the author. Little, Brown, 1991 (0-316-04264-1). 32 pp. Picture book.

   Interest level: Ages 4–7

When a little girl learns that her mother is expecting a baby, although her family assures her that she should feel fortunate, she doesn't feel particularly lucky. She is bored waiting for the baby to be born and is much more interested in her own activities. When the baby arrives, she can't understand what the fuss is all about. Although most of the time she is pleased to share her parents' attention, there are times she feels left out, such as when her mother is breast feeding. She tries lots of coping strategies, begging her mother to play with her or trying to entertain her brother. When he cries during his bath, she and her father snuggle together to read. Finally the parents utilize the girl's skills as a care giver, which makes her feel rewarded and important. She is gratified when people say that it is the baby brother who is the lucky one. The whimsical illustrations make this story about a common situation lively and engaging. There's no magical ending, and just taking care of the baby doesn't release the elder sibling from her problems with the baby. But a collaborative solution is modeled and the family is presented as well-meaning and recognizable.

4. Arnold, Eric H., and Jeffrey Loeb, eds. *I'm Telling: Kids Talk about Brothers and Sisters.* Illus. by G. Brian Karas. Little, Brown, 1987. o.p. 160 pp. Nonfiction.

Interest level: Ages 8–13

The producers of a National Public Radio children's issues show have put together preteens' taped observations about family life from the radio program "Hole in the Sock" and presented it with all its natural humor, pathos, and idiosyncratic wisdom. The editors hardly interject at all; their words only appear in a brief introduction alerting children to read the book for guidance or for curiosity's sake. Chapters cover such issues as family position, negatives and positives, jealousies and competition, tattling, sharing rooms, and good times. The book also ventures into such special spheres as being an only child or becoming part of a stepfamily. It's all very exuberant and, with next to no changes by the editors, childlike, filled with normal kids who trick their sibs with fibs, bribe them, look up to them and down on them, and otherwise do very normal brother-sister things. The full range of life's experience is here, and on balance, being part of a family is very enjoyable, as this book is too.

Genuine and down-to-earth, this reassuring book is likely to get passed around from child to child and occasionally brought to a parent with a plaintive plea for change or a self-justifying "I told you so."

5. Asch, Frank, and Vladimir Vagin. *Dear Brother.* Illus. by the authors. Scholastic, 1992 (0-590-43107-2). Unpaged. Picture book.

Interest level: Ages 5–10

Joey and Marvin, two mouse brothers, discover some old letters in the attic while their mother is getting rid of unwanted old "stuff." The mother tosses out two portraits and other things, but the boys take the letters and stay up all night to read them. It turns out that the letters are a correspondence between the boys' great-great-granduncles Henry and Timothy. Joey and Marvin—whose general mode of relating to each other is to banter and call each other names and whose styles of behavior are very different from each other—are so touched by the love evidenced between the brothers in their letters that they retrieve the portraits and feel much fonder of each other. The great-great-granduncles' letters demonstrate not only their love for each other, but also their differences and the problems they have resolving them. They finally accept each other's life-styles and ways of looking at the world, and they maintain their correspondence until they are both old. One lives in the city and the other in the country, but their bond is strong. The book is a lovely model of accepting differences and affirming affection between siblings.

6. Bode, Janet. *Truce: Ending the Sibling War*. Watts, 1991 (0-531-15221-9). 144 pp. Nonfiction.

Interest level: Age 12+

About one fourth of the siblings the author interviewed revealed that their relationships with their siblings were violently negative, even to the point of being dangerous. In this book, aimed at those youngsters whose sibling relations are causing crises, teenagers report on their problems with siblings. For some of them, particularly because their parents feel helpless to intervene, the situations are intolerable and will only be resolved when the siblings are separated or when they grow up and move away. The author recommends that youngsters who are having serious problems with their siblings first work on their self-esteem, then try to "rework the family script." Perhaps the most beneficial advice is to find support and resources outside the family. A list of resources and suggested readings is provided.

7. Bogart, Jo Ellen. *Daniel's Dog*. Illus. by Janet Wilson. Scholastic, 1990 (0-590-43402-0). 32 pp. Picture book.

Interest level: Ages 5–7

Daniel, a bright and affectionate member of an African-American family, feels displaced when his sister is born. To help himself cope with his feelings, he invents Lucy, an imaginary dog with whom he plays and for whom he is special. Daniel's mother understands his feelings and includes him in many of the activities the baby requires, such as holding the baby after she has eaten, reading to his mother and the baby, and singing to the baby while she waits for their mother to change her diaper. His mother shows her appreciation and is very affectionate to both Daniel and the baby. The imaginary animal is never an obsession; Daniel engages in many other play activities. But it is a way of handling his negative feelings, and he is wise enough to recommend an imaginary animal to his friend Norman when Norman expresses anxiety over the imminent business trip his father has to take. The endearing illustrations realistically and affectionately capture the sense of unity in the family. Daniel and his mother and sister are African American; Norman is Asian American; no father appears in the pictures or the text.

8. Brisson, Pat. *Your Best Friend, Kate*. Illus. by Rick Brown. Bradbury, 1989 (0-02-714350-3). 40 pp. Fiction.

Interest level: Ages 7–10

Kate and her brother, Brian, bicker endlessly, causing their parents considerable distress. Their extended automobile tour through 11 states does nothing to alleviate the siblings' arguments. When Brian decides to stay for a visit at their aunt's house, Kate writes a note letting him know that

she cares about him and that his feelings are important to her. The reader
has no doubt that the two siblings really do love each other.

9. Brown, Marc. *Arthur's Baby*. Illus. by the author. Little, Brown,
   1987 (0-316-11007-8); pap. (0-316-11074-4). 32 pp. Fiction.

   Interest level: Ages 4–7

Although Arthur would prefer the surprise to be a bicycle, the fact is that
his parents are going to have a baby. Arthur has enough trouble coping
with his younger sister, D.W., but his parents and D.W. are thrilled.
Arthur's friends warn him about the problems of an infant, including the
noise, the odor, and the infringement on Arthur's free time.

When the baby comes, Arthur is still not delighted. He is reluctant to
have anything to do with the baby until one day the baby starts to cry and
no one can stop her. Then Arthur holds the baby so that she burps, and she
is happy again.

The ending is predictable: Arthur is the instrument of the baby's satisfaction. The burp is an amusing surprise. The illustrations and the dialogue between Arthur and the other characters make this a sibling book
that stands out above the rest.

10. Buckley, Helen E. *"Take Care of Things," Edward Said*. Illus. by
    Katherine Coville. Lothrop, 1991, LB (0-688-07732-3). Unpaged.
    Picture book.

    Interest level: Ages 3–6

When Edward goes off to school, his younger brother, Tom, misses him
dreadfully. As the school bus pulls away, Tom calls wistfully, "Don't go,
Edward . . ." Edward tells Tom to "take care of things" while he is gone.
His parents go to work, and Tom manages to occupy his time, chatting
with the swings and taking his bike for a ride. His babysitter suggests he
take care of the pets and compliments him on the parade of stuffed animals he sets up in Edward's room. Finally, it is time for Tom's lunch and
nap. He fears that he has not "taken care of things"; his babysitter, a nurturing and accepting older woman, assures him that he has managed well.
When the school bus returns, the brothers have a joyous reunion. This
book is an example of a tender, loving sibling relationship.

11. Bulla, Clyde Robert. *The Christmas Coat*. Illus. by Sylvie
    Wickstrom. Knopf, 1989 (0-394-89385-9). 48 pp. Picture book.

    Interest level: Ages 7–10

Hans and Otto continuously and needlessly fight with each other. Despite
their mother's importuning, and perhaps exacerbated by the fact that their
father has recently died, the two boys seem able to agree on absolutely

nothing. Finally their mother separates them from each other by drawing a line down the middle of their room. Each is forbidden to cross the line into the other's section of the room. One day, without permission, they open a box and find a handsome coat. They fight over whose it will be, and inadvertently tear the coat in two. Much to their dismay, they discover that the coat was a Christmas gift for their next-door neighbor, so they work together to have the coat repaired. They finally come to the awareness that they have been hurting their beloved and generous mother and that their fighting must cease. Although the story is not quite realistic, it is, nevertheless, a well-told parable that makes its point in an entertaining manner.

   12. Cole, Joanna. *The New Baby at Your House.* Photos by Hella
       Hammid. Morrow, 1985 (0-688-05806-X); pap. (0-688-07418-9). 48
       pp. Nonfiction.
       Interest level: Ages 3–7

Preparing for life with a new baby is sensitively handled here. In a full, detailed note to parents is the warning "a parent's job is not to 'fix things' so the negative feelings will go away and everyone will be happy all the time." Rather, it's to acknowledge the scope of feelings, make siblings feel included, and allow time for adjustment. The note gets down to helpful specifics, for example, "Experts urge parents to say good-bye to their children before they leave for the hospital, even if it means waking them up to do so." The note also recommends pressing for sibling visits in hospitals through intercession by the doctor or midwife.

   The children's portion of the book has large black-and-white photos showing several families of varying races. There are few words on each page. The process is laid out chronologically, from siblings "talking" to the baby in the uterus, to visits in the hospital, to picking up Mommy there. It immediately becomes apparent that siblings are involved with the pregnancy at every point. The observations of siblings are a strong focus, such as the still-attached umbilical cord and infants' initial lack of tears. The emphasis is on fascination with development and becoming an active scientific participant in what is observed—for example, seeing baby's sucking capacity firsthand with a clean sibling finger. This aspect of being participants distinguishes Cole's book from others in the field, where children are merely encouraged to be helpers.

   The emotional sphere is not left out, however, as children's jealousies and angers are expressed and parents make time for explanations, reassurances, and time with the sibling alone. The book shows good modeling for a family where "love can grow as big as it has to." An excellent job.

13. Corey, Dorothy. *Will There Be a Lap for Me?* Illus. by Nancy Poydar. Whitman, 1992, LB (0-8075-9109-2). Unpaged. Picture book.

Interest level: Ages 4–6

Kyle grows increasingly unhappy as his mother's lap grows increasingly less accessible, due to the fact that she is going to have a baby and her swelling abdomen makes for less and less lap space. Kyle's father, grandmother, and baby-sitter try to provide substitutes, but they are not acceptable to him. Even after the birth of baby Matt, Kyle's mother's lap is unavailable because she is so busy with the new baby. One day, when the baby is asleep, Kyle's mother invites him to do a project just with her and then sit in her lap while they watch a bird at the feeder. All is again right in Kyle's world. The story models realistic accommodations to new infants while making time and space available for elder siblings. The family is shown as African American.

14. Dorris, Michael. *Morning Girl.* Hyperion, 1992, LB (1-56282-285-3). 74 pp. Fiction.

Interest level: Age 8+

Although Morning Girl and Star Boy are siblings, they are very different from each other in temperament, interest, and behavior. They are both part of a tightly knit community of Tainos, whose main values include hospitality, courtesy, and cooperation. The setting is the Bahamas in the late fifteenth century. Star Boy and Morning Girl take turns telling their story, a chapter each at a time. Readers get to know the siblings and the entire family very well over the course of the book. The sibling relationship is central to the action, as is the birth of a new baby sister. The perspective of both siblings is reasonably and effectively conveyed. The children are sometimes naughty, sometimes angry, often sensitive and reflective. They help readers to see how, although they are so different, they are each talented, intelligent, and worthy. It is, therefore, all the more painful when, at the end, the reader realizes that Columbus and his men are landing on the island, and that this means the end of life for Star Boy, Morning Girl, and their entire community.

15. Dragonwagon, Crescent. *I Hate My Brother Harry.* Illus. by Dick Gackenbach. Harper, 1983. o.p. 32 pp. Fiction.

Interest level: Ages 3–8

The little girl who narrates this story vividly describes her brother's teasing and practical jokes. She reiterates how much she hates him and provides evidence for the validity of her feelings. Harry truly is a big tease, but he can also be tender and thoughtful. The little girl realizes this and wishes he were like that all of the time. She does have hope, however, because he responds positively to her question about whether he wants to be friends.

This story is unusual because it is told from the perspective of the younger, rather than the older, sibling. Both elder and younger siblings will empathize with the characters while they are chuckling over the diabolical ways Harry dreams up to torment his little sister.

16. Edelman, Elaine. *I Love My Baby Sister (Most of the Time)*. Illus. by Wendy Watson. Puffin, 1985, pap. (0-14-050547-5). 32 pp. Fiction.

 Interest level: Ages 4–7

In this amiable book, the older sister fully understands the positive and negative features of having a baby sister in the house. For the most part, the older sister can tolerate the baby's yanking of hair, nose grabbing, and lack of speech. She also knows how to attract her mother's attention when the baby is receiving too much of it. All in all, the entire family, including the parents, is actively involved in the nurturing and the management of the family's activities.

Watson's illustrations contribute enormously to the appeal of the book. A sense of affable mess pervades each picture. Clothing, toys, food, and household utensils are strewn around the house; leaves and pebbles clutter the outdoors. The overall effect is that of a busy, informal life-style in which people matter much more than things and neatness is not the primary goal.

17. Galbraith, Kathryn O. *Roommates and Rachel*. Illus. by Mark Graham. Macmillan, 1991 (0-689-50520-5). 42 pp. Fiction.

 Interest level: Ages 5–8

Although the focus is on the two older sisters' responses to baby Rachel's arrival, the story tells of the entire family's accommodation to the birth of the baby. The parents are busier than ever, but Daddy manages to help the two older girls bake holiday cookies. Mommy is tired and somewhat irritable (though not at all abusive), and she consents to bring the new baby to the girls' classrooms for special sharing time. The baby is a big hit, and the older girls become somewhat more reconciled to her presence, especially when they learn how to comfort and amuse her. The picture here is of a family somewhat harassed by the new arrival but able to cope with the extra work and increased pressure because of their loving feelings for each other.

18. Greenwald, Sheila. *Alvin Webster's Surefire Plan for Success (and How It Failed)*. Illus. by the author. Little, Brown, 1987 (0-316-32706-9); Pocket Books, pap. (0-671-67239-8). 95 pp. Fiction.

Interest level: Ages 9–12

Alvin's parents are going to have a new baby, and Alvin is jealous and anxious about it. His parents are eager for him to love and want the baby. They show Alvin the ultrasound of his soon-to-be baby brother, and they place the picture on the bulletin board next to Alvin's math test. Alvin's parents give him all sorts of books on how to be a big brother. They also go off to take a birthing and parenting course.

Alvin is in the gifted program at school, and he is very competitive, as are his parents, particularly his mother. She wants him to be the best in everything he does. When Alvin is assigned to tutor a child in math, he determines to be the best tutor of all. He learns a lot from Bone, the child he tutors, because Bone is happy with himself and doesn't even mind an occasional failure.

Everything Alvin does turns into an occasion for intellectual analysis. Thus, he writes a book about how to be a tutor. Bone is upset when he sees the book because he feels that Alvin has dehumanized and exploited him. By the end of the story, Alvin hasn't exactly reformed, but he is much more comfortable with the idea of possible failure. His parents have become somewhat more open as well.

Greenwald pokes fun at parents who go about the process of parenting intellectually rather than intuitively. She also implies that gifted children are anxious and competitive. On the other hand, she portrays Bone as a character who is very talented and bright, but whose values are more cooperative and style more easygoing. Bone's mother is as delighted with his ability to draw birds as are Alvin's parents about his grades. One wonders if, in the end, both sets of parents aren't more alike than different. Alvin is given a guinea pig to care for so that he may experience firsthand a process analogous to parenting. It works. He understands what it means to accept and love a creature no matter what it looks like or what its talents are. The story is humorous, and the reader is interested in what happens to the characters. There may even be some lessons to be learned here.

19. Havill, Juanita. *Jamaica Tag-Along*. Illus. by Anne Sibley O'Brien. Houghton, 1990 (0-395-49602-0); pap. (0-395-54949-3). Unpaged. Picture book.

Interest level: Ages 5–8

Jamaica thinks it's very unfair that her older brother, Ossie, doesn't permit her to play basketball with him and his friends, especially because one of the boys who is allowed to play is shorter than she is. When, in her disappointment, she goes alone to the adjoining sandlot and starts to play in the sand, she is annoyed by a little boy who wants to play with her. She suddenly realizes that she is treating the boy as her brother treats her, so she welcomes the boy into her play. Ossie drifts over after he is finished playing with his friends and joins the two younger children. Jamaica magnanimously permits him to play. The dilemma of the younger sibling's always wanting to be with the older one is well portrayed here from both perspectives. The solution is a reasonable and equitable one. All of the characters except for one of Ossie's friends are people of color. The illustrations add to the feeling tone of the plot.

20. Hazen, Barbara Shook. *If It Weren't for Benjamin (I'd Always Get to Lick the Icing Spoon).* Illus. by Laura Hartman. Human Sciences, 1979 (0-87705-384-7); pap. (0-89885-172-6). 32 pp. Fiction.
    Interest level: Ages 3–6

Told from the perspective of the younger brother, this book explores the child's feelings about his relationship with his older brother, Benjamin. He is jealous of Benjamin's prowess and position in the family. He fears that he is not loved as much as his brother, but his parents and grandmother reassure him of their love. They all explain to him that it is not necessary for him to be and do the same as his brother; he is loved for who and what he is.

The child is also helped to respond appropriately to his negative feelings. He learns to channel his anger into constructive actions, such as kicking a ball. He learns to deal with his frustration at being excluded from Benjamin's games by inviting over a friend of his own. And he learns to savor the rare times when he beats Benjamin in a game, rather than sulking over losing most of the time.

This book is helpful in showing children ways to defuse their negative feelings while acknowledging their validity. It is also helpful to see that both older and younger siblings have problems. The book also shows that younger siblings are entitled to their own point of view.

21. Hendrickson, Karen. *Getting Along Together: Baby and I Can Play.* Illus. by Marina Megale. Parenting, 1985. o.p. 23 pp. Nonfiction.
    Interest level: Ages 3–7

The narrator of this book speaks directly to older siblings in a respectful and informative tone. The book celebrates the importance of older brothers and sisters, acknowledges both their positive and negative feelings, and recommends specific activities for older children to do in response to their negative feelings. It also presents some excellent ideas for how to play with babies when the older children are in the mood to do so.

The activities progress from such relatively passive ones as playing where the baby can see the older child to cuddling and stroking, picking things up that the baby drops, playing peek-a-boo with toys and people, and crawling and chasing. The author wisely recommends thinking ahead to when parents are too busy to attend to the older children. Hendrickson recommends that older children create a special box of items to play with and do while their mother is nursing the baby. She discusses a number of negative feelings and how to handle them, ending with the assurance that the baby is lucky to have such a special and important older brother or sister.

Included at the back of the book is a set of notes to parents to guide them in the use of this book and to help them with the issue of sibling relationships in general.

22. Hest, Amy. *The Mommy Exchange.* Illus. by DyAnne DiSalvo-Ryan. Macmillan, 1988 (0-02-743650-0); pap. (0-689-71450-5). 32 pp. Fiction.

Interest level: Ages 4–7

Jessica thinks that Jason's house is infinitely preferable to hers, and Jason feels that way about Jessica's. Jessica has twin siblings, toddlers who seem to dominate her household. Jason's house is quiet and orderly. Both Jason and Jessica are angry and impatient with their mothers. They decide to arrange an exchange, one in which fathers will be permitted to visit, but not mothers. They view the exchange as a permanent one, although their parents, who go along with the idea, assure them that they will be welcomed back when they decide to come home.

Of course, it turns out that neither child is happy away from home and that they prefer their own mother's style of managing and nurturing. The child's perspective is clearly transmitted, but the resolution is not as convincing as it could be. The sibling relationship is never resolved, and, as a matter of fact, it turns out that Jason's potential problems are about to begin because his mother is pregnant with twins. The book is amusing and well illustrated and could be the spark for children's discussions of their family's life-style and their methods for coping with younger siblings.

23. Lakin, Patricia. *Don't Touch My Room.* Illus. by Patience Brewster. Little, Brown, 1988 (0-316-51230-3); pap. (0-316-51228-1). 32 pp. Fiction.

Interest level: Ages 4–8

Aaron's room is being torn apart and redone because his parents are expecting a new baby. Aaron is not happy about the new baby or his room change. It seems as if he is no longer in control of his world. He tells people not to touch his things, but they do anyway. He still has some misgivings after his new room is all ready, but it has a special small compartment that he loves. Into this compartment, he puts his treasures.

After the baby, Benji, is born, Aaron relies increasingly on the sanctuary of his secret compartment. Benji has displaced him, and Aaron feels most secure in his own special place. After a number of months, Benji grows old enough to get into mischief and to have people call him a bad boy. Now it is Aaron who comes to his brother's defense, and, ultimately, he rescues Benji from being punished by bringing him into the security of his secret place.

Aaron progresses through the sequence of "Don't touch my room" to "Don't touch my things" to "Don't touch my baby." His parents don't seem to understand either of their children's feelings at any point in the book. They summarily override their children's wishes and contribute to the children's sense of displacement. They appear to be well-meaning but inept. Perhaps they can serve as examples of what not to do when expecting a baby.

The story is told from a decidedly childlike perspective, and young children will probably identify with Aaron. The author does not make the mistake of having Aaron's negative feelings suddenly disappear. It takes quite a while before Aaron considers his baby brother a suitable companion. He takes on the protector's role in a believable way. The book is filled with humor. The illustrations show us the specifics of the children's many wonderful possessions as well as capturing the feelings of the youngsters.

24. Lakin, Patricia. *Oh, Brother.* Illus. by Patience Brewster. Little, Brown, 1987. o.p. 32 pp. Fiction.

Interest level: Ages 4–8

Aaron, who was introduced in *Don't Touch My Room*, is now eight years old, and he is still resentful of Benji, his younger brother, who is now three. Benji gets lots of attention and special favors, while Aaron is expected to be responsible for himself now. Even when Aaron tries to behave like a three-year-old, it doesn't work out well for him. His attentive parents respond to his unpleasant feelings by once again rearranging his room. This time, they build him a treehouse bed and provide him with a space for his work. When Benji is frightened by Aaron's stories of monsters, Aaron invites his younger brother to join him in bed, and he reassures him that there are no monsters lurking.

Lakin is well aware that sibling rivalry does not end with the adjustment of the older sibling to the baby. It is an issue that must be confronted in an ongoing manner. This family tackles the situation with a change of environment. It works for them, and it may provide a solution for some readers as well.

25. Lasky, Kathryn. In the words of Maxwell B. Knight. *A Baby for Max*. Photos by Christopher G. Knight. Aladdin, 1987, pap. (0-689-71118-2). 48 pp. Nonfiction.

Interest level: Ages 3–7

This book is the story of Max Knight, a five-year-old child whose mother is going to have a baby. The story is told in Max's own words, with the text written by his mother and the photos taken by his father.

The book is an excellent presentation of the "new baby" issue. It can serve as a model for both the adjusting child and the parents expecting their second child. Max is involved with his sibling's arrival from the start. He goes to the doctor with his mother, visits the hospital where she will have the baby, is given a lesson by the nurse on how to diaper the baby, visits other newborns in the hospital nursery and helps his father make a changing table. All of these activities involve Max in the birth of the baby, provide him with a sense of his own importance, and show him how he can help the family.

Max's experience is related in realistic language easily understood by the young child. He talks to the baby through his mother's belly button. When he accompanies his mother to the doctor, he hears the baby's heartbeat, which he describes as being like the "ocean water washing and somebody hammering and fish splashing."

Although the book focuses on his excitement, Max's apprehension and resentment about his new sibling are also shown. On the day the baby is born, Max is happy at first, but he becomes sad later in the day because his parents are not there and because of all the excitement the new baby's arrival has caused. After the baby has been home for a few days, Max tells about his anger because people are not paying enough attention to him. When his mother shows him how to zip the baby into the carrying sack, Max wonders if, after they zip the baby into the sack, they could sell it.

Max looks forward to when the baby will be old enough to play with him. Although he sees and acknowledges his feelings of anger and jealousy, Max often reminds himself of the things he is able to do that the baby cannot.

The photographs add to the book's realistic nature. By reading this book, children are helped to understand that feelings of jealousy and misplacement are normal.

26. Little, Jean. *Revenge of the Small Small.* Illus. by Janet Wilson. Viking, 1992 (0-670-84471-3). Unpaged. Picture book.

Interest level: Ages 4–7

Patsy hates being the youngest. Her brothers and sister tease her endlessly, even though she brings them special treats when they are sick. When Patsy has chicken pox, they do not reciprocate. Her father brings her a box filled with art supplies to use as she recovers. Her siblings suggest things she should create, but Patsy has her own ideas. She spends hours creating a village, complete with a library, a church, and a cemetery whose graves bear the names of her siblings. As she becomes more absorbed in her task and less concerned with her siblings, they gradually begin to appreciate Patsy's attentions. They finally each make a special gesture to Patsy to show their love. Patsy agonizes about putting her siblings' names on the gravestones. Her father acknowledges her frustrations and Patsy manages to assuage everyone's feelings in the end.

27. McCully, Emily Arnold. *New Baby.* Illus. by the author. Harper, 1988. o.p. 32 pp. Fiction.

Interest level: Ages 3–6

In this wordless picture book, children can see themselves in the next-to-youngest member of the mouse family's reaction to the newborn baby mouse. Nothing the mouse child does distracts others' attention from the baby. Even behaving like a baby doesn't work. Finally, with the help of a loving older sibling and the discovery of some interest in the baby, the jealous sibling is permitted to help with the baby and the household returns to normal.

The images of this busy family are cheerfully depicted, and the jealous older sibling is never in terrible trouble, even when she runs off to be by herself (to a spot where she can see but not be seen). The amiability of the family augurs well for the harmony of the family to be restored. Again, including the older siblings in the care and feeding of the newborn is a good way to dispel negative feelings. Young children will enjoy inventing their own dialogue for this story.

28. Manushkin, Fran. Created by Lucy Bate. *Little Rabbit's Baby Brother.* Illus. by Diane de Groat. Crown, 1986. o.p. 29 pp. Fiction.

Interest level: Ages 5–8

Little Rabbit fears that she will be displaced by her expected baby brother. Her parents are very busy planning for the new arrival, and they seem to be paying less and less attention to Little Rabbit. After the baby arrives, he is too noisy, he can't eat the food Little Rabbit wants to feed him, and their parents are so solicitous of the new baby that they seem always to be reprimanding Little Rabbit. Finally, Little Rabbit hops outside and threatens to hop around the world. She hops right outside their house until after the sun goes down. At last, her parents make it clearly and loudly known that they miss her and want her to come home. Little Rabbit then hops into the house and is welcomed by her parents as a Big Sister. She decides that she will designate her robe a Big Sister Robe to wear when she helps with the baby. Her father decorates the robe with medals, bells, and stars for her having been such a wonderful baby and maker of snow angels, and now a wonderful big sister. She helps quiet the baby, holds him, and dreams of the day when she can play with him outdoors.

Manushkin wisely does not have the character really run away from home to attract her parents' attention. Little Rabbit stays within the range of her parents' vision and hearing. She adopts a ritual that helps her to overcome many of her jealous feelings. She is a Big Sister only when she is wearing her special robe. At other times, she is simply herself. Her role is also aided by the knowledge that she is competent in her parents' eyes—hence, the symbolic medals. Children going through the throes of sibling rivalry may be able to take from this book some good ideas on how to overcome their negative feelings.

29. Naylor, Phyllis Reynolds. *The Baby, the Bed, and the Rose.* Illus. by Mary Szilagyi. Clarion, 1987. o.p. 32 pp. Fiction.

Interest level: Ages 3–6

David and Tom try to comfort their baby sister, Molly, when she is crying. The boys help entertain her, change her, and feed her, but when she is returned to her crib the crying begins again. Finally, they realize that Molly is fascinated by the pink rose painted on the footboard of her crib.

In this simple story, the family models how a new baby is incorporated into the family by enlisting the aid of her siblings, her mother, and her grandfather. Research has demonstrated that when older siblings are encouraged to take responsibility for some of the nurturing of the new baby, they form a close relationship. It is clear that Molly's brothers are delighted by her progress toward standing up and creeping. They willingly interrupt their games to take care of the baby.

The father is absent from all of the pictures, including the one at bedtime when the rest of the family is standing around the crib. No mention is made of him. Nor is there a grandmother. Older children might want to discuss the possible reasons for their absence. Younger children will enjoy and benefit from the joyousness of the family's appreciation for one another.

30. Ormerod, Jan. *101 Things to Do with a Baby.* Illus. by the author. Lothrop, 1984, LB (0-688-03802-6); Puffin, pap. (0-14-050447-8). 27 pp. Nonfiction.

Interest level: Ages 5–8

This catalog of activities, all doable and practical, is a merry romp for siblings, from saying "good morning" to exercising, bathing, whispering, and tickling (including some things to watch out for, such as ankle biting and Granny's glasses), and finally to the good-night kiss. The book exemplifies a helpful and loving relationship in a family whose members clearly care a lot for each other.

The illustrations make it clear that the older sibling is every bit as valued and attended to as the infant. The author obviously understands that the more an older sibling is involved constructively with the new baby, the easier it will be for the child to bond with the baby.

31. Pankow, Valerie. *No Bigger Than My Teddy Bear.* Illus. by Rodney Pate. Abingdon, 1987. o.p. 28 pp. Fiction.

Interest level: Ages 4–8

Dustin is a little boy whose mother has just given birth to a premature baby. Through Dustin's eyes, we learn how hospitals care for premature babies. This approach also lets readers understand how older siblings and the family feel about the new baby. It helps Dustin to compare the baby with his teddy bear and to treat the teddy bear as a surrogate baby sibling.

The information in this book is given in an accurate and straightforward manner. The comparison with the teddy bear is a good one, and it makes the facts more interesting and accessible.

32. Patent, Dorothy Hinshaw. *Babies!* Photos. Holiday, 1988, LB (0-8234-0685-7); pap. (0-8234-0701-2). 40 pp. Nonfiction.

Interest level: Ages 4–9

A noted author and zoologist, Patent tackles the human development of babies and achieves glorious results. She is abetted in her task by intriguing, appealing photos produced by some of the most well-known photographers of children: Suzanne Szasz, Bruce McMillan, and others. The babies are multiethnic.

Birth, the biggest change one goes through in life, is the start of the book, and the reader is instantly involved: "Have you ever seen a newborn baby?" Patent has simple ways of explaining the baby's beginning and growing traits: "Its tongue is designed for sucking. The baby can wrap it around a nipple and pull the milk out easily." Without being stuffy, Patent taps what are obviously the interesting results of scholarly studies: "By the time it is six weeks old, it can tell the difference between the touch of its mother and father. It knows if its brother or a stranger has picked it up." Always the reader is invited to participate, as regarding babies' many forms of communication: "You can learn what it is trying to say if you watch and listen closely."

The development focuses mostly on the first year, but travels into the second as well. Particular attention is paid to the second half-year of life, when babies get upset if the mother leaves the room. "No one else, even a brother or sister, can ease the pain. This stage can be difficult for everyone. Mother can't always be with the baby, and other family members may feel hurt that they can't provide comfort." Patent shows a great deal of understanding regarding the development of babies. And she gives advice, too, like this, about babies who don't seem to talk at the so-called right time: "Each family needs to be patient and accept the pace set by its own toddler." A delicious book for sharing and learning about the new sibling.

33. Polushkin, Maria. *Baby Brother Blues*. Illus. by Ellen Weiss. Bradbury, 1987. o.p. 26 pp. Fiction.

Interest level: Ages 4–7

The little girl's baby brother is a mess and a nuisance as far as she's concerned. He can't talk or even stand up, he is sometimes smelly, he is often noisy, and he throws things on the floor and gets into everything. All the grown-ups adore him and think he is wonderful. At last, when the baby is crying and no one can comfort him, the little girl makes him stop crying. This endears him to her, and she acknowledges that he is likable after all.

The book is charmingly and amusingly illustrated in cheerful cartoonlike pictures, with some of the characters' reactions floating out of their mouths in comic-strip balloons. The contrast between the child's reactions to the baby and the adults' adoration is amusing and telling. The ultimate shift is predictable and not quite believable, but it is, by now, an accepted happy ending for a sibling rivalry book. Adults might want to discuss with children how to handle their negative feelings and, perhaps, indicate that they understand that siblings feel differently toward new babies than adults do.

34. Rogers, Fred. *The New Baby*. Photos by Jim Judkis. Putnam, 1985 (0-399-21236-1); pap. (0-399-21238-8). 32 pp. Nonfiction.

Interest level: Ages 3–8

Rogers's approach to a new sibling, as expressed in the introduction to adults, is to assure the older sibling that he or she has a special place in the family that no one else can ever take; to find special time to be alone with the older child; to encourage talk about feelings; and to enable the older child to feel active and important in the care of the newborn.

In the text, Rogers engages the reader by asking questions like "Is it hard to imagine what your family will be like with a new baby there?" Using two families to illustrate—one black, one white; one with an older sister-to-be, one with an older brother-to-be—he brings the older children back to their baby pictures and points out how good the parents feel about being parents and proud of their child. "They like taking care of you and they like taking care of the new baby." The underside is noted, though: "But moms and dads sometimes spend so much time looking at their new babies and holding them and making faces at them . . . that they seem to have less time with you." Rogers goes on to comment about the presents babies get, older siblings' wish to be babies again, and new restrictions (for example, be careful, be quiet). "A person could get very grumpy." If that happens, Rogers recommends doing angry things that don't hurt anyone (Judkis's photo illustrates knocking down blocks). Selfhood is emphasized when a child sees his crib used by another but doesn't have to share his teddy. At the close, Rogers tells of the many things an older sibling can teach someone younger. "Soon you'll even be able to help the baby understand about pretending and sharing." In the end, this book is about feeling—feeling good and feeling bad—and both are all right.

35. Root, Phyllis. *Moon Tiger*. Illus. by Ed Young. Henry Holt, 1988, pap. (0-8050-0803-9). 32 pp. Fiction.
   Interest level: Ages 5–8

The little girl is angry at her mother and younger brother. She feels that it is unjust that she should have to go to bed at the same time as her brother just because she refused to read him a story. She was busy playing with her tiger, and now she uses the tiger as her vehicle for an imaginary journey far away from her house. During the journey, she resolves her anger and decides to tell her little brother the story of her journey.

The illustrations evoke the feelings of magic and power that the little girl needs to overcome her anger. The text helps readers to experience the little girl's feelings of anger, escape, and competence. Together, the blend of words and pictures creates a mood, a story, and an experience that is very satisfying.

36. Ross, Dave. *Baby Hugs*. Illus. by the author. Crowell, 1987. o.p. 32 pp. Nonfiction.
   Interest level: Ages 4–8

One of a series of general hug-humor books, this one starts off, "You can hug a lot of things . . . but everyone agrees the best hugs of all are when you hug a baby." Ross goes on to explain what hugs do for the baby's health and happiness—moreover, what they do for the hugger. He claims, probably rightly, that it is almost impossible to frown while hugging a baby. Hugs are then classified, such as in welcome for newborns and newly adopted babies. Then there are meet-the-new-baby hugs, in which everyone from siblings to office buddies likes to participate. Also, among feeding hugs are nursing hugs reserved "just for Mommy and baby." Sharp-edged black-and-white cartoons really show off the essence of the varied hugs, as in a bleary-eyed 3:00 A.M. feeding hug given by a dad. Additional hugs include wake-up, going-places, play, baby-sitter, comfort, and family hugs that are aptly named (sandwich, reach-around, and so on). As if these weren't enough, there are special hugs for twins, triplets, and quintuplets. Ross includes a most enjoyable small segment on ways babies ask for hugs, from flirting to lip quivering. One only wishes siblings were pictured more often in the book.

37. Samuels, Barbara. *Faye and Dolores.* Illus. by the author. Bradbury, 1985 (0-02-778120-8); Aladdin, pap. (0-689-71154-9). 36 pp. Fiction.

Interest level: Ages 4–8

Faye and her younger sister, Dolores, sometimes argue, but most of the time they are very kind and loving to each other. The story tells of some of their arguments (for example, Dolores breaks Faye's crayon and Faye hurls several insults at Dolores). It also describes a number of incidents where they care about each other's feelings and play happily together. The book can serve as an affectionate and amusing model for sibling interaction.

38. Schaffer, Patricia. *How Babies and Families Are Made: There Is More Than One Way!* Illus. by Suzanne Corbett. Tabor Sarah, 1988, pap. (0-935079-17-3). 64 pp. Nonfiction.

Interest level: Ages 5–9

This book's intention is to help children from various backgrounds feel welcome and included. The author calls it an "updated facts of life." As such, the narrative discusses a wide range of circumstances and loses its focus. In these pages are descriptions of miscarriage, twins, in vitro fertilization, stepparents, adoption, prematurity, stepchildren, babies with disabilities, and artificial insemination. Some pages have the simplicity of a first-grade basal reader; others offer more science and technology than most children of the age group want or can grasp. In trying to create a large umbrella, the author may have created confusion instead.

39. Shreve, Susan. *Lily and the Runaway Baby.* Illus. by Sue Truesdell. Random, 1987, pap. (0-394-89104-X). 62 pp. Fiction.

Interest level: Ages 7–10

Lily believes that no one in her family loves her or cares about her. Her parents have acknowledged that the birth of their "sweet surprise" baby would be hardest on eight-year-old Lily, but they still seem to pay more attention to the baby and to the twins than to Lily. When Lily reasons that they might not miss her, but they will miss the baby, she decides to take the baby with her.

She and the baby board a train from Scarsdale to New York City. On the way, an elderly woman helps Lily with the baby, and while Lily is in the bathroom washing up, the woman steals her baby sister. The police, her parents, and many other people are involved in the search for the baby, but Lily is the one who finds her. Lily then solemnly promises never to run away again. It is important that Shreve points out how dangerous it is to run away or to leave a baby in the care of a stranger.

Although Shreve based her story on an incident that happened to her when she was six years old, in print it does not ring true. Lily's emotions are certainly understandable, but her actions as presented in the story are not believable. Young readers might benefit from discussing Lily's alternatives.

40. Smith, Anne Warren. *Sister in the Shadow*. Avon, 1988, pap. (0-380-70378-5). 69 pp. Fiction.

    Interest level: Ages 11–15

Beset by confusion and jealousy when her younger sister becomes more popular than she, Sharon tries to take a break from the family tension by getting a summer job as a mother's helper 60 miles away. Preschooler Tim is precocious and miserably spoiled, but more challenging is his cold mother, who wants to care for him but won't let him live a normal life. Why is she so tense and overprotective? In unfolding the tragedy of crib death that lies behind the mystery, Sharon gains perspective about her own past year. Smith gives the characters both quick-paced action and sharp, cerebral dialogue and internal monologue. Tim, the world's original monster, is totally credible, and although Sharon is occasionally too wise and can solve the problems of the adults around her, she is usually believable, too. Sharon's funny introspection is exemplified by her questions to herself: "What would Mary Poppins have done?" An excellent book about the effects of family constellations.

41. Smith, Dian G. *My New Baby and Me*. Illus. by Marie Madeline Franc-Nohain. Scribner, 1986, pap. (0-684-18712-4). 44 pp. Nonfiction.

    Interest level: Ages 3–8

This clever album is designed to include older siblings in the practice of recording special firsts, talents, events, and activities. Instead of focusing on the baby, there are spaces in this book for the older sibling to insert his or her accomplishments. The new sibling is always referred to as "my baby." Comparisons are invited that help the older sibling to put things into perspective. There are spaces for indicating the number of teeth, books, stuffed animals, cousins, rattles, freckles, and siblings both the baby and the older sibling have. This is an excellent strategy for helping children overcome their feelings of loss of attention and gain respect for their attributes.

42. Steptoe, John. *Mufaro's Beautiful Daughters: An African Tale.* Illus. by the author. Lothrop, 1987 (0-688-04045-4). 32 pp. Fiction.

   Interest level: Ages 7–11

In this retelling of a Kaffir folktale, Steptoe presents readers with a gift of lavish paintings that convey a palpable sense of the beauty and majesty of the southern African people and setting. The text respectfully tells the story of two beautiful young women, Nyasha and Manyara—one gentle and thoughtful; the other competitive, selfish, and vain—who respond to the invitation issued by the king to appear before him so that he may choose a wife. Of course, Nyasha, the generous and loving one, is selected.

The story has value beyond its exquisite illustrations. It is refreshing that the selfish woman is beautiful. Children need to get the message that one cannot tell from physical appearances what the character of a person is like. It is also a valuable factor that the king knows Nyasha and what she is like. He has lived near her, in the guise of a snake, before issuing his proclamation. This is not love at first sight for him; it is love born of knowledge. One wonders why he had to invent the ploy of the competition, but it suits the story to have the nasty sister try to become queen and fail because of her own behavior and character.

The competition between the sisters is not really resolved. Undoubtedly, Manyara will cause trouble in the castle unless she has learned her lesson. Perhaps children can discuss how they would help Manyara to become a better person. This is a deeply satisfying book because of its beauty, its respect for the people and culture of the story, and its careful wording.

43. Titherington, Jeanne. *A Place for Ben.* Illus. by the author. Greenwillow, 1987 (0-688-06493-0). 24 pp. Fiction.

   Interest level: Ages 4–7

When Ben's baby brother is moved into Ben's room, he decides that he needs a place of his own where no one will intrude on him. He fixes up such a place in the garage, but then he gets lonely and wants company. His baby brother is the only one who responds to his wish, and Ben is glad to see him. The simple story carries a familiar and perhaps simplistic message, but the illustrations of Ben and his family are wonderfully realistic and appealing, and the look of genuine joy on Ben's face as he greets his baby brother is unmistakably authentic.

44. Tyler, Linda Wagner. *My Brother Oscar Thinks He Knows It All.* Illus. by Susan Davis. Puffin, 1991, pap. (0-14-050947-X). 32 pp. Picture book.

    Interest level: Ages 3–6

Oscar's younger sister tells this story about sibling relationships that are sometimes rocky and sometimes warm. She complains that Oscar wins at checkers all the time, dominates the treehouse space, and is better able to skate and ride bikes than she. Worst of all, he ignores her when he has a friend over to play and then shows off when her friends are around. On the other hand, when she races and wins, her biggest supporter is Oscar, who can be seen cheering at the finish line with all of his friends. The characters are illustrated as birds, which adds a touch of absurdity to this story about typical sibling rivalry.

45. Voigt, Cynthia. *Sons from Afar.* Atheneum, 1987 (0-689-31349-7); Fawcett, pap. (0-449-70293-6). 214 pp. Fiction.

    Interest level: Age 12+

This story is another in the Tillerman family saga. This time, we learn much more about Francis Verricker, the father who deserted Dicey, Maybeth, Sammy, James, and their mother. James and Sammy search for their father in an attempt to find out more about themselves. They never quite catch up with him, but they do find out all sorts of information, not only about him and their family but also about themselves and their relationship as brothers.

Readers can appreciate the protagonists' stamina and determination at the same time that they empathize with their feelings of self-doubt and conflict. Here are two siblings who manage, despite their antagonism and tensions, to carve out a working relationship with each other.

As always, Voigt presents us with characters and situations that are far from the ordinary, but that contain elements that every reader can relate to. We are not permitted the luxury of hating villains unalloyedly;

there are no real villains. All of the characters are notable for their fallibility as well as their virtues, and what emerges is their humanity.

46. Von Königslöw, Andrea Wayne. *That's My Baby?* Illus. by the author. Firefly, 1986 (0-920303-56-0); pap. (0-920303-57-9). 24 pp. Fiction.

    Interest level: Ages 3–7

Lexi, told by Mom and Dad that there will be a new baby, is very excited—what a great toy to show off, she tells her stuffed dinosaur, confusingly named Teddy. As the months go on, Teddy and Lexi count off the days and watch the changes in Mommy's belly (there seems to be no lap left for them to sit on). They visit the female doctor with Mommy, and soon it is time to be brought to a friend's house late one night. There is some humor as Lexi asks, "Am I going to be a brother if it's a boy?"

Teddy becomes the voice of reason as the action unfolds. When Lexi is jealous and wants to leave the baby at the hospital, Teddy tells her, "Mommy and Daddy love us more than ever. They're just busy." Lexi tries nursing but doesn't like it; in general, she's unhappy with this new baby who can't yet play. Again Teddy reminds her that her new sister will be bigger soon and encourages Lexi to hold the baby when she isn't so sure about that. And what Teddy said would take place, does. Soon they do play and bathe together. And then she won't trade her for anything. The action is a bit hard to follow, but this is an affectionate story nonetheless.

47. Walker, Mildred Pitts. *My Mama Needs Me.* Illus. by Pat Cummings. Lothrop, 1983 (0-688-01670-7). 32 pp. Fiction.

    Interest level: Ages 3–7

Jason's mama comes home from the hospital with his new baby sister, and Jason is eager to help his mama. He refuses all invitations from friends and neighbors with the response "My mama needs me." But it seems to be only wishful thinking that his mother needs him. The reality of the situation is that Jason's mama and baby sister want to sleep most of the time. When the baby wakens briefly, Jason rubs her back and both baby and mother are appreciative. Afterward, Jason is permitted to help bathe the baby. For the most part, Jason feels unwanted and unloved until his mother assures him that he can go and play with his friends because he is needed all the time, but he can also enjoy himself. When his mother gives him a big hug and tells him she loves him, Jason realizes that this reassurance was what he was really looking for; he wanted his mother to need him, want him, and love him.

In addition to verbalizing the fears and behaviors of young children who feel displaced by their new siblings, the book has beautiful illustrations of a close and loving African-American family that add to its value.

48. Watson, Jane Werner, Robert E. Switzer, and J. Cotter Hirschberg. *Sometimes I'm Jealous.* Illus. by Irene Trivas. Crown, 1986. o.p. 32 pp. Fiction.

   Interest level: Ages 2–8

Newly illustrated and revised in content, this book offers parents guidance in the preface and gives sound advice and thoughts for its young listeners who now have a baby to contend with. As doctors Switzer and Hirschberg intone, "Gradually Baby learns that even though he may have to wait for what he wants, he can count on Mommy and Daddy." The unisex child in the story to be shared is right up front, starting off with: "Do you know what I like? I like having my own way . . . I like having Mommy and Daddy pay attention to me—nobody else, just me!" The child then takes the listener through some of the development that has already been accomplished—for example, slowly learning that some things make parents happy, others do not. Attention is paid to children's inner lives, as when the child comments that when Daddy and Mommy were angry, "they seemed further away." And now, after all this development, there's a new baby. And what do you know, it's not a "plaything" for the child.

49. Wilhelm, Hans. *Let's Be Friends Again.* Illus. by the author. Crown, 1986. o.p. 32 pp. Fiction.

   Interest level: Ages 3–7

When the little boy's sister releases his pet turtle into the pond, the little boy is furious. In general, he has a good relationship with his sister, but this time he wants to kill her. He dreams of all sorts of dire punishments for her, notices that she is enjoying herself while he is seething, and decides to go and make up with her. When she suggests that they buy a new turtle, he declines and decides to buy two hamsters instead, one for each of them. The hamsters will live in the turtle's old aquarium.

   The idea of the story is a good one, but there seems to be no explanation for why the brother is so willing to forgive his little sister. His replacement of his lost pet so quickly is another flaw in the book. If he were so devastated by his pet's loss, how is it that he is going to be satisfied so easily with a new pet? Children will benefit from discussion of these questions.

   The illustrations are charming and convey the children's emotions very well, perhaps more so than the text.

50. Young, Ruth. *The New Baby*. Illus. by the author. Puffin, 1987, pap. (0-670-81304-4). Unpaged. Picture book.

Interest level: Ages 3–5

The New Baby is always characterized that way, capitalized, and referred to as "It." The elder sibling is about three years old and has fairly positive feelings about his new sibling, largely due to the careful approach the parents take. They provide special individual time with each child, provide opportunities for the elder sibling to help out, and share pleasurable times, such as singing and lap time with both children at the same time.

51. Zolotow, Charlotte. *Timothy Too!* Houghton, 1986 (0-395-39378-7). 32 pp. Fiction.

Interest level: Ages 4–7

Timothy adores his older brother, John, and he emulates his every word and act. John is impatient with Timothy and considers him a pest, but Timothy continues to worship his older brother. When Timothy finally begins to play with a little boy his own age and does not need to shadow his older brother all the time, John misses the attention and invites Timothy and his new friend to join him.

Although the message is a familiar one, the story is presented in an amiable and positive manner. It is, perhaps, a little too pat, but the idea is believable, and the book may help younger children in this situation decide to try to find friends of their own.

Moving

Moving means the loss of friends and surroundings that have grown familiar. The move may necessitate separation from people, schools, neighborhoods, habits, customs, and attitudes that have been taken for granted. In order to cope, children must eventually accept these changes and take at least partial responsibility for adjusting to them. Although many of the challenges presented by moving are similar, different situations involve a variety of adjustments. Transferring to a new school will necessitate breaking into already established cliques of friends and becoming acquainted with new teachers and their styles of teaching. A new neighborhood or community also requires becoming accustomed to new expectations of behavior. Historical accounts of moving westward involve pioneering in many ways, including trying on new roles and acquiring new responsibilities. Moving from a different country, because of adoption or out of political or economic necessity, intensifies these demands and is sometimes exacerbated by the need to learn a new language. Loneliness, challenge, and pressure to adjust to the physical and emotional differences of the new situation form the dramatic tension in many of these books about moving.

General

52. Artenstein, Jeffrey. *Moving: How to Be Sure that Your Child Makes a Happy Transfer to a New Home.* Illus. by Neil Yamamoto. Tor, 1990, pap. (0-8125-0579-4). 118 pp. Fiction and nonfiction.

Interest level: Ages 6–12

This Parent/Child Manual combines useful, down-to-earth advice for parents with fictionalized case studies about kids who are coping with moving. The author is well aware of both the small and large issues involved with changing homes. For example, the author advises parents to let the child decorate his or her new bedroom, thus involving the child in some of the decision-making about the new home. Serious symptoms of unhappiness, such as regressive behavior exemplified by bed-wetting, are discussed as well. The realistic stories enhance the book and end with questions that are designed to keep parent and child communicating. The illustrations are not great art but do serve to punctuate the points the author makes. This book is most useful for children ages 5 to 12. The particular problems that teenagers experience when facing a traumatic move are not really addressed except in a general way.

53. Banks, Ann, and Nancy Evans. *Goodbye, House: A Kids' Guide to Moving.* Illus. by Marisabina Russo. Crown, 1988, pap. (0-517-53907-1). 64 pp. Nonfiction.

Interest level: Ages 5–8

A combination of advice book, journal, and scrapbook, this slim volume is a helpful stimulus to activities and discussions that can help children cope with the trauma of moving. Starting with preparations for the move, such as looking at a map to locate where they are moving and how far away it is, children are encouraged to make all sorts of lists, to give friends self-addressed postcards to ensure getting mail, to create an address book so that they can keep in touch with friends, and to decide on ways to be helpful to their parents. The focus is on the child's feelings, but the book wisely acknowledges that the move is a family event and that children must learn to be part of the family enterprise.

Banks and Evans also recommend helpful activities to do after the move has taken place, such as drawing a map of the new neighborhood so that the children won't get lost; planning their first day of school; making more lists; and, perhaps, finding a secret hiding place in the new house.

Part of the coping strategy is to collect a list of pleasant memories of the old house and to also think of the things children are glad to be rid of.

The parents' notes are as thoughtful as the primary content. Banks and Evans have themselves experienced many moves and have talked to many children in their research. They remind parents to be honest about the reasons for moving and give a reasoned analysis of the debate about timing for moving: Should it be in the summer or during the school year? They offer ways to include the child that parents might not have thought of—for example, getting enough change-of-address postcards from the post office in order to give some to the child. The authors also offer ideas that can reassure the child, such as allowing the child to fantasize and suggesting a flashlight for the first night in a new room. And they're very practical in their reassurance, too, as when they suggest having the van filled with the children's things last so they can be emptied first. The kids' rooms can then be set up reassuringly quickly and thus give the children a place to stay out of the way; the children can do final arrangements of the rooms while the rest is unpacked. This book is a wonderful helpmate for a difficult time!

54. Booher, Dianna Daniels. *Help! We're Moving.* Messner, 1983. o.p. 144 pp. Nonfiction.

Interest level: Ages 12–16

In this entry in the Teen Survival series, Booher tells of her own fright at moving during high school, in her case from a junior class of about 25 to one of more than 500. Booher weaves stories to get her points across, particularly about resiliency, which she brightly calls "snapbacktivity." There is an emphasis on the positive, true, but there is also good advice on wrapping up loose ends. Insightful self-quizzes can help youngsters decide if they want to stay behind when the family moves if the school year is not over: "Have you ever been with the relative's or friend's family when they've been upset or angry?" The chapter on adjustment to the new locale is filled with practical ideas ("call the Y," for example), as is the chapter on coping with newcomer blues ("give your pets extra care"), making friends, and finding one's way around the school. The aim throughout is ego-building and finding lots of ways to feel good, and Booher presents a bouncy, lively list. Bibliography, index.

55. Greenwald, Dorothy. *Coping with Moving.* Rosen, 1987 (0-8239-0683-3). 140 pp. Nonfiction.

Interest level: Ages 11–15

With snappy chapter titles like "Pity Party or Great Adventure," free-lance writer and real estate agent Greenwald sets out the mixed emotional luggage moving may represent. Reminding readers of other good-byes (visits, summer camp, and so on), she sets the stage for making moving less devastating.

Greenwald puts the teenage love relationship and the prospect of leaving it up near the front of the book. At first, this seems to be disjointed organization, but perhaps she is really right on target about what truly matters to teens who must leave. She is also very concrete about additional losses other books of this type haven't covered—for example, leaving a favorite teacher. Other topics include possibilities of staying behind, making sure the school transition is smooth with all courses credited, using community resources such as the YMCA or YWCA, planning ahead, garage sales, getting ready for the big day, the actual day, and beyond, when one must adjust to a new school, home, and town. Making new friends is the subject of not one chapter but two, with practical ideas for joining established groups. Index.

56. Nida, Patricia Cooney, and Wendy M. Heller. *The Teenager's Survival Guide to Moving.* Macmillan, 1987, pap. (0-02-044510-5). 148 pp. Nonfiction.

  Interest level: Ages 12–16

Nida runs a consulting firm specializing in helping families and organizations deal with the human side of moving. Heller is a journalist. Together, they make strong emotions the centerpiece here, being admirably cognizant of the losses involved in moving. Breaking the process into phases (for example, disconnect, change, reconnect), the authors try to make the inevitable less stressful. They also rightly regard moving as a family affair and address the likely concerns of others in the group besides the teen reader, thus giving that reader insight into the five-year-old, a grade school child, and the child's parent. Influenced by rational-emotive therapy and its proponents, the authors advocate "thinking straight" to control emotions and make the situation turn out for the best. Readers are given minitraining in not jumping to conclusions.

Helpful sections relate to saying good-bye, preparing to say hello, and getting oriented to the new surroundings. In keeping with the rational-emotive point of view, readers are told to talk to themselves continuously to remind themselves that their new vulnerability is only a fleeting condition. Of particular value is the discussion of boarding and *not* moving along with the family. As this is often an option chosen by teens close to their high school graduation date, it's a welcome addition. Other unique features of this book include a section on moving overseas, returning from overseas (which is often regarded as harder), and guidelines for forming a Welcomers Club at a high school.

This unusual book is at once appropriately chatty and blessed with quite a bit of depth to its exploration. Clearly, the authors have been around.

57. Rogers, Fred. *Moving*. Photos by Jim Judkis. Putnam, 1987. o.p. 32 pp. Nonfiction.

Interest level: Ages 2–6

Like the other titles in the Mister Rogers' First Experience Books series, this one boasts a sensitive introduction for parents, similarly understanding content within, and outstanding photographic work. Rogers recommends including children in some of the moving process in order to give them a sense of continuity. He also advocates talking about their feelings so that they can join in some of the adventure of moving, not just be overwhelmed by the hectic pace.

The book begins, "It's a good feeling to know the neighborhood where you live and to know some of the people who live there . . . but families don't always live in the same house forever." Pictured, looking at the for-sale sign, is a toddler dragging a blanket. Explanations of what's brought along and what's left behind, the inconvenience of packing, the crankiness that everyone feels, and finding time to talk and hug are helpful. The young reader is brought into the discussion: "Are there a few things you'd rather *not* pack so that you can play with them on the trip to your new home?" Then the moving van comes and that process is shown. Again, children are encouraged to ask questions. And again, children are given signals for decision making. "You may be able to help decide where your bed and clothes and books and toys will go in your new room."

The sense of discovery is paramount here, made possible by acknowledging that leaving is hard and by bringing the child in the story into the process. The book ends with a discussion of identity. The old house is still there. Your old friends are still your friends. And wherever you are, "You're still the same person—the same person your old friends will be remembering."

New School

58. Adler, C. S. *Always and Forever Friends*. Avon, 1990, pap. (0-380-70687-3). 164 pp. Fiction.

Interest level: Ages 9–12

Wendy, age 11, is bereft because her best friend has moved away. Wendy's mother has recently remarried, and, although Wendy likes her stepfather, she is having lots of difficulty with her new stepsister and step-brothers. Both her mother and stepfather work, and Wendy is burdened with many responsibilities in addition to her personal problems. She is depicted as a cheerful, ingenious girl, but the other children in her class are either members of previously established cliques (Wendy is a relative newcomer to the school) or have personality problems of their own. One girl, Honor, seems to be a likely candidate for friendship, but she is mysteriously standoffish.

Wendy fixes on Ingrid, a new arrival at school, as the most likely person to be her best friend. The reader quickly sees that this is a mistake, but Wendy doesn't discover this until the end of the book. Finally, after countless demonstrations of friendship, loyalty, and excellent advice on Honor's part, Wendy realizes that Honor is her friend. It is unfortunate that it takes her so long to come to this recognition.

Issues such as the trials and tribulations of stepparenting and being a stepsibling are also explored, as is Honor's dilemma of being a biracial child whose white mother has emotionally abandoned her. (Honor lives with her paternal grandmother. Her father is dead, and her mother's new husband doesn't want Honor because she is black.) Wendy's stepsister, Ellen, is disruptive and sullen throughout most of the book, but this situation is resolved as she and Wendy begin to get along. The story moves along briskly, and Wendy and Honor are likable and interesting characters. Wendy's lack of perception occasionally becomes annoying, but, in general, the reader can empathize with her plight.

59. Buehler, Stephanie Jona. *There's No Surf in Cleveland.* Clarion, 1993 (0-395-62162-3). 136 pp. Fiction.

Interest level: Ages 7–10

Philip hates Los Angeles, where he and his mother have relocated after his parents' divorce. He misses his grandparents and, to everyone's astonishment, the weather in Cleveland. He attends a new school and manages fairly well, especially because he has a good friend, Washington, who joins him in all of his escapades. He encounters a bully, bilks other students out of quarters by performing "magic" tricks, is called to task by the principal, and finally adjusts to his new situation. The writing is light-hearted. No character is demeaned, not even the bully, and most of the adults are quite fair-minded and tolerant of Philip's occasional whining and complaining.

60. Bulla, Clyde Robert. *The Chalk Box Kid.* Illus. by Thomas B. Allen. Random, 1987 (0-394-99102-8); pap. (0-394-89102-3). 59 pp. Fiction.

Interest level: Ages 7–10

In a story somewhat reminiscent of Eleanor Estes's *The Hundred Dresses* (Harcourt, 1974), Gregory—a nine-year-old boy whose family has had to move to a new neighborhood because his father has lost his job—draws with chalk the garden he would love to have if he had ground on which to plant it. Gregory's artistic ability is the only thing that saves him from despair. His self-centered young uncle monopolizes his room; his parents are too preoccupied with trying to make ends meet to pay much attention to him; and the children at school reject him.

A visit from a local nursery owner gives Gregory the idea for his garden. Although his classmates have not been welcoming and he doesn't feel as if he belongs, one child in school, Ivy, who has won a prize for her artwork, recognizes Gregory's talent and succeeds in bringing it to other people's attention. In the end, even Gregory's uncle appreciates his ability, and the children in school become friendly.

The book avoids sentimentality because of its unadorned style and characterization. Gregory is not a wimp; he is a sensitive, motivated, and coping boy. The reader knows that he will go far.

61. Carey, Mary. *A Place for Allie.* Dodd, 1985. o.p. 250 pp. Fiction.

Interest level: Age 11+

It is the turn of the century in Nova Scotia. Allie and her sister, Gertrude, are happy and active girls who adore their father, love their mother, and feel secure in the midst of their extended family. But in the year that Allie is 12 and Gertrude is 9, their father is killed in a boating accident and their lives change completely. Their mother cannot abide remaining with her husband's family in her husband's country. She moves with her daughters to her sister's apartment in Boston, and the two girls enter a new school there.

The school is a disaster. Children are cruel to the two sisters, and Gertrude is constantly harassed by a bully. Their only friend is Rosa, whose Italian heritage makes her the butt of the other children's jibes. Schoolwork is dull and focuses on American history, with which the girls are unfamiliar.

Their Aunt Susan is a sympathetic listener and their only comfort. Their mother is withdrawn and unhappy until she finds a position 50 miles away as a housekeeper and cook for a wealthy man. She plans to place the girls in a Catholic academy, which is fine with them, until Rosa's aunt requests that Allie be permitted to come and live with her. To the girls' and Susan's dismay, their mother consents because she thinks that Allie will have a wonderful opportunity.

In order to escape separation, Allie and Gertrude run away to their grandmother's house in Nova Scotia. When their mother comes to claim them, the family arranges that Allie and Gertrude will, after all, go to the academy, and come home to Nova Scotia for the summers. The arrangement is a satisfactory one for everyone.

Many issues are examined in this book. The mother's reaction to her husband's death is to reject and resent all things that relate to her life with her husband. She is a bitter and ungiving person. She has not gotten past the denial and anger stage of mourning. The girls, on the other hand, grieve for their father but go on with their lives, as they know he would have wished. The themes of adjustment to a new school, coming to terms with loss, and running away are also handled in a thoughtful and helpful manner. The story moves quickly. The characters are all three-dimensional, and the author weaves them skillfully into the plot.

62. Caseley, Judith. *Starring Dorothy Kane.* Greenwillow, 1992 (0-688-10182-8). 154 pp. Fiction.

Interest level: Ages 5–8

Dorothy starts at her new school on the wrong foot by placing her little brother, Harry, into the wrong class. How was she to know that the sign on the door that said "2K" stood for second grade, not kindergarten? The principal publicly humiliates her, and the neighborhood bully laughs loudly at her. The experience makes her reluctant to participate in class, or even to attend school. At last she finds a friend, and her sympathetic and pleasant teacher helps ease the process of adjustment.

63. Cone, Molly. *The Big Squeeze.* Houghton, 1984 (0-395-36262-8). 114 pp. Fiction.

Interest level: Ages 9–12

Dudley is a high school sophomore, but he looks more like a seventh grader. What is more, he and his family are constantly on the move. His father fixes up old houses, sells them, and moves on. Dudley has never been a part of any of the schools he has gone to, and he feels this loss keenly. He is very sociable and makes friends easily, however. This time, he develops a crush on a girl named Donna, whom all the boys ogle because she has large breasts. Dudley is attracted to her because of the role she plays in the school production of *The Fantasticks.* He takes part in the play and is sure that Donna is attracted to him, but in the end she selects another boy for her affection. Dudley is not dismayed; he realizes that he loved the character in the play, not the girl. And he also finds out that his family is moving again, this time to a brand new city.

Dudley is a competent young man. Despite his longing for some sort of permanence, he comes to understand that he is fortunate to be with parents who love each other and him. They are his security; they are his permanence. Cone provides for young readers a different perspective on the problem of moving because of this awareness of the importance of the family structure.

64. Delton, Judy. *Kitty from the Start.* Houghton, 1987 (0-395-42847-5). 141 pp. Fiction.

   Interest level: Ages 8–11

The story is set during the Great Depression. Kitty's family must move to a new neighborhood because their landlord is selling their house. Kitty loved her old school and is so terribly apprehensive about going to a new one that she has nightmares about it. When the time comes, despite a mix-up at the outset, she settles in well at the school. The nuns are similar to those in her former school, the children are friendly, and she is a good student.

Much of the story deals with the climate of the Catholic school in the 1930s. When a lay teacher comes to substitute for Sister Charlene, Kitty is astonished to discover that she is of normal health and intelligence and that she is a good teacher. Some other encounters with Catholicism and its tenets (such as a trip to the movies, where one of Kitty's friends mortally fears they are witnessing a "B" rated film) form the basis for some amusing and provocative incidents.

The book is engagingly written, and the protagonist is an attractive one. Although adjusting to a new school is the major theme and Kitty gets a chance to make another newcomer feel at home at the end of the book, there is much more to the story. The look at Catholic life in the Midwest of the 1930s flavors the book enormously.

65. Magorian, Michelle. *Back Home.* Harper, 1984 (0-685-08449-3); pap. (0-06-440411-0). 375 pp. Fiction.

   Interest level: Age 12+

Magorian, author of *Good Night, Mr. Tom* (Harper, 1982), has again given us a thoughtful and dramatic story with strong characters and a plot that contains themes of loneliness, coming of age, knowing oneself, abuse, and the aftermath of war. The book also treats the issues of clashing values, adjusting to a new school, and striving for independence and understanding.

The protagonist is a feisty girl nicknamed Rusty by the foster family with whom she stayed in America when she was evacuated from England during World War II. She left her parents when she was seven, and now, five years later, she has been forced to return. She has loved her foster family and her life in America and has become thoroughly Americanized in outlook, speech, and manner, but the war in Europe is over and her mother wants her back.

Her new life in England is a difficult one for her. Her mother, Peggy, has changed over the five years from a passive, helpless creature into a woman who is an adroit auto mechanic and has friends of her own. Peggy lives in Devon with her four-year-old son, Charlie. She has been stationed here as part of her Women's Voluntary Service group, and it is to this place that Rusty has come and where they remain until the Japanese surrender.

They return to their permanent home, where Rusty's grandmother lives. Her grandmother is a snobbish, unbending woman who disapproves of everyone but her own son. When her father returns from the army, he is cold, punitive, and removed. One person who has been kind to Rusty, and whom Rusty has grown to love, dies and leaves her house in Devon to Rusty's mother.

Rusty is forced to go to an oppressive boarding school where no one likes her. She takes refuge in a bombed-out cabin in the woods and retreats there regularly. After a set of minidisasters, Rusty runs away from school and returns to Devon. Although she goes back to the school, she is expelled. In the end, her mother and father separate, and she and her mother and brother move into the small house in Devon. Rusty and her brother go to a day school that is Summerhillian in philosophy, where Rusty and her brother are welcomed and will flourish.

For some reason, Rusty is not angry at her father. She does hate her grandmother, but she is strangely sympathetic to her father. She wishes that her father would come with them; nevertheless, she is happy to be in Devon. She realizes that she loves her mother and that she would probably not fit in anymore in America. This conclusion is a little too pat, but the power of the rest of the book makes up for the small flaws in the logic of the narrative.

66. Robinson, Nancy K. *Veronica the Show-off.* Illus. by Sheila Greenwald. Macmillan, 1984 (0-02-77360-4); Scholastic, pap. (0-590-42326-6). 128 pp. Fiction.

Interest level: Ages 8–11

Veronica desperately wants friends, but no one in her new school seems to be interested in becoming her friend. Veronica tries her best to attract children by inventing what she thinks are interesting stories about how rich she is and how many things she has. She can't understand why the children are not interested.

As the story progresses, we realize that Veronica's father never comes to see her, even when he is in town. He also doesn't invite her to come to visit him. Veronica's mother is also too preoccupied with her own interests to pay any attention to Veronica. So Veronica is really a deserted child, even though she lives with her mother. Her showing off is a way of getting attention, but it doesn't work.

Quite by accident, Veronica does become friends with an understanding classmate who defies stereotyping. She is petite and gentle, and she takes karate lessons. Her house becomes a haven for Veronica.

Veronica also practically lives in the public library. She loves to read, and she is furious when a book that she has been waiting for is renewed by another child. Veronica and the girl, Melody, engage in a sort of warfare for a while; but when they meet each other, they discover more similarities than differences, and they become friends. They are both distraught and angry when they learn that their library has been closed due to lack of funds. Together they send a letter to the newspaper to demand the reopening of the library.

Because she now has friends and some real issues and interests to share with these friends, the other children in the class begin to view Veronica differently. There may be little hope of her receiving satisfaction at home, but in school and in her social life Veronica has made great gains.

The story may help children better understand those of their peers who always seem compelled to brag about their exploits and possessions. It may also provide a mirror for those children whose behavior is inappropriate if their aim is to establish friendships.

67. Smith, Jennifer. *Grover and the New Kid.* Illus. by Tom Cooke. Random, 1987 (0-394-88519-8). 32 pp. Fiction.

Interest level: Ages 3–7

In something of a reversal of the usual situation, Barry, the new child in school, is the one who doesn't want to share and who is mean to the other children. Grover tries to befriend Barry, but the new boy doesn't seem to appreciate it and goes so far as to ruin Grover's painting. At last, Barry sees that Grover is unhappy and apologizes to him, and begins to share. He confides in Grover that he was afraid to come to this new school and tells him how much he appreciates his friendship.

The story's use of the popular Sesame Street Muppets serves as a good stimulus for talking about the plight of the new child. In this story, it is not only the new boy but also Grover and the other children in the class whose feelings we are invited to understand. Admittedly, Grover is extraordinarily empathic for a young child, and Barry does come to his senses a bit suddenly. But the story is gentle and positive.

68. Soto, Gary. *Taking Sides.* Harcourt, 1991 (0-15-284076-1). 138 pp. Fiction.

   Interest level: Ages 9–12

Lincoln Mendoza has a problem: He has just relocated to a new neighbor-hood and new junior high, and he is torn between feeling that he must demonstrate loyalty to both his old and new friends, schools, and commu-nities. He is on the basketball team, and the next game is one between his old and new schools. He decides to play his best, no matter what. The Spanish phrases and the setting of the two schools, in the urban barrio and in the suburbs, add dimension to this fast-paced book.

69. Stolz, Mary. *Ivy Larkin.* Harcourt, 1986 (0-15-239366-8); Dell, pap. (0-440-40175-5). 226 pp. Fiction.

   Interest level: Age 11+

The story deals with the changes that Ivy goes through as she confronts going to a snooty private school and her family's deteriorating situation during the time of the Great Depression. The characters in the book are well developed. They could easily have become stereotyped. The father is a jovial and poetic Irishman whose love for his family sometimes suffers because of his pride. The mother is a hard-working nurse who is willing to sacrifice anything so that her children will get good schooling. Frank, the independent older brother, hangs around with the local gang, but he refuses to miss his family's weekly outings, is sensitive to his youngest sister's fears, and gives his lunch to a poor man on the street. Megan, Ivy's younger sister, is so beautiful and sensitive that no one can deny her anything, yet she is so fearful that one of her siblings must always be with her. Ivy, the main character, is 13 years old. She is not as attractive or as outgoing as her siblings. She is jealous of their talents, but her love for all of them always keeps her balanced.

   The story tells of how difficult it is for the family when the father is out of work for a number of months. It also details the problems that Ivy encounters in the private school to which all three siblings have won scholarships. Although Ivy sees the advantages in the school, she finally decides, despite her father's prejudice against it, that she will go to a parochial school. She pledges, however, that she will always think for her-self.

70. Wirths, Claudine G., and Mary Bowman-Kruhm. *I Hate School: How to Hang In and When to Drop Out.* Illus. by Patti Stren. Harper, 1987 (0-690-04556-5); pap. (0-06-446054-1). 128 pp. Nonfiction.

Interest level: Age 12+

This is a most unusual, needed book that can help kids make decisions that might lead to attending a new school. At last, someone (in this case, two people with teaching, administering, and writing experience) has addressed the needs of alienated students. In a question-answer format, the authors address issues as varied as building concentration ability, stepping out versus dropping out, alternate routes to degrees, and dealing with authority figures. Accompanying cartoons are sophisticated and meaning-ful (for example, a character saying "I wouldn't mind school if it was just a few weeks a year"). Successfully chatty, this book has great value: how to get over homework hurdles, study skill buildups, tips for reading faster and writing better, ways to remember material, report outlines, and test-taking strategies.

Wirths and Bowman-Kruhm also attend to deep personal problems that students may be having, realizing that they influence attitudes toward school and the ability to function there. In this section, they switch from the question-answer format and wisely become more authoritative in their discussion. Example of a heading: "Serious Family Problems (physical abuse, sexual abuse, divorce, abandonment, criminal or racial threats to family safety, illness, money, and so on)." And underneath that heading are guidelines: whom to talk to, and agencies to call—for example, "Call the main number for county offices and ask the operator who answers to connect you with a family service agency." This is a down-to-earth treat-ment that will appeal to many alienated students because it doesn't view staying in school as the only possibility.

New Community

71. Auch, Mary Jane. *The Witching of Ben Wagner.* Houghton, 1987 (0-395-44522-1). 132 pp. Fiction.

Interest level: Age 11+

Because their father has a better opportunity in another town, the family must move. None of the children is happy about the move, and the ride in the car to the new town is an agony for all of them, as they squabble and suffer from the heat. Ben's first day at school is equally disastrous. He cannot find his way to his first class, is embarrassed about telling anyone, and is reprimanded for cutting class. Ben's older and younger sisters seem to make a better adjustment than he does, but in reality, Ben's sister Susan is so anxious about making friends that she lies to her friends about where she lives and how much money she has. She also tells stories about Ben to get him into trouble.

Then Ben meets Regina near the lake and becomes friendly with her. He suspects that she may be a witch, because he has heard that witches haunt this area. She knows a lot about herbs and cures, and she speaks of trances and brews. Both her parents have deserted her, and she lives with her grandmother. Ben believes that it is Regina's magic that is helping him to do better at school and to feel less unhappy there. He also believes that it is Regina's spell that enables him to rescue his younger sister, Liz, from drowning.

In the end, Ben discovers that Regina is not a witch, that his accomplishments have been his own, and that his family can get along together once the truth about all of their behavior is uncovered.

The story is believable, even to the point where the reader is not sure whether Regina is a witch. The family is an ordinary family trying its best to get along. The mother has no individuality, but Ben's plight is worthy of investigation, and young readers will empathize with him.

72. Brimner, Larry Dane. *A Migrant Family*. Photos by the author. Lerner, 1992, LB (0-8225-2554-2). 32 pp. Picture book.

Interest level: Ages 5–8

Juan is a migrant child living with his family in a tent camp in California. Juan's daily life is chronicled through the text and, more importantly, through the black-and-white photos that tell far more of his story than any words can. The family is seen cooking over an open fire, crowding around the catering truck that sells breakfast, and ultimately rebuilding at a new campsite when the old one is razed. Juan's difficulties at school and his worries about missing so much of his education are as much part of his existence as are sharing a bus stop with a reluctant classmate whose mother spat at him when he first began waiting there for the bus. Included also is much information about migrant workers in general; but it is Juan's story that the reader cares about, and it is Juan's face that remains in one's memory long after the book is closed.

73. Carlson, Nancy. *Loudmouth George and the New Neighbors*. Illus. by the author. Carolrhoda, 1983 (0-87614-216-1); Puffin, pap. (0-14-05515-6). 28 pp. Fiction.

Interest level: Ages 5–8

When he finds out that his new neighbors are a family of pigs, George, a rabbit, decides he will have nothing to do with them. But he changes his mind after he sees all of his friends playing happily with the Pig children. When a family of cats moves into the neighborhood not long after, George grudgingly agrees to play with them despite his prejudices about cats.

The issues here include not only the difficulties of moving into a new neighborhood but also the prejudices that people have about each other. George would perhaps never have overcome his bigotry if he weren't abandoned by his friends in favor of the new neighbors. The message here is intended to be a positive one.

Children should take care to avoid thinking that just because a bigot decides to try out the company of people he formerly despised, that that constitutes a victory for equality. George is very much the "Archie Bunker" type: tolerated for reasons unknown and loud in his defaming of other groups.

The book is charming enough that children will enjoy tackling a discussion of George and his bigotry.

74. Carlstrom, Nancy White. *I'm Not Moving, Mama!* Illus. by Thor Wickstrom. Macmillan, 1990 (0-02-717286-4). Unpaged. Picture book.

Interest level: Ages 4–7

The little mouse in the story is anguished at the thought of moving. He threatens to remain behind, even though many of his treasures will be going on to his new home. His mother accepts the mouse's unhappy feelings, gently reminding him that there will be another climbing tree at his new house, wild birds who will need to be fed, unexplored secret corners where he can read, and new mirrors where they can make funny faces. More importantly, she reassures him that the family's life would be empty without him. The charming watercolors show the mother packing the family's belongings while her son expresses his dismay at the move. The illustrations show the mouse gradually accepting the inevitable and the story ends as the family approaches its new home and friendly neighbors. Children who are having difficulty accepting an anticipated move may see themselves in the agonized mouse. Parents would do well to imitate the mouse mother's patient acknowledgement of her son's pain.

75. Dowling, Paul. *Meg and Jack's New Friends.* Illus. by the author. Houghton, 1990 (0-395-53513-1). 32 pp. Picture book.

Interest level: Ages 5–8

Meg and Jack can't wait to meet all the children in their new neighborhood. Jack plans to offer them a smorgasbord of toys to play with, but Meg is reluctant. When the next-door neighbors come over for an arranged visit, Meg hides behind her mother and ignores Guy, who eagerly awaits her attention. When Jack and Rosa eventually go outside to play, Guy follows and joins them. Finally, Meg becomes more interested in the games than in her anxieties and allows herself to enter the group. A minor flaw is that both Meg and Rosa are portrayed as initially shy while Jack and Guy are outgoing; however, all the children play actively and creatively. A related book, *Meg and Jack Are Moving*, is a lighthearted look at the trials of moving as seen by preschoolers.

76. Fleming, Alice. *Welcome to Grossville*. Scribner, 1985. o.p. 104 pp. Fiction.

Interest level: Ages 9–12

Not only are Michael's and Jenny's lives changed by the sudden news that their parents are getting a divorce, their anguish is compounded when their mother tells them that they are moving from Glenville to a new town, selling much of their furniture, and dismissing their housekeeper and gardener. Their new house is much smaller than the one in which they have lived all of their lives (Michael is 11; Jenny is 8). The third bombshell explodes when their mother tells them that she will have to find a job. Michael finds it difficult to make friends in the new neighborhood. Although both their former and present towns are suburbs of New York, Glenville is a high-income area, and Humboldt, the new town, is middle-class. Michael calls it "Grossville." A group of boys in the new neighborhood think he is snooty because he has a fancy bike and wears trendy clothes. Jenny, on the other hand, makes a friend right away, which causes Michael to be envious and resentful. He spends most of his time snacking and watching television. When he is with his father on Sundays, he is sullen and argumentative.

At last, he starts to meet children his age who are friendly and with whom he enjoys himself. With his new friends' help, he eventually becomes friends with the group of boys he first encountered as a hostile group. At the end of the story, he has adjusted happily to life in Humboldt, and he is well on his way to coping with the divorce.

The book is helpful in many ways. Through the elements of a good story, the reader is able to build a repertoire of strategies for coping with divorce and with the stresses of moving to a new neighborhood. Positive thinking, permitting others to get to know you, and letting go of petty resentment and preconceptions are all part of the process. And Fleming presents it with humor and balance.

77. Griffith, Helen V. *Georgia Music*. Illus. by James Stevenson. Greenwillow, 1990, LB (0-688-06072-2); Morrow, pap. (0-688-09931-9). Unpaged. Picture book.

Interest level: Ages 5–8

The girl and her grandfather enjoy each other's company when she visits him for the summer at his cabin in Georgia. They engage in all sorts of activities there, like gardening, fishing, lying on the grass, and listening to the grandfather play "Georgia Music" on his harmonica. The next summer, they take the old man back with them to Baltimore because he is clearly in need of help. He is tired and depressed. But the grandfather languishes in his new home until his granddaughter attempts to play his music and it looks as if the old man has a chance to recover. The mood created by the author and illustrator underlines the affection and respect the grandfather and granddaughter have for each other. The grandfather's difficulty in adjusting to his move to a new home is understandable and is sympathetically handled.

78. Grove, Vicky. *Good-Bye, My Wishing Star*. Putnam, 1988 (0-399-21532-8); Scholastic, pap. (0-590-42152-2). 128 pp. Fiction.

Interest level: Ages 9–12

Grove's intent in writing this book was to help make children aware of what is happening in the country today and to convey the resilience that people have, even in a time of hardship and loss. The story tells of Jens, a 12-year-old, whose letter, to whoever moves into her house, begins the book. In her letter, Jens tells of the people of the community that she and her family are now leaving. She tells of the hardships that other people endure, and she describes her own difficulties with her friends and her family. Most of all, the thread of her family's serious economic problems runs through the story, leading to the family's decision to leave their beloved farm and move to the city.

Each of the characters comes alive through the author's perceptive eye. When Jens and her friends try to do something nice for Brenda, a child whose father has just died, they present her with a gift that they think she will enjoy, and instead of reacting with pleasure or thanks, Brenda asks them why they did this. The memory of this incident comes back when, on learning that Jens is leaving, her friends give her a surprise party. Jens is so distraught over the fact that she must move that she feels that a party is totally inappropriate. She asks her friends why they did this, and then she leaves. But she recovers her good sense when she learns that her friends gave the party because they wanted to show her how much they will miss her. One lesson to be learned is that good intentions do not always make up for insensitivity. Another is that different people grieve in different ways.

With the help of her family and friends, Jens is finally reconciled to the fact that she must go. She knows that she will keep this home in her heart forever, but she also knows that wherever she and her family are will be home to her.

The story is well told and refreshing in its directness. The characters are neither petty nor stereotypical. They are interesting people with recognizable traits and problems, but they transcend these problems by their determination not to let these difficulties defeat them.

79. Lasky, Kathryn. *Beyond the Divide*. Macmillan, 1983 (0-02-751670-9); Dell, pap. (0-440-91021-8). 254 pp. Fiction.

   Interest level: Age 12+

Meribah Simon chooses to join her father, Will, who has been excommunicated by the Amish community, in his westward journey. The story tells of the hardships of the wagon train in its attempt to reach California. But the story tells far more: It is the story of Meribah's strength of character and personal courage and her anger at injustice; it is a portrait of the values and attitudes of nineteenth-century America; and it is a tale of tragedy and survival.

Meribah, like her gentle father, finds the punitive, restrictive, and rigid atmosphere of their Amish community stifling. She and her father are disappointed to find the same sorts of attitudes prevalent among their fellow pioneers. When times grow difficult, Meribah sees "civilized" people who are quick to criticize low-class behavior performing acts of cruelty and cowardice. Until they reach the Great Divide, they share food and labor, and spirits are high. But once these mountains loom, they are not only a physical barrier but the symbolic separation of what is veneer from what is real among the travelers.

Rape, death, selfishness, theft, and wanton destruction as well as illness, abandonment, and broken promises are part of their everyday existence now. Finally, when Meribah's father becomes very ill and they lose one of their oxen and most of their wagon in a landslide, they are heartlessly abandoned by the consensus of the group.

Death and the loss of friendship and loved ones are important themes in this book. Death becomes more and more familiar to Meribah, and then, alone, she experiences the death of her father. It is then that she understands the words spoken by another pioneer who died, "Dying is horrible, death is not." Eventually, in order to prevent being raped, she kills a man.

The book describes how Native Americans are viewed as savages by the emigrants. Will helps Meribah to understand their plight, and George Goodenough, an artist, vividly describes to her the inhumane treatment of the Native Americans by the white settlers. Meribah's personal experience provides her with her own basis for respecting this group of people. She is adopted into the Yahi tribe after they save her life.

Despite all Meribah's ordeals, the book ends hopefully for her. She discovers who she is and what she wants. *Beyond the Divide* is a useful book for young readers. It raises issues of separation from cultural background; it critically examines the pioneer experience for those who might otherwise over-romanticize this period of American history; and it brings an understanding of the pain of dying and the possibility of coping with death.

80. Lovik, Craig. *Andy and the Tire*. Illus. by Mark Alan Weatherby. Scholastic, 1987. o.p. 32 pp. Fiction.

Interest level: Ages 7–10

When no one becomes his friend in the new school or neighborhood into which Andy, his sister, and his parents have moved, Andy is unhappy and resentful. He finds an old tire on his way home from school and spends almost all his time learning to ride on it and do tricks with it. Although Andy does become quite accomplished at everything except stopping, no one seems to appreciate his performance. His mother makes him take the tire out of the bathtub, and his grandmother exiles the tire outdoors after Andy gets tread marks on her carpet. Things come to a head when Andy and his tire wreck the Founders' Day parade. The officials are very tolerant, however, and explain to him that next year he had better apply for a parade permit. When Andy's parents realize the reason for his exhibitions, they help Andy tie the tire to a tree and convert it into a swing. Now many children come to play in the swing, and Andy acquires some friends. But he also unties the tire from time to time and practices on it to be ready for next year's parade.

In a charming and amusing story, the message is communicated that there are many ways to attract friends, that parents can help, and that being a new person in school and in the neighborhood is hard. Andy is a competent and inventive boy whose sense of self is well established.

81. McLerran, Alice. *I Want to Go Home*. Illus. by Jill Kastner. Tambourine, 1992 (0-688-10144-5). 30 pp. Fiction/picture book.

Interest level: Ages 8–10

Marta is very unhappy in her new house. Although her mother speaks encouragingly about new friends, Marta is unconvinced. Then Marta's mother gets her a cat that cannot move with its owners. The cat, called Sammy, is very suspicious of his new surroundings, refusing to eat or play. When Marta discovers the cat in her closet, she is delighted to see him, but Sammy hides under her bed. Marta speaks to him reassuringly, telling him many of the same things her mother told her. Eventually Sammy begins to eat and then Marta finds him cuddled up on her bed. Sammy's adjustment seems to mirror that of Marta, who now believes she is really home. Marta's mother is encouraging and hopeful but not saccharine in her discussions about the new home.

82. Mohr, Nicholasa. *Felita*. Illus. by Ray Cruz. Bantam, 1990, pap. (0-553-15792-2). 112 pp. Fiction.

Interest level: Ages 9–12

For a month, eight-year-old Felita is terribly anxious because of her family's impending move from the barrio that has been her home since infancy. Felita is unhappy to be leaving her friends. Even when everyone tells her she is going to a "better" neighborhood, she is not at all comforted. Her parents believe that she and her brothers will have the opportunity to attend better schools in the non-Hispanic neighborhood they are moving into. Unfortunately, although Felita is at first accepted by the children on her block, their parents force the children to stay away from Felita because of her Puerto Rican heritage. Some of the bigger boys even accost her physically. Because of the bigotry, Felita and her family decide that the new neighborhood is not better than their old one and that they will return to where they know they will have a supportive community.

83. Murrow, Liza Ketchum. *West Against the Wind*. Holiday, 1987 (0-8234-0668-7). 232 pp. Fiction.

Interest level: Age 10+

Abby and her family are journeying westward in a wagon train, hoping to rejoin Abby's father, who has gone on ahead to pan for gold. Now he sees great promise in the new land and has urged his family, including his brother, to come and settle in the West. The group takes on Matthew as a hired hand to help with the driving of the wagons and with the chores. Matthew, whose father was killed in a fight, is a mysterious but attractive young man. The wagon train encounters many hardships and tragedies along the way. Abby recounts the details of their journey in a series of letters to her sister, which she accumulates in a diary. Her strength of will and her determination to reach her father carry the rest of her family through the hard times.

The story is one of survival and determination rather than one of homelessness. Throughout the book, the importance of family and loyalty are stressed. The spirit of the young woman is an inspiration.

84. O'Donnell, Elizabeth Lee. *Maggie Doesn't Want to Move.* Illus. by Amy Schwartz. Macmillan, 1987 (0-02-768830-5); pap. (0-689-71375-4). 32 pp. Fiction.

Interest level: Ages 5–8

Charming illustrations complement the amusing and authentic text in this book, in which a young boy, Simon, tries desperately to persuade his mother not to move. He uses the ploy that his baby sister, Maggie—a cheerful toddler who never utters a sound in the story—is the one who does not want to move. Their mother and all the neighbors are sympathetic and understanding. Mother takes the children to see the new neighborhood and Simon's new school. The fact that he will have some friends and that his new teacher is a man, plus his mother's wisdom in acquainting him with how the neighborhood looks, convince Simon that Maggie will be happy there and that she doesn't want to stay in the old neighborhood without their mother.

The household is obviously a single-parent family. The mother is wise and understanding of her son's anxiety. Simon's feelings and the ploy he uses to express them are respected and handled well. This is a useful model book that is both entertaining and thoughtful.

85. Park, Barbara. *The Kid in the Red Jacket.* Knopf, 1987 (0-394-88189-3); pap. (0-394-80571-2). 113 pp. Fiction.

Interest level: Ages 7–11

Ten-year-old Howard Jeeter has to move from Arizona to Massachusetts despite his protests. The book covers his moving and his handling of the most humiliating (and scary) position of his whole life: being the new kid! He has to make new friends and also deal with his six-year-old new neighbor, Molly Thompson, who desperately wants his friendship.

Howard narrates the story. It is consistently humorous and believable. The book portrays the anxieties of moving, making friends, relating with siblings (Howard has an infant brother, Gaylord, with whom he has serious talks), and the problem of desertion (Molly has been deserted by both parents after a divorce and is now living with her grandmother). Molly's attachment to Howard is explained by her circumstances. The book ends with Howard's writing a positive letter to his best friend in Arizona.

Readers will enjoy the humor and wit of the story, while at the same time sympathizing with the plight of the characters.

86. Pevsner, Stella. *The Night the Whole Class Slept Over.* Clarion, 1991 (0-89919-983-6). 162 pp. Fiction.

   Interest level: Ages 9–12

Eleven-year-old Dan is tired of his parents' choice of life-style: always moving somewhere new in order to gain inspiration for their artistic pursuits. When the family moves in with his mother's parents in the town where she grew up, Dan begins to establish himself once again, to make friends and enjoy a more stable life, which includes pot roast dinners and a library card, one symbol of stability for Dan. As he adjusts to his new home, Dan feels constantly threatened by his mother's proposed next move: to an abandoned artists' colony near the Canadian border. He does not feel that he can speak out, but hopes that either his grandmother or some unforeseen event will delay or even cancel the move. The family is warm, and its members clearly love each other; however, there are gaps in understanding that they all must work through before the story resolves itself in Dan's favor. Young readers might want to discuss how they would speak out if they were in Dan's shoes.

87. Rabe, Berniece. *A Smooth Move.* Illus. by Linda Shute. Whitman, 1987 (0-8075-7486-4). 32 pp. Fiction.

   Interest level: Ages 5–9

Gus shares with us his journal detailing a month and a half of events from the time he hears that he has to move from their Portland, Oregon, home to after he and his family are settled in Washington, D.C. Gus and his family experience very little trauma; the worst things that happen are that the moving men mistakenly pack an unbaked clump of dough, some wet laundry, and some dirty dishes from the sink, and that the moving van gets stuck in Utah, delaying their move from a hotel to their house for more than a week.

   The whole family is very good-tempered about the move; it must be a step up in the father's career. Gus is a gregarious, bright boy, and his family is clearly a loving and cheerful unit. Many details of the plane trip, the hotel, and the move itself are included. Gus leaves a large group of friends, but despite his early anxieties, he meets a new friend almost immediately. This book certainly provides a model for a smooth and pleasant move.

88. Sharmat, Marjorie Weinman. *Gila Monsters Meet You at the Airport.* Illus. by Byron Barton. Macmillan, 1980 (0-02-782450-0); pap. (0-689-71383-5). 32 pp. Fiction.
   Interest level: Ages 6–9

A young boy must move with his parents from New York to someplace "out West." He has many preconceived notions of life in the West, and these ideas add to his fears of moving. The boy arrives at the airport and briefly meets a youngster moving to New York. This boy's fears of life in New York bring about an understanding that life in the West will be neither as different nor as bad as our hero first imagined.

This is an enjoyable book written with humor. It has a lesson for all of us. Sometimes our imaginations create situations far worse than reality.

89. Shura, Mary Francis. *The Search for Grissi.* Illus. by Ted Lewin. Putnam, 1986 (0-399-21705-3); Avon, pap. (0-380-70305-X). 128 pp. Fiction.
   Interest level: Ages 9–12

Peter, his sister, DeeDee, and their parents have just moved from Peoria to Brooklyn, and Peter is very unhappy about it. To make matters worse, it is November, and all of the children already know each other and are settled into their routines. He has always been teased by his peers because he likes to draw, but now he is teased because of his former hometown and because he has to walk his younger sister home from school every day. She makes friends quickly and even finds a cat named Grissi to have for her own pet. Peter doesn't make one friend and must endure a school he hates and the jibes of the boys in his class. His teacher proves to be very understanding of his situation and even explains to Peter the phenomenon of being the new boy in school. He assures him that all will be well as soon as the newness wears off, and he commends Peter's courage. When Grissi runs off, the search leads the children to an area where there are many stray cats. During a series of events, DeeDee manages to find homes for all of the stray cats, an old man who has been a benefactor to the cats dies, and Peter not only finds a friend but also receives much praise and respect for his talent.

Although the story deals with many issues, it works well as a story and the characters are interesting.

90. Singer, Marilyn. *Archer Armadillo's Secret Room*. Illus. by Beth Lee Weiner. Macmillan, 1985. o.p. 32 pp. Fiction.

Interest level: Ages 4–7

Archer Armadillo loves the burrow in which he and his large family live. He loves its many rooms, and especially he loves his own secret room, where he can go to curl up and get away from everyone and everything. His grandfather is especially understanding of Archer and his feelings, and Archer is happy. Then one day, Archer's father announces that their water hole is drying up and they must move. He goes off and finds a suitable new place, but Archer is very unhappy about moving. He runs back to their old house and determines to stay there alone. He has recognized that his plan is not a feasible one when he hears noises in the old burrow. It is his grandfather who has also decided to run away from the others and return to the old burrow. Archer persuades his grandfather that there will be no one to get food and take care of them if they stay at the old place, and so he and his grandfather go together to their new home where, the grandfather assures him, he is certain that Archer will again find a secret place for himself.

The pictures and text blend well to portray a very realistic and attractive story of the pains and pleasures of moving. The characters and the experience are easy to identify with. The solution of running away is presented not as one that stirs up the rest of the family, but rather as an episode in which Arthur figures out for himself that this is not a wise thing to do. The grandfather's ploy is, perhaps, gratuitous, but it does establish a link between the youngest and oldest family members, and it communicates well that moving is not only difficult for young children, but is a potentially traumatic event for older people as well.

91. Slote, Alfred. *Moving In*. Harper, 1988, LB (0-397-32262-3); pap. (0-06-440294-0). 167 pp. Fiction.

Interest level: Ages 8–11

Robby and his sister, Peggy, hate the idea of moving yet again. Their father has been offered a partnership in a company; their mother died two years before, and this looks like a very good opportunity for him. His new partner is a woman, and Robby and Peggy are convinced that she wants their father to marry her. The two children behave rudely and concoct all sorts of plots to prevent this marriage from occurring. It turns out that although their father does, indeed, want to marry his new partner, she is in love with someone else.

Despite their anxieties, the children grow to enjoy their new town. They make friends, and they get used to the different environment. They even understand that their father needs female companionship, and they start to plot how they will find someone for him to marry.

Some helpful hints are given here about how to adjust to a new neighborhood. Robby knows that moving vans are attractions for neighborhood kids, and he looks forward to meeting some people on the day that they move in. When none show up, he goes to the nearby park, where he meets a number of potential friends. He is outgoing, unselfconscious, and a good model for children who are anxious about moving.

92. Tsutsui, Yoriko. *Anna's Secret Friend*. Illus. by Akiko Hayashi. Puffin, 1989, pap. (0-14-050731-0). 32 pp. Fiction.

   Interest level: Ages 3–6

Anna and her family have moved to a new location, near the mountains. It is very beautiful, but Anna is lonely and bored. She receives mysterious, anonymous gifts of flowers, a letter saying that friends are nice to have, and a paper doll. When she sees the paper doll being inserted into the mail slot, Anna is finally quick enough to call out to the little girl who is the giver of these gifts. Then Anna and the little girl play actively and happily, and it is clear that they will become good friends.

Readers might want to discuss why the little girl didn't wait for Anna's response to her earlier gifts. If she was adventuresome enough to send a letter and to come regularly to Anna's house, why didn't she at least wait a few moments to benefit from Anna's reaction? Even though readers may not quite believe the behavior of the secret friend, they will enjoy the outcome. The appealing illustrations greatly enhance the text.

93. Turner, Ann. *Dakota Dugout*. Illus. by Ronald Himler. Macmillan, 1989 (0-02-789700-1); Aladdin, pap. (0-689-71296-0). 32 pp. Picture book.

   Interest level: Ages 4–8

This poetic tribute to the pioneers who settled the West identifies the feelings and challenges faced by those Americans who chose to relocate to an unknown part of the country. The narrator tells how she cried when she first arrived and describes the conditions present in her sod home: dirt falling on her bed, wind blowing through the hide doorway, snakes, and so on. Winter means dead cattle and hard ground. Summer provides a welcome respite from the harsh life as the corn furnishes food and resources to build a clapboard home. The ingenuity and patience needed by these pioneers is revealed through the translucent lines. Himler's drawings bring the prairie to life.

94. Turner, Ann. *Stars for Sarah*. Illus. by Mary Teichman. Harper, 1991 (0-06-026186-2). Unpaged. Picture book.

Interest level: Ages 3–7

Sarah is going to move and needs reassurance from her mother that the family will be together. The mother is gentle and honest, telling Sarah what will be at the new house and what will not. This book's poetic phrases soothe the natural nighttime fears that Sarah has.

95. Voigt, Cynthia. *Dicey's Song*. Atheneum, 1982 (0-689-30944-9). 196 pp. Fiction.

Interest level: Age 11+

It is difficult to place this 1983 Newbery Medal–winning book in a particular category of loss. It is the sequel to *Homecoming* (Atheneum, 1981), which describes the journey that Dicey and her younger sister and brothers made when their mother abandoned them in the parking lot of a supermarket. They are now with their grandmother in the tidewater area of Maryland, and they are secure in the knowledge that their grandmother loves them.

The book deals with the issues of abandonment, displacement, coming to terms with differences, adjusting to a new community and a new school, learning about themselves, and, finally, accepting their mother's death. Dicey, her siblings, and her grandmother are all strong and unique characters. But so is every other character in the book. They are not eccentric; they are real. Each has his or her own story to tell, as does every human being. Each deals with loss and challenge in different ways, but all are valid. This book should be read by everyone because there is something for everyone in It. It is told with beauty, empathy, warmth, and wisdom.

96. Wallace-Brodeur, Ruth. *The Godmother Tree*. Harper, 1988 (0-06-022457-6). 120 pp. Fiction.

Interest level: Ages 8–11

Laura is the daughter of an itinerant farm worker. Although she has learned to adjust to the family's continuous moves, she yearns for stability. Her brothers have their own difficulties in adjusting. The family has now moved to a situation that includes a run-down farmhouse of their own. Here Laura learns how to create her own feeling of home. The family is close-knit, and the characters are very much individuals, each with his or her own set of needs.

97. Yolen, Jane. *Letting Swift River Go.* Illus. by Barbara Cooney. Little, Brown, 1992 (0-316-96899-4). Unpaged. Picture book.

Interest level: Ages 5–8

Sally Jane recalls many details of growing up in a town on the Swift River in Massachusetts. She remembers friends visiting, walking past the Old Stone Mill and the Grange Hall to go to school, fishing in the river, picnicking in the cemetery, sleeping under the stars, and catching fireflies. She also particularly remembers having to let the fireflies go. Years after the towns are all "drowned" to create the Quabbin Reservoir to provide water supply for Boston, she remembers the pain of losing her friends, because everyone had to move away. However, she understands that she has to let go of her sorrow over all that was lost. The story is told in lyric verse, and the illustrations provide an incandescent backdrop to the poignant story.

New Country

98. Angell, Judie. *One-Way to Ansonia.* Bradbury, 1985. o.p. 183 pp. Fiction.

Interest level: Age 11+

This story conveys an authentic sense of the hardships and life-style of some of the poor immigrant Russian Jews on New York City's Lower East Side at the turn of the century. Far from romanticizing the poverty-stricken, crowded, dehumanizing environment where children were expected to work to help support the family and where people jammed themselves, their families, and their friends into small tenement apartments, this book introduces us to the reality of the situation. Angell also does not fall into the trap of idealizing the people. Although we meet kindness, honesty, and intelligence, we also note the weaknesses and selfishness of many of the characters.

The story's protagonist is Rose Olshansky, who, at eight years of age, was sent to earn money as a housekeeper and was known as "The best housekeeper in Neschviz." At the beginning of the book, she and her three sisters and brothers have just arrived from their small village in Russia to join their father, Moshe, in America. He is something of a scoundrel, having married two women in Russia since his wife died three years earlier. Having divorced neither of them, he is now getting married again, on the very day that his children arrive. He keeps them a secret from his new wife, Mume, until after the wedding. Then, when he tells her about the children, she firmly informs him that there is room for only the youngest girl, Celia. The others will have to find other places to live. Moshe appeals to all of his landsmen at the wedding, extolling his children's virtues. He manages to find beds for all of them but his son, Meyer, who has to sleep in a stable with the peddler's horse.

The children know their father's faults, yet they obey him unquestioningly and they love him. To his credit, he responds appropriately when Rose comes to him and lets him know that the father of the family she is staying with has tried to molest her. He immediately arranges for her to be placed in another home. Although she now has to share a bed with her sister, she finds it more palatable and manages to maintain her energy and thirst for knowledge. She attends night school, learning English and math, works during the day, and does piecework at night and on weekends. She gives her father most of her money, as do the other children. It is not until several years later, when he tries to arrange a marriage for Rose that she does not find appealing, that she disobeys him, and instead, at age 14, marries Hyman Rogoff, a young man whom she has been dating.

The story contains many details of the tragedies of the era. One of Rose's dearest friends is killed accidentally by a policeman because she happened to be observing a labor dispute. Women die from bearing too many children and not having the proper nourishment. But there is also the more positive side of their existence: the parties where they meet together as a community, the excitement of the new wave of unionism, the genuine opportunity for education and advancement, the maintaining of certain of the old and cherished rituals, and the fact that they are free from the terror of the pogroms.

At the end of the story, Rose leaves her husband, her father and siblings, and her friends. She takes her infant with her and buys a one-way ticket to Ansonia, Connecticut. She plans to find work and send for her husband when they can be assured of some financial security. Hyman never attempts to stop her; in fact, he recognizes that this spirit is what he loves in her. The reader must wait for a sequel to see what happens.

In this story the author provides us with the many facets of leaving home. The heroic act of coming from Russia to America without knowing what awaited them was a common experience for many immigrants. Once they arrived in New York, it was difficult for them to go further, and it was not until the second and third generation that people began to feel that they had freedom of movement. But Rose, in this story, is determined to make a better life for herself. Some of the questions readers are sure to ask concern the people she leaves behind. How will they communicate with each other? What will happen to Rose and her child in a place where there are few, if any, Jews, let alone immigrants? What is the reader's judgment of Rose's action? This book is certain to spark much research, discussion, and interest.

99. Bode, Janet. *New Kids on the Block: Oral Histories of Immigrant Teens*. Watts, 1991, pap. (0-590-44144-2). 128 pp. Nonfiction.

Interest level: Age 12+

The author has interviewed 11 young people ranging in age from early to late teens about their experiences in leaving their countries of origin and emigrating to the United States. Their backgrounds vary, but they have come, by and large, from developing countries—India, China, Vietnam, Afghanistan, El Salvador, and Cuba, for example—to seek political or economic refuge. Each of the teens talks candidly about his or her reactions to the new country and to their parents' desire to maintain their values. Each of the young people emerges as an individual rather than a representative of a particular population. The author provides an informative introduction on immigration and a description of each country before reporting on the interviews. The reader is made to understand how complex is the process of adjusting to a new country, community, language, and set of standards and customs.

100. Bresnick-Perry, Roslyn. *Leaving for America*. Illus. by Mira Reisberg. Children's Book Pr., 1992, LB (0-89239-105-7). Unpaged. Picture book.

Interest level: Ages 7–10

In this autobiographical picture book, the author tells of when she and her mother left their *shtetl* in Russia to join her father in America. Details such as the mother packing her favorite quilts and underthings because she fears she won't find any as good in the new country add to the authenticity of this bittersweet tale. The young narrator is filled with excitement and hope for the future, but she is also heartbroken that she may never again see her friends and family, especially her beloved cousin, Zisl. An end note informs readers that, in fact, Zisl and the others all perished in the Holocaust. This book substantively adds to the literature about immigrants by inviting the reader to experience with the main character the palpable loss of community, family, and culture in the decision to come to America.

101. Brown, Tricia. *Hello, Amigos!* Photos by Fran Ortiz. Henry Holt, 1986 (0-8050-0090-9); pap. (0-8050-1891-3). 48 pp. Nonfiction.

Interest level: Ages 5–9

A day in the life of one San Francisco first grader is the focus here. Frankie Valdez takes a long bus ride from his Mexican-American neighborhood. At his school, he and his sister are happy in a bilingual environment. Brown gives a full flavor to the book by showing the dual cultural life Frankie has in his large family. Spanish words are intermixed with

English—for example, *piñata, mariachi,* and *corona.* A realistic, well-photographed essay.

102. Crew, Linda. *Children of the River.* Delacorte, 1991 (0-440-50122-9); Dell, pap. (0-440-21022-4). 213 pp. Fiction.
    Interest level: Age 12+

Sundara fled Kampuchea (Cambodia) with her aunt and uncle and their children, leaving behind her own parents and siblings. The complexity of how to honor one's heritage while at the same time adapting to new demands and mores is well conveyed here, as is the tension between adapting to new ways in a new country and maintaining a respect for the old. The plot is over-involved with Jonathan, a too-good-to-be-true football hero who falls in love with Sundara, and she with him, but the story is competently told. There is so little written about Cambodian Americans, that despite its flaws, the book is worth listing.

Jonathan's parents provide yet another wrinkle to the plot: Jonathan's father is a physician who decides to carry through on his principles and go to Thailand to minister to refugees in the camps there.

Sundara carries the secret and heavy guilt of not having been able to save the life of her baby cousin when they were escaping. Her aunt carries the same burden, because she, too, wasn't able to take care of her child. They both make peace with themselves and each other at the end of the story, and there is a hopeful note because a family member arrives with the news that Sundara's younger sister has survived and is in a camp in Thailand.

103. Fisher, Leonard E. *Ellis Island: Gateway to the New World.* Photos and drawings by the author. Holiday, 1986 (0-8234-0612-1). 64 pp. Nonfiction.
    Interest level: Age 10+

By all means, join Fisher on his majestic journey, the "largest movement of human beings in history." Through his evocative writing, along with the immigrants, we too "fall silent with excitement and expectation." On the way, there's the area's history from colonial times until today and stories and remarks by individuals who went through the process there: the first to arrive on the actual island (Annie Moore, Ireland, 1892), the fire that destroyed all records from 1855 through 1897, the painful eye exam, the heartbreak of being sent back. Perhaps most lingering, the "hollow din . . . the talk, laughter, tears, sobs, and screams all melting together like a wavy sigh." Well-chosen National Park Service photographs of varied ethnic groups, in combination with Fisher's dark scratchboard drawings, effectively convey emotion, making this a wonderful book.

104. Fritz, Jean. *Homesick: My Own Story.* Illus. by Margot Tomes. Dell, 1984, pap. (0-440-43683-4). 176 pp. Fiction.

Interest level: Ages 9–12

Fritz tells about her life growing up in Wuhan, China, as if it were a story. She decided to fictionalize her life in order to be able to draw freely upon what might have been inaccurate memories and to create conversations as she remembered them or as they might have occurred. Fritz is homesick for America, a land she had never been to but still identified as her home. When she does come to the United States, it is every bit as familiar as she thought it would be. She is elated to see cows grazing in a perfectly imagined pastoral scene. Her grandmother looks and sounds exactly as Fritz thought she would. She is enchanted with the wildflowers she finds. However, she is unprepared for the prejudice she encounters as, not simply a "new" girl, but a new girl from China. She must deal with the ignorant questions of her peers and others. Finally, she makes a friend who is truly interested in her experiences. Most children who move must deal with a change in their concept of home; in this book, Fritz comes to the realization of a home that had been only a dream.

105. Garland, Sherry. *The Lotus Seed.* Illus. by Tatsuro Kiuchi. Harcourt, 1993 (0-15-249465-0). Unpaged. Picture book.

Interest level: Ages 7–10

The story, in spare but strong language, tells of the resettling in the United States of a Vietnamese family forced to flee their home because of war. The focus here is on adjusting to a new country rather than on their refugee status. The grandmother takes with her a precious lotus seed that she has carried since she was a young girl. For her, the seed symbolizes life and hope and is a remembrance of her home country. When, after many hard years in this country, her young grandson steals the seed and plants it, the grandmother, fearing that the seed is lost, is bereft. The following spring, the seed sprouts and blossoms, eventually yielding seeds for each family member and thus carrying on the heritage.

The extraordinary illustrations extend the emotional impact of the story by providing a historical context and a feeling for the different settings of Vietnam and the United States. The endurance of the grandmother is especially palpable through the luminous paintings.

106. Geras, Adele. *Voyage.* Atheneum, 1983. o.p. 193 pp. Fiction.

Interest level: Age 10+

Mina is a spirited young woman, just entering adolescence. She has many burdens to shoulder: She, her mother, and her young brother, Eli, are on a ship journeying from Eastern Europe. They are traveling in steerage along with hundreds of other passengers, all of them too poor to pay for better passage, all of them pinning their hopes on what they will find in America.

We become familiar with a number of these passengers: Clara, a wise and brave old woman; Mr. Kaminsky, an old man who has seen his family and friends destroyed in a pogrom and who no longer wants to live; Mrs. Katz and her son, Yankel, two nasty, selfish, small-minded characters; and several young men and women, all of whom we come to know and respond to. We learn about the history of some of the characters, and we become familiar with their hopes, fears, virtues, and flaws.

In all, it is a moving story of the displacement of people and their eventual accommodation to a new place and a new society. It is also the story of coping with such massive losses as death and the devastation of persecution. Geras is a gifted writer. Her books are all well worth reading, and she has much to say through her stories and characters.

107. Hesse, Karen. *Letters from Rifka.* Henry Holt, 1992 (0-8050-1964-2). 148 pp. Fiction.

   Interest level: Age 10+

This story details the physical and emotional hardships endured by immigrants on their journey to the United States as seen through the eyes of Rifka, a 12-year-old Russian Jew escaping the pogroms in 1919. Rifka's journal is in the form of letters to her cousin, Tovah. She writes them on the blank pages of a book and doesn't plan to send them. Rifka becomes separated from both her homeland and her family, first when she comes down with typhus in Poland and again when she is detained at Ellis Island because she has ringworm. Because of this, her head is shaved, and even after she is cured, her hair is slow to grow back. The officials try to deny her request for immigration because a bald girl, they say, would have few marriage prospects and would wind up on the dole. On Ellis Island, she proves herself to be intelligent, resourceful, and hard-working, so she is finally allowed to rejoin her family. This vivid, realistic portrayal of the immigrant experience shows a courageous, independent young woman who overcomes many obstacles and keeps her spirit intact.

108. Hoyt-Goldsmith, Diane. *Hoang Anh: A Vietnamese-American Boy.* Illus. with photos by Lawrence Migdale. Holiday, 1992, LB (0-8234-0948-1). 32 pp. Nonfiction.

   Interest level: Ages 8–11

Hoang Anh's family escaped by boat from South Vietnam for political reasons. They stayed for a time in a relocation camp in Malaysia, where Hoang Anh was born. Now living in San Rafael, California, the father is a fisherman and the mother works full time at a beauty shop. Hoang Anh and his family enjoy traditional Vietnamese cooking and the annual Tet festival held on the San Jose, California, fairgrounds. The family members are all citizens now and are trying to master English. Hoang Ah attends a multicultural junior high school and has friends from many backgrounds, but he is clearly proud of his heritage and wants to learn more about it. He tells of a visit with a distinguished traditional Vietnamese scholar and recounts two important folk tales. The book manages to convey the importance to the family of maintaining traditions while becoming fully engaged in the new country. The fact that it is narrated in the first person makes this book more personalized and authentic. Captions for each photograph are in the third person. A map, glossary, and pronunciation guide are provided.

109. Kraus, Joanna Halpert. *Tall Boy's Journey.* Illus. by Karen Ritz. Carolrhoda, 1992 (0-87614-746-5). 48 pp. Fiction.

Interest level: Ages 7–10

Kim returns from picnicking in the Korean hills to find his uncle waiting with sad news. Kim's grandmother has died, and now Kim has no one who can care for him. He learns he has been adopted by an American couple and must leave his homeland. His uncle, a soldier in the Korean army, tells him to be brave, a "Tall Boy" who can go on this important mission. Kim flies to the United States, a frightening place where flash cameras cause him to crouch to the floor for protection and where he must sleep on a high bed and eat strange food. Worst of all are the pasty-faced, long-nosed people who are everywhere! Kim refuses to wear American clothes or eat American food until his parents wisely ask a Korean friend to intervene. Hearing his native language spoken by Mr. Cho, a man who works with Kim's adopted father, and eating the familiar noodles and kimchi, help relax Kim, and he gradually begins to show signs of adapting to his new land and his new family. There are some minor flaws in the plot (e.g., his uncle vanishes from the story after Kim boards the plane), but the story is told entirely from Tall Boy's viewpoint, and there are many comic twists as he misinterprets what he sees and hears. The author and her husband adopted a Korean boy, which helps add authenticity to the story. The illustrations are stunning.

110. Lester, Alison. *Isabella's Bed.* Illus. by the author. Houghton, 1993 (0-395-65565-X). Unpaged. Picture book.

Interest level: Ages 4–7

Grandmother is reluctant to speak about her native South America. Her grandchildren are eager to hear stories about her bed with the silver pieces decorating the headboard. Yet every night, she sings a sad song to the children, a song about a broken-hearted widow who sailed to America with her child. One night, the bed mysteriously takes the children on a journey to places reminiscent of the figures on the bed. When they return, they have guessed their grandmother's secret: She is the widow, Isabella, in the song. This discovery releases her. She now agrees to share the stories of her past life with them, and she is finally able to accept her own losses.

111. Levine, Ellen. *I Hate English!* Illus. by Steve Bjorkman. Scholastic, 1989, pap. (0-590-42305-3). 30 pp. Picture book.

   Interest level: Ages 5–8

Mei Mei understands, but resents, English. She was never included in the family's decision to move from Hong Kong to New York, and she doesn't understand the reasons for their relocation. Although they move to Chinatown, where everyone in her new community looks and talks in a familiar way, in school Mei Mei is subjected to what she considers an unpleasant-sounding language. Mei Mei's cousin introduces her to the Chinese Learning Center, an after-school facility to help Chinese people increase their skills. Mei Mei loves the center. She tutors younger children in math, helps set up activities, and writes letters, all in Chinese. After a while, much to Mei Mei's resentment, Nancy comes to the center to tutor her in English. Nancy overcomes Mei Mei's negative attitude by reading to her from storybooks that catch Mei Mei's interest. But Mei Mei is terrified that if she learns English, she will no longer have her own identity and will lose her affiliation with her Hong Kong Chinese roots. Finally, when Mei Mei wants to communicate with Nancy, she does so in English. Mei Mei continues to speak both languages and will be encouraged to maintain her original culture while adding new customs and experiences.

112. Levine, Ellen. . . . *If Your Name Was Changed at Ellis Island.* Illus. by Wayne Parmenter. Scholastic, 1993 (0-590-46134-6). 81 pp. Nonfiction.

   Interest level: Ages 8–12

Using a question-and-answer format, this book explores what happened to immigrants to the United States who entered the country at Ellis Island. The book gives detailed information on the actual process of immigration, including how the physical examinations were done, what the new arrivals had to eat on the island, and what happened when someone in your family was turned away. The immigrant experience was not always pleasant after leaving Ellis Island, and the trials that awaited them are mentioned too. There is a section on the contributions from the many nationalities who arrived at Ellis Island and some of the common words—like *alligator* (Spanish) and *prairie* (French)—that they introduced to the American vocabulary. Especially illuminating are the beautiful paintings that illustrate the book.

113. Levitin, Sonia. *The Return.* Atheneum, 1987 (0-689-31309-8). 213 pp. Fiction.

Interest level: Age 12+

It is unusual to find the topic of Ethiopian Jews in a book for young readers. This story tells of a rescue mission called Operation Moses, in which thousands of Ethiopian Jews were airlifted secretly from the Sudan to Israel during a six-month period in 1984–1985. The Ethiopian Jews are persecuted in their own country and called *Falashas,* which means *stranger.*

The story tells of three siblings who leave their home to find religious freedom in Israel: Desta; her brother, Joas, who is killed before they arrive at their destination; and their younger sister, Almaz. It is at Joas's insistence that Desta consents to leave her beloved homeland and her extended family. But after Joas is killed, Desta assumes leadership and protects her sister on their strenuous journey.

Levitin skillfully blends factual information with story so that the effect is one of a true-to-life adventure that instructs and inspires the reader. The characters seem drawn from life, and the fact that this is based on a true event makes the book all the more compelling.

114. Lord, Bette Bao. *In the Year of the Boar and Jackie Robinson.* Illus. by Marc Simont. Harper, 1984 (0-06-023003-2); pap. (0-06-440175-8). 169 pp. Fiction.

Interest level: Ages 9–12

Shirley Temple Wong is the heroine of this story of moving to a new land and adjusting to new customs and circumstances. Shirley and her mother have just come to Brooklyn to be with Shirley's father. He has been in America for a long time preparing the way for the rest of the family to be together again. Shirley misses her extended family and home in China. She has trouble learning English, and she faces the problem of some antagonistic and pugnacious classmates. And to compound matters, she is placed in a class with children a year or two older than she, because of the difference in the Chinese way of counting age (that is, she was considered a year old at birth and a year older each New Year's Day).

Shirley is bright, feisty, and imaginative. She is generous and enthusiastic and cares deeply about people. The author introduces us to Chinese customs and to Shirley's feelings through her escapades and her interactions with people. The story is full of humor, information, excitement, and sentiment. The triumphant moment, when Shirley is introduced to her idol, Jackie Robinson, has an authentic ring to it, as does the rest of this endearing book.

The book demonstrates how children can cope with separation from homeland and family and with the challenges of moving to a new neighborhood, entering a new school, and dealing with differences in heritage and customs.

115. Pettit, Jayne. *My Name Is San Ho.* Scholastic, 1992 (0-590-44172-8). 149 pp. Fiction.

Interest level: Ages 10–14

San Ho flees his tiny village in Vietnam when his mother feels it is too dangerous for him to remain. He stays in Saigon with a family friend and loses touch with his mother until a letter arrives instructing him to come to the United States. San Ho's journey and his eventual reunion with his mother and her new husband, as well as his gradual adjustment to life in the United States, are all seen through his eyes. San Ho learns that his mother spent years making the necessary arrangements for his arrival; she was not able to come and get him herself. He finds he must get used to his stepfather, Stephen, who must also adjust to having a new son. Dramatically portrayed are San Ho's first months at school, his bewilderment at baseball, and his devastation when his garden is vandalized. Issues of learning a new language, fitting in to a new culture while retaining identification with the old one, confronting prejudice, and adjusting to a country that has little understanding of what it means to live in a war-torn land are all presented in this book.

116. Rosenberg, Maxine B. *Making a New Home in America.* Photos by George Ancona. Lothrop, 1986 (0-688-05824-8). 48 pp. Nonfiction.

Interest level: Ages 6–10

Through the words of four seven- and eight-year-old children, the author reveals mixed emotions about the changes involved in coming to the United States. The children have left Japan, Cuba, India, and Guyana; two are here temporarily, and two have come to stay. The reasons range from a parent's job transfer to the need for freedom of speech.

The children's reactions are explored with candor that is authentic, engaging, and easy to identify with. Japanese Jiri's misbehavior in school is given as much attention as Guyanan Carmen's awe at the material splendor she finds here. Rosenberg has intertwined the four profiles to look at central themes of adjustment. We see the commonalities of the four experiences.

Ancona's top-notch, sharp, slick photos draw us into natural home, neighborhood, and school scenes. The children's sparkling eyes look terrific on exceptionally fine paper, adding to the desire to view, re-view, and understand.

117. Sandin, Joan. *The Long Way Westward.* Illus. by the author. Harper, 1989, LB (0-06-025207-3); pap. (0-06-444198-9). 64 pp. Fiction.
    Interest level: Ages 6–9

With Ellis Island in the background, Carl Erik remarks that the streets in America are not paved with gold. He and his family pass through immigration and board trains to other parts of the United States. Carl Erik and his brother mistakenly enter a first-class train and believe that this will be their accommodation. When the porter orders them out, they find themselves sleeping on the floor of a car with other immigrants. As the train travels through Pennsylvania and Ohio, the immigrants speculate about their lives in a country that has no king. In Chicago, they are almost swindled by a man who preys on immigrants; they are saved by a member of the Svea Society who is there to help Swedes who are in need. They are reunited with extended family members when they finally reach Minnesota. The family's challenges as they make their way to a new home provide them with chances to strengthen their bonds with each other.

118. Say, Allen. *Grandfather's Journey.* Illus. by the author. Houghton, 1993 (0-395-57035-2). 32 pp. Picture book.
    Interest level: Ages 6–10

Based on the author's own family and experience, this story of belonging to two cultures and loving two lands is told movingly. The grandson describes how his grandfather journeyed to many places before settling in California. After he marries and has a daughter he returns with his family to the land of his youth, but always misses California. When the grandson grows up he too journeys to California and settles there, and understands his grandfather's feelings because when he is in one place he misses the other. The paintings portray the people and the settings through a filter of nostalgia and memory. The luminous portraits of each of the people in the family, through their stance on the page and their faces gazing straight at the viewer, involve the reader in their lives and feelings. The spare language evokes a deep emotional response in the reader. The dilemma of the sojourner is presented with passion and empathy.

119. Stanek, Muriel. *I Speak English for My Mom.* Illus. by Judith Friedman. Whitman, 1989 (0-8075-3659-8). 32 pp. Picture book.
    Interest level: Ages 6–9

Lupe, a Mexican-American girl, occasionally resents, but mostly feels pride in, her role as an interpreter for her Spanish-speaking mother. She has a great deal of responsibility providing not only translation but emotional support to her mother, who has a difficult time adapting to life in the United States. In the end, she encourages her mother to enroll in English classes so she will be able to get a better job. Although the mother's seeming weakness and insecurity are not very believable in a woman who has overcome as many obstacles and taken as many risks as this woman has, the book is still valuable because it addresses a very real situation for many children of immigrants. It also demonstrates that moving to a new country can be daunting unless one actively acquires some survival skills.

120. Surat, Michele Maria. *Angel Child, Dragon Child.* Illus. by Vo-Dinh Mai. Raintree, 1983 (0-940742-12-8); Scholastic, pap. (0-590-42271-5). 32 pp. Fiction.

　　Interest level: Ages 5–9

Written poetically and with almost overwhelming feeling, this is the story of Ut, who has come with her sisters, brother, and father to the United States from Vietnam. There is no money yet for her mother to join them. School is a misery, where instructional methods are different and she is teased mercilessly by Raymond, a classmate who (naturally) turns out to be as insecure as she. "Pajamas," he calls out to her, mocking her clothes. The seasons proceed this way, with Ut finding solace in her mother's photo. She is less able to be the Angel Child or brave Dragon Child her mother had told her to be. Instead, she is an Angry Dragon. When Raymond goes too far, the principal intervenes, cleverly creating a task whereby he must write down Ut's story as she tells it to him. The principal, now the hero—a weakness in the story—then rallies the student body to raise money for Ut's mother to come to the United States through a Vietnamese Fair. The writing is as gentle and poetic as Ut herself: "We slid through icy winter . . . We splish-splashed through spring rain."

121. Winter, Jeanette. *Klara's New World.* Illus. by the author. Knopf, 1992 (0-679-80626-1). 38 pp. Fiction/picture book.

　　Interest level: Ages 7–12

A touching and realistic story about a family's immigration to the United States in the second half of the nineteenth century. Jeanette Winter is the daughter of Swedish immigrants, and her familiarity with the situation lends authenticity to the story. The family's sadness at leaving their home is well captured, as are the details of the arrival at Castle Garden and their subsequent journey to the Midwest. Their filing of a claim and settling on the land seem a little too effortless, but this does not seriously damage the impact of the story. Klara reflects the apparent ability of an immigrant child to realize her role in the family and to not be absorbed in what will happen to her but focus on how the whole family will manage in the new world.

Temporary Separations

A great number of separations during childhood, many of them temporary, evoke feelings of loss in children. A child loses a valuable object, or a pet, gets lost for a time, goes away for an overnight or extended stay or to summer camp. Even going on a trip or visiting can cause anxiety related to separation from the familiar. Lacking a large body of experience in the world, some youngsters are unsure of eventual reunions. If not handled properly, terror can be the result.

When visiting or going to camp becomes a regular, predictable event and the situation is a secure and pleasant one, it can serve as a model of reassurance for young readers. When children are included in planning and decision making, their emotional balance is better maintained. Happy endings or model solutions should reflect this understanding.

Lost and Found

122. Delton, Judy. *I'll Never Love Anything Again.* Illus. by Rodney Pate. Whitman, 1985 (0-8075-3521-4). 32 pp. Fiction.
    Interest level: Ages 6–10

A young boy develops allergies and must therefore give up his dog. He is distraught, and he imagines that no one will be able to love and understand his dog the way he does. The boy's mother is very understanding because she is also unhappy about having to give their dog away. She arranges for a good home for the dog, on a farm where the boy will be able to visit in the summer.

The details of the relationship between the boy and the dog, the specifics of the dog's attributes, and the loving and intelligent help the boy's mother gives him combine with the boy's authentic responses to this unhappy situation to form a very helpful and well-crafted book.

123. Havill, Juanita. *Jamaica's Find.* Illus. by Anne Sibley O'Brien. Houghton, 1986 (0-395-39376-0); pap. (0-395-45357-7). 32 pp. Fiction.
    Interest level: Ages 4–8

From start to finish, this is a story about feelings. Jamaica finds a toy dog on the playground. She loves it and wants to keep it, but her parents help her to empathize with the child who has lost the dog. She returns it to the office of the park administration. Later on, she meets a little girl who is looking for her lost dog. Jamaica takes the little girl to the office, where she is reunited with her toy. Jamaica has lost the dog, but she has found a friend.

The illustrations are wonderfully realistic and warm. The plot is filled with interesting details (parents who express their opinions but let their child find her own way to a decision) and speaks to readers' hearts without moralizing. The children have personality and make the situation an interesting and believable one. An added plus is that Jamaica is portrayed in the watercolors as an African-American child, but being African-American has nothing to do with the story line. A useful book to spark discussion about values and socializing.

124. Murrow, Liza Ketchum. *Good-bye, Sammy.* Illus. by Gail Owens. Holiday, 1989, LB (0-8234-0726-8). 30 pp. Fiction/storybook.

Interest level: Ages 5–9

Sammy is a toy rabbit who is accidentally left on an airplane by his devoted owner. The boy is heartsick and, along with his mother, tries everything he can think of to get Sammy back. Despite all of the family's efforts, Sammy remains lost. The boy goes through various stages of grief and even dreams about playing with Sammy. His parents are sympathetic and let him grieve. His mother accepts his angry refusal to buy a replacement bunny. Eventually, the boy agrees to get a new bunny and prepares for its arrival by making a house for it. As he plays with the new toy bunny, Roger, the boy invents stories about Sammy and gradually begins to accept his new toy. Although the story is simple, it is very true-to-life. The illustrations are textured and engaging and depict the full range of the boy's emotions.

125. Schubert, Dieter. *Where's My Monkey?* Illus. by the author. Puffin, 1992, pap. (0-8037-1071-2). 24 pp. Fiction.

Interest level: Ages 3–6

In this wordless book, a young boy takes his toy monkey everywhere. It is clear that the boy loves the monkey very much. One rainy day, when the boy has been on a bicycle outing, the monkey falls from his arms without his noticing it. He and his mother search for the monkey, but they can't find him. They don't see that he has fallen into an opening near a large tree. A family of mice, then a hedgehog family, and finally a bird claim the monkey. After he has been dropped into a lake, a man who, fortuitously, is the proprietor of a doll hospital fishes him out, repairs him, and places him in his shop window, just as the unhappy young owner of the monkey comes by. Of course the reunion is a joyful one.

Not many toys are so miraculously found, and young readers will have to learn to cope with irretrievable losses. But this lovely fantasy is so much the fulfillment of children's dreams that it would be ungracious not to acknowledge its wonderful happy ending.

Getting Lost

126. Cowen-Fletcher, Jane. *It Takes a Village.* Illus. by the author. Scholastic, 1993 (0-590-46573-2). 32 pp. Picture book.

Interest level: Ages 5–8

Yemi's mother asks her to take care of her younger brother, Kokou, at the village marketplace. Yemi sets her brother down for a moment to get him something to eat. When she turns around he is gone. The rest of the afternoon Yemi searches frantically for her brother, fearing that he is hungry, thirsty, tired, and frightened. In fact, he is being attended to by a succession of people in the marketplace who feed him, give him drinks, play with him, provide a place for him to take a nap, and return him happily to his mother and sister at the end of the day. The mother is never concerned because she knows that the entire village is there to protect him. The author/illustrator developed the story from the West African proverb, "It takes a village to raise a child." She became acquainted with the people and customs of Benin when she served there in the Peace Corps.

127. Crary, Elizabeth. *I'm Lost.* Illus. by Marina Megale. Parenting, 1985, LB (0-943990-08-4); pap. (0-943990-09-2). 32 pp. Nonfiction.

Interest level: Ages 4–8

This title is an entry in the Children's Problem Solving Book series, in which the child gets to choose solutions to problems. The books in this series are best read along with a parent, and there is no right or wrong response. This story focuses on the alternatives facing Amy, who has become separated from her father at the zoo. Amy can think of seven ideas, all of which the child can follow in a sequence chosen by the reader. The ideas are: stay where she is, go hunt for her dad, cry, look for a police officer, find a woman with children, ask a clerk for help, or wait at the front gate. The child, in following the various options, gets to interact with the parent, responding to such activity questions as "How does Amy feel now?" or "What do you think Amy will do next?" As in the other books in the series, a final page is left blank for the child to fill in his or her own ideas.

128. Hines, Anna Grossnickle. *Don't Worry, I'll Find You.* Illus. by the author. Dutton, 1986. o.p. 32 pp. Fiction.

Interest level: Ages 3–6

Three females go shopping at the big, confusing mall: Sarah; her mother; and, at Sarah's insistence, her doll Abigail. "Well, if you lose her, don't complain to me about it," Mama warns, adding that Sarah should stay put if *she* gets lost. All hands are held tightly as the reader eagerly anticipates one of the three getting lost; each pastel picture becomes a "what's missing" search. Suspense mounts as they choose clothing and have lunch. A pair of red sneakers is finally exciting enough to distract Sarah, and Abigail is left behind. Sarah runs back, and Abigail is indeed in the same spot. When she then can't find her mother where she'd left her, Sarah stays put, just as her mother had advised and just as Abigail had done. In a cute twist, it's the doll's presence that brings the mother and daughter back together. Spare, soft illustrations simultaneously show the dizziness of a mall and reassure readers that parents and child may be temporarily separated but will eventually reunite.

129. Johnston-Hamm, Diane. *Laney's Lost Momma.* Illus. by Sally G. Ward. Whitman, 1991 (0-8075-4340-3). Unpaged. Picture book.

Interest level: Ages 3–7

Laney and her mother lose each other in a department store. Their actions mirror one another's as they frantically search for the one who is "lost." Their reunion is very realistic and typical of such a common occurrence.

130. Paulsen, Gary. *Hatchet.* Bradbury, 1987 (0-02-770130-1); Puffin, pap. (0-14-032724-X). 195 pp. Fiction.

Interest level: Age 11+

Brian Robinson's plane crashed, and he is the only survivor. He had been on his way to visit his father; his parents are divorced, and he is obsessed with the secret that he carries: He saw his mother embracing and kissing another man before his parents were divorced, and he knows that that is the reason for the divorce.

Brian matures through the course of the book. He is forced to rely on his intelligence, strength, and instincts in order to survive. The language is specific and graphic, especially when it describes human bodily functions and reactions and the sensations and odors of the wilderness. For example, when Brian catches a bird and is faced with the problem of cleaning it before he can eat it, he pulls the skin off and likens it to peeling an orange. The bird's insides fall out, and a "steamy dung odor" arises from its entrails. There is much retching and flatulation in the book, but the language is appropriate and respectful of the reader.

In addition to its being an adventure and survival story, the book also helps the reader to empathize with Brian, who is trying to come to grips with his parents' behavior before, during, and after the divorce. Contrary to what Brian had originally anticipated, he returns to his mother; and his father, after an initial show of interest and concern, returns to his self-centered ways. This is a good, realistic book on many levels, and it will be appreciated by many young readers.

Camp

131. Carlson, Nancy. *Arnie Goes to Camp.* Illus. by the author. Viking, 1988, pap. (0-670-81549-7). 32 pp. Fiction.

  Interest level: Ages 5–8

Arnie is reluctant at first to go away to summer camp, but his mother assures him that it is only for two weeks. When he arrives at camp, he is somewhat homesick, but he quickly overcomes this feeling and enjoys all of the activities the camp has to offer. The camp is one that anyone who has ever been to camp will recognize. Nothing of significance, except for some bee stings, happens to Arnie. He not only survives the experience, he thrives on it. Perhaps this book can help youngsters who are anxious about their first summer camp experience to feel better.

132. Cole, Brock. *The Goats.* Farrar, 1987 (0-374-32678-9); pap. (0-374-42576-0). 184 pp. Fiction.

  Interest level: Age 12+

The details of the story are dramatic: An adolescent boy and girl are brought to a small island by their summer campmates, stripped naked, and left to fend for themselves. Apparently it has been a tradition at this particular camp to select the least popular campers, label them as "goats," and abandon them on the small island overnight. The two goats (they don't discover each other's names until almost the end of the book) decide not to wait for the other campers to come and claim them. They manage, by their wits and determination, to get off the island, steal some clothes, and survive for a week until the girl's mother comes to get them.

  During their odyssey, they gain greatly in strength and self-esteem. They help each other and come to love and depend on each other. They are both, in a sense, abused children, although the abuse is emotional rather than physical. Laura's mother is a single parent whose work occupies so much of her time that she has little left to give to her daughter. Howie's parents, archaeologists, have made it clear to their son that he was unplanned and unwanted, and that he is a nuisance and a burden to them.

They do not mean to be unkind, but their work is the overriding feature of their lives.

During the course of the book, the reader is introduced to another summer camp where the campers are very helpful to Howie and Laura. These campers are poor, from the city, and wise in the ways of survival. For them, the camp represents an opportunity, not a frivolous taking up of time.

The novel is just as much a coming-of-age story as it is one of survival. Cole realistically portrays different kinds of abuse that youngsters are subjected to. The reader is never tempted to disbelieve, because the writing is powerful and graphic. The issue of nudity is handled delicately, as is the relationship between the two adolescents. Other problems—such as Laura and Howie stealing clothing and money and deceiving a motel owner into permitting them to stay in a room rented by someone else—are tackled in an ethical manner. The two youngsters steal, but they know they are doing something against their moral code, and they keep track of everything they are taking so that they can eventually reimburse the owners.

Cole masterfully demonstrates how the two main characters and Laura's mother develop and change for the better. He also introduces memorable minor characters in the person of the girls' head counselor and some of the campers in the "good" camp. The police, deputy sheriff, and camp director fare badly and are one-dimensional, but they are foils who are designed to lend drama to the situation. They do not damage the integrity of the story. The reader is left to speculate about what will happen at the end, but there are sufficient clues to reassure us that the ending has every possibility of working out for the best.

133. Delton, Judy. *My Mom Made Me Go to Camp.* Illus. by Lisa McCue. Delacorte, 1990 (0-385-30040-9); Bantam, pap. (0-553-37251-3). Unpaged. Picture book.

Interest level: Ages 5–8

The narrator of the story is a little boy who is not at all sure that he wants to go to camp. His mother describes camp to him, identifying activities she is sure he will enjoy, like roasting marshmallows and gathering firewood. The boy doesn't like the idea of being labeled, although his mother is referring to sewing name tags on his clothes. She matter-of-factly waves good-bye to him on the bus, calling out instructions for him to write her a postcard. At first, the boy hates camp. He doesn't like to sing, he sinks instead of swims, and he gets a rash. His postcards home are very negative. Eventually, he makes friends and then is not so eager to come home.

By the end of camp, the boy is the only one who isn't homesick. He returns home to his mother somewhat more mature, but disappointed that no marshmallow roast had occurred. This tongue-in-cheek look at the camp experience seems at first to confirm children's fears about their stay away from home; however, the light touch adds a realistic bit of humor that should help dissipate anxieties about going to camp.

134. Gauch, Patricia Lee. *Night Talks*. Putnam, 1983. o.p. 156 pp. Fiction.

   Interest level: Age 12+

In this study, a group of overprivileged teenagers attend camp with a group of poor teenagers, and all of them learn about stereotyping and living together. The camp counselor is a well-respected, competent young woman who motivates the campers to rise above their differences and to cooperate with and care for each other. One camper, Margaret, is particularly difficult. She is transformed by the end of the summer from a sullen, silent person to someone who trusts her friends and who is almost destroyed by that trust. The girls mistakenly try to interfere in her life at home by sending her mother a letter. They finally come to the conclusion that they should not interfere in matters that they do not understand.

   The atmosphere of a summer camp is well portrayed here. The author communicates the intensity of the summer experience and the creation of a community set apart from the rest of the world.

135. Martin, Ann M. *Bummer Summer*. Holiday, 1983 (0-8234-0483-8); Scholastic, pap. (0-590-43622-8). 152 pp. Fiction.

   Interest level: Ages 9–12

Kammy is upset about her new stepsiblings. They badger her constantly, and they ruin her things. She is also not very happy about her new step-mother, Kate. Although Kate tries to get along with Kammy, nothing she does seems to be right. Kammy's father is powerless to fix the situation, so he suggests that Kammy go to a summer camp. Kammy pleads with her father not to send her away, but they strike a bargain: Kammy will go for two weeks, and if, at the end of that time, she wants to come home, she will be permitted to do so.

   Kammy goes to camp, and it is worse than she imagined. She is constantly in trouble. She has one friend, but she has one enemy, too. After some conversations with a sympathetic counselor and a remarkably understanding director, Kammy begins to enjoy camp. After two weeks, when her family comes to visit and offers to take her home with them, she informs them that she wants to stay for the rest of the summer. She has reconciled with her stepmother and siblings and made up with her enemy.

One of the benefits of a camping experience is that children learn to adjust to difficult situations. That is the case for Kammy. The book is fun, and Kammy's coping strategies are useful.

136. Voigt, Cynthia. *Come a Stranger.* Atheneum, 1986 (0-689-31289-X); Fawcett, pap. (0-449-70246-4). 190 pp. Fiction.

Interest level: Age 11+

Mina wins a scholarship to an otherwise all-white dance camp in Connecticut the summer she is ten years old. She loves the camp and is praised for her dancing ability. When she returns home, she is critical of her old friends and of almost everything about her close-knit Maryland community. Her father, a minister, and mother try to help her see herself more clearly, but she only lives for the next summer, when she can again go to camp and be with her white friends.

Over the year, Mina grows and develops physically at a rapid pace. When she gets to camp, she cannot help but see some slights and attitudes that she never noticed before. Although the other girls and the teachers are friendly to her, she has no roommate, and she detects subtle evidences of racism. To make matters worse, she is no longer a good dancer and is sent home.

Over the next few years, Mina develops a deep love for the summer minister in their community. His name is Tamer Shipp, and those of us who have read *The Runner* (Atheneum, 1985) remember him as Bullet Tillerman's friend. He is married and has named one of his children for Bullet. Through her friendship with Dicey Tillerman, Mina brings Tamer together with the Tillerman family. Everyone is deeply moved by the encounter, and 14-year-old Mina is at last free to be her own woman and move toward relationships with men her own age.

This story, like every story by Voigt, is a complex one. In addition to welcoming this book to the rich store of connections we have with the Tillerman family, the reader is given the opportunity to grapple with pre-conceptions, assumptions, philosophy about people and life, and the moral behavior of people toward each other. The characters are full-blooded mixtures of goodness and meanness, bigness and smallness. Mina changes as she grows older and wiser, but her essence remains the same, and most readers can identify with her humanity, while enjoying her individuality.

137. Weyn, Suzanne. *My Camp Diary.* Illus. by Ann Iosa. Bradbury, 1986. o.p. 128 pp. Nonfiction.

Interest level: Ages 9–15

This spiral-bound book is meant to be a fill-in companion to take along to camp. By using it, youngsters will have both a record of their experiences to turn back to in later years (for example, names of bunkmates) and a way to sort out feelings. There are funny quotes from the books of well-known children's book authors (for example, Judy Blume and Ellen Conford) on the challenges of growing up and being independent. Also, there are charts for scoring every aspect of camp life and then rescoring at the end to see how the scores compare. Weyn includes games for rest hour, tips for getting into and out of trouble, and self-analysis sections on such things as the homesick blues (for example, "The person I most want to see is . . ."; "Sometimes I start to feel homesick when . . ."; and "When I feel homesick, this is how I cheer myself up . . ."). A number of pages can be torn out and sent as instant letters, and a number of others are pages for private notes to oneself. There's understanding of the minicrises that come about, such as getting an award but having your name misspelled on the certificate, or worse, not getting one at all. To these letdowns, the author provides solace in the form of imagined revenge: "If I gave the awards . . ." With places for addresses, photographs, and important scraps, this chronology of the camp experience from arrival to departure will surely be worth its cost as a summer gift. A fine idea happily brought to fruition.

Travel

138. Bernstein, Joanne E. *Taking Off: Travel Tips for a Carefree Trip.* Illus. by Kathie Abrams. Lippincott, 1986. o.p. 190 pp. Nonfiction.

Interest level: Age 12+

Ours is a time when youngsters desire and need to travel independently. It may be that they need to board a plane, train, or bus to visit a parent who doesn't live with them. It may be that they are ready to leave home on a tour, traveling with other youngsters under supervision. Or perhaps they want to go off with friends by bike, car, or bus on a first jaunt without parents. This is a guide to those first travel experiences and adventures.

Topics are both psychological and practical. Along psychological lines, Bernstein develops questions readers can ask themselves regarding their likes and dislikes: How long should you be away? Should you have a schedule? Would you be better off traveling alone or with a companion? If with a companion, there are questions useful for choosing a compatible person. There is also guidance on how to keep from feeling lonely while on the trip, how to stay in touch with relatives back home but still be independent, how to stay safe and healthy while traveling, and how to meet people.

Practical information includes full information on all means of travel: train, bus, plane, and car. There is also discussion on how to get a ticket, how to get the best price, and luggage needs. Various places to stay are detailed, including advantages and disadvantages: hotels and motels, guest houses, colleges, YMCAs/YWCAs, and camping. There is a chapter on vacation ideas: theme parks, resorts, package plans, teen tours, hostel stays, and international education. The nitty-gritty is addressed in detail: getting passports, finding out about locales, and packing. An especially helpful section on caring for emergencies rounds out the material. Abrams's drawings add wry humor with just the right balance for teens serious about their new responsibilities. A full, annotated list of travel organizations is appended. Index.

139. Brisson, Pat. *Your Best Friend, Kate.* Illus. by Rick Brown. Bradbury, 1989 (0-02-714350-3). 40 pp. Fiction.

Interest level: Ages 7–9

During her family's extended automobile tour of 11 states, Kate and her brother, Brian, fight. Although the arguments distress the children's parents, Kate shows that she cares about her brother's feelings by leaving him an encouraging note when he stays behind to visit an aunt while Kate and her parents return home. Car travel can be an ordeal for many families; this one reacts with a fair degree of good humor and inventiveness.

140. Brown, Laurene Krasny, and Marc Brown. *Dinosaurs Travel: A Guide for Families on the Go.* Illus. by the authors. Little, Brown, 1988 (0-316-11076-0); pap. (0-316-11253-4). 30 pp. Picture book.

Interest level: To Age 9

This engagingly illustrated book about the popular Dinosaurs is bright and cheerful and motivating by design. The Dinosaurs look like they are having a wonderful time as they take the subway, sleep in a hotel room, and come home to share their experiences while traveling. The book is filled with helpful hints about all manner of travel, as well as acknowledgments of common fears that children might experience. Also included are suggestions about ways to make travel more enjoyable and encouragement to readers who might not understand why travel can be educational and fun. There are even postcards that children can send to share their experiences with friends and family. This book will be reassuring to children who are nervous about going on a trip and will no doubt elicit positive responses from seasoned travelers as well.

141. Faulkner, Matt. *The Amazing Voyage of Jackie Grace.* Illus. by the author. Scholastic, 1991, pap. (0-590-44860-9). 42 pp. Fiction.

Interest level: Ages 5–8

Jackie goes on a fantasy voyage in his bathtub, during which time he encounters the noisy crew of a sailing ship, a wicked storm at sea, and pirates. He leaves his tub on hearing his mother call him, and we hear a small "yoho" from the ship that has now been returned to its original toy size.

The illustrations are a wonderful blend of exaggeration and reality. The imaginary adventure lets children know that their fantasies are acceptable and prepares them for the eventual real-life adventure of leaving home.

142. Fleischman, Paul. *Time Train.* Illus. by Claire Ewart. Harper, 1991, LB (0-06-021710-3). Unpaged. Picture book.

Interest level: Ages 4–9

The Rocky Mountain Unlimited is a special train that takes a group on a field trip back in time. As the children pass through Philadelphia, they notice horses and buggies and realize that this is no ordinary field trip. As they continue, their teacher gets anxious, but the children become more and more excited as they go through what is apparently the Ice Age and wind up in a forest populated by dinosaurs. The children use the time wisely: They study the dinosaurs' eating habits, take photographs while riding a pterodactyl, and enjoy scrambled eggs for breakfast. Miss Pym seems greatly relieved when the train makes a return trip. This is a fun look at travel and may relieve children who have "field trip anxiety" because of its sheer absurdity. The illustrations are well executed and humorous, especially those of the harried teacher.

143. Fritz, Jean. *China Homecoming.* Photos by Michael Fritz. Putnam, 1985 (0-399-21182-9). 143 pp. Nonfiction.

Interest level: Ages 9–12

Jean Fritz grew up in China and always harbored a fierce desire to return. For years, it seemed as if this would be impossible. Finally, the relationship between the United States and China made it feasible for Fritz to initiate the permissions and paperwork necessary for her to revisit her childhood home. This is the story of her sometimes emotionally wrenching trip to Hankou and Wuhan, where she was aided and escorted by the Foreign Affairs Bureau. Fritz tries to find her own house but is discouraged when she realizes that the street names have been changed. She wonders about her memory and whether or not her home has been torn down. In a highlight of the book, Fritz serendipitously discovers it and is overjoyed when she is allowed to go inside. This book is a wonderful example of the role that memories, both accurate and imagined, play in traveling.

144. Howard, Elizabeth Fitzgerald. *The Train to Lulu's*. Illus. by Robert Casilla. Bradbury, 1988 (0-02-744620-4). 32 pp. Fiction.

Interest level: Ages 4–8

Beppy and Babs take the train to Great-Aunt Lulu's, going from Boston to Baltimore, mirroring a trip the author took as a child each summer. They are on their own on this nine-hour trip, packed up for the entire summer. Their parents have given them detailed instructions: The conductor will take care of them, Travelers' Aid will see to it that only Lulu picks them up, and so on. The 1930s setting is painted beautifully in full color, each watercolor setting the mood as they change on the long trip—fear, excitement, and impatience. Beppy takes good care of her younger sister Babs and monitors the activities: eating, drawing, reading, resting, and eating again. When they arrive, not only is Great-Aunt Lulu there, but a large extended family as well, creating a warm circle. The parents and grandparents of the children reading or hearing this book will enjoy the feelings and adventures of these two African-American girls—in a time when milk could be bought on a train for 10 cents. And the book provides an excellent model for children traveling alone for the first time.

145. Huff, Barbara A. *Welcome Aboard! Traveling on an Ocean Liner*. Illus. and photos. Clarion, 1987. o.p. 128 pp. Nonfiction.

Interest level: Ages 9–14

Huff is a children's book club editor and an ocean crossing enthusiast-fanatic. Here she presents a jubilant account of what such a crossing might be like, specifically based on her adventures on the *QE2*. She draws the reader into a day-by-day diary right from the start: "You are among the hundreds of passengers who crowd the ship's railings. Some, like you, look down on the dock fifty feet below." In this brief passage, one can see both the attention to a cruise's excitement and the accuracy of her research. (Youngsters feeling fretful about their trip away from home may be comforted to learn that the *QE2* carries enough ice cream to create 24,000 cones.)

Along with the diary of her trip, there are historical looks at cruising, stories of famous ships of the past and present, and innovations in today's cruising (theme trips, Mark Twain country, visiting Hawaii and Alaska, and so on). Throughout, Huff talks about games, activities, and opportunities for children; she tells interesting, real stories about children she has met on voyages—for example, the girl (shown in a photograph) who can knot a cherry stem inside her mouth. With the exuberance that only a person in love with her subject can bring, Huff has created a delightful book that will get both youngsters and their older relatives ready to pack their bags and leave the usual behind. List of resources, index.

146. Krementz, Jill. *Jamie Goes on an Airplane*. Photos by the author. Random, 1986. o.p. 14 boards. Nonfiction.

   Interest level: Ages 1–5

Bright photographs make it fun to visit Grandma and Grandpa. This is not a first visit, as preschooler Jamie tells us: "We fly there on a big airplane." He seems to know the routine well: Mommy helps him pack his own suitcase the night before, the skycap puts tags on the suitcases so that they won't get lost, and the family of three gets seat numbers at the counter. Photographs show security and its necessity ("to be sure we're not taking anything dangerous"), loudspeaker announcements, meeting the smiling pilot, fastening the seatbelt, take-off safety procedures, meeting the stewards, snacks on board, a very adult-looking meal, a little nap, and then a happy-landing reunion with Grandma and Grandpa. "I love plane trips," says Jamie, in this happy introduction to temporary separation from the comforts of home.

147. Neville, Emily Cheney. *The China Year*. Harper, 1991 (0-06-024384-8). 243 pp. Fiction.

   Interest level: Age 11+

Henrietta, called Henri, goes to Beijing, China, for a year while her father takes a position as a visiting professor at the university. The move is very strange for Henri, with its combination of unusual Chinese food and pseudo-American fare; a lack of peers, except for Caitlin, who is several years younger; and some disquiet about her mother's well-being. Henri ventures out and finally meets Minyuan, a boy whom she befriends, and it is through him that she begins to realize the deepening unrest in China. The author infuses the text with the aura of China; but readers will identify with Henri, whose problems reflect those of young teenagers worldwide.

148. Roffey, Maureen. *I Spy on Vacation*. Illus. by the author. Four Winds, 1988. o.p. 28 pp. Nonfiction.

   Interest level: Ages 4–7

With so much to see on vacation, the details readers must look for on these pages will make any earlier worries simply disappear. Each double spread shows a busy scene, and the few words start with the phrase "I spy. . ." The first page, for example, says: "I spy the sea." The family (two parents and three children) is shown arriving at a hotel, with other people looking out windows, boats on the ocean, palm trees, and so on. Subsequent pages let the child fill in the words—for example, "I spy a pair of sunglasses on the. . ." They are pictured on the floor, and the reader must spot them. And on it goes: "I spy the waiter bringing two . . . (ice cream sodas)." On and on goes the fun, ending with a plane ride bringing the family back to Grandma and Grandpa. This book will be enjoyed again and again, both before a trip and afterward.

149. Trivas, Irene. *Annie . . . Anya: A Month in Moscow.* Illus. by the author. Orchard, 1992 (0-531-05452-7). Unpaged. Picture book.

Interest level: Ages 5–8

Annie is to spend a month in Moscow, and she is not a bit happy at the thought. Although she finds some of her trip interesting, she is tired from jet lag and is unable to get a familiar peanut-butter-and-banana sandwich. The children at the day-care center that she visits stare at her. Red Square isn't red. Annie misses her home. There are some bright spots, however: Annie is entranced at the circus; she loves the huge escalators; and finally, she meets Anya, a little girl at the day-care center. The two girls develop a friendship, sharing Russian and English words. Annie becomes fascinated by Russian words and learns several. She visits Anya's cramped but happy apartment, takes ballet lessons, and goes on field trips with the other children at the center. Predictably, Annie is sad to leave, but she has had a wonderful travel experience.

150. Walsh, Jill Paton. *When Grandma Came.* Illus. by Sophy Williams. Penguin, 1992 (0-670-83581-1). Unpaged. Picture book.

Interest level: Ages 3–6

Beautiful illustrations grace this gentle story about a little girl and her world-traveling grandmother. Even though Grandma has been to such exotic places as the Arctic Circle, Australia, and the Nile River and seen strange animals in the wild, nothing can compare with the awe she feels when she visits with her granddaughter, Madeleine. Each time she returns from a trip, Grandma is delighted to discover something new about Madeleine. In addition to the tender relationship that Madeleine and her grandmother share, the book conveys a message that travel is exciting and enriching, but home has its own beauty. The illustrations are nothing less than exquisite.

Visiting/Sleeping Over

151. Crews, Donald. *Bigmama's.* Illus. by the author. Greenwillow, 1992 (0-688-09950-5). 32 pp. Picture book.

Interest level: Ages 5–8

Every summer, the young narrator and his family journey to the country and spend a happy reunion at their grandmother's farm. The furniture in the house, the layout of the house and farm, the details of everyday activities—like getting water from the well and hunting for eggs—and above all the congeniality and communication of family members make the visit memorable each year. Young readers are brought into the family and the farm setting through the pictures and text. The family is African American.

152. Godden, Rumer. *Great Grandfather's House.* Illus. by Valerie Littlewood. Greenwillow, 1993 (0-688-11319-2). 76 pp. Fiction.

Interest level: Ages 7–10

Keiko is a feisty, somewhat spoiled, thoroughly modern Japanese girl who is sent to stay with her Great Grandfather and "Old Mother" while her parents are on an extended trip to England. Keiko doesn't want to go and makes up her mind that she will not enjoy either her visit or her younger cousin Yoji, also a visitor. Soon after her arrival, Keiko finds that her hoydenish ways make it difficult for her to adapt to the very traditional household. She drops a freshly laid egg, spills Great Grandfather's paints, and makes loud noises when she eats. Her great-grandparents are understanding but firm; they give her suggestions about how to avoid her frequent accidents. Yoji, although portrayed a little too perfectly, is a gentle child who relishes the outdoors and helps Keiko to realize the beauty of nature. He introduces her to his toad, which she almost kills, and a friendly titmouse, which she eventually rescues from the cold. Gradually, Keiko begins to respond to the serenity of the home and learns to tune in to her environment. At the end of the visit, she is reluctant to leave the beauty she has discovered. The book not only conveys the Japanese appreciation for natural beauty and harmony, but is reassuring to children that an openness to new experiences can lead to a satisfying visit.

153. Griffith, Helen V. *Grandaddy's Place.* Illus. by James Stevenson. Greenwillow, 1991, LB (0-688-06254-7); Morrow, pap. (0-688-10491-6). Unpaged. Picture book.

Interest level: Ages 6–9

Janetta meets her grandfather for the first time when she and her mother go to visit him on his farm. At first, Janetta is very unhappy because she is intimidated by all of the animals and the unfamiliar activities on the farm. But she and her grandfather turn out to be kindred spirits: Both of them like to tell tall tales and have an affinity with nature, so they enjoy each other's company. The visit is a successful one, and the relationship between Janetta and her grandfather is an important by-product. Readers may want to invent stories about why Janetta and her grandfather never met before. They may also enjoy speculating about the mother and why her approach to life is so very different from her father's.

154. Havill, Juanita. *Leroy and the Clock.* Illus. by Janet Wentworth. Houghton, 1988. o.p. 30 pp. Fiction.

Interest level: Ages 5–8

Leroy goes for his first overnight stay away from home to his grandfather's house while his parents go on vacation. It is clear that grandfather has no idea about what a young boy needs. At one o'clock, grandfather falls asleep in the chair, leaving Leroy without anything to do. Leroy does manage to amuse himself, but the old grandfather clock bongs and ticks loudly and frightens him.

Grandfather is a clock maker, and he doesn't want Leroy to play with the delicate clockworks. He gives Leroy a block of wood and nails, but Leroy soon becomes bored with aimlessly pounding nails into the wood.

At night, Leroy finds it difficult to sleep and wishes that the big clock would stop. Lo and behold, it does! In the morning, grandfather reassures Leroy that wishing can't make a clock stop; lack of winding does it. He then realizes how Leroy has been feeling and offers to refrain from winding the clock. Leroy asks if he can wind the clock himself, which he does. Having conquered his fear, he is further delighted when grandfather informs him that they will go to the park together.

The book realistically points out that grandparents do not necessarily know how to be good baby-sitters for their grandchildren. In this pleasant and beautifully illustrated book, the grandfather and grandson eventually accommodate each other's needs, and all ends well.

155. Hest, Amy. *Weekend Girl.* Illus. by Harvey Stevenson. Morrow, 1993 (0-688-09690-5). Unpaged. Picture book.

Interest level: Ages 4–7

It is the end of the summer, and Sophie's parents are ready to go on their "no-kid" vacation. Sophie is brought to her grandparents' apartment in New York City. Her parents are clearly looking forward to their weekend in Honeymoon Cottage, but they acknowledge that they will miss Sophie very much and will need her back at the end of the weekend. Sophie's grandfather is a photographer whose pictures are an inspiration for the family stories. Her grandmother tells her about Honeymoon Cottage as she prepares for a special surprise trip for Sophie. The surprise turns out to be a picnic in Central Park under the stars while they reminisce about their family and the loving relationships that have resulted from it. Sophie is enveloped by the love expressed by her parents and grandparents both for her and for each other.

156. Hooker, Ruth. *At Grandma and Grandpa's House.* Illus. by Ruth Rosner. Whitman, 1986. o.p. 32 pp. Fiction.

Interest level: Ages 3–6

Soft full-color watercolors portray the magical, cherished nature of things at two children's grandparents' house: a closet light that goes on when you open the door, a junk drawer for exploring, a long hall for running. Perhaps best of all, besides a staying-overnight room, there are toys and games, all on hand because their grandparents think of them, set aside space and time, and relish their role. Junk drawer and closet light or not, youngsters will nod in recognition.

157. Howard, Elizabeth Fitzgerald. *Aunt Flossie's Hats (and Crab Cakes Later).* Illus. by James Ransome. Clarion, 1991 (0-395-54682-6). 32 pp. Picture book.

Interest level: Ages 5–8

The setting is Baltimore. Aunt Flossie, an elderly African-American woman whose loving and extended family likes to come and visit her, recalls lively incidents of her youth. The two protagonists are young girls who enjoy hearing Aunt Flossie's stories and who regularly visit her house, try on her numerous hats, and join with their parents afterward to eat crab cakes. The ritual of the visit and the gathering of the family is a fine model. Children may be surprised that the two young girls enjoy so thoroughly a visit with an elderly aunt. The paintings are luminous, natural, and beautifully convey the ambiance of the loving family.

158. Leonard, Marcia. *Little Kitten Sleeps Over.* Illus. by Karen Schmidt. Bantam, 1987. o.p. 24 pp. Fiction.

Interest level: Ages 3–6

Hoping to lure an entirely new generation into the "choose your own adventure" genre, this book gives children a chance to participate actively with animal characters. In addition, there are really two stories in one! Some parents and teachers may question whether three-year-olds can handle this concept, but at least there are only two stories, not the several offered for older children. This particular entry is truly participatory in asking children to imagine themselves as the protagonist: "Pretend you are a little kitten and you're at your grandma and grandpa's house." Homesickness ensues on this sleepover, and on page 4 the child must make a choice. "If you want to get up and find someone to keep you company, go on to page 5." Alternatively, "If you want to stay in your room and call for your grandma, turn to page 11." (Notice both these alternatives result in company.) In the first alternative, the kitten doesn't have grandma in mind and would have been happy with brother or even the goldfish. A story from Grandma does the trick. In the second story, fear suddenly intrudes and the kitten sees danger where there is none: "There's something hiding in my closet!" Grandma explains the several frightening possibilities under the bed, out the window, and so on, but then partially ruins it by lacking understanding: "There's nothing to be afraid of." She comes through, however, offering a toy that had belonged to the kitten's father: "Now it can be your special friend and keep you company all through the night."

159. Mohr, Nicholasa. *Going Home.* Dial, 1986, LB (0-8037-0338-4); Bantam, pap. (0-553-15699-3). 192 pp. Fiction.

Interest level: Ages 8–11

Felita, now 12, experiences hostility when she visits Puerto Rico one summer. Confused about why she is not welcomed, she longs to go home to her family and friends. Through perseverance, she finally makes friends and brings home with her a different perspective of her native land and a better sense of her identity.

160. Nilsson, Ulf. *If You Didn't Have Me.* Illus. by Eva Eriksson. Trans. by Lone Thygeses Blecher and George Blecher. Macmillan, 1987 (0-689-50406-3). 113 pp. Fiction.

Interest level: Ages 7–10

A young Swedish boy and his little brother stay at their grandmother's farm while their parents are completing the building of their new house. In a series of chapters, each a complete story in itself, the boy explores the world and learns about it and himself. He engages in rituals of controlling his fears as he tries to gain dominance over natural phenomena, such as the singing of birds and the rising of the sun. He confronts the farm animals and tames his fear of them. He visits elderly people in an old-age home and acquires some insight into his little brother's feelings. He finds a friend in the hired man and learns about books and history. And he tests his parents' need and love for him and finds them satisfyingly responsive.

The book is simply but profoundly written from the perspective of a young child, but with the insight of a wise adult.

161. Nomura, Takaaki. *Grandpa's Town.* Illus. by the author. Kane/Miller, 1991 (0-916291-36-7). Unpaged. Picture book.

Interest level: Ages 6–9

The setting is a town in Japan. The grandfather has lived alone since his wife died, and his daughter and grandson are worried about him. They visit him and attempt to persuade him to come and live with them. The child and his grandfather go to the fish store, the greengrocer, and the public bath, where they socialize with many of the grandfather's friends. The child recognizes that the grandfather is neither alone nor lonely, and they are less anxious about leaving him. Their visit has been a successful one. The text is in both Japanese and English. The illustrations of the Japanese town convey a flavor of the special setting and provide universal messages about families and about old people and their survival.

162. Roberts, Sarah. *I Want to Go Home.* Illus. by Joe Mathieu. Random, 1985 (0-394-87027-1). 32 pp. Fiction.

Interest level: Ages 3–6

When Big Bird goes to visit his grandmother at the seashore for his first-ever trip away from home, he enjoys himself for a day. But then he grows terribly homesick. Granny wisely recognizes what is wrong with Big Bird and gives him picture postcards to send to his friends at home. She also listens to his stories about his friends, without feeling defensive or making Big Bird think that his feelings are not valid. Eventually, he finds a friend, and his feelings of homesickness diminish.

Children will probably enjoy seeing their beloved Sesame Street characters experiencing the same sorts of feelings that real-life children do. The topic is lightly, somewhat simplistically handled, but the book can be helpful in preparing a child for going away for an extended visit or to camp.

163. Rockwell, Anne, and Harlow Rockwell. *The Night We Slept Outside.* Illus. by Harlow Rockwell. Macmillan, 1983. o.p. 48 pp. Fiction.

Interest level: Ages 6–9

An entry in the Ready-to-Read series, this "chapter" book concerns two brothers and their new sleeping bags. After asking and being refused on a school night, they get permission to sleep outdoors on the weekend. Their sense of the special experience is captured in their plans not to bring pajamas—"You don't wear pajamas on an adventure." What begins as fun turns to higher adventure, of course, when in the darkness strange sounds become frightening. Ensuing escapades with a raccoon, cat, mouse, owl, and even a skunk bring out the two personalities: The younger sib is ready to call it a night and return home, the older one becomes protective. And in the morning, after a rainstorm does bring them inside, there's plenty of bravado from both of them. A good vehicle for discussions about sharing or hiding feelings.

164. Rockwell, Anne, and Harlow Rockwell. *When I Go Visiting.* Illus. by the authors. Macmillan, 1984. o.p. 24 pp. Fiction.

Interest level: Ages 3–6

A little boy enjoys visiting his grandparents and tells readers what he packs. He's eager to see them because of the differences: He lives in a house, they live in an apartment. The authors capture the joy in differences, such as riding in the elevator. The grandparents are ideal—they make a special room for him (he has to sleep on a cot in the living room); they shower him with attention such as taking him to the park; they show him photos of his mother as a child; they share interests with him, exemplified by grandfather's seashell collection and a visit to the library with grandmother. They sing. Both grandparents cook. Clear paintings show each aspect of the sleepover in appealing, calming fashion. The book has a feeling of real grandparents, perhaps a real relationship. And as it should be, the boy has a great deal of fun. "I almost don't want to leave when it is time for me to go. But if I stayed, my mother and father would miss me. So I do go home, until it is time to visit again."

165. Rodowsky, Colby. *Jenny and the Grand Old Great-Aunts.* Illus. by Barbara J. Roman. Bradbury, 1992 (0-02-777785-5). 36 pp. Fiction/picture book.

Interest level: Ages 7–9

When her parents have plans that do not include her, Jenny is brought to visit her great-aunts for the afternoon. She is unhappy about the thought of spending several hours with her elderly aunts by herself. What will she do for an entire afternoon? What will happen if Jenny can't remember her way to the bathroom? The aunts, who live in a large Victorian house, are delighted to see Jenny, but they do not seem to have any special plans to entertain her. Jenny feels even worse when Aunt Abby suggests a trip to the attic. The attic turns out to be a place full of treasures. Jenny and her aunt play with a Victrola, a Noah's Ark toy set, and some hats. As she realizes that her aunt has a lot to share with her, including stories about each of the items, Jenny relaxes and has a wonderful time. Jenny's aunts are true-to-life, and children may recognize relatives in this story.

166. Slote, Elizabeth. *Nelly's Grannies.* Illus. by the author. Morrow, 1993 (0-688-11315-X). Unpaged. Picture book.

Interest level: Ages 3–6

Nelly has two grannies, one who lives in the mountains and one who lives in the city. Every year, Nelly visits both of them and enjoys special experiences with each. With Granny Gussy, who calls her "my little onion," she swims in the pond, eats corn and blueberry pie, and watches fish swimming in the clear water. Granny Lou, wearing pearls and fur, calls her grandchildren "my precious jewels." There, Nelly watches city life, eats at fancy restaurants, and visits art museums. When it's time to leave, Nelly is sad. Even though they are vastly different, Nelly misses both of her grandmothers. The book ends with the grandmothers at Nelly's front door, all set for a visit with her. Nelly is seen having a variety of experiences and enjoying each visit for its uniqueness.

Disrupted Friendship

A common, but often traumatic, loss for children occurs when a dear friend moves away, or, for some reason, becomes an antagonist. Sometimes the rift is caused by a misunderstanding, sometimes by a third person interfering in the relationship, sometimes by one friend developing more rapidly than the other. In any case, the separation, whether temporary or permanent, is painful. Books can help young readers acknowledge the universality of the experience, and can sometimes provide a vicarious situation that can begin the process of problem solving.

167. Ackerman, Karen. *The Tin Heart*. Illus. by Michael Hays. Atheneum, 1990 (0-689-31461-2). 32 pp. Fiction.

Interest level: Ages 8–10

Mahaley and Flora each wear half of a tin-heart necklace to demonstrate their friendship. When the Civil War starts, the girls stop seeing each other because Mahaley's father supports the North while Flora's favors the South. The girls know it will be a long time before they will see one another again, but they are sure that their friendship is secure. The story is well written and realistic. The illustrations do a good job of conveying its mood. Unfortunately, except for an appearance by Flora's mother to serve cocoa, adult women are absent. Politics seems to be men's domain. The girls don't express any opinions about the war or slavery; they care only for their friendship.

168. Bergstrom, Corinne. *Losing Your Best Friend*. Illus. by Patricia Rosamilia. Human Sciences, 1988 (0-87705-471-1). Unpaged. Picture book.

Interest level: Ages 4–9

Jenny and Robin enjoy being together exclusively, although Jenny loves to pretend and Robin does not. When new children move into the neighborhood, Robin decides to become best friends with Sandy. Jenny's feelings of being left out are valid; she realistically senses that she is not wanted and must find others with similar interests to fill the gap that Robin has left.

169. Brooks, Martha. *Paradise Cafe and Other Stories*. Little, Brown, 1990 (0-316-10978-9). 124 pp. Fiction/short stories.
    Interest level: Age 12+

This sensitively written collection of short stories depicts a variety of losses, big and small. Although many of the issues involved are typical of adolescence, the freshness and style lift them out of the ordinary and give these experiences the dignity and compassion they deserve. The title story, for example, tells of the beginning and breakup of a romance. The reader experiences with Lulie the ecstasy of new love, the slow dissolution of the union, and the pain of recognition that the friendship is over. The detail of Lulie's peeling off the adhesive tape, now tattered and gray, that once functioned to make Graham's ring fit her finger, serves as a metaphor for their frayed relationship. The story ends on a note of hope: Lulie agrees to go out on a date with a boy who will be more appreciative of her than Graham was. Other stories in the book deal with the death of a pet, leaving childhood, and absent parents.

170. Eriksson, Eva. *Jealousy*. Illus. by the author. Carolrhoda, 1985. o.p. 24 pp. Fiction.
    Interest level: Ages 4–8

When Rosalie recovers after having been in bed with the mumps for two weeks, she is dismayed to discover that her best friend, Victor, is enjoying playing with another little girl, Sophie. Rosalie is terribly jealous of the newfound friendship between Victor and Sophie, and she tries to get rid of Sophie. None of her schemes works. Through a misunderstanding, the two girls find themselves together, each trying to emulate the other. They gain enough perspective to laugh at their own behavior, and when Victor reappears on the scene, they are ready to share him and to be three best friends together.

Just as it is with sibling rivalry—where children must learn that their parents' love is expandable and all-inclusive—so, too, they must come to adapt to maintaining multiple friendships. This is a difficult concept, and this book, although somewhat simplistic, can be used as a starting point.

171. Greenfield, Eloise. *Koya DeLaney and the Good Girl Blues*. Scholastic, 1992 (0-590-43300-8). 124 pp. Fiction.
    Interest level: Ages 10–12

Koya is a joyously happy girl who has a close relationship with her sister, Loritha, and their best friend, Dawn. When Koya's cousin Del, a rock star, arrives in town, this causes a split in the girls' friendship. Koya is distressed that nobody is keeping Del's visit at her house secret and is offended by the rude fans on her front lawn. When Koya learns that Dawn has betrayed Loritha by not teaching her a new step for an important jump-rope competition, this rocks Koya's faith in people. She is fiercely loyal to her sister and orchestrates the reconciliation between the other two girls. Greenfield is a wonderful writer, who has portrayed a loving African-American family with ordinary problems.

172. Hansen, Joyce. *Yellow Bird and Me.* Clarion, 1986 (0-395-55388-1). 155 pp. Fiction.

Interest level: Age 10+

In this sequel to *The Gift-Giver* (Houghton, 1980), Doris, a sixth grader living in New York, pines for the companionship of her friend Amir, who left the Bronx and was sent to a group home in Syracuse when his foster family moved to California. Doris's fellow classmate Yellow Bird also misses Amir's supportive friendship and asks for her assistance with his homework. Through his letters, Amir encourages Doris to help Yellow Bird battle his dyslexia. As Doris's friendship with Yellow Bird deepens, her mourning the loss of Amir lessens, and she learns to place his friendship in perspective as they continue to correspond through the mail.

Hansen uses humor and insight into her characters' feelings in this lively story of friendship. The setting of the African-American community adds depth and reality, while reminding the reader of the universality of the characters' responses.

173. Jones, Rebecca C. *Matthew and Tilly.* Illus. by Beth Peck. Dutton, 1991 (0-525-44684-2). 32 pp. Picture book.

Interest level: Ages 5–8

Matthew and Tilly are best friends who enjoy cooperating in all of their activities. Like most friends, however, they occasionally get tired of each other and even have arguments in which they hurt each other's feelings. After one of these disagreements, each child tries to play alone but doesn't enjoy it. They each apologize and resume their close friendship. The illustrations provide an urban setting for the story. The friendship is biracial: Matthew is white, and Tilly is black. It is also good to see a friendship between a boy and a girl, with non-gender-linked activities or characteristics.

174. Murrow, Liza Ketchum. *Dancing on the Table.* Illus. by Ronald Himler. Holiday, 1990 (0-8234-0808-6). 128 pp. Fiction.

Interest level: Ages 9–12

Jenny has enjoyed a close connection with her grandmother; they have been good friends and share some characteristics of creativity and rebelliousness. Jenny feels very jealous of her grandmother's relationship with Charlie and resents the fact that her Nana is now getting married. She wishes that something will intervene to block the wedding. When her wish comes true (a hurricane sweeps through the area), she must deal with her guilt over the consequences. She manages to make amends, and her grandmother eventually goes away with her new husband, assuring Jenny that their relationship will remain intact.

175. Okimoto, Jean Davies. *Take a Chance, Gramps!* Little, Brown, 1990 (0-316-63812-9). 135 pp. Fiction.

Interest level: Ages 11–14

A light-hearted story about a young girl who helps her grandfather cope with the pain he feels after his wife dies. At the same time, she manages to adjust to the loss of her best friend, who has moved far away. Jane is desolated when Alicia moves to a new city. Her identity seems gone. Jane's mother asks her to spend some extra time with her grandfather, who is withdrawn and is developing such bad habits as refusing to put in his teeth. When Jane and Gramps visit the Seattle Center, they happen upon a senior-citizens dance, where they meet a young man who has accompanied his grandmother for the day. Both pairs are somewhat awkward, particularly Jane and Brady. The development of their parallel relationships is the focus of much of the story. In the end, both Jane and her grandfather have learned to take a chance, have gained self-esteem, and have gained an appreciation for their own nurturing relationship.

176. Ottens, Allen J. *Coping with Romantic Breakup.* Rosen, 1987 (0-8239-0649-3). 148 pp. Nonfiction.

Interest level: Ages 12–16

This book, about the throes of adolescence, is most welcome. Ottens, a university psychologist, intends the book to speed the injured party's recovery from unilateral breakups. He speaks to both sexes and is quite practical, separating healthy emotions and desirable behavior from the negative emotions that can make you feel you're stuck in mud. Wisely, Ottens refers to two types of loss in the breakup: the loss of the individual and the loss of personal power implied when you are rejected. His understanding of loss extends to other areas of life, as he has readers understand parallels in losing a job, for example. Both are investments, and both may have presented illusions of fair treatment.

Ottens seems to understand the language young adults sometimes resort to in expressing their hurts, from spying and threats, to promises, even to harassment and physical abuse of the other person or oneself. He presents a good analysis of relationships as they cool off and makes suggestions on how youngsters can assess the present state of a romance.

For those who must cope with the end of a relationship, Ottens recommends avoiding hanging on by asking friends about him or her, looking for him or her to appear and just happening to be where that might happen, and so forth. Instead, Ottens recommends a clean break made possible by imagery exercises—for example, imagining an embarrassing consequence from the spying. Also recommended are drawing up a list of irritating habits and bad points to keep up your resolve, developing diversionary tactics for the hardest times of the day or week, and mental exercises that can soften the image of the person in one's mind, keeping both the good and bad aspects of the relationship in perspective. Ottens understands the feelings of loss, and his hints will be useful indeed.

177. Perl, Lila. *Fat Glenda's Summer Romance.* Clarion, 1986. o.p. 144 pp. Fiction.

Interest level: Ages 9–13

Thirteen-year-old fat Glenda finds herself newly thin but waiting watchfully for the threatening ghost of her former self to return. The fast-paced action revolves around this and other changes: how to get along in an adult world away from home as a waitress at an inn, how to respond to a new boy's attention, how to get her mother to stop coddling, and most important, how to adjust when a dear friend is suddenly rejecting. Glenda's hopes for a glorious summer with her old friend Sara quickly crumble in lively, funny, and readily identifiable incidents, but other good things happen, such as being convinced by her new boyfriend to abandon the old fat self-image. It's a fast and thoroughly enjoyable read.

178. Samton, Sheila White. *Jenny's Journey.* Illus. by the author. Viking, 1991 (0-670-83490-4). 32 pp. Picture book.

Interest level: Ages 4–7

Jenny's friend Maria has moved away and writes Jenny that she is lonely. Jenny responds by describing the journey she plans to take to visit Maria. The journey will take Jenny through the crowded harbor, past the Statue of Liberty, into the open sea. There Jenny describes to Maria her feelings when Maria moved away. Jenny has many adventures: She weathers a storm at sea and sings to keep herself cheerful. Finally, she greets Maria on an island, presumably Puerto Rico, where they have a joyous reunion. The book ends when Jenny finishes her letter, promising Maria that she will come and see her one day on the island. This is an effective coping strategy for Jenny. Children in similar situations might like to write about their own fantasy adventures traveling to see a faraway loved one.

179. Savin, Marcia. *The Moon Bridge.* Scholastic, 1992 (0-590-45873-6). 230 pp. Fiction.

Interest level: Ages 8–10

Ruthie and Mitzi are friends even though they live in San Francisco during World War II and the prejudice against people of Japanese heritage is virulent. They become friends after Ruthie confronts her long-time friend Shirl for persecuting Mitzi, a Japanese American who is a newcomer to the school. Ruthie and Shirl stop being friends because of this. As the war continues, anti-Japanese behavior escalates. A curfew is declared for Japanese Americans, and they are beaten up for simply walking down the street. The policy of internment is brought home in a very direct and chilling manner when Mitzi and her family are removed to camp. The two friends try to maintain their contact through letters, but they lose touch with each other after Mitzi and her family are forced to move to another camp. After the war, Mitzi and Ruthie meet again, but each has changed over the four years' separation and their relationship can never again be what it was.

180. Smalls-Hector, Irene. *Irene and the Big, Fine Nickel.* Illus. by Tyrone Geter. Little, Brown, 1991 (0-316-79871-1). 32 pp. Picture book.

Interest level: Ages 5–9

Irene, an independent seven-year-old, spends a summer morning with her friends. She has an unpleasant encounter with one friend, Charlene, who violates a rule of playing "the dozens" and provokes Irene so that she wants to have a physical fight. When Irene finds a nickel on the sidewalk, enough to buy a raisin bun to share with her best friends, Charlene asks to be included. Irene magnanimously forgives her, and all is well. The author portrays a strong, tightly knit African-American community built on trust. The neighbors don't lock their doors, and the children are free to come and go as they please. Irene avoids a fight, learning that forgiveness is often better than holding a grudge.

181. Voigt, Cynthia. *Izzy, Willy-Nilly.* Atheneum, 1986 (0-689-31202-4); Fawcett, pap. (0-499-70214-6). 262 pp. Fiction.

Interest level: Age 12+

The book contains powerful insights into the emotions experienced by a young person who has undergone an amputation. It discusses the difficulties and challenges of adjustment and the contribution that family and friends can make to this process. It also raises the issue of friendships lost and found.

Izzy, a junior in high school and a popular member of the "in" crowd, is devastated when she loses the lower half of her leg in an accident caused by the drunken driving of a date she didn't even like. Voigt, with great sensitivity and well-researched accuracy, explores the pain and success of Izzy's adjustment.

Izzy's sense of loss is compounded by the virtual abandonment by her three long-standing friends, also pretty, popular members of Izzy's crowd, who are unable to comfort her during her crisis. Symbolized by the uselessness and frivolity of her friends' gifts, which are brought to the hospital, Izzy realizes that these friendships were based on her looks rather than her essence.

A sincere friend enters her life in the person of Rosamund, an awkward and outspoken classmate whom Izzy had previously ignored. It takes time for Izzy to appreciate her, but it is with Rosamund's care and support that Izzy recovers. Izzy learns to face her feelings and to appreciate and value her strengths and those of others with greater clarity and maturity.

182. Waber, Bernard. *Ira Says Goodbye.* Houghton, 1988 (0-395-48315-8); pap. (0-395-48413-2). 40 pp. Fiction.

Interest level: Ages 5–8

Ira (of *Ira Sleeps Over,* Houghton, 1972) is losing his best friend, Reggie. Not only is Reggie moving away, but he seems to be happy about the fact and not aware that Ira is devastated by the impending loss. Not until the actual day of the move does Ira discover that Reggie, too, is overwhelmed by the knowledge that he and Ira are being separated. Only then can the two boys acknowledge that they will miss each other. They exchange precious gifts: two turtles and a favorite baseball card. That night, Reggie calls Ira and invites him to spend the weekend at Reggie's new house. Of course, Ira accepts, and we know that the boys have not lost each other's friendship after all.

Using humorous dialogue, Waber has put his finger on a common fear and problem of childhood: the possible loss of a friend, not because of moving away, but really because of misunderstanding each other's feelings. If Ira and Reggie had not displayed their true emotions, they would have harbored great resentment toward each other. The story is powerful and provides an outlet for children who need to learn to express their feelings of concern about friendship or, for that matter, about any relationship.

183. Winthrop, Elizabeth. *The Castle in the Attic.* Illus. by Trina S. Hyman. Holiday, 1985 (0-688-09686-7). 179 pp. Fiction.

   Interest level: Ages 9–12

William is crushed that Mrs. Phillips—his housekeeper and companion of ten years, ever since he was born—is now leaving him to return to her original home in England. She thinks he is old enough to do without her and that her absence will make his parents spend more time with him. As a going-away present, she gives him a wonderful castle that has been in her family for generations. It is a lifelike replica of a castle with a drawbridge and many rooms. One silver knight comes with the castle. William tells Mrs. Phillips that he would rather have her stay than have the castle and that he will think of some way to keep her with him.

   Before Mrs. Phillips leaves, William discovers that his touch has made the little knight come to life. He learns that the knight has an amulet that shrinks living things until they are tiny. He uses the amulet on Mrs. Phillips and places her in the castle, believing this is a way to keep her with him forever. But Mrs. Phillips refuses to speak to him until he is her size.

   Because of his guilt over what he has done to Mrs. Phillips, William decides to permit himself to become small so that he can save the knight's kingdom and restore Mrs. Phillips to her proper size. He embarks on a long and dangerous journey, but, due to Mrs. Phillips's excellent influence, he succeeds in his quest. He vanquishes the wicked wizard, retrieves the amulet that restores people to their proper size, and returns home, magically arriving at exactly the same time that he left, with no one knowing he was gone.

   His quest is, of course, one that will win him his independence. Once he recognizes that he can be brave and strong, he knows that he must permit Mrs. Phillips to return to her home. This is a part of growing up for him, and he does it well.

   Winthrop has handled a delicate subject well. No one is blamed for his or her feelings. The silver knight is not zapped back and forth from toy to human because of the whim of the child. He is a real person who has been enchanted and who retains his dignity at all times. The story works very well.

184. Woodson, Jacqueline. *Last Summer with Maizon.* Doubleday, 1990 (0-385-30045-X). 106 pp. Fiction.

   Interest level: Ages 4–6

Margaret is devastated when her father dies and further agonized when her best friend, Maizon, goes away to Blue Hill, a school for the gifted in Connecticut. Much of the book is about how the girls survive the anticipation of Maizon's leaving. Margaret is not sure how she will manage without her friend, especially after the jolting loss of her father. Maizon eventually leaves, and Margaret is on her own. At school, a teacher discovers Margaret's gift for writing; a poem she writes about her losses is selected to be read aloud to the mayor. When Margaret recites the poem to her classmates, they are appreciative, although Margaret must learn that not all audiences respond the same way. A host of intriguing characters bring the warm and nurturing urban neighborhood to life: Ms. Dell, who can see the future; her daughter Hattie, 19 and unimpressed by Maizon; Maizon's grandmother, a Native American; Margaret's mother, who spends the summer learning to cope with her own loss; and her father, whose spirit permeates the household. When Maizon returns from Blue Hill, she and Margaret break new ground in their relationship. Both girls have changed: Margaret's self-esteem has risen, while Maizon's has plummeted due to her feelings of unacceptance at school. It seems their friendship will survive and be enriched by the changes.

Understanding Fears

Young children experience many fears: darkness, going to bed, monsters, pressures of parental and other adult expectations, and new situations, such as attending day-care or school for the first time. These fears should be respected and not denied, trivialized or treated punitively. Books can be helpful when they portray children taking part in overcoming their fears. Books may also model how sympathetic family and friends may help without assuming the entire responsibility.

When youngsters first enter school they must separate themselves from the familiar. The comfort and security of home seems lost. The fear is that there will be no friendly faces to welcome them in a new situation. Books should acknowledge the developmental element of this milestone and should not confuse it with an abusive environment. Teachers should be portrayed realistically, not as saints or devils.

185. Bunting, Eve. *Ghost's Hour, Spook's Hour.* Illus. by Donald Carrick. Clarion, 1987 (0-89919-484-2); pap. (0-395-56244-9). 32 pp. Fiction.

Interest level: Ages 3–7

When Jake is awakened in the middle of the night by some strange noises, he tries to turn on the light, but finds that the electricity doesn't work. He and his dog, Biff, cling to each other fearfully as they make their way to Jake's parents' room, only to find that his parents are gone. The noises of the wind, the branches of the trees scraping against the windows, the moaning of the dog, and the ordinary noises of the clock are frightening in the context of the time of night and the missing parents. When Jake's parents appear, they explain that they had been bothered by the noise of the branches so they decided to sleep on the sofa bed. And Jake explains that Biff was very frightened. They reassure Jake that everyone gets frightened sometimes, and they invite both Jake and Biff to spend the rest of the night with them on the sofa bed.

Bunting's prose, graphically describing the scary sounds, works well with the expressive illustrations to convey the sense of the child's fears. A plausible explanation of the parents' absence is important for the young reader. Some experts might frown on taking the child and the dog into bed, but it really is the humane thing to do in this case.

186. Bunting, Eve. *Sixth-Grade Sleepover.* Harcourt, 1986 (0-15-275350-8); Scholastic, pap. (0-590-42882-9). 96 pp. Fiction.

   Interest level: Ages 8–12

Bunting combines a story about school readathons with a drama about overcoming fears. The Rabbit Reading Club's plan for an all-night session frightens Janey, who desperately wants to go but can't seem to shake her trauma-induced terror of the dark night. Will this turn into the evening when everyone finds out she still uses a night light? The action mixes in preteen crushes and the embarrassment of puberty, giving a rounded feeling to the plot, and Janey's dread is finally resolved when another person in the class has an equally vexing problem. Newcomer Rosie also must move away from her fears, for she has thus far been able to hide her first-grade reading level. The events have a natural flow to them, so when the girls team up to be open about their problems, it is perfectly believable. Both girls come out of their darkness and into the light in this subdued, elegant ode to the literacy theme.

187. Canty, John. *Shadows.* Illus. by the author. Harper, 1987. o.p. 20 pp. Fiction.

   Interest level: Ages 4–7

"Benjamin hates the dark. Fierce creatures live there. Late at night, he sees one move. Or at least he thinks he does." And so, in darkness, Benjamin tests the night, and in his mind, shapes form and grow. What was once a rabbit shadow becomes a monster. He tries to reason. "If I run, . . . it will always chase me. Always and forever. But this is my room, and I won't run from anything!" And with this assertion, Benjamin calms the room down; shadows whirl, swirl, and melt away, vanishing "into the farthest corners, back to where dark shadows belong." The boy conquers his fear of separation himself and makes his own safety from his bravery.

188. Gridley, Sally. *I Don't Want To!* Illus. by Carol Thompson. Little, Brown, 1990 (0-316-32893-6). Unpaged. Picture book.

Interest level: Ages 3–6

Jim does not want to go to school. He refuses to get up. He is not helpful when it's time to get dressed. He throws his toast on the floor. When he arrives at school, Jim insists that he wants to go home. He hugs his father rather than looking at all of the intriguing activities going on in the room. The other children are curious and seem friendly, but Jim shies away from joining in the painting. Finally, when he cannot resist painting a picture, Jim agrees to participate. As he relaxes, he enters into more activities, and by the end of the afternoon, Jim decides he wants to come back the next day. School is pictured as a nonthreatening, relaxed place where there are many enjoyable things to do. Jim needs some observing time before he feels comfortable joining the others. This is accepted by his teacher and the other children. The illustrations are whimsical but true-to-life.

189. Grifalconi, Ann. *Darkness and the Butterfly.* Illus. by the author. Little, Brown, 1987 (0-316-32863-4). Unpaged. Picture book.

Interest level: Ages 4–7

Osa is terrified of the dark of her African jungle home. Even though she is strong and brave when it is light, darkness causes Osa to tremble and hide. One afternoon, Osa loses her way and finds herself at the hut of the Wise Woman. She confesses her fears, exploring them with the Wise Woman who tells her the story of the yellow butterfly, a tiny being who flies straight through the night no matter what. Osa dreams that she also can fly. The image of the butterfly will help her face her fears. Osa runs down the path to her village that night, rejoicing that she now can embrace the night.

190. Guthrie, Donna. *Not for Babies.* Illus. by Katy Keck Arnsteen. Simon & Schuster, 1993, pap. (0-671-79362-4). Unpaged. Picture book.

Interest level: Ages 4–7

Andrew is tired of his noisy siblings, so he decides to set up a tent in his backyard and sleep outside all night. He packs a survival bag with plenty of sandwiches and a book to read. When his mother wishes him good night and offers to leave the porch light on, Andrew is indignant; however, once it gets dark, Andrew discovers that he is a little lonely and somewhat scared. Andrew conquers his anxiety, stays outside the entire night, and emerges ready to interact with his family again.

191. Howe, James. *When You Go to Kindergarten.* Photos by Betsy Imershein. Knopf, 1986 (0-394-97303-8). 48 pp. Nonfiction.

Interest level: Ages 3–6

Husband and wife Howe and Imershein worked at New York-area schools for this photoessay, including the famed Little Red Schoolhouse. It is unique in presenting a variety of schools, rather than just one. An introduction to parents suggests discussing differences between what is shown and what the child's situation will be. More important, they also discuss the difficulty for the parent in letting go of the child's hand as well as the child's difficulty in taking the big step.

The narrative talks to children directly: "This book will tell you about kindergarten—and what it's like to go there." Children are shown both walking to school and going by bus. Some schools have long halls, some have stairs; most have a principal's office, we're told. Parents reading aloud may have to explain what a principal is, as well as a custodian, but this book is meant for sharing aloud. The photographs capture tense children on the first day: "They're all starting out—just like you." Howe emphasizes the nitty-gritty. There is an introduction to the bathroom, water fountain, cubbies, taking attendance, fire drill, and so forth. Also such concepts as getting in line, sharing, and learning the alphabet are introduced. Some perhaps unnecessary pressure is placed on the kindergarten children to learn to read. Adults can reassure children that everybody reads when he or she is ready.

The photos are large and clear, and in one of the classes, the teacher is a man. Mostly, the attempt to show everything, everywhere, at home, at school, and so on, works. One problem is that there is an attempt to show too much, such as a fire drill and a birthday party, and some children who can't prepare in one sitting (who can?) might be a bit overwhelmed. This is a book to share over and over so that its many pieces can be absorbed.

192. Impey, Rose. *The Flat Man.* Illus. by Moira Kemp. Dell, 1991, pap. (0-440-40504-1). Unpaged. Picture book.

Interest level: Ages 5–8

A little boy scares himself at bedtime with stories about the Flat Man, who slips into the boy's room and crushes him in an icy embrace. The boy can rid himself of the Flat Man at will, but his antics cause his father to chastise him. When his father leaves, however, the boy is ready to conjure up another fearful creature. The text of this story has a light touch, but the illustrations, although well executed, could be frightening. Although the father is rather insensitive, the book convincingly portrays a common nighttime fear in a humorous, engaging way.

193. Johnson, Dolores. *What Will Mommy Do When I'm at School?* Illus. by the author. Macmillan, 1990 (0-02-747845-9). 32 pp. Fiction.

    Interest level: Ages 4–7

A little girl, about to start school for the first time, worries that her mother will be lonely because they have never been apart for very long. When her mother tells her that she will be beginning an adventure of her own, a new job, the little girl is relieved. Mother and daughter look forward to telling one another about their new experiences at the end of each day. The theme of this loving, gently reassuring book is universal. The family shown in the illustrations is African American.

194. Kraus, Robert. *Spider's First Day at School.* Illus. by the author. Scholastic, 1987. o.p. 32 pp. Fiction.

    Interest level: Ages 4–7

Spider experiences all the anxieties and negative feelings about the first day of school that most children suffer. His teacher and the children are, for the most part, friendly, with the exception of one group, the bedbugs. The school activities are relevant and fun for him. Spider is a friendly person who shares generously with his classmates. When the class has a football game, Spider is the hero of the game. At the end of the game, all the children are admiring of Spider, and are all friends.

    School is depicted as a place where problems can be solved by positive social interaction. It is also filled with activities that make sense and that are appropriate to the children's needs and interests. It is unfortunate that Spider must become a hero in order to be totally accepted. In fact, he is happy before the game, but the game becomes the icing on the cake. Lots of good ideas are incorporated into the book about how to make school a successful experience.

195. Krementz, Jill. *Katharine Goes to Nursery School.* Photos by the author. Random, 1986. o.p. 14 boards. Fiction.

    Interest level: Ages 2–5

In this photoessay, Krementz follows a young girl to school. Katharine speaks directly to her audience, and though this is not a first experience at nursery school, the narration sensibly balances delighted independence with contact and reminders of Mommy and Daddy. Specifics are explained through chronology: the teacher's greeting, parent's good-bye, games and activities, snack, story, nap, reunion. Katharine speaks like a three-year-old.

Most pages have two or three photographs, all well composed, asplash with hearty color, joyful, and caring. Katharine's love for school will be contagious, just as Krementz intended.

196. McCully, Emily Arnold. *School.* Illus. by the author. Harper, 1987, LB (0-06-024133-0); pap. (0-06-443233-5). 32 pp. Fiction.

Interest level: Ages 3–6

This wordless picture book treat tells the tale of a curious little mouse who watches his many siblings trek off to school on a fall day. He sneaks off to follow them, is welcomed in, and becomes part of the large class. (All the mice are brown and without clothes, but he can be identified by his size and a watch on his wrist.) Of course, his mother has missed him. She comes hurriedly in, sees he is safe and happy, and they leave together to go back home. Children use books to get their first idea of what a new experience will be like, and this one, in its unique form, offers a peaceful view of a school in which everyone learns and gets along.

197. Magorian, Michelle. *Who's Going to Take Care of Me?* Harper, 1990, LB (0-06-024106-3). 32 pp. Picture book.

Interest level: Ages 4–6

Eric enjoys going to day-care with his older sister, Karin. She shows him where to get art supplies and invites him to sit beside her at music time. They make sand castles in the sandbox. When Eric learns that Karin is going to school, he feels left out. Not only does Karin get new clothes, but she is obviously excited about her new challenge and doesn't play with Eric as often. Worst of all, Eric worries that there will be no one to watch over him at day-care. After Karin skips gaily off to school, Eric must face day-care alone. He learns that he, too, can help others when a new child enters the center and Eric takes over, doing what Karin did for him. The clever illustrations depict the loneliness felt by a sibling who is left behind.

198. Mayle, Peter. *Sweet Dreams and Monsters: A Beginner's Guide to Dreams and Nightmares and Things That Go Bump under the Bed.* Illus. by Arthur Robins. Harmony, 1986 (0-517-55972-2). 32 pp. Nonfiction.

Interest level: Ages 7–12

With droll, sly humor, author and illustrator actually bring the reader to the brink of monstrous nightmares half remembered. The cockroach nightmare with which the book starts tells you right away if this is the book for you. Not afraid to venture forth? If so, there are subject headings like "Free Movies Every Night," which explores dream physiology and our ability to remember nightly separations from those we love. Also included is information about what winds up in our dreams, our subconscious store-house, and a beginning list of common dreams—for example, forgotten dreams, memory, the future, and nightmares. Mayle explains how real life actually influences dreams that seem to come true. Once you get past that eerie cockroach, this book is sort of fun and can help ease children's minds for that daily time we must be alone.

199. Mayper, Monica. *After Good-Night.* Illus. by Peter Sis. Harper, 1987. o.p. 32 pp. Fiction.

Interest level: Ages 4–8

This unusual book pays attention to the daily separation children must endure after they are sent to bed. Focusing on sensations, particularly what little Nan experiences, the author brings a rare insight into children's imaginations. "Nan is the eyes of the house: The dark is dark-dark in the corner where her chair has rocked her animals to sleep." There's a passing car, whose lights reflect on her ceiling, causing her to hold her breath until it passes. There's father's night walk, when he locks the door and jiggles the toilet handle. And as this and more go on, Nan starts an imaginative ocean journey on a bed-boat, her way of greeting sleep.

Children reading this book may, in a discussion with a parent, bring to consciousness all they hear and see as they drift off. They are not alone. Others have similar journeys. They can even improve theirs.

200. Rogers, Fred. *Going to Day Care.* Photos by Jim Judkis. Putnam, 1985, (0-399-21235-3). 32 pp. Nonfiction.

Interest level: Ages 2–6

Acknowledging that increased numbers of children are attending day-care, Rogers has written about the situation's differences from school (mixed age groups, for example). He also calls the adult staff *day-care givers*, as opposed to *teachers*. In his note to parents, Rogers emphasizes taking the time (and he acknowledges it may take a lot of effort) to find a good day-care situation about which both parent and child can be happy. Also important are talking about feelings, being reassured they *will* come home at day's end, and letting children know how loved and valued they are at home. With these steps, new attachments can begin to be forged.

In this book, two children (boy and girl; black and white) are pic-tured going to day-care centers or day-care homes. The settings look warm, colorful, cheerful. Rooms in the day-care center are shown—kitchen, bathroom, and so forth. The emphasis is on balance—some things children can do by themselves (for example, washing hands); other things children need help with (for example, shoe tying). Children are shown helping grown-ups and each other, eating, resting, playing inside and out, and being in a group and playing alone. They have the day-care giver to themselves, too: "It feels good to know that there are times when you can have someone you love all to yourself." The day ends happily with a father picking up a child and a proud day-care giver discussing the child's activities during the day. And then at home, there's a lot to talk about, too. This book is recommended for its warmth, clarity, and respect for early-childhood development.

201. Rogers, Fred. *Going to the Potty.* Photos by Jim Judkis. Putnam, 1986 (0-399-21296-5); pap. (0-399-21297-3). 32 pp. Nonfiction.

Interest level: Ages 2–4

In his introduction to this particular volume in his First Experiences series, Mr. Rogers of the "Mister Rogers" television program stresses that parents apply a balance of gentleness and persistence in their toilet-training approach. He uses those very qualities in his writing as well, explaining that children need help in many ways, but as time goes on they need less help. First, several babies are shown being helped to dress and eat, and then Rogers moves into the ideas behind training, explaining the seat and stressing children's readiness: "Children need to take their time about things like that." He's cognizant of aspects of the big toilet that can be frightening, such as the noise of the flush and the forbidding nature of the seat: "At first it may feel a little hard and cold." He involves his reader, too: "Do you have a chair or seat like that?"

Rogers uses adult words in the book (urine, bowel movement), but in his introduction for adults understandingly states, "You may be more comfortable substituting the words with which your own family is familiar." The full-color photographs of two families going through the training process are sharp and pleasant. They also show older children, age four or five, sitting on the toilet. One wonders how these models felt at being asked to be photographed this way, but knowing the care and sensitivity with which the Mr. Rogers Neighborhood projects are undertaken, one is reassured that it was likely done with the utmost intelligence, perhaps explained by Mr. Rogers himself. This is indeed the book they hoped to have, one which would promote the mastery and stronger sense of self that the toilet-training process, ideally realized, accomplishes.

202. Roth, Harold. *Babies Love Nursery School.* Photos by the author. Grosset, 1986. o.p. 14 boards. Nonfiction.

Interest level: Ages 2–6

This small-sized book shows a multiethnic classroom with close-up shots of children painting, drawing, eating, and participating. The reader is drawn in with such sentences as: "Nursery school is a busy place. You can draw with crayons . . . or try sponge painting." It's an all-day affair, it seems, with children eating lunch, and it's a happy place. The children shown are not babies but preschoolers, as the nursery population is. The title is cause for wonder, as babies might be in day-care, which usually starts at around age 3, but not nursery school. Recommended. Children will enjoy the book's size—tiny like themselves—and the colorful presentation will keep them interested.

203. Waddell, Martin. *Can't You Sleep, Little Bear?* Illus. by Barbara Firth. Candlewick, 1988 (1-56402-007-X). Unpaged. Picture book.

Interest level: Ages 3–5

Little Bear is frightened of the dark. No matter how many lanterns Big Bear places by his bedside, Little Bear cannot go to sleep. When Big Bear shows Little Bear the moon and stars, the knowledge that there is light outside the cave helps lull Little Bear to sleep. The illustrations are winning, especially of Little Bear's attempts to get himself to sleep. Big Bear is a wonderful male nurturer. This is a simple, repetitive story, but it will be reassuring to a toddler or preschooler.

204. Watanabe, Shigeo. *I Can Take a Walk!* Illus. by Yasuo Ohtomo. Putnam, 1991, pap. (0-399-21847-5). 32 pp. Fiction.

Interest level: Ages 2–6

As a book in the I Can Do It All by Myself series, this volume features Bear, a character seen in other books. This time, he decides to take a walk by himself, and he's full of bravery and adventure. Wherever he goes, his imagination is at work, too, just as younger children's imaginations are. As he walks across a park bench, he says, "I can cross this high bridge." It is likewise with other happy adventures, such as shooing away birds that to him are flying dragons. But when he gets stuck on the edge of what to him seems like a cliff, he's very relieved when Daddy comes walking by, and he's most happy to join him for the walk home. This book beautifully captures the essence of the preschool child, who needs to step away but simultaneously needs to know that he or she can always come back and the parent will be there, just when a helping hand is needed.

Leaving Childhood

Developmental issues of loss occur when children move from one stage of childhood into the next or when they undergo the experience of reaching adolescence or young adulthood and must leave behind them their dependence and protected position. Emotions of excitement at achieving a new status sometimes war with anxieties provoked by new responsibilities. Authors often demonstrate their understanding of the developmental dilemma when they respect characters' feelings of ambivalence and confusion and treat the issues within the context of the story.

205. Alexander, Sue. *Dear Phoebe.* Illus. by Eileen Christelow. Little, Brown, 1984. o.p. 32 pp. Fiction.

Interest level: Age 9+

It's time for Phoebe Dormouse to leave home and be out on her own. She and her mother outwardly pretend that everything is just fine. They hide their true feelings from each other, but both are actually very anxious and unhappy about this move. Once Phoebe is in her own place, they miss each other very much, but keep up the pretense that nothing is wrong. They write cheerful letters to each other until in one letter Phoebe's mother confesses that she misses her daughter. This admission helps Phoebe to feel better about being away from her mother, and she can now look forward to visiting her in the spring. This book is in picture-book format and appears to be aimed at a young audience. But it really concerns the older teenager's issue of leaving home and living independently. Perhaps the author wants to prepare youngsters for their impending move far in the future, or perhaps she wants younger siblings to understand the fears and feelings of their older, more independent family members.

The text and illustrations are well crafted, but certainly too simplified to be of great use to a young person now in the main character's shoes. The story might also be used to show how important it is for people to communicate their true feelings to each other, and in that case, as a story about two characters, it would be appropriate for its young audience.

206. Banks, Jacqueline Turner. *Project Wheels.* Houghton, 1993 (0-395-64378-3). 107 pp. Fiction.

Interest level: Ages 9–12

Sixth grade is a year of changes, and Angela learns that changing friendships is part of the process of growing up. Angela is close to twin boys, Judge and Jury, and is offended when they play a trick on her. Their intention is harmless, but Angela sees it as underlining a distance that has been growing among them. She is somewhat friendly with Faye, whom she feels is overly competitive. Gradually, the two girls begin to build a more trusting relationship. When the class decides to buy a motorized wheelchair for Wayne, a rather cranky classmate, the friends manage to redefine their relationships.

Angela, an African American, is a wonderful character, down-to-earth and good-humored. Other people tend to make big issues out of simple situations, such as when her mother overreacts to Angela's question about her skin color, which happens to be darker than her parents'. She explains that, rather than having to deal with teasing at school, she had been studying about genes and she had been curious. Angela and her classmates are good examples of nice kids who are experiencing bumpy times in their relationships as they begin to mature physically and emotionally.

207. Cole, Joanna. *Asking about Sex and Growing Up: A Question-and-Answer Book for Boys and Girls.* Illus. by Alan Tiegreen. Morrow, 1988 (0-688-06927-4); pap. (0-688-06928-2). 128 pp. Nonfiction.

   Interest level: Ages 8–12

In a matter-of-fact tone, Cole packs a punch in her openness with preteens. In sections on girls' and boys' development, masturbation, crushes, intercourse, birth and birth control, homosexuality, and self-protection from abuse and disease, she provides nitty-gritty information that parents would wish they could offer as smoothly—for example, about how many women enjoy having their breasts caressed, how a tampon is removed, how each sex masturbates, how a girl can view her sexual organs by using a mirror. There's an occasional fact parents might not know, too—for example, why one testicle hangs lower than the other. The section on child abuse is strong and helpful for this age group, as the author delineates more types of abuse than are commonly acknowledged, such as being kissed in an adult way and being unable to stop it. The material on AIDS is up to date, and, although the readers are young, Cole trusts them with precautionary strategies against AIDS (for example, using condoms and washing the sexual organs before and after intercourse). Cole's comforting manner reassures and, most important in a book of this kind, makes it absolutely, positively all right to want to know. Bibliographies for parents and children.

208. Curtis, Robert H. *Mind and Mood: Understanding and Controlling Your Emotions.* Scribner, 1986. o.p. Nonfiction.

   Interest level: Age 12+

Among this book's strengths is its historical approach to emotions, ranging from biblical and ancient Greek observations of human feeling to Darwinian explanations. To show the relationship between mind and body, internist Curtis uses unique cases, such as "Tom's Stomach," in which doctors literally had a window into the coloration of one man's emotions. Curtis also deftly shows emotion's rich spectrum—for example, how trepidation, fear, dread, terror, panic, and horror differ from one another. Sections covering psychotherapy, behavior modification, endocrines, and the nervous system are commonly found in other volumes; the chapter on personality tests is fresh and will be of interest. A weakness, however, is the distant, formal tone that doesn't make contact with the individual reader.

209. DeClements, Barthe. *I Never Asked You to Understand Me.* Viking, 1986. o.p. 144 pp. Fiction.

Interest level: Age 12+

DeClements's novels for preteens have been immensely popular. This novel for an older group concentrates on students who have chosen or been forced to attend a casual alternative high school, a group DeClements understands from her work as a counselor in such a school. Didi is there because she becomes truant during her mother's terminal illness, terrified at being left with a distant father and a great-grandmother who sees illness as something we will on ourselves. The action revolves around Didi's struggle to see her own truth. How responsible are we for our destinies? Didi tries to find answers in the context of her new circle: teachers who stress self-actualization with kids who have seen the world through drug abuse, detention centers, and other tragedies. When she is able to help her desperate friend Stacy out of the dilemma of incest, Didi begins to find direction. Whether it's when Didi's father forgets a Christmas present or her friends party with drugs, DeClements creates memorable incidents with her large group of well-delineated characters.

210. Glenn, Mel. *Class Dismissed II: More High School Poems.* Photos by Michael J. Bernstein. Clarion, 1986 (0-89919-443-5). 96 pp. Fiction.

Interest level: Age 12+

Glenn has written 70 new poems about high school life, accomplishing the admirable task of sounding like each person who speaks. Glenn, a high school teacher himself, records words, feelings, and manner powerfully in these first-person vignettes. Bernstein's close-up photographic portraits of a multiethnic high school student body heighten the effect, whether the emotion is fear, despair, ebullience, pride, bravado, or one of many others.

Among the poetic-photographic portraits in this volume are Paul Hewitt, who wants books that can help him deal with real life ("I'm never going to fight the Civil War. And I certainly don't live in the Dust Bowl."); Candie Brewer, who has heard every line in the book at the rock club she frequents; and Veronica Castell, who has seen schools in seven states, courtesy of the Air Force. Many will identify with Robert Ashford, whose parents have usurped his power in picking out colleges for him, and Juan Pedro Carrera, who wants to return to his home country, where he doesn't "have to act so strong." A strong book all around.

211. Johnson, Julie Tallard. *Making Friends, Finding Love.* Lerner, 1992 (0-8225-0045-0). 64 pp. Nonfiction.

Interest level: Age 10+

This book explores the issues of friendship, love, and growing up for teenagers. It is never pedantic, nor does it make light of the intense need for teenagers to connect with their peers. This is not a book on how to be popular. This is a book that acknowledges the need that teenagers have to find a kindred spirit and frankly states that this might not always be possible. One chapter includes a list of key ingredients in evaluating friendships. In addition, the book discusses broken friendships, including suggestions on how to break off a relationship; dealing with family members; and coping with jealousy. Honest quotes from young people that appear throughout each chapter supply a veracity that supports the text. There is an ample reading list at the end.

212. Klein, Leonore. *Old, Older, Oldest.* Illus. by Leonard Kessler. Hastings, 1983. o.p. 48 pp. Nonfiction.

Interest level: Ages 6–10

Old, Older, Oldest is a concept book about the relative nature of age. The author takes a humorous approach that gets right to the heart of that relative nature. For example, "Is 'old' when your bones feel achy and cold?" The next page shows that eight-year-old Michael must therefore be old because he has the flu and his bones feel achy and cold. Next, "Is 'young' when you kick up your heels and dance?" In that case, Grandma is young although she is 65 years old, and the jaunty illustration shows her kicking up her heels. The rest of this useful book examines different animals, explaining their typical life spans. Additional concepts are examined, the most interesting of which is "How old would you like to be?" Well done and likely to provide the perspective the author and illustrator tried to offer.

213. McGuire, Paula. *It Won't Happen to Me: Teenagers Talk about Pregnancy.* Delacorte, 1983 (0-385-29244-9); pap. (0-685-06445-X). 244 pp. Nonfiction.

Interest level: Age 13+

Fifteen young women from varied backgrounds are interviewed by the author, who is a writer and editor of educational materials. All seem to want to talk so that others can benefit from their experiences. Some have decided to have abortions, some get married very young and keep the baby, some opt for adoption. The interviews are broad in scope, covering the varied roles and nonroles the fathers of these children have chosen to play in the unfolding drama. Other topics include pregnancy by rape, reasons the teens had sex, and discussion of venereal disease. The interviews are made into first-person narrations, with the editor's words hardly appearing at all. Occasionally, others participate in the narration, such as a young woman's mother. As the narrations are based on real people talking, they have a poignant power that simple information dispensing is less likely to offer. Bibliography, resource list, index.

214. Mills, Claudia. *The Secret Carousel.* Bantam, 1987, pap. (0-553-15499-0). 138 pp. Fiction.

Interest level: Ages 8–12

Lindy Webster lives with her grandparents because her parents were killed in an automobile accident. Her sister, Joan, has gone to New York to live with an aunt, because Joan is a ballerina and needs the city for her career. Lindy must decide what she wants for her own life, and that is what the process of the story is about. She builds a knowledge of herself and her grandfather, as well as an appreciation of the small town in Iowa where they live.

The story is a good one for young people to read. Not only does it move well, but the characters are interesting and have depth. Lindy suffers from loneliness, boredom, self-doubt, and jealousy, but she is also generous, loving, talented, and introspective. The family support system is an honest one. The problems and issues include the grandfather's retirement, the grandmother's concern, and the envy of the older sister who has a passion for ballet. A very satisfying book.

215. Rosenblum, Richard. *My Sister's Wedding.* Illus. by the author. Morrow, 1987. o.p. 32 pp. Fiction.

Interest level: Ages 6–9

A nostalgic look back to the 1940s gives this book charm as it touches on a common theme: big sister's getting married. Will her younger brother get her room? And how can that younger brother make friends with his new brother-in-law and his intriguing army and navy cohorts? The first-person account, speaking from the vantage point of an 11-year-old, harkens back to the author's actual experience, and each memory of planning and being at the wedding feels real, from the much-listened-to radio in the living room and the synagogue traditions to the servicemen's uniforms and conga line at the wedding. Oh, and brother never gets the room, because sister's husband goes overseas and sister stays home after all.

216. Skorpen, Liesel Moak. *Grace*. Harper, 1984. o.p. 87 pp. Fiction.

Interest level: Ages 9–12

Sara is suffering from loneliness. Her friends have all progressed into a stage that Sara is not yet ready for. She feels isolated and alienated, not only from her peers, but also from her family. She meets Amy, whose mother has run off and who is contemptuous of all things conventional. Under Amy's influence, Sara participates in rude behavior to Grace, an old, senile woman who lives alone next door to Sara's family.

Not until Sara is forced by her parents to apologize to Grace does Sara realize how lonely and afraid the old woman is. Sara befriends her throughout the summer. She visits the old woman regularly and promises to keep secret the fact that she is ill and almost helpless. In turn, Grace teaches Sara some old songs and serves as a friend to the lonely girl. Grace is terrified of dying in an institution; she wants to die in her own bed in her own house. At the end of the summer, she has her wish, and she bequeaths to Sara her Bible, her hymns, her Grimms' Fairy Tales, and the pearl her father gave her for her wedding day.

After Grace's death, Sara can make contact with her old friends again and determines to tell her parents about her experience with Grace. Sara has come of age.

The story is written in a style that is spare but flavorful. The reader is invited to fill in some of the details, but the implications and tone are sufficient to carry the story. Both Grace and Sara are characters who will stay with the reader after the book is ended.

217. Yolen, Jane. *The Girl Who Loved the Wind*. Illus. by Ed Young. Harper, 1992 (0-690-33101-0). 32 pp. Fiction.

Interest level: Ages 9–12

Danina is a protected princess whose concerned father never allows her to see or experience anything sad. Despite his efforts to insulate Danina from the world, she encounters the wind, whose sometimes powerful, sometimes sweet voice beckons her. The wind tells her about the world outside her walls, and Danina finds she cannot resist its invitation to break out of her loving prison and embrace the real world. This original folk tale is a lyrical allegory about breaking the bonds of childhood and entering adulthood, with its danger, its excitement, and its satisfactions.

4

Who Will Take Care of Me?

The Baby-Sitter

For many children, the first loss they experience is the mundane one of being cared for by someone other than their parents when their parents go out for an evening. Baby-sitters and other care givers are also needed when both parents (or the single parent) need to work outside the home. Baby-sitting arrangements vary, and children need to be prepared with sensitivity and understanding of their reasonable anxieties.

218. Crary, Elizabeth. *Mommy Don't Go*. Illus. by Marina Megale. Parenting, 1986, LB (0-943990-27-0); pap. (0-943990-26-2). 32 pp. Nonfiction.

Interest level: Ages 4–8

Part of the Children's Problem Solving Book series, this volume presents Matthew's problem: His mother is going on a trip, and he is staying with a baby-sitter. Matthew wants his mother to stay home. It's a solve-it-yourself book, with no right or wrong answers. The parent must read it with the child and go through the book based on the child's responses. To the opening question, "What can Matthew do so he will feel better?" there are nine answers, among them: cry, tell the sitter he is sad, keep something special of Mom's, make a surprise for his mom, ask for loving, try to make Mom stay home, and pretend he doesn't care that she's going. When parent and child turn to the page appropriate to the child's response, they can read a ministory that demonstrates the action and its consequences. The bottom of the page asks, "What will he do now?" which leads to another ministory. After some stories, the child is asked, "How do you like this ending?" And at the end, there's a blank page for writing and drawing your own ideas. Perhaps a bit complicated, but thinking is a complicated activity.

219. MacLachlan, Patricia. *Seven Kisses in a Row.* Illus. by Maria Pia Marrella. Harper, 1983 (0-06-024083-0); pap. (0-06-440231-2). 57 pp. Fiction.
    Interest level: Ages 7–10

Emma, an outspoken and engaging seven-year-old, and her older brother, Zachary, who knows her idiosyncrasies and understands her needs, spend five days with their aunt and uncle, who are baby-sitting for them while their parents go off to an "eyeball convention." When her aunt and uncle first arrive, Emma is not happy. She has special routines and rituals, and she is sure that her aunt and uncle won't understand her. At first, they don't. The very first morning that her aunt and uncle are there, they don't make Emma a divided grapefruit with a cherry, and they don't give her seven kisses in a row. So Emma "runs away" to a neighbor's house, where she always goes when she's running away. Zachary comes to pick her up, and he takes her back home, where her aunt and uncle are ready to begin practicing being parents.

One of the reasons Emma's aunt and uncle turn out to be such good baby-sitters is that they respect their niece and nephew and are willing to learn from them. They also enjoy engaging in the activities the youngsters invent. When Emma decides to sleep in a tent in the yard (in order to avoid the "night rumbles"), first her brother, then her aunt, and finally her uncle come out to join her, and they all sleep in the tent together.

Emma finds, to her surprise, that she's enjoyed her aunt and uncle so much that she doesn't want her parents to come home. Her aunt and uncle, who are expecting their first child, are so grateful to Emma and Zachary for teaching them about parenting that they give the children two bus tickets, so that they can come to visit as soon as the new baby is born.

This MacLachlan story contains all of the elements that make her such a popular writer. The humorously told story touches on serious themes of adjustment, separation, and preparation for parenthood. The happy combination of the inventive and lively children with the attentive and responsive adults makes a week they will all remember fondly—and so will the readers.

220. Orgel, Doris. *My War with Mrs. Galloway.* Illus. by Carol Newsom. Viking, 1985. o.p. 80 pp. Fiction.
    Interest level: Ages 8–11

Rebecca has had a succession of baby-sitters since her parents' divorce. Her mother is a physician, and her father is an artist who now lives in Portland, Oregon, far away from Rebecca and her mother, who live in Brooklyn, New York. Most of Rebecca's sitters have been pleasant and relaxed, leaving Rebecca to her own devices. But Mrs. Galloway, Rebecca's new sitter, is more attentive and structured and not as tolerant as Rebecca is accustomed to. Rebecca, therefore, declares war on Mrs. Galloway.

The story describes a series of misunderstandings and mishaps, most of which end up with Rebecca's being angry at Mrs. Galloway. But in the end, Mrs. Galloway proves to have been a responsible and competent sitter, and Rebecca learns to adjust to her style.

The story is humorously told and is sympathetic to Rebecca even when she is acting like a spoiled child. The story is fun, in and of itself, but children who are left regularly with baby-sitters will probably appreciate the book, as will parents who are trying to teach their children how to get along with their baby-sitters.

221. Richardson, Jean. *Thomas's Sitter*. Illus. by Dawn Holmes. Four Winds, 1991 (0-02-776146-0). Unpaged. Fiction.

Interest level: Ages 3–7

After new baby Katy Victoria arrives, Thomas learns that his mom plans to return to work outside the home and that his parents have decided to hire a baby-sitter. During interviews with prospective baby-sitters, Thomas misbehaves so that none of them will want to stay with him. But one day, he is completely disarmed by Dan, who is creative, fun to be with, and accepts Thomas as he is. Thomas thrives under Dan's guidance and manages to work out some of his frustrations about having to share the spotlight with a new baby. Dan is a nurturing, positive model. Can any baby-sitter measure up to this one?

222. Rockwell, Anne, and Harlow Rockwell. *My Baby-Sitter*. Illus. by the authors. Macmillan, 1985 (0-02-777780-4). 22 pp. Fiction.

Interest level: Ages 3–8

Martha is an ideal baby-sitter. This little book simply recounts the routine in which Martha engages when she is baby-sitting for the five-year-old narrator of the story. Martha makes a delicious dinner, dances with the little boy, makes sure that he brushes his teeth, watches television with him, reads to him, and puts him to bed. If he can't sleep, she talks to him and soothes him. He looks forward to her coming.The book is designed to help children feel comfortable with the fact that their parents occasionally leave them in the care of someone else. Martha, a 15-year-old, is competent without being spectacular. The little boy doesn't expect much from her except for a certain amount of attention and security. This is a useful statement and model for children.

223. Viorst, Judith. *The Good-bye Book.* Illus. by Kay Chorao. Macmillan, 1988 (0-689-31308-X); pap. (0-689-71581-1). 32 pp. Fiction.
    Interest level: Ages 3–7

The young boy tries to cajole, threaten, bully, frighten, and nag his parents into staying home or taking him with them when they go out for dinner. He imagines his baby-sitter as an unattractive person who will compel him to do terrible things, like eat vegetables. His parents stoically proceed with their preparations for going out, and when, at last, his attractive young male sitter arrives, he happily becomes engaged in activity with the sitter and cheerfully waves good-bye to his parents.

Both the text and Chorao's illustrations are amusing, true, and effective. It is unfortunate that the imagined sitter is a middle-aged heavy woman. Perhaps the "dreaded" fantasy sitter would have best been left to the child-reader's imagination, thus eliminating some negative stereotyping. But on the whole, this book is sure to be useful in homes where a child makes a fuss about parents leaving for the evening.

Parents at Work

Sometimes parental employment requires separation and becomes a loss situation for a child. If parents must travel or work at a distance from home children left behind feel the absence deeply. They miss the company of a necessary adult in their lives. In today's economy it is more than likely that both parents in a two-parent family work outside the home. Books that demonstrate how children cope with this phenomenon can be useful guides.

224. Banks, Ann. *Alone at Home: A Kid's Guide to Being in Charge.* Illus. by Cathy Bobak. Puffin, 1989, pap. (0-14-032689-8). 56 pp. Nonfiction.
    Interest level: Ages 7–10

A manual for children who, through choice or necessity, must spend significant blocks of time alone at home. Topics include safety, communication, siblings, and activities to do. The book begins by inviting children to paste a picture of themselves on the page so as to establish a sense of ownership in the book and its activities. The author then asks children to fill in information about themselves, their family, and their feelings, particularly about having to stay at home alone. Simulations are provided, such as acting out what to say and do if a stranger rings the doorbell, claims his car has broken down, and asks to use the phone. There are also such helpful hints as keeping a spare key at a neighbor's so as to avoid getting locked out. For more dramatic situations, children are urged to hold a wet towel to their faces if there is lots of smoke. For emotional support, the author recommends routines, selecting favorite radio or TV stations, playing with pets, or preparing a special, festive meal. The authors also suggest keeping a log and exploring fears in order to talk them out and handle them. Advice for parents is also provided.

225. Bauer, Caroline Feller. *My Mom Travels a Lot.* Illus. by Nancy Winslow Parker. Puffin, 1985, pap. (0-14-050545-8). Unpaged. Picture book.

Interest level: Ages 5–8

In a format that invites young readers to create their own text, the book explores the positives and negatives of having a mom whose work takes her away from home much of the time. The book's pattern consists of "The good thing about it is . . . ," followed immediately by "The bad thing about it is . . ." Some of the bad things include that "Mom misses special events, such as the birth of a puppy or a school play." The book ends with two good things: The children get gifts, but the best thing is that the mom always comes home to them. The title of the book can be changed to *My Dad Travels a Lot* to see how the good and bad things might change. It is helpful, however, to have a story that acknowledges that moms as well as dads can have jobs that necessitate travel.

226. Jarrow, Gail. *If Phyllis Were Here.* Houghton, 1987. o.p. 132 pp. Fiction.

Interest level: Ages 9–12

Libby's grandmother, Phyllis, has won the lottery and is now going to move to Florida with her boyfriend. Libby is bereft because her grandmother has been her primary caretaker, confidante, and source of emotional comfort. Although Libby's parents are both at home, they are preoccupied with their work, and they, too, rely on Phyllis to manage the house and to be there for Libby.

The mother is depicted as someone who is a competent lawyer but an inept homemaker. When Phyllis leaves, she hires a housekeeper who is more concerned with keeping the place neat than with Libby's feelings. Eventually, after several near disasters and some emotional trauma caused by a nasty girl at school, all is resolved, and it looks like Libby and her parents will manage well. The story is written with a light touch, but it provides young readers with some excellent insights into the dynamics of a working family as well as helping to blast some stereotypes about old people.

227. Kleeberg, Irene Cumming. *Latchkey Kid.* Illus. by Anne Canevari Green. Watts, 1985 (0-531-10052-9). 102 pp. Nonfiction.
    Interest level: Ages 9–13

Kleeberg opens the book by combining statistics with her helpful point of view: "Imagine! Between two and six million kids coming home after school and managing things just fine." Topics include snacks, chores, homework, neighbors, telephone calls, brothers and sisters, occupying oneself (chapter heading: "What Is There to Do?"), friends, illness, joining after-school clubs, summer, housekeeping, safety and emergencies, and when to call a parent. The advice is simply stated and clear—for example, how to receive a call for a parent without saying the parent isn't home. There are some original ideas, too, such as using office memo pads to take messages, beneficial because of their easy-to-fill-in boxes. Another area for original ideas is the author's activity section—for example, building an obstacle course that doesn't present a safety hazard as an afternoon activity. The safety measures are broad in coverage, showing good thinking regarding potential occurrences in a house. Besides the obvious—fire and the like—there is information about a toilet overflowing, no lights, thunderstorms, and water in the cellar. Helpful, respectful, and fun. Glossary.

228. Kyte, Kathy S. *In Charge: A Complete Handbook for Kids with Working Parents.* Illus. by Susan Detrich. Knopf, 1983. o.p. 128 pp. Nonfiction.
    Interest level: Ages 8–12

Suggesting a family conference to get rules and procedures under way, Kyte recommends master lists and contact persons. Her guide is divided into such sections as child care, cooking, caring for your clothes, and coping with a crisis. She's big on charts that elucidate daily schedules and chores, certainly matters that can become more easily accomplished if put in writing.

The crises to which she attends are both little and big—little exemplified by a power outage, big by fire and crime. Her section on crime prevention is especially good, telling readers to do a homecoming check and helpfully reminding them that such sections deserve rereading from time to time. Her hefty section on cooking includes easy recipes that are very appealing (for example, apple toast).

This is a lively book. Kyte writes with chatty gusto and builds self-confidence in her readers. "You will astonish yourself with your In

Charge, crisis-coping ability." In her illustrations, Susan Detrich provides reassuring laughs about what might otherwise seem overwhelming. In the section on plumbing, a boy is shown dressed in goggles and fins swimming in his basement trying to find the water valve. Bibliography.

229. Leiner, Katherine. *Both My Parents Work.* Photos by Steve Sax. Watts, 1986. o.p. 48 pp. Nonfiction.

Interest level: Ages 5–9

Part of the My World series, this volume does what the series claims: open up new experiences and horizons. The families portrayed demonstrate varied patterns—night, day, home, and office jobs. The people, of various races, hold jobs ranging from ones children are familiar with (police officer, farmer, manager of a fast-food restaurant) to vocations that will be very new to children (arbitrator, city planner).

The children who narrate the sections range in age from 5 through 12 and describe their parents' jobs and the schedule the family as a whole keeps. Varying child-care arrangements are discussed: relatives, day-care, baby-sitting, and so on. They also describe feelings, exemplified by David, who feels left out sometimes when his psychologist mother and musician father keep him out of the rooms where they are practicing. The author and photographer maintain interest throughout, although they are profiling ten children and their weekly family schedules.

230. Stanek, Muriel. *All Alone after School.* Illus. by Ruth Rosner. Whitman, 1985 (0-8075-2078-2). 32 pp. Fiction.

Interest level: Ages 5–8

Josh's mother can't afford a baby-sitter for him and she has to work, so she helps Josh prepare to be alone in the house after school. She discusses an important set of rules for his safety and security; she tapes a list of useful phone numbers on the wall; and she informs all the necessary people about the situation. She also demonstrates her empathy for Josh by giving him a special stone to hold, a talisman to help him feel brave.

On his first day alone, he immediately calls his mother at work and they have a good, though short, talk. When his mother comes home, they are both overjoyed to be together, and his mother tells Josh how proud she is of him.

Now, a year later, Josh is able to use his own good experience to help Becky, a new classmate, to overcome her anxieties about being a latchkey child. He is so secure now that he can give Becky his security stone.

The details of Josh's and his mother's preparations for his being alone, and the specifics of the activities Josh engages in when he is alone, help enormously. The book has an authenticity and respectful tone that make it very effective.

Marital Separation and Divorce

Marital separation and divorce constitute loss for the child, not only because of the destruction of the parents' marriage, but also because of the added element of rejection, especially because children perceive that their parents have *chosen* to separate. Divorce and separation are additionally difficult for all concerned because society offers no rites to engage in to ease the bereavement.

Although it sometimes happens in real life that parents reunite, this reconciliation is not germane for a book trying to help children cope with divorce. It is often the sought-after happy ending, but it is better for a child to see that there is life after divorce than to be encouraged to go on vainly hoping for parents to get back together. Children need to learn to cope with the separation, not to expect that it will magically end. Authors should avoid painting either parent as a total victim or oppressor. Sudden or complete adjustment to the separation is unrealistic. Authors serve their audiences better when they convey the understanding that coping comes with time and hard work.

231. Banks, Ann. *When Your Parents Get a Divorce: A Kid's Journal.* Illus. by Cathy Bobak. Puffin, 1990, pap. (0-14-034340-7). 62 pp. Nonfiction.
    Interest level: Ages 7–10

A useful workbook for helping children vent their feelings and understand that they are not alone in these feelings. Questions and activities are open-ended, including such items as comparing the mother's home with the father's home, listing people they can talk to, and determining what makes them happy. The message to parents at the end of the journal succinctly summarizes good, practical advice. Unfortunately, cartoonlike illustrations include predominantly white, middle-class children in limited family constellations. This can be partially offset by having young readers draw their own illustrations. The authors invite children to paste a photograph of themselves on the first page; perhaps this can help the book to be more inclusive.

232. Baum, Louis. *One More Time.* Illus. by Paddy Bouma. Morrow, 1986 (0-688-06587-2); pap. (0-688-11698-1). 24 pp. Fiction.
    Interest level: Ages 4–8

Simon and his father spend an idyllic Sunday together, and the reader is surprised when Simon's father says good-bye to him after depositing him at his door. Only then is it clear that Simon's parents are divorced and Simon spends only one day a week with his dad.

There is a bittersweet element about the joy that Simon and his father experience during their day together. At the end, Simon is reluctant to let his father go, but he is more willing to do so knowing that he will see him again soon. This issue is a difficult one with young children. Even when parents have demonstrated that they are trustworthy, the fact of the separation causes anxiety. This book may serve as a catalyst for discussion and the airing of feelings.

233. Boegehold, Betty. *Daddy Doesn't Live Here Anymore: A Book about Divorce.* Illus. by Deborah Borgo. Western, 1985 (0-307-12480-0). 28 pp. Fiction.

Interest level: Ages 4–8

As in the other Golden Learn about Living books, this has a note to parents in the preface, advising on how to reassure their children during a difficult adjustment period. The story concerns Casey, who returns from school wondering if her mom and dad will be fighting. She thinks, "No. They'll pretend everything is okay. As if I didn't know better!" But Casey returns to find Dad's car gone and Mom crying again. Trying to forget that her father has left by playing the scene out with her dolls in a dollhouse helps for the moment. At dinner, though, Casey's mother informs her that her father isn't going to live with them anymore and her parents are going to divorce.

Casey's mother tries to reassure her that her father loves her a lot, but the two adults don't love each other anymore and can't get along. "I don't want to have no daddy," Casey cries. Again, her mother tries to comfort: "Daddy will always be your daddy. He'll just live in a different place. You'll see him lots of times, but most of the time, you'll live with me." It's too much to hear at once, and Casey runs to her room and her own doll children. There she tries to bargain and get Daddy to come back by being sick. Mom does call Dad, and he explains that they just can't live together anymore. The next ploy is to run away, but not so far that mother can't come and woo her back. This time, the mother reassures her that her father's leaving wasn't because of anything Casey did. Casey's next doll play involves putting the father doll in a separate place and exclaiming: "And you better have the kids come over to visit a lot—I'm telling you." And it's Casey's turn to reassure her dolls. The usual emotional reactions are explored, however briefly, and the resolution is realistically not complete at book's end; the device of using dolls is helpful.

234. Brown, Laurene Krasny, and Marc Brown. *Dinosaurs Divorce: A Guide for Changing Families.* Little, Brown, 1986 (0-316-11248-8); pap. (0-316-10996-7). 32 pp. Nonfiction.

Interest level: Ages 5–10

Starting off with a glossary cum invitation, the authors say, "The starred (*) words are in the book. See if you can find them." And then readers are off into a comic strip-style assessment of divorce, culled from the authors' experiences as "a parent, stepparent, and for Laurie [the author], as a child herself." Marc Brown's children gave numerous ideas, too.

It's hard to put the many complex ideas about divorce, remarriage, and stepsiblings into a picture book, but these authors succeed in touching children's hearts and feelings. They do this in several ways. First, their point of view is stated squarely in the first sentence: "Divorce takes place between mothers and fathers. You are not to blame if your parents get divorced." Second, humorous dinosaur children and parents portray the action, bringing an amazing repertoire of emotions with them, from ashamed to angry, from relieved to confused. Through the fine wedding of words with illustrations, a great deal is brought out that children can infer. For example, the words say, "If you feel angry, tell your parents why and look for ways to show anger that don't hurt others or yourself." Accompanying pictures show a child dinosaur in animated hostile dramatic play with dolls and an airplane. The illustrations also convey jokes that can be enjoyed on rereading—for example, the logo on a truck: "Tyrannosaurus Truckers/Since the Jurassic Period." Third, the authors touch on such complicated issues as scapegoating and self-destructive behavior.

The book assumes helpful parents who, although getting divorced, can sit calmly and answer questions. It also offers good advice and words to say that children can adopt and adapt. For example, "You don't have to listen when parents say bad things about each other. Say you love them both and hearing this upsets you. You may have to tell them more than once." On occasion, the authors gloss over difficult issues or expect too much of children's capability for maturity. For example, "Living with one parent almost always means there will be less money. Be prepared to give up some things" (an illustration shows a child longingly looking in a toy store window). Another example is: "Some parents feel too guilty or unhappy to visit you. Sometimes you can keep in touch by calling or writing." A third example is: "Try to be open to these changes."

Perhaps adults sharing this book with children can bring their own ideas to it, reassuring children that they don't have to be that mature and giving. Other than these occasional shortcomings, this is a book of deep understanding that is highly admirable: "It may feel strange at first to show your love for one parent in front of the other. Try to remember it's okay to love both and to show that you do."

235. Christianson, C. B. *My Mother's House, My Father's House.* Illus. by Irene Trivas. Atheneum, 1989 (0-689-313-94-2); Puffin, pap. (0-14-054210-8). Unpaged. Picture book.

Interest level: Ages 5–8

Joint custody is explored in this story, where the child shuttles back and forth from one parent to the other every three or four days. Her parents differ from each other in many ways: One is messy, the other neat. One has a large house, a car, and two dogs; the other has three large rooms, rides the bus, and owns a cat. One is a photographer, the other seems to be a professor or a writer. Both parents, however, demonstrate their love and concern for their daughter. The situation is understandably a difficult one for the child, and she wistfully dreams of a time when she can own a combination of what her parents have, enjoy visits from her parents and, above all, stay in the same place all the time.

236. Cleary, Beverly. *Dear Mr. Henshaw.* Illus. by Paul Zelinsky. Morrow, 1983 (0-688-02405-X); Dell, pap. (0-440-21366-5). 134 pp. Fiction.

Interest level: Ages 8–11

Leigh Botts has been writing to an author named Henshaw since second grade. He is now in sixth grade, adjusting to a new school in a new town because his parents have been divorced. He is angry at Mr. Henshaw because in his last letter Mr. Henshaw asked Leigh to answer some questions about himself. Although Leigh claims to want to be a writer, he resents having to do added work; his letters to Mr. Henshaw have usually been prompted by a school assignment.

During the course of his correspondence with Mr. Henshaw, Leigh writes about what bothers him and what he wishes, which mostly has to do with his father, although he hardly sees or hears from him. His father is a truck driver and on the road a lot, but most of the problem is that his father is not a very attentive or loving person to Leigh or his mother. Another of Leigh's problems is that someone is stealing his lunch at school. He's also lonely, especially because his father has custody of their dog, Bandit.

Leigh's continuing correspondence with Mr. Henshaw reveals that the author is too busy to read much of what Leigh writes. He suggests that Leigh keep a journal, perhaps in the form of letters to someone. So Leigh writes letters to Mr. Henshaw in his journal rather than mailing them. He does manage to send some fan mail in response to the author's new book.

And Mr. Henshaw answers with postcards from wherever he happens to be.

Meanwhile, things are going badly for Leigh and his father. When Leigh calls his father one night, he hears a boy's voice asking when they will go out for pizza. To add to Leigh's misery, Bandit has been lost.

In the process of becoming a writer and adjusting to his new school and to his new situation as a stepbrother, Leigh learns a lot about himself. He manages to solve his new-school problems; Bandit is found; and his mother comes to terms with the fact that her ex-husband will probably never change.

The book is written in Cleary's inimitable style. It is truthful but light; important issues are not sidestepped; and the characters are respected. Divorce is presented as a wrenching experience for everyone involved, but it is also clear that the problems can be surmounted. Leigh learns, develops, and succeeds in his efforts to become better adjusted to his situation.

237. Dragonwagon, Crescent. *Always, Always.* Illus. by Arieh Zeldich. Macmillan, 1984 (0-02-733080-X). 32 pp. Fiction.

   Interest level: Ages 6–10

The young girl lives with her mother in New York for most of the year, but every summer she visits with her father, who is a carpenter in Colorado. Her parents' life-styles and values are very different from each other, but they are wise enough not to catch their daughter in the middle. They do, however, do things that they ask her not to tell the other parent about, such as permitting her to chop wood and giving her a manicure.

When the girl asks her parents why they ever were married, they each tell her that their marriage was a mistake, but that she wasn't and they love her dearly. Despite her parents' differences, the girl seems very well adjusted. She has a fine relationship with each parent; accommodates to each life-style with ease; and has friends and possessions in each place. It looks as if she will continue to live a balanced and secure life.

Dragonwagon is good at helping children to understand and respect differences in life-style as well as opinions and values. She is nonjudgmental and conveys the notion that life is joyous and to be savored.

238. Galloway, Priscilla. *Jennifer Has Two Daddies.* Illus. by Ana Auml. Women's Educational Press, 1985. o.p. 32 pp. Fiction.

   Interest level: Ages 3–8

Jennifer is very fortunate. She has two of almost everything, and her mother and father and stepfather love her very much. Her parents have joint custody, so Jennifer commutes weekly from one place to the other.

She's generally content until her father has to go away for three weeks. He tries to prepare her for his absence, but she becomes terribly anxious and tries to call him in the middle of the night. Even though she has dialed a number in Bombay, India, her mother and stepfather are very understanding, and they help her to dial her father's number. He helps her to deal with his absence in a loving and practical way. Jennifer is enveloped in love and concern, and the reader knows that she will be fine.

239. Girard, Linda Walvoord. *At Daddy's on Saturdays.* Illus. by Judith Friedman. Whitman, 1987 (0-8075-0475-0); pap. (0-8075-0473-4). 32 pp. Fiction.

   Interest level: Ages 3–8

Katie's daddy and mommy separate, and they will be divorced. They are both very solicitous of Katie and discuss all of her worries with her in an open and loving way. She goes to visit her father in his new apartment, and he assures her that he will always love her, always be her father, and always tell her the truth. Katie's mother is also in tune with Katie's feelings. She lets Katie know that it is not Katie's fault that her father doesn't live with them any more. Both parents seem respectful of each other as well as of Katie's feelings. The narrator of the book acknowledges that Katie may never be free of a hurt feeling about the divorce, but at least she knows that she is loved and wanted by both her parents.

   The author is clearly aware of the criteria for helping children deal with divorce. She is in touch with children's anxieties and reactions, and she does not fall into any of the traps of "happy" endings or false hopes. This book may help serve as a model for some parents who wonder how to handle the topic of divorce with their young children.

240. Herzig, Alison Cragin. *Shadows on the Pond.* Little, Brown, 1985. o.p. 200 pp. Fiction.

   Interest level: Age 12+

Jill's parents' marriage is deteriorating, and Jill and her mother go to their summer home in Vermont for the first time without her father and sister. Her sister has detached herself from the situation. Jill cannot do that, but she is able to resume her friendship with her neighbor, Megan, and to work together with her to defeat the cruel trapping of beavers in their secret pond. When an accident keeps Megan at home, Jill continues the work with the help and friendship of a new friend, Ryan, who is on vacation in this same area.

   Ryan and Jill's friendship blooms while her mother and father's once loving marriage has cooled to the point of estrangement. Jill's mother is learning to live alone and finds difficulty managing the tasks that were once the province of her husband. The tension that exists between her parents is overwhelming and frightening for Jill, who must guess at much of what is going on because her parents do not confide in her. She is hurt and confused and constantly longs for the way life used to be. Ryan, whose parents divorced many years previously, represents a person who has become reconciled to a similar situation and has come out of the pain. He is able to help Jill gain a different perspective on her agonizing situation.

The book deals with many issues, but the overriding theme is reconstruction. The beavers will rebuild their dams, Ryan and Jill will continue their friendship in New York, and it also seems hopeful that, with effort, Jill's parents can resolve their own crisis. The book concludes with Jill's recognition that despair can be overcome through acceptance.

241. K   Krementz, Jill. *How It Feels When Parents Divorce*. Photos by the author. Knopf, 1988, pap. (0-394-75855-2). 128 pp. Nonfiction.

Interest level: Age 8+

This book contains 19 profiles of children's views and experiences. The children range in age from 7 to 16, and their parents encouraged photojournalist Krementz to speak to and photograph the children. Krementz thanks the children: "It took courage for them to talk openly about their fears, their sorrows, their confusions, knowing full well that what they were revealing about themselves would not only be read by strangers but by the very people whose actions had caused much of their pain."

And talk to this author (a child of divorce) of their pain they certainly do. She has captured the real thing, and in the rawness of the children's experience, she touches home. There is the child who gets caught in the middle of money problems; the divorced mother who embarrasses her former husband and child by wanting to kiss her ex-husband "good night" at a class play; the exploited child who is kidnapped and, so that the parent doesn't have to produce records that would expose location, is left back in school; and that very exploited child who still misses the parent who kidnapped him (he's back with the other parent now). Children's feelings are very strong: wanting half siblings, not wanting them; wanting stepparents, not wanting them. One child asks for broadening of the Catholic Church's views: "Being divorced is bad enough, but feeling God is mad too only adds to the feeling of guilt and makes the situation worse."

The families are of varied races. The family constellations are varied—some remarried, some live-ins, some boy- and girlfriends. Custodial arrangements vary, too, with nearly every conceivable plan included (parents switch, children switch, brief spans, long spans). Here's one reasonable holiday solution: "During the summer we alternate every six weeks, and we always spend Christmas with my father and Easter with my mother. On our birthdays it's whoever we're with and then the other parent calls."

The profiles are lengthy, with few pictures, usually an individual portrait of the child and a portrait or action shot with at least one parent. The leisurely length allows for the expression of deep feelings—for example, one boy's idea of what a custody battle would be like: fighting over a restaurant check, when secretly neither party wants it. Such haunting images are frequent in Krementz's book, making it compelling, instructive reading for both children and adults.

242. McGuire, Paula. *Putting It Together: Teenagers Talk about Family Breakups.* Delacorte, 1987, pap. (0-385-29564-2). 184 pp. Nonfiction.

Interest level: Age 12+

McGuire interviewed 20 adolescents and social service professionals who specialize in family problems, and the end result "tells it like it is" in feelingful vignettes. Raw emotion with little held back of the pain felt after death, separation, or divorce is the rule. The kids' fantasies touch the heart (brothers Peter and Quentin wanted to follow Mom to a 100-acre farm; "it was going to be really good"). Reality was disappointing (Mom was never reliable, so it probably never would come to pass). Some of the teens involved come from middle-class homes and are college bound; others are those more on the periphery, who have run away, live in shelters, or are flirting with a lengthy future in the prison system.

The sadness of such a broad panorama becomes the book's power, reflecting on not just one group of teens and making it different from most books of this sort. It shows us various aspects of this generation and the one to follow.

243. Nickman, Steven L. *When Mom and Dad Divorce.* Illus. by Diane de Groat. Simon & Schuster, 1986, LB (0-671-60153-9); pap. (0-671-62878-X). 80 pp. Nonfiction.

Interest level: Ages 8–14

Pediatric psychiatrist Nickman uses seven stories of typical situations to present generalized insights: The subjects include analysis of what leads to divorce, how it feels at first, joint custody, stepfamilies, and actions that can help. Nickman's central thrust might be: "Kids have a right to be kids." And with this in mind, he offers concrete suggestions for getting through a tough time. Letting kids in on the reality that things will likely get worse before they get better, Nickman describes what happens in separation for kids who haven't yet gone through it. His ability to capture that reality is down-to-earth—for example, "Your eyes may fill with tears when you least expect it." He also gives a full account of one child's therapy and what she derived from it. Among Nickman's many practical suggestions for coping with a situation that seems out of control are remembering other tough things you've navigated and *yelling* if you're stuck in the middle.

Although similar in tone to Eda LeShan's *What's Going to Happen to Me? When Parents Separate or Divorce* (Four Winds, 1978), this book has something new to say in its author's emphasis on looking at and insisting on each party's rights and his willingness to share with youngsters adult insights about the pathways of marriage.

244. Okimoto, Jean Davies. *Jason's Women.* Little, Brown, 1986 (0-316-63809-9); Dell, pap. (0-440-20000-8). 210 pp. Fiction.

Interest level: Age 11

The main character is a shy 16-year-old boy with divorced parents who are both very involved in their own lives. The story concerns his close relationships with an 80-year-old woman who is dying of cancer and a young Cambodian girl, Thao, who has escaped her country, leaving behind her family.

This book was a lovely surprise. The jacket leads one to believe it will be about a shy, lonely boy learning to face social challenges. That it is, yet it is also about a remarkable old woman whom Jason learns to respect and love and the Cambodian girl she has sponsored. In helping Thao and learning her brave story, Jason learns more about himself. Interracial and intercultural relationships are sensibly and sensitively developed. Jason lives with his father, and their relationship is clearly and realistically portrayed. The mother seems more one-dimensional. There is humor; the characters are interesting; the plot is fun.

245. Pfeffer, Susan Beth. *Dear Dad, Love Laurie.* Scholastic, 1990, pap. (0-590-41682-0). 120 pp. Fiction.

Interest level: Ages 8–11

Laurie's twelfth year is full of traumas. Although she has fairly well recovered from her parents' divorce, she is upset by her mother's dating. She is also angry and jealous because her friend has been accepted into a gifted-and-talented program and she has not. The book consists of Laurie's letters to her dad, who has moved to Missouri. Laurie's mother and father maintain a friendly and mutually respectful relationship. They are both intelligent and warm people and love Laurie very much. No blaming is even hinted at in this book, which reflects many children's feelings and anxieties. Laurie is an open, responsive child who communicates both her negative and her positive reactions in each of her letters. She feels free to tell her parents when she hates them as well as when she loves them. The story provides a model of how successful a divorce can be. The humor, screamingly funny at times, enhances the plot, and the characters emerge as real and sympathetic. It is too bad that the author does not pay as much attention to the needs of reporting accurately about gifted students or programs for them. The author confuses educational models and does nothing to illuminate either the special qualities of academically talented students or the practices and principles of programs for gifted students.

246. Pomerantz, Barbara. *Who Will Lead Kiddush?* Illus. by Donna Ruff. Union of American Hebrew Congregations, 1985, pap. (0-8074-0306-7). 32 pp. Fiction.

Interest level: Ages 4–8

Divorce occurs in all groups, and this book's purpose is to reflect on how parental separation might affect a religious Jewish household. The author tries to find predictable, reliable aspects for a child to hold onto, and in the Sabbath there is such stability. The tradition can help strengthen a child, she says, while other traditions are less stable. As such, holiday traditions can also be a source of continuity.

The first-person story begins with a single-parent family already past the marital separation. "Tonight, it is my turn to lead Kiddush with Mommy." The female protagonist then remembers how it was when Daddy lived with them. Then Daddy moved away. This is a portrayal of a father who plans to be active in the life of his daughter (phone calls every night, visits together several times a week)—in fact, in the life of his wife, too, as he will still be partially responsible for building the *sukkah*, an outdoor structure for the Feast of Tabernacles. And the child spends every other Sabbath with her father; on their first together, he gives her a present: her own kiddush cup to make the wine benediction. The kiddush becomes a way to think of one another, even if they are apart. A loving, thoughtful portrait that can help many families bridge distances.

247. Simon, Norma. *I Wish I Had My Father.* Illus. by Arieh Zeldich. Whitman, 1983 (0-8075-3522-2). 32 pp. Fiction.

Interest level: Ages 5–8

The little boy dreads Father's Day. Every year, he is forced to make something for Father's Day, and he feels terrible because he never sees or hears from his father. He doesn't really know anything about him except that his father left his mother and him a long time ago.

His teachers always say that he can make something for any man he knows, but that doesn't alleviate his longing. He knows one child whose father is dead, and he knows another whose parents are divorced. It helps him to have other children in his situation. It also helps that he has several adult males who are surrogate fathers to him, but he wishes that he could have his own father with him, even if it were for only one day a year.

The story helps adults and children to understand the difficulties of coping with nontraditional family situations. How sad that so many teachers and adults assume that all children live in traditional surroundings. This book clearly presents the lives of those children who, in increasing numbers, do not live in two-parent families. Perhaps the book will help adults to become more sensitive to all the children they serve.

248. Slepian, Jan. *Getting On with It.* Four Winds, 1985. o.p. 171 pp. Fiction.

Interest level: Age 11+

The story tells of 13-year-old Berry Brice and the summer she spends at her grandmother's cottage while her parents arrange to get a divorce. Berry is furious at her parents and feels that she has been exiled to her grandmother's house. She is a romantic dreamer who creates scenarios in her mind for herself and everyone she meets. She leaps to conclusions and lets her first impressions color her responses to people. As the story unfolds, her impressions change and she realizes that there is more complexity to people and their interactions than she had ever imagined.

In the process of telling the story, the author blasts a number of stereotypes. The older woman next door is not a mouse; she is emotionally and sexually involved with Sonny, the younger man who was adopted into her family by her older sister. The recluse in the woods is not a crazy man or a thief, but a person who feels that he causes trouble for people and who is afraid to harm anyone else. He is Sonny's father, and, although Sonny wants to take care of him, he goes off by himself at the end of the book. Berry becomes friends with an 11-year-old boy, much against her initial intent. And Berry's parents do not reconcile, even though Berry does not understand the cause of the divorce. She is especially taken aback by her parents' decision because she has never heard them fighting. All these stereotypes are dispensed with, not only for Berry but also for the reader.

Berry's grandmother is another interesting character. She is a Holocaust survivor who never discusses her story. In a moment of weakness, she discloses that her family sent her to safety, but all of them were killed. She cannot understand why she survived. She doesn't like to talk about her emotions or her experiences, and she never permits Berry to talk about hers either. She doesn't change at the end of the story, but Berry does. Here again, the author lets us know that everything doesn't always come out as we wish it to, that life is often unpredictable because people are unique.

249. Stinson, Kathy. *Mom and Dad Don't Live Together Anymore.* Illus. by Nancy Lou Reynolds. Firefly, 1984, LB (0-920236-92-8); pap. (0-920236-87-1). 23 pp. Fiction.

   Interest level: Ages 3–7

The book opens with the picture of a sad child thinking about the fact that her mom and dad do not live together anymore. It deals with this little girl's feelings—her wish for them to get back together, her desire to see both parents every day, her anxiety about her dad's relationship with another woman, and her worry about where she and her brother will celebrate Christmas. It deals with separate residences, vacation spots, and days on which the parents see them. She even asks, "Mom, when I grow up, will I get married and then get apart?" In the final pages, both parents tell her that she makes them happy, and she realizes that she likes to be with both of them and that they love her, "just not together."

   This simple, well-written, and realistically illustrated book presents a reassuring approach to children of divorce. Young children reading this book will feel more comfortable about separated parents and realize that they are still loved by both, even though they don't live together anymore. One flaw is that the author has paid little attention to the brother. Boys have feelings too!

250. Vigna, Judith. *Grandma without Me.* Illus. by the author. Whitman, 1984 (0-8075-3030-1). 32 pp. Fiction.

   Interest level: Ages 4–8

A young boy feels cut off from his paternal grandmother after his parents' divorce. He particularly hates celebrating Thanksgiving without her. To help make each other feel better, the boy and his grandmother initiate a correspondence. The boy keeps a scrapbook of letters and memorabilia that his grandmother sends him. He also hits on an excellent idea to help lessen his grandmother's sadness at his absence from the Thanksgiving dinner. He has his mother trace his shape on a large piece of paper. He sends the shape to his grandmother's house so that he will be represented there in a tangible form.

   His mother is very angry at his father. His father has remarried and will be at the grandmother's dinner with his new spouse. The boy lives with his mother, who is clearly very bitter about the divorce. But after seeing the boy's anguish, she promises him that he will be permitted to attend his grandmother's Thanksgiving celebration next year.

The author honestly and clearly portrays a family in the throes of bitter and unhappy feelings after a divorce. The child and the grandmother are the victims of the situation. No one wants them to be unhappy, but that, nevertheless, is the result. The boy and his grandmother do their best to cope with a bad situation, and the reader is left with hope because of the genuine bonds between them that they are working hard to maintain.

251. Vigna, Judith. *Mommy and Me by Ourselves Again.* lllus. by the author. Whitman, 1987 (0-8075-5232-1). 32 pp. Fiction.

Interest level: Ages 4–8

Here is a sad tale of today's times. Amy has lost not once but twice. Her parents have divorced, her father doesn't come to see her, and now her mother's romance with Gary has ended. But Gary was kind; he gave Amy a charm on her last birthday and promised her one every year for the rest of her life. Or *was* he kind? Amy misses Gary, and so does her mother. Mom tries to help on this crucial day, knowing Gary will not come. She takes Amy on an outing, and she exclaims, "Lots of times it's fun, Mommy and me by ourselves." But the pain lingers, as there is no father figure. She berates herself and vows never to love again. She worries, too. Will Mommy leave? The book ends with six relatives arriving, each bearing a charm and each better able to keep a promise.

Amy's mother tells the painful truth: "It's hard to find someone who's special enough to be a good husband for me and a good father for you, but I hope I will someday." Many families live through this situation—impulsive behavior that unintentionally causes hurt and confusion. The book offers a sensitive, realistic treatment of this situation with brief sentences and illustrations in soft pastels.

Stepparents and Stepsiblings

When parents remarry children often experience conflicting emotions, ranging from relief that their parents are happier to jealousy of a parent's new partner. They must learn to get along with the additional parent or two, and sometimes siblings and an extended family. Books reflecting blended families can be helpful in acknowledging the challenges, joys, and conflicts that arise in these new family constellations. Characters should be realistically complex, and the central situation should not be the only substance of the book. Stereotypes that should be avoided include the wonderful/terrible stepfather, the bratty/long-suffering stepsibling, the victimized/super-strong mother, and the put-upon/spoiled-rotten child.

252. Bauer, Marion Dane. *Face to Face.* Clarion, 1991 (0-395-55440-3); Dell, pap. (0-440-40791-5). 176 pp. Fiction.

Interest level: Age 11+

Michael is small for his age, frequently victimized by bullies, and resentful of his stepfather, who he suspects married his mother so that he could have his own farm. Although Dave, his stepfather, is a good man who loves him, Michael craves the company, attention, and love of Bert, his birth father, who deserted him and whom he has not seen in eight years. When Bert suddenly calls and invites Michael to spend time with him white-water rafting in Colorado, Michael jumps at the chance. But after being with him for a short while, he discovers that his father is not the man he longed for all of his growing-up years. In the end, after despairing and almost killing himself, Michael becomes his own person and appreciates Dave in a way he has not been able to before.

253. Craven, Linda. *Stepfamilies: New Patterns of Harmony.* Simon & Schuster, 1983, LB (0-671-49486-4). 192 pp. Nonfiction.

Interest level: Ages 11–16

The author reveals her own crises in living in a stepfamily, moments they thought they wouldn't make it through, and this brings the book immediacy. Youngsters tell first-person stories, and this, too, brings immediacy. Topics include myths about the stepfamily proposition (happily ever after, ugly stepmother, and so on); dealing with change by being good to oneself (creating a private space); roles and possibilities for stepchildren and stepparents; making roles clear; and confusions, hurts, and complexities in stepfamilies. A section on stepsiblings offers good practical advice on how to stay balanced when a stepparent's kids come by and there is a threat of displacement.

   Her background as a stepparent gives Craven special insight into the particular problems of stepsiblings who are almost the same age. With openness, Craven discusses advantages and disadvantages of the stepfamily and doesn't shy away from the thorniest of issues: discipline and sexuality in a stepfamily. She seems to understand the pain youngsters can go through in watching a parent be lovey-dovey, for example. Craven never said living in a stepfamily was easy, but with her honesty about such issues as child abuse, incest, jealousy, and individuality, it may become less hard. Appendix of resources, index.

254. Gay, Kathlyn. *Changing Families: Meeting Today's Families.* Enslow, 1988. o.p. 128 pp. Nonfiction.

Interest level: Age 12+

In what could also be an accessible reference work for adults, the author lays out the scope and breadth of the issues surrounding today's family structures. She points out that a significant percentage of all American families (43.4%) are headed by single parents. The book handles issues of interracial families, older families, single-parent families, working families, and looks at such arrangements as religious communities and communes. A few chapters are of particular interest. One, "Split Families," deals with divorce; there are personal feelings expressed on divorce by those who have been affected by it, but the chapter ends on a hopeful note. Another chapter, "Families on the Edge," focuses on families whose economic situation has had a profound impact on their lives. There are statistics, but not so many as to burden the text. Foster families and adoptive families are also examined. Important assets of the book are its balanced tone and its positive look at what makes families strong.

255. Getzoff, Ann, and Carolyn McClenahan. *Step Kids: A Survival Guide for Teenagers in Stepfamilies . . . and for Stepparents Doubtful of Their Own Survival.* Walker, 1984, pap. (0-8027-7236-6). 182 pp. Nonfiction.

Interest level: Age 11+

Meant primarily as a book for children of divorce, one or both of whose parents have remarried, this book is a compendium of brief but very valuable, practical advice. Because of its breadth, depth may suffer a bit, but the breadth is nevertheless to be applauded for giving food for thought. For example, "When You Don't Like Your Stepbrother or Stepsister" is given but a page worth of attention, but its attendant section, "How to Cope," in only three fourths of a page manages to fit in four different ideas. Breezy? Maybe, but the subject is complex, and if but one good idea is gleaned, the book is worthwhile.

Topics covered include sending messages, how to talk about feelings, why parents divorce, accepting your own feelings (including not loving or loving your stepparent), and getting along with stepsiblings. Also covered is how stepparents feel—with careful attention to pet peeves suffered by both sexes (for example, borrowing clothing without asking, complaining about food, and irresponsibility). Hints are given on how to get along with specific kinds of stepmothers (Mrs. Smother, Mrs. Clean) and stepfathers (the Dictator, Mr. Hot Pants), adding a touch of humor to what could be a grim situation. As can be seen from the epithet, problems of sexuality are openly addressed, and readers are given examples of words to say to counter overtures. Special situations are also given attention, such as not seeing one parent, being forbidden to see one parent, mental illness, sexual assault, parents in a homosexual relationship (an especially sensitively handled, informative section). Worthwhile and to the point. Appendixes include information on how to hold a family council meeting, nine ways for stepparents and stepkids to become friends, when to seek professional help, a bibliography, and material on the Stepfamily Association of America.

256. Glassman, Bruce. *Everything You Need to Know about Stepfamilies.* Rosen, 1991 (0-8239-0815-1). 64 pp. Nonfiction.

Interest level: Ages 7–10

In simple and succinct language, the author defines terms relating to changing families and provides information about the causes and consequences of the changes, including death and divorce. He particularly focuses on how children can make their feelings known. He acknowledges such difficulties as stepparents' wanting to replace rather than supplement a child's absent parents, and the issue of surnames and whether they should be changed. The layout of the book is attractive, with both color and black-and-white photos, interesting boldfaced subtopics ("Name-Calling," "Feeling Guilty"), and sample diary entries. The author challenges readers to think about their feelings, including identifying their own expectations. There is a glossary of common terms and a readable index. The emphasis is not so much on dispensing advice as on reassuring children that their feelings are valid.

257. Henkes, Kevin. *Two Under Par.* Illus. by the author. Greenwillow, 1987 (0-688-06708-5). 116 pp. Fiction.

Interest level: Ages 8–11

Wedge's mother, Sally, has just remarried, and her new husband, King, who wears a crown instead of a hat, has opened a miniature golf course, complete with castle, just outside their home. Ten-year-old Wedge is embarrassed by his stepfather and confused over many events in his life, including why his father deserted him and his mother even before Wedge was born. He also does not like his five-year-old stepbrother, and he wonders why his mother married King.

Sally decides that it would be a good idea for her to go on a trip with Andrew, King's son, and for Wedge and King to be together so that they will get to know each other better. Everyone but Wedge is delighted at the idea. Sally returns home early because Wedge gets hysterical when he hears that his mother is pregnant with King's baby. King naively thought that Wedge would be pleased to hear this news.

Because King is such a loving and generous man, he eventually wins Wedge over, and Wedge's dream of one day having a real father comes true. The author paints portraits of real people grappling with real problems, and he does it well. Wedge's winning over is believable and satisfying.

258. Jukes, Mavis. *Like Jake and Me*. Illus. by Lloyd Bloom. Knopf, 1984 (0-394-85608-2); pap. (0-394-89263-1). 30 pp. Fiction.

Interest level: Ages 7–10

Alex is a young boy, approximately seven years old, living out West with his mother and stepfather, Jake. Jake is a cowboy—complete with Stetson hat, silver longhorn belt buckle, tattoo of an eagle on his chest, and boots with yellow roses and "Jake" stitched on the sides. Virginia, Alex's mother, is pregnant with twins. Alex's father is an important although unseen character; Alex still cares for his father and sees him regularly, and his father has enrolled him in a ballet class when he stays with him. Alex feels he does not have much in common with his stepfather, who seems fearless and "macho."

Alex begins a discussion with Jake about wolf spiders (his father is an entomologist), without specifically mentioning the wolf spiders. Jake mistakenly thinks the conversation is about Virginia, Alex's mother. Their talk goes on for quite a while, making sense until Alex informs Jake about the spider that is in Jake's coat. Jake goes berserk; he is terrified of spiders. At this point, Alex is able to help Jake. Through this humorous exchange, a real bond forms between the boy and his stepfather. The last scene shows them "dancing" on the porch. Virginia says she feels the twins dancing inside her, too. "Like Jake and me," says Alex.

The differences between the father and stepfather make Alex's dilemma interesting. Different life-styles are presented as to be equally valued. The "bonding" between stepfather and son is accomplished humorously yet convincingly.

259. Kaplan, Leslie S. *Coping with Stepfamilies*. Rosen, 1991, LB (0-8239-1371-6). 176 pp. Nonfiction.

Interest level: Age 11+

After defining what a stepfamily is, the author describes specific subcategories—those formed after the death of one parent differ in specific ways from those coming together following divorce. Attention is also paid to the differences that are likely to come about in children of varying ages, as well as the specific dynamics of how each gender might respond to a stepmother or a stepfather. The reader is encouraged to understand why parents might date or remarry and what the remarriage is likely to represent to the children. There is full discussion of the problems of lost dreams of reunion, social confusion, privacy, sexuality, getting along, being loyal or disloyal, and so on. Most helpful are the suggestions for making individual rules to fit individual families, not living by stereotypical expectations. Although the insights are good, the writing is somewhat disjointed, sometimes almost presented backward. An instance of this occurs in the discussion of the specific problem of restricted mourning before launching into a general discussion of the stepfamily formed after a death. Bibliography.

260. Lowry, Lois. *Switcharound.* Houghton, 1985 (0-395-39536-4); Dell, pap. (0-440-48415-4). 118 pp. Fiction.

Interest level: Ages 9–12

Eleven-year-old Caroline and her 13-year-old brother, J.P., have seen their father only twice in the past nine years. He has not seemed interested in them, and they have reciprocated his negative feelings. Because their parents' divorce settlement stipulates that their father can have the children for the summer, they have no choice but to go to him now that he has summoned them for the entire summer. He is living in Des Moines, has remarried, and has six-month-old twins and a six-year-old boy they call "Poochie."

It becomes clear at once to Caroline and J.P. that their father has invited them for the summer so that they can take care of the children. They agree to put aside their usual bickering and feuding in the face of their common enemy, and they begin to plot their revenge.

After a while, as they learn more about the family, Caroline and J.P. begin to change their opinions about their father and stepmother. Their father also changes his behavior and his misconceptions about them, once he gets to know them better. Through a series of misadventures and escapades, everything and everyone get straightened out, and the siblings enjoy their summer with their father and his family. Even their schemes of revenge turn out not to be as disastrous as they had feared.

The story is an amusing plea for people to listen to and sympathize with each other, no matter how difficult the task seems at first glance. It also makes readers think twice about assigning blame when they may not know all of the facts.

261. MacLachlan, Patricia. *Sarah, Plain and Tall.* Harper, 1985 (0-06-024101-2); pap. (0-06-440205-3). 58 pp. Fiction.

Interest level: Age 8+

This 1986 Newbery Medal winner can be read at many different levels by readers from 8 to 80. It deals with the feelings of two children whose mother has died; it alludes to the loneliness of life on the prairie; it palpably presents the feelings of displacement caused by leaving home.

Sarah is a mail-order bride. She becomes very important to Papa, Caleb, and Anna, who fear that she will never recover from her longing for the ocean of her native Maine. Sarah's recovery takes a while; she manages to bring some of the sea to the prairie by her colored-pencil drawings and by using the simile of the grain looking like the ocean. She will probably never totally lose her sadness over having to leave her home, but she has added a set of people and things that she loves here in her new home.

Anna, the oldest child, is capable and sensitive. She harbors a secret pain whenever she sees her brother, Caleb. After all, it was as a result of Caleb's birth that her mother died. But she loves Caleb, and she never lets him know that she blames him for their mother's death. All the characters convey a depth of emotion that readers resonate to.

The language, though simple, is passionate. For example, when Sarah returns from a shopping trip, much to Caleb's relief, "Caleb burst into tears. 'Seal [the cat] was very worried!' he cried. Sarah put her arms around him and he wailed into her dress. 'And the house is too small, we thought! And I am loud and pesky!'" The child's anguish over the thought that Sarah might leave the family is communicated in his outburst, and the reader and Sarah understand that he needs to be reassured.

The book is a small gem that will be treasured by all who are fortunate enough to read it.

262. Mark, Jan. *Trouble Half-way*. Illus. by David Parkins. Atheneum, 1985. o.p. 129 pp. Fiction.

Interest level: Ages 10–12

Amy is uncomfortable with her stepfather of six months. She doesn't know what to call him; he isn't like her father, who died fairly recently at a very young age; and his truck-driving job keeps him away much of the time. When she is forced to accompany him on one of his trips because her mother and baby sister had to go to help her grandparents, she learns a lot about him and herself, and she comes to admire, enjoy, and respect him. She even grows to think of him as her dad.

The story is set in England, and some of the words need defining in the glossary that is included. But the situation and the feelings of the characters are not bound by the setting. This is a respectful and unusual book in its exploration of the growth of the relationship between the girl and her stepfather.

263. Pevsner, Stella. *Sister of the Quints*. Clarion, 1987 (0-89919-498-2). 177 pp. Fiction.

Interest level: Age 10+

Natalie has chosen to live with her father and his new wife after her parents' divorce. Natalie's mother has moved to Colorado and is a teacher.

She is crushed when Natalie refuses to go with her. But Natalie likes living in her familiar house with her father and Jean, her new stepmother. She is pleased when Jean gives birth to quintuplets. But after a while, she begins to think that her father and Jean care nothing about her and are using her to help them with the quints. She revises her opinions when one of the quints is "borrowed" for a while by a disturbed young woman. She realizes then how much her mother must miss her and, in fact, how much she misses her mother.

Natalie's father is very upset that Natalie is now choosing to return to live with her mother, but Natalie is firm in her decision. She knows how important her mother is to her, and she will continue to visit her father and his new family, but her place is with her mother.

Natalie's quandary is one with which a number of young readers will identify. Her decisions are each reached according to a reasonable process, and the author is convincing in the unfolding of the story.

264. Rosenberg, Maxine B. *Talking about Stepfamilies.* Bradbury, 1990 (0-02-777913-0). 145 pp. Nonfiction.

   Interest level: Ages 9–12

The author interviewed many stepchildren (from age 8 to 41) in order to find out how they felt about being part of a stepfamily. She found, in general, that children of blended families view their families as different from the norm, even though this arrangement is so much more common now than it ever was before. The people interviewed also agreed that they were more flexible people because of the necessity of conforming to different sets of rules and adapting to a variety of personalities. Further, they began at an early age to think about marriage, relationships, and the importance of family.

265. Seuling, Barbara. *What Kind of Family Is This? A Book about Stepfamilies.* Illus. by Ellen Dolce. Western, 1985 (0-307-12482-7). 28 pp. Nonfiction.

   Interest level: Ages 4–8

This contribution to the Golden Learn about Living series asks readers to imagine themselves part of a new family—"with a new stepfather or stepmother, with a new stepbrother, or a new stepsister, or even a new stepbrother and a new stepsister, and maybe even a new pet or two—pets that didn't get along with your pet." Whew! But, then again, for Jeff, the fictional character who demonstrates the principles here, as well as for innumerable others, life is no less complicated.

The topics covered include appellations (Jeff resents it when his stepfather calls him "son"), new rooms, crowded conditions, and different household rules. Finally, Jeff erupts: "What kind of family is this? . . . I can't even go to the bathroom when I want to!" An argument with his stepbrother, Scott, results in a string across their shared bedroom, delineating territory. This and other familiar childhood tribulations are calmed a bit by his mother, who explains the only way she and Henry could live together with each other and with their children is if they all learned to be a family together.

In the end, an idea for playing brings Jeff and Scott to better terms. It was, as his mother said, taking time, but he was getting used to it. A realistic resolution, not all sweetness and light, and using common children's situations and dialogue.

266. Vigna, Judith. *Daddy's New Baby.* Illus. by the author. Whitman, 1982. o.p. 32 pp. Fiction.

Interest level: Ages 3–6

Many of the results of Daddy's having a new baby are negative ones for the young narrator of this story. She no longer has her own room at her daddy's house; her outings with her father are sometimes canceled because, for one reason or another, they have to stay home and watch the baby; and the baby seems to be ever-present, so that the little girl never gets to be alone with her daddy anymore. Further, her mother is anxious about the added expenses that the baby may cause, and she is fearful that her ex-husband won't have enough money for her and his first child. The little girl does, however, like to help take care of her baby sister, and she enjoys entertaining her. She also feels a kinship with this new child because they share the same daddy.

The issues brought up in this simple book are accurate and real. The story would be a good catalyst for discussion with children in the same situation.

Adoption

Authors should take care to avoid the use of the term *real* to describe birth or biological parents. Adoption should be seen as permanent, as contrasted to foster care, which is designed to be temporary. All characters should be portrayed as complex human beings with identities beyond their family roles.

267. Awiakta, Marylou. *Rising Fawn and the Fire Mystery.* Illus. by Beverly Bringle. Iris Pr., 1983, pap. (0-918518-29-6). 48 pp. Fiction.

Interest level: Age 10+

Rising Fawn's family has been killed by marauding whites, and she has been adopted by a well-meaning Christian white couple who are ignorant of her culture and background. Told through the perspective of Rising Fawn, a Choctaw child, customs and beliefs of native people and white people are compared and connected. Although the ending cannot be happy (all of Rising Fawn's family are dead), there is hope that Rising Fawn and her newfound parents will love, trust, and understand each other. This story is a dramatic one, especially because it is whites who killed Rising Fawn's birth family and now it is whites who adopt the native child. The Cherokee author is a fine poet.

268. Banish, Roslyn, and Jennifer Jordan-Wong. *A Forever Family.* Photos by Roslyn Banish. Harper, 1992 (0-06-021673-5); pap. (0-06-446116-5). 44 pp. Nonfiction.

   Interest level: Ages 5–8

Eight-year-old Jennifer leads the reader through photos that are landmarks of her life. Through the vehicle of the album, Jennifer talks about herself and the events leading up to her adoption and her new "forever family." Jennifer's new family is large, extended, biracial, and loving. Jennifer's experiences in foster homes, and now in her permanent home, have been positive. The reader gets a sense of Jennifer's good fortune as well as her questions about her birth parents and the circumstances of their relinquishing her for foster care and ultimately permanent adoption.

269. Caines, Jeannette. *Abby.* Illus. by Steven Kellogg. Harper, 1973, LB (0-06-020922-4); pap. (0-06-443049-9). 32 pp. Picture book.

   Interest level: Ages 5–8

Abby is an adopted child loved by her parents and her older brother, Kevin, although he upsets her sometimes with his teasing about her being a girl and his only liking boys. Abby goes through a regular ritual with her mother about where she came from (Manhattan), how old she was when her mom and dad got her (11 months and 13 days), and what she was wearing (the clothes her doll is wearing now.) Her brother really loves her and is proud of her. He even wants to take her to school for show-and-tell, to tell that she is adopted and that he gave her a fire engine as a gift. Adoption is depicted as a loving, warm event. The illustrations of this African-American family add to the impact of the book.

270. Cohen, Shari. *Coping with Being Adopted.* Rosen, 1988 (0-8239-0770-8). 136 pp. Nonfiction.

   Interest level: Ages 11–15

Cohen discusses the common feelings about being adopted ("Why did she give me away?" for example), but goes a step further in offering ways to cope with offhand remarks that may unintentionally hurt, with the longing to know the biological parents, with the extra frustrations adopted children might have.

Young people are interviewed, and through them the reader learns the fantasies adopted children may have. ("*They* would let me go on the trip.") To counter fears and anger, she recommends removing the expression "because I'm adopted" from the inner and exterior vocabulary and searching for other explanations in events instead. Practical suggestions for handling anger and talking out feelings are offered. She also recommends using nonjudgmental responses to upsetting remarks, setting the situation straight, not ignoring what has been said.

There are brief sections on transracial and disabled adoptees, reflecting some of the prejudices that they may encounter and how to handle them. In handling actions by family members who favor the birth children in a family (say, grandparents who give better gifts to them), Cohen is less strong, advising children to view the problem as that of the relative and ignore it. One would think the adoptive parent could play a role here. The sense of humor Cohen recommends may not be enough.

Cohen recommends finding out who you are before searching for biological parents and gives exercises to start the process going. The conflicts teens have with their parents are examined in light of adoption, and means of communicating better without running away are listed. As for the search that may ultimately be undertaken, studies show that if the subject is treated positively and honestly, the adoptee can be more at peace. Cohen gives examples of both positive and negative characteristics. Finally, there are informative chapters on parents' views (particularly on letting go) and how the mechanics of the adoption system works in this country. Although sometimes too brief on the depth and complexity of issues (such as accidental revelation of adoption and secret keeping), this book is somewhat unique in the literature, and thereby its many strengths will offer help to those who need it. Bibliography, index.

271. Freudberg, Judy, and Tony Geiss. *Susan and Gordon Adopt a Baby.* Illus. by Joe Mathieu. Random, 1986 (0-394-88341-1). 20 pp. Fiction.
    Interest level: Ages 3–7

This story tells how Susan and Gordon become the parents of Miles by adopting him. The book emphasizes that now they will be Miles's parents forever, and that when someone new enters the family the love just grows and grows—so there is plenty of love to go around.

272. Gay, Kathlyn. *Adoption and Foster Care.* Enslow, 1990, LB (0-89490-239-3). 128 pp. Nonfiction.

   Interest level: Age 11+

The author uses interviews and anecdotes to convey the situations of adoptive families and children. The book describes several placement procedures and airs the many debates engendered by this emotional process. Children whose race is different from their potential parents, some with special needs, children who are born overseas, and foster parents who wish to adopt are all discussed. Included are statements from both sides of many issues, case studies, and lists of helpful organizations. The book is a balanced one; the author's tone is reasoned and empathic.

273. Girard, Linda Walvoord. *Adoption Is for Always.* Illus. by Judith Freeman. Whitman, 1986 (0-8075-0185-9); pap. (0-8075-0187-5). 32 pp. Fiction.

   Interest level: Ages 4–8

When Celia finally hears the words her parents have been telling her since she was a little girl, that she is adopted, she reacts with anger. She goes through various stages: grief, anger, pain, loneliness, fear, curiosity about her birth parents, resentment, longing, self-doubt, and, finally, acceptance. Her parents and the other adults around her give her support, firm but loving responses, and understanding. They also reassure her that they will always be her parents and that she belongs with them.

   One of the things the parents do is get a book from the library on adoption. Celia rejects the book at first, but she soon uses it to comfort and inform herself. Her parents also do not make the mistake of coddling her; they understand her anger, but they do not permit her to break the rules that they have consistently set forth. She must still pick up her things and behave constructively. They remind her of how they felt when they first adopted her. They assure her that it was through no fault of her own that her birth parents gave her up for adoption. And an adult friend indicates that her birth mother must have loved her very much to let her go to a family that would love and care for her better than her birth mother could.

   Some critics might argue that this is a somewhat didactic and simplistic book, but coupled with books presenting other perspectives, this book can probably be very useful not only for children who are adopted but also for children who want to understand how adoption works.

274. Girard, Linda Walvoord. *We Adopted You, Benjamin Koo.* Illus. by Linda Shute. Whitman, 1989 (0-8075-8694-3); pap. (0-8075-8695-1). 32 pp. Picture book.

Interest level: Ages 6–10

In accurate, respectful language (including *birth mother* and *first mother*) nine-year-old Benjamin Koo Andrews narrates the story. His mother had deposited him at the door of the orphanage in Korea when he was an infant. Benjamin wonders about her, but is comforted by the knowledge that she left him in a place where he would be cared for. The long process of adoption is described, as is the fact that Benjamin became a U.S. citizen when he was four months old. His large extended family welcomes him heartily, and his parents tell him early on about his adoption. Benjamin is open about his feelings of anger at his separation from his birth parents and about his resentment at the physical differences between him and his adoptive parents. He is aided by a counselor who helps him appreciate his situation and his parents. Benjamin is involved in the decision to adopt another child, and his sister Susan is then adopted from Brazil. The parents are careful to include cultural celebrations from each child's birth country. The narrative deals honestly with the issues of intercultural adoption, especially outsiders' manifestations of bigotry. It also discusses the joys and concerns of ordinary adoption.

275. Greenberg, Judith E., and Helen H. Carey. *Adopted.* Photos by Barbara Kirk. Watts, 1987. o.p. 32 pp. Nonfiction.

Interest level: Ages 5–9

Sarah and Ryan are adopted siblings, both adopted beyond the newborn stage. A friend asks Sarah if adopted babies can be taken back if they cry too much. "Nobody can send Ryan back . . . We adopted him and he's part of our family now." Sarah's mother overhears this and works to help her daughter, explaining, "Sometimes a healthy baby can't grow in a mother's uterus . . ." She continues that both children were born in the hospital, but she didn't see them until the adoption agency brought them together. Later, when Sarah asks who her real mother is, she tells Sarah, "I am . . . I didn't help you to be born, but I am your mother because I take care of you and love you." She also tells of the goodness of her birth mother, who perhaps was alone or too young to care for her but let her be adopted so she "could have all the things she needed to grow up happy and healthy."

In a side note, it is mentioned that Sarah has two friends who are adopted also, one of whom is Vietnamese and came here at age six. The picture of Sarah's extended family is warm and her grandfather advises, "Being adopted doesn't make you different or special. You are special because you are Sarah." He then tells what makes her special, and too much of it seems to hinge on kindness and sharing. But the photographs in this section are especially strong, allowing the extra sweetness to glide by.

276. Holland, Isabelle. *The Journey Home.* Scholastic, 1990 (0-590-43110-2). 212 pp. Fiction.

Interest level: Ages 9–14

Irish immigrants Maggie and Annie cannot stay with their fatally ill mother, so she arranges for them to join a group of orphans who are traveling out west in hopes of finding a family. Both girls want to stay with their mother until the end; Maggie prays fervently to the Virgin Mary for help. Maggie is firm in her belief that she and her sister must remain together.

After almost being adopted at one stop, but refusing to be separated from one another, both girls are taken in by a prairie couple whom they call Aunt Priscilla and Uncle James. Annie seems to fit right in, but Maggie is unhappy; she feels distressed at having to abandon her Catholic faith. She worries that she won't measure up to the family's expectations. She is reluctant to embrace farm life. When Aunt Priscilla's mother, a difficult woman, comes to stay, she and Maggie clash but gradually begin an important friendship. Through this relationship, Maggie begins to accept her situation and feel part of her new home. Although Maggie's constant prayers to the Virgin Mary may seem obsessive, they are reflective of the coping strategies used by many Catholic immigrants of the time.

277. Koehler, Phoebe. *The Day We Met You.* Illus. by the author. Bradbury, 1990 (0-02-750901-X). 48 pp. Picture book.

Interest level: Ages 4–7

Every child likes to hear the story of his/her birth; adopted children love to hear the story of the day they were adopted. This loving book is a warm, gentle retelling of the story of one child. The specifics in this book are wonderful. When the parents receive a call telling them they can pick the baby up, they immediately get ready for the long-awaited moment. They borrow a car seat. They buy tiny socks and an elephant mobile. The new grandfather gets a teddy bear. There are wind chimes in the window. The reader can almost feel the anticipation of the new parents as they go to meet their baby. The poetic phrases are almost like a lullaby and are complemented by the pastel illustrations. An Afterword gives suggestions about talking over adoption with young children.

278. Krementz, Jill. *How It Feels to Be Adopted.* Photos by the author. Knopf, 1991, pap. (0-394-75853-6). 110 pp. Nonfiction.
    Interest level: Age 10+

Nineteen children, ages 8 to 16, tell in their own words how they feel about being adopted. One child reports finding her birth mother and responding to a friend's query, "When you're adopted by people, these people are your real parents. Finding your birth mother is just filling up a gap that makes you feel you belong." Another child whose birth mother found her says, "In my view I have only one mother and that's the mother who raised me and mothered me—who gave me food and shelter and love while I was growing up." A number of the children are from different heritages than their adoptive parents. They discuss the situation openly, acknowledging some problems, but focusing on the universality of love and family. The author's photographs underline the book's authenticity. The author's intent is to affirm and acknowledge each adoptee's response. Both concerns and benefits are discussed, and although each person tells a different story, the net effect is one of self-acceptance and security in the midst of a loving family.

279. Lindsay, Jeanne Warren. *Open Adoption: A Caring Option.* Morning Glory, 1987 (0-930934-22-9); pap. (0-930934-23-7). 256 pp. Nonfiction.
    Interest level: Age 14+

Equally useful to pregnant teenagers and their parents, this book explores current outlooks in adoption. The author is a teacher in a Teen Mother program for pregnant teens who don't wish to remain in the regular classroom during their pregnancy. Through use of vignettes of various cases, the author presents changing drama in families, the law, and society. The chapters look at closed adoption, open adoption, the respective rights of birth parents and adoptive parents, the role of the church, and how an agency can move from closed to open adoption. Specific agencies are profiled to give readers an idea of the counseling and services they might expect and results that can come from the new honesty. A special chapter looks at teen pregnancy. In its attentive look at such complex issues as confidentiality, reactions of birth grandparents, and grief, the author provides details of a new avenue teenagers might not have considered. A rich examination throughout. Annotated bibliography.

280. Mills, Claudia. *Boardwalk with Hotel*. Bantam, 1986, pap. (0-553-15397-8). 131 pp. Fiction.

Interest level: Ages 9–12

After a baby-sitter inadvertently discloses to 11-year-old Jessica that her parents thought they couldn't have children, which was why they adopted her, Jessica thinks that perhaps she is second-best to her siblings, who are her parents' children by birth. From that moment on, Jessica questions and mistrusts everything her parents do or say. She is convinced that they love her sister and brother more than they love her. She becomes sullen, argumentative, and nasty.

As the story progresses, Jessica comes to learn more and more about herself. When she is a sore loser at Monopoly, she seeks solace from her best friend, who tells her affectionately that she is, indeed, regularly a sore loser. When she finally tells her father what has been bothering her, he is not effusive in his reassurance, but he is clear about his love for her.

Finally, when Jessica realizes that she loves her brother, even though she resents and dislikes him at times, she comes to terms with her feelings of rejection and understands how her parents feel. The author honestly and humorously presents a family's way of dealing with children, both natural and adopted, and makes it clear that it is not the fact of adoption, but the actions and character of the child, that determine the parents' reactions.

281. Paterson, Katherine. *Come Sing, Jimmy Jo*. Dutton, 1985 (0-525-67167-6); Avon, pap. (0-380-70052-2). 178 pp. Fiction.

Interest level: Age 11+

James's family has been a singing group for many years, but James only sings for the family. He has terrible stage fright. When James is 11 years old, an agent discovers his wonderful voice, and he is drawn into the singing profession despite his fears. He acknowledges that he has a gift when the fans go wild about him.

James feels closest to his grandmother and father. His mother is a flighty young woman who James later discovers is having an affair with his uncle, his father's brother, also a member of the singing group. One day, a stranger tells James that he is really James's father, which turns out to be true, and James is dismayed to find that the two people he loves most in the world are not his blood relatives.

It takes some thought and some help, but James finally comes to realize that his grandparents and "adopted" father are his real relatives, and his biological father is no more than an accident of biology. He reconciles with his family and even begins to understand his mother's needs, as he joins the family publicly in singing, "Will the Circle Be Unbroken?"

Katherine Paterson is masterful with language and characterization. She demonstrates again the ability to take a particular set of characters in their own special circumstances and transform them into universal representatives, while taking care that they retain their individuality and vitality. The issue of raising a child who is not your biological offspring is powerfully conveyed, as is the practice of understanding and forgiving people their weaknesses.

282. Pelligrini, Nina. *Families Are Different*. Illus. by the author. Holiday, 1991, LB (0-8234-0887-6). 32 pp. Picture book.

Interest level: Ages 4–7

Nico, the young child who narrates the story, at first is uncomfortable with the obvious physical differences between her and her parents, but she comes to realize that everyone she knows is different in some way. Therefore, she fits in because she and her sister are different from their mom and dad. Nico and her sister are of Korean heritage. Their adoptive parents are Caucasians. The intent of the story is to communicate that differences are fine if the family is loving. The language and illustrations are very simple, and the story works well.

283. Pursell, Margaret Sanford. *A Look at Adoption*. Illus. by Maria S. Forrai. Lerner, 1978. o.p. 36 pp. Nonfiction.

Interest level: Ages 7–10

Down-to-earth truthfulness characterizes this explanation of adoption. Yes, parents do give up children because they aren't ready to be parents. Yes, disabled, older, and multiracial children are in need of homes. And yes, if you want to adopt a healthy infant, there is often a long waiting list. Many actual families posed for the photos in this book. The stance is taken that adopted children should be told that they are adopted and should be helped to understand that their adoptive parents are their "real" parents. It is, perhaps, a reflection of the book's publication date that it does not at all mention open records or the adoptive children's curiosity about their birth parents.

284. Rosenberg, Maxine B. *Being Adopted*. Photos by George Ancona. Lothrop, 1984 (0-688-02672-9). 48 pp. Nonfiction.

Interest level: Ages 7–10

Three children are introduced who have been adopted into three different American families: Rebecca, a 7-year-old Cheyenne girl; Andrei, a 10-year-old boy from India; and 8-year-old Karin, a Korean child adopted by the author into a family where there are already three biological sons.

Through sensitive text and wonderful black-and-white photographs, the book brings out many issues pertaining to adoption that are not unique to these youngsters.

The fear of a new environment and family structure, the period of initial adjustment, the inevitable questions about birth mothers and the reason children were given up, and feelings of rejection and low self-worth are all functions of any adoption. The book also discusses the additional problems that pertain to multicultural adoptions: the issue of looking different from their adoptive parents and siblings; daydreams about life in their culture of origin; and the desire to look and be like the dominant culture. Rosenberg tempers the difficulties encountered by these children with the constant reassurance that it is the love and cooperation among family members that binds them rather than physical appearance or place of birth.

The author's perspective is clear, particularly because she is one of the adoptive parents. But she does not minimize the challenges that face both the families and the children in these augmented families.

285. Rosenberg, Maxine B. *Growing Up Adopted*. Bradbury, 1989 (0-02-777912-2). 128 pp. Nonfiction.

Interest level: Age 10+

This is a well-documented account of how adopted children view their situations. Details include how the adopted person learned his or her story and felt about the adoption. Each of the interviews includes many details of the adoption plus the feelings and perspectives of all concerned parties. The interviewees are of various ages and have different perspectives. Amy, age 12, wonders about her birth parents but doesn't want to meet them face to face. Ten-year-old Mark is more upset about being the only boy in his family than about being Korean in a family of Caucasians. Adults who are still dealing with their own adoptions seemed to have more feelings of anger or discomfort; presumably, the secrecy surrounding adoption in years past contributed to these feelings. The experiences of the subjects interviewed were largely positive; the author stresses that adoption is just one facet of a full life.

286. Sobol, Harriet Langsam. *We Don't Look Like Our Mom and Dad*. Photos by Patricia Agre. Coward, 1984. o.p. 32 pp. Nonfiction.

Interest level: Ages 5–9

Eric (age 10) and Joshua Levin (age 11) are brothers by adoption; they have different biological mothers; and both are Korean by birth. They were adopted as babies. Their Caucasian parents keep their Korean heritage alive by cooking Korean food, by reading books about Korea and

Korean culture, and by saving the clothing in which they arrived. Both boys still have Korean middle names. Like children everywhere, they enjoy hearing their baby stories—in this case, about their arrival at the airport to join the Levins.

The Levins sought out Korean children because of the recognized need of children in Korea for parents. They were aided by an agency. Eric and Joshua do feel slightly different from the other children in their community, but they spend little time thinking about their origins. They're too busy with school and playing with friends. When in anger Eric says, "You're not my brother," their mother answers, "In this family, you're brothers."

Like many adopted children, Eric wonders why his mother gave him up for adoption. He is bothered that he didn't grow inside his American mother. For some of the boy's questions, there are no known answers. His adoptive mother can only speculate that his biological mother cared about him and realized that she could not properly care for him. She assures him that his mother must have felt sad for a long time after she gave him up for adoption. Also discussed are the negative and inquisitive looks this family gets when they are shopping. This book honestly addresses both the joys and the problems that arise.

This seems to be a model book, addressing honestly both the joys and problems that arise. The Levins are not a typical family. No one in the family is biologically related to any of the others. Nevertheless they are a family because they choose to be one.

Foster Care

To provide a balanced and accurate picture, the collection of books should contain a variety of foster care situations. Not all of the books need include abusive experiences. Foster parents as well as children should appear in all shapes, sizes, and personalities, and their backgrounds should vary. The resolution of permanent adoption should be used sparingly so as not to convey a false picture to readers.

287. Bunting, Eve. *If I Asked You, Would You Stay?* Harper, 1987, LB (0-397-32066-3); pap. (0-06-447023-7). 151 pp. Fiction.

Interest level: Age 12+

Crow has been rejected by his mother and has been in a series of foster homes. He has run away from the last one, not because they were unloving to him, but because he was afraid of yet another rejection, so he left before that would happen. He finds a secret place to stay, behind a carousel. Into his hiding place, he brings Valentine, whose life he has saved. Valentine, too, has been rejected. She has also been abused by her mother's new husband and by the man to whom she ran in order to escape from her stepfather.

Crow and Valentine fall in love with each other and, in the process, learn to become more self-preserving. They leave, each of them for a different safe place, but this time they are going *to* a better life, not running away from anything. It is a measure of Crow's evolution that he is able to return to the foster home where he was loved and to trust that he will continue to be loved.

Foster care is, in general, a difficult situation for both the foster child and the foster parent. It is difficult to feel secure when the placement is, by definition, a temporary one. Both the characters in this story have been betrayed by their mothers and by their subsequent caretakers. It is important for them each to develop a feeling of self-worth before they can accept and give love again. The book helps readers to understand this fact.

288. Myers, Walter Dean. *Me, Mop and the Moondance Kid.* Illus. by Rodney Pate. Delacorte, 1988 (0-440-50065-6); Dell, pap. (0-440-40396-0). 154 pp. Fiction.

Interest level: Ages 9–12

The story is about a group of boys and girls, some of whom live in a Catholic institution for orphans. The children, of different races, are all friends and play on the same Little League team. Two brothers, Moondance and T.J., yearn to be adopted, and it finally happens. Even after they are placed with a permanent family, they remain close friends with the children on the team. The happy ending is satisfying and not beyond believability.

289. Nixon, Joan Lowery. *Caught in the Act.* Bantam, 1988 (0-553-05443-0); pap. (0-553-27912-2). 150 pp. Fiction.

Interest level: Age 11+

Mike Kelly has been adopted by the Friedrichs, a family of German immigrants. Mr. Friedrich is hard and punitive and beats Mike. Gunter, the Friedrichs' son, resents Mike and does all sorts of dreadful things to get Mike into trouble. After a series of mishaps and misunderstandings, Mike succeeds in getting himself extricated from the Friedrichs' farm and going to live at Fort Leavenworth, Kansas, with a family he admires greatly.

This second novel in the Orphan Train Quartet continues the story begun in *A Family Apart* (see entry below). Mike is the boy who stole in order to feed the family, and, by coincidence, there is a tragedy in the Friedrich family involving a son who also stole to feed them. The flavor of the era is conveyed well, as is the setting of the Midwest in the mid-nineteenth century. The story is well told, and the dilemma of the foster family is as dramatically presented as is Mike's situation. The issue of poverty and the heartbreak of deciding to send children away to what is hoped will be a better life for them are poignantly portrayed in this series.

290. Nixon, Joan Lowery. *A Family Apart.* Bantam, 1987 (0-553-05432-5); pap. (0-553-27478-3). 162 pp. Fiction.

Interest level: Age 11+

The six Kelly children, ranging in age from 6 to 13, are sent west, in 1860, on a train filled with orphans to be adopted by families, some of whom want cheap labor and some of whom genuinely want children to love. Although the children are aware of the impoverished state their widowed mother is in, they feel that she has abandoned them. They feel even worse when they discover that they are to be separated from each other.

This book is the first in a series of four books that chronicles the adventures of the Kelly children. The story begins with modern-day Jeff and Jennifer, who are visiting their grandmother's house and are bored. Their grandmother entertains them by telling them the story of her great-grandmother, Mary Frances Kelly, the oldest of the six Kelly children.

As the six children are assembled before embarking on the train that will take them to new homes in the West, Mary Frances overhears the adults talking about the fact that families want to adopt no more than two children at a time, and that boys are much more desirable as adoptees than girls. Mary Frances decides to masquerade as a boy so that she and her youngest brother can be together. The Children's Aid Society is managing the adoptions as humanely as it can. Eventually, all six children are adopted, and Mary Frances's ruse works: She and Petey are adopted together by an attractive couple from New England who have come west partly to farm and partly to fight slavery. They are a part of the Underground Railroad.

All through the book, Mary Frances fixes on the word *sacrifice.* Her mother uses it, and many other adults use the word. She finally comes to understand the meaning of the term and to forgive her mother for sending the children away. At the end of the book, she has proven her stamina, has forgiven her mother, and has regained her true identity. The reader has hopes for her and for young Petey. The book ends with the promise of another story about one of the other Kelly children.

291. Radley, Gail. *The Golden Days.* Macmillan, 1991 (0-02-775652-1); Puffin, pap. (0-14-036002-6). 160 pp. Fiction.

Interest level: Ages 9–12

Corey is a foster child who has been placed in a succession of homes. In his present home, Corey fears that because the foster couple is expecting a baby they will send him back to the orphanage. He has become close to Carlotta, an elderly woman who hates being confined to a nursing home. The two run away together and struggle to survive. They manage for a while, but Corey and Carlotta both realize that they cannot manage on their own. The happy ending is satisfying because it is plausible and because the characters have endeared themselves to the reader. Corey and Carlotta both learn what it means to be part of a family.

292. Ruby, Lois. *This Old Man.* Houghton, 1984 (0-395-36563-5). 192 pp. Fiction.

Interest level: Age 12+

Greta has been placed in a group home for young women whose domestic situations are intolerable. Greta's mother is a prostitute who is in love with her pimp. Thankfully, she has the good sense to remove Greta from their home when her pimp decides that it is Greta's turn to enter his "stable." She befriends most of the young women in the home and becomes friendly with a 15-year-old Chinese-American boy. She accompanies him daily when he takes dinner to his aged grandfather in the hospital. Greta's therapist helps her to see that she views the old man in many complicated ways, including imbuing him with power that she would like to attain. The old man is revered by his family, and although they are poor, he is well cared for. No character in this well-crafted book is stereotypical. Readers are invited to draw conclusions and make judgments about the major characters. Even the pimp is treated even-handedly. The only thoroughly irredeemable character is a young thug from China who exhibits no concern for his family or his heritage.

293. Thesman, Jean. *When the Road Ends.* Illus. by Robert Wisnewski. Houghton, 1992 (0-395-59507-X). 184 pp. Fiction.

Interest level: Age 10+

Mary Jack, the narrator, is 12 years old, strong and competent beyond her years. She takes care of another foster child, Jane, who has been horribly abused. Mary Jack helps maintain the delicate balance of stability at the home of their foster parents. The three foster children (the third child is Adam, a 14-year-old boy who is angry and often on the edge of violence) endure the sullen, neurotic Mrs. Percy and the well-meaning but weak Father Matt Percy (an Episcopal priest.) The story never crosses the line into sentimentality, although the situation is sometimes heartrending. The plight of foster children and the blundering of well-intentioned but ineffectual adults are underlying threads in the well-paced and well-drawn plot. Although the ending is a happy one, it is not far-fetched. The author does a fine job laying the foundation for resolution of the characters' problems.

Absent Parent(s)

There may be many reasons for one or both parents to be absent from the home. Sometimes the absence is of short duration, sometimes it is extended. The absence may be of no serious consequence, such as a brief trip, or it may be as grave a circumstance as a parent in prison. Parents may be on military duty, away at school, or fulfilling an ambition. The resulting situation is that, at least for a time, the child has a single parent or other family caretakers. For many youngsters there has always been only one parent. The unique support of a mother or father is missing, causing the child to wonder or fantasize about the unknown or absent parent.

Some books portray the absent parent as one who wishes to maintain contact with the child. In some cases, the father may never have acknowledged the child or may be unknown. Even when a parent is absent, the remaining family should be seen as a unit rather than incomplete or "fractured." The relationships of the people maintaining the family should be respected.

294. Bailey, Marilyn. *The Facts about Single-Parent Families.* Crestwood, 1989 (0-89686-437-5). 48 pp. Nonfiction.

    Interest level: Ages 8–10

Comforting, realistic information about the circumstances, problems, and "bright side" of living in a single-parent household. Although most of the book refers to divorce, other causes for single-parent families are also discussed. The photographs make clear that this arrangement is not restricted to any particular ethnic group.

295. Butterworth, Oliver. *A Visit to the Big House.* Illus. by Susan Avishai. Houghton, 1993 (0-395-52805-4). 48 pp. Fiction.

    Interest level: Ages 7–10

Willy and his sister, Rose, are apprehensive about visiting their father in prison for the first time. They are uneasy about how he might look, what the building will look like, and what to say when they see him. Their mother is honest but reassuring; she tells the children that their father took something that did not belong to him and is making up for the deed. She hopes that he will learn something while he is incarcerated. On the ride to the prison, Willy nervously asks about the conditions there, recalling what he has heard about dungeons. Once at the gate, the guard is pleasant to the family as they bravely enter the "Big House." Their father initially seems ill at ease; the illustrations do not show him embracing his family. After some time spent talking, the family relaxes and begins to rebuild the strained relationship. The visit ends happily, with more visits promised for the future. Although at times the dialogue is stilted, this book could be a useful tool for explaining what happens when someone goes to prison. It also acknowledges the ambivalent feelings that would be quite natural under the circumstances.

296. Emerson, Kathy Lynn. *Julia's Mending.* Avon, 1990, pap. (0-380-70734-9). 160 pp. Fiction.

   Interest level: Age 10+

When Julia's parents go to China to be missionaries, they send her to her cousins' house in upstate New York. Julia would have preferred to have stayed with her grandmother in New York City, but her parents want her to be with people who hold the same religious beliefs they do. Julia immediately hates her new surroundings and dislikes her cousins. They feel the same negative way about her. On her second day there, she falls and breaks her leg. Julia begins keeping a journal with the intention of sending it to her parents so that they will see how she is suffering and either send for her or permit her to go to her grandmother's.

   Life in a rural community in the nineteenth century is not easy, and Julia misses the coddling and luxury of her New York grandmother's home. During and after her convalescence, Julia engages in some energetic self-reflection and decides to change her attitude and behavior. She makes friends with her cousins, helps to solve a mystery, and looks forward to a much happier stay.

   Emerson has written the story from materials and memories from her own family. The situation and characters have the ring of truth. The characters are all three-dimensional and interesting. Julia's predicament and separation from her family will probably strike chords in a number of readers who have had to endure a prolonged separation from their parents.

297. Gifaldi, David. *One Thing for Sure.* Clarion, 1986 (0-89919-462-1). 172 pp. Fiction.

   Interest level: Age 10+

Dylan is a 12-year-old whose father is in prison. He faces the usual stigma attached to families of convicted people. His former "friends" torment him. Fortunately, he meets Amy, who is spending some time with her grandparents while her mother and stepfather are vacationing in Europe. Amy and Dylan become good friends, and together they overcome the nastiness of Dylan's tormentors.

Dylan is not only confronted with external abuse but also worried that perhaps he has inherited his father's bad traits—that he has "bad blood." He resents his father so much that he refuses to visit him in prison. His mother is understanding and clear about her feelings. She does not press Dylan to visit his father, but she does insist that he respond appropriately and not with violence when he is teased about his father.

It is somewhat difficult to understand why Dylan was ever friends with the bullies. It seems as if they were never worthy of his attention. Amy is almost too good to be true, but her character is an engaging one. The author successfully portrays the pain of separation and the ensuing bitterness and misunderstanding surrounding the families of convicted prisoners.

298. Gilbert, Sara. *How to Live with a Single Parent.* Lothrop, 1982, LB (0-688-00633-7). 128 pp. Nonfiction.

   Interest level: Ages 9–12

The product of a single-parent family herself, Gilbert bases her book on her own experiences, the results of a questionnaire and interviews, and the opinions of experts. The book is peppered with lots of quotations, advocacy of exploration, and expression of feelings. One of the especially valuable aspects of this book is its inclusion of a wide variety of real situations and real people. Acknowledging that single parenthood is not only the result of divorce, the author presents many anecdotes that reinforce feelings and assure readers that they are not alone. Gilbert speaks directly to the young people who are experiencing a single-parent family. Her advice is sensible and sympathetic, and children's worries—real and unreal—are given credence.

299. Hickman, Martha Whitmore. *When Andy's Father Went to Prison.* Illus. by Larry Raymond. Whitman, 1990, LB (0-8075-8874-1). 40 pp. Fiction.

   Interest level: Ages 8–10

Andy and his mother have relocated in order to be closer to his father, who is in prison. Andy deals with his conflicting emotions of family loyalty and fear that his classmates will ostracize him if they find out about his father. He encounters an understanding teacher and good friends. He also learns that other people have problems, too, for his best friend's father is dying of cancer. Andy feels good about himself despite his family's problems. When the story ends, his father is about to be paroled. The book allows children a look into a prison, showing the family sharing a picnic on visitors' day. This story could be useful for children in Andy's situation or who know someone in his situation. It's unfortunate that Andy's

younger sister is hardly mentioned. It would have been nice to have had
her point of view included as well.

300. Hort, Lenny. *How Many Stars in the Sky?* Illus. by James E.
   Ransome. Tambourine, 1991 (0-688-10103-8). Unpaged. Picture
   book.
   Interest level: Ages 5–8

The mother is away, and the young boy and his father can't sleep. They
start counting the stars in the sky and continue by taking a ride through the
city where mother's office is and then out to the country, where they fall
asleep under the stars. They both look forward to the mother's return and
to telling her about their adventure. It is clear that this African-American
family is a loving and happy one. The universal feelings of missing the
absent parent and looking forward to her return are warmly communicated.

301. Isadora, Rachel. *At the Crossroads.* Greenwillow, 1991 (0-688-
   05270-3). 32 pp. Picture book.
   Interest level: Ages 5–8

The setting is South Africa. A group of children eagerly await their
fathers' return from work in the mines, some entertaining themselves by
forming a band and playing music. Their fathers have been gone for ten
months, and some of the children have the stamina to wait all through the
night for their return. Although apartheid and the severe poverty the families endure are not specifically mentioned, the illustrations show the clusters of corrugated tin shacks that form their community. The reunion is,
predictably, a joyful one.

302. Lash, Michelle, Sally Ives Loughridge, and David Fassler. *My Kind
   of Family: A Book for Kids in Single-Parent Homes.* Waterfront,
   1990 (0-914525-13-1). 208 pp. Nonfiction.
   Interest level: Ages 6–11

An excellent workbook for children living with a single parent, no matter
what the reason. The problems, special circumstances, hopes, feelings, and
wishes of children in these families are presented here in a format that
invites children to contribute their own responses and ideas. A good guide
for adults to follow in communicating with children.

303. Levinson, Nancy Smiler. *Snowshoe Thompson.* Illus. by Joan Sandin.
   Harper, 1992 (0-06-023801-1). 64 pp. Easy-reader picture book.
   Interest level: Ages 5–8

Danny's father has gone away to dig for gold. Danny desperately wants him to come home for Christmas and writes him a letter to tell him that. Unfortunately, there's no chance that his letter will reach his father because the snows have come and isolated their community from the rest of the world. Snowshoe Thompson constructs skis (the first seen in this part of the country), delivers Danny's letter, and brings an answer back to the lonely boy. This easy-to-read story is based on a real person, John Thompson, a Norwegian immigrant who delivered mail on skis through the harsh Sierra Nevada winters.

304. Lewin, Hugh. *Jafta's Father.* Illus. by Lisa Kopper. Lerner, 1989, pap. (0-87614-496-2). 24 pp. Fiction.

Interest level: Ages 4–8

Jafta's father works in the city and must be away most of the time. Through the illustrations and the narrative, it is clear that Jafta's father loves him very much and that his mother trusts his father. Jafta remembers every detail of the activities he and his father engage in when his father is home. These memories sustain him during the time that his father is away. Nevertheless, although he knows his father will return, there is always an edge of anxiety until Jafta sees his beloved father again.

This beautifully illustrated book tells, in simple but evocative language, of the feelings of a young child about his father's enforced absence. The flavor of the community and family come through in this story set in South Africa. Although the setting and some of the details are of a land far away, the interaction and emotions are universal.

305. Lichtman, Wendy. *Telling Secrets.* Harper, 1986. o.p. 243 pp. Fiction.

Interest level: Age 13+

Toby's father is in jail for embezzlement, and Toby's mother has sworn her to secrecy about it. Her mother even forbids Toby to tell Sharon, her college roommate and best friend. During the course of the four months that her father is in jail, Toby explores her feelings about herself, her family, and the world. She is desperate to talk about her father, and one night she tells the secret to a young man with whom she engages in sexual intercourse for the first time in her life.

Eventually, Toby tells Sharon and feels better for it. During the course of the story, some thefts get solved, a cousin confesses to having tried to kill himself, and other secrets get revealed. In the end, Toby and her family are much closer and more self-knowledgeable and the future looks bright.

Too few books exist on the problem of separation from a parent who is in prison. This story helps readers to see the issues involved in keeping secrets of this sort.

306. Lindsay, Jeanne Warren. *Do I Have a Daddy? A Story about a Single-Parent Child.* Illus. by Cheryl Boeller. Morning Glory, 1991 (0-930934-45-8); pap. (0-930934-44-X). 48 pp. Fiction.

Interest level: Ages 4–7

Erik and Jennifer are playing together happily until they have an argument. When Erik says he'll tell his daddy about it, Jennifer points out that he doesn't have a daddy, upon which Erik goes home. When he tearfully reports the incident to his mother, she informs him that he has a daddy, but that she and his dad were too young to get married, and that his dad went away because he wasn't ready for the big job of taking care of a baby. She also helps him to see that other men in his life perform some of the functions that daddies do. The book includes a special section of advice for single parents. It provides one model for how to respond to questions when a child wants to know about a parent he or she has never seen.

307. Lyon, George Ella. *Cecil's Story.* Orchard, 1991 (0-531-05912-X). Unpaged. Picture book.

Interest level: Ages 4–6

This lyrical story about a boy who waits for his father to come home from the Civil War is both gentle and poignant. When his mother receives word that her husband has been hurt in battle, the boy must go to a neighbor's home to wait while his mother goes to fetch his father. He worries about his father's injuries, what will happen if he dies, and how he will cope if that happens. The neighbors reassure him until his mother brings the injured father home. Although the father has lost an arm, the boy realizes that the family will survive. The mother is a strong woman, and the boy seems relieved to be able to let her support him when she returns. The paintings evoke a pastoral mood and bring this gentle masterpiece to life.

308. McKinley, Robin. *My Father Is in the Navy.* Illus. by Martine Gourbault. Greenwillow, 1992 (0-688-10639-0). 20 pp. Picture book.

Interest level: Ages 5–8

Sara's mother is eagerly anticipating the father's return home from the navy. She reads his letters to Sara and seems to assume that Sara is excited as well. But Sara has no recollection of her father, although she always says good-night to his picture when she goes to bed. Sara feels left out when the ship returns; she is not connected to all of the excitement that surrounds her. When her father finally arrives and hugs Sara and her mother, Sara looks into his eyes and is able to remember him in a real sense.

309. Maury, Inez. *My Mother and I Are Growing Strong; Mi Mamá y Yo Nos Hacemos Fuertes.* Illus. by Sandy Speidel. Trans. by Anna Muñoz. New Seed, 1979 (0-938678-06-X). 28 pp. Fiction.

Interest level: Ages 5–10

The left side is in English, the right side is in Spanish, and each page is given a title—for example, "My Mother Keeps Secrets." The narrator, Emilita, introduces herself and her mother. We meet them working in a garden and taking over a job the father had before he went to prison. (The secret is that the mother has taken over the father's jobs. The daughter approves when her mother keeps friends' confidences but not that she is keeping this important information from the father.)

Much of the book is commentary: "be fair to others," her mother says; how her mother and she are becoming self-sufficient and can now fix machinery; and so on. In this story, Emilita's father has been jailed for getting into a fight after being ethnically insulted. The man fell to the sidewalk and hit his head, and Emilita's father must spend a year in prison. Emilita and her mother hope for parole. The mother visits the prison but does not take Emilita. "I wish she would take me, but she says a prison is too sad for children. I say why is it worse for children than for grown-ups?" A few pages later, under the heading "A Mother Can Change Her Mind," the mother does allow her daughter to visit. Sure enough, it is terrible. It even smells scary. Emilita is surprised at how pale her father has become. Their visit is described emotionally and realistically in terms of today's society—the females cry, the male merely grows paler. Nonetheless, Emilita hopes to go again and plans to think of something funny to do on the next visit.

Alas, when there are family problems, too often children think they must make themselves responsible for making things right. That aspect of children's nature is shown well here. And what do you know, on the next visit, Emilita's attempt to bring fun into the prison by carrying a bouquet of radishes brings about an emotional torrent from the father and he does cry. His tears mix with joy when he reveals that he will be freed in a week's time. This is a loving story about a loving family caught up in life's circumstances.

310. Monfried, Lucia. *The Daddies Boat.* Illus. by Michele Chessare. Dutton, 1990 (0-525-44584-6); Puffin, pap. (0-14-054938-2). Unpaged. Picture book.

Interest level: Ages 4–7

The story's narrator is a little girl who spends the summer on an island. She enjoys going to camp, having picnics, and taking showers outside in her bathing suit. She looks forward to Friday, when she can meet the ferry that brings many working people from the city to the island. The ferry is called the Daddies Boat because of the large number of fathers who use it. Despite her enjoyment of her weekdays at the shore, the little girl eagerly anticipates the boat's arrival so that she can spend the weekend with her mother. The story is slight and predictable, but it is charmingly illustrated, with an androgynous figure (whose head is never shown) as the daily care-taker of the child.

311. Myers, Walter Dean. *Somewhere in the Darkness*. Scholastic, 1992 (0-590-42411-4). 168 pp. Fiction.

Interest level: Age 12+

Jimmy hasn't seen his father since he was a baby. His father, Crab, has been in prison, convicted of murder, and now he claims to be out on parole. Although Jimmy has adjusted to and is happy living with Mama Jean, his mother's friend, Jimmy decides to accompany his father on a road trip. Eventually, in a wrenching conversation with his father, he learns that they are running from the police because his father has escaped from prison. Crab escaped because he knows he is dying and wants this last opportunity to establish a relationship with his son. Unfortunately, he makes promises that he cannot keep, although he wants to; and Jimmy misses the stability of his home and Mama Jean. Their tenuous relation-ship develops slowly. Inevitably, Crab is caught, and later he dies. Jimmy returns home, sad, but feeling as if he has connected with his father.

312. Rosenberg, Maxine B. *Living with a Single Parent*. Bradbury, 1992 (0-02-777915-7). 114 pp. Nonfiction.

Interest level: Age 10+

Seventeen children are interviewed about the way they manage their life with their parents. Although each case differs, the similarities are striking. Logan's parents split up after an argument about a seemingly insignificant incident. Logan's father moved to Florida, and Logan sees him only occa-sionally. Logan spent a great deal of time brooding about his situation and his schoolwork suffered. His mother arranged counseling for the whole family. Now Logan views his mother a little differently and appreciates the work she does around the house. He copes with a shortage of pocket money and he recognizes that his parents will not get back together.

Sakeeya has been raised by her mother since birth. She entered coun-seling with her mother and sister when the school alerted her mother that

Sakeeya was fantasizing about having a father. Her mother was in college, and money was a serious problem. She felt incomplete without a father. Now household chores are shared in an organized way. Sakeeya's mother plans to start graduate school. Her father, whom she finally met, lives at a distance but maintains a relationship with her. Most of the children profiled express a desire for a two-parent family, but most accept their situations with courage and common sense. The book ends with some useful guidelines for living with a single parent.

313. Stowe, Cynthia M. *Dear Mom, in Ohio for a Year.* Scholastic, 1992 (0-590-45060-3). 180 pp. Fiction.

Interest level: Ages 9–13

When her mother goes back to college, Cassie is sent to live in rural New England with her aunt and uncle. Besides having to adjust to a new school, new friends, and relatives she hardly knows, Cassie has to deal with the anger she feels toward her mother. Cassie vents her feelings by writing angry letters to her mother, but then she destroys them so that her mother never hears from her. Gradually, Cassie learns to like living in the country, and she and her aunt and uncle make efforts to adjust to one another. However, Cassie's anger takes some time to subside. Her mother is rather self-absorbed and insensitive. She is unable to visit Cassie at all during the year, and plans are not made for Cassie to travel to Ohio. Still, the anguish that her mother feels is apparent even to Cassie. By the book's end, Cassie and her mother are able to make strides toward resolving their hurt and better communicating their feelings to each other. Children might want to be problem solvers after reading this book. For example, they could brainstorm ways in which Cassie and her mother can visit during the school year. Or they might role-play some of the advance discussions that Cassie and her mother could have had in order to forestall some of the separation conflicts.

314. Wright, Betty Ren. *Christina's Ghost.* Holiday, 1985 (0-8234-0581-8); Scholastic, pap. (0-590-40284-6). 105 pp. Fiction.

Interest level: Ages 9–12

Christina and Jenny are supposed to stay with their grandmother on her farm when their parents go off to Alaska for the summer. But when the girls get to their grandmother's farm, they find that she has been hospitalized, so Chris must go with her grumpy old uncle to an out-of-the-way cottage he has consented to take care of as a favor to a friend. Chris already feels abandoned by her parents, and now she must face the rejecting behavior of a man who clearly prefers to be alone. When Chris and her uncle arrive at their destination, they discover that there is a mystery about the cottage. As it turns out, two ghosts haunt the place and a murder was committed there.

Wright cleverly presents the story of an alienated child who gains self-acceptance and self-confidence by befriending a mournful young ghost, solving a mystery, and learning to get along with her gloomy uncle. The story is full of suspense. The mystery is handled adroitly, so that the reader is very willing to suspend disbelief. The mixture of fantasy and reality works well here.

Desertion

Look for books where the deserting adult is not a one-sided villain and the deserted family members are not simply designated as victims. The desertion should not be the entire substance of the plot. Anger and hurt of the people left behind should be acknowledged and not miraculously or easily expunged.

315. Adler, C. S. *Roadside Valentine.* Macmillan, 1983. o.p. 185 pp. Fiction.

Interest level: Age 12+

Jamie's mother deserted him and his father. After a few years, she dies in an automobile accident. Bereft of her loving and exuberant warmth, Jamie tries to please his strict, hard-working father, but nothing seems to work. His father is a silent, undemonstrative man who has found it difficult to express his emotions. After a stage of drug taking and alcohol abuse, Jamie settles into a more constructive life, but he still cannot seem to please his father. After Jamie builds a gigantic snow valentine expressing his love for a young woman who has another boyfriend, Jamie and his father get into a terrible argument and Jamie moves out. Not until Jamie gets a job, rents an apartment, and sends out college applications do he and his father reconcile and begin to understand each other better. With his newfound independence and self-esteem, Jamie wins the girl he loves, is accepted to college, and establishes a solid relationship with his father.

The author demonstrates that moving out of one's parents' home is not necessarily the worst or most destructive thing to do. It is only when Jamie is truly independent that he can forge an interdependent relationship with his father. All the characters in this story are believable and authentic. Readers can identify with both the situation and the people.

316. Blue, Rose. *Goodbye, Forever Tree.* Signet, 1987. o.p. 155 pp. Fiction.

Interest level: Age 13+

Heather seems to be the only person in the trailer park who is stable and has a vision of the future. Few of the families have both parents living there, and there is much sexual promiscuity among the inhabitants. Heather is part of a large crowd of teenagers who are aimless, bitter, and self-destructive. She is an attractive young woman who is talented in art. Her teachers support and encourage her to achieve her ambition of becoming an art therapist. She wins a scholarship and makes plans for a secure future, the symbol of which is a tree that she dreams about and that an elderly friend of hers paints: the "forever tree."

The book has the patterns of a romance novel, because it focuses heavily on the characters' romantic entanglements and on their physical appearance. But the theme of desertion and its effects on the families of the deserted ones is consistent, and it provides readers with a perspective that goes beyond the thinness of the plot. We come to know several characters, although there are a number of characters who seem to be present more as parts of the scenery than parts of the plot. Heather somehow manages to rise above her background, her mother's neglect, and her father's and brother's desertion. She manages to resist the sexual pressures her boyfriend puts on her, and she is also able to become involved with two potentially appropriate partners for her future.

The author conveys Heather's dilemma well. The issue of transience and its attendant complications is clearly described. Although some of the characters are cardboard figures, those whom we get to know have attractive as well as self-destructive qualities. This could be a useful book to help teenagers who are in this situation find some support. It could also be a help to young people who have never had to deal with the issue of abandonment and uncertainty to become more empathic with those who are in this circumstance.

317. Brooks, Bruce. *Midnight Hour Encores.* Harper, 1986 (0-06-020709-4); pap. (0-06-447021-0). 263 pp. Fiction.

Interest level: Age 13+

Sib's mother deserted her when she was 20 hours old. Her father, Taxi, has brought her up, but Sib feels that although her father has been a good father, she has brought herself up. She has never asked him about her mother or wanted to see her until now, at age 16. Now she not only wants to know all there is to know about her infancy and her mother, but tells Taxi that she wants to see her mother.

So Sib and her father begin an odyssey, visiting the places of her father's youth and meeting people who were important to him during the 1960s. Her father tells her of how he nurtured her when she was an infant. She learns things about the care and feeding of babies that she had never thought about before. She learns about her father, and she also learns about her mother as seen through her father's memory.

Before they get to San Francisco, where her mother lives, Sib informs her father that she really wanted to go on this journey in order to audition for a new music school in San Francisco. Sib had originally intended to go to Juilliard. She is a champion cellist, of international reputation. Her father is crushed that she wants to leave him, but he understands her wishes and is gracious about her decision.

Both Sib and her father are surprised when they discover that her mother, Connie, is no longer a drug-taking, impoverished hippie. She is a very wealthy businesswoman. She accepts Sib into her home, buys her expensive clothes, and assumes that Sib will stay with her when she is accepted into the music school. Sib is accepted into the school, but at the last moment she decides to return with her father. The reader is left to wonder what she will do with her considerable musical talent and with the rest of her life.

Interesting issues are raised in this compellingly written book. We expect to hate the mother; and in truth, we never love or admire her, but rather understand her. More important, her daughter understands her. Some of the relationships are dealt with too cursorily. And many specific questions about some of the characters and their eventual outcomes remain. However, the ending is satisfying, and the reader ends up more informed about important matters than in books where the endings are neatly tied up packages.

318. Cleaver, Vera. *Sweetly Sings the Donkey.* Harper, 1985, LB (0-397-32157-0); pap. (0-06-440233-9). 150 pp. Fiction.

Interest level: Age 10+

Fourteen-year-old Lily is the anchor of the Snow family. Her father, Judson, is a junk collector and a dreamer. He has never managed to support his family adequately. Martha, their mother, is pretty, delicate, and dependent. Lily is the most practical member of the family, and it is she who carries most of the responsibility for caring for her two brothers. After they move to Florida, because Judson has inherited some property there, they discover that Judson is ill, the land does not have any dwelling on it, and the impoverished family will have to scrape for a living.

Martha finally leaves them; she runs off with a man who has befriended the family. Lily and her friends build a house for the family, and by the end of the book we know that, thanks to Lily, the family will survive and even, perhaps, prosper.

It is ironic but true to life that Martha was deserted by both her parents when she was a child. She tells Lily that she has stayed with Judson because she didn't want to do to her children what was done to her. Yet she does it. In the end, she cannot withstand the same sort of self-centeredness that her own parents exhibited.

This book contains the same ingredients that the other books by Cleaver and her late husband have always contained: a strong and individualistic female protagonist, an accurate sense of setting, and a cast of memorable characters woven into a gripping story.

319. Furlong, Monica. *Wise Child.* Knopf, 1987 (0-394-99105-2); pap. (0-394-82598-5). 228 pp. Fiction.

Interest level: Age 12+

The story is an interesting combination of fantasy and reality. Wise Child's mother is a witch who deserted her when she was very young. Her father has left on a voyage, and it is unlikely that he will return soon. Wise Child is placed with a mysterious woman, an outcast named Juniper, who instructs her in languages and expects her to work hard.

When Maeve, Wise Child's birth mother, discovers that she is with Juniper, she comes to try to woo her away. Wise Child does go to her mother, but runs back to Juniper when she discovers that Maeve is a wicked witch. She realizes that your true mother is not so much the mother who bore you, but rather the person who nurtures and loves you.

There is magic and mystery in this story set in Scotland in early Christian times. The values of loyalty, hard work, and education come through, and the fantasy is engaging.

320. Grant, Cynthia D. *Kumquat May, I'll Always Love You.* Macmillan, 1986 (0-689-31198-2); Bantam, pap. (0-553-26416-8). 182 pp. Fiction.

Interest level: Age 10+

Livvy's father died, and now her mother has deserted her. She receives an occasional postcard from her mother that says her mother loves her and will return, but it has been more than two years now, and still her mother has not come home. Livvy is now 17. She has not told anyone except her two best friends that her mother is gone. She does not want to be sent to other relatives; she wants to wait in her own house for her mother's return. She lies to family and other adults, and she devises elaborate schemes for making people think that her mother is living with her. When her boyfriend (a third person she has told that her mother is gone) pushes her too far, she sends him away and he tells the authorities that her mother is gone and that she is living alone. They come to investigate, and her mother returns home at that moment.

Livvy's mother is portrayed as a disturbed and limited woman who is, nevertheless, a survivor. Her daughter is much stronger than she. The end of the story is ambiguous: The mother has once again left the house on an errand, and it is not certain that she will return. But the reader knows enough about Livvy to feel confident that Livvy will manage.

The story is a strange one. The author is persuasive enough to have the reader suspend disbelief up to a point, but the intrusion of the boyfriend, Raymond, weakens the story, as does the less-than-full depiction of Livvy's best friend, Rosella. Livvy herself is an interesting and strong character, and her predicament involves the reader in her problems.

321. Hahn, Mary Downing. *Tallahassee Higgins*. Houghton, 1987 (0-89919-495-8); Avon, pap. (0-380-70500-1). 180 pp. Fiction.

Interest level: Age 10+

Tallahassee's mother, Liz, has sent her daughter to live with Liz's older brother and his wife in Maryland, while she goes off with the latest in her string of boyfriends to seek an acting career in Hollywood. Twelve-year-old Tallahassee (Tally) fears that her mother will forget her, as she seems to have forgotten her past boyfriends, the family cat, and her family of origin. At the same time, she loves her mother deeply and is fiercely loyal and protective of her. Indeed, her mother does not communicate regularly with her, and the Hollywood plans fall apart.

Most of the story involves Tallahassee's learning to cope with her mother, her nasty aunt, and, especially, her feelings about herself and her situation. One of the interesting features of this book is its exploration of different life-styles and the choices people make. We come to know a number of characters, each of whom manages everyday living in a different way. Tally's best friend and her family, Tally's aunt and uncle, Tally's mother, her grandmother, and the other children at school all provide distinct options.

Tallahassee discovers for the first time who her father is when she sees some pictures in an album belonging to a former friend of her mother's. She meets her grandmother, who until now never knew of her existence. She learns some facts about her mother as well as her father. And ultimately, she comes to terms with her own situation.

The mother here is reminiscent of the mothers in Cynthia Voigt's *A Solitary Blue* (Atheneum, 1983) and Katherine Paterson's *The Great Gilly*

Hopkins (Crowell, 1978). All three women are physically attractive, terribly self-centered, and totally unreliable. All three have children who love them and want to be with them. And all three ultimately disappoint and desert their children. Like Jeff and Gilly, Tallahassee is intelligent, introspective, and hopeful that her mother will somehow become a person who can be counted on. Like the other two, Tally must learn to adjust to a family life without her mother.

322. Hamilton, Virginia. *A Little Love*. Philomel, 1984. o.p. 207 pp. Fiction.

Interest level: Age 12+

Sheema lives with her grandparents. Her father left her immediately after the death of her mother. She attends a vocational high school and has a talent for cooking. She is a generous-hearted, obese young woman who, until she became involved with a young man named Forrest, was promiscuous and self-deprecating. Forrest loves and admires her. He sees in her qualities that she doesn't even know exist. Her grandparents, too, love her dearly, and she is fiercely loyal to them.

Sheema decides that she must see her father and come to terms with her grief over his not remaining with her when her mother died. She has long ago accepted her mother's death, but her father is alive; he sends money for her support, but she never hears from him. She and Forrest drive off together, with her grandparents' blessing but without Forrest's father's knowledge, to seek her father. They find him, and Sheema at last lays to rest the expectations she had of him. He is a sad man who mourns his losses and has not really recovered from them, even though he has a new family and is successful in business.

With new knowledge and self-respect, Sheema returns to her grandparents, and she and Forrest pledge to marry each other. All the characters are well drawn and rich, as might be expected in a Hamilton novel. Forrest, in particular, is a remarkably insightful, gentle, and loving person. The book deals with the complexity of people's responses to loss and recognizes that desertion is but one of these responses.

323. Hermes, Patricia. *Mama, Let's Dance*. Little, Brown, 1991 (0-316-35861-4). 168 pp. Fiction.

Interest level: Ages 9–12

Mary Belle, Callie, and Ariel have been abandoned by their mother. Ariel works nights at a gas station to keep the family afloat financially; Mary Belle is in charge of the household. Seven-year-old Callie is nurtured and protected by her two older siblings. The children were deserted by their father years before. They are determined that no one discover that they are unsupervised for fear of being separated. Mary Belle struggles to maintain some sort of order in the house, stretching Ariel's small salary as far as she can and keeping up the facade of living with a parent. They get help from their friend and neighbor, Amarius, an older black man, who suspects their situation and quietly assists them. However, when Callie gets sick, their secret is discovered and Amarius and his sister, Miss Dearly, become the children's chief source of support. Callie dies. Mary Belle, broken and exhausted, is finally able to surrender her problem to Miss Dearly, who manages to convince the authorities that she and Amarius should have custody of the children. This book reflects an unusual solution to a painful situation, yet the characters are so well drawn and believable that the ending is plausible and uplifting. The mother is not seen as a villain but as a troubled woman. The connections among the siblings are strong and account for their deep devotion to each other. Miss Dearly and Amarius are calmly accepting of the situation; their actions show their deep love for humanity, and one could imagine them creating a loving home for Ariel and Mary Belle.

324. Highwater, Jamake. *I Wear the Morning Star.* Harper, 1986 (0-06-022356-1). 148 pp. Fiction.

Interest level: Age 12+

Sitko is a frightened, isolated, and unhappy boy whose parents have deserted him and whose older brother, Reno, is ashamed of being a Native American. The two boys have been placed in a home called Star of Good Hope, but it is an abusive and terrifying place for Sitko, who is a sensitive artist and who has a love for his Cherokee heritage that was instilled in him by his beloved grandmother. Reno, on the other hand, hates being a Cherokee, denies that he is, and tries to bully his younger brother into rejecting his heritage.

In poetic prose, the author conveys the complexity of desertion and the agony of self-hatred. The story is filled with people who hate, not only Native Americans but also Jews. No noble beings emerge. Even the grandmother, who is a brave and wise person, is so filled with hatred for the white man who gives her and her family shelter that she poisons any possibility of a truce among them. Sitko is the last hope. The story is a tragedy in one sense, because the boys' father kills their mother, and their lives are seldom more than painful exile. But there is triumph here, too, because the grandmother transfers her store of knowledge and tradition to the young artist, Sitko, and the reader knows that he will carry it on.

325. MacLachlan, Patricia. *Journey.* Delacorte, 1991 (0-385-30427-7); Dell, pap. (0-440-40809-1). 83 pp. Fiction.

Interest level: Age 10+

The summer that his mother leaves, 11-year-old Journey has a difficult time adjusting. He agonizes over why she is gone, examining photo albums, trying to repair a ripped-up picture that she left behind, and resuscitating memories of both his parents. His grandparents are his real family, and it takes Journey a long time to recognize it. Both of his parents have deserted him and his sister; for too long, Journey yearns for his mother's return. He is helped in his healing and comprehension by his grandfather's photographs. Through them, he learns to focus on what is real and acknowledge what is imagined. As with all her work, the author challenges the reader's depth of perception at the same time that she opens new pathways to understanding.

326. Mahy, Margaret. *The Catalogue of the Universe.* Macmillan, 1986 (0-689-50391-1). 185 pp. Fiction.

Interest level: Age 13+

Angela May has heard many stories about her father, whom she has never known. Her mother has tried to help Angela feel loved, and she has succeeded. But when Angela finally meets her father, she discovers that her mother did not tell her the truth, and she is furious. Over the course of this novel, Angela falls in love, battles with her mother, and finally reconciles with her. Both she and her mother are strong and independent women. By the end of the book, Angela has come of age; she can function as her own person and perhaps even come to terms with her father and grandmother. The story's interest is heightened by its New Zealand setting.

327. Rodowsky, Colby. *Julie's Daughter.* Farrar, 1985 (0-374-32963-5); pap. (0-374-43973-7). 231 pp. Fiction.

Interest level: Age 12+

Using the strategy of telling the story with the voices of the three main characters, the author has successfully conveyed the necessity to view a situation from different perspectives. The three characters are Julie, Slug, and Harper. Julie ran away from her mother's home when she was 17, leaving her newborn baby, Slug. Now that her mother has died, Julie returns to take Slug to live with her. The two of them find a common ground in their caring for Harper, their neighbor, who is dying of cancer. The chapters alternate among the three characters, and each has her own story to tell. It is to the author's credit that although the stories blend, each one remains individual, like the themes in a fugue.

Harper is an artist and keeps creating art until the cancer kills her. The book tells not only of the losses caused by desertion of a child but also of the loss of ability and the contemplation of the loss of one's own life. None of the characters is a stereotype; the reader learns that none of them can be judged, although they have been guilty of harmful acts. Perhaps the most powerful feature of this book is its invitation to consider the subtlety and pain of these acts rather than to leap to pat conclusions.

The plot is an interesting one, but the holes are a little too numerous and deep for the reader to stay absorbed and willing to suspend disbelief.

328. Stolz, Mary. *Go and Catch a Flying Fish.* Harper, 1992, pap. (0-06-447090-3). 213 pp. Fiction.

Interest level: Age 12+

Taylor and Jem are tired of the escalating arguments between their parents, Tony and Junie. They are worried about their little brother's reaction to the fighting and wonder what will happen if their parents get divorced. Still, they are unprepared when their mother leaves. More than anger, they feel confusion and abandonment. Tony does his best to cope, and each child finds a certain measure of relief in the now quiet household. When it becomes apparent that Junie intends to stay away for a long time because she has decided to go back to school in New York, the family pulls together and begins to create a new life. The Florida setting provides a lot of flavor and underscores the differences between the mother, who feels a need to become her own person, and the father, who enjoys the relaxed life-style that living by the sea offers. The tone is not condemnatory toward Junie; Tony is somewhat bumbling but is a capable and loving father.

329. Voigt, Cynthia. *A Solitary Blue.* Macmillan, 1983 (0-689-31008-0); Scholastic, pap. (0-590-47157-0). 240 pp. Fiction.

Interest level: Age 12+

Deserted by his mother, Melody, at the age of seven, Jeff Greene lives with Horace, his distant, scholarly, and considerably older father. Four years later, while he is recuperating from a debilitating illness, his mother reenters his life and invites him to spend the summer with her. Oblivious to her faults, Jeff is infatuated with her beauty and charm. When he returns to his father, he is lonely and aches for his mother and her family, even though he knows that she is dishonest and superficial. A friend of the family, Brother Thomas, helps Jeff and his father to reach out to and appreciate each other. Together, they renovate a property overlooking the marshes of Chesapeake Bay. There Jeff meets Dicey Tillerman, and they develop a strong bond. Decisively choosing to remain with his father when Melody sues for custody and the divorce is finalized, Jeff is able to develop a strength and eventual detachment that enables him to see Melody's immaturity and selfishness clearly, and to value the honesty of genuine relationships.

Jeff is the victim of self-centered emotional manipulation by Melody. Neglected from a very early age, Jeff is expected to feel guilty about wanting his mother to stay with him. His father is preoccupied with the academic world of the university, and Jeff is constantly apologizing for his existence, careful to disguise his feelings lest his father desert him too.

Although Horace never speaks ill of Melody, she sabotages Jeff's relationship with his father by undermining and devaluing him as a person and as a father. Once Horace recognizes the depth of Jeff's suffering and loneliness, he becomes more open with his son and takes responsibility for helping him to heal. He reassures Jeff that he is wanted and loved and apologizes for his neglect. Once he and his father have been emotionally reunited, Jeff is able to become independent and strong. The lesson is an important one. The story is a moving one.

330. Zindel, Paul. *The Amazing and Death-Defying Diary of Eugene Dingman*. Harper, 1987 (0-06-026862-X); Bantam, pap. (0-553-27768-5). 186 pp. Fiction.

Interest level: Age 12+

Eugene Dingman is a sensitive, intellectual, and passionate 15-year-old who lives with his mother and older sister. His emotional outpourings are too much for his mother, who sends him away to a summer resort to work as a waiter. Eugene's father never comes to see him, although Eugene writes poignant letters pleading for his father's advice, understanding, and presence.

Eugene's peers are no more empathic than his parents. He is an oddball. His summer is filled with put-downs and betrayals, including two that are the most painful: The girl he has a crush on lies to him and goes out with many other males; and his father "sweeps" through the resort without even speaking to him. The ultimate blow is revealed to him in a letter from his mother: She will not be there when he returns home; she has married someone Eugene does not like, and she indicates that she feels that Eugene must change if he is to be a happy person.

Eugene is an open, aching wound, but his brilliance and his willingness to confide all to his diary make this a book that attracts the reader to him. Zindel's perception of young people communicates well. He conveys the results of Eugene's parents' physical and emotional desertion of the boy in a style that engages the audience. His use of the diary form is an excellent strategy for involvement. Eugene's problems, painful though they are, become wryly amusing because of the context and format of the story. Adolescents will probably identify with Eugene and his situation.

Running Away

Running away is a serious issue, not to be taken lightly. Especially in today's society, where abuse has been publicized and few people can ignore the dangerous consequences of children separated from their homes and families, it is irresponsible of authors to pretend that running away is a harmless act of juvenile rebellion. Caring parents in books as well as in real life need to respond to children's threats of running away with firm and loving assurances that they will not be permitted to do so and that their complaints must be resolved in other ways.

331. Artenstein, Jeffrey. *Runaways. In Their Own Words: Kids Talking about Living on the Streets.* Illus. by the author. St. Martin's, 1990 (0-312-93132-8); Tor, pap. (0-8125-1354-1). 170 pp. Nonfiction.

  Interest level: Age 12+

This is a difficult book to read because it deals with such painful situations. However, teenagers who choose to run away are indeed confronting such threats as drug dealing, prostitution, and gangs. Artenstein interviewed runaways at the Los Angeles Youth Network and used excerpts from these interviews in this book. Except for some interspersed comments about his own feelings while doing the interviews, what you read is straight from the runaways themselves, and it is powerful stuff. The language is strong and the descriptions are graphic. The reasons that these teenagers have left their homes or foster homes range from mental, physical, and sexual abuse to extreme feelings of isolation. Two of the teens have forged a strong, albeit seemingly impossible, relationship since they have been at the shelter. Artenstein ends the book with epilogues about each of the interviewees, some of which seem hopeful. There is no doubt that this author cares deeply about these teenagers and wants to enlighten others about the reality of running away.

332. Blos, Joan W. *Brothers of the Heart.* Macmillan, 1985 (0-684-18452-4); pap. (0-689-71166-2). 162 pp. Fiction.

  Interest level: Age 12+

The story tells of a pioneering family in which Shem, the only son, runs away from home in anger over an argument with his father. Shem has a disability: One leg is shorter than the other, and he has found it difficult to find work. But when he runs away, he finds work immediately, has many adventures, proves his manliness, and is able to return home to his family and the young woman who eventually becomes his wife.

The story tells of the strength necessary to endure the hard times and many losses the pioneers faced. It also conveys the indefatigable spirit of the unlikely hero. The author, who won the 1980 Newbery Medal for *A Gathering of Days* (Macmillan, 1979), brings authenticity and scholarly research to her story.

333. Landau, Elaine. *On the Streets: The Lives of Adolescent Prostitutes.* Messner, 1987 (0-671-67135-1). 112 pp. Nonfiction.

Interest level: Age 12+

Landau writes frequently about social issues, and with the gaze of a reporter she has taken on the several worlds of teen prostitution. She offers an understanding perspective, combining in-depth sociological and psychological information with moving first-person profiles. She tells it honestly but somehow doesn't overwhelm her reader with the tragedy that abounds. There's the ugliness of a man who visits 13-year-old Lynn and insists on calling her by his own daughter's name. And the sadness of Chad, who had been repeatedly abused by his grandfather and gradually sold into prostitution by his own family. And there's the frightening story of a 15-year-old abducted into slavery until her escape six months later. How about 16-year-old Samantha who is back home, but already has needed a hysterectomy. About 50 percent of teen prostitutes live at home, it seems.

Landau's informative chapters on male prostitution, child pornography, and pimps are highly revealing, and the actual nonglamour of escort services is exposed. The long American history of prostitution, particularly on the frontier, where suicide before age 18 was frequent, is instructive, particularly because it reveals that the technique of getting girls drug-addicted is an old one. The chapter on pimps' methods of wooing teens into dependency and keeping them there is so highly detailed that readers may be more savvy if they are approached. It may just save some lives. Health problems are discussed, including venereal disease, but surprisingly, AIDS, already hot in the media by publication time, was not given attention.

Landau offers an intelligent look at reasons kids become prostitutes. These are multitudinous, ranging from being thrown out (perhaps for promiscuity, homosexuality, so-called incorrigibility, and so on) to escaping a home of physical/sexual abuse, from abduction to economic destitution. Landau writes without an air of hysteria, yet her words serve indelibly as a warning to those who might be individually tempted or those who might be abducted into prostitution rings.

334. Levoy, Myron. *The Magic Hat of Mortimer Wintergreen.* Harper, 1988 (0-06-023842-9); pap. (0-06-440335-1). 211 pp. Fiction.

   Interest level: Ages 8–12

This comic fantasy has serious overtones: Joshua and his younger sister, Amy, have been orphaned and forced to live with their evil and abusive Aunt Vootch. Amy, who is an artist, has stopped drawing human beings. She does not trust anyone over the age of 15.

   Then, one day, the children meet the magical and eccentric Mortimer Wintergreen. He owns a magic hat that has a mind of its own and is very unpredictable. The children run away with Mortimer Wintergreen and have many adventures, all of them amusing and imaginative. With the aid of the magic hat they finally locate their grandparents, with whom they feel loved and secure.

   This is really a book about running *to* rather than away. Aunt Vootch is a cartoon villain. For those people who might be tempted to compare this book with some of Roald Dahl's fantasies, the differences are palpable. Although the characters have the flavor of a Dahl romp, the heroes are not vicious or cruel to others. No one is mutilated or seriously hurt. The magician is eccentric, but he is more the captive of his magic than the master of it. He is good-hearted and willing to confess his shortcomings. His values are clear and constructive. Although the characters in the book fall into certain stereotypical categories (the wicked aunt, the kind and quirky grandparents), the story is not one that teaches intolerance.

   Levoy returns at the end of the story to the neighborhood he so lovingly draws in his earlier work, *The Witch of Fourth Street and Other Stories* (Harper, 1972). His style is respectful of his audience and of his characters. This book may be helpful, because its fantasy format is an unusual one in helping children sort out their feelings about an abusive situation, and their responsibility for extricating themselves from it.

335. Miller-Lachmann, Lyn. *Hiding Places.* Square One, 1987, pap. (0-938961-00-4). 208 pp. Fiction.

   Interest level: Ages 12–16

Seventeen-year-old Mark Lambert has seen too much: his parents' divorce, the death of his physician father in a drug-induced automobile crash, school failure, ulcers, physically abusive treatment from his perfectionistic stepfather, a suicide attempt, and retreat from his timid mother, who can't seem to protect him. Now his stepfather wants him to learn discipline at military school. "No way," Mark insists, and runs off to New York's East Village shortly after being released from the hospital following a brush with death from drinking.

There, after his widowed stepmother can't help him, he lands at Harbor House, a home for runaways, but can't make good use of the counseling offered there. Always a poet, and a capable student when he wants to be, Mark enrolls in the local high school and eventually gets his own apartment and supports himself with a free-lance typing business.

This gritty novel from an alternative press is highly readable and, in spite of its subject matter, rather tame, sweet, and clean-cut. It is blessed with smooth writing, action, and believability, as Mark establishes himself as a young adult, making friends, meeting a girl, and finding adults he can trust. A central character, Dr. Sam, an administrator in the New York high school, becomes a guiding figure. When he dies of a heart attack right after an argument with Mark, Mark's guilt over his own father is reawakened and reinforced. Over the course of the novel, Mark learns to take responsibility for what is his (for example, his poetry, his aspirations) and leave behind responsibility for events beyond his control.

336. Nelson, Theresa. *The Beggars' Ride.* Orchard, 1992, LB (0-531-08496-5). 243 pp. Fiction.

Interest level: Age 12+

Clare disguises herself and flees her Tennessee home, her drunken mother, and her mother's abusive boyfriend. She takes a bus to Atlantic City, New Jersey, in search of Joey, a former lover of her mother's who had been kind to her. Joey has long since left the area, so Clare manages to hook up with a group of other homeless teenagers. Led by Cowboy, each member is named for a Monopoly playing piece; Clare becomes Hat after she joins the gang. When her initiation task—robbing a fast-food place—fails, Clare is befriended by the owner, Mr. Morgan, who turns out to be Joey's father. Mr. Morgan's kindness and nurturing help heal Clare physically and emotionally, but she feels great loyalty to her friends. When Cowboy is injured, it is Mr. Morgan to whom Clare turns, and it is Mr. Morgan who supports Cowboy's contention that Griffey, a social worker, is an abuser. Clare is reunited with Joey by telephone, but she is wise enough to recognize the limits of that relationship. After Clare talks with her, her mother promises to try to conquer her alcoholism. Clare is gratified that her mother believes her tale of abuse at the hand of her mother's boyfriend. She finally decides to return to Tennessee, stronger and wiser, thanks to her friends—and especially Mr. Morgan.

337. Roberts, Willo Davis. *To Grandmother's House We Go.* Atheneum, 1990 (0-689-31594-5). 192 pp. Fiction.

    Interest level: Ages 8–10

Rosie and her two brothers run away to find their estranged grandmother because they fear they will be sent to separate foster homes while their mother recuperates from a stroke. The book is a page-turner, although much of the story line is a bit too pat. (They fortuitously get transportation practically to their grandmother's door and find her house even though they have never been there or met her.) The suspense is nicely built, and the characters (except for the mother, whom we never meet) engage our sympathy and attention. The children are models of sibling cooperation and concern. Their decision to run away, while based on rumor and innuendo, is a carefully planned enterprise with many built-in safeguards. The lesson of how tragedies are constructed is clear here in the lack of communication between adults and children. In this story, it is manifest in three generations.

338. Rylant, Cynthia. *A Fine White Dust.* Bradbury, 1986 (0-02-777240-3); Dell, pap. (0-440-42499-2). 106 pp. Fiction.

    Interest level: Age 10+

Thirteen-year-old Peter Cassidy tells his story in retrospect to help himself finish an episode in his life that has taught him many hard lessons, among them that he can count on his parents, but not to expect anything, and, "If somebody loves you, it's because he wants to. And it's never because it's what he's supposed to do."

    Peter has always loved going to church, even though his parents do not accompany him. When he meets an itinerant revivalist preacher, he falls under his spell and plans to abandon his best friend and parents and accept the preacher's invitation to go away together. However, instead of meeting Peter at their appointed time and place, the preacher runs off with Darlene Cook, a young woman who works at the drugstore.

    Crushed, Peter returns home; his parents and loyal best friend provide him with love and understanding, and his life returns to normal, except that he is now wiser about people and what can be expected of them. The story moves quickly and is accessible to readers aged ten and up, even though the topic is one that might be more appropriate to older readers who are grappling with issues of whom to choose as heroes, how different to be from one's parents, and how to establish a value system. Unfortunately, Cynthia Rylant does not let us in on what motivates Peter, either to his religious fervor or to his willingness to abandon his friends and family for the preacher. His religious convictions remain unshaken, but he now attends church less regularly and certainly less passionately.

"But it's a real quiet thing for me now. Sort of like a nice swim in the lake."

Rylant never clears up the mystery of why Peter's parents feel as negatively as they do about going to church. At one point, when Peter confronts them, his father says, "There's more to it than you can see, Pete . . . things you might not understand." Peter is alarmed, because he is afraid to learn his parents' secrets. Peter's mother intervenes just as his father is about to explain it to him, and so neither Peter nor the reader ever find out what the secret is.

Such deep issues as autonomy and independence, religious fervor, hero worship, and betrayal are explored in this book. Rylant has a gift for conveying the voices of the characters and for providing the reader with an authentic sense of place.

339. Springstubb, Tricia. *Which Way to the Nearest Wilderness?* Little, Brown, 1984 (0-316-80787-7); Dell, pap. (0-440-99554-X). 166 pp. Fiction.

Interest level: Ages 9–12

Eunice gets a knot in her stomach every time her parents argue, and they argue more and more with increasing hostility. Eunice's younger brother is a disturbed child; her older sister seems to be totally preoccupied with her current boyfriend, but she, too, is frightened about the prospect of her parents getting a divorce. Eunice is a very bright child, whose mother overly relies on her and calls her "my sensible child."

The story is about running away, but not in a conventional sense. Although it is Eunice who plans throughout the course of the book to emulate Thoreau and create her own Walden, it is Eunice's mother who runs away for a while. The family is jolted into the reality of life without their mother. Surprisingly, they manage very well, but equally surprising to them is that they miss her very much, even with all the fighting that their parents did.

When the mother, at last, returns, the author wisely does not provide a facile reconciliation and elimination of all the family's problems. It becomes clear that everyone will have to compromise a little and that each person must bear the burden of anxiety about what will happen to the family. There are no guarantees, but there is hope.

340. Switzer, Ellen. *Anyplace But Here: Young, Alone and Homeless: What to Do.* Atheneum, 1992 (0-689-31694-1). 162 pp. Nonfiction.

Interest level: Age 12+

This is a readable book about a difficult subject. The author begins with anecdotes about her own life. Told in a chatty, confidential style, they nonetheless have a substantial impact and increase the desire to keep on reading. She examines the population that constitutes most runaways—unhappy, abused adolescents—and discusses where they go and how they get there. In one chapter, the reader is introduced to a group who live together in an abandoned building in New York. The teenagers in the group are able to manage if they work together (culling food from garbage cans at restaurants), but they cannot survive independently. Another group of teens live in a cardboard and plastic tent city in Venice, California. Another chapter is devoted to Aggie, called a success story because she managed to survive several years on the streets and is now the owner of a social security card, has a job, and lives in an apartment. Although Aggie is coping with a difficult life-style, it seems that many of the psychological scars from her past have not faded.

The second half of the book gives practical advice on how to cope and where to find help. Included here are hotline numbers and addresses, information on unplanned pregnancy and AIDS, and suggestions for sticking it out at home. Finally, there is a chapter on how to get off the streets, followed by an update on many of the people who have been mentioned throughout the book. This author projects a matter-of-fact attitude about the problems of runaways and creates an atmosphere of practical caring. A book like this one would be an important addition to shelters all over the country.

341. Thomas, Jane Resh. *Courage at Indian Deep.* Houghton, 1984 (0-89919-181-9); pap. (0-395-55699-6). 108 pp. Fiction.

Interest level: Ages 9–12

Cass is angry at his family for having to move to the wilderness of the Lake Superior shore. He misses their home and his friends in the city. He does not make friends here; as a matter of fact, he has enemies. He stays more and more by himself and frequently goes to a cave where he has hidden some food and supplies. When an incident happens at school that causes Cass to fear his father's anger and punishment, he runs away. A storm arises and he is almost killed, but he and his former enemy manage to save most of the crew of a boat that was in danger of being wrecked by the storm. In the end, Cass and his family are reunited in more ways than one. They have developed a new awareness of each other's feelings and needs.

Although Cass feels that he has to run away in order to solve his problems, and although the running away does seem to be the catalyst for the resolution of all his trouble, the author makes the reader aware of the danger of this act and of the anguish that the family feels at the loss of their son. Young readers might benefit from trying to invent other ways that Cass could have behaved.

Economic Loss

In the past several years, children have been more and more exposed to the issues of rising unemployment and poverty through newspapers and television. Many children are themselves suffering from the effects of the economic depression. Books have begun to reflect these conditions and to present them in ways that help some children empathize and others see that they are not alone.

Some situations might invite creative ways of dealing with the economic deprivation and maintaining the family structure despite the hardship. Also included in this topic are books that portray the devastating effects poverty may have on family life and relationships. Care should be taken to avoid blaming the victim. It is also not constructive to imply that hard work and pure thoughts will lift a family out of poverty. Homeless people should have identities beyond their circumstances. They should not be objects of pity or symbols of a failed society. Dehumanizing language should be avoided.

Unemployment

342. Cleary, Beverly. *Ramona Forever.* Illus. by Alan Tiegreen. Morrow, 1984 (0-688-03785-2); Dell, pap. (0-440-47210-5). 182 pp. Fiction.
    Interest level: Ages 7–10

Now in third grade, Ramona Quimby is experiencing a difficult year. Some of the problems that Ramona and her sister, Beezus, have are: They hate going to Mrs. Kemp, their baby-sitter, because they feel that she dislikes them; they discover that their mother is pregnant; their friends tease them because their father is still going to school, studying to be an art teacher, and does not yet have a "regular" job; money is scarce, and everyone is worried about it; their cat dies of old age; and their beloved Aunt Bea is going to marry a man they don't like. To compound their problems, their father receives an offer to teach in a one-room schoolhouse far away from their present home, and they don't want to move.

Everything turns out for the best, of course. Ramona's baby sister is born, and Ramona survives her initial worries about being displaced. She and Beezus grow to appreciate their new uncle. Their father accepts a full-time job at the supermarket rather than uprooting his family. And Beezus and Ramona are permitted to take care of themselves, rather than having to go to the baby-sitter they feel uncomfortable with.

It is strange that the girls do not mourn their cat, who, after all, was with the family for ten years. They bury him and have a funeral, but then he is all but forgotten. The children do, however, freely express their anxieties and delights about all of the other happenings in this eventful year.

Cleary has produced a winner of a story about Ramona and her family. Children will certainly empathize with and enjoy the characters' escapades. They may grieve for Picky-Picky, the cat, more than Ramona and Beezus do, because the cat has been an integral part of many of the stories in this series. Nevertheless, the book deals well with most of the losses and displacements that normally occur in the life of a young child.

343. Delton, Judy. *My Mother Lost Her Job Today.* Illus. by Irene Trivas. Whitman, 1980. o.p. 32 pp. Fiction.

Interest level: Ages 4–8

When Barbara Anne's mother loses her job, the little girl is worried that everything is going to be different. She's afraid that all of the celebrations and happy rituals of her life with her mother will change. At first her mother is angry and upset that she has lost her job. However, when she sees how anxious Barbara Anne is, she comforts her daughter and reassures her that everything will turn out fine.

The relationship between mother and child is clearly a close and supportive one. The author and illustrator combine to show the characters' emotions and to help young readers identify with this single-parent family.

344. Quinlan, Patricia. *My Dad Takes Care of Me.* Illus. by Vlasta van Kampen. Firefly, 1987, LB (0-920303-79-X); pap. (0-920303-76-5). 24 pp. Fiction.

Interest level: Ages 4–8

"My stomach hurt when the kids in school asked, 'What does your dad do?' I didn't know what to say, so I said, 'He's a pilot.'" Actually, Luke's father is unemployed. Both of them have mixed feelings about this—it's good that Luke can come straight home instead of going to a baby-sitter, they can play games and cook together, and they talk more about feelings, but both wish he were employed.

The layoff from a factory job has meant a move from the country to the city, where the mother has gotten a new job with computers, at which she sometimes works nights. Luke likes both city and country living, but there are sometimes difficulties in this adjustment, like when he wants a bike and is told they can't afford it. And it's difficult to see his father grumpy and sad. Once, he cried when he didn't get the job he wanted. Luke tries to comfort him at times like this. The book has the ring of truth but doesn't develop gracefully. In spite of what are probably the world's most sensitive parents (who are made all the more attractive with the use of watercolors), Luke's shame doesn't clear up until he meets a classmate whose father is home, too. That father says his job is taking care of Jillian, and now Luke has something to say, too, and his stomach stops hurting when he is asked what his father does.

345. St. Pierre, Stephanie. *Everything You Need to Know When a Parent Is Out of Work.* Rosen, 1991 (0-8239-1655-3). 64 pp. Nonfiction.
   Interest level: Ages 9–12

This book indeed tells readers everything they might like to know about out-of-work parents in a clear, nonthreatening manner that is suitable for preteenage children. Beginning with reasons why a parent is out of work, the book provides concise information abut coping strategies, effects on the family, and how to prepare for the future. Interspersed among the text are italicized stories about children who have had related experiences, such as being separated from their parents due to a faraway search for employment. There are suggestions for keeping morale up and getting counseling. There does not seem to be enough information provided concerning financial assistance and what to do in emergencies, but there is a list of agencies provided for further information. The black-and-white photographs seem authentic and are representative of realistic scenes of parents scouring newspapers for job leads, sitting sullenly and unseeing in a chair, and, ultimately, grinning for joy. Glossary.

Poverty

346. Allison, Diane Worfolk. *This Is the Key to the Kingdom.* Illus. by the author. Little, Brown, 1992 (0-316-03432-0). Unpaged. Picture book.
   Interest level: Ages 5–8

The traditional chant is adapted for this story about a young African-American girl who lives in the inner city. She carries a small bag of groceries through her gray, littered neighborhood. Her imagination takes her to a lush, multicultural world filled with warmth and opulence. Her trip washes her with serenity and security, especially when she arrives at a comfortable home and joyously embraces an old woman, probably her grandmother. When she returns to reality, she manages to make a homeless man who is huddled on her street a little warmer and happier. The child is not an object of pity; she serves as an excellent model for coping with hard reality in an unusual way. The little girl's face is memorable; the watercolor illustrations are delicate and detailed.

347. Ashabranner, Brent. *Dark Harvest: Migrant Farmworkers in America*. Photos by Paul Conklin. Dodd, 1985. o.p. 160 pp. Nonfiction.

Interest level: Ages 9–14

This book provides portraits of farm workers and their families, along with an explanation of migrant workers' way of life. There are maps of individual travel patterns, along with an analysis of why these workers are needed. The emphasis is on sociology and economics, with amplification of how the crew leader system works. An often bleak picture of farm life is portrayed: shorter than average life spans; above average infant and maternal death rate; health and workplace hazards; pesticide poisoning; status as the poorest paid workers in the country, including the youngest workers permitted by law. Many farm workers' children drop out of school early.

The sharp, cheerful photographs almost belie the above statistics, showing happy family groupings, but chapter subtitles such as "Being Poor" bring back the larger feeling of the book as a whole. Segments on migrant childhoods are especially poignant, and the book ends with chapters on the future. Informative and moving. Bibliography, index.

348. Bograd, Larry. *Poor Gertie*. Illus. by Dirk Zimmer. Delacorte, 1986, pap. (0-385-29487-5). 103 pp. Fiction.

Interest level: Ages 8–11

Gertie is the narrator of this story, and her voice is clear and true. She is a spunky, funny girl, even though her father has deserted her and her mother. Her mother's job not only doesn't pay enough but is unpleasant. Things come to a head when the landlord threatens to evict them if they can't pay the back rent. Gertie and her grandpa hold a sale of Gertie's artwork and materials that he has repaired, and they earn the money needed to pay the rent. Gertie's mother gets a better-paying job, and it looks as if the family will survive.

The seriousness of the story is lightened by the humor and quirkiness of the characters, but the message comes through that it is no fun to be poor. The ending is believable and satisfying, especially because Gertie's good fortune does not change her solid character traits.

349. Coil, Suzanne. *The Poor in America*. Messner, 1989, LB (0-671-69052-3). 126 pp. Nonfiction.

Interest level: Age 12+

This book looks at historical and recent conditions of poverty in a matter-of-fact manner that does not seek to point a finger of blame. There is a chapter that focuses on the poverty of the twentieth century including the effects of immigration and the Depression. Another chapter describes the "chronic poor," a category that includes migrant workers and people from Appalachia, Native Americans, and African Americans. Also included in a special chapter are women and children, now considered among the poor in increasing numbers. The book concludes by identifying the challenges for the next few years, but it offers few solutions. There is an extensive bibliography.

350. DiSalvo-Ryan, DyAnne. *Uncle Willie and the Soup Kitchen.* Illus. by the author. Morrow, 1991 (0-688-09165-2). 32 pp. Fiction.

   Interest level: Ages 7–10

Uncle Willie is a model of an older person who continues to be productive and community-minded. He shares a close, loving relationship with his young nephew and teaches the boy that there are humane ways to help the hungry and homeless. The book is narrated by the young boy, who describes working in a soup kitchen with his uncle, and feeling sad and scared when he sees a woman sleeping on a bench and a man gathering cans to cash in.

351. Greenberg, Keith Elliot. *Out of the Gang.* Lerner, 1992, LB (0-8225-2553-4). 32 pp. Nonfiction.

   Interest level: Ages 9–12

Two people, a 28-year-old man and a young Hispanic boy, recount their frightening experiences with gangs in New York City. Butch is recruited by the the 21 Black Jacks. He goes through an initiation, allows the gang to become the focus of his life, and gets involved in a brawl when a fellow gang member is challenged for using a convenience store in another gang's territory. When Butch joins a gang for older teenagers and his best friend is stabbed, he decides he has had enough. Butch is fortunate: When he makes the decision to leave the gang, he is not challenged. He manages to create a life for himself with wife, children, and a steady job.

   Gino is much younger than Butch. After joining a "posse" called Kings of Graffiti, he is suspended from school for constant fighting. Gino, too, leaves his gang, after one fight too many.

   Both former gang members seem to have shed their former lives: Butch is a member of the Guardian Angels, Gino becomes active in the El Puente community center. This book illustrates that there are alternatives to gang life; however, it also clearly shows that the attractions of joining a gang are difficult to resist, especially for young men who see gang life as their only option. The black-and-white photographs are an important supplement to the text.

352. Hicyilmaz, Gaye. *Against the Storm.* Illus. by Diana Zelvin. Little, Brown, 1992 (0-316-36078-3). 200 pp. Fiction.
      Interest level: Ages 10–13

Eleven-year-old Mehmet does not understand why his parents want to move from their beautiful village in the Turkish countryside to Ankara, although he realizes they wish to better themselves and possibly become rich like Mehmet's uncle, Yusuf Amca. In Ankara, the family must live in a poor apartment with no running water. They are devastated to learn that their uncle expects a high rent from them. While in the city, Mehmet befriends Muhlis, a homeless boy, who further opens Mehmet's eyes to the struggle of city life. When Muhlis dies, Mehmet decides he must return to his village, although his parents do not join him. The book uses language effectively to give a flavor of Turkish culture. However, it does not reflect the range of heritages that must exist in a city as large and varied as Ankara.

353. Kaufman, Curt, and Gita Kaufman. *Hotel Boy.* Photos by Curt Kaufman. Atheneum, 1987 (0-689-31287-3). 40 pp. Nonfiction.
      Interest level: Ages 4–8

After an apartment fire, five-year-old Henri and his brother have to live in a hotel with their single-parent mother. This book tells of the crowded conditions and the loss of the usual amenities of home—the clothes, toys, and books are gone. Henri must also go to a new school (Gita Kaufman actually was Henri's kindergarten teacher). This much starting over often seems like too much starting over.

Henri tells the story of the city help his family received, of how hotel children make their own meager entertainment, and how the wide-open streets often are more appealing than the single room that the three must share. And yet, while the family endures as Mom searches for a job and they await a new apartment, other family traditions and milestones of growth remain: a trip to the zoo, buying pizza, learning to tie a shoe. When the big day comes and the family gets a new apartment, there's excitement all around. This book is a valuable look at an increasingly prevalent problem.

354. Mazer, Harry. *Cave under the City.* Harper, 1986 (0-690-04559-X); pap. (0-06-440303-3). 152 pp. Fiction.
      Interest level: Ages 9–12

This book may be a painful one for young readers, even though it has a happy ending. It tells of Tolley and his five-year-old brother, Bubber, and their survival for a number of weeks on the streets of the Bronx during the Great Depression. The boys' father has gone to Baltimore to look for work. Their mother is in the hospital suffering from pneumonia and probably tuberculosis; she works in a sweatshop where the air is always filled with bits of thread and dust. Their grandmother is also hospitalized, and the boys don't want to be placed in a children's shelter.

For a while, they live in their own apartment, buying groceries on account and finding whatever bits of change they can. Then, when the grocery owner won't allow them any more credit and the social worker keeps coming around to look for them, they take to the streets. They hide in a basement, try to earn money whatever way they can, and often are reduced to begging. Tolley steals two doughnuts and a bottle of milk when Bubber is sick, and this tortures his conscience.

After a number of weeks, when Tolley becomes too sick to function, the boys once again return to their own apartment. They are astounded and delighted when their father comes home and rescues them with the news that he will be staying home with them from now on.

The neighborhood in the Bronx is authentic. Mazer's detailed description of the setting and the burdens the boys bear makes the reading hard. But it is the kind of difficulty that comes from reality, not from elaborate prose or turgid description. The story brings home the pain and desperation that people felt during the time of the Depression, feelings from which children were not exempt.

355. Mitchell, Margaree King. *Uncle Jed's Barbershop*. Illus. by James Ransome. Simon & Schuster, 1993 (0-671-76969-3). Unpaged. Picture book.

Interest level: Ages 6–10

Sarah Jean narrates the story about her favorite relative, Uncle Jedediah Johnson, her granddaddy's brother. He is an itinerant barber whose dream is to own his own shop. The family lives in the South during the Depression and is part of a larger African-American community of sharecroppers and those who own small parcels of land. Although he is very frugal and saves money regularly, Uncle Jed has to postpone buying his shop when he helps Sarah Jean's family pay for her emergency surgery. Then, after he has accumulated more money, the banks fail and he loses his money. Finally, at age 79, he opens his shop and everyone celebrates with him. The author includes information about the economic and social systems prevailing in the United States at that time. The illustrations are particularly striking. Each of the characters connects visually and emotionally with the others; the bond is plain to see. James Ransome's father always aspired to have his own barber shop, and achieved his dream late in his life, so the story could have been his as well. The partnership of author and illustrator works wonderfully in this book.

356. Myers, Walter Dean. *Scorpions.* Harper, 1990 (0-06-024364-3); pap. (0-06-447066-0). 160 pp. Fiction.

Interest level: Age 12+

Twelve-year-old Jamal Hicks's older brother, Randy, is in jail for a gang-related murder. Although Jamal does not want to participate in the gang, he and his best friend, Tony, are lured into taking Randy's place in his street gang, the Scorpions, and running drugs in order to pay for Randy's appeal. Even though the amount of money needed for the appeal is small, no one in the family can raise $500. Tony and Jamal get involved in a gun-fight, and Tony inadvertently kills a gang member. He is emotionally wounded by this act. The friendship breaks up when Tony leaves for Puerto Rico. Randy is still in prison, and there is still no money for an appeal. Jamal leaves the gang, but he knows that the temptation will always be there to join, have power, and be a part of a group. He hopes he will be able to resist the temptations. This graphic portrayal of gang life by a gifted author is an important exploration of a neglected subject.

357. Sachs, Marilyn. *Call Me Ruth.* Doubleday, 1982. o.p. 128 pp. Fiction.

Interest level: Age 9+

Ruth and her mother emigrate from Russia to New York City. Ruth's father had worked for nine years to save enough money to send for them. Ruth loves America from the moment she arrives. Her mother hates it. They are poor; their apartment has no toilet or bath; the father is ill and soon dies. Afterward, the mother becomes active in the labor movement, causing enormous embarrassment to Ruth. Ruth is a very bright, academically talented child. She works hard at school, loves to read, and is considered a model child. The author presents several points of view clearly and sympathetically. She also conveys an accurate historical view of early twentieth century labor and immigrant issues.

358. Wolff, Virginia Euwer. *Make Lemonade.* Holt, 1993 (0-8050-2228-7). 200 pp. Fiction.

Interest level: Age 11+

LaVaughn is 14. In order to augment her college fund, she agrees to baby-sit for Jolly, an older girl with two babies who barely manages to eke out an existence in her small, squalid apartment. LaVaughn is efficient and accepting; gradually, she becomes attached to the mother and her two children. Her own mother, whom Jolly calls Big Mama, is a no-nonsense character who believes Jolly should straighten out her life. Jolly is fired from her job at a factory after making an accusation of sexual abuse; LaVaughn helps out, baby-sitting free so that Jolly can find another job. Even though Jolly adamantly refuses to accept welfare, LaVaughn manages to convince her to attend a program for teenage mothers where she can get a high school degree while her children are in daycare. Academics are difficult for Jolly, but fortunately she pays attention in her CPR class and is able to save her baby from choking.

The book is divided into 66 conversational chapters; it flows smoothly, and all the issues do not crowd the plot. It is unfortunate that the author uses a somewhat trite device, that of having Jolly save her baby's life, to make it possible for Jolly to become a hero. However, the engaging narrator, LaVaughn, is a sensible balance for the dramatic characterization of Jolly. The story's main focus is always on her and her responses.

Homelessness

359. Aaron, Chester. *Lackawanna.* Lippincott, 1986. o.p. 210 pp. Fiction.

   Interest level: Age 12+

It is difficult for many young readers in today's affluent society to comprehend what life was like for children their age during the time of the Great Depression. In this disturbing novel, six children of varying ages meet in a "Hooverville," constructed of shacks. All their parents have either died or deserted them in hopes that orphans would be more eligible for welfare than children with able-bodied parents. The children band together and declare themselves a family. They name themselves Lackawanna, for the freight trains they hop in search of food and money.

The six children find shelter in an abandoned building where Carl's father used to do bookbinding. They are warm and dry and somewhat comfortable there until the day that Herbie, the youngest of the group, gets kidnapped. Deirdre, Herbie's sister, is frantic. Willie, the leader of the group, gathers information from a railroad worker, and the five children go off in search of Herbie. He has been kidnapped by a hobo whose own son died. When the group finds Herbie, he is reluctant to leave the hobo, who has been like a father to him for several weeks. One of the children freezes to death; another is hospitalized because a policeman attacked him. In the end, the remaining five survive because they help each other.

The details of the life of a hobo during the Depression are shockingly specific. During this era, many people starved to death and many more were homeless. The story succeeds as a story, but it is also a history text from which young readers can learn.

360. Ackerman, Karen. *The Leaves in October.* Atheneum, 1991 (0-689-31583-X). 128 pp. Fiction.

Interest level: Ages 8–11

Children need to know that people of all sorts of backgrounds and circumstances can end up homeless. This story involves a father and his two children who are forced to live in a public shelter for several months. The author does not condemn anyone. She tries to make the reader appreciate the problems and issues that arise when a family is homeless. Livvy, the protagonist, is a little too perfect to be believable, but she certainly demonstrates what an active, assertive young girl can accomplish. The "happy" ending is feasible and open-ended enough for readers to design some sequels of their own.

361. Berck, Judith. *No Place to Be: Voices of Homeless Children.* Houghton, 1992 (0-395-53350-3). 148 pp. Nonfiction.

Interest level: Age 11+

With a compelling Foreword by Robert Coles, this look at the lives of homeless children is searingly honest, not only because of its straightforward prose, but especially because of the words of the children interviewed by the author. In each of the 13 chapters, the reader is given important factual information about such topics as the reasons for the prevalence of families who have become homeless; types of available shelter; how families handle inevitable stress; basic health risks; and feelings homeless children express about school. Even more significant than the author's prose is her selection of thoughts, poems, and comments from the group of homeless children she spoke with. In the chapters about stress and school, their conversation is simply punctuated by the author's comments; Berck wisely realizes that their words say far more than she ever could. Most poignant of all is the chapter "Dreams and Visions." The children speak about their desires for careers as police officers, actors, and reporters; their wishes for "two closets full of clothes"; and their advice to the President. Berck ends with a somewhat pessimistic prognosis for the children she worked with; although a few are doing well, some have been shattered and others have disappeared.

362. Bunting, Eve. *Fly Away Home.* Illus. by Ronald Himler. Clarion, 1991 (0-395-55962-6). 32 pp. Picture book.

Interest level: Ages 5–8

Andrew and his father live in an airport. Bunting tells a story that makes a seemingly unbelievable life-style come alive with a poignant realism. Each day, Andrew and his father have a routine that includes regular bathroom times and an organized schedule that Andrew's father keeps in a notebook to ensure they are not discovered frequenting the same terminals and airline waiting areas. There are other inhabitants of the airport whom Andrew and his father know. One family looks after Andrew on weekend days, when his father goes to a part-time job. Although Andrew's father frequently tries to get an apartment, he is unsuccessful because rents are too expensive. When Andrew sees a small bird that has been imprisoned in the airport fly away free, he remembers the image and uses it as a metaphor for his own life. The relationship between Andrew and his father is loving; clearly these victims of circumstance are valiantly trying to cope until better times arrive.

363. Fox, Paula. *Monkey Island.* Orchard, 1991, LB (0-531-08562-7); Dell, pap. (0-440-82408-7). 152 pp. Fiction.

Interest level: Ages 10–13

Clay Garrity's life has changed drastically in the past several months. His father, once an art director for a magazine, has left the family; Clay's pregnant mother leaves him alone in a hotel room with just over $28. Now Clay must survive on the streets if he is to avoid being discovered by Social Services and, he believes, losing his only chance to reunite with his mother. In a park inhabited by street people, he is befriended by two men, and the three of them form a kind of family unit. Life in the park is horrific: Clay is freezing cold and frightened, especially by the Stump People, gangs who enjoy destroying the shelters that the people have built and beating up any occupants they find. Clay is hospitalized with pneumonia and must cope with the woman from Social Services, but by this time he is exhausted and beaten down by his physical condition. It is through the help of his social worker that Clay is placed in foster care and ultimately reunited with his mother and new sister.

The book poses some unanswered questions. Why did Clay's father leave in the first place? Why does Clay's mother seem only slightly remorseful over her abandonment of her son? How did Clay's street friend, Buddy, manage his miraculous recovery, find employment, and amass a nest egg? Why did Buddy visit Clay in the hospital only once? Despite these mysteries, this is a powerful, searing story about life as a homeless person. Professional helpers are seen in balance: Some of them are inadequate, some are very competent. The author never glamorizes homelessness and suggests that help is available to those who ask.

364. Holman, Felice. *Slake's Limbo*. Scribner, 1986 (0-684-13926-X); pap., Aladdin (0-689-71066-6). 117 pp. Fiction.

Interest level: Age 11+

Orphaned and alternately teased and neglected, clumsy Slake nears despair after his sole friend is killed by a car. At age 13, Slake escapes from his strangulating life into the subways of New York City. There he creates a makeshift home and quickly fashions ways to survive. When his subway hideaway is taken from him four months later, Slake has proven to himself that—previous indications to the contrary—he is clever, competent, creative, and able to have relationships with others. Triumphant, he knows he can survive aboveground as well. The intricate, eloquent detail of Slake's ingenuity involves the reader. The book is especially useful in eliciting feelings from withdrawn youngsters.

365. Hyde, Margaret O. *The Homeless: Profiling the Problem*. Enslow, 1989, LB (0-89490-159-1). 96 pp. Nonfiction.

Interest level: Age 11+

This thoughtful book is an important contribution to the literature about homelessness. Hyde begins with an overview of the homeless and identifies categories of people who are most likely to be in this situation, ranging from young and/or abused mothers to the mentally impaired to ex-offenders. Many are given names and their life stories are shared. Chapters are devoted to the special needs of homeless babies and children, runaways, and the mentally ill. The final chapter gives ideas for action, including the story of Trevor, a young man who was so moved by the condition of the homeless in Philadelphia that he created a shelter called Trevor's Place. Ideas about where to go for help, addresses and hot-line numbers, and a useful bibliography are included.

366. Landau, Elaine. *The Homeless*. Simon & Schuster, 1987, LB (0-671-53492-0). 112 pp. Nonfiction.

Interest level: Ages 11–16

The brutality of being homeless comes through on the first page in the story of Mama, a homeless woman who is found dead in New York's Grand Central Station on Christmas morning. The varying reasons for being homeless are explored (mental illness, destitution, housing shortages, eviction, fires, alcoholism, eccentric preference, and so on). Landau shows sympathy for their plight. ("It is nearly impossible for someone in extremely dire circumstances to remain neat and clean.")

As in her other books, Landau combines research into public policy and statistics with individual first-person stories to make her story come alive. An example is Marybeth, who had four children in five years of marriage, then became widowed, was ill, then evicted. In telling the stories, Landau weaves in material about public shelters, treatment facilities, and so forth. Landau seems to have come to know homeless individuals and tells of their habits, again sympathetically: "Life on the street forces homeless people to become aware of the hours at which public rest rooms open and close. Whenever possible, they try to regulate their food and liquid intake in order to avoid middle-of-the-night emergencies."

A special chapter is devoted to homeless youth and their attempts to survive, albeit through illegal trading of body and substance, after running away or being thrown out. Like the rest of the book, it is moving and disturbing. To read that a nine-year-old prefers the abuse of a sex ring to the home environment tells of astounding levels of violence in this society. Unfortunately, according to Landau, the crisis is likely to continue, bright lights appearing from private and local sources, not the federal government. Bibliography, index.

367. Paulsen, Gary. *The Crossing.* Orchard, 1987, LB (0-531-08309-8); Dell, pap. (0-440-20582-4). 114 pp. Fiction.

Interest level: Age 13+

Manny is an orphan struggling to survive on the streets of Juarez, Mexico. Robert is a hard man, an alcoholic, a veteran of the Vietnam War, and an Army sergeant, stationed just across the border at Fort Bliss, Texas. The two meet several times and touch each other's lives in a significant way. At the end of the story, the boy who could not ask for favors asks for one, and the man who could not grant favors grants one, and there is hope for them both as a result. The story is told dramatically, and Paulsen's use of the border as a symbol of a spiritual as well as physical crossing works well.

368. Schertle, Alice. *Little Frog's Song.* Illus. by Leonard Everett Fisher. Harper, 1992 (0-06-020059-6). Unpaged. Picture book.

Interest level: Ages 3–6

Little Frog sleeps through a rainstorm and awakens to discover his beloved home, the pond, has disappeared. Little Frog searches for his home and is helped by kind-hearted creatures, but he remains homeless until befriended by a human who returns Little Frog to the pond. This is a gentle, repetitive story, especially suited to being read aloud.

5

Coping with Critical Loss

Death

Euphemisms should be avoided in books dealing with death, partly because they deny feelings of loss, but mostly because they are misleading and potentially frightening for a child. Phrases such as "going to sleep," "going on vacation," and "passing on" confuse the issue and sometimes make the child wary of going to bed or taking a trip. Children are often very literal and believe the language without discerning the intent. Authors should try to reflect the normal reactions to the death of a loved one: denial, guilt, anger, and depression. Individuals grieve in different ways; these differences should be respected and presented as acceptable.

When suicide is a factor in a story, try to find books that avoid assigning blame to friends and family. Usually, unless there is active abuse involved, the suicide is not any particular individual's fault. Children should not feel that they have to bear the burden of a friend's death.

In all cases, whether the death is of a close relative, friend, or pet, the child's feelings must be acknowledged and respected. Books should be sought that help children to see that they are not wicked, strange, or unique in their reactions. Wherever possible the stages of mourning should be reflected in the actions of the characters and an understanding should be conveyed that the mourning process takes time.

General

369. Bernstein, Joanne E. *Loss: And How to Cope with It.* Clarion, 1977. o.p. 160 pp. Nonfiction.

Interest level: Age 10+

This book regards life as a series of losses. The author seeks to help young people deal with one of life's most serious losses, the death of a loved one. In order to celebrate existence, loss must be faced, grappled with, and managed. Utilizing research data, personal anecdote, and the opinions of individuals ranging from Shakespeare to Dick Cavett, the following topics are covered: what happens when someone dies, children's concepts of death, feelings of bereavement, living with survivors, handling feelings, the deaths of particular individuals (parent, grandparent, friend, pet, and so on), unusually traumatic death (suicide, war, murder, and so forth), and the legacy of survivors. The author tries to achieve a warm and reassuring manner as she deals with practical issues. Bibliographies of nonfiction and fiction titles treating death are appended, as well as listings of film resources and service organizations. Index.

370. Dolan, Edward F. *Matters of Life and Death.* Watts, 1982. o.p. 128 pp. Nonfiction.

Interest level: Ages 12–16

Today's controversies as they reflect on our concepts of life and death are explored here: abortion, contraception, euthanasia, in vitro fertilization, artificial insemination, and cloning. For each, free-lance writer Dolan instructs on the core of the procedure, then investigates the heart of the controversy, as it has existed over long periods of time and as it existed in the 1980s in the United States. The many controversies are presented fairly and in depth, as exemplified by examining abortion in history, as seen by churches, through the eyes of the law, and as a political arena. Newspaper stories on these issues are part of Dolan's story—for example, the story of Karen Ann Quinlan. Bibliography, index.

371. Gerstein, Mordicai. *The Mountains of Tibet.* Illus. by the author. Harper, 1987 (0-06-022149-6); pap. (0-06-443211-4). 32 pp. Fiction.

Interest level: Age 7+

The book begins with the birth of a little boy—high in the mountains of Tibet—who grows to enjoy flying kites. He lives out his life in one place, but he always longs to visit different lands and come to know different sorts of people. When he dies, he is given the choice of rebirth, and he takes it. He is given one choice after another and consistently chooses that which feels most like home to him. His last choice is whether to be a boy or a girl, and he chooses to be a girl because he seems to remember that he was once a boy. The book ends with the birth of a little girl in the same high mountains of Tibet, and she also enjoys flying kites.

Aside from the notion of reincarnation, the book deals with the philosophical issue of choices and how we make them. Children will certainly enjoy speculating about what their choices might be if they were given the option of rebirth again on any spot in the galaxy, in any universe, on any planet, in any country, as any creature of either gender.

The illustrations in this beautiful picture book are framed almost as snapshots in the real world and take the form of mandalas when the story takes place in the world beyond. The details of the options the main character is offered are interesting and attractive. Truly an unusual book.

372. Guernsey, JoAnn Bren. *Should We Have Capital Punishment?* Lerner, 1993, LB (0-8225-2602-6). 96 pp. Nonfiction.

Interest level: Age 11+

This book is one of the Pro/Con series from Lerner, which brings controversial issues to older children in order to guide them in developing perspective and understanding an issue more completely. As promised, *Should We Have Capital Punishment?* presents a clear look at both sides of the issue. The book explores what it's like on death row; what happens to the families of those who are executed; methods of execution; and what happens in the courtroom prior to the event. There is also a chapter about the people who perform the executions and how they handle what would seem to be a distasteful profession. The colorful maps and charts make the design of the book appealing. The photographs of the convicted, their families, and the victims are not sensational, but they add to the understanding of the topic. One particularly poignant photograph shows two death row inmates, one white and one black, playing checkers through their cell bars. Unfamiliar terminology is explained in the text and in the glossary. Extensive footnotes and a bibliography add to the matter-of-fact presentation of the material but do not interfere with the attractive design.

373. Heegard, Marge Eaton. *Coping with Death and Grief.* Lerner, 1990, LB (0-8225-0043-4). 64 pp. Nonfiction.

Interest level: Ages 9–12

Starting with a chapter about moving to a new city and progressing through the deaths of animals, friends, siblings, and various beloved family members, the book explains and describes such factors as funerals, cremation, different ways people die (suicide, accidents, etc.), and other details that children are inquisitive about. The author helps readers to understand that their negative feelings are normal and that there are a number of ways that they can cope with their loss. The tone of the book is neither abstract nor condescending. The information is provided in gradual, small doses. Children are given permission to remain children rather than having to suddenly become adults. They are assured that they can't "fix" people's grief, but that they can listen and respond.

374. MacLachlan, Patricia. *Unclaimed Treasures.* Harper, 1984 (0-06-024094-6); pap. (0-06-440189-8). 118 pp. Fiction.

Interest level: Ages 10–12

Although the book describes a summer that begins with a death and a funeral and nearly ends with one, this treasure of a story is about life and helps readers contemplate and value life's ordinary and extraordinary events. As with all of MacLachlan's books, the characters are individuals who capture readers' attention with their particular actions, observations, and feelings and move the reader with the universality of their situations and the thoughtful and appropriate way in which they handle their problems.

In this story, Willa, twin sister to Nicholas, searches continuously for her true love. They have just moved into their new home, and they soon meet Horace Morris, the boy next door, who lives with his tall, solemn artist-father and several aunts whom he calls Unclaimed Treasures because they are elderly women who never married (that is, they were never claimed). One of the aunts has just died. Horace's mother has deserted him and her husband. She's "out in the world looking for something that needs her." Willa is not happy with her mother at the moment, because after 11 years her mother is pregnant, and Willa wishes that her mother were out in the world doing something extraordinary.

Other characters in the book include Old Pepper, who demonstrates that old age need not be synonymous with self-centeredness and crotchety behavior. Old Pepper teaches Willa to do more than "just look." He pays attention. He helps the children to think about and cope with the idea of death as he contemplates the fact of his eventual death.

Love and death and friendship and understanding are interwoven. Although the reconciliation of Horace's parents is a romantic rather than realistic outcome, it is appropriate for this book, whose tone is gentle and wise and extraordinary in its valuing of the ordinary.

375. Marsoli, Lisa Ann. *Things to Know about Death and Dying.* Photos and illustrations. Silver, 1985. o.p. 48 pp. Nonfiction.

Interest level: Ages 7–12

Short chapters on many subjects inform the reader about death's basics. Some of the topics are the usual found in nonfiction today: what death is physically, funerals, suicide, death of a pet, death of a relative, death of a child. Others are more unusual: dying in a hospital, at home, or in a hospice; death as portrayed on television; ceremonies at military funerals or for police or fire personnel who die on duty; obituaries; and afterlife.

Marsoli manages to give a great deal of information, but she also attends to emotions, with a fine tone at that. She tells readers death is not a punishment, but a natural, eventual end for every living thing. She reminds them that death can never be caused by people's thoughts. She alerts children to the idea that not everyone will know how to comfort them if they have had a death in the family and that anger the children may feel when they see this deficit in those around them is perfectly acceptable. She reminds children that dying people also have emotional needs, that if someone in their home is dying, they can help that person with emotional needs by sitting and talking, reading to him or her, and so on. Marsoli is unafraid to talk about difficult subjects. Bibliography, index.

376. Mellonie, Bryan. *Lifetimes: The Beautiful Way to Explain Death to Children.* Illus. by Robert Ingpen. Bantam, 1983, pap. (0-553-34402-1). 48 pp. Nonfiction.

Interest level: Age 5+

Exquisite paintings are the centerpiece of this Australian import, immediately stirring inspiration and appreciation for life and lifetimes, no matter how long. Each illustration is captioned in tiny print (for example, Young Apple Growing), framing it as a work of art. And the words? They are simple, poetic, and inviting: "There is a beginning and an ending for everything that is alive. In between is living. All around us, everywhere, beginnings and endings are going on all the time."

The paintings show animals and plants going through the process, explaining that although most of the time living things recover, illness or accident can hurt living things so much that "they die because they can no longer stay alive. This can happen when they are young, or old, or anywhere in between." But, reassuringly, the author adds: "Each one has its own special lifetime." For trees, therefore, it's one hundred years or more. For flowers and vegetables, it's a seasonal existence. Butterflies live as butterflies only a few weeks. In each of these and other instances, the repetitive line appears: "That is their lifetime."

Toward the end, the author asks, "And people?" A painting showing four generations of women is accompanied by the answer: "Well, like everything else that is alive, people have lifetimes, too. They live for about sixty or seventy years, sometimes even longer, doing all the things that people do like growing up and being grown up." Then the reminder is repeated that sometimes illness or hurt interferes to cause earlier death. "It may be sad, but that is how it is for people. It is the way they live and it is their lifetime. So, no matter how long they are, or how short, lifetimes are really all the same." Quietly philosophical, this is a book that, in its beauty, contributes to acceptance.

377. Rofes, Eric E., ed., and the Unit at Fayerweather Street School. *The Kids' Book about Death and Dying: By and for Kids.* Little, Brown, 1985 (0-316-75390-4). 128 pp. Nonfiction.

Interest level: Age 10+

"The Unit" is a voluntary discussion group/class in the private Fayerweather Street School, Cambridge, Massachusetts. Rofes, a teacher, and his pupils created a course of study that resulted in this book. The youngsters, ages 11 through 14, shared ideas, saw related movies, read related books, and interviewed kids, parents, and other adults. They visited and talked to professionals in hospitals, suicide prevention centers, hospices, funeral homes, and cemeteries. To start off, they talked about the responses they had to the first deaths they were aware of; those responses form the introductory material. They also did exercises, the results of which are here to be learned from. For example, what would death look like if it were a person or an animal?

The chapters cover causes of death; what death is; legal death; euthanasia; autopsies; funeral customs; burial; cremation; death of a pet, parent, or sibling; suicide and other violent deaths; death caused by illness; and life after death. The tone is chatty, and children are quoted frequently. What the authors have provided is a summation of real feelings, not the experts' feelings disguised in children's voices. As such, the authors offer good ideas. For example, when a child has lost a parent, the teacher should consult with the child before discussing it with the class. The book is also filled with dramatic specifics that are very memorable— for example, a girl whose father had always had sherry and a slice of bologna after dinner. When that tradition was gone, it was hard for her to sit at the table at the close of the meal. The ideas throughout give an insight into childhood—from the discussion of mounting Roy Rogers's horse Trigger to children with cancer learning not to ask their parents certain questions if those questions brought tears to the parents' eyes. Very worthwhile. Bibliography.

378. Sanders, Peter. *Death and Dying.* Watts, 1991, LB (0-531-17278-3). 32 pp. Nonfiction.

Interest level: Ages 7–10

The book explores such questions as What is death? What is dying? What is a funeral for? Is death the end of life? What do people feel when they know they will die? Why are people afraid of death? What happens after death? The language is simple, but the answers are presented in enough depth to be worthwhile. The photographs showing a diverse population add to the effectiveness of the book.

379. Simon, Norma. *The Saddest Time*. Whitman, 1986 (0-8075-7204-7); pap. (0-8075-7203-9). 40 pp. Fiction.

Interest level: Ages 4–8

In poetic prose and with faultless understanding of children's development, Simon recounts three situations in which people die and are mourned. In each case, there are knowledgeable and sensitive adults to help the children cope with their loss. The deaths of a young child, an old woman, and an adult but not-quite-middle-aged man are dealt with honestly but delicately.

When Teddy, an eight-year-old, is killed in an accident, the children recall with sadness the times they weren't nice to him or quarreled with him. Their teacher explains that no one is perfect and that the children's feelings are natural. He helps them to express their feelings on paper in letters to Teddy's parents. When Emily's grandmother dies, Emily cries with her grandfather, but she also remembers the good times with him. Similarly, with Michael's Uncle Joe, who dies after a long illness, Michael is frightened at the thought that perhaps his parents will die young, too. His family helps him to feel more secure and to think of ways to help his aunt, and in that way to handle his own grief.

The stories are the stuff of which literature is made. They are gentle and true. The language is strong and flowing; the characters are appealing.

Suicide

380. Bunting, Eve. *Face at the Edge of the World*. Clarion, 1988 (0-89919-399-4); pap. (0-89919-800-7). 158 pp. Fiction.

Interest level: Age 12+

Seventeen-year-old Jed Lennox is a bright, sensitive young man. He is an outstanding photographer and has won several prizes for his photographs. But he must contend with problems that would overwhelm a mature adult: His best friend, Charlie, has just committed suicide; Jed's mother died when she gave birth to him, and his father blames him for her death. As a consequence, Jed's father is rarely at home, leaving Jed to fend for himself.

Charlie's suicide is not the only one in the story. Another boy at Jed's high school kills himself, and a retarded young man attempts suicide. Such issues as drug abuse, media hype, bigotry, guilt, and fear of punishment emerge as contributing factors. Guilt, anger, and despair lead the list of reactions to the suicides. A variety of young people are presented to the reader, supporting the understanding that each person is an individual. Peer pressure is strong, but individual relationships are stronger.

The story takes the form of a mystery to be solved, with Jed the protagonist and detective. Through a series of events and a building up of clues, Jed uses his powers of observation and his love for his friend to uncover the answer to why Charlie killed himself. The ending is positive but realistic. A masterful book.

381. Gardner, Sandra, with Gary Rosenberg. *Teenage Suicide.* Simon & Schuster, 1990, LB (0-671-70200-9); pap. (0-671-70201-7). 128 pp. Nonfiction.

Interest level: Age 12+

A free-lance writer and a psychiatrist collaborate to tell the stories of six people who tried to commit suicide and the signals they gave. The narrative is concrete and thus affecting: "Every night for a month, Debbie cut skin off her wrists with a razor blade. The only way she knew she was alive, she says, was when she saw the blood."

Gardner and Rosenberg wisely relate a lot of suicide feelings to previous losses, such as death and divorce, loss of childhood, and loss of self-esteem. Rich with psychological concepts (for example, "the expendable child," trying to kill off unwanted portions of the self), these ideas are useful in trying to find reasons for suicide. Pressures for success are also attended to here, as well as social and cultural factors (for example, fear of pregnancy).

Some adolescents participate in other self-destructive risk taking, which the authors examine. Perhaps some readers will identify themselves in the stories of anorexia, sexual acting out, and so forth. There is also a chapter on the romance of suicide in the media, including suicide clusters. This insightful book concludes with a section on prevention, highlighted by the travails of Kim Fields, an actress on the television program "Facts of Life." Her own feelings made her become active in suicide prevention work. Prevention programs are described, along with warnings not to keep secrets of suicide intentions if one knows someone is feeling that way. Resources for help, bibliography for adult readers, suggestions for further readings, index.

382. Kolehmainen, Janet, and Sandra Handwerk. *Teen Suicide: A Book for Friends, Family, and Classmates.* Lerner, 1986, LB (0-8225-0037-X); pap. (0-8225-9514-1). 72 pp. Nonfiction.

Interest level: Ages 10–16

Kolehmainen and Handwerk, counselors and developers of community programs on suicide prevention, offer an analysis of what is known about suicide, including the statistics, myths, and warning signs. Narrative profiles of attempters, friends of attempters, and those who succeed demonstrate through dramatic specifics what can happen. For example, with Steve, a boy with suicidal thoughts, the value of a friend and counselor listening comes through. Other chapters demonstrate involving an adult, anger, regrets, risks, the aftermath of a suicide attempt, and grief shared by a community. A final chapter discusses ways we can help ourselves and others, professional help, and community resources. Of books in the genre, this one is simply structured and not laden with sociological analysis. The stories are readable and make their points smoothly. Those who are not deep readers will find its straightforward information and advice valuable.

383. Langone, John. *Dead End: A Book about Suicide.* Little, Brown, 1986 (0-316-51432-2). 176 pp. Nonfiction.

Interest level: Age 12+

In Langone's tradition (*Goodbye to Bedlam*, Little, Brown, 1974, and so on), *Dead End* is both scholarly and thoughtfully expressive (for example, suicide is "murder's blood brother"). Chapters on history, psychology, social attitudes, and suicide notes are given added punch by citing such unusual sources as high school newspapers and interspersing comments of teen attempters and survivors. Its considerable superiority over other recent volumes about the second leading cause of teen death lies in several areas: lengthy, informed discussion of the role of biochemistry and genetic links in depression and impulsive behavior; inclusion of a wide range of research results (for example, stress is greatest at the start of a school term, not at exam time); differentiations between attempters and committers; and highly detailed checklists, warning signals, and guidelines for prevention. Perhaps most important is the investigation of such controversies as the right to die and the possibly contagious influences of music and media, even daring to ask if and how we can openly talk about the topic without causing an increased number of suicides through our focus.

384. Peck, Richard. *Father Figure.* Viking, 1988 (0-670-30930-3); Dell, pap. (0-440-20069-5). 182 pp. Fiction.

Interest level: Age 11+

Byron and Jim's mother takes her life when she can no longer tolerate her cancer. The boys and their mother have been living with their well-to-do grandmother, who now finds that she cannot deal with her grief and the boys' needs. She sends them to their estranged father for the summer. The story tells how 17-year-old Jim finally lets go of his rage at his father's desertion, his mother's death, and his grandmother's aloof and controlling behavior. He also finds it possible to relinquish his role as a hovering father figure to eight-year-old Byron. Through Jim's telling of the story, the reader understands each of the characters, even the grandmother. It helps that the author is such a master at injecting humor into even the most serious topics.

385. Peck, Richard. *Remembering the Good Times.* Delacorte, 1985 (0-385-29396-8); Dell, pap. (0-440-97339-2). 181 pp. Fiction.

Interest level: Age 12+

Buck, Katey, and Trav are inseparable friends. Buck lives with his divorced father, and Katey lives with her great-grandmother and her divorced mother. Trav's parents are together, but he resents them, and their relationship is a tense one. The story focuses on the friendship that the three build over the course of a few years, with Trav the newcomer at the beginning of eighth grade.

Trav is a disturbed young man, and his problems reach a head when he is caught shoplifting. He is sent away by his parents, and when he returns he is greatly upset by a number of changes that have occurred in the town, among them the killing of Scotty, a family friend who owned a gasoline station. Trav gives his friends two possessions that he values highly, and then he kills himself, leaving his friends, his parents, and the town angry, guilty, and confused.

The issue of suicide is dealt with well, as are the other themes in this swiftly moving and poignant book. Humor and warmth temper the chilling effect of the suicide. Katey and Buck are bereft but determined to make themselves heard after the tragedy. They will endure.

386. Pevsner, Stella. *How Could You Do It, Diane?* Clarion, 1989 (0-395-15041-4); Pocket, pap. (0-671-70897-X). 192 pp. Fiction.

Interest level: Age 12+

The story begins five days after the sudden suicide of Bethany's pretty, lively, and popular 15-year-old stepsister, Diane. She has left no note explaining her decision. The family is shocked and devastated by the tragedy. Bethany is obsessed with finding an explanation for the suicide. It turns out that Diane had taken an overdose of sleeping pills one time, and her mother had kept it secret from Diane's father. Diane claimed that she was depressed but would never make that mistake again. After agonizing over Diane's suicide, Bethany makes it her mission to discover the real cause. She talks to Diane's friends and former boyfriends, gathers some clues, but finds no satisfactory answers. All of the family members are plagued with grief and guilt. The plot is intricate, partly because this is a blended family. Diane was the father's birth daughter; her mother and father were divorced. Bethany's biological father died; her mother and new dad were married when Bethany was about four years old and Diane was five. The two were best friends from the start. Two young children, Nell and Ned, are the offspring of the new couple. They, too, are distraught over the death of their half-sister, and their behavior deteriorates. Finally, after entering therapy, all of the family members are able to stop blaming themselves and each other and move on. The characters are well developed, and the plot is realistic and engrossing. The lessons learned here are that communication is important, that help should be sought as early as possible when a problem has been detected, and that it is important to move on with one's life, even after so terrible a trauma as suicide has occurred in a family.

387. Smith, Judie. *Coping with Suicide: A Resource Book for Teenagers and Young Adults.* Rosen, 1990, LB (0-8239-1052-0). 128 pp. Nonfiction.

Interest level: Age 12+

Smith, an expert on suicide and crisis intervention, begins her book with the story of a teenager who committed suicide, told by her mother. Then she looks at the issues: suicide over history, statistics, the legal issue, rational suicide, and dispelling the myths (all suicidal people want to die, for example). Theories of why a person would want to die are explored (for example, crisis theory). Other reasons for attempting suicide are also looked at: sociological factors, suffering a loss, depression, rebellion, low self-esteem, and loss of communication. Warning signs are carefully laid out.

The second half of the book, which makes this particular volume so unusual, is a manual on crisis intervention communication skills. Smith explains about feelings and their importance, letting readers in on the possible strength or mildness of each potential feeling. Exercises help the reader separate thoughts from feelings. Once that concept is grasped, the reader is ready to learn what a teenager can and cannot do: how to promote understanding in speaking with people who are in crisis and how to get additional help. Exercises help build up skill. A final chapter deals with surviving the loss of a friend or relative who has committed suicide. Each chapter has a summary, discussion questions, and references. Resource list, bibliography, index.

388. Thesman, Jean. *The Last April Dancers.* Houghton, 1987 (0-395-43024-0); Avon, pap. (0-380-70614-8). 206 pp. Fiction.

Interest level: Age 12+

Cat St. John's sixteenth birthday is marked by ecstasy and agony. She receives beautiful and exciting gifts, spends most of the day with Cameron, the young man she loves, and earns her driver's license. But this is the day that she lets her father know how angry she is at home; and this is the day that her father commits suicide. Cat's father is a shadowy character throughout the book. Together with Cat, the reader discovers more and more about him and about Cat's mother and grandmother. Cat also discovers more about herself as this engrossing, well-crafted novel unfolds.

One of the major discoveries in the book is that things are not necessarily as they seem. A number of mysteries are presented in the book; many characters are introduced along with their conflicts; no issue is completely resolved. The reader is not left dissatisfied, however. The ambiguity of the resolutions acts in the book's favor, because the reader is respected enough to work out the possible endings. For example, we know that the relationship between Cat and her mother is strained and volatile. We are furious with Cat's mother for pushing her out of the house after her father's death. The mother is afraid that Cat will become sexually involved with Cameron in reaction to her father's death. Cat's mother is also very self-involved, and she can't handle her own grief and guilt. But there is enough evidence of both Cat's and her mother's conscious willingness to change to indicate that they may be able to resolve their difficulties. On the other hand, we suspect that Cat's grandmother will never accept the reality of her son's act.

All of the characters are believable and interesting. Even the minor characters command our attention. Cat is a strong, intelligent, and attractive individual, and Cameron is a worthy companion for her.

The issue of serious mental illness is dealt with in the context of the story. No new information is transmitted, but the author clearly conveys the dangers of ignoring symptoms and creating a fantasy in which there is the pretense that nothing is really wrong. Cat's feelings of guilt over her feeling certain that she has killed her father are presented in an authentic manner. We feel with Cat, even when we know she is mistaken. Adolescent readers will take much from this book. It deals with many of the concerns in their lives.

389. Yolen, Jane. *The Stone Silenus*. Philomel, 1984. o.p. 127 pp. Fiction.

Interest level: Age 11+

Melissa adored her father. Now, a year after his death (probably a suicide), she still remains in the denial stage. She meets a young man whom she calls Gabriel, who believes himself to be possessed by her father's spirit, and for a while Melissa believes it too. The story takes us through

Melissa's near suicide and her memories and veneration of her father, to her eventual realization that Gabriel is psychotic and that her father is truly dead.

For Melissa, the most difficult task is to relinquish her romanticized vision of her father and to see him as the man he was. Until she can acknowledge his imperfections, she cannot accept his death. It takes some dramatic and dangerous encounters with Gabriel to finally bring Melissa to her senses.

Yolen uses her considerable poetic skill to convey to the reader the dual pictures of Melissa's real father and the idealized version that her father wanted the world to have of him. Melissa's mother colluded with him in his attempt to fool not only the world but also his own children. The message here is an important one, and it comes through to the reader by means of Melissa's awakening to the truth and her ability to bear it.

Death of a Parent

390. Adler, C. S. *Carly's Buck.* Clarion, 1987. o.p. 166 pp. Fiction.

Interest level: Age 10+

Carly's mother has died of cancer, and Carly blames herself and her father for not having been as good to her mother as she thinks they should have been. Carly asks to leave her father after her mother dies. She goes to stay with her aunt, her father's younger sister. Carly's home is in California; her aunt and uncle live in the Adirondack region of New York.

When Carly starts attending the school near her aunt's home, she finds, to her surprise, that she is having trouble making friends. She has always been a gregarious and popular girl, and she is puzzled and disturbed by her lack of success. She also refuses to have anything to do with her father, although she recognizes that she still loves him. She feels that his cold-hearted treatment of her mother is too great a sin for her to forgive. At last, with the help of her friends and her aunt and uncle, she decides to change her style of interacting with her peers, and she can begin again to build a relationship with her father.

One factor that helps Carly to change her ways is her preoccupation with a deer, which she hopes to save from a hunter's bullet. The father of her closest friend accidentally kills the buck, and Carly must cope with her own anger and grief over the death of the buck. Her friend helps her to see her father and herself in a different light, and the pain that has engulfed Carly for so long starts to recede.

Deer lore was carefully researched by the author, and its authenticity is one of the book's excellent qualities. Carly's pain over her perceived failure to be good enough to her mother is palpably described. We feel with Carly her guilt, as well as her disappointment and anger at her father. We also become involved enough with her to hope fervently that she will be able somehow to resolve her feelings and come to terms with her pain and self-hatred. Adler accomplishes these aims masterfully and engagingly. The book is a welcome addition to the literature on mourning and coping with the death of a loved one.

391. Adler, C. S. *Daddy's Climbing Tree*. Clarion, 1993 (0-395-63032-0). 134 pp. Fiction.
    Interest level: Ages 9–12

Jessica refuses to believe that her adored, lively, nurturing father is dead. Even his funeral and the comments of visiting friends and family fail to persuade her of the truth of this awful and sudden loss. It is only after making an odyssey to the family home they have just moved from that Jessica acknowledges her father's death and understands that she must adjust her way of thinking and living. She will be responsible for maintaining a balanced relationship with her mother and brother, and she will keep her father's memory alive within her heart and soul. The story is all the more poignant because, even though the reader meets him only briefly, the father's personality and place in the family are firmly established. Each character's individual perspective is well handled here, and the reaction to death-by-accident is accurately and sensitively depicted.

392. Boyd, Candy Dawson. *Circle of Gold*. Scholastic, 1984, pap. (0-590-43266-4). 124 pp. Fiction.
    Interest level: Ages 9–12

Mattie Benson, an 11-year-old black girl, lives with her mother and her twin brother, Matt. Her father died six months ago in a car accident. From that day on, everything changed in Mattie's life. Her mother is always tired and angry, having lost all interest in anything. Her mother has also had to work two jobs since her husband died. Mattie wants to help her mother and make the family happy again. She does the housework and baby-sits for extra money. She also works hard in order to win the local newspaper's writing contest on the subject of what your mother means to you. She reasons that if she wins, she can earn enough money to buy a beautiful pin for her mother for Mother's Day. Warm memories about her father help her through every hard time. Her best friend is also a great support. Finally, she wins the contest and buys the pin. Mattie's courage touches her mother deeply, and they become a happy family again.

The family's sorrow over their loved one's death and how they try to build a new life as a family are presented sympathetically in this book. The author tells the reader that death can bring gigantic sorrow to a family, but that the other family members can share love among themselves and try to soothe each other. It is unfortunate that so much responsibility is placed on Mattie's shoulders. Why isn't her brother as involved as she in helping out? What sort of relationship do they have with each other? It is not a good idea for a book to continue the myth that only females can be nurturing. Otherwise, the book succeeds in presenting the image of a caring family reacting to a massive loss with strength and dignity.

393. Brooks, Martha. *Two Moons in August.* Little, Brown, 1992 (0-316-10979-7). 199 pp. Fiction.

Interest level: Age 12+

A year after her mother's death, 16-year-old Sidonie, her older sister, Roberta, and their father are still disjointed. The father has buried himself in his work, often distancing himself from his daughters. Nineteen-year-old Roberta has overburdened herself by attempting to fill the shoes of her mother. She feels very guilty because she argued with her mother before her death from tuberculosis. Sidonie has become very introverted, but finally she tires of grieving alone and vows to bring the other survivors out of their shells. She arranges a reunion with her mother's sisters and acknowledges that long-term healing is a collaborative effort. The book is somewhat complicated by side relationships: between Sidonie and a young man named Kieran, whose parents were in an abusive marriage, and by Roberta's somewhat bumpy interactions with her boyfriend, Phil. The theme of mourning and overcoming one's grief is appropriately complex, and the author does a fair job of communicating this.

394. Clifford, Eth. *Leah's Song.* Illus. by Mary Beth Owens. Scholastic, 1989, pap. (0-590-42193-X). 112 pp. Fiction.

Interest level: Ages 9–12

Leah and her little brother, Daniel, rely strongly on each other after their father's death. Leah reads to Daniel and answers all his questions as well as she can. They sorely miss their affectionate, imaginative, nurturing father. Their economic circumstances and their emotional stability are shaky. The mother has moved them into a two-room apartment and furnished it with secondhand furniture. She sews for a living and has made the apartment as attractive as possible, but the stairways and halls are dark and the children are afraid to climb the steps alone. Their neighbor, a blind man, at first inadvertently frightens Leah, but eventually he gains her confidence as well as her mother's love. The ending, with Leah appreciating the new man in their lives, and the mother finding a new lifetime partner is romantic but satisfying. The characters must grapple with their real problems, and they solve them believably.

395. Clifton, Lucille. *Everett Anderson's Goodbye*. Illus. by Ann Grifalconi. Henry Holt, 1983 (0-8050-0235-9); pap. (0-8050-0800-4). 32 pp. Fiction.

Interest level: Ages 5–8

Written, like all the Everett Anderson books, in poetic form, the story takes us through the five stages of grief: denial, anger, bargaining, depression, and acceptance. Everett Anderson's mother is with him throughout the process, but she cannot help him actively until he emerges from his depression. She is always there to accept his feelings and to guide him to his next step, but he must come to the understanding himself that just because his father died does not mean that love dies.

Grifalconi's illustrations are enormously expressive of both the mother's and the child's feelings. This is a loving and helpful book.

396. DeFelice, Cynthia. *Devil's Bridge*. Macmillan, 1992 (0-02-726465-3). 95 pp. Fiction.

Interest level: Ages 9–12

Set in Martha's Vineyard, Massachusetts, the book centers on Ben, who has recently lost his father, and Ben's eagerness to win the annual Striped Bass Derby in order to break his late father's record. Ben learns that someone has been cheating and may unfairly win the contest. He is infuriated by what he thinks is a slur on his father's memory. Ben challenges the cheaters and risks his life to turn them in. This experience causes Ben to face some of his own resentment toward his mother, who seemed to be less affected by his father's death than Ben. Eventually, Ben and his mother each come to terms with the father's death and Ben is able to let go.

397. Dragonwagon, Crescent. *Winter Holding Spring*. Illus. by Ronald Himler. Macmillan, 1990 (0-02-733122-9). 32 pp. Picture book.

Interest level: Ages 7–10

After Sarah's mother dies, Sarah and her father spend time together walking, working in the garden, rocking on the porch glider, and, in general, helping each other to heal the hurt of the mother's death. Sarah's father is a loving and intelligent man. Sarah is a thoughtful and sensitive 11-year-old. Sarah and her father find the seeds and evidence of the next season in the midst of each current season, and they determine that, although they will always miss their loved one, they hold her in their lives and she will never be totally lost to them. The pattern of the book helps readers to see the cycle of grieving that Sarah and her father weather.

398. Fenton, Edward. *The Morning of the Gods*. Delacorte, 1987. o.p. 184 pp. Fiction.

Interest level: Age 12+

Carla Lewis has come to Greece to spend some time with her great aunt and uncle, who raised her mother. Carla's mother has recently died, and Carla needs this time to come to terms with her mother's death and her own grief. She is visiting the people who knew her mother best, and she wants to see and touch all the places her mother told her about as she was growing up. Carla becomes very much involved in the Greece of the 1970s, as well as the place that her mother knew and loved. And she discovers things about her mother that she had never known, such as the fact that she wrote poetry.

The political situation cannot be avoided because Greece is now ruled by a dictatorial junta. Carla helps to prevent the military from capturing a poet who is a national hero. She risks her own safety by doing so, but she is deeply gratified to have been successful. She returns to America, but only for a while. The next autumn finds her back in Greece, where she has made spiritual contact not only with her mother, but with herself. Fenton has done a masterful job of blending the setting with the emotional tone of the work. Carla's conversion is the reader's as well.

399. Fleischman, Paul. *Rear-View Mirrors*. Harper, 1986, LB (0-06-021867-3). 128 pp. Fiction.

Interest level: Age 12+

A cryptic telegraphic invitation begins Olivia's journey to meet the reclusive father she's never known. It seems he wants an heir, and Olivia is given the doubtful privilege of auditioning. Their visit starts with a volley of hyperarticulate one-upmanship-type barbs, he digging at Olivia's mother, Olivia digging at him. Bright high school kids—equally standoffish, cynical, and needy in turn—will appreciate the characters' glib tongues; they will also enjoy the inspired description ("legs stiff as beef jerky") and unexpected slapstick humor.

Olivia is a junior in high school when she hears from her father for the first time. Her mother and father were divorced when Olivia was eight months old, and she and her mother have lived in the San Francisco area of California, while her father has remained in New England. After all these years, he has written to invite her to come to spend the summer with him. She goes, and during the summer Olivia's father acquaints her with who he is, what he likes, and, especially, what he doesn't like. She also discovers that he feels that he will die soon, partly because his heart is weakening, and partly because of an inner contest he wages with death that he knows he will lose. Indeed, he does die, shortly after the summer that he and Olivia share, while he is fixing the roof during an electrical storm.

Part of the story is told in flashback, and part of it is in the present as Olivia returns to her legacy, the house and land that her father left her. She undertakes a ritual bicycle ride that her father used to do, with special rules and conditions. She encounters a number of obstacles, but she succeeds in completing the ride and upholding all of its conditions. She now feels that she can lay her father to rest and go on from there, the stronger because she knows both her parents, is like both of them, but has an individuality of her own.

The idea of a ceremony or ritual to complete the process of mourning is a valid one, especially when a person decides for herself what that ritual will be. The marathon bicycle ride is the symbol of Olivia's father's life and spirit. It is something that she can claim as her own as well, and it works well in this story. The first-person narrative is also effective. The book is unblemished by the intrusion of an artificial romance, and none of the characters is glorified.

400. Fosburgh, Liza. *Mrs. Abercorn and the Bunce Boys.* Illus. by Julie Downing. Four Winds, 1986 (0-02-735460-1); Dell, pap. (0-440-40154-2). 115 pp. Fiction.

Interest level: Age 10+

Otis and his older brother, Will, are close friends. They understand each other and are always in each other's company. Ever since their father died of cancer, and Bink, a beer-drinking construction worker, moved in with their mother and them, they have been unhappy and unsure of their mother's deep concern.

Bink has found a construction job in the Berkshires, so they all go there from their home in Ohio. The boys are at odds and lonely because their mother has taken a waitressing job. They are fortunate to meet Mrs. Abercorn, a lusty, hardy, fast-driving old woman who has made a good living as a mystery book writer and who opens her home and heart to the two boys. She teaches them to fish, lends them books, and takes them places. They spend every day together and grow to love each other. Mrs. Abercorn's son and grandson never come to see her; they are waiting to inherit her money. But she understands enough about human beings to help the boys see their mother and Bink in a more sympathetic light and to help them deal with their father's death. At the end of the summer, when the boys must return home to Ohio, they leave their cherished puppy with Mrs. Abercorn.

The book is very well written. The characters are appealing and three-dimensional. Their situation is realistic. There is much to be learned from each of the incidents that the boys and Mrs. Abercorn encounter, and the author builds each of their characters so that as the book progresses we get to know and like each of them more and more. It is to be hoped that we hear more about the boys and Mrs. Abercorn.

401. Garland, Sherry. *The Silent Storm*. Harcourt, 1993 (0-15-274170-4). 240 pp. Fiction.

Interest level: Age 12+

Alyssa has not spoken a word since her parents were washed overboard during a hurricane. Although Alyssa, then ten years old, had been with them on board their charter boat, she survived. Alyssa lives with her grandfather, a crusty Scotsman who yearns to return to his homeland to die. Her younger brother, Dylan, lives with their aunt and uncle in Houston. When her grandfather determines that Alyssa must join her brother so she'll be able to live in a more typical family structure, she is horrified. Her aunt is still grieving over the accidental death of her own son and so she overprotects Dylan. Alyssa tries to run away but is herself caught in a hurricane. She is aided by her new friend, Ty, whose sympathetic, friendly nature has drawn Alyssa out. She returns after the storm to find her grandfather near death. The doctors say Alyssa might help him recover if she will speak to him. This circumstance enables Alyssa to remember her parents' deaths and relive the situation that caused her silence. She manages to speak, and her grandfather eventually recovers. Like after a storm, the air has been cleared. The book ends optimistically, but it is not known whether Alyssa will remain with her grandfather, move to Houston to live with her aunt and uncle, or even relocate to Scotland. The reader is left with the distinct impression that no matter what happens, the family members have renewed their affiliation to one another and will survive. The trauma Alyssa suffered as a result of her parents' horrific deaths is over, and it is clear that healing has begun. The book is a plausible example of the extreme reactions resulting from the trauma of the death of loved ones.

402. Hathorn, Libby. *Thunderwith*. Little, Brown, 1991 (0-316-35034-6). 214 pp. Fiction.

Interest level: Age 12+

Set in the Australian Outback, Thunderwith provides an exotic locale for a story that rings true no matter where the setting. Lara's mother dies, and after a long search for her father, she is reunited with him and taken to live with his family. Resented by her stepmother, Lara is lonely and feels root-less. Her stepsiblings are wary of her, and her father is away much of the time. When Lara befriends a dog on one of her solitary walks, she finally begins to enjoy her surroundings. She looks forward to seeing the dog, whom she has named Thunderwith, and sharing her feelings with it. At school, Lara makes adjustments and begins to feel comfortable in her new life as her relationships with her stepsiblings gradually warm up. When Thunderwith is killed by its owner, a local teenage bully, Lara is devas-tated. However, this event serves as a catalyst to confronting her deepen-ing feelings toward her new family and to accepting their newfound love for her. She is particularly validated by her stepmother's admission of need, which has been stifled by her waspish personality. This is a many-layered book. The relationships are complex and imperfect, which is what makes the ending all the more satisfying.

403. Hermes, Patricia. *You Shouldn't Have to Say Goodbye.* Harcourt, 1982 (0-15-299944-2); Scholastic, pap. (0-590-43174-9). 117 pp. Fiction.

Interest level: Age 10+

Although dealing with the death of a 13-year-old girl's mother from can-cer, the author also deals with the affirmation of life. Love and courage are the themes here. While Sarah goes through the stages of mourning for the life she once had, her mother prepares her for the inevitable. Even after death occurs, Sarah's mother helps her by means of a diary that she (the mother) has kept throughout her illness. This is good fiction, told through Sarah's eyes and feelings. The plot moves quickly; there are very few flashbacks, which can be confusing to less able readers; the print is large; and there is enough white space so that the book is not intimidating.

404. Juneau, Barbara Frisbie. *Sad, but O.K.—My Daddy Died Today.* Blue Dolphin, 1988, pap. (0-931892-19-8). 112 pp. Fiction.

Interest level: Ages 9–12

Told through the language of nine-year-old Kelly, the book details the dying of Kelly's father from a malignant brain tumor. Dennis Frisbie was 34 when he died. His close and loving family did everything they could to make his last weeks comfortable. The book describes every part of the sequence of the father's illness and eventual death. Every aspect of his deterioration is included, even his loss of bladder control, but the book is not grisly or maudlin. The family is religious, involved with church, fam-ily, and friends, and very open in discussing and accepting the reality of the fact that the father is dying. The details of the funeral are included, as is the obituary, a particularly poignant addition, because the father's photograph pictures him as a handsome, affable-looking young man. The children are fully involved with all aspects of their father's final days. The book provides an excellent model of how to cope with the impending death of a close family member.

405. Krementz, Jill. *How It Feels When a Parent Dies.* Photos by the author. Knopf, 1991, pap. (0-394-75854-4). 128 pp. Nonfiction.

Interest level: Ages 9–14

Intended as a support for children who have lost a parent or who know someone who has, this book contains the experiences of 18 children, between the ages of 7 and 16, who have lost a parent. The stories, told in the children's own words, are honest and often moving. The children speak about their feelings about the loss and about how their families handled the experience. They mention some of the rituals associated with death in which they and their families participated. They discuss how they have managed to continue their own lives after their losses. All of the narrators are honest about their reactions to events that have been a result of their parent's death, such as the restructuring of their family through remarriage. As always, the author has captured the spirit of her subjects in poignant black-and-white photographs.

406. Lanton, Sandy. *Daddy's Chair.* Illus. by Shelly O. Haas. Kar-Ben, 1991 (0-929371-51-8). 32 pp. Fiction.

Interest level: Ages 5–8

Michael's dad has died of cancer. Michael makes a sign, placing it on his father's chair so that no one else will sit on it. The family comes to sit shiva (a Jewish custom of mourning for seven days) and tell stories about Michael's dad. Finally, Michael decides that he will sit in his father's chair whenever he wants to have special memories of him. The book respectfully describes Jewish customs of mourning. It is an honest, sensitive confrontation with death, simply told, but in no way condescending.

407. Lasky, Kathryn. *Home Free.* Dell, 1988, pap. (0-440-20038-5). 252 pp. Fiction.

Interest level: Age 11+

Fifteen-year-old Sam and his mother return to New Salem, Massachusetts, after his father's death in a car accident. He becomes involved with Gus Earley and the reintroduction of eagles into Quabbin. It is through this project that Sam meets Lucy, an autistic girl with whom he works to help overcome her handicap.

The book revolves around the theme of Sam's adjustment, not only to his life in New England, but also to his problems with life and death. It penetrates the mind and actions of the adolescent Sam and his discovery of the purpose and meaning of life through his relationships with his mother—who is struggling to recover from the loss of her husband; with Lucy—who has already died once from the cruelties she experienced in an earlier existence; with Quabbin Valley; with Gus—whose life is purposeful although he is dying; and with the eagles themselves. The reestablishment of the eagles becomes important and meaningful to each character as a symbol of faith in the future.

The book sensitively discusses the issue of death in the violent and untimely demise of Sam's father and Gus's slow, painful bargaining with death as he dies of cancer. Although both deaths seem to be final, the very existence of Lucy, and Gus's sitting on the hill after his demise, suggest to the reader that nothing is really final. Sam's father is very much alive in his continued influence on Sam's intellect and interests, and Gus's work will be continued by Sam and others in Quabbin.

Sam is portrayed as a compassionate and sensitive boy. He is able to see beyond Lucy's disability, recognizing that her spirit cannot be limited by the psychologists' tests and labels. He is courageous, can face solitude, enjoys hard work, and is able to plan and organize his own time. Although his father has obviously influenced his thinking, his mother's strengths are never belittled, even though he does not share her enthusiasm for restoring their New England home and finds it hard to relate to her family.

Sam cares for and communicates with his mother; each understands the other's grief but cannot penetrate or assuage it—each has to work it out alone. The eagle project and Lucy are the catalysts for Sam's self-realization and the reconciliation of life and death.

This wonderfully written story can convey to the reader a sense of the purpose and integration of life—past with present, nature with man, life with death—and is highly recommended.

408. Little, Jean. *Mama's Going to Buy You a Mockingbird*. Viking, 1985 (0-670-80346-4); Puffin, pap. (0-14-031737-6). 213 pp. Fiction.

Interest level: Age 11+

For the first half of the book, the story tells about Jeremy, his younger sister, Sarah, their mother, and their dying father. The father, a teacher, has cancer, and the children are not informed about this until they overhear someone else talking about it. In general, the children are excluded from much that goes on. They are not permitted to visit their father in the hospital, except for occasional Sundays, and then not for very long. Isolated and uninformed, they are, therefore, confused and angry about the whole situation. Once the father is hospitalized, he seems to be already dead, because there is no interaction and no real communication going on. Before his hospitalization, however, the reader comes to know him as a kind and thoughtful man. He gives his family some gifts that later become symbols for his presence.

After the father's death, the children, especially Jeremy, are required to take more and more responsibility for their welfare. They move to an apartment, and their mother goes to school to equip herself with skills to earn money. Jeremy becomes friendly with a girl, Tess, whom his father had especially wanted him to befriend. Tess's mother has deserted her, and she is an outcast in school because she looks, dresses, and behaves differently from the other children.

During the course of the story, the author deals with small losses of material objects and a pet. All of the lost items are found. When Jeremy finds it in his heart to give his mother a ceramic owl his father had given him, the message is conveyed that Jeremy has finally been able to accept the loss of his father and to share his memories and grief with his mother.

The support of other people is an important element in this book that deals with many losses, massive and slight. Tess cannot cope with her mother's desertion until she is befriended by Jeremy and his mother. Jeremy needs Tess's support. Tess's grandfather offers himself as a substitute grandfather to Jeremy and Sarah. They accept his offer, but Jeremy knows that although they are all a family now, it will never be the same as when their father was alive. He does not view a new "grandfather" as a replacement.

Little writes well. Interspersed in the story are references to other children's books, such as Kipling's *Kim* (Penguin, 1987), and Paterson's *The Great Gilly Hopkins* (Harper, 1987). The idea of using books therapeutically is accepted as beneficial here. The withholding of information from the children seems to be accepted as common practice, but the reader can certainly see the harm in it. And even though the mother offers the children the option of staying away from the funeral, they are wise enough to decline. The funeral, however, is not a personally tailored one; it seems to be a time of distress rather than healing. Children can be invited to discuss these problems and to come up with their own solutions. In general, and because the story is such a good one, the book is a good one.

409. Madenski, Melissa. *Some of the Pieces.* Illus. by Deborah Kogan Ray. Little, Brown, 1991 (0-316-54324-1). 30 pp. Fiction/picture book.

Interest level: Ages 6–10

To mark the first anniversary of the father's death, Dylan and her mother and sister travel to the river to remember him through stories and to sprinkle his ashes on the water. The stories continue as they drive home. Dylan recalls wrestling, skipping rocks, and sharing his dreams with his father.

At home, Dylan remembers how it felt when his father died, how achingly lonely it was. Dylan's eventual recovery, which he notes bit by bit, is helped by the rituals his mother has created for remembering. This book, with its poignant illustrations, is a treasure.

410. Martin, Ann M. *With You and Without You.* Holiday, 1986 (0-8234-0601-6); Scholastic, pap. (0-590-40589-6). 179 pp. Fiction.

Interest level: Age 11+

Liza's father has been told that he will die in the next six months to a year. His heart is failing, and nothing can be done to save him. The entire family responds by vowing to make his last days memorable and pleasurable. Their energy becomes focused on their last Christmas celebration together. When he dies, each of the family members responds differently to the loss. Liza, the protagonist, seems to be the most affected. She cannot visit her father's grave; she is angry at him for dying; she feels guilty about accepting invitations from friends because she doesn't think it's appropriate to enjoy herself. Further, she thinks that the other members of her family have forgotten their father and are not grieving. Once Liza realizes that her siblings and her mother are also mourning their loss, but in their own ways, she permits herself to accept the fact that she must, indeed, go on with her own life.

Martin realistically portrays a loving and normal family coping with an incalculable loss. The father and mother form a partnership to do all they can to prepare the children for his death. They do not pretend that there are no problems, but they try to create an idyllic time for everyone to remember. They try to ensure that there will be no guilty regrets later on.

But it is also made clear that no matter how carefully people prepare, the reality of this massive loss is larger than the expectation. The financial burdens and the pressure of time and obligations are difficult for everyone. Martin does her audience a service by providing characters at different developmental levels: Hope, the four-year-old, finds it difficult to believe that her father won't return; Brent, the eldest, must work hard in order to be able to afford to go to college; Carrie, the next oldest, baby-sits to earn money and plunges herself into activity so that she won't have time to think; the mother tries to pretend that she is stoic and strong enough for all of them.

Through constant communication and mutual affection, the family works out its problems. They make some hard decisions, such as moving from the home that has been in their family for generations, but they are together and they are functioning. The story is well written, realistic, and inspiring.

411. Mills, Lauren. *The Rag Coat.* Illus. by the author. Little, Brown, 1991 (0-316-57407-4). 30 pp. Fiction/picture book.

Interest level: Ages 6–10

The Rag Coat is the story of Minna, a poor girl from the Appalachian Mountains, who wears a homemade rag coat to school and faces derision from her classmates. When Minna's father dies, there is no money for a school coat, but the Quilting Mothers donate scraps for a coat modeled after Joseph's coat of many colors. In despair, Minna leaves school in tears, but she then seems to feel her father's presence as she recalls his words to her. She confronts her classmates and tells them the story of each piece in the patchwork coat, winning their admiration and feeling again connected to her father. Although the theme of this story has been heard before, Mills refreshes it with her detailed watercolor depictions of Minna and her coat. The children's change of heart seems realistic, and the message that family and friendship can flourish in poverty is well taken.

412. Oneal, Zibby. *A Formal Feeling.* Viking, 1982 (0-670-32488-4); Puffin, pap. (0-14-034539-6). 162 pp. Fiction.

Interest level: Age 12+

The title is taken from an Emily Dickinson poem that describes the feelings that come after great pain, until finally the person who is suffering can let go. The story revolves around 16-year-old Anne, who has so idealized her dead mother that she cannot tolerate the idea of her father's remarriage. Her mother died only a year before, and she resents the idea that her father has been able to remarry in so short a time. She is now at home for her first vacation from school since her father's remarriage, and she is cold and unresponsive to her father and her stepmother.

The real problem is that Anne has not yet come to terms with her mother's death. In the year that has passed since her mother's death, she has cried only once, and she is determined not to do that again. She and her brother, Spencer, differ over what life was like when their mother was alive. Anne remembers only the good; Spencer remembers more dissent and errors.

At last, Anne remembers how difficult life with her mother really was. She remembers the time that her mother left them and how she felt that she was to blame. She remembers her mother's insistence on self-control and no display of emotion. In the end, she can let go of her hurt and anger and begin to live her own life again.

Oneal's prose is crisp and clean. She paints images for the reader of the characters, the setting, and the emotions of all of the characters. We get to know and understand even the minor players in this drama, and they all contribute to the impact of the story. Anne develops important insights during the brief period that she is at home, and the reader knows that they will serve her in good stead.

413. Paterson, Katherine. *Park's Quest.* Lodestar, 1988 (0-525-67258-3); Puffin, pap. (0-14-034262-1). 148 pp. Fiction.

Interest level: Age 11+

The book's title prepares us for the actual and symbolic quest that Park, the 11-year-old protagonist, undertakes. Park's father was killed ten years ago in the Vietnam War. His mother refuses to talk to Park about his father or, indeed, even about his father's family. Park yearns to hear about his father. He longs to know about his own background. Park has always felt multiple loss, because not only is his father dead, but when his mother refuses him any information, it's as if he never existed. Paterson ably demonstrates what an error it is to try to keep the truth from children. In the end, the mother recognizes her mistake, which helps the mother as well as Park.

Ever since he was little, Park has actively fantasized that he is a knight who lives in the time of quests and daring, chivalrous acts. He plays out these fantasies in scenarios with courtly language and knightly deeds. He reads voraciously, mostly books of high fantasy.

Park has found a picture of his father in a book of poetry. He resolves to unlock the mystery of his father's (and his) identity, first by reading his father's books, and second by finding his father's name on the Vietnam Veterans Memorial in Washington, D.C. A librarian has told Park that people can be known by the books that they read, and he has seen evidence that this belief holds true. His father's books include all of Conrad's work, and when Park has read his way through his father's books, he goes to the memorial and does, indeed, find his father's name. This gives him the courage to confront his mother, who finally consents to contact his paternal relatives and arranges for Park to visit them.

During this two-week visit, Park discovers that he has an uncle and a grandfather. He also finds out, eventually, that his mother divorced his father after she learned that he had had an affair with a Vietnamese woman and that they had had a child. After this divorce, Park's father returned to Vietnam for a second tour of duty, during which time he was killed. The child now lives with Park's Uncle Frank, who has married the child's mother.

Park comes to recognize that he has been feeling guilty all these years for his father's death. But Park also discovers that his grandfather and his mother have also felt guilty about the same thing. Only when Park can ask the question of Parsifal, the archetype of grail-seeking knights, "What ails thee?" can he set himself and his grandfather free. There is also the hope that he can do the same for his mother. He has accomplished every knight's quest: He has reached the holy grail.

Religion plays an important role in Paterson's life. And her books reflect this religious and philosophical base in their ability to ask the deepest of questions and to examine the most profound of human emotions. They deal with issues of morality, life and death, guilt, and the way people choose to live their lives. Her characters are often called on to be more than themselves, to rise to greater levels than what can reasonably be expected of them. And they do. Park's quest is an individual one, but it echoes the search that everyone must conduct, for one's own sense of self, and the expiation of one's own culpability for the errors of the past.

414. Powell, E. Sandy. *Geranium Morning*. Illus. by Renee Graef. Carolrhoda, 1990, LB (0-87614-380-X). 40 pp. Picture book.

Interest level: Ages 5–8

Timothy's dad has died in an automobile accident. Frannie's mother has died after a long illness. Both children help each other go beyond their guilt and grief. This is not a great work of literature, but it is a simple narrative that accomplishes its intent of helping children to know that they are not alone in their mourning, and that "if-onlys" won't bring back people who have died.

415. Schwandt, Stephen. *Holding Steady*. Henry Holt, 1988 (0-8050-0575-7); Avon, pap. (0-380-70754-3). 161 pp. Fiction.

Interest level: Age 12+

Brendon Turner is the only person in his family who has not yet come to terms with his father's death. His younger brother seems to have accepted it almost immediately, and his mother—although she misses her husband, feels numb, and sometimes cries when she thinks of him—has resumed most of her usual activities. But Brendon has cut off most of his old friends and refuses to go on vacations. Now he has reluctantly consented to spend a month with his mother and brother at a remote island resort where they have gone before as a family and where his mother and father first met.

On the island, he meets Courtney, a girl to whom he is very attracted, and he meets a number of his father and mother's old friends. Over the course of the summer, he realizes that he is jealous of his younger brother because he thinks that his father favored him. He almost kills himself proving that he is brave and worthy, and he realizes that he has been a fool. His brother sets him straight about his father's true feelings—he loved and admired Brendon—and Brendon ends the summer having come back to a sense of himself and having forgiven himself for his father's death.

Other issues in the book include Courtney's father's alcoholism and Courtney's desire to have a good relationship with her father, who is divorced from her mother because of his problem with alcohol. A bully, coming of age, and ecology are also part of the plot, but the major theme is that of coming to terms with the death of a loved one.

416. Shusterman, Neal. *What Daddy Did*. Little, Brown, 1991 (0-316-78906-2); Harper, pap. (0-06-447094-6). 230 pp. Fiction.

Interest level: Age 12+

What Daddy Did is a story with a powerful theme that needs to be acknowledged as an unfortunate but occasional tragedy in our society. Preston Scott is leading what he considers to be an ordinary life when his father, apparently enraged by his mother's dating during their separation, murders her. Preston's father is ashamed and contrite; he is sentenced to prison. Preston and his younger brother live with their maternal grandparents and are bathed in love. When the father returns, the family must make adjustments to the situation. It is clear that, despite the murder, Preston truly loves his father and will work to make the family function again. The father is portrayed as a sympathetic character, yet the mother, who clearly wanted some independence, was loved as well. It is the grandparents— through their relationships with Preston, his brother, and his father—who model unconditional love and who hold the family together, even though it was their daughter who was murdered. Everyone in the story practices some denial, and this makes the story more believable. A jarring note occurs when Preston's father meets Sarah, a single parent, who clearly would like to marry him. That relationship seems doomed from the start and doesn't add much to the understanding of the characters or plot. Shusterman hints that this is a true story by giving information about "Preston" before and after the story. If Preston is a real person, he is a very loving young man.

417. Stevenson, Laura C. *Happily After All*. Houghton, 1993 (0-395-50216-0). 256 pp. Fiction.

Interest level: Ages 8–12

When Rebecca's adored father dies, Rebecca is stunned to learn that she must now live with her mother, Rachel. Rebecca has been told that Rachel deserted her when she was a baby. As the story unfolds, the truth emerges: Her father lied, kidnapped her, and used his influence as a prominent attorney to deny custody to Rachel. Rebecca must adjust, not only to her father's death, but also to an entirely new life-style with her mother. The author provides detailed and insightful portraits of each of the characters, even the minor ones. The issues of bereavement, sudden change, and adjustment to different people and circumstances are well drawn. The sub-plot of a foster child who is exploited and abused by his father adds to the fullness of the story. Although all is resolved in a rather neat package in the end, the resolution is believable.

418. Stolz, Mary. *The Edge of Next Year.* Harper, 1974. o.p. 224 pp. Fiction.

Interest level: Age 12+

A moving story of the devastating effects of a mother's death on her family. The husband becomes an alcoholic, and the two boys must try to fend for themselves. In the end there is hope that the father will recover.

419. Vigna, Judith. *Saying Goodbye to Daddy.* Illus. by the author. Whitman, 1991 (0-8075-7253-5). 32 pp. Picture book.

Interest level: Ages 6–10

In this realistic and moving book, Clare deals with her feelings of guilt, anger, denial, and grief after her father's death in a car accident. The day her father died, her mother and grandfather told her, very simply but directly, "A very, very sad thing has happened to Daddy. His car skidded in the rain and fell off the road. He hurt his head so badly that he died." There is no attempt here at euphemisms, and no one is blamed. The funeral process is explained in detail, and Clare is reassured that the other adults in her family are planning to live for a long time and will care for her. Clare experiences denial and anger, and she is supported by her understanding mother and grandfather, who give her her father's wallet full of mementos and periodically play with the dollhouse he built before he died to comfort her when she felt especially sad. The adults' behavior is a model of appropriate and understanding response to the death of a close family member.

Death of a Sibling

420. Adler, C. S. *Ghost Brother.* Clarion, 1990 (0-395-52592-6). 160 pp. Fiction.

Interest level: Age 10+

Jon-o, age 15, has died while trying to save a drowning boy. His adoring younger brother, Wally, keeps seeing and talking to Jon-o's ghost. The spirit of Jon-o urges Wally to become more outgoing and adventuresome, qualities that Jon-o enjoyed. Wally starts to behave like Jon-o rather than himself. He violates rules, takes risks that make him injure himself, and tells lies. Wally's mother is in a deep depression because of the death of her son. She has relied on him ever since her husband died eight years before. Now his death has made her so distraught that she needs her sister, Aunt Flo, to come to stay with Wally and her and oversee the daily running of the house. Despite Aunt Flo's badgering and his mother's tearful entreaties, Wally continues to behave as he thinks Jon-o would have, until he escapes potentially serious injury in a skateboard accident. He realizes that he can keep his brother's spirit alive not by being just like him, but by being himself and being as strong and loving as possible. The figure of Aunt Flo is a little too overbearing, but the characters' emotional responses are understandable in light of the enormity of the loss. Wally's behavior is believable, as is the visitation by Jon-o.

421. Alexander, Sue. *Nadia the Willful.* Illus. by Lloyd Bloom. Pantheon, 1983, LB (0-394-95265-0); Knopf, pap. (0-685-55461-9). 46 pp. Fiction.

Interest level: Ages 7–10

Nadia, a feisty Bedouin girl—called Nadia the Willful because of her stubbornness—is bereft when her father decrees that the name of his dead son, her brother, Hamed, must not be spoken. Nadia's father, the Sheik Tarik, is known as a kind and good man, but he cannot face the reality of his son's death, and he does not understand that silence prolongs grief.

At first, Nadia unwittingly mentions Hamed's name, because she notices that her brothers are making errors when they play the games that Hamed taught them. Nadia reminds them of the right way. She then moves on to share with the women, as they sit at their looms, the stories that Hamed told her. Once she begins, Nadia cannot stop. She goes all over the camp, talking with everyone about Hamed and her loving memories of him.

One evening, after Tarik has exiled a shepherd who said Hamed's name, Nadia confronts her father. She confesses to him that she has been reminding everyone of Hamed's life and thereby has kept his image alive. The sheik is moved and persuaded by her good sense, and he renames her Nadia the Wise. The shepherd is returned to the group, and Hamed is permitted to live again in everyone's heart.

The story is beautifully told, and the pencil drawings by Bloom add dimensions of flavor and emotion.

422. Ellis, Sarah. *A Family Project.* Macmillan, 1991 (0-689-50444-6); Dell, pap. (0-440-40397-9). 144 pp. Fiction.

Interest level: Ages 9–12

Jessica's mother is 41 years old and a successful engineer; her father has worked at many jobs and is now a cab driver, but mostly he stays home and takes care of the household. The family consists of Jessica, age 11, and her two older brothers, the elder of whom lives independently from the family. Most of the story tells of the happy anticipation and genuine pleasure the entire family experiences at the birth of Lucie, an unplanned but welcome baby. Jessica has a particular affinity for her new baby sister. When Lucie dies of sudden infant death syndrome, her mother succumbs to a "nervous breakdown" and the rest of the family becomes depressed. The minutiae of the funeral arrangements and the activities of the family after the baby's death make the sense of mourning all the more palpable to the reader. Little by little, the children and father support and comfort each other, and the mother begins to get back to her former tasks and abilities. The image of the collaborative family structure rallying around to help each other is sympathetically and realistically presented.

423. Grant, Cynthia. *Phoenix Rising*. Atheneum, 1989 (0-689-31458-2); Harper, pap. (0-06-447060-1). 160 pp. Fiction.

    Interest level: Age 11+

Jess's adored older sister, Helen, has died of cancer at age 18, and Jess is inconsolable. She has nightmares, feels physically ill, and finds it difficult to concentrate. A combination of a helpful friend's visits and reading her sister's diary finally helps her to begin to come to terms with her sister's death. The story details Helen's feelings about having cancer and Jess's extreme emotional response. It also reveals how each family member unsuccessfully tries to deal with Helen's death. This is not a comforting book, but it is a strong and compelling portrait of a family in crisis, suffering from an all too real, cruel loss.

424. Greene, Constance C. *Beat the Turtle Drum*. Illus. by Donna Diamond. Viking, 1976 (0-8446-6598-3); Dell, pap. (0-440-40875-X). 120 pp. Fiction.

    Interest level: Ages 9–12

"Nothing will ever be all right again," says 13-year-old Kate, after her 11-year-old sister, Joss, is killed instantly in a fall from a tree. Joss was a unique, gay, ethereal child—the family favorite, thinks Kate—especially devoted to horses. In celebration of her birthday, Joss accumulates enough money to rent an old horse for a week. Ironically, it is in looking after the nag that she falls and loses her life.

    The story is exquisitely crafted. Unlike most stories of loss, the character dies almost at the end; instead of treating the family's adjustment in detail, the author spends most of the pages creating a picture of the loving, warm family. In fact, in the end, readers are left at the height of acute grief—mother is looking toward pills for solace, father toward alcohol, and Kate is miserably isolated in her home. Yet the hint that grief will fade—found in the comfort of condolence, in overtures made by adults outside the family, and in Kate's expression of feeling in poetry—is enough.

Without equal are the passages in which bereavement is described. So few words are used, but those chosen are almost unbearably precise and sensitive, never hitting a false note. About the immediate shock: "I don't know how we got home, my mother and I. One minute we were in the emergency room at the hospital, the next we were standing in our living room." On the somatic symptoms of grief, as experienced by Kate: "My bones feel hollow with loneliness." And as experienced by Joss's friend: "Tootie was huddled on our back steps." On denial: "I imagine I can hear her breathing in the next bed. It's all in my mind. I know that, but I can't stop myself from turning on the light to make sure." Finally, the handling of unspeakable pain, when Tootie asks Kate if Joss knows how much she is missed: "I have to turn away and pretend I'm tying my shoe or something. I don't want him to see how much he upsets me." Also: "I weep inside my head." Each and every character in this outstanding novel is memorable.

425. MacLachlan, Patricia. *Baby.* Delacorte, 1993 (0-385-31133-8).130 pp. Fiction.

Interest level: Age 11+

Larkin is the narrator of this touching story. Her father is taciturn by day and mellow in the evening. Her mother is an artist who withdraws from her family because she cannot accept the death of her newborn baby boy. The whole family is wounded by the death to the extent that they cannot address their grief, and the mother, in particular, withholds her nurturing from Larkin. One day at the end of summer, a toddler is left in a basket, with a note explaining that the child's mother is entrusting her to the family's fostering for a while, until conditions improve in her life. Sophie's arrival changes all their lives. They love her so much that the thought of her mother's reclaiming her is a constant cause of anguish to each family member. Sophie enriches their lives, engages them all, and serves as a catalyst for their mutual affection and eventual understanding of each other's feelings. When the inevitable happens, and Sophie's mother returns and reclaims her, the family finally confronts the death of their baby boy. They name him, remember him, and mourn him. The author, with her distinctive depth of character and unusual viewpoints, portrays a foster family's challenge as well as the difficulty of transcending the tragic loss of a newborn.

426. Richter, Elizabeth. *Losing Someone You Love: When a Brother or Sister Dies*. Photos by the author. Putnam, 1986. o.p. 80 pp. Nonfiction.

Interest level: Age 10+

The grief of 15 adolescents is expressed in their own words. The passages vary in length, and the teens differ in their stages of bereavement and ability to verbalize agony, but the halting quality of their narration enhances the book's piercing reality. Their siblings have died from crib death, vehicular and drowning accidents, cancer, blood disorders, murder, and suicide. The person lost was usually a teen (in one case, a twin), but sometimes a younger child, toddler, or infant. Some of the deaths were recent, others many years ago. Regardless of the circumstances, Richter allows survivors to speak whatever is on their minds now. The composite, edited result is an unobtrusive, natural overview of likely emotions: fear for one's health, guilt at survival, abandonment, pervasive sadness or depression, the need to try to recover.

Except for recommending the sibling and teen groups of The Compassionate Friends (see Appendix under Death, Bereavement), Richter wisely doesn't give step-by-step procedures for that recovery. What she offers instead are the details other survivors and their friends want over and over again as reassurance that they're not alone: a father's scream on hearing the news, watching a crypt be sealed, having trouble falling asleep. As she did in *The Teenage Hospital Experience* (Coward, 1982), Richter provides one compelling doorway out of loneliness.

Death of Extended Family

427. Burningham, John. *Granpa*. Illus. by the author. Crown, 1985 (0-517-55643-X); pap. (0-517-58797-1). 32 pp. Fiction.

Interest level: Ages 3–8

Most of the book explores the loving and active relationship between a little girl and her grandfather. They garden together, play at make-believe, argue, go to the park and the beach, and go fishing and sledding. The grandfather reads to the little girl, tells her stories, and respects her questions and concerns. Then the grandfather gets confined to the house, and, ultimately, we see his empty chair and a sad, pensive little girl taking her baby sibling for a walk, and we assume that she will pass on to her sibling the love and companionship she enjoyed with her grandfather.

The text is sparse but evocative. The whimsical crayon-and-ink pictures have a spontaneous, expressive line quality and a childlike style full of action and texture. *Granpa* is a loving book to share with young children.

428. Gould, Deborah Lee. *Grandpa's Slide Show*. Illus. by Cheryl Harness. Lothrop, 1987 (0-688-06973-8). 32 pp. Fiction.

Interest level: Age 6+

This story will arouse memories and stir emotions in the many children and adults who fondly remember a family member, particularly a father or grandfather, who entertained them with slides of vacations and family gatherings. In this case, the grandfather, who has been the primary photographer and master of ceremonies for the slide shows, has died. After the funeral and after all of the well-wishers have left, the immediate family gathers around for a slide show of the miscellaneous vacations the family has taken. The slides and memories are cathartic for everyone, especially the little boy who goes to sleep and dreams of his smiling grandfather.

The brothers' reactions are depicted well. For example, Douglas is confused by the fact that his grandfather is dead, and, in his confusion, he acts silly. Later, he tries to grab his grandfather's image from the screen. The details demonstrate what children are likely to notice during a family gathering and throughout a family crisis. The author and illustrator demonstrate that rituals and happy memories help in the process of mourning a loved one. This tender and true book will be a treasure in many homes.

429. Hazen, Barbara Shook. *Why Did Grandpa Die? A Book about Death*. Illus. by Pat Schories. Western, 1985 (0-307-12484-3). 24 pp. Fiction.

Interest level: Ages 5–8

Molly has much in common with her grandfather: They both have dimples and enjoy pink lemonade, and they spend time in the park together. One day when she finds a dead butterfly, she asks her grandfather why it is not moving. He explains that it will never move or fly again because it is dead. They bury it.

The next day, Grandpa was going to take Molly sailing, but he has chest pains. He is taken to the hospital, where he dies. Molly denies this fact. She cannot believe her beloved grandfather is dead. Her father holds her and explains that her grandpa was old and could not be fixed up despite the best care. Molly wriggles away and goes into her room, where she feels awful and frightened, but she does not feel like crying. Her father reminds Molly that Grandpa was his father, whom he loved very much. He adds that he knows that the love between Molly and her grandfather was very strong. In these statements, he binds them all together with the enduring, common bond of love. When Molly asks why her grandfather died, her father explains that everything that lives must die eventually and that death is the end to everyone's life.

When Molly's mother later brings her some pink lemonade, Molly rejects it because she misses her grandfather too much. Her mother acknowledges Molly's grief and joins in it. She affirms that they can never see him again except in pictures and memories.

Molly, her family, and the many friends, relatives, and colleagues of her grandfather go to the graveyard, and Molly picks daisies for his grave. She still thinks he will return sometime.

As time passes, Molly misses Grandpa less painfully, but there are still reminders: pink lemonade, the leaves falling. . . . When school starts, she tells her classmates about her grandpa's death. That night, at last, she cries. By the next summer, when the flowers she and Grandpa planted are blooming, she is not as sad. As Molly grows up, she keeps her loving memories of grandfather and shares them with other members of her family.

This is an excellent book about death and grieving. It could serve as a model for all people. The information to parents in the blurb at the front is accurate and helpful. Euphemisms for death and dying are not used. Molly's parents are available to her and supportive of her feelings. The process of grieving, including the postponed crying, is quite accurate. The illustrations support the narrative. The expressions in the pictures complement and expand our appreciation for the feelings and content in the narrative. The notion developed in the last part of the book is important: Storytelling is a means of holding onto and passing on a family's traditions and connections.

430. Hesse, Karen. *Poppy's Chair*. Illus. by Kay Life. Macmillan, 1993 (0-02-743705-1). Unpaged. Picture book.

Interest level: Ages 4–8

Leah is constantly reminded of her grandfather's absence on her first visit to her grandmother's house since his death. She misses him sorely and has a difficult time adjusting to his death. She tries to avoid confronting the fact of his death by refusing to look at his picture, and she doesn't go near his chair. When she discovers her grandmother asleep in her grandfather's chair she unleashes her fears and confesses she is now afraid her grandmother will die. Her grandmother reassures her about the state of her health and her intentions, but she also warns that one day she *will* die and she helps Leah to deal with her feelings of loss and fear. Together they remember the grandfather and comfort each other.

431. Hickman, Martha Whitmore. *When James Allen Whitaker's Grandfather Came to Stay.* Illus. by Ron Hester. Abingdon, 1985 (0-687-45016-0). 48 pp. Fiction.

Interest level: Ages 4–9

After James Allen's grandmother dies, his grandfather comes from Massachusetts to North Carolina to stay with James Allen's family. He is a wonderful old man who keeps busy and is genuinely helpful. He detects when his daughter, James Allen's mother, is being patronizing or overly solicitous, and he puts things into context for everyone. Even though he tries to make the best of it, he misses his home dreadfully. And, perhaps even more, he misses his independence.

The grandfather lovingly builds a birdhouse that is a replica of his house in Massachusetts. When it is completed, he presents it to James Allen and his parents and informs them that he is returning to his home. He has made arrangements to have renters stay there with him so he won't be alone, and he invites his family to spend summers with him. His decision is based on his own needs, and he is caring and firm about it. There is no acrimony, but there is the ability to face the situation with dispassion and clarity.

The grandfather is an excellent model of a senior citizen who is not senile or infirm but is temporarily displaced because of the loss of his life-long partner. It is clear that his decision is a good one and that his life will continue to be a fulfilling, active one.

432. Jukes, Mavis. *Blackberries in the Dark.* Illus. by Thomas B. Allen. Knopf, 1993 (0-394-87599-0); Dell, pap. (0-440-40647-1). 48 pp. Fiction.

Interest level: Ages 8–11

Austin is a nine-year-old boy who has visited his grandparents every summer for a number of years. This summer, however, is different. Grandpa will not be there; Grandpa died. With constant reminders of what summers used to be like, fishing gear hanging on the barn wall, tractor sitting in the barn, Austin painfully remembers his grandfather. With his grandmother's help, Austin is able once again to take part in family traditions.

Jukes does an excellent job dealing with a child's reaction to death. She creates a touching scene in the barn that had not been cleared of Grandpa's things: Austin and Grandma hug each other and think back to the promise Grandpa made to teach Austin to fly-fish this summer. The stage of acceptance is portrayed by Austin and his grandmother using Grandpa's fishing gear and eating blackberries in the dark for supper—a family tradition.

Besides revealing the pain and joy of a relationship, Jukes also does a wonderful job of nonstereotypical writing. Grandma is not a feeble, broken-down woman dependent on her family to take care of her. Rather, she is old but spunky and capable of taking care of herself. She is willing to take on a grandson for the summer, fish with waders in the stream, and run the tractor to cut the tall grass.

433. Jukes, Mavis. *I'll See You in My Dreams.* Illus. by Stacey Schuett. Knopf, 1993 (0-679-82690-4). Unpaged. Picture book.

Interest level: Ages 6–9

A young girl is preparing to visit her beloved uncle in the hospital where he is dying. Her mother warns her about the unpleasant and even frightening scenes she may encounter and gives her the option not to go, but she is determined to say good-bye to her uncle. She prepares for the experience by imagining herself as a skywriter piloting her plane across the sky and writing her good-bye in the sky, adding the words, "I love you" and "I'll see you in my dreams." In reality she flies with her mother in a plane to see her uncle, not sure if he is aware she's there, but knowing in her own heart that her visit is important. The book is a tribute to the strong bonds a child can form with a beloved relative, and to the power of performing the ritual of a last good-bye.

434. Khalsa, Dayal Kaur. *Tales of a Gambling Grandma.* Illus. by the author. Tundra, 1991 (0-88776-179-8). 32 pp. Fiction.

Interest level: Ages 7–10

The author-illustrator has given young readers a colorful story about her grandmother and their special relationship. Her grandmother emigrated from Russia as a very young girl and settled in Brooklyn. She married a plumber and had two children. In order to supplement their income, Grandma learned to play poker. She won by marking the cards and hiding aces up her sleeve. In later years, after the death of her husband, Grandma moved into her daughter's house in Queens. This coincided with the birth of her granddaughter, Dayal (the author). Because both of her parents worked outside the house, the girl and her grandmother were always together.

Grandma's activities included sitting and knitting, telling stories, giving advice, and taking her granddaughter to Coney Island, vaudeville shows, movies, Chinese restaurants, and the Sunshine Ladies Card Club, a gambling club for the local elderly women. She also taught her grand-daughter how to play poker. One day when Dayal came home from school, her grandmother was ill. Then she died, leaving the young girl with her memories of a vibrant woman and a special relationship.

The beautiful color illustrations lend a kind of fairy-tale quality to the book. This is appropriate because the reader gets the sense that the grandmother was an accomplished weaver of tales, and that the book is somewhere between fiction and nonfiction and, therefore, a fitting tribute to this vibrant, warm, loving, strong-willed, and nonstereotypical woman.

435. MacLachlan, Patricia. *Cassie Binegar.* Harper, 1982 (0-06-024034-2); pap. (0-06-440195-2). 120 pp. Fiction.

Interest level: Ages 8–11

Cassie mourns for her grandfather and dreams about him all the time. She bitterly regrets her behavior the last time she saw him, because she yelled at him and didn't apologize when he asked her to. She thinks that had she apologized he might not have died. She keeps this as a bitter secret to herself for a long time.

To compound Cassie's problems, her family has moved to a place near the sea, where her father and brothers can fish and her mother can tend a group of cottages in order to make a living. The members of Cassie's family are all unconventional in some way, and Cassie longs for a more traditional sort of family, one more like that of her new friend, Margaret Mary. Margaret Mary's parents ask polite, dull questions; their house is very neat; and they use matching dishes at every meal. Margaret Mary wears matching clothes with matching ribbons and socks.

Cassie is a poet. She can express in writing some of the fears and feelings that she does not dare to express out loud. When her grandmother comes for an extended visit, Cassie is able, at last, to talk about her bad feelings, and her grandmother helps her to overcome them.

MacLachlan is an expert at character creation. Each one is unique, yet each carries a universality that communicates itself to the reader. The author respects her characters and their situations. She accords them permission to express themselves in deep and thoughtful ways. The reader benefits from the product of the characters' thoughts and from the questions that they ask. Often the questions are not answered, but they are nevertheless important to explore.

436. Pomerantz, Barbara. *Bubby, Me, and Memories.* Photos by Leon Lurie. Union of American Hebrew Congregations, 1983 (0-8074-0253-2). 32 pp. Fiction.

Interest level: Ages 5–9

In the foreword, early childhood educator Pomerantz says: "When children ask questions, they need answers. When children feel grief, they need comfort. When children see us mourn, they need our open permission to comfort us. When children are curious about death, they need to be shown the purpose of life." With these aims in mind, her protagonist, a young girl of eight or nine, tells the story of her *Bubby*, the Yiddish word for grandmother. Large photos illustrate the girl's memories: walking in the park, being hugged and read to, receiving presents, baking challah together, and sharing jokes. Then, "A few days ago my Bubby died." The girl relates what her parents have told her, among which are the concepts "It's okay to cry" and "Everything that is alive dies some day. That means old people and very, very sick people, and plants, and animals." Some may question limiting death to the old and sick and wonder if a qualifier such as "usually" would have been more courageous, but the rest is on target. The child then tells of her feelings and how her parents responded (for example, denial relating death to sleep, to which her father responds, "Bubby will not wake up again"). The child also shares Jewish mourning customs of the Shiva condolence period and the Kaddish prayer for the dead, and the book concludes with an honest appraisal of what grief is like and how we work through it: "Sometimes she feels lonely, but she remembers the things they did together and begins to feel better."

437. Rylant, Cynthia. *Missing May*. Orchard, 1992 (0-531-05996-0). 96 pp. Fiction.

Interest level: Age 11+

Aunt May and Uncle Ob have made Summer feel that she is a beloved part of their family ever since she was six years old. When Aunt May dies, Summer and Uncle Ob find it difficult to survive the loss. Uncle Ob retreats to his bed, goes on a spiritual odyssey, and ultimately decides to return to an active life. The author is good at creating characters with whom readers can empathize. The death is a difficult one to deal with, not only for the characters in the book, but also for the readers.

438. Thomas, Jane Resh. *Saying Good-bye to Grandma*. Illus. by Marcia Sewall. Clarion, 1990 (0-89919-645-4). 48 pp. Fiction.

Interest level: Ages 7–10

This book provides young readers with the anatomy of mourning. The mother, father, and young girl drive for two days from their home to the home of the grandparents in order to attend the grandmother's funeral. During the drive, the parents reminisce about the grandmother's characteristics and activities. They join their relatives, who greet them lovingly, but sadly. From the breakfast the family eats while they are in the motel, to the exquisitely painful, bittersweet memories each of the family members contributes, to the step-by-step progression of the funeral, the author's careful details help the reader to experience and understand the process of mourning and provide a model of interaction and conversation that are beneficial.

439. Tomey, Ingrid. *Grandfather's Day*. Illus. by Robert A. McKay. Boyds Mills, 1992, LB (1-56397-022-8). 62 pp. Fiction.

Interest level: Ages 7–10

Raydeen's grandfather has come to live with her and her family after his wife of 49 years has died. Raydeen's room has been relegated to the hall closet because grandfather now occupies her room. He never washes or combs his hair, and he stays in his pajamas all day. Nevertheless, Raydeen determines to help mend his broken heart. She is an optimistic, perky, constructive child, but nothing she does seems to pull her grandfather out of his deep depression. Even her idea of instituting a Grandfather's Day at school fails to draw him out. One night, when her parents are out and a storm knocks out the electricity, the grandfather does respond to Raydeen's cries for help, holding her in his lap and calming her fears. Realistically, this does not magically mark the end of his depression, but it does help him to improve, responding to Raydeen's questions about her grandmother and becoming a little less disagreeable and glum. He explains to Raydeen that just as she is afraid of storms, he is now afraid to be with many people. He declines her invitation to come to the end-of-school picnic, but he finally appears, and it looks as if his heart is somewhat mended.

Raydeen is an almost too perfect child. She does express some negative emotions, but essentially she is cheerful and sensitive. One wonders why her parents couldn't have found a better solution than making Raydeen live in a windowless room. It is also difficult to understand why Raydeen never got to know these grandparents. They lived far away, but it is hard to imagine grandparents not seeing their son or grandchild in nine years. Despite these flaws, the book is touching and demonstrates the deep depression a grieving survivor can undergo.

440. Whelan, Gloria. *Bringing the Farmhouse Home*. Illus. by Jada Rowland. Simon & Schuster, 1992 (0-671-74984-6). Unpaged. Picture book.

Interest level: Ages 6–9

The entire extended family comes together a year after the matriarch of the family dies to divide the material goods she left. They devise a plan of creating five stacks of things (there are five surviving children) as equitably as possible. They will then draw lots. They create the piles as a group, after having circulated around the house, locating their favorite items. Then, once the lots are drawn they barter for individual items they want. The child narrator has her heart set on her grandmother's quilt, but her aunt wins it, and won't trade it for anything but a platter with pink and red roses painted on it. This was her mother's heart's desire, and it was in the pile her mother won. To the child's joy, her mother agrees to relinquish the platter for the quilt. After every family member has amassed a collection to his or her satisfaction, the family members depart for their various homes, feeling that they have taken the farmhouse home. The nitty-gritty of dividing up a legacy is rarely mentioned in a children's book. This story invites readers to consider how they might have done this and to comment on how tolerable or fair was the process that this family undertook.

Death of a Friend

441. Bauer, Marion Dane. *On My Honor.* Houghton, 1987 (0-89919-439-7); Dell, pap. (0-440-46633-4). 90 pp. Fiction.

Interest level: Age 10+

A summer afternoon's escapade turns to tragedy when Tony, challenged by Joel to swim in the treacherous Vermillion River, drowns. After desperately and unsuccessfully trying to rescue Tony, Joel is overwhelmed with grief and guilt at the loss of his best friend. He fears telling the truth about the accident to his and Tony's parents. His father had expressly forbidden him to swim in the river. Joel concocts a story that hides his involvement, but he becomes obsessed with his guilt and, at last, confesses.

In this swiftly moving 1987 Newbery Honor book, the author explores Joel's dilemma with extraordinary insight and sensitivity. Joel perceives the world as a punitive one. He feels powerless to exercise control over his own behavior when Tony persuades him to disobey their parents' injunctions, and they go on a treacherous bike path. He then feels so frightened at what happened that he conceals the truth. He is angry at Tony for goading him into his behavior, and he is angry at his father for being duped into permitting him and Tony to go on their bicycle trip.

Joel is astounded when his father, on learning the truth, apologizes for misjudging the situation. Although this response alleviates Joel's pain, the reader cannot help but wonder when and how Joel will learn to take responsibility for his own decisions and actions.

442. Boyd, Candy Dawson. *Breadsticks and Blessing Places.* Macmillan, 1985 (0-02-709290-9). 210 pp. Fiction.
   Interest level: Age 10+

Toni has two best friends, Susan, who is flighty and fun, and Mattie, who is serious, loyal, and academically minded. Mattie is musically talented and knows that she must work hard to earn a scholarship to college, because her widowed mother cannot afford to pay tuition. Toni and Mattie want to get accepted to King Academy, an excellent public preparatory school in Chicago. Mattie's parents impress on her the importance of black people getting a good education.

When Susan is struck down and killed by a drunken driver, Toni is inconsolable. She goes through all of the stages of mourning: She denies that Susan is dead; then she pleads and bargains with God to make her be alive. She is angry at her classmates and her teacher for removing Susan's things from the classroom. She cannot eat or sleep. Mattie helps her to ease her grief by admonishing her to do the hard work of mourning for herself. When Toni conducts her own special funeral service for Susan, she is finally ready to come to terms with her grief and set about the business of her own life. At the end of the story, both Mattie and Toni are accepted into King Academy.

The book conveys an authenticity, not only of voice, but also of character, setting, and situation. The grappling that the characters must do over the death of people dear to them is a model for readers.

443. Carlstrom, Nancy White. *Blow Me a Kiss Miss Lilly.* Illus. by Amy Schwartz. Harper, 1990 (0-06-021012-5). 32 pp. Picture book.
   Interest level: Ages 7–10

Miss Lilly, an elderly woman, is young Sara's best friend. The two spend a lot of time together telling stories, gardening, and canning jam. One day, Miss Lilly goes to the hospital, where she later dies. Sara's family adopts Miss Lilly's cat, which helps Sara with her grief. The next spring, Sara visits Miss Lilly's garden and feels as if Miss Lilly is blowing her a kiss.

The relationship between the two protagonists is a wonderful intergenerational friendship, but it is strange that neither character seems to have any other friends. A stereotypical expectation is confirmed when the elderly protagonist dies at the end. Nevertheless, the story has substance and the characters are strong.

444. Clardy, Andrea Fleck. *Dusty Was My Friend: Coming to Terms with Loss.* Illus. by Eleanor Alexander. Human Sciences, 1984 (0-89885-141-6). 32 pp. Fiction.

Interest level: Ages 5–10

Benjamin, the eight-year-old narrator, describes in detail his feelings when he learns of the death of his friend, Dusty. He goes through the stages of mourning and discusses his reaction during each stage. He talks to his parents, and they respond helpfully and informatively. He never stops missing and loving Dusty, but he goes on with his life and remembers the good times he and Dusty shared.

Although this is clearly a didactic book aimed at helping children cope with the loss of a young person, it is well crafted and gentle in its approach. Young readers will identify with Benjamin's feelings and take to heart his message of permission to grieve and to mourn.

445. Cohn, Janice. *I Had a Friend Named Peter: Talking to Children about the Death of a Friend.* Illus. by Gail Owens. Morrow, 1987 (0-688-06686-0). 32 pp. Fiction.

Interest level: Ages 4–8

The first section of this sensitive book is for parents, answering questions about children's development of separation/loss concepts, how to explain death in general and particularly of a young child, and pitfalls to avoid (for example, comparisons with sleep, or a concept of heaven wherein the dead look over a potentially naughty child). Social worker/consultant Cohn stresses the importance of honest simplicity and describes children's emotional reactions, from the giddiness of anxiety to boisterousness and sadness.

In the children's section, Betsy, a child of about six, is told by her parents that her best friend, Peter, has been hit by a car. Her parents are attentive and models of what to say and do. "Peter was hurt so badly that the doctors couldn't make him better, and he died." Betsy wants to go to the funeral, so they describe the service and burial. Betsy shows the varied reactions likely: a stomachache, a bad dream, guilt about their fights, a short sadness span, and then back to grief. Her parents share their sadness, explaining that they, too, can't sleep. A lovely feature of this book is the tapping of a child's natural capacity and desire to comfort. It's not syrupy but real when Betsy offers to help Peter's parents, and when the children in school the next day remember Peter with discussion and drawings. The sad pastels heighten the emotion in this finely tuned, valuable book.

446. Deaver, Julie Reece. *Say Goodnight, Gracie.* Harper, 1988 (0-06-021419-8); pap. (0-06-447007-5). 214 pp. Fiction.

Interest level: Age 12+

Morgan and Jimmy have been friends all their lives. Their parents are close friends, too, and the two families are always together. Jimmy and Morgan love each other, communicate directly to each other, and depend on each other for support. They are both interested in the theater, and both experience setbacks that make them rely even more on each other's nurturing.

When Jimmy is killed in an automobile accident by a drunken driver, readers experience the sense of a genuine loss. This is no literary device; it is real. Morgan refuses to acknowledge her feelings. She is numbed by the extent of her loss. She cannot go to Jimmy's funeral or speak to his parents. She feels withdrawn from the world and thinks that she cannot go on without Jimmy.

Morgan's parents are very understanding. They permit her to stay home from school and to try to engage in theatrical activities, and they take turns sitting up with her when she cannot sleep. They finally take her to her aunt, who is a psychiatrist and who has prescribed tranquilizers and sleeping pills, but who now refuses to permit her to take any medication. She helps Morgan to confront her denial, anger, guilt, and fear. Morgan finally decides that she will choose life and try to cope with Jimmy's death in a more constructive manner.

Deaver conveys the sense of loss very well. Because Jimmy is so alive and vibrant, we commiserate with his family and friends when he is killed. We also respond to each of the characters in their grief. Deaver is adroit at describing the everyday events that affect a grieving person, such as the encounter with people who have not yet heard of the death or having to deal with disposing of the deceased's possessions. This novel is a well-crafted, moving story.

447. Kaldohl, Marit. *Goodbye Rune.* Illus. by Wenche Owen. Kane/Miller, 1987 (0-916291-11-1). 32 pp. Fiction.

Interest level: Ages 7–10

Sara and Rune are best friends, playing, planning, and imagining a future romance together. One day, not paying their best attention to Sara's mother's instructions, they venture too near the lake and Rune is drowned. Sara is blessed with understanding parents who try to help. She's filled with questions that might be expected: "Can I see Rune again?" "No, he can't talk to anyone, see or hear." But Sara discovers that she can remember Rune and see him smiling, just the way he always did. But when she remembers that she can never play with Rune again, her sadness returns.

Sara attends Rune's funeral, along with nearly all the townspeople. Later, when winter has come and gone, she visits his grave, where, her mother explains, Rune's body is slowly turning into earth. Despite the factual information, this experience brings Sara a great longing to have Rune again as her friend.

The author is a poet, and her collaboration with painter Owen is felicitous; the ethereal paintings demonstrate empathy with a little girl's needs. A flaw, however, is that Sara does not question her possible role in the death, although she was there and did not insist that Rune stay away from the water. This detracts somewhat from an otherwise masterful job.

448. Payne, Bernal C., Jr. *The Late, Great Dick Hart.* Houghton, 1986. o.p. 133 pp. Fiction.

Interest level: Age 10+

Dick Hart, Tom's idolized best friend, has died of a brain tumor at age 12. Six months later, Tom is still grieving over his friend's death. One night, Tom is taking a lonely walk to the town square when he meets Dick, looking as though he were alive. Dick explains that the world in which he now resides is filled with former residents of their town, all of whom have died, and all of whom have selected the age at which they wish to remain, no matter how long the passage of time. Thus, while Tom is now 13 years old, Dick is still 12.

Dick and Tom enter Dick's world through a special opening in a tree. After they have spent some time together, Tom becomes aware of the gap between him and Dick and the changed perception he is developing about his relationship with Dick. When Dick gives Tom the opportunity to accept a sudden, early death and to come to stay in Dick's world forever, Tom realizes that he must decline. He wants the opportunity to find out what his life will be in his own world. He knows that Dick's company is not sufficient for him any longer. He reenters the world of the living and says good-bye to his friend for what he knows will be many years, but he is comforted by the knowledge that they will meet again. Dick reluctantly returns to his world beyond the living, and the special exit that he used is closed forever by the One in charge.

The book invites a consideration of such philosophical issues as what happens to people when they die, and if there is an afterlife, what does it look like? Readers will undoubtedly ask such questions as "How did Dick get away with his escape and his bringing Tom into the afterlife? Where was God?" and "If all the people who died from this town were supposed to be in this small location, why wasn't it enormously overpopulated?"

Tom's supernatural encounter with his friend helps Tom to value and appreciate life. Perhaps young readers will also take this opportunity to look at their own lives. The author also invites a look at changes that occur without our even recognizing that they are happening. Tom tries to deny that he is taller and stronger than Dick. He wants to keep within himself the image of the friend who outshone, outran, and outsmarted him. This may lead readers to ponder the issue of friendship.

Payne deals well with the issue of coping with the death of a dear friend. Tom's mother is very understanding and helps Tom to name his emotions and to accept his angry and negative feelings. Although the book contains a number of logical inconsistencies, it is well worth reading because it is well written, contains an interesting premise, and will stimulate much thought on the part of readers.

449. Taha, Karen T. *A Gift for Tia Rosa*. Illus. by Dee DeRosa. Bantam, 1991, pap. (0-553-15978-X). 40 pp. Fiction.

Interest level: Ages 4–8

Carmela is delighted when her beloved neighbor, Tia Rosa, comes home from the hospital. Despite signs to the contrary, including the sad face of Tia Rosa's husband, Tio Juan, Carmela is sure her friend will get better and is determined to see her as often as she can. Tia Rosa and Carmela spend time together, knitting and conversing. Tia Rosa is making a pink blanket for her expected grandchild, whom she is sure will be a girl. When Tia Rosa inevitably dies, Carmela is grief stricken, but she is helped by her family. She is reluctant to see Tio Juan because she cannot endure his sadness. The story ends when Carmela sees Tio Juan and acknowledges her compassion for him. She decides to finish making the baby blanket for Tio Juan's new grandchild, Rosita. This is Carmela's gift to Tia Rosa. The relationships in this story, particularly the intergenerational friendship between Carmela and Tia Rosa, are warm, accepting and realistic. Carmela's refusal to accept the signs of Rosa's impending death rings true, as does her reluctance to face Tio Juan. The ending is pat, but satisfying.

450. Varley, Susan. *Badger's Parting Gifts*. Illus. by the author. Lothrop, 1984, LB (0-688-02703-2); Morrow, pap. (0-688-11518-7). 24 pp. Fiction.

Interest level: Ages 7–10

In poetic prose and illustrations reminiscent of Ernest Shepard, the story tells of Badger, who was much loved by all of the woodland creatures. He tries to prepare his friends for his death, but when he finally dies they grieve. During the springtime, Badger's friends gather and remember the kind and good things that Badger did. From cutting out paper figures to skating, from knotting a tie to baking, Badger had given his friends many gifts that they could now recall with love and gratitude. And whenever his name was mentioned, it brought happiness. That is a legacy many people would covet.

The book is helpful in conveying a process of preparing for death and in affirming the value of a life well lived.

Death of a Pet

451. Cohen, Miriam. *Jim's Dog Muffins*. Illus. by Lillian Hoban. Greenwillow, 1984 (0-688-02564-1). 32 pp. Picture book.

Interest level: Ages 5–8

After Muffins is killed by a car, Jim has a hard time dealing with his grief. He becomes withdrawn and pushes away classmates who try to comfort him. His teacher realizes he "needs time to feel sad," but this is difficult for his friends to understand. His friend Paul finally helps him to cry, laugh, and get on with his life. The text and pictures present a reassuring message that life goes on and that it's okay to feel sad in your own way.

452. Greenberg, Judith E., and Helen H. Carey. *Sunny: The Death of a Pet*. Photos by Barbara Kirk. Watts, 1986. o.p. 32 pp. Nonfiction.

Interest level: Ages 5–9

Sunny, Ken's dog, likes to nap in a sunbeam—hence, her name. One day, she doesn't get excited at the sight of the leash, and she's barely wagging her tail. She hardly eats. An appointment at the veterinarian is scheduled, and she is given medicine for old-age heart ailments.

Sunny dies while Ken is in school, and the photographs appropriately show him thinking of her while he has to be away. Ken's mother tells him with feeling, "I have some sad news for you. Sunny died this afternoon." Ken's emotions are shown well—he doesn't feel like playing. His friend Bill comes over to keep him company, an appropriate action for children who seem to be about age nine. The two friends talk about times with Sunny, and she is later buried in the yard. Other emotions and actions given attention here include dreams about the dead and imagining seeing the loved one. Another good idea is shown when Ken puts Sunny's leash and toy bone in a box and looks at them when he misses her.

In this story, boy gets dog in the end, but it's handled with understanding. Bill's aunt's dog has had puppies, and Ken is offered one. "I want Sunny, not a dumb new dog." But then looking at Bill's new pet makes him think a puppy would like Sunny's bone, too. This wise mother tells her son, "Getting a new dog doesn't mean you have to stop loving Sunny." And the new puppy is allowed her own personality, being named Lacey "because she chased his shoelaces."

453. Kuklin, Susan. *Mine for a Year*. Photos by the author. Coward, 1984. o.p. 80 pp. Nonfiction.

Interest level: Ages 8–12

Loss is preordained in this unusual book. Doug, a black labrador puppy, is meant to spend only a year with George and his family. Afterward, Doug will become trained to be a guide dog for a blind person. George is part of the preliminary training, getting Doug to be congenial and mannerly. This he accomplishes through pouring affection and good feeling onto the dog. The dog-boy duo is part of a project called Puppy Power, which places young pups with families through the auspices of the 4H.

The subjects of this particular book are doubly interesting. Besides taking on the training project, George is a foster son. Just barely a teenager, George has had three eye operations. He knows it is possible that one day he'll be a candidate for ownership of a guide dog. In a first-person narrative, Doug movingly tells of his training procedures, sharing his experience with others, visits to the vet, and more training procedures. Finally, there is the parting. Now that George is so good at training dogs, Yuri, a new puppy to train, arrives.

The Puppy Power project enables children to see that loss is not just a negative experience—rather, part of growing up. In loving the dog and then having to relinquish it, children have a counterbalanced experience. Usually, it is not a good idea to replace a pet immediately when one is lost. In this case, as the loss was inevitable from the start and part of a service venture, it seems entirely appropriate.

454. Pank, Rachel. *Under the Blackberries*. Illus. by the author. Scholastic, 1992 (0-590-45481-1). Unpaged. Picture book.

Interest level: Ages 5–8

When Sonia's beloved cat, Barnie, is killed by a car, Sonia moves through the stages of grief before accepting his death. The ritual of a funeral is comforting to her, and she plants a rosebush on his grave. When the family gets a new kitten, it is not used as a replacement for the cat, but simply as a new pet. Sonia loves it and allows it free run of the garden, except for Barnie's rosebush, which will remain his alone.

455. Rogers, Fred. *When a Pet Dies*. Photos by Jim Judkis. Putnam, 1988, pap. (0-399-21529-8). 32 pp. Picture book.

Interest level: Ages 4–6

Mr. Rogers discusses common feelings and reactions resulting from the death of a pet and encourages families to talk about these feelings. He is well aware of the developmental level of the child audience and presents his material with clarity, describing the process and stages of mourning and the rituals surrounding death. He avoids euphemisms and assures children that their feelings of anger, guilt, sadness, and acceptance are normal, and that in time, they will feel better. The photographs illustrate the feelings of the children and the parents' comforting behavior.

456. Wahl, Mats. *Grandfather's Laika.* Illus. by Tord Nygren. Carolrhoda, 1990, LB (0-87614-434-2). 32 pp. Picture book.

Interest level: Ages 5–8

Matthew and his grandfather spend a lot of time together playing with Laika, a golden retriever. Laika grows very old and sickens, and it is clear that she is not going to get well. The grandfather, as gently as possible, explains to Matthew that he will take Laika to the vet, where she will be given an injection and die. Matthew and his grandfather visit Laika's grave and mourn together. The book deals with euphemisms, the inevitability of death, and the importance of memories.

457. Wilhelm, Hans. *I'll Always Love You.* Illus. by the author. Crown, 1985 (0-517-55648-0); pap. (0-517-57265-6). 32 pp. Fiction.

Interest level: Ages 4–7

Elfie and her young master grow up together, but, as a dog's life is much shorter than a human's, Elfie grows old and dies when her master is still quite young. His grief over her death is ameliorated by the knowledge that every night he has engaged in a ritual of telling his dog that he'd always love her. And now, even in death he knows that his love will continue. He refuses an offer of a new puppy, even though he knows that Elfie wouldn't mind. He is not yet ready for a new pet but when he does decide to have a new pet he knows that he will tell the new pet every night, "I'll always love you."

The story meets many of the criteria that are recommended for helping children to cope with loss. The child knows that Elfie will not return; he is permitted to mourn, together with his family; he does not accept a new pet as a replacement for the one that died; and he takes comfort in the relationship that he had with his dog while the dog was still alive.

The illustrations admirably convey the sense of love and caring that the boy and his dog share.

Kidnapping

The bombardment in the newspapers and on television of stories of kidnapping has captured children's attention. They fear being kidnapped, even though the incidence is not terribly high in the general population. Recognizing that this topic, by definition, is frightening, authors should try to avoid sensationalism and lurid detail. It is less threatening to young readers when the motivation for the kidnapping is communicated.

458. Duffy, James. *Missing.* Scribner, 1988 (0-684-18912-7). 144 pp.
Fiction.
Interest level: Ages 9–12

Ten-year-old Kate has a history of wandering away from home. She lives with her mother and 12-year-old sister, Sandy. Their parents are divorced, and her father is an alcoholic. The story revolves around Kate's abduction by an emotionally disturbed man who has been watching Kate for a long time because she reminds him of his own daughter, who disappeared several years ago. His wife has left him, and he has fixed on Kate as the means of his salvation. He tricks Kate into getting into his car and holds her prisoner at his house. With the help of a woman who is a retired police officer, Sandy is finally the instrument of Kate's rescue.

The story is suspenseful. We get to know each of the characters very well, and, as in any good detective story, we are invited as readers to predict what will happen next and to imagine what we would do if we were any of the protagonists. The reader is also given some good advice about staying away from strangers, no matter what they tell you. Kate behaves in an intelligent way once she has been captured. She catches on to her sister's plan quickly and cooperates in her own rescue.

Although the book does not inform us quite enough about the background of the characters, enough clues are given for us to construct much of their history for ourselves. Why Kate and Sandy don't have friends is something of a puzzle; they are likable and bright. That they are from a single-parent family and that their mother works are not reasons enough, particularly because Sandy plays several sports. Kate's previous runaway escapades are not sufficient explanation either. Children might be asked what they would do to help someone like Kate, if they had the opportunity. They can certainly discuss rules of self-preservation when accosted by strangers.

459. Hyde, Margaret O., and Lawrence E. Hyde. *Missing Children.* Photos.
Watts, 1985. o.p. 112 pp. Nonfiction.
Interest level: Ages 11–16

Who are the missing? They are runaways, victims of parental abduction, victims of stranger abduction, and lost children. This book explores the attempts to find such children and such problems as a lack of cooperation among agencies involved. The Hydes evaluate changing attitudes toward these problems from colonial times until the present. Case studies punctuate the narration and point up the use of such community social tools as hot lines and shelters. Causes of runaways and family abductions are looked at in depth, with ample attention to the psychological impact on a child. Likewise, profiles of various strangers who might abduct a child are helpful (pedophiles, childless psychotics, profiteers involved in pornography and sex rings, serial murderers). From this book, readers can learn of common lures used by child abductors (asking for help, saying a parent is hurt, and so on) and ways to thwart would-be assailants.

Such controversial issues as fingerprinting programs are discussed, as are the efforts of such individuals as the families of Etan Patz and Adam Walsh, the latter being influential in having the Missing Children Act enacted into law. This very helpful, informative book ends with programs and legislation designed to get at the heart of the problem, including a section on how teens can help in their schools. An appendix of resources includes hot lines, action agencies, and organizations that assist. Bibliography.

460. Marsano, William. *The Street Smart Book: How Kids Can Have Fun and Stay Safe!* Illus. by Richard White. Messner, 1985. o.p. 80 pp. Nonfiction.

Interest level: Ages 8–12

A serious book about a most serious subject: kidnapping. The author respectfully addresses children who are on their own for the first time in playgrounds, malls, school yards, and elsewhere. Marsano explains that there are several types of kidnappers (noncustodial relatives, people who actually like children and neurotically act out their need for a child, strangers who want a ransom and endanger life, and child molesters). He then alerts children to tips for staying safe (keeping eyes open, being especially careful on stairways, not emblazoning one's name on clothing, and so on). A section tells a child how to get away if he or she feels in imminent danger (whom to tell, how to tell, the value of noise, and so forth). The book concludes with several stories of children who found themselves in danger and what they did. Appended resources include the FBI and various missing-children's bureaus.

461. Martin, Ann M. *Missing since Monday.* Holiday, 1986 (0-8234-0626-1); Scholastic, pap. (0-590-43136-6). 165 pp. Fiction.

Interest level: Age 11+

Courtenay, the four-year-old half-sister of Maggie and Mike, has disappeared. She was in her older siblings' care because their parents were away on vacation. The rest of the book describes the search for the little girl. Along the way, we meet other characters and learn of Maggie and Mike's mother, who was not granted visitation rights after her divorce from their father.

It turns out that Maggie and Mike's mother was the person who kidnapped Courtenay. She did not harm the child, but she is a disturbed woman who needs extensive psychiatric treatment. There were hints that she might have been the one who took Courtenay, so it was not an enormous shock when this turned out to be the case.

Included in the narrative is a set of instructions of what to do if a child is missing and what to do to prepare children to protect themselves from would-be kidnappers. The book is a good blend of story and information.

462. Morris, Judy K. *The Crazies and Sam.* Viking, 1983. o.p. 136 pp. Fiction.

Interest level: Age 10+

Sam, who has been living with his father since his parents' divorce, feels both neglected and overorganized through lists, schedules, and routines by his protective but busy father. He has little contact with his mother, but he loves and admires his adventurous and high-spirited Aunt Kristen. He has a friend, a Burmese boy who is an expert artist and reckless cyclist. Sam often has the urge to follow the "crazies" (the tramps, homeless, and mentally ill people). Sam considers himself somewhat crazy, too, and he is fascinated by what he perceives to be their freedom.

Disappointed at being left alone one Saturday, Sam hitches a ride with a "crazy" lady who takes him to her small apartment. He enjoys her erratic and eccentric behavior, until it dawns on him that she intends to keep him. He uses his wits to free himself. Through this traumatic experience, he comes to understand the true strength and value of his father's love and the real meaning of freedom.

Sam is a casualty of divorce. His mother is too busy with her job to maintain contact with him. Although Sam's father is sensitive to the problems of being a single parent—he makes a genuine effort to create a healthy and efficiently organized environment for his son by joining a food co-op and planning nutritious meals, in addition to maintaining his job outside the home—Sam resents his father's "mental notepad" and misses the element of mothering that his father cannot supply. The end of the story provides no panacea, but Sam's father does promise to try to be home more on weekends, and Sam realizes that he cannot force his mother to be something she isn't.

Judy K. Morris brings to the readers' attention some problems of single parenthood that are as much societal as personal, and she presents the issues well.

463. Rardin, Susan Lowry. *Captives in a Foreign Land*. Houghton, 1984. o.p. 218 pp. Fiction.

Interest level: Age 12+

An important conference on nuclear arms control is being held in Rome, Italy. While the adults are meeting, the families of the delegates tour the city. An Islamic group takes some of the American children hostage to try to force a ban on nuclear arms. They take the children to a desert hideout in the Middle East, and the children are kept there until they are rescued.

The author vividly reflects the children's fears and responses while they are being held captive. She also describes, somewhat less clearly, the people who took the children hostage. The children are treated in a more humane manner than they expect, and it is through the children's efforts that one of their group manages to be brought out of captivity and tells where the rest of the children are being held.

The book succeeds best when it describes the children's reactions. It is well paced and transmits suspense to the reader. It is not as successful in conveying its message of antinuclear idealism. The children's message to the world and the Islamic group's supposed idealism deteriorate to slogans and rhetoric, noble though the intent is.

464. Sebestyen, Ouida. *The Girl in the Box*. Little, Brown, 1989 (0-316-77935-0). 166 pp. Fiction.

Interest level: Age 12+

Jackie has been kidnapped and tossed in a cellar. She has no idea why she has been abducted, although she speculates as to possible reasons. It is clear that Jackie comes from a loving though economically struggling family, and she worries about their reaction to her kidnapping. She also wonders about what effect her abduction will have on her former best friend, April. Because Jackie was carrying her typewriter and some paper when she was kidnapped, she is able to write about her experiences in the dark hole. In addition to letters to her parents, the police, and strangers who might help her, Jackie also writes a story about herself, April, and Zach, a boy who had become close to both girls, that reveals why the trio ended their friendship. Jackie writes very dramatically about her efforts to survive in the "box"; her descriptions about bodily functions and food and water rationing are graphic yet effective. Sebestyen is a compelling writer, but unfortunately, the reader never learns what ultimately happens to Jackie. We can assume that Jackie is rescued; her written chronicle of events is organized as she has promised it would be if she survives. Still, this disturbing element mars an otherwise powerful book.

465. Thesman, Jean. *Rachel Chance.* Houghton, 1992 (0-395-50934-3). 175 pp. Fiction.

Interest level: Ages 10–12

Rachel Chance is a feisty 15-year-old whose brother, Rider, has been kid-napped. Rider is an adorable toddler, and Rachel has great affection for him. She suspects the revivalists who had been camped in town are responsible, but she knows she is up against insurmountable odds. Her family is poor, and many townspeople are disdainful of the Chances. The preacher holds a grudge against the family. Her mother is so distraught over the loss that she is unable to help. Rachel enlists the aid of Druid Annie, a matriarchal figure; her elderly grandfather; and Hank, a hired hand. They manage to track down Rider and return home with him. Although the storyline seems somewhat melodramatic, the action is believable and the conclusion is satisfying.

Chronic or Serious Illness

Miraculous cures are devices for avoiding the issues attendant upon chronic and serious illness. They usually signal the author's inability to resolve the plot in a believable fashion. Research findings, medical vocab-ulary, and treatment should be accurate for the time depicted in the book. People, rather than the illness, should be the focus. Characters should be well rounded, whether or not they are ill, and the illness should be pre-sented as a facet of their characterization.

General

466. Bernstein, Joanne E., and Bryna J. Fireside. *Special Parents, Special Children.* Photos by Michael J. Bernstein. Whitman, 1991 (0-8075-7559-3). 64 pp. Nonfiction.

Interest level: Ages 8–10

The stories of four families in which one or both parents have special needs are told here. John Kavanaugh is blind; Bob Holdsworth uses a wheelchair because his legs are paralyzed, the result of a mysterious virus. Connie and Bob Rigert are achondroplastic dwarfs, and Carmen and Bob Stewart are deaf. All of the families function well and do all of the typical things that families do: they go on outings, participate in sports activities, and talk to each other about their circumstances and their feelings. Unkind or ignorant remarks from strangers are discussed, and each family has its own way of dealing with these. The black-and-white photographs add personalizing detail to the text.

467. Frandsen, Karen G. *I'd Rather Get a Spanking Than Go to the Doctor.* Illus. by the author. Childrens, 1987 (0-516-03498-7); pap. (0-516-43498-5). 32 pp. Fiction.

Interest level: Ages 3–8

With a snappy title like this, the choice of cartoons to illustrate one little girl's feelings is not surprising and right on target. She's too busy to get her shots, and besides, she doesn't need them. (As she says this, her back is to her mother and the reading audience—she wants nothing to do with this business, but all the while she's adding humor and helping kids who see her laugh at themselves.) Other tactics include feigning illness, getting busy with chores, crying, wanting ice cream to feel better, even asking for the titled spanking instead. Finally, they get in the car to go, and she is still crying. The doctor says "Hi" and that she's getting big. Too big for shots, perhaps, she muses. Then the doctor (unseen on the pages, by the way) distracts her by asking her to count the balloons on the wall. It's over in a flash and then, probably, they are off for the ice cream that the little girl had asked for. Different and effective.

468. Kosof, Anna. *Why Me? Coping with Family Illness.* Watts, 1986. o.p. 96 pp. Nonfiction.

Interest level: Age 11+

A serious illness is a family affair, says the author, a writer with an anthropology background. Through firsthand stories of adults and children, Kosof explores the world of cancer and heart patients, accident victims, and those born with birth defects, such as spina bifida. The emphasis is on coping mechanisms, which are spelled out—overcompensation, intellectualization, anger, and so forth. In each case, we are brought into the family of the ill adult or child, with opinions expressed by all involved. The changes in daily routines are discussed (extra chores, perhaps) as well as the more emotional, internal changes. The lesson chronically ill people have learned—how to be encouraged and live one day at a time—comes up time and again in the book, in varied forms as the cases differ. Each person in the book has changed as a result of the illness, and the doctors have changed as well. Highly readable and not at all depressing, this book wisely recommends honesty, keeping everyone informed, and considering emotional as well as physical needs. Index.

469. Krementz, Jill. *How It Feels to Fight for Your Life*. Photos by the author. Little, Brown, 1991 (0-316-50364-9). 132 pp. Nonfiction.

Interest level: Ages 9–12

The author focuses here not on children who are dying, but rather on those who are dealing with a special kind of adversity in a non-self-pitying, courageous, and graceful way. At least one million children in the United States today have illnesses severe enough to require lengthy hospitalization or that interfere on a regular basis with the child's usual activities. The children's conditions vary from heart malformations, cancer, spina bifida, anemia, arthritis, asthma, kidney failure, diabetes, and conditions caused by serious spinal damage. Each child tells his or her story, with details of the condition, treatment, and aftermath. Family members are important to these children, and some of them greatly help the children tolerate the sometimes awful pain of their condition and its treatment. Social interactions often become uncomfortable, which is where friends and family can be of great help. The photographs help make this book a very personal one, in which the reader becomes closely acquainted with each child.

470. Kuklin, Susan. *When I See My Doctor*. Photos by the author. Bradbury, 1988 (0-02-751232-0). 32 pp. Nonfiction.

Interest level: Ages 4–7

Full, happy color accentuates the first-person account of a four-year-old named Thomas, a child of Asian background who, with longish hair, doesn't clearly look like a boy. He also has a Caucasian mother. One wonders why this very accomplished author-photographer added extraneous issues such as adoption to the content of the book. On the one hand, by having interracial families merely an incidental fact, it does reinforce the idea that families come in all flavors—see, no big deal. On the other hand, it might take interest away from the action. Let the reader decide!

On to the real action: Thomas does the talking about procedures involved in his checkup, but somehow he sounds like his mother, using sentences such as: "A fresh sheet is put down for the next patient." Few preschoolers would speak in this manner. Nevertheless, the book is extremely pleasing visually, and new instruments (lancet and hemoglobinometer) are given pictorial insets with pronunciation guides alongside. Dr. Mitchell is a most considerate doctor, warming up the stethoscope and taking other steps to make Thomas comfortable. Most important, Kuklin has Thomas explain the purpose of doctors' strange behavior—why they feel for bumps, and so on. If one gets beyond a little boy talking alternately in four-year-old sentences and mouthing the words of an older speaker, this is a book of great value.

471. Lee, Sally. *Donor Banks: Saving Lives with Organ and Tissue Transplants.* Photos. Watts, 1986 (0-531-10475-3). 96 pp. Nonfiction.
     Interest level: Ages 10–14

Broader than blood donor banks in scope, this book covers bone, corneas, skin, hearts, and other organs as well. In order to put in perspective the computerized networks that track, record, and bring substitute materials to needy patients, Lee first explains a bit about cell theory to show why substitutes can work when needed. With this in mind, the modern-day magic becomes more understandable—for example, why cadaver bone can be inserted, then disappear after serving as a framework for new bone to grow into. For each type of donation, the process is detailed—with blood, from donor's decision through tests, identification, receiving, and transmission to a recipient. Specifics related to donation type are discussed, such as questions about AIDS as related to blood donation. This is an entry in the First Book series; technical words are printed in boldface.

Lee describes the astounding opportunities in today's medical field very dramatically: On a small level, readers learn that the temporal bone can help people with hearing or balance problems; looking at the larger picture, a harvest of organs can take place—one person's organs can benefit four people. The delicate care taken in preserving organs is discussed, as are controversies (sale of organs, animal experimentation, and levels of consent, for example). Photographs are dull in color but interesting in content (for example, rows of bones in differing sizes).

Lee ends with a plea for organ donation. Lee's dramatic details make the book work, so young readers will remember to plan for donation when they grow older and will talk to their parents, too. When Mary, going blind before her transplant, must bring her children to neighbors for care, they will grasp her need and the miracle that donor banks perform. List of organizations, glossary, index.

472. LeShan, Eda. *When a Parent Is Very Sick.* Little, Brown, 1986 (0-316-52162-0). 112 pp. Nonfiction.
     Interest level: Age 8+

With a warmhearted arrow right to children's hearts, LeShan gives them license to feel and encouragement to talk when faced with the confusion of parental illness. Knowing that angry, worried questions of "Who will take care of me?" predominate, LeShan clears the air about common happenings in families inexorably altered by accidents, cancer, heart disease, multiple sclerosis, and other sudden, chronic, or degenerative illnesses.

Events include being scapegoated, having less money, school failure, and feeling shunted aside. Unafraid to look at both sides of the issue—recovery *and* death—LeShan also relates likely consequences for children who are only children or from single-parent homes. Her belief that feelings have an impact on the immune system (perhaps influenced by the work of her psychologist husband, Lawrence LeShan, who works with cancer patients) is interesting, albeit controversial. Parents should model the conversational style of most of the adults in the book—they are ingenious, understanding, and helpful people.

473. Levine, Saul, and Kathleen Wilcox. *Dear Doctor.* Lothrop, 1987, LB (0-688-07094-9); pap. (0-688-07095-7). 256 pp. Nonfiction.

Interest level: Age 12+

A compendium of advice by two Toronto physicians, one a psychiatrist with a newspaper column for youth, the other a specialist in adolescent medicine. Taking turns and giving lengthy responses, Levine and Wilcox air rather complex problems concerning physiology, growth and development, sex and sexuality, schooling, relationships, family life and problems, drug abuse, and psychological difficulties. Each chapter begins with an antiquated, now amusing quote from a guidebook used in the late 1800s. The doctors are strongest on the physical questions; on psychiatric issues, they are highly sympathetic, but they occasionally don't look deeply enough at causes, skip steps, or don't provide enough specific advice. In one case, a boy who has humiliated his younger, handicapped brother and regrets it is told by the authors to apologize and that his brother needs help. Where is the help for the older boy in terms of understanding why he may have laughed at the handicap? In another example, a girl who has been "flogged" during much of her growing up complains she's too shy to get medical help with the scars on her legs. The answer assumes she may be able to approach her parents, which may not be so.

On balance, though, *Dear Doctor* is a solid piece of work that will be consulted often. Its encyclopedic nature allows for exploring many concerns not found in other books, from meeting potential stepparents to morning-after pills. The nitty-gritty answers found here are needed.

474. Rogers, Fred. *Going to the Doctor.* Photos by Jim Judkis. Putnam, 1986 (0-399-21298-1). Nonfiction.

Interest level: Ages 2–6

Part of the Mister Rogers' Neighborhood First Experience series, this book centers on young patients visiting two doctors—a black male and a white female. Starting with the premise that there are many ways parents help children take care of themselves, the narrative moves into the health sphere by discussing doctors. Doctors were once children themselves, Rogers tells his young audience. "They grew up and wanted to help take care of people." Covering where doctors work—offices, clinics, emergency rooms—the clear, sharp, easy-to-read photos then bring us into the waiting room (realistically crowded) and office, showing such instruments as the stethoscope.

Rogers brings to the action his usual understanding of children's notions—for example, regarding the stethoscope, the doctor can "look and listen, but can't see or hear what you're thinking or feeling." A lovely feature is Rogers's attention to the often unexplained. In doing so, he gives parents words. An example is the explanation of why we get undressed at the doctor's. "Doctors need to make sure children's bodies are healthy all over." Now, how often does that go unspoken! Rogers encourages children to ask questions of their doctors and parents and to use the real and play tools to explore their functions and have dramatic play.

475. Wolfe, Bob, and Diane Wolfe. *Emergency Room.* Photos by Bob Wolfe. Carolrhoda, 1983. o.p. 40 pp. Nonfiction.

Interest level: Ages 6–10

Captioned black-and-white photographs show the busyness of the emergency room (E.R.). In this visit, the staff is delineated and a potential registrant is shown the E.R. process with the explanation: "Long waits are common here since more serious cases are taken care of first and may require a lot of time, so don't think that you have been forgotten." Sample cases include Scott, an elementary schoolchild who fell from a tree, injuring his wrist; Joel, a teen who broke his finger in karate class; toddler Mike, who needs stitches over his eye after a cut suffered in a fall; grade school student Denise, who has a high fever; a girl a little older, Gretchen, who has burned herself on a barbecue grill. Each is shown according to his or her needs: an X-ray for Scott and Joel, a throat culture and other examination for Denise, bandages for Gretchen, a restraining board for screaming Mike so he can be sewn up. (His stitching process is shown in steps, too.) There is an adult, as well—a man who arrives with chest pain and is tested for signs of heart attack.

The text also explains much of the machinery available for use in the E.R.: an airway, oxygen, and trauma and burn equipment. The work of paramedics is also part of this information-rich, realistic look at the whirlwind activity of the E.R.

Hospitalization

476. Brooks, Bruce. *The Moves Make the Man.* Harper, 1984 (0-06-020679-9); pap. (0-06-447022-9). 280 pp. Fiction.

  Interest level: Age 12+

Jerome Foxworthy is the single black student in an otherwise all-white high school. He is very bright, very happy with his family, and an excellent athlete as well. He befriends a boy named Bix Peters, who is also an excellent athlete, but who is by no means as well adjusted as Jerome. Bix cannot compromise; he cannot tolerate uncertainty or deception. When Bix's mother is hospitalized because of her emotional problems, Bix and his stepfather handle the entire situation badly. A visit to his mother (after he and his stepfather engage in a vicious competition to determine whether Bix will be permitted to visit her) is disastrous. Bix runs away, and Jerome is left to speculate about what happened to his friend.

  The differences between the way Jerome and his brothers deal with the temporary loss of their mother when she is hospitalized after being in an accident and how Bix and his stepfather handle Bix's mother's hospitalization provide an instructive contrast. Bix and his stepfather have an antagonistic, closed relationship. They do not seem to care about each other. And they blame each other for the mother's emotional problems.

  The story is told in Jerome's voice. Bix is his first best friend. The friendship is the primary factor in his narrative, but issues of differences between black and white people, the relationship between parents and children, and the emotional upheaval of adolescence are also themes in this well-written, engrossing novel.

477. Carter, Sharon, and Judy Monnig. *Coping with a Hospital Stay.* Rosen, 1987 (0-8239-0682-5). 110 pp. Nonfiction.

  Interest level: Ages 10–16

This is a truly valuable book written in an easy, straightforward style by a free-lance writer and a nurse. Its chatty tone and slim size seem just right for the concentration ability of those facing hospitalization. The authors cover a variety of topics, ranging from the expected (for example, what to bring to the hospital and pertinent questions to ask the doctor) to the pleasantly surprising, perhaps even more useful (for example, getting along with a roommate, depressing visitors and how to turn them off, and how to handle dumb questions about such things as cancer). Even in its few pages, there is considerable depth of exploration about attitudes, such as people who seem to tell the hospitalized it's their fault. And throughout, the authors admirably give young readers assertive lines to say back: "Hey, I don't like that! That doesn't make me feel very good!"

Along with instructions on assertion are guidelines for being a good patient as well, ensconced in a chapter titled "Don't Be a Patient the Nurses Want to Kick." This alerts readers to the scope of a nurse's job and ways to develop patience. Other chapters include checking into the hospital; long-term stays; ideas to avoid boredom; ways to keep up with schoolwork; admissions from an emergency room; hospitalization for cosmetic surgery, cancer, and psychiatric care; accidents; and having an uncertain medical future. There's also a diary of a typical hospital stay, this one caused by a car accident.

The chapter organization is not the best and chapters contain more than their heading describes (there's a full discussion of guilt and other feelings in the chapter on the emergency room). Readers should therefore be advised that skipping around is fine. From page one on, this book is a fine mix of information and acknowledgment of the many feelings attendant to a sudden hospitalization.

478. Delton, Judy, and Dorothy Tucker. *My Grandma's in a Nursing Home.* Illus. by Charles Robinson. Whitman, 1986 (0-8075-5333-6). 32 pp. Fiction.

Interest level: Ages 6–10

Jason finds it very difficult to adjust to his grandmother's Alzheimer's disease. He misses her and wants her to come home, where they can garden together the way they used to. She is in a nursing home, and when Jason and his family go to visit, there are people who discuss their fantasies, people without teeth, and his grandmother who does not remember his name. Jason's mother keeps shushing him when he tries to correct people's misimpressions. Eventually, Jason learns to be quiet when it is appropriate, talkative in response to the old people's needs, and accepting of his grandmother's condition.

Although the presentation is somewhat oversimplified, the message is a useful one: People with Alzheimer's disease and people who are old, lonely, and need institutional care have their own human needs and can enjoy the company of their loved ones. The illustrations are realistic and informative.

479. Hautzig, Deborah. *A Visit to the Sesame Street Hospital.* Illus. by Joe Mathieu. Random, 1985, LB (0-394-97062-4); pap. (0-394-87062-X). 32 pp. Fiction.

Interest level: Ages 2–7

An introductory note in this "pictureback" volume talks about parents and children sharing calmly together. The story concerns Grover, a Jim Henson Muppet, who has had one sore throat too many this year. His doctor (not a Muppet, but a human) recommends a tonsillectomy and arranges for a tour of the hospital for the Sesame Street gang. A nurse explains about the funny smell of disinfectant and allows them to visit the pediatric ward and get close to the children, which might not take place in an actual prehospital tour. There Grover tries out the call button and looks at a menu. The group visits the playroom, where a child explains about the hospital bracelets. The group also sees X-ray machinery and the operating room and tries on special surgical clothing. The visit closes with a visit to the gift shop, where it's hinted someone might bring Grover a present. The doctors shown are male, female, black, and white. There's also an emphasis on reasons for things, such as the reason for sterile clothing. Each hospital visitor on this tour thinks a different thing is best about the hospital, but Grover knows "the best thing about the hospital is getting well!"

480. Richter, Elizabeth. *The Teenage Hospital Experience: You Can Handle It.* Photos by the author. Coward, 1982. o.p. 128 pp. Nonfiction.

Interest level: Ages 11–16

Nineteen teenagers relate their experiences, hopes, fears, and disappointments. Some have been in and out of hospitals repeatedly, others are facing new problems, such as cancer. Also interviewed are professionals in the hospital: a surgeon, a nurse, a psychiatrist, and a specialist in adolescent medicine. Elizabeth Richter has used the expertise of staff from numerous hospitals on the East Coast.

The professionals speak about the mechanics and what you can expect: getting admitted, how to deal with doctors and nurses, not being embarrassed to ask questions, and so forth. Richter also includes a position statement on the care of adolescents and provides a question checklist that teenagers may want to use, for example, "What's wrong with me? Is there a name for it? How did I get sick? What will be done about it? Will the treatment hurt? Will I look any different?" This last question is extremely important, as teens are just forming their self-image regarding looks, and hospitalization threatens that.

The patients are identified by name, hospital, and age, and their diagnosis and treatment are discussed matter-of-factly. Included are a ninth grader with gonorrhea and another teen who has been pregnant. Other ailments include broken bones, surgery, spinal damage, paralysis of a leg after a camping accident (and the adjustment that entails for the rest of one's life), and internal injuries. Each vignette feels real (for example, a girl with scoliosis relates that when her boyfriend found out about her condition, he dropped her). The teens' frustrations with their illnesses and with the system come out in first-person narratives that are sensitively recorded: "It took more than five doctors to figure out what's wrong with me." (He has blood clots.) The dramatic specifics of hospital life and being in a place you don't want to be make this a very worthwhile book to have on hand. The close-up photographs handsomely show off a group of teenagers who were willing to tell their stories. Glossary, index.

Alzheimer's

481. Bahr, Mary. *The Memory Box*. Illus. by David Cunningham. Whitman, 1992, LB (0-8075-5052-3). 32 pp. Picture book.

    Interest level: Ages 6–9

The first part of the story acquaints the reader with Zach's grandparents, especially his grandfather, with whom he shares an idyllic day of fishing. Gramps talks about a special box for memories that an old person and a young person fill together so that "no matter what happens to the old person, the memories are saved forever." Zach becomes uneasy, but for the rest of the summer Zach and his grandparents remember the good times they have had together, and they stock the memory box with souvenirs of these times. They add new memories, too. Then, after Zach notices his grandfather talking to people who aren't there and wandering off and needing to be led home, his grandmother reveals that Gramps has Alzheimer's disease. The symptoms of the disease are clearly spelled out in the course of the touching story. The focus is on dealing with the situation—not dwelling on the sadness, although the sadness is there—as well as on the strength of the family's love and its reliance on the preservation of the happy memories.

482. Frank, Julia. *Alzheimer's Disease: The Silent Epidemic*. Illus. with photos and diagrams. Lerner, 1985 (0-8225-1578-4). 80 pp. Nonfiction.

    Interest level: Age 11+

Sarah, a hypothetical older woman who is victimized by Alzheimer's disease, is the focus of this book by Julia Frank, a professor of psychiatry. Medical procedures, progression of the disease, and the state of current knowledge are explained through her case. We become interested in all this, starting with Sarah's growing confusion and moving into more advanced stages of the disease. Frank makes the material memorable by tagging it to Sarah's hypothetical experiences. For example, she relates that at the beginning Sarah could find her way to the store because it was familiar, but she had trouble navigating the zoo with her grandchildren.

Brain physiology, heredity, diagnosis, and controversies of causality become easier for readers to navigate because intermittent anecdotes about Sarah make the path easier.

The book will be particularly valuable for youngsters trying to understand their relatives who have changed, for ample attention is given to fluctuations in temperament, loss of bodily functions, and such psychological problems as paranoia. From the book, they will also glean understanding of the kinds of help Alzheimer's victims and their families need and the kinds of community resources that are developing to provide that help. The book closes with a moving poem-essay by Dr. Marguerite Rush Lerner, a victim in the early stages of Alzheimer's. (Dr. Lerner may be known to some as an author in the Lerner Publications backlist.) Dr. Lerner feels she has lost everything: her career as a physician, her ability to write, aspects of her family. "I've lost a kingdom," she says. Glossary.

483. Graber, Richard. *Doc.* Harper, 1986. o.p. 150 pp. Fiction.

   Interest level: Age 12+

Brad adores his grandfather. He finds it impossible to acknowledge that his beloved grandfather, who is suffering from Alzheimer's disease, is any less competent than he always was. When his Aunt Susan tells him how terrible a husband and father his grandfather was, Brad does not want to hear it. He makes all kinds of excuses for his grandfather.

When there is a terrible car crash and Brad and his grandfather are at the scene of the accident, Brad is gratified to see that his grandfather marshals all of his energies and is able to handle much of the first aid that is necessary. But the effort is too much for the old man, and he dies. The family is more relieved than grieved that his death comes when and as it does.

The story is interesting in its raising the issue of how we idealize the people we love and find it difficult to believe that they are fallible. It is also painful to see our loved ones deteriorating, and sometimes we like to pretend it is not happening. The book is honest and revealing and invites thought.

484. Guthrie, Donna. *Grandpa Doesn't Know It's Me: A Family Adjusts to Alzheimer's Disease.* Illus. by Katy Keck Arnsteen. Human Sciences, 1986 (0-89885-302-8). 32 pp. Nonfiction.

   Interest level: Ages 4–8

This book was produced in cooperation with the Alzheimer's Disease and Related Disorders Association. The note to parents that precedes the text states that the book is designed to answer young children's questions: "What is wrong? Is this an illness that happens to lots of grownups? Did I do anything to cause it? Will *you* get it? Will I get it? Why did it happen to us? What do I tell my friends?"

In the text, young Elizabeth remembers happy times with her grandfather. But when Elizabeth was in first grade, Grandpa started forgetting things and liked to sit and watch instead of do. The narrative describes specific kinds of losses: remembering the distant past as if it were yesterday, the mounting forgetfulness that eventually becomes dangerous (for example, leaving a pot boiling), leaving independent living to live with relatives, and hostility in the face of growing deficits. The book ends with the grandfather still alive, living with his children. He doesn't know Elizabeth, but with the guidance of her parents, she remembers and still loves him.

All the questions above are answered gracefully, and additional information is nicely interspersed, such as existence of day-care respite centers. Illustrations in peach, black, and white gently complement this sad but necessary story.

485. Sakai, Kimiko. *Sachiko Means Happiness.* Illus. by Tomie Arai. Children's Book Pr., 1990 (0-89239-065-4). 32 pp. Picture book.

Interest level: Ages 5–8

Young Sachiko's grandmother, also named Sachiko, has Alzheimer's disease. She does not know her family and believes she is five years old. Young Sachiko is sent to entertain her and becomes angry and frustrated until she figures out that she can help her grandmother by playing along with her fantasies. She learns how to accept her grandmother's limitations and communicate her love.

486. Schein, Jonah. *Forget Me Not.* Illus. by the author. Firefly, 1988 (1-55037-001-4); pap. (1-55037-000-6). 24 pp. Fiction.

Interest level: Ages 4–9

Schein, who is 12 years old, has based the story on his family's experience as his grandmother lapsed into Alzheimer's disease. A photograph of his grandmother is included on the dedication page.

The story, written from the point of view of a young child, concerns a visit from the child's critically ill grandmother. Neither the child's brother, Matthew, nor the child likes the grandmother. They manage to avoid her at the start of the visit, but they soon notice her confusion. When the parents have the grandmother's condition diagnosed, the children come to understand that she isn't mean or crazy but sick. Soon after, the grandmother is placed in a home. A postscript tells us that the grandmother has died. The child writes, "She may not have always been the Grandma most children hope for, but I know now in her own way she cared about me and my family." A photograph of Jonah Schein and his family follows the narrative.

The strengths of this book are many. The habits of those in the first stages of Alzheimer's disease are accurately portrayed (for example, suspiciousness of theft), and Schein is certainly on target about his feelings. On the negative side, though, for a 24-page picture book there are a few too many words; and perhaps a professional should have done the pictures—the artwork is uneven.

Other Illnesses

487. Ackerman, Karen. *Just Like Max.* Illus. by George Schmidt. Knopf, 1990, LB (0-394-90176-2). Unpaged. Picture book.

Interest level: Ages 4–7

Aaron is very fond of his Uncle Max, who lives on the fourth floor of their brownstone and spends his days sewing and telling stories. One day, Aaron sees Max being taken away in an ambulance; he is heartbroken until Max returns home. Uncle Max has suffered a stroke and now must be cared for by Aaron's mother. Every day, Aaron visits Max and waits for him to respond. Finally, Aaron takes down some curtains and awkwardly creates a dress from them for his mother; he hopes his re-creation of one of Uncle Max's stories will help the old man recover. Aaron's retelling of Max's story affects his uncle and his whole family. The book ends with a grown-up Aaron, now a writer, telling his own nephew stories about Uncle Max. This gentle tale demonstrates the emotional impact that children can have on adults. Aaron cannot cure Max's stroke, but he can communicate his affection and admiration.

488. Casely, Judith. *When Grandpa Came to Stay.* Illus. by the author. Greenwillow, 1986 (0-688-06128-1). 32 pp. Picture book.

Interest level: Ages 5–8

Benny handles with aplomb Grandpa's coming to stay after Grandma dies, and he adjusts well to helping Grandpa recuperate from a stroke. Benny and his grandfather engage in many activities together and truly enjoy each other's company. Benny does not seem to mind any of his grandfather's physical problems. Then, one day, Grandpa cries, and this sends Benny into a tizzy. He berates his grandfather for behaving like a baby and storms out of the room. Afterward, he is very ashamed of himself. Grandpa understands Benny's behavior and explains that he, too, has behaved badly in his time. The two then take a trip to the cemetery to visit Grandma's grave and to renew their mutually satisfying relationship.

489. Fleischman, Paul. *Path of the Pale Horse.* Harper, 1983, LB (0-06-021905-X); pap. (0-06-440442-0). 144 pp. Fiction.

Interest level: Age 11+

It is the year 1793, and a plague of yellow fever has erupted in Philadelphia. Dr. Peale and Lep, his 14-year-old apprentice, go there to gather supplies and to rescue Lep's sister, Clara, who is in the city to help the family's benefactor, Mr. Botkin. The inhabitants of Philadelphia and its environs are in a panic because of the plague. Lep becomes separated from Dr. Peale and finds that Mr. Botkin has moved from his house, taking Clara with him. It turns out that Mr. Botkin is an impostor who sells magical rings guaranteed to cure the plague. Lep is contemptuous of people who are quacks and who hold out false promises. But his medical treatment turns out to be no more curative than the quacks' remedies. Lep and Clara return home with Dr. Peale sadder and wiser than when they went to Philadelphia. The brother and sister will strive to remain honest and kind, but their illusions are gone.

As the author points out in his note at the end of the book, people did not know the cause of yellow fever until 1902, when Walter Reed discovered that it was not contagious and that it was caused by mosquitoes. Until that time, the disease was a scourge. It killed 4,000 people in Philadelphia during the time this story takes place. The same helplessness and panic that accompany any unexplained fatal illness were present at that time and are ably described in this story. Ultimately, the story depicts the coming of age of Lep, the idealistic and courageous young protagonist who must come to terms with the lack of knowledge that his chosen profession of medicine must cope with.

490. Grollman, Sharon. *Shira: A Legacy of Courage.* Illus. by Edward Epstein. Doubleday, 1988. o.p. 96 pp. Nonfiction.

Interest level: Ages 8–13

Shira Putter died of a rare form of diabetes while still in elementary school. For three and one-half years, she suffered, spending months on end in hospitals all over the United States and Canada, undergoing many operations and, for most of that time, moving about with a foot pole and insulin pump attached to her, a last resort because she didn't benefit from more-standard approaches. She was surrounded by love throughout her ordeal, and she tried to make the best of her ever-worsening situation. In the hospital, she would put on plays, go trick-or-treating, and attempt to do schoolwork. She also wrote poetry and intermittently kept a journal, and those sometimes funny, sometimes confused, sometimes sad writings became the basis for this book. Grollman, a psychologist and author, took Shira's writings—and after interviews with her family reconstructing the illness and the child's point of view—created a fuller diary of what Shira might have said and thought.

The result is a most moving piece, in which we see the many ups and downs of a girl and her family in agony: A teacher doesn't understand she must snack when she needs to and scolds her. Shira changes schools. Shira experiences the attempts of her classmates at the new school to include her; but as her condition worsens, her classmates eventually withdraw. Shira gets close to hospital personnel and children as well, keeping her sense of humor enough to play a trick on a newcomer to the hospital. Shira is treated insensitively at a roller rink—"Why don't you stay home, where you belong?" someone shouts. In response, her friends skate around her in a circle of love, a thrilling moment. Shira comes home for the Passover Seder, and she and her family are unafraid to cry together at the predicament of her illness. Shira's emotions are many. She faces fear, not just the fear of pain and death, but the fear of losing her parents' love because she is a burden and the fear of being forgotten after death because her short life was so sad.

With the help of a psychiatrist, Shira learns visualization techniques and tries to master pain. The doctor also helps her talk about death. In time, as she weakens, she is eager for death because life seems so hard. In discussions with her mother, she helps her parents get ready to let her go, something children often do, according to the introduction by Rabbi Harold Kushner. Unlike many unfortunate children, Shira had not needed to keep her feelings bottled up so as not to upset her parents. Instead, there was much openness. This story of love, hope, and courage will help readers realize the truth of the "Song of Songs" phrase "Love is stronger than death." The book closes with an epilogue by Shira's mother. Glossary, bibliography, index.

491. Haas, Jessie. *Skipping School.* Greenwillow, 1992 (0-688-10179-8).
181 pp. Fiction.

Interest level: Age 12+

Philip's family has changed drastically since his father's emphysema has become critical. Now that he is on an oxygen machine, his father stares at the television set and rarely communicates with the family. His mother, always a capable woman, is now obsessed with running the house so that the father can rest. Worst of all, the family has moved to a suburban home from their working farm. There's nothing for the father to do but wait to die. Philip is in the throes of adjusting to a new school and cultivating a friendship with Kris, a rather reserved girl. Philip loves his part-time job at the veterinary clinic. He rescues two kittens from being put to sleep, and they become the focus of his attention. He even leaves school to tend to them at an abandoned house he discovers. When his sister, Carrie, away at school, loses her boyfriend and asks for her mother's company, Philip and his father respond to the sense of freedom they feel without the mother's well-meaning but stifling rules. As they relax and begin to communicate, they are able to make some decisions about the quality of life they both want.

492. Howard, Ellen. *Edith Herself.* Illus. by Ronald Himler. Atheneum, 1987 (0-689-31314-4). 132 pp. Fiction.

Interest level: Ages 9–12

After Edith's mother and father die, her siblings send her to live with an older married sister. Edith is devastated at being sent away, even though her siblings live in the same general geographic area. She has a very difficult time adjusting, especially because John, her sister Lena's husband, is a very serious and stern person. John and his mother, who lives with them, are devoutly religious. Lena and her father-in-law are less strict in their religious observance. The story is set in the late nineteenth century and is flavored with customs of the period.

Although the adjustment is very difficult for young Edith, she finally manages to make friends with Lena's surly little boy, Vernon, and to tolerate the frequently nasty old grandmother. Edith is subject to epileptic seizures, but eventually even this disability does not deter her from going to school with Vernon, making friends, and even surmounting the negative effects of her seizures at school. Surprisingly, it is John who insists, over Lena's tearful resistance, that Edith attend school. He points out that Edith is bright and capable and that she needs to feel competent and independent.

This book is successful in a number of ways. It provides the reader with a number of complex characters who defy stereotyping. It presents a story in a historical context that is relevant to today's children. It reminds us that no person is all good or all bad and that sometimes people can smother others in the name of love. It also gives some accurate information about epilepsy. It treats the issue of mourning with compassion and wisdom. There is much for the young reader to discuss in this interesting and fast-moving book.

493. Kipnis, Lynn, and Susan Adler. *You Can't Catch Diabetes from a Friend.* Photos by Richard Benkof. Triad, 1979. o.p. 64 pp. Nonfiction.

Interest level: Ages 7–11

Using a series of photographs and simple, but specific, text, the book follows the experiences of several children who have diabetes through their daily routines. The children are of different ages and backgrounds, but they all handle their condition competently. For one, this means making careful eating decisions—for example, choosing a piece of fruit over cookies. For another, this may involve managing daily insulin injections. Another child has to make sure his friends know how to help if he has an insulin reaction. The effect of diabetes on family members is also explored. The appealing photographs add to the attractiveness of the book.

494. Mulder, Linnea. *Sarah and Puffle: A Story for Children about Diabetes.* Illus. by Joanne H. Friar. Magination Press, 1992 (0-945354-41-X); pap. (0-945354-42-8). 32 pp. Fiction.

   Interest level: Ages 5–8

The information provided here is accurate and helpful to children who must deal with juvenile (type 1) diabetes, as well as to their friends and family. It is presented in the guise of a story about Sarah, who hates the idea of having to constantly watch the clock and monitor her food intake and blood sugar level. Even though she knows that the insulin shots have helped her to feel better, she resents the fact that she has a condition that requires her to do so many special things. Her stuffed sheep comes to life for a while to tell her in rhyme about the facts of her condition: It is not her fault that she has it, it will not go away, she has a support team who will help her, and everyone is different, so she shouldn't feel bad about being unlike her friends and family in this way. The rhyming sheep is a bit too precious, but the material is valuable enough to overcome some of the reader's antipathy to the trite device.

495. Ostrow, William, and Vivian Ostrow. *All about Asthma.* Illus. by Blanche Sims. Whitman, 1989, LB (0-8075-0276-6); pap. (0-8075-0275-8). 32 pp. Nonfiction.

   Interest level: Ages 7–10

Written by a boy who has experience coping with asthma, the book offers a clear, authentic perspective about what it means to be afflicted with this disease. Ostrow explains what asthma is and what it is not (e.g., personal punishment for something); he gives insight into possible causes, although these vary between individuals; and he mentions some famous people who also had asthma, like Teddy Roosevelt and Jackie Joyner-Kersee. Best of all, he gives several practical, tested suggestions about ways that readers afflicted with asthma can help themselves. He recommends that children participate in their health care, avoid things that trigger attacks, exercise, and relax. He recommends that asthma sufferers consider attending an asthma conference, where they might be able to glean techniques for handling asthma as well as offer help to those people who are not as able to cope as they are. This upbeat book offers a useful perspective on a disease that affects many children.

496. Pirner, Connie White. *Even Little Kids Get Diabetes.* Illus. by Nadine Bernard Westcott. Whitman, 1991 (0-8075-2158-2). 24 pp. Picture book.

   Interest level: Ages 6–8

The narrator of the story, a five-year-old child who has diabetes, tells how she came to be diagnosed and the impact the illness has had on her life. She describes her feelings about the frequent blood tests, insulin shots, dietary restrictions, and family fears in a nonthreatening way. The book could reassure children with diabetes or children who know someone with diabetes that someone with this condition can lead a normal, active life.

497. Roy, Ron. *Where's Buddy?* Illus. by Troy Howell. Clarion, 1986. o.p. 96 pp. Fiction.

   Interest level: Ages 7–10

Buddy is seven years old and has diabetes. Mike, his older brother, is in charge of him when their parents go to an auction. Mike wants to play football and he arranges for Buddy to play with a friend. However, Buddy is missing when Mike returns home after the game. He and several friends search for Buddy and his friend and ultimately find them in a cave near the sea. Buddy has had an insulin reaction, but Mike is able to revive him. Although Buddy has not taken his medicine, it is clear to the reader that he knows what regimen is required and can cope with his condition. Mike realizes that he should not have put his own enjoyment before his responsibility to Buddy; however, it is apparent that the whole family needs to reevaluate the way they treat Buddy. Spoiling him because he is afflicted with diabetes is not ameliorating his situation. This is an exciting story that incorporates important information about coping with diabetes.

498. Tiger, Steven. *Diabetes.* Illus. by Michael Reingold. Messner, 1987 (0-671-63273-6). 64 pp. Nonfiction.

   Interest level: Ages 8–12

Tiger, a physician's assistant and an author in the Understanding Disease series explains that diabetes is not a single disease and then gives a picture of who is likely to get diabetes. He also explains diagnosis and what can be done. Readers get a good idea of the role of metabolism and diet in various types of diabetes, each handled separately. The book is up-to-date, referring to laser procedures to fix burst blood vessels in the eye and other modern techniques. Prevention is also discussed in terms of diet. The illustrations are found in the center, in vibrant, attractive colors. On occasion they are confusing: A picture of a pregnant woman, for example, is captioned: "Pregnancy causes a temporary diabetes—it disappears when the pregnancy is over." A check of the text indicates that only 1 percent to 2 percent of pregnant women develop diabetes. Glossary, index.

Psychological/Emotional Conditions

499. Adler, C. S. *Good-bye Pink Pig.* Avon, 1986, pap. (0-380-70175-8). 176 pp. Fiction.

Interest level: Age 10+

Although Amanda spends much of her time dwelling in fantasy, as the story unfolds it is clear that Amanda will be fine. Her "perfect" mother, who is beautiful, elegant, and mindful of all the necessary ingredients for success, turns out to be the disturbed person. Amanda's friend, Libby, and her grandmother, Pearly, help Amanda come to the point where she can relinquish her fantasy life and manage well in the real world.

500. Adler, C. S. *The Shell Lady's Daughter.* Coward, 1983. o.p. 140 pp. Fiction.

Interest level: Age 11+

Fourteen-year-old Kelly has been her mother's best friend for a long time. Her father is a pilot and is away more often than he is home. Kelly has noticed certain danger signs of her mother's mental illness, but her father prefers to make light of them. Kelly's mother's lethargy; her mentioning that it feels as if her skin is crawling; her pricking her hand with a needle so that the needlework becomes bloodied; her telling sad stories about a doomed shell lady all come to a head one day, and she is hospitalized. Kelly is sent off to stay with her grandparents in Florida despite her protests and her concern that no one will visit her mother in the hospital. According to her father, it is the doctor's orders that she not see her mother. Kelly feels very guilty, certain that she has been the cause of her mother's illness.

Kelly's grandparents are wealthy. Her grandfather had been a college president, but is now senile. Despite her ferocious loyalty to her husband, her grandmother is, to the rest of the world, a detached, rigid, snobbish, somewhat cold woman who does not want to discuss anything that has to do with feelings. She disapproves of Kelly's mother because her background is not as upper class as Kelly's father's. She angrily tells Kelly that her mother didn't think enough of her to refrain from attempting suicide. Kelly is shocked and even more guilt ridden, but she is angry, too.

Fortunately, Kelly makes friends with the next-door neighbor, Evan, a wealthy man confined to a wheelchair because of polio. He reassures

Kelly that her mother's illness is no one's fault. He also helps Kelly to see that physical disabilities need not affect a person's relationships. He tells Kelly that love and support made him strong enough to be independent and happy. Largely because of what Evan has told her, but also because she has matured, Kelly makes the decision to return home to help her mother get well. Kelly will have a life of her own and will be there for her mother and for her own self-esteem.

Adler has written a novel that is strong enough to stand on its own as a good story. She has also incorporated some sound psychological information about mental illness, people with disabilities, abusive families, and the normal process of growing up. This book is a winner.

501. Bennett, James. *I Can Hear the Mourning Dove*. Houghton, 1990 (0-395-53623-5). 224 pp. Fiction.

Interest level: Age 12+

Grace is hospitalized for a psychotic condition and receives excellent treatment. Grace's thoughts and feelings are presented to the reader in a dramatic and highly understandable first-person narrative that never lets the reader's attention wander. The issues of death, attempted suicide, and emotional disability and its treatment are all authentically presented in the context of a gripping story. Perhaps because the author is an experienced mental health professional, the characters are believable in their behavior as well as their words. The therapist is not godlike, although she is very understanding and insightful; the patients have personalities in addition to their problems, and the ending is not an unrealistic panacea. This is a book well worth reading, both as a good story and as a way of helping students to understand some of the issues that emotionally disturbed people confront.

502. Cooney, Caroline B. *Don't Blame the Music*. Putnam, 1986 (0-448-47778-5). 172 pp. Fiction.

Interest level: Age 12+

The blackmail power of a person out of control is an unusual theme. High school senior Susan has an older sister, Ashley, who had dropped out of sight several years earlier. Now she's back, age 25, but ragefully infantile. Failing to achieve the only thing that matters—fame—Ashley vengefully lashes out. Is punk rock to blame for her bizarre, violent history? While coping with the everyday snide hostilities of her preppy school environment, Susan must also endure the ravages of her sister's tragic mental illness. How long will her parents deny Ashley's illness as she destroys their safety? One might wish for deeper exploration of character motivation, but that's because each and every character—Susan, her parents, boyfriends, school rival, and, of course, Ashley—is memorable and their intriguing actions are consistently on the mark.

503. Dinner, Sherry H. *Nothing to Be Ashamed Of: Growing Up with Mental Illness in Your Family.* Lothrop, 1989, LB (0-688-08482-6); pap. (0-688-08493-1). 160 pp. Nonfiction.

Interest level: Age 10+

This book contains lots of no-nonsense information and advice about how to help young people take charge of their lives when a member of their family is suffering from a mental illness. Topics covered in this book include mood and anxiety disorders, post-traumatic stress disorder, Alzheimer's disease, and eating disorders. The book is not directed at the people suffering from these conditions, but rather at their family members and close friends. The author points out that even if young people understand the reasons for the behavior of some mentally ill people, they may still be annoyed by it. She recommends that they try to establish outside activities so that they will avoid spending too much time with the person who is annoying them. The author cautions readers to avoid self-destructive behavior, such as abusing drugs or alcohol in an attempt to hide from their problems. She emphasizes two points: that readers adopt the philosophy of the serenity prayer used in most 12-step programs ("God grant me the serenity to accept the things I can't change, the courage to change the things I can, and the wisdom to know the difference between the two.") and Sydney Harris's observation that everyone has the choice of either acting or reacting, but that acting is more productive. Although the author focuses on what young people ought to do to help themselves, she also offers some suggestions for how to help other people in the family.

504. Gordon, Sol. *When Living Hurts.* Photos. Union of American Hebrew Congregations, 1985, pap. (0-8074-0310-5). 140 pp. Nonfiction.

Interest level: Age 12+

Sex and family life educator Gordon offers an inspirational guide on what to do when one feels depressed, lonely, or suicidal, trying to help youngsters look seriously at what they deem the purpose of life. The concept that we are all our brothers' keepers is entwined in the pages, and as such, the author wisely recommends talking to someone immediately if a teen feels terrible, before reading the book. He also gives step-by-step instructions to readers on how to help others who are having anxiety attacks or expressing suicidal thoughts.

After emergency measures are taken, the reader may be ready to learn why depression occurs and how it relates to either bad or good happenings. The art of giving caring messages while sharing the secret suicidal feelings with an adult who can help is stressed.

Short-term ways to help oneself or a friend get out of a depression (go to a park, write to someone who will be surprised to hear from you, and so on) are coupled with suggestions for long-term help (therapy, seeking help from the clergy, and so forth). Other topics covered include substance abuse, minimal self-esteem, sexual worries, anger, and boredom as they may have an impact on depression. The book offers exercises to think and write about—for example, look at the worst thing that ever happened to you and reflect on what you learned and whether anything good came out of it.

Additional areas of exploration are disappointments in religion, not getting along with parents (and here, he offers advice to parents as well as children on how to keep communication avenues open), and special family situations (divorce, stepfamily, and so on). The individual segments are short but neither glib nor empty. Instead, Gordon is reassuring in his terse, forthright presentation and trustful manner in presenting philosophies to children. The ideas of Frankl, for example, are related to help teens find meaning in life. Gordon also doesn't fear to recommend additional reading and inject his own life: anecdotes, poems, and sayings he values in trying to recover from life's batterings. Renewal, forgiveness, and being kind to oneself are folded into every page, and the message will uplift teens.

505. Hahn, Mary Downing. *Daphne's Book*. Clarion, 1983 (0-89919-183-5); Bantam, pap. (0-553-15631-4). 178 pp. Fiction.

Interest level: Age 10+

Daphne and her younger sister, Hope, live with their grandmother. Their parents are dead, and their grandmother is growing increasingly psychotic. Daphne is afraid to let anyone know about her grandmother because she doesn't want to be sent to an orphanage. But when Daphne's friend, Jessica, who is the narrator of this book, realizes that Daphne and her sister are in danger of being seriously hurt, she tells her mother about the situation. Daphne's worst fears are realized. She and her sister are placed in an institution. Her grandmother is hospitalized, and she dies soon after. Daphne feels terribly guilty. In the end, Daphne and her sister will go to live with a couple who sound as if they will care for the girls well. They are cousins, found by the social worker. Jessica is relieved that there will be a happy ending, and she reassures Daphne that they will always be friends.

The book describes a desperate situation, but perhaps readers will realize that sometimes children who seem to be different from the rest, who are shy or withdrawn, need some special understanding. The story is well told. The incidental issues of single-family parenting (Jessica's parents are divorced, and she lives with her mother, who is at work most of the day) and adjusting to new situations are well handled.

506. Naylor, Phyllis Reynolds. *The Keeper*. Atheneum, 1986 (0-689-31204-0). 212 pp. Fiction.

   Interest level: Ages 11–15

Honesty is the best policy, even when it hurts, perhaps especially when it hurts. Nick's father has changed jobs frequently; they are living in Chicago for only a couple of years when he slumps rapidly into paranoiac mental illness. At first, Nick and his mother are baffled by his mysterious dropping out of work. As they realize what the problem is, they first try to ignore it, then cover for him, but tensions caused by his suspicions, sleeplessness, and a suicide attempt soon overtake everyday life.

   Nick's collapse in his junior high school gym class results in the vital contact that the family needs—the school and hospital staff finally get his father to consent to being hospitalized. Based on the author's experiences with her first husband, the book succeeds in moving the reader, especially when Nick realizes that he can call the school nurse in his emergency. Nick's final openness is not without consequence: He loses his first girlfriend. But without that realism, the story would be inauthentic.

507. Osborne, Mary Pope. *Love Always, Blue*. Dial, 1983 (0-8037-0031-8). 183 pp. Fiction.

   Interest level: Age 12+

Blue adores her father and is devastated that he now lives in New York, while she remains with her mother in North Carolina. Blue is an intelligent, lonely, and anxious young woman who can't let go of her fixation about her father. Even on her fifteenth birthday, when he has clearly forgotten about it, she calls him and is happy just to talk to him, and he claims to miss and love her.

   Blue persuades her mother to let her visit her father in New York during school vacation. When she arrives in New York, Blue sees that her father is in bad shape, physically, economically, and emotionally. He cries a lot, is clearly very depressed, and cannot sleep or eat. Blue can't do anything to help him. She meets the son of one of her father's friends, and they immediately "click." Blue's father is jealous, becomes even more depressed, and leaves the house. Blue gets hysterical, runs out of the house without her keys, calls her mother, and is upset when her mother sends her uncle to New York to bring her home. When Blue's father returns, he seems to finally see that he needs help and he promises Blue that he will seek it. She returns home wiser about her father's situation and clearer about herself and her relationship with her parents.

Blue's mother tries to help Blue understand her father and feel good about herself, but until Blue has seen for herself how ill her father is, her mother can't break through the barriers that Blue has erected. Now, perhaps, Blue won't blame her mother so much for her parents' divorce. She has been praying for her parents to get back together again, and the author has left the door open for a reconciliation, which may not be realistic. But the situation is one that young readers may find compelling, that may cause them to think about how they would advise Blue and her parents.

Alcohol/Drug Dependency

508. Adler, C. S. *With Westie and the Tin Man*. Macmillan, 1990, pap. (0-02-041125-1). 194 pp. Fiction.

Interest level: Age 12+

Greg's mother is an alcoholic, and Greg has been jailed for a year for repeated offenses, notably shoplifting. On his release from jail, he finds that his mother, who hasn't had a drink in a year, and a friend whom she met at AA, Manny Horowitz, have set up a business. Greg doesn't feel welcome or comfortable, except with Manny's dog, Westie. As the days go by, Greg learns that Manny has much to offer him, that his mother has changed for the better, and that telling the truth is an important task he must learn to do.

Adler is a prolific and popular writer. She manages, in the space of this one story, to convey a lot of information about alcoholics and their families. She also presents a believable picture of a 15-year-old boy who is angry at the world and at himself, yet manages to overcome his problems. This book is well worth reading.

509. Berger, Gilda, and Melvin Berger. *Drug Abuse A–Z*. Enslow, 1990, LB (0-89490-193-1). 128 pp. Nonfiction.

Interest level: Age 12+

This helpful dictionary of terminology associated with drugs and drug use includes more than 1,000 entries. Slang phrases as well as medical and pharmacological terms are defined. The authors' perspective seems to be one of moderation and lack of hysteria coupled with as many facts as possible. Drugs are divided into five classifications, ranging from cough medicines with codeine that may be sold over the counter to people over age 18 (with a record of the buyer's name), to those drugs—such as heroin, LSD, and mescaline—that have a high potential for abuse and no known medical use in the United States. These drugs may be obtained only for limited research purposes. The information needs some updating, and readers might conduct some research to see what the latest terminology, laws, findings, and attitudes are about drugs and drug use.

510. Birdseye, Tom. *Tucker.* Holiday, 1990 (0-8234-0813-2). 120 pp. Fiction.

Interest level: Ages 9–12

Eleven-year-old Tucker Renfro lives with his alcoholic father. His relationships with both his father and his friend Joe are seriously eroded when Livi, his younger sister, comes to visit for a couple of months, after seven years of estrangement. Both parents seem to have left their children out of any decision making or communication with each other. Livi's unfailingly cheerful and loving behavior is not quite believable, but she is an appealing character. Duane Renfro's alcoholism and its debilitating effects on him might cause the reader to wonder why he was granted custody of his son and why his estranged wife would permit her daughter to visit. On the other hand, he is not an abusive alcoholic, and the story provides a good literary model of effects of the disease when it doesn't lead to violence and physical abuse. The ending is realistically hopeful.

511. Bunting, Eve. *A Sudden Silence.* Harcourt, 1990 (0-15-282058-2). 112 pp. Fiction.

Interest level: Age 10+

Bry Harmon is killed by a hit-and-run driver, partly because Bry is deaf and cannot hear the oncoming car, but mostly because the driver is drunk. Jesse, Bry's brother, feels horribly guilty because he was walking with Bry the night of the accident, and he could not save his brother's life. Through assiduous investigation, he discovers that the killer is the alcoholic mother of a young woman he is involved with emotionally. Throughout his investigation, he (and the reader) acquires much information about alcoholism and its effects. The book is dramatic and suspenseful, and the plot brings out how relationships are damaged because of people's substance abuse.

512. Cohen, Susan, and Daniel Cohen. *A Six-Pack and a Fake I.D.: Teens Look at the Drinking Question.* Evans, 1986 (0-87131-459-2); Dell, pap. (0-440-21297-9). 180 pp. Nonfiction.

Interest level: Age 12+

Teenagers will make their own decisions, the Cohens know, so their attempt is to give a balanced picture with "reliable and believable information." Their task is difficult because while it's generally agreed that alcoholism is a serious national problem and drunk-driving deaths are rampant, alcohol is also an integral and accepted part of our culture. Their wisdom is in acknowledging this paradox. Then, without moralizing, the authors examine the role alcohol plays in our culture and educate teens about the effects of drinking. They use science in describing the chemical changes that occur in the body, and they tap social science as well, including a short history of the laws that have been created (and sometimes uncreated) around alcohol consumption.

A strength of this book is the Cohens' tips for dealing with the kinds of situations teens are likely to find themselves in: the party that threatens to go overboard, peer pressure, and so forth. They give practical hints for successfully preventing situations from escalating and for confronting pressure. A section deals with communicating with parents, another with knowing when help is necessary and where to get it. This matter-of-fact approach will appeal to both teenagers and their parents. A recommended handbook.

513. Cohen, Susan, and Daniel Cohen. *What You Can Believe about Drugs: An Honest and Unhysterical Guide for Teens.* Evans, 1988 (0-87131-527-0). 180 pp. Nonfiction.

Interest level: Age 12+

Starting off by asking readers to imagine a world in which tobacco is banned, the Cohens offer a balanced look at drugs: From coffee and tea through steroids, heroin, speed, cigarettes, and marijuana, they answer teens' likely questions. Can cocaine kill? Looking at the example of Len Bias, yes, occasionally, but it's rare. They thereby confront the hysteria seen in the media. One might say their outlook is: There is no such thing as a devil drug, although there are excellent reasons not to use them. This is an erudite book, offering the history of marijuana, hallucinogens, and narcotic use and the various fashions through the decades, including why and how they became illegal. Through its pages, the Cohens weave allusions to literature and the arts (for example, *Long Day's Journey into Night*).

Also included is an overview of ways these substances are ingested, which, although informative, might seem to give new ideas: "Some affluent teenagers play around with heroin by injecting it under the skin or sniffing [snorting] it. Either method is less likely to lead to addiction than injecting heroin directly into a vein. Others try to avoid addiction by injecting themselves intravenously only occasionally, say before a party." One hopes teens will also read the red-alert signals the Cohens add to these antics: "But playing with narcotics is like playing with fire. It's like speeding along in your car with your foot pressed down on the accelerator, surviving, and telling yourself, 'Hey I'll never crash.' People who drive wildly often end up dead and people who use heroin often end up addicted." Other topics include drug testing and, most important, ways to find highs without drugs. Alcohol is not included because it was the subject of their earlier *A Six-Pack and a Fake I.D.* (see entry above). Sources of help are appended. Bibliography, film list.

514. Fox, Paula. *The Moonlight Man*. Bradbury, 1986 (0-02-735480-6); Dell, pap. (0-440-20079-2).179 pp. Fiction.

Interest level: Age 12+

Catherine calls her father the moonlight man, in contrast to her mother, whom she considers the daylight woman. Each of her parents has remarried, and Catherine spends most of the year at a Canadian boarding school. Her father is a charming man, a writer. He is also an alcoholic and irresponsible. He lies and cheats and cannot be counted on to keep his word, even to his daughter. The month that she spends with him is like a ride on a roller coaster. She loves his company; she hates his vices. Fox's writing is as vivid and empathic in this book as in her other fine books. The dialogue, the characterizations, and the situations compel the reader's attention. This is no clinical case study of an alcoholic, but it is as authentic as any text, and it has the advantage of being clothed in the truth of story. A worthwhile book.

515. Hall, Lindsey, and Leigh Cohn. *Dear Kids of Alcoholics*. Illus. by Rosemary E. Lingenfelter. Gurze, 1988, pap. (0-936077-18-2). 96 pp. Nonfiction.

Interest level: Ages 7–10

Told in the first person by the young son of an alcoholic, the story is a blow-by-blow description of the progress of the child's father from abusive to recovering alcoholic. An intervention, where family members and friends confront the father, is also meticulously described. Although the story is designed to inform people about this condition, the details are well integrated into the plot, and the reader's attention and sympathy are always with the young boy.

516. Halvorson, Marilyn. *Cowboys Don't Cry*. Dell, 1986, pap. (0-440-91303-9). 160 pp. Fiction.

Interest level: Age 11+

Shane's mother was killed in an automobile accident when he was ten years old. The terrible thing about the accident is that Shane's father was driving and he had had too much to drink. After his wife's death, Shane's father does not stop drinking. As a matter of fact, his problem worsens.

When Shane is 14, his maternal grandfather dies and leaves him a ranch. Shane hopes against hope that they will now be able to settle down and be a family again.

Although Shane's father embarrasses him on his first day of school, and Shane gets into a fight with a bully, the other students are welcoming and pleasant, and he is encouraged about the prospects of making a success of it. He does make a success of school, but his father cannot hold to his intent to remain sober. It takes an almost fatal accident to make his father realize that he seriously needs to take hold of himself.

At the end of the story, it looks as if Shane and his father will try harder to express their feelings to each other. The main point is that they love each other, and they are able to say so.

Marilyn Halvorson vividly demonstrates how painful it is to feel responsible for the death of a loved one. She also details well the healing process and the importance of loving friends in that process.

517. Harris, Jonathan. *Drugged Athletes: The Crisis in American Sports.* Four Winds, 1987 (0-02-742740-4). 104 pp. Nonfiction.
    Interest level: Ages 11–16

A highly intelligent book, this examination of a current problem broadly brings together the concerns of the professional athlete with the aspiring high school team member. Drugs seem to be everywhere—drugs to relax muscles, drugs to improve performance, drugs to mask pain, and drugs for sheer pleasure. Using statistical evidence of abuse of cocaine, steroids, and other drugs, social science writer Harris relates these to the stories of people who died from drugs (for example, Mercury Morris), athletes who came back, and those who came close to abuse but escaped. The stresses of sports contribute to the problem—starting young, being pampered, getting injured, being pawns in the larger money-making goals of college and professional sports, and so forth.

Harris points to national shames: racism that exploits black athletes but fails to prepare them academically, coaches who stress winning over everything, shaving points, and so on. Chapters deal effectively with drug tests (and the controversies surrounding them) and treatment programs. How interesting it is to see the intense effort that goes into treating a valuable commodity on the playing field: daily therapy sessions, group sessions several times a week, and so on. Harris hopes the future will come from policymakers aiming at prevention. Glossary, bibliography, index.

518. Lee, Essie E. *Breaking the Connection: How Young People Achieve Drug-Free Lives.* Photos. Messner, 1988, LB (0-671-67059-X). 172 pp. Nonfiction.

Interest level: Ages 12–16

This book examines how young people from all social classes—lower, middle, upper—have easily become involved with drugs and what some of them have done to get out of their predicaments. Lee, a professor of health education, relates stories of dependency on various drugs but emphasizes cocaine and crack because of their prevalence in today's society and their immense danger. It is surprising how simply crack is made, by combining cocaine with household baking soda. It is almost like a fast food: compact, popular, and profitable. Lee provides superb analysis of societal pressures that cause people to try the drugs and subsequently need treatment. Among them are the appetite suppressant qualities cocaine is reported to have, the high salaries some rather young adults command without concomitant maturity, and so on. She visits Phoenix House and other treatment centers and tells in depth about their procedures for accepting or declining to treat a particular patient. The detail-filled, fascinating stories of numerous young people who have overcome their drug problems are realistic and gritty and can serve as inspiration, for these people have used the many self-help programs and approaches she lists. Lee's list of agencies offering help is broader than that found in most books and will be very useful. Resource list, drug charts, index. Highly recommended.

519. McFarland, Rhoda. *Coping with Substance Abuse.* Rosen, 1990 (0-8239-1135-7). 160 pp. Nonfiction.

Interest level: Age 12+

McFarland, a certified alcoholism and drug abuse counselor, here looks at the effect of chemical abuse (all drugs, including alcohol and prescription drugs) on the body, the person, the family, and society. Part of the book discusses teenagers who abuse chemicals; the other part discusses living with a parent who is an abuser. The media, says McFarland, make it seem that drug use is acceptable, and from that attitude a myriad of social and emotional problems ensue.

McFarland is especially strong in discussing the implications for the family when a parent is addicted. Her exploration of the types of roles children may take—hero, scapegoat, mascot, lost child—is especially insightful. One unusual feature of this book, found almost nowhere else, is a chapter on coping with a sibling who is the abuser. Likewise, there is one on friends. In each case, just as McFarland did with the parents and the teen who is the abuser, she examines the addiction and its problems from early to late stages. And, as she did with the parents, for siblings and friends, she explores codependent issues: how not to aid in the addiction, how to help get intervention, how to detach oneself from the need to save the person (which is impossible for another person to do anyway), and by doing so, becoming part of the solution, not part of the problem. There are also helpful quizzes to assess one's own attitude and behavior patterns toward chemicals and one's roles in others' patterns. Index.

520. Osborne, Mary Pope. *Last One Home.* Dial, 1986 (0-8037-0219-1). 180 pp. Fiction.
   Interest level: Age 11+

Bailey's mother left her family three years ago to be institutionalized for alcoholism and now lives in Florida. Bailey's brother is joining the army, and her father will soon marry Janet, a woman who has twin boys. Bailey is very upset. She doesn't want her brother to leave or her father to get married. Although Bailey is 12 years old, she begins behaving like a small child, complete with temper tantrums.

   Bailey often stays at home with her brother while her father sleeps at Janet's house. Bailey is invited to sleep there, too, but she doesn't want to. She feels deserted. Her emotions become so difficult to manage that she drinks a lot of wine, gets drunk, and becomes violently ill. Later, she tries to run away, but her soon-to-be stepmother and her father find her and take her .home. The reader is left with the assurance that Janet will take care of Bailey and that Bailey will flourish from her nurturing.

   The book brings out how children of alcoholic parents can be damaged. It also uncovers the issue of the insensitive father who loves his children, but is more concerned with his own activities than with their welfare. He means well, but he seems incapable of responding in a way that his daughter wants and needs. The story is believable and consistent with what is known about families where a parent is an alcoholic.

521. Porterfield, Kay Marie. *Coping with an Alcoholic Parent.* Rosen, 1990 (0-8239-1143-8). 148 pp. Nonfiction.
   Interest level: Age 12+

Starting with a checklist to see if a parent might actually be alcoholic, Porterfield moves on to the multiple complications in the family because of the drinking, the alcoholic's many tricks, and the scope of children's feelings. In a section on myths, she reiterates the book's focus: "Alcoholism is a family disease."

Chapters cover what alcohol does to the body, why various people may be alcoholic, family genetics, and how the problem affects various family members. A particularly interesting section concerns the often destructive unwritten rules families may live under—for example, "Don't trust yourself, don't let your feelings get hurt, and don't discuss the problem with the family or outsiders."

Also included is up-to-date information on coping styles and strategies that are common to alcoholic homes—for example, perfectionism, peacemaking, withdrawing, distracting, and rebelling. The pitfalls of these coping mechanisms are explained simply through profiles of youngsters. The book fully discusses better ways to thrive, including specific lists of tactics to let go of deficient strategies. In addition, Porterfield lets readers in on overall strategies for better functioning: guided imagery, controlled relaxation, and exercise. The book culminates in hearty sections on getting help for oneself through Alateen and other organizations and ways to form a new, less responsibility-taking relationship with the alcoholic parent. There is also a good section on the new household with a recovering alcoholic and a helpful, tell-it-like-it-is chapter on the alcoholic's child as a potential alcoholic. Appendix of organizations, bibliography. Thoughtfully done.

522. Reading, J. P. *The Summer of Sassy Jo.* Houghton, 1989 (0-395-48950-4). 182 pp. Fiction.

Interest level: Age 11+

Sara Jo is spending the summer with her estranged mother, Joleen, who abandoned the family when Sara Jo was five. Joleen is a recovering alcoholic. Joleen has gotten her life together and wants nothing more than to win her daughter back. Slowly and believably, they begin to find common ground. At the end, Sara feels comfortable with her life with Joleen, her new friends, and her first boyfriend. Joleen is not excused for the pain she caused by abandoning her family, but her situation is explained by the fact that she was an extremely depressed alcoholic who could not even take care of herself. She sought treatment, and continues to go to AA meetings years later. The issue of alcoholism is particularly well handled.

523. Ryerson, Eric. *When Your Parent Drinks Too Much: A Book for Teenagers.* Facts on File, 1985 (0-8160-1259-8); Warner, pap. (0-446-34692-6). 144 pp. Nonfiction.

Interest level: Age 12+

Eric Ryerson is the pseudonym of an author who has written many other books for teenagers. Here, he writes a personal story as the son of an alcoholic. Ryerson has taken an investigative approach, however, not limiting himself to his own family experience. Topics include why alcoholism is a disease, the limits of responsibility that a teen can take for that disease (in other words, you can't cure your parent's drinking problem), how family members may unintentionally aid the alcoholic in getting liquor, and how to stop that behavior. Also covered are how to find ways to detach yourself from someone else's problem; how to get over your own feelings of isolation, shame, and guilt; and how to deal with a crisis. In addition, Ryerson discusses several approaches to getting help for the alcoholic and the family.

There is much information here: why alcoholics drink, how to tell if someone is truly an alcoholic, how family members hole up and change their lives around the disease, understanding the sober parent's point of view, the role of intervention, the parent who becomes sober, and so on. But there is also a deep feeling side, understanding the many roles children of alcoholics can take: "If you are the super-responsible one, you may be angry at how the others aren't helping or aren't trying nearly as hard as you are to keep things from falling apart completely." Then Ryerson tells why others may be behaving differently. Throughout, there's a balance of the author's own story and what he knows of other families—for example, before he learned detachment, how he screamed, cried, and pleaded with his mother to stop. He talks about himself and then becomes more general. It's a technique that works well and will help many readers. List of resources, index.

524. Sebestyen, Ouida. *On Fire.* Little, Brown, 1985 (0-87113-010-6); Bantam, pap. (0-553-26862-7). 207 pp. Fiction.

Interest level: Age 12+

It is 1910. Twelve-year-old Sammy adores his 16-year-old brother, Tater. The two boys have a desperate time trying to get along with their alcoholic father. Tater had killed a man (the saintly black father from *Words by Heart*, Atlantic, 1979), mistakenly thinking he was defending his father, but "Pap" is continuously abusive to the boy and often says that he wishes Tater were dead. The boys' mother and their four younger siblings are passive and victimized.

Tater and Sammy run away to a town where mining is the major industry and where there is a terrible, bloody conflict between the union and the owners. The plot becomes very complex and more characters are introduced, among them a young woman who rescues her dead sister's baby and who becomes a guardian to the two boys. Tater sets a destructive fire and almost kills another man, but Sammy prevents him from doing so. At the end of the book, the father has committed suicide; it looks like the mother has finally begun to make some decisions for herself; Tater seems to have reformed; and there is the hope that the family and the young woman will form an alliance and survive.

The ugliness of Tater's bigotry festers like a sore in this book. In the end, he professes to have learned from the old black man, who, he confesses, was a better man than most. The family is pictured as the dregs of humanity, with no member having much of an identity except for Tater and Sammy. These are not lovable characters. But the seaminess of their existence and the desperation of their poverty may make some young readers think about the times in which this story takes place, as well as the time in which we now live.

525. Seixas, Judith S. *Drugs: What They Are, What They Do.* Illus. by Tom Huffman. Greenwillow, 1987 (0-688-07399-9); Morrow, pap. (0-688-10487-8). 48 pp. Nonfiction.

Interest level: Ages 7–10

Seixas has written about complex subjects in the easy-to-read format before, notably alcohol and tobacco. Here she covers psychoactive drugs, explaining that they are usually illegal but have been known for thousands of years as painkillers. The book's concrete style will help children understand the nature of drug use. For example, in discussing buildup of tolerance, she uses the example of jumping into cold water and then getting used to the cold.

Topics include how stimulants, sedatives, hallucinogens, and narcotics enter the body and work; their side effects; and difficulties with addiction. Dangers are clearly spelled out: Stimulants can cause heart attacks; sedatives can confuse you into an overdose that may stop breathing. She also covers why kids try drugs and introduces such terminology as *gateway drugs* (tobacco, alcohol, and marijuana). Probably most convincing to this age group as reasons not to begin are Seixas's reliance once again on the concrete: "You won't be good at computer games" and "You won't be able to catch or kick a ball." Continuing in the same concrete game, she lists ways to say no—actual excuses and words to say. Well done.

526. Stevens, Sarah. *The Facts about Steroids.* Crestwood, 1991 (0-89686-606-8). 48 pp. Nonfiction.

Interest level: Ages 8–12

This book provides a balanced look at steroids, why people might choose to use them, and the health problems they can cause. It avoids relying on scare tactics, but it does not mince words when describing the effects of these potentially dangerous drugs. It is sympathetic to the reasons why young people might be attracted to them and points out such alternatives as exercise and diet.

527. Tapp, Kathy Kennedy. *Smoke from the Chimney.* Macmillan, 1986 (0-689-50389-X); pap. (0-689-71323-1). 169 pp. Fiction.

Interest level: Ages 9–12

Erin and her friend Heather want to go away to camp together, but Erin's family can't afford the fee, so Erin decides to earn the money herself. She and Heather write and present a series of puppet shows based on the Tarzan books they love. They earn a good amount of money, but Erin's father, an alcoholic, has hit a new low, and he and Erin's mother have separated. Erin's mother now needs money for necessities, and Erin gives up her dream of going to camp.

The author clearly describes the issues that beset the family of an alcoholic. The family pulls together in the end, and there is even some hope that the father can overcome his condition. But it is not falsely optimistic hope: The mother knows that he has made this effort before and failed. She is not again going to live her life based on what she wishes her husband would do. Erin does not go away to camp, but instead goes camping with her mother and two sisters, and it looks as if the family will function well.

528. Vigna, Judith. *I Wish Daddy Didn't Drink So Much.* Illus. by the author. Whitman, 1988 (0-8075-3523-0). 40 pp. Fiction.

Interest level: Ages 3–7

Lisa's daddy is an alcoholic. She is often afraid of her father, especially when he shouts at her and when he storms around the house looking for something to drink. After her father has ruined their Christmas celebration, her mother explains to her that although Lisa sees that her father is drunk, he is really sick, and that her "true, kind Daddy" loves her and is a good person.

Lisa and her mother take their Christmas dinner to the house of their friend Mrs. Fields, who helps Lisa acquire some strategies for feeling happier. Mrs. Fields explains that she understands very well what is happening because she, too, used to drink too much. She also invites Lisa to come to visit her whenever she likes. Lisa knows that she can feel safe at Mrs. Fields's house.

The author tells this story from the point of view of a three- or four-year-old child. She uses simple illustrations and examples to help young readers understand that they are not alone in suffering from the problem of an alcoholic parent. The two suggestions she gives—that Lisa do something that she really enjoys, and that she visit a good and kind friend whenever possible—are helpful coping strategies for children.

Eating Disorders

529. Erlanger, Ellen. *Eating Disorders: A Question and Answer Book about Anorexia Nervosa and Bulimia Nervosa.* Lerner, 1988 (0-8225-0038-8). 64 pp. Nonfiction.

Interest level: Ages 12–16

The author, a school counselor and administrator, effectively latches onto the reader's attention by introducing her book with a list of famous women who have struggled with eating disorders. Next comes an individual story, through which basic concepts of the disorders are explored. Questions and answers come to the fore afterward, encompassing signs and symptoms, causes (emotional, physical) and cautions, and help and hope. A range of therapies is explained, from nutrition counseling and behavior modification to individual and group therapy and support groups. Besides offering information on helping oneself, there is advice on how to aggressively encourage someone else to get help. The effectiveness of helping others is seen in some of the first-person stories in the book. The illustrations are black-and-white drawings of women from earlier periods—an interesting choice for modern problems that had antecedents before they were given names. The information is thorough and thoughtful, hard to achieve in a book that is so short. Its brevity will attract many readers who might be intimidated by more detail. List of relevant organizations, bibliography, index.

530. Kolodny, Nancy J. *When Food's a Foe: How to Confront and Conquer Eating Disorders.* Little, Brown, 1987 (0-316-50167-0); pap. (0-316-50181-6). 224 pp. Nonfiction.

Interest level: Ages 12–16

Kolodny, a social worker, takes on the eating disorders of bulimia and anorexia nervosa (obesity is not a subject here). Written for boys as well as girls, the book compares having an eating disorder to entering a maze alone. A special feature is the many self-quizzes and charts to fill out. Through these, readers examine their self-esteem and self-image and can begin to ascertain if habits are turning into obsessions—in other words, warning signs. She recommends defusing the disorder—usually with professional help—one step at a time, by isolating negative triggers. Kolodny compares a therapist who deals with eating disorders to a coach working with an athlete, probably a very apt analogy.

Lively and strong on practical advice (don't get a job in a food-related business if you may be susceptible), the book does not delve quite as deeply into causes. She speaks of power issues as important but does not stress perfectionism, which for many people with eating disorders plays a major role. She also talks about the social costs of being anorexic or bulimic—for example, becoming an outcast or self-imposed exile. This consequence is well worth pondering, especially for those who aren't yet fully caught up in the syndromes. Unique features include advice for helping those who are anorexic/bulimic, word-for-word suggestions on how to tell your family you need help, charts of calorie/fat content of fast foods, and insightful cartoons from the comic strip "Cathy." It will be helpful to those who, in the author's words, are finding the "dining table a battleground."

531. Landau, Elaine. *Why Are They Starving Themselves? Understanding Anorexia Nervosa and Bulimia.* Simon & Schuster, 1983, LB (0-671-45582-6); pap. (0-671-49492-9). 128 pp. Nonfiction.
    Interest level: Ages 11–16

"Mirror, mirror, on the wall, who's the thinnest one of all?" Each anorectic hopes it is she, according to Landau. The book is strong on describing the obsessions that bring this about and keep it going. The perfectionistic strains of people with these problems are given special attention, showing why they are so hard to treat, going through a hospital revolving door in their persistent attempts to starve and vomit. Individual stories complement general outlines and patterns, creating a narrative that remains interesting and brings the reader to understanding. The theories regarding reasons are well explained: "Some therapists believe that the anorectic's unconscious desire not to grow up but to remain a little girl is a factor in her illness."

The concluding chapters describe help that is available and approach it broadly, including self-esteem development, assertiveness training, self-help relaxation techniques, and organizational outreach. One treatment program described is designed by Ellen Schor, a recovered food disorder patient. Bibliography, index.

532. Stren, Patti. *I Was a 15-Year-Old Blimp.* Dutton, 1986, pap. (0-451-14577-1). 185 pp. Fiction.
    Interest level: Age 10+

Told in the first person by Gabby Finkelstein, this is the story of a young woman who so thoroughly dislikes herself that she becomes obsessed with her weight, goes on fad diets, and becomes bulimic, making herself vomit every morsel of food that she eats. The story is most effective when the author is describing Gabby's weight problem. It becomes somewhat less so when the focus is on Gabby's wish to be admired by the "in" crowd. The young people in the supposedly popular group are shallow and cruel. Gabby has two friends who love her dearly and who are much worthier of her admiration than the group she craves acceptance from.

Gabby's parents are intelligent and concerned, but Gabby's mother is somewhat less capable of expressing her feelings than Gabby's father. The parents are well characterized here; the author escapes the trap of making the parents into cruel and uncaring stick figures. They help Gabby by reacting immediately when they discover that she is bulimic. They send her to a camp that focuses on healthful diet and exercise. And when she returns, thinner and healthier, they follow up with securing her some professional therapy.

The camp experience helps Gabby to put her problem into perspective. She is among girls who have the same issues to contend with that she does. Her counselor empathizes with her because she suffered from the same problem.

The book is engagingly written and moves quickly. The sections describing Gabby's condition in graphic terms are very effective. Unfortunately, weight and physical appearance, despite the characters' disclaimers about what really counts about a person, seem to be the major factors that make a person attractive and worthwhile. The book is, nevertheless, a great discussion starter and source of information.

Loss of Physical Function

533. Bergman, Thomas. *Seeing in Special Ways: Children Living with Blindness.* Photos by the author. Gareth Stevens, 1989, LB (1-55532-915-2). 54 pp. Nonfiction.

Interest level: Ages 7–10

The children who are interviewed in this book attend the Tomteboda School for the Blind in Stockholm, Sweden. The children openly discuss their blindness and how they cope with it. Andrew, for example, uses his cane as "a long finger" and loves to sit in cars. Katie, who has limited vision, shares her worries about being taken advantage of by strangers, such as shopkeepers who might cheat her by giving her the wrong change. The author's questions are mostly of the yes-no variety, but the children make up for his lack of expertise by amplifying their answers. Each child emerges as an individual with special thoughts, ideas, reactions, and hopes.

534. Butler, Beverly. *Light a Single Candle*. Dodd, 1964. o.p. 256 pp. Fiction.

Interest level: Age 12+

In learning to accept her newly sightless condition in order to lead a full, rich life, 14-year-old Cathy Wheeler encounters not only such obstacles as doors and curbs but also people's prejudices and fears. Through her own determination and hard work and the help of her very supportive family and friends, Cathy manages to get through her initial depression and a semester at a dismal school for the blind. The author, who is blind, vividly describes how Cathy learns to have confidence in herself, get around with her guide dog, Trudy, make many friends, and achieve in her classes at the public high school.

535. Coutant, Helen. *The Gift*. Illus. by Vo-Dinh Mai. Knopf, 1983. o.p. 48 pp. Fiction.

Interest level: Ages 7–10

Anna, a shy young girl, moves into a new town and befriends Nana Marie, an old woman who has also recently moved there to live with her son and daughter-in-law. Anna and Nana Marie have lengthy conversations and see each other every day. When Anna finds her friend absent from the house one day, she fears that Nana Marie has been taken to a nursing home and that she will never see her again. Instead, it turns out that Nana Marie has been in the hospital with some mysterious illness that has left her blind.

When Anna discovers the news of her friend's blindness, she is devastated and spends the rest of the day trying to think of an appropriate gift to take to her friend. She finally decides to take her a complete, detailed description of her day as Nana Marie has taught her to see it. In essence, she is continuing to bring Nana Marie the priceless gift of friendship.

The story reminds us that friendship knows no age barriers, that old and young people can contribute to each other's happiness just as importantly as people the same age can. It is unfortunate that Nana Marie's family did not think about informing Anna of her friend's hospitalization. The temporary separation could have been made easier for both friends had Anna been told earlier.

536. Dugan, Barbara. *Loop the Loop*. Illus. by James Stevenson. Greenwillow, 1993 (0-688-09647-6). 32 pp. Fiction.

Interest level: Ages 5–8

Mrs. Simpson, a very old woman, and Anne, a girl about seven years old, spend their summer together enjoying such activities as feeding the ducks in the pond, playing cards and Scrabble, and playing with Mrs. Simpson's cat and Anne's favorite doll. Mrs. Simpson also demonstrates her remarkable prowess as a yo-yo player. The story is told from Anne's point of view, and the reader feels her anguish when Mrs. Simpson is hospitalized with a broken hip and seems more out of touch with reality than usual. Later, Anne visits her in the nursing home where she will stay for the foreseeable future. Anne smuggles in Mrs. Simpson's cat for a forbidden visit and leaves her beloved doll with Mrs. Simpson. The portrait of the vigorous old woman is an engaging one. The ending raises many questions about how to handle some of the problems attendant upon extreme old age and physical disabilities.

537. Johnston, Julie. *Hero of Lesser Causes*. Little, Brown, 1993 (0-316-46988-2). 194 pp. Fiction.

Interest level: Age 11+

Twelve-year-old Keely and her older brother, Patrick, enjoy a bantering, competitive relationship; one is always daring the other to take risks, such as standing in a bloodsucker-infested pond for 15 minutes. Both are becoming interested in the opposite sex, and this new preoccupation has added a layer of complication to their lives. It is 1946, the start of the polio epidemic. Patrick contracts polio and becomes paralyzed. This event has a catastrophic effect on him, his rage at this circumstance souring his disposition and making him suicidal. After a long stay in the hospital, Patrick returns home; the doctors feel they cannot help him and that he must try to improve his physical condition on his own. The family hires Peggy, a practical and amusing nurse, and she manages to make some inroads in Patrick's deep depression. Keely frantically tries to cheer Patrick up; she and Peggy rig up slings to enable him, once a talented artist, to draw. Keely brings friends to visit, including Alex, whose no-nonsense attitude affects Patrick and who ultimately convinces Patrick to use a wheelchair. By the book's unsentimental end, Patrick, after a feeble attempt at suicide, decides that there is much he can still enjoy, largely thanks to Keely, the spunky heroine of the story. The story's setting, just after World War II, provides a framework for the effects of the polio scare on the characters.

538. Levinson, Riki. *DinnieAbbieSister-r-r!* Illus. by Helen Cogancherry. Bradbury, 1987. o.p. 96 pp. Fiction.

Interest level: Ages 6–8

The title characters are siblings whose nicknames are always slurred together as one name in this atmospheric story of a Jewish family in Brooklyn during the 1930s. In those times, boys seemed to have everything, according to the five-year-old girl, Jennie. They took the elevated train to go to yeshiva, and they ran and hopped down the streets, seemingly "full of beans," while Jennie and her mother stayed behind talking.

The action takes place over a year's time, during which Abbie falls sick with an unnamed illness that keeps him from walking. The caring shown by all the family as Abbie is nursed back to health is movingly shown in vignettes—for example, Dinnie is unable to put his heart into going to school without his brother. Likewise, the tone of real conversations—whose toes can reach highest on the wall, who can be funny with bananas across one's teeth—brings home even more strongly the bonds of family affection. And, in spite of the times that said, "Girls do this, boys do that," Jennie, too, becomes more than just little "Sister-r-r"—she's soon full of beans, too.

539. Marsden, John. *So Much to Tell You . . .* Little, Brown, 1990 (0-316-54877-4). 117 pp. Fiction.

Interest level: Ages 10–12

Marina was disfigured by her father and has not spoken since. She is sent to a private school where a teacher encourages her to write about her feelings. Gradually, she begins to develop a relationship with a few of the girls, as well as the teacher, although she does not speak to them. Her contact with her mother and stepfather is confined to some breezy letters and a short home visit. Finally, she is taken to a hospital, but she determines that she would like to go back to school and see Cathy, who has become a special friend. Ultimately, Marina realizes that she must see her father, who is imprisoned not too far from Cathy's home. Marina manages to journey to find her father and is finally able to speak at their reunion. Although the plot sounds somewhat melodramatic, the story is written as a journal, which lends balance to the dramatic events. Marina is courageous and determined, and she overcomes incredible odds in a believable fashion. The reader is heartened by the reunion with her father. Despite the horrible events that preceded the story, it becomes evident that this is the parent with whom Marina should live.

540. Osofsky, Audrey. *My Buddy.* Illus. by Ted Rand. Holt, 1992 (0-8050-1747-X). Unpaged. Picture book.

Interest level: Ages 5–8

Buddy is a golden retriever who has been trained as a Service Dog. The young, unnamed narrator has muscular dystrophy and uses a wheelchair. In the two weeks of their training, he was literally linked to Buddy in order for the two of them to bond emotionally. Buddy and the narrator learned 60 commands during this program. Buddy can fetch items, click the light switch on and off, push elevator buttons, go to the store, and open and close doors. He regularly accompanies his master to school as well. Some parts of the story are a little confusing: Why does Buddy retrieve an empty milk carton from the trash? And how does he know which book to take from the library shelf? Young readers might be motivated to research the Service Dog program more thoroughly after being exposed to this book.

541. Thiele, Colin. *Jodie's Journey.* Harper, 1990, LB (0-06-026133-1). 170 pp. Fiction.

Interest level: Age 10+

Jodie's dream of being a champion horseback rider is shattered when the pains in her joints turn out to be rheumatoid arthritis, a debilitating illness that leaves her in severe pain and in a wheelchair until she is old enough for joint replacement surgery. She begins to accept flare-ups and remissions as a part of life. In the Afterword, we see Jodie several years later, still in chronic pain but leading a fulfilling life, including a career and helping young girls who are interested in horses. The author has had rheumatoid arthritis for over 40 years, so he speaks with authority when he describes the progression of Jodie's illness and the adaptations she makes. A fire and Jodie's heroism are based on fact, but they add an unnecessary melodramatic burden to the story. Nevertheless, the value of the book survives.

Cancer

542. Amadeo, Diana M. *There's a Little Bit of Me in Jamey.* Illus. by Judith Friedman. Whitman, 1989 (0-8075-7854-1). Unpaged. Picture book.

Interest level: Ages 6–9

Brian, the narrator, is Jamey's older brother. Jamey has leukemia, and he frequently gets sick during the night and has to be rushed to the hospital. The specifics of what happens at the hospital are described: A device is placed in the back of Jamey's hand for repeated drawing of blood; he is connected to an IV that drips medicine into his arm; and all visitors must wear masks so they don't contaminate Jamey with germs. When Jamey returns from the hospital, everyone fusses over him and Brian feels left out and unvalued. He erupts in anger one day, causing his parents to try to pay more attention to him. More details are given about the effects of chemotherapy and radiation on Jamey, but it becomes clear that the treatments are not helping. Brian is asked to donate some of his bone marrow to his brother so that Jamey's leukemia may be arrested. Again, details of the procedure are presented, and the book ends with the hope that Jamey will one day be well. Unfortunately—although the reader is made aware of

Brian's feelings and personality—there is little the reader learns about Jamey other than his illness and the fact that he collects baseball cards. This book is definitely from the perspective of the sibling of a very ill child, and it is useful in that function.

543. Bergman, Thomas. *One Day at a Time: Children Living with Leukemia.* Photos by the author. Gareth Stevens, 1989, LB (1-55532-913-6). 32 pp. Photo essay.

   Interest level: Ages 5–8

The words "Don't turn away" appear on the title page of this book, and it would indeed be tempting to close the book without seeing children who are suffering. This is a painful book. Yet Bergman, who is a photographer from Sweden, has carefully chronicled the illnesses of two small children and presented his essay in a powerful framework of matter-of-fact text. Hanna and Frederick go through the stages of treatment for leukemia. The reader is not spared their tears or pain. But it is marvelous how they cope with their illnesses, how, even at their young ages, they begin to take charge of their health care—for example, by giving themselves injections. Their families are also affected: When Frederick's nose bleeds profusely, the family cannot go on vacation. Hanna's baby brother is born while she is ill. The doctors and nurses at the Karolinska Hospital show genuine compassion for their young charges. The book does not promise cures, but it does say that both children must undergo more treatment before it is known whether they will get better. Still, the beautiful photographs of Hanna with newly grown hair and of Frederick playing with his brother give the reader hope that the children will survive. The question-and-answer page at the end of the book gives important factual information about leukemia and chemotherapy. Readers will be glad they did not turn away.

544. Brack, Pat. *Moms Don't Get Sick.* Illus. by Ben Brack. Melius, 1990, pap. (0-937603-07-4). 106 pp. Nonfiction.

   Interest level: Age 10

Ben's mother has breast cancer. The devastating news shakes up the entire family, especially when the cancer recurs. This book tells the story of one family's bout with cancer from two perspectives: Ben's and his mother's. The chapters, which have such titles as "The World Turned Upside Down" and "Bad Gets Worse," feature events as seen through their eyes. (To make it easier for the reader to tell who is speaking, Ben's thoughts and reactions are in italics; his mother's are in regular print.) Ben's anger, fear, and confusion are well expressed, acknowledged, and accepted. For example, at Christmas, Ben is delighted to have his mother home. In his exuberance, he rushes to give her a bear hug. Everyone in the room shouts a warning to prevent what might be a painful embrace. Ben is truly hurt, and his entry for that day reflects this. His mother's entry describes her reaction to the same scene, ending with "Both of us hurt." Ben's mother is recovering when the book ends. Obviously, writing the book was therapeutic for them both. This book is particularly useful because of the dual perspective, making it a wonderful communication tool for any family experiencing a similar situation.

545. Ferris, Jean. *Invincible Summer.* Farrar, 1987 (0-374-33642-3); Avon, pap. (0-380-70619-9). 167 pp. Fiction.

Interest level: Age 12+

Robin is diagnosed as having leukemia. When she is in the hospital for tests, she meets Rick, a charming young man who also has leukemia. Rick helps Robin through the hardest time of her condition: from first discovery through chemotherapy. When it is discovered that Rick's cancer has spread so that it is irreversible, it is Robin's turn to try to help him and herself.

The story is explicit in its description of both the physiological and the psychological effects of this serious illness. The story is more than a clinical description. The reader gets involved with Robin and her family. Although Rick dies, Robin has learned to value herself and life, and the story ends on a note of hope.

546. Fine, Judylaine. *Afraid to Ask: A Book about Cancer.* Lothrop, 1986, LB (0-688-06195-8); Morrow, pap. (0-688-06196-6). 177 pp. Nonfiction.

Interest level: Age 12+

A highly valuable resource on a difficult subject; Fine offers solid information through a writing style that enables her to make complex concepts understandable and memorable. Originally a Canadian imprint, the book has material that is up-to-date and future-oriented, including trends in prevention, palliative care, and treatment techniques (pion radiation, monoclonal antibodies, and so on).

Information about more than 20 specific types of cancer is offered in question-and-answer format. For each, there is a description of the body part and its function, what the particular cancer involves, who is at high risk, symptoms, diagnosis, and treatment. Fine's admirable gift for simile helps harness the scientific puzzlements of how cancer cells function. Her useful comparison objects are diverse, ranging from Indian corn and photocopy machines to "multicoloured marble cake before it has been baked," the last image describing cancer cells under a microscope.

Though potentially frightening and depressing, the material is not, because the author joins the reader as a student herself, always learning. Although the author's voice is heard throughout, she never intrudes. Instead, she asks the same logical questions her readers would ask, tries to solve the same problems, and airs the same confusions. Whether relating the anger of bereaved teens or explaining the scientific basis for body pain, she is the teenager's ally.

Some will read this excellent reference volume in its entirety; others will check out only the sections that concern them because of their own illness or those of relatives. A book that makes things so clear and treats readers so respectfully should certainly be on hand. Bibliography.

547. Gaes, Jason. *My Book for Kids with Cansur: A Child's Autobiography of Hope.* Illus. by Tim Gaes and Adam Gaes. Melius and Peterson, 1987 (0-937603-04-X); pap. (0-937603-09-0). 32 pp. Nonfiction.

Interest level: Age 6+

At age six, Jason comes down with Burkitt's lymphoma. As time goes on, he copes by recording his thoughts for other similarly afflicted children. His aim is to say kids don't always die. He relates how his cancer was discovered and describes operations, radiation, and chemotherapy. He gives advice on what to do in the hospital. He sounds candid and like a real little boy, albeit one blessed with fine, understanding parents. Jason tells one good effect of baldness: no shampoo in the eyes! Yet he doesn't play down the bad parts of cancer, such as endless blood tests. He's wise—kids who laugh at baldness are not very good friends anyway. Along the way, he folds in ideas for parents, such as get your mom to rock you when you're afraid. He even leaves his phone number for readers to call. The childish illustrations by his twin and older brothers and his squiggly beginning writing are effective. Allowing Jason's early-school spelling is overly cute; words like *toomer* (tumor) are distracting. Children deserve editors, too. Three years later, Jason is considered cured, but his dedication to another child touches home: Regarding the purgatory that living with cancer implies, "We're both waiting to see if our cancer comes back." Readers will root for him to indeed attain his aspiration to be a cancer doctor. On the whole, this book is well done and deserves wide attention by families who need it.

548. Gravelle, Karen, and Bertram A. John. *Teenagers Face-to-Face with Cancer.* Messner, 1987, LB (0-671-54549-3). 128 pp. Nonfiction.

Interest level: Ages 11–16

The authors, a science editor and a hospital psychologist, tell the stories of a group of teenagers who have had cancer. The point of view is one of adolescence normally being a time of tumultuous change resulting (one hopes) in some control over the changes, a reasonable self-image, and plans for the future. Cancer throws a monkey wrench into all of this, both for the teenage patient and for his or her family and friends.

Chapters cover the initial shock, varied treatments, surgery (including amputation), and types of cancer. Feelings are attended to throughout, and the chapter on dealing with doctors should also be read by the doctors themselves. Possibilities of recurrence are looked at statistically and from an emotional point of view. The chapters on relationships are especially rich with nuance (for example, taking on the hero image and then having it backfire with friends by seeming to be on another plane). Specific relationships are looked at individually—with parents, friends, siblings, school officials, and so forth. With an air of hope, the book offers a hefty section on planning for the future: career, marriage, and family. All are looked at realistically—for example, the medical aspects of having children while on chemotherapy or afterward.

Finally, coming to terms with possible death is explored, again realistically, and the words of the teens are picked up most eloquently here, echoing many frames of mind, from denial to fighting spirits to philosophies. Glossary, bibliography, index.

549. Greenberg, Jan. *No Dragons to Slay.* Farrar, 1984 (0-374-35528-2); pap. (0-374-45509-0). 152 pp. Fiction.

Interest level: Age 12+

Tommy Newman goes through the stages of denial, anger, and depression when he discovers he has cancer. The therapy he must undergo requires all of Tommy's stamina and strength and results in unpleasant side effects such as hair loss, nausea, and ultrasensitive skin. His family never comes to terms with his illness, but Tommy does; this results in a confrontation between Tommy and his father that ultimately opens the door to renewed communication. Tommy decides to join an archaeological dig as a summer project. While on the dig, he makes friends and finally accepts the possibility of his own death, making the decision to go on to college if he can. The book ends on a hopeful but unsentimental note as Tommy goes to Dartmouth, determined to keep meeting the challenges that lie ahead. The author manages to include the life-threatening disease without making this a didactic, single-issue book. Tommy is a teenager who must confront many issues other than cancer, and his relationships with his friends and mentors form an important part of the story.

550. Hughes, Monica. *Hunter in the Dark.* Atheneum, 1983 (0-689-30959-7); Avon, pap. (0-380-67702-4). 131 pp. Fiction.

Interest level: Age 12+

Mike's parents have protected and pampered him for all of his 16 years. They continue to try to protect him when it is discovered that he has leukemia. They keep the news from him, but Mike wants to know what is wrong. He finds out for himself what his illness is by researching his symptoms and treatment in the library. He handles the situation well, telling his parents that he knows and getting support and comfort from his closest friend, Doug.

Mike's treatments and his response to them are graphically described, but this is no clinical study. Mike's feelings of panic and desperation communicate to the reader. Mike doesn't want to die. He rages against his body, the illness, the treatments, and the world. He goes in and out of remission, and he determines to accomplish a goal of his or die in the attempt: He wants to hunt and shoot a white-tailed buck.

Doug and Mike had planned this hunting expedition for a long time, but now Mike wants to go alone, as a rite of passage, as a talisman against death. His solitary hunt serves as the setting for the story, which is told in a series of flashbacks. Mike does find a deer, and he has the opportunity to shoot it, but he decides not to. He returns home, having made his peace with death and having learned that no matter what happens he will have the courage to face it.

551. Hyde, Margaret O., and Lawrence E. Hyde. *Cancer in the Young: A Sense of Hope.* Westminster, 1985 (0-664-32722-2). 96 pp. Nonfiction.

Interest level: Age 11+

This accounting of the state of cancer treatment for young people offers balanced facts and, despite its age, an amazingly up-to-date picture of the outlook victims currently face. This book includes a description of cancer cells and how they multiply and spread and elaborates on specific cancers, including leukemia, bone cancer, brain tumors, lymphoma, neuroblastoma, retinoblastoma, and others. A large section of the book is devoted to diagnosis and treatment plans, and the reader is given a helpful description of how medical procedures might be conducted—a spinal tap, for instance. Because many seeking this book will already be diagnosed or have relatives/friends in that situation, this comprehensive quality is very helpful. Throughout, the words and feelings of young cancer patients give the book humanity and help the reader make a connection. The increasing attention given to support of cancer patients and their families is also elucidated, in discussion of special hospitals, support groups, camps, and so on. An extensive glossary and lists of cancer centers, organizations, camps, and hot lines are appended. A fine reference tool.

552. Krishner, Trudy. *Kathy's Hats: A Story of Hope.* Illus. by Nadine Bernard Westcott. Whitman, 1992 (0-8075-4116-8). 32 pp. Picture book.

Interest level: Ages 5–9

As a small child, Kathy loved hats. Then she develops cancer, her hair falls out, and hats become a necessity. Kathy's feelings about having to wear her hat reflect her natural concern about what her classmates will say and how they will react. She confides her fears to her mother, who is comforting and accepting. Then Kathy decides to put a favorite teddy bear pin on her hat; her friends and family respond by giving her other pins: one shaped like a valentine, another like the state of Minnesota. Soon she has a collection and feels much better about wearing her hat. The book ends on a hopeful note: Kathy's treatments are over, and it appears that her cancer has gone into remission. She celebrates at school with a party. The colorful illustrations are simple but exude a certain charm, especially when Kathy begins to dream about the hats in her future. This book is based on a true story about the author's daughter, which makes it even more useful for children who may be in similar circumstances.

553. Mazer, Norma Fox. *After the Rain.* Morrow, 1987 (0-688-06867-7); Avon, pap. (0-380-75025-2). 290 pp. Fiction.

Interest level: Age 11+

Rachel's grandfather, Izzy, is dying. He has a cancer caused by exposure to asbestos. Rachel goes to his house almost every day and walks with him. Until recently, she has not really known her grandfather, but now that she spends so much time with him they get to know each other very well. Even though her grandfather is often irritable and sometimes nasty, they develop a close connection. The author builds the relationship slowly, so that its intensity engulfs the reader.

The details of the inexorable disease are described with almost clinical precision, but they are as much a part of the story as any of the characters. As the disease progresses, Izzy gets weaker and weaker. His last days are spent in the hospital with Rachel at his side. She is with him when he dies. Her memory of him and the time they shared together enriches Rachel. She mourns, but she celebrates his life as well.

554. Naylor, Phyllis Reynolds. *The Dark of the Tunnel.* Atheneum, 1985 (0-689-31098-6). 207 pp. Fiction.

Interest level: Age 12+

Two themes are developed in parallel in this moving story. The major issue is that of Craig's mother, who is dying of pancreatic cancer. This is the more effective of the themes as it relentlessly details the mother's physical deterioration and its effect not only on her but also on Craig, his brother, and their uncle.

The other theme is an important one rarely found in books for young readers: the preparation for a nuclear attack. Craig's uncle is the county's civil defense chief, and he is responsible for preparing a safe place to evacuate the people of the county in the event of a nuclear attack. He is very much involved in the planning of a drill that the entire county will participate in.

Other people agitate more toward influencing the government that it is futile to plan for survival of a nuclear blast, that it is more important to work for peace. This cause is led by a man who has been devastated by war; his brother died in Vietnam, and he has been institutionalized because of his emotional response to his brother's death. He kills himself in a blast that destroys the tunnel that was to have been the shelter used in the drill.

It is clear that this is the author's message: It is better to work for peace than prepare for war. Although it has global implications, this message is less powerful here than the one of coping with the dying and eventual death of a parent.

555. Paulsen, Gary. *Tracker.* Bradbury, 1984 (0-02-77022-0); Puffin, pap. (0-317-62280-3). 90 pp. Fiction.

Interest level: Age 10+

John's grandfather is dying. The doctors have said that his cancer is so advanced that there is nothing they can do. John weeps and then spends lots of time denying that his grandfather will die. He has been raised by his grandparents; they are his closest friends, and he cannot bear the thought of losing his grandfather.

John and his grandfather have gone deer hunting together each season. Now John must go alone. He strikes a bargain with himself: If he can get close to a deer, not kill it, but touch it, then his grandfather will not die. He stalks a doe, one that has come to his grandparents' farm just before hunting season begins. He does not kill her, but he touches her, and returns home to tell his grandparents of the experience. His grandfather is impressed and proud of John's feat, but John realizes that the bargain was a false one—his grandfather will die.

The spiritual conflict with and acceptance of death drives the story. It is poetically and sometimes mystically told. The inevitability of death and the mourning that precedes the actual death are palpably conveyed here.

556. Swenson, Judy Harris, and Roxanne Brown Kunz. *Cancer: The Whispered Word.* Illus. by Jeanette Swofford. Dillon, 1986. o.p. 40 pp. Nonfiction.

Interest level: Ages 6–9

Part of the Understanding Pressure series, this volume is very worthwhile. A child tells the story of his mother's cancer and her treatment. The upheaval the family goes through is well portrayed (for example, the child's embarrassment over the mother's loss of hair). Questions of contagion and inheritability are answered. Up-to-date resources for getting through the trauma, such as support groups, are used.

Advice is given on protection from cancer (for example, sun protection), and the warning signs are explained. New concept words are highlighted, and the book has a glossary, an adult resource guide, and two unique inclusions: activity suggestions, such as writing down feelings and methodically sharing responsibilities, and a short recipe section for easy cooking that children can do to help out. Very helpful.

557. Trull, Patti. *On with My Life.* Putnam, 1983. o.p. 144 pp. Nonfiction.

Interest level: Age 12+

This extremely moving story tells of an adolescent's struggle with a sarcoma that cost her a leg. Trull was diagnosed around her fifteenth birthday, but she went on to beat a highly malignant disorder, becoming a hospital worker with young cancer patients. Down-to-earth and honest, the various chapters deal with the family's shock, her own very intense feelings, and her uphill battle with schools that didn't want to let her study toward her goal in occupational therapy. Trull tells of trying to be happy, although there is unhappiness in her life. She lets readers in on her world travels and romances as well as ways she found to get around with one leg. Each child whom she has helped as a therapist becomes vibrant, and through her work with them the reader comes to deep understanding of the trauma of cancer and the courageous sense of adventure meeting that trauma can bring.

AIDS

558. Check, William A. *AIDS: Encyclopedia of Health.* Chelsea, 1988 (0-7910-0054-0); pap. (0-7910-0481-3). 128 pp. Nonfiction.

Interest level: Ages 12–16

This look at AIDS is written by the former editor of the *Journal of the American Medical Association,* who previously won the American Medical Writers Association Book Award for *The Truth about AIDS.* The volume boasts a lengthy, insightful introduction by former Surgeon General C. Everett Koop.

Check offers the necessary biological understanding, but his entry in the growing adolescent AIDS bookshelf is primarily an epidemiological, sociological perspective. One third of the book is devoted to tracing the early cases as they turned up in New York, San Francisco, Africa, and other places around the world, discussing the patients and pioneering doctors involved and examining the roles of various medical centers in putting the pieces of the puzzle together. The stories are told in a fascinating manner, even though they are tragic—fights between the United States and France over honor, nations reluctant to share statistics for fear they'll be labeled country of origin, and the power of denial making it difficult to provide information for prevention. Chapters are devoted to the search for drugs and a vaccine, blood testing and its attendant controversies, and the heartbreaking dilemmas AIDS has wrought—how to give medical care to such large numbers; how to help drug addicts in the face of a federal government that talks about a war on drugs yet won't pay for treatment; and how to care for dying infants whose parents are dying as well. The author emphasizes behavior change (safe sex only with partners who are known well and in a caring relationship) as the only hope to avert worldwide disaster, believing that this can come about through information, counseling, and the brave societal response we are already seeing, as exemplified by the gay community and people of influence in film and other media.

Check is a graceful writer, and his sympathies won't elude the adolescent reader, who is likely to read this book from cover to cover. One hopes readers will take up his idea of the only preventive treatment available today: "behavioral vaccination." List of resources, glossary, index.

559. Colman, Warren. *Understanding and Preventing AIDS.* Photos and illus. Childrens, 1988 (0-516-00592-8); pap. (0-516-40592-6). 128 pp. Nonfiction.

   Interest level: Age 12+

Stories of individuals (such as Ryan White) and the question-and-answer chapters give invaluable information teens may not have thought of: You can't tell by looking; the virus inactive in a partner can become active in you; sharing razor blades might be unwise. It's a caring, daring treatment that bends toward the conservative but is aware of adolescent behavior. Thus in one and the same book is discouragement of sexual involvement ("Most experts believe that teens really aren't emotionally ready for a deep, committed relationship—the kind of relationship many feel should accompany sex") and instructions on how to put on and take off a condom. The color photographs are medical, sometimes grisly—closeups of Karposi's sarcoma, a sad picture of a hospital boarder baby, and a microscopic view of AIDS. A unique feature is the accounts of plagues from other eras. Here is a mature, technically informative yet feelingful account, fully cognizant that knowledge is rapidly changing. The presentation is scientific and statistically thorough. A first-class, highly recommended book on the subject. List of organizations and hot lines, bibliography.

560. Durant, Penny Raife. *When Heroes Die.* Atheneum, 1992 (0-689-31764-6). 136 pp. Fiction.

   Interest level: Age 12+

Gary is devastated to learn that his adored Uncle Rob is dying of AIDS. His mother tries to help Gary understand but is understandably absorbed in caring for her brother. Rob's friends, particularly Christie, an older next-door neighbor, are supportive when they learn about the situation. Rob dies near the end of the book, and Gary must not only come to terms with the death but also with his newfound knowledge that Uncle Rob was gay. Although Gary doesn't question how Rob contracted AIDS until well after he hears the bad news, when the author introduces the topic of homosexuality, she does so in an accepting manner. Gary's feelings of bewilderment and initial horror are acknowledged; he is able to continue the loving relationship with Uncle Rob until the end.

561. Fassler, David, and Kelly McQueen. *What's a Virus, Anyway? The Kids' Book about AIDS.* Waterfront, 1990 (0-914525-14-X); pap. (0-914525-15-8). 85 pp. Nonfiction.

   Interest level: Ages 5–8

For the very youngest of readers, this workbook-type presentation outlines simply and clearly what the AIDS virus is and how it manifests itself. Some pages contain children's drawings and questions, such as "What's a virus, anyway?" and "How does someone get AIDS?" Answers, in the simplest of terms, are then given on the following pages. In answer to how one gets AIDS, the author lists four statements, explaining that people get AIDS from those who have HIV in their blood, and that drug users may also get it from sharing needles. He also points out that babies can get it even before they are born if their mothers have the virus. He then goes on to list seven ways people can't get AIDS: from mosquito bites, toilet seats, drinking fountains, touching or hugging, shots from the doctor, coughing and sneezing, or sharing food or toys. The strongest message is one of dispelling fears and myths about AIDS.

562. Girard, Linda Walvoord. *Alex, the Kid with AIDS*. Illus. by Blanche Sims. Whitman, 1993, LB (0-8075-0245-6); pap. (0-8075-0247-2). 32 pp. Picture book.

   Interest level: Ages 5–9

Alex joins the fourth grade three days after the start of school and is assigned a seat next to Michael, the narrator of the story. The children have already heard about Alex, who contracted AIDS through a blood transfusion. A nurse prepares the children, telling them about the disease and reinforcing the doctor's and principal's message that it is safe to attend school with a child who has AIDS. Alex's teacher tolerates misbehavior from him and treats him as a special case. Alex takes full advantage of his special status. Finally, after he has been hurtful and rude, his teacher acknowledges her error in treating him differently and lets him know that he will be expected to behave like a typical member of the class. Although not much is imparted about AIDS in this book, the reader learns that children with serious illnesses need to be treated like other children, not as if their condition is their only characteristic. In this story, Alex becomes a boy in the class, not just "the kid with AIDS."

563. Greenberg, Keith Elliot. *Magic Johnson: Champion with a Cause*. Lerner, 1992, LB (0-8225-0546-0). 64 pp. Nonfiction.

   Interest level: Ages 8–11

A well-paced biography of the talented basketball star that focuses on his handling of the fact that he contracted the AIDS virus. Most of the book describes Magic's early years and his experiences and talents as a basketball star. The author tells how Johnson decided to inform the world about his condition shortly after he learned of it. Known for his generosity of spirit on the court (Magic often passed the ball to teammates rather than try to score points himself), it is no surprise that he would choose to devote his energy to educating about AIDS. He has been an important factor in changing many young people's behavior and thus has perhaps prevented some from acquiring the virus.

564. Hausherr, Rosmarie. *Children and the AIDS Virus: A Book for Children, Parents, and Teachers*. Photos by the author. Clarion, 1989 (0-89919-834-1); pap. (0-395-51167-4). 48 pp. Nonfiction.

   Interest level: Ages 5–9

The major part of the text, written in larger type, is directed toward young children. Additional text, in smaller print, adds information of a more spe-

cific and advanced nature for older children and adults. The author's intent
is to be as informative and as comforting as possible so as to allay children's fear of contracting the AIDS virus. She points out that in the not-
so-distant past virally caused diseases such as measles, mumps, and polio
were also deadly and unpreventable. She holds out hope that a vaccine
may be found to prevent AIDS as well. The author focuses on the causes
of AIDS as well as situations where there is no danger, such as playing
with animals or toys, touching doorknobs or toilet seats, kissing, insects,
sharing food, holding hands, or handling money. She assures children that
they may play with children who have the virus, even swimming in the
same pool or enjoying snacks together. The black-and-white photographs
underscore the information in the text.

565. Hyde, Margaret O., and Elizabeth Forsyth. *AIDS: What Does It Mean
to You?* Walker, 1986 (0-8027-8202-7). 128 pp. Nonfiction.

Interest level: Age 12+

A "catastrophic collapse of the immune system"—the authors' definition
bespeaks compassion. Theirs is a difficult task: to reassure in midst of battle while governmental response remains hopelessly inadequate. The picture may be too rosy in early comment, "It seems likely that most people
have nothing to fear from AIDS." News stories about inaccurate statistics
and rapid spread among heterosexuals give pause, supported by even the
authors' own estimate: "Each day . . . as many as two thousand people . . .
who belong to the high risk groups, may be acquiring the virus." Aiming
at balance between sensible precaution and concern for sufferers, information on spread, medical progress, and research studies are given human
dimension through profiles of sufferers, comparisons with plagues in other
times, and controversies (for example, testing by insurers and employers).
Scientific yet journalistically accessible—a very worthwhile overview.
Glossary, organization list, index.

566. Hyde, Margaret O., and Elizabeth Forsyth. *Know about AIDS.* Illus. by
Debora Weber. Walker, 1987 (0-8027-6920-9). 80 pp. Nonfiction.

Interest level: Ages 8–12

The authors of a book on the same subject for teens, *AIDS: What Does It
Mean to You?* (see above entry), this prolific reporter-psychiatrist team
also brings the message to a younger group. Their aim is to answer children's questions and help teachers in that task. Most of the time, they succeed, as the book explains the possible origins of AIDS, virus mechanisms
and how this particular virus seems to work, the primary risk groups, who
might need a test, and the search for a cure. On occasion, however, they
falter, as in their statement (which might be misconstrued): "People do not

get better when they have AIDS." This doesn't allow for small improve-
ments or small recoveries, only a steady decline. Also not reassuring is the
story of the child afflicted with AIDS who lets herself cry only during
therapy sessions. Why can't she cry at other times? She certainly has
something to cry about. On the whole, though, the individual stories
strengthen the work and help children to have beginning empathy (for
example, foster care of an AIDS child, and a child whose bisexual father is
afflicted). The book has another strength: crediting the gay community for
its role in creating awareness. Interestingly, adults who read this book may
discover new information, such as the fact that the disease has different
characteristics in varying geographic locations, or that pregnancy can
bring about full-blown AIDS in a woman infected with AIDS-Related
Complex.

567. Jordan, Mary Kate. *Losing Uncle Tim.* Illus. by Judith Friedman.
Whitman, 1989, LB (0-8075-4756-5); pap. (0-8075-4758-1). 30 pp.
Fiction/picture book.

Interest level: Ages 9–11

Uncle Tim—a favorite of the story's main character, Dan—has AIDS.
When his mother tells him, Dan is angry and confused, but he seems to
understand the ramifications of what he has been told. As spring progresses, Uncle Tim weakens. Dan and his father discuss Uncle Tim's disease; the father is reassuring and accepting about Dan's fear that he may
catch AIDS. Dan visits Uncle Tim, plays checkers with him, and tells him
he loves him. Uncle Tim loves Dan, too. When Uncle Tim dies, Dan is
comforted by the legacy that his uncle has left behind. The pictures are
somewhat washed out—probably due to the printing process, rather than
to the watercolors themselves—but they add to the quiet tone of the book.

568. Kesden, Bradley. Produced by Oralee Wachter. *Sex, Drugs and AIDS.*
Photos. Bantam, 1987, pap. (0-553-34454-4). 76 pp. Nonfiction.

Interest level: Age 14+

This is a book based on a film produced by the New York City Board of
Education. It was scarcely shown to its students because, in the opinion of
some of its critics, it did not stress abstinence enough. As a film adaptation, it has a magazine format and approaches AIDS from several viewpoints. There are first-person stories and worries; friendly advice from
Rae Dawn Chong, who starred in the film; and common questions and
responses. Throughout, the message "AIDS is hard to get" is repeated.
That does not mean precaution is not necessary, and the book discusses
drug abuse and straight and gay sex. Homophobia is also discussed, and
the short magazine format makes the material easily digestible, somehow

retaining the active voice that film allows—for example, "Remember, just one fix with an infected needle can give you the AIDS virus." Some of the profits from this sensible book have been set aside for AIDS research.

569. Kittredge, Mary. *Teens with AIDS Speak Out.* Messner, 1992, LB (0-671-74542-5). 119 pp. Nonfiction.

   Interest level: Age 12+

The author communicates in strong, direct, sometimes colloquial language what AIDS is, how it is contracted, and what is currently being done to prevent and treat it. She highlights teenagers' stories as examples. Dawn used drugs and had unprotected sexual relations with people using drugs when she was a young teenager. By the time she was 19, she had settled down, gotten married to a responsible young man, and had a baby. The baby died of AIDS when she was 18 months old. Dawn now is an advocate for AIDS prevention. Jim contracted AIDS through unsafe sexual relations with a male friend when he was 15 years old. Not all of his family and friends know that he is a homosexual or has AIDS. Mike got infected at age 13 by a man who assured Mike that he was healthy. And so the stories go. The book reports on the specifics of treatment and advises young people on how to avoid the deadly disease.

570. Landau, Elaine. *We Have AIDS.* Watts, 1990, LB (0-531-10898-8). 126 pp. Nonfiction.

   Interest level: Age 12+

The deadly disease is dramatically personalized through first-person accounts by nine teenagers of their ordeal with AIDS. Interspersed between narratives is factual information about the virus and its means of transmission. Some of the stories are also grim accounts of abuse and betrayal. It is painful to read about children who have turned to prostitution or have been hooked on drugs by people they trusted. Other stories, like Paul's, are sad in a different way: Paul and his brother Danny contracted the virus through contaminated blood products they received during treatments for hemophilia. Each of the young people knows that no one has survived the disease, but those with supportive families and friends have the comfort of knowing that people care about them and that they are not alone.

571. Lerner, Ethan A. *Understanding AIDS.* Illus. Lerner, 1987 (0-8225-0024-8). 64 pp. Nonfiction.

   Interest level: Ages 8–12

The author, a doctor with a Ph.D. specializing in immunology, makes a head-on attack on AIDS and all the tension and fear it has brought to the world. Starting with a tittering classroom discussion about swollen lymph glands and strep throat, soon the sick child's classmates are asking if he has AIDS. And what is AIDS? "It's something that queers get," yells a classmate. And so we get the idea this is going to be a book that doesn't skirt issues as they may be felt by countless people—one issue being denial: putting AIDS into just one category of people, not at all "like us." Soon enough, though, Lerner teaches readers not to be so confident that they are not at risk. By framing similar stories and supplementing them with question-and-answer paragraphs, the author provides full discussions of homosexuality and its connection to AIDS, transmission by blood transfusion, becoming infected through sharing drug needles, how children become infected, and so on. The chapters address most of today's newspaper issues as well, such as a description of condom use and questions about children with AIDS being allowed to attend school. (The answer here is that they can as long as they are mature enough.)

In one riveting chapter, a young man named Stefan tells of his own life cut short. Not yet finished with college, he has AIDS, even though as a gay person he tried to be careful. Stefan tells of his earlier wish to believe it couldn't happen to him, of his shock, and of his current treatment. Through the device of Stefan (whether he is a real person or not we do not know, but the author has actually worked with AIDS victims), we learn of other people's reactions: Most people stayed on the swim team when Stefan told them of his illness, but a couple thought the pool was permanently infected. He tells also of his growing weakness and eventual need to stop swimming, even of his AIDS dementia. Throughout, new concept words are highlighted. For the age group, this is a sensible discussion that is unafraid. As the months and years go on, however, it may become dated in its highlighting of special groups and de-emphasis on the general population.

572. LeVert, Suzanne. *AIDS: In Search of a Killer.* Messner, 1987, LB (0-671-62840-2). 140 pp. Nonfiction.

   Interest level: Age 12+

LeVert offers a combination of reporting on epidemiological research and compassionate visits with affected individuals. Opening with questions and answers about AIDS, she covers the basics as known in 1987—who gets AIDS, how, and the biological basis of its spread. She follows with a scientific analysis of immunology, a history of the disease, and case studies. The book is especially strong on the heroic efforts of the gay community to fight for their survival and on discussions of civil rights regarding insurance, housing, jobs, and testing. The author occasionally fails to meet issues head-on, as when she says, "Homosexual men contract AIDS more often (in this country) than heterosexuals because they frequently perform a certain sexual act common, but not exclusive, to the homosexual lifestyle."

Because of AIDS, parents are forced to discuss sex in much more graphic detail with their adolescents than they'd ever imagined they would, trying to give both warning and understanding. Those parents unable to muster the nerve to discuss sexual issues may rely on books to give the full story and say real phrases like "anal intercourse." It's a shame the author and/or publisher skirted the issue here.

LeVert refers to AIDS as a clever disease. She makes an analogy between the search for its cure and a mystery, what with its killers, victims, false leads, modus operandi, and doctor detectives. Her analogies give the book its interest, heartbeat, and challenge. Index.

573. Miklowitz, Gloria D. *Good-Bye Tomorrow*. Delacorte, 1987 (0-385-29562-6); Dell, pap. (0-440-20081-4). 150 pp. Fiction.

Interest level: Age 12+

Told through the voices of three of the characters, Alex, Shannon, and Christy, the story treats a topic of high interest in today's society: AIDS. Alex is a clean-cut teenager who is neither gay nor a drug user. He has, however, had two blood transfusions because of an automobile accident. It turns out that Alex has AIDS-Related Complex (ARC) and that he will have to be careful to avoid infections, but he does not have AIDS. His doctor tries to explain the difference to him and his family. Then Alex must explain the difference to his friends, teachers, and principal.

Miklowitz includes many details about AIDS and ARC within the context of the story. She also describes the reactions of Alex's friends and family. For a while, it looks as if Alex will be ostracized, but in the end his closest friends stand by him, and the reader can hope for the best.

Abuse

Physical, sexual, and emotional abuse are coming more and more to the forefront of our attention. Whether this is true because of greater incidence or better reporting strategies, it is still a problem of concern. Abused children experience a terrible loss of self-esteem and of confidence in adults. The loss may be compounded if the abusing adult is a parent and that parent is removed from the house, or if the child is sent to a foster home as a result of the abuse being discovered. Children need to know that they are not at fault and that they have the right to be heard. They also need to know that they are not alone. As with other emotionally charged themes, this one should attempt to avoid sensationalism and lurid detail. Victims need to be seen as real people with characteristics other than those inflicted by abuse.

General

574. Boegehold, Betty. *You Can Say "No": A Book about Protecting Yourself.* Illus. by Carolyn Bracken. Golden, 1985 (0-307-12483-5). 28 pp. Nonfiction.

Interest level: Ages 4–9

In this book, part of the Golden Learn about Living series, the first-person narration of varied youngsters covers numerous anxiety-producing situations. For example, "I'm shopping with Mom—and Mom disappears! I can't find her anywhere. Either she's lost—or I'm lost!" Then the boy must choose among alternatives, including going with strangers, to which he says, "No. Absolutely not!" Other situations include: being approached by a stranger in the park and told his mother wants him home and he'll take him there; and countering abduction by running, yelling, hitting, kicking, and/or fooling the abductor.

A segment involves discriminating among people one knows. A girl will say "Hi" to the mailman and apartment building superintendent, but not to the man who sweeps the sidewalk. "I don't like him. I don't like the way he talks to me. Or looks at me." The story goes on to this man's attempt to "comfort" her by patting her between her legs, her running away, and discussing her fear with mother. Mother says, "Nobody is allowed to touch me that way—nobody. This is my own special body and nobody can fool with it." The second child talks of playing "funny games" with an uncle and, through a friend, getting the nerve to tell her mother.

This book has many situations covered in brief pages. Parents will want to share the book numerous times so youngsters can grasp the message, perhaps sharing only one segment at a time. The note to parents, always included in this series, tells parents what to teach their children for self-protection, including letting you know if someone wants to give a present or keep a secret between himself/herself and the child. Also included are signs of sexual abuse and what to do if a child is indeed assaulted.

575. Chlad, Dorothy. *Strangers.* Illus. by Lydia Halverson. Childrens, 1982, pap. (0-516-41984-6). 32 pp. Nonfiction.

Interest level: Ages 3–7

Simply, a girl named Susie tells readers about strangers. "A stranger is someone you don't know. Be careful when you go to school . . . your friend's house . . . the playground . . . or the park." On subsequent pages, a stranger beckons her into a car. She warns, "Never get in!" Beyond saying no, she tells readers, try to remember what the stranger and the car looked like, the license plate, and so on. And tell your parents, brother (sexist?), or teacher. Instructions are also given for a stranger offering gifts. Say no, and if the stranger touches you, "Scream as loud as you can. Kick as hard as you can. And run away as fast as you can." The book closes with the guidance that it's safer to stay with your friends and family than be off on your own. The illustrations show multiethnic children and adults. Strangers are both men and women.

576. Cleaver, Vera, and Bill Cleaver. *Hazel Rye*. Harper, 1985, pap. (0-06-440156-1). 178 pp. Fiction.

Interest level: Age 10+

When we first meet Hazel, she is content to remain ignorant, unlettered, and unambitious. Her mother has abandoned her. She is her father's darling and his sole companion. She is dirty, quick-tempered, and self-indulgent. By the time we reluctantly leave her, she has begun her quest for knowledge and a wider circle of friends and interests. What is more, she now knows the extent to which her father has been involved in keeping her isolated and restricted. We wonder how Hazel will manage to overcome his destructive intervention in her life, but we are given some clues when we hear her planning how she will become more and more independent and self-sustaining.

The book's characters are all well drawn and memorable. Felder, a young boy who assists in Hazel's awakening, is a gentle, extraordinarily intelligent, talented person, reminiscent of Dickon in *The Secret Garden* (Lippincott, 1987), except that Felder is a voracious reader. He is particularly gifted in making things grow and in understanding human beings. We must believe that he and Hazel will meet again and that she will have the courage and strength to overcome her father's abusive and insidious hold on her.

577. Dolan, Edward. *Child Abuse*. Watts, 1992, LB (0-531-11042-7). 128 pp. Nonfiction.

Interest level: Age 12+

This careful look at child abuse has been expanded due to the apparent increase in cases of child abuse over the past several years. The author provides a chronological look at the practice of child abuse along with some reasons for current trends. Particularly effective is "How Can You Help?," the chapter on ways in which readers can respond to child abuse. Although they are difficult to read, the suggestions about identifying specific times that abuse occurs and patterns of behavior that trigger attacks are extremely practical and helpful. Unfortunately, at times the author skirts dangerously close to the issue of blaming the child for the abuse. The most useful way to share this book would be for an adult to discuss it with a child and emphasize that abuse is never an acceptable response to anything a child says or does. An extensive, thorough bibliography reflects the latest research in this area.

578. Girard, Linda Walvoord. *Who Is a Stranger and What Should I Do?* Illus. by Helen Cogancherry. Whitman, 1985 (0-8075-9014-2). 28 pp. Nonfiction.

   Interest level: Ages 4–9

The book is almost a manual for young children on how to deal with strangers. It points out that it is perfectly all right to talk to strangers if you are in the company of an adult. But when you are alone there are certain rules to follow. It explains the reasons for the rules, and phrases the rules in clear and simple language, so that children will not be frightened but will understand exactly what is being said.

   The book provides a definition of strangers and tells where strangers may be encountered, including those who telephone or come to the house. There are rules such as "Never get into a car with a stranger" that must be followed. The book also provides a set of exercises for children to try that invite them to simulate what they would do in certain situations. All in all, the book, although not imaginative or entertaining, is a useful guide.

579. Hyde, Margaret O. *Know about Abuse.* Walker, 1992 (0-8027-8176-4). 94 pp. Nonfiction.

   Interest level: Ages 8–11

This book is full of general information about abuse written for a younger audience. There is a historical overview followed by an explanation of the forms that abuse may take at different ages in a child's life. The author describes such types of abuse as prenatal drug addiction and sexual abuse. One side effect of abuse in the home—running away—is also explored. Fictionalized accounts of abuse enhance the statistics and factual information presented. This serves to sharpen the awareness that this is a problem all too often faced by real people, as do the photographs of people who have been affected by this problem. Although the book does not go into detail about agencies that can help those confronting some form of abuse, there is a page of helpful telephone numbers to call for advice.

580. Landau, Elaine. *Child Abuse: An American Epidemic.* Messner, 1990, LB (0-671-68874-X). 128 pp. Nonfiction.

   Interest level: Age 11+

Concentrating on child abuse in the family setting, Landau gives admirable in-depth attention to varied causes that might turn otherwise loving parents into abusive ones, among them past deprivations of the parents, familial isolation, and unwritten societal sanctions. Psychological abuse can be as devastating as physical abuse, says Landau. And because the book is geared toward teens, she pays special attention to the particular concerns of abused teens, a broad variety of topics ranging from overly heated arguments to sexual abuse. Most important, she gives readers ideas as to why their parents might be acting as they do. Because finding a way to get help often presents a double bind (Am I disloyal? Will I be further abandoned?), Landau offers helpful information about ways to seek help without running away or becoming a suicide statistic. Readers may find practical routes here, such as group living arrangements. A hefty portion of this level-headed book is also devoted to discussion of organizations that can be of service, such as the Clearinghouse on Child Abuse and Neglect. Bibliography.

581. LeShan, Eda. *When Grownups Drive You Crazy.* Macmillan, 1988 (0-02-756340-5). 144 pp. Nonfiction.

Interest level: Ages 8–12

Noted parent educator LeShan here takes on the foibles of parents, bringing her knowledge to children so they can with open eyes learn to love themselves, try to be good people, and try to understand themselves and others, albeit in their limitations. The chapters concern many kinds of interactions between children and adults, going beyond parents to teachers and others. Some are serious types of "craziness," such as abuse; others are persistent aggravations. Her information and advice center on adults who make children angry, frightened, or embarrassed. The range of the book is broad: from parents who keep secrets or lie, to those who are out of control when drunk or otherwise abusive of those in their charge.

As in earlier books, LeShan shows great respect for children's capacity to understand. She therefore dares to share stories of her own parenting mistakes and her own sexual abuse by a trusted family doctor. Her many anecdotes about families will help readers differentiate between idiosyncrasies and serious problems. Whichever kind children face, LeShan provides alternative ideas for action and samples of actual words children can say to show how they feel.

Surprisingly, LeShan makes little reference to outside help, and most of her focus is on becoming a good reader of behavior instead. In her attendance to subtle matters that are nonetheless important (overprotection, immaturity, unpredictable mood changes, interference with privacy), LeShan speaks about points that haven't been addressed much in children's books. Because youngsters are the ones most likely to bear the brunt of small problems as well as large, she performs a needed service.

Physical Abuse

582. Anderson, Deborah, and Martha Finne. *Robin's Story: Physical Abuse and Seeing the Doctor.* Illus. by Jeanette Swofford. Macmillan, 1986 (0-87518-321-2). 48 pp. Nonfiction.

Interest level: Ages 5–9

The fictional child used to relate information about child abuse is Robin, whose early grade teacher notices she has a cut on her forehead. Robin's mother has thrown a cookie tin at her, causing the injury. She does that sort of thing when she gets angry, then she gets remorseful, but it happens again. And she instructs her child not to tell. "If anyone asks what happened tomorrow at school, tell them you ran into a door." But with gentleness, the teacher elicits the real story. The sequence of referral is then from teacher to social worker to doctor to child protective services worker. All the workers in this case are female. They are also all understanding, knowing how hard it is to tell the story over and over. Robin expresses her fears: Will she be sent to a foster home? The ending is not a foster home, of course, but help for both child and mother, so that the abuse doesn't continue. As is the case with the other books in this Child Abuse Books series, extensive end matter includes a discussion of physical abuse: differences between discipline and abuse, places to get help, and a list of whom to tell. Glossary, note to adults.

583. Froelich, Margaret Walden. *Reasons to Stay.* Houghton, 1986. o.p. 181 pp. Fiction.

Interest level: Age 12+

In a tangled story, three children live together with a weak mother and an abusive father. In actuality, the man is father to two of the children and the woman is mother to two of them. Babe, the eldest, has been taking care of the family as best she can, and when her mother dies, she tries to keep the two younger children from being further abused. Only after her mother dies, when Babe hears the neighbors shouting at her "father," does she discover that he is, in reality, not her father, and that her mother was not her "sister" Florence's mother. This confusing turn of events is as incomprehensible to the reader as it is to Babe.

Somehow, after a strange journey by mule and wagon, the children are deposited with a remarkably kind and generous family. This family, the Shaws, takes them in; the wicked stepfather is killed in a flood; Babe finds her family of origin; and all three children become a permanent and happy part of the Shaw family.

Despite the confusion and the needlessly tangled prose in some parts of the book, and despite the idyllic ending, there is strong writing here. Some of the sections are so painful as to cause the reader to have to pause in the reading. Babe is a heroic figure, and her character makes the book worth reading.

584. Kurland, Morton L. *Coping with Family Violence.* Rosen, 1990 (0-8239-1050-4). 141 pp. Nonfiction.

Interest level: Age 12+

The psychiatrist author of this book tells of individuals who wisely sought counseling for problems of violence in the family. Episodes include examples of children caught in the crossfire of divorce; children victimized by confused, frightened parents who married or bore children too early; and families where drug abuse is the source of out-of-control behavior. Also discussed are murderous impulses and actions; sexual violence perpetrated within the family and on children who are not within the family by teachers, coaches, friends, and so forth. In an unusual section not found in books about abuse, Kurland pays attention to those occasions in which sibling rivalry exceeds normal bounds and becomes dangerous to those involved.

Woven into the case stories are pieces of information about psychology and how the human mind works (for example, when discussing sibling rivalry, Kurland notes that Freud was "Golden Siggy" to his mother). Each story also includes names of relevant organizations (Al-Anon, for example) that could be of help to readers, and the book culminates with steps to identify violence that is threatening, including recognition of the behavior, validation, and confronting those involved. An overview of the kinds of people who can be of service is included.

The book is broader than many often seen, reminding readers of experts they might otherwise overlook, such as religious experts. The stories are interesting and the lesson repeated throughout is valuable—violent behavior usually cannot be changed by family members alone. Professional help is a must.

585. Magorian, Michelle. *Good Night, Mr. Tom.* Harper, 1986, LB (0-06-024079-2); pap. (0-06-440174-X). 336 pp. Fiction.

Interest level: Age 10+

Willie Beech—an eight-year-old who has never slept in a bed, taken a bath, played, or had other basic experiences—is placed in a home in the country in order to escape the bombing of London in World War II.

Willie's stay with Tom Oakley is a dream compared to the nightmare of his abused life with his mother. Just when Will's sores are healed, he has learned to read and write, has grown to love the country, and has his first friends, his mother calls him back to London, claiming she is ill. She *is*, but her illness is not physical, and she tortures Will and kills a baby she has had in his absence. Will is saved from death by Tom, who comes to London especially to rescue him. First printed in England, this story is graced by distinguished writing. Will's relationships with Tom, his teacher, and others are delicately touching. Although Tom is portrayed as almost too good to be true, the author makes the reader want so much for Will to succeed that one is ready to forgive this minor flaw. The book provides a special, memorable experience for its readers.

586. Rench, Janice E. *Family Violence: How to Recognize and Survive It.* Lerner, 1992, LB (0-8225-0047-7). 64 pp. Nonfiction.

Interest level: Age 10+

Each chapter contains a brief but specific description of a form of family abuse. The contents include details of abusive behavior and ways children can get help when they discern that they are being subjected to abuse. Physical abuse, for example, is listed as slapping, punching, burning, pushing, or biting. Children are informed of their rights and are helped to recognize the difference between discipline and abuse. They can be distinguished from each other partly by the reasonableness of the action and partly by the intent. When an act is meant to teach acceptable behavior, it is not likely to be hurtful. Physical punishment is not seen as an acceptable means of discipline. Emotional abuse includes neglect and the denial of love or affection. Each chapter contains a short vignette illustrating the particular kind of abuse focused on in that section. In addition to physical, verbal, and emotional abuse, are sexual, elder, sibling, and domestic abuse. The last chapter discusses the importance of self-esteem and recommends some strategies for the improvement of self-esteem. A list of resources and hot lines completes this informative, simply stated book.

587. Roberts, Willo Davis. *Don't Hurt Laurie!* Illus. by Ruth Sanderson. Aladdin, 1988 (0-689-30571-0); pap. (0-689-71206-5). 176 pp. Fiction.

Interest level: Ages 9–12

The well-publicized syndrome of the parent who was abused in childhood and grows up to abuse his or her children is presented here. Laurie's mother lies to teachers and hospital staff when suspicions are aroused; she even moves when necessary. Wherever they go, Laurie is not permitted friends, for she might leak the secret. Her mother reasons that Laurie deserves to be burned, have her bones broken, and chased with a kitchen knife because she resembles her deserting father. Laurie, meanwhile, entertains fantasies that her mother will be crippled and her father will return to rescue her. Almost no one realizes what Laurie's mother is doing, not even her new husband, a traveling salesman. An exception is Laurie's younger stepbrother, who at seven is on adolescent Laurie's wavelength. Laurie's dawning realization that she may one day be killed brings about sudden resolution: She seeks refuge in her stepgrandmother's house. Although at first her stepfather cannot believe what he is hearing, his decent nature comes through and he protects everyone and ensures an intact family at the end. This book can evoke discussions about blind spots. In what circumstances do we deny reality? Do we have choices when we fail to see the truth? When are blind spots lifted? Is it always healthy to remove blind spots?

588. Sachs, Marilyn. *A December Tale*. Doubleday, 1976. o.p. 87 pp. Fiction.

Interest level: Age 11+

Myra and Henry Fine have been placed as foster children in the home of an abusive woman and her dysfunctional family. Their father is remarried, and he doesn't want anything to do with the children. Myra is forced to do all sorts of menial labor and is physically abused, along with her brother. Myra is angry because she thinks that if Henry weren't around, her father would permit her to come home. When Henry is beaten so brutally that Myra fears for his life, she realizes that she loves him and she finally takes hold of their situation. Together, the children find a sympathetic older woman who consents to harbor them. The major message in this painful but well-written book is that abused children must, like Myra, take their fate into their own hands and not permit themselves to be abused any longer.

589. Stanek, Muriel. *Don't Hurt Me, Mama*. Illus. by Helen Cogancherry. Whitman, 1983 (0-8075-1689-9). 32 pp. Fiction.

Interest level: Ages 6–10

After her father deserts her and her mother, life changes drastically for the young girl. She and her mother move to a city where no one knows them, and they are isolated. The mother can't get a job, and she begins to drink too much and to hit her daughter. One day, she beats her daughter with a belt and admonishes her not to tell anyone. When the child gets to school, her teacher notices that something is wrong and sends her to the nurse, who discovers what is wrong, informs a social agency, and gets help for the family.

With today's focus on helping the abusive parent and keeping the child at home with the parent, this book helps readers understand that abusers are often victims too. As a matter of fact, it is the mother whose feelings we can empathize with. The little girl seems to manage unusually well, and she does not share her emotions with anyone. It would have been helpful for the author to let us in on how she feels. Although the ending in this book is somewhat unrealistic in its swiftness and total resolution of the problem, it serves to bring up the issue of abuse in a hopeful context.

590. Stark, Evan. *Everything You Need to Know about Family Violence.* Rosen, 1991 (0-8239-1314-7). 64 pp. Nonfiction.

Interest level: Ages 8–12

Despite its title, this book points out that abuse is not limited to physical violence, but includes emotional, sexual, and economic abuse as well. It also includes two other forms of abuse: isolation and gender roles. Isolation is described as controlling someone's behavior in terms of freedom to move about one's daily life and cultivate friendships. Gender roles include unfair treatment based on sexual discrimination. The design of the book is inviting: different fonts, black-and-white and color photos, bold-face print, and bullets for statistics are combined to attract the reader and make the information presented as clear as possible to the young reader. Although much of the information is very basic, the tone is suitable for a younger audience. Glossary, brief bibliography, and a list of resources.

591. Voigt, Cynthia. *The Runner.* Atheneum, 1985 (0-689-31069-2); Fawcett, pap. (0-449-70294-4). 192 pp. Fiction.

Interest level: Age 12+

Set in Maryland in the late 1960s, the story describes Bullet Tillerman, a strong 17-year-old long-distance runner. He trains regularly, is the best on the school team, and has been the state champion for two years. But he is a loner. His relationship with his father is an ugly and combative one. His father is an overbearing, abusive authoritarian who has repressed and subdued his wife into silence and has driven Bullet's older brother and sister from their home. For Bullet, running is his outlet, and he values it above everything else in the world.

The product of a Southern white segregated and bigoted society, Bullet refuses to coach a promising black athlete, Tamer Shipp, and as a consequence is thrown off the team. Then Bullet discovers that his employer and only close friend, Patrice, is of black heritage. No longer so certain that his view of the world is the right one, he now realizes that his feelings for Patrice transcend any boundaries of color, so he agrees to work with Tamer. He neither offers nor expects friendship, but in the process of running and working together the two young men come to understand and respect each other, and together they win the state championship for their team.

Bullet's anger at his father never abates. He may know that his mother adored him, but if he does it is not because she reveals it openly to him. She travels miles to watch his last race, but she leaves without congratulating him. Bullet leaves home on his eighteenth birthday, enlists in the army, and is sent to Vietnam, where he is killed in action. When his mother hears of his death, she erupts into passionate anger at herself and the world.

The Runner gives us information about what happened before the events in *Homecoming* (Atheneum, 1981), *Dicey's Song* (Atheneum, 1982), *A Solitary Blue* (Atheneum, 1983), and, particularly, *Come a Stranger* (Atheneum, 1986). As with the other Tillerman family stories, it presents the reader with powerful insights into the relationships within families and the forces, internal and external, that shape the thinking and behavior of young people.

592. Woolverton, Linda. *Running before the Wind*. Houghton, 1987 (0-395-42116-0). 152 pp. Fiction.

Interest level: Age 10+

The story is an insightful and, at times, moving exploration into the feelings of a girl in early adolescence who experiences conflicting emotions on the death of her abusive father. Kelly Mackenzie, who is 13, has a father who, on his good days, can be charming and fun to be with, but more often than not he displays a disagreeable and violent temper, which is mostly directed at Kelly. The explanation for the father's behavior includes the fact that he was abused by his family's housekeeper; that he is very unhappy in his work because he keeps getting passed by for promotion; and that he was once a very gifted runner but was stricken with polio and never came to terms with his disability.

Kelly loves running and has been invited by the junior high school track coach to join the team. Her father violently forbids her to do so. The idea that Kelly can be successful when he cannot seems to be too much for him to tolerate. Kelly is unable to find support from her mother or sister, both of whom are subdued by Mr. Mackenzie's outbursts as they desperately attempt to keep peace in the household at any cost. It seems to Kelly that they consider her to be at fault for her father's outbursts. She cannot discuss the situation with any of her friends; they are all involved with their own problems. Her only outlet is her running, which she does secretly.

When Kelly's father dies in a boating accident after a particularly violent incident during which Mr. Mackenzie beat both Kelly and her dog, Kelly is torn between her relief that the abuse has ended and her grief at losing the father she often loved and enjoyed. Her mother and sister are immersed in grief over their loss. Kelly is further confused and dismayed when she recognizes how alike she and her father were in many ways, and she sees in herself the potential for violence. Fortunately, Kelly confides in her gym teacher, an athlete and excellent coach, who both trains and counsels Kelly so that she can come to terms with her anger and guilt, understand and forgive her mother and sister, and bring closure to her rage at her father.

In addition to having written an engrossing story, the author has contributed enormously to helping young readers acknowledge the complexity of such a painful issue as abuse.

Emotional Abuse

593. Hunt, Irene. *The Lottery Rose.* Berkley, 1987, pap. (0-425-10153-3). 100 pp. Fiction.
    Interest level: Age 11+

Georgie is an abused child. His mother and her boyfriend have mistreated him for all of his seven years. He eventually goes to a Catholic school, where he is treated better than he ever was before. He slowly begins to heal emotionally and eventually establishes a loving and permanent relationship with a woman whose life has been full of tragedies. Although the book contains some clichés (a mentally retarded boy dies), the language and power of the book are extraordinary. Be prepared to cry; this is a very touching story.

Sexual Abuse

594. Anderson, Deborah, and Martha Finne. *Margaret's Story: Sexual Abuse and Going to Court.* Illus. by Jeanette Swofford. Dillon, 1986. o.p. 48 pp. Nonfiction.
    Interest level: Ages 5–9

Few books exist on helping children cope with the process of testifying in court, a frightening ordeal for most. Using the fictional device of Margaret, who narrates, the authors (administrators of a child abuse service center) tell about a typical child's encounter.

Margaret tells her mother that Thomas, a man who lived across the street, put his hand in her shorts and wanted her to touch him. Her mother explains there is something wrong with Thomas. She is very angry with Thomas, but not with her daughter. And she's glad her daughter told her. Both loving parents support their child and enable Thomas to come before the law, assuring Margaret that she is in no danger. A social worker helps get Margaret ready to testify by showing her the court and explaining procedures. An understanding lawyer has Margaret draw about her experience and shows her the details of the courtroom, having her sit in the chair to answer practice questions. Thomas lies about the abuse and is sent to jail, where he is given treatment. "That meant that people would help him learn that he shouldn't hurt children." Margaret expresses fears that continue through the difficult trial period and beyond. "Mom and Dad said when I feel that way, I should ask for a big hug and a little talk."

The story is followed by information for the young reader about sexual abuse, explaining: "No one has a right to touch you on your private parts without a good reason." Good reasons include going to the doctor or being touched by parents or guardians if you are sick, hurt, or have gotten dirty. Other rights are explained in the context of the story, for example, Margaret saying "no." A list of places to get help is appended, plus a glossary and a note to adults regarding believing the child, being calm and reassuring, and reporting the abuse. The courtroom preparation Margaret receives is caring, competent, and thorough, a good model for professionals and families involved in abuse trials.

595. Bass, Ellen. *I Like You to Make Jokes with Me, but I Don't Want You to Touch Me.* Illus. by Marti Betz. Lollipop Power, 1985, pap. (0-914996-25-8). 28 pp. Fiction.

Interest level: Ages 3–8

The supermarket clerk, Jack, comes too close to protagonist Sara; his tickling and teasing become frightening. Jack claims, "Who me? I'm just a silly old man." But Sara's mother tells her, next time "you can tell Jack that you like him to make jokes with you, but you don't want him to touch you." When the child is too shy, her mother practices with her in a humorous fashion until she feels confident. Then, when the time comes, Sara carries it off, Jack understands, and the situation is solved. The story is developed believably and can teach children gently about one of the most irritating annoyances of childhood: Encountering the adult who, while not really dangerous, is not adequately cognizant of boundaries between people and, particularly, between adults and children. A good job on an unexplored subject that deserves mention.

596. Benedict, Helen. *Safe, Strong, and Streetwise: The Teenager's Guide to Preventing Sexual Assault.* Illus. Atlantic, 1986 (0-316-08899-4); pap. (0-87113-100-5). 192 pp. Nonfiction.

Interest level: Age 12+

This manual is blunt and to the point. It can save lives because it gives clear advice and doesn't shy away from difficult issues. Crisis counselor Benedict writes for girls *and* boys with an acceptance of possible teenage sex before marriage; she's also knowledgeable about youngsters' concerns as vulnerable beginners in adult life. The difficult subjects she deals with range from incest to doctors, teachers, and other professionals who betray their power of authority, yet she remains positive and empowering: "You can change that." Direct guidelines are offered for safety, from not working in a store alone, to safe places to park with a date. Also shown are physical self-defense techniques (for example, the Power Yell) and guilt-evoking date mind games ("You know you want it") and how to turn them off. More broadly useful than just against sexual attack, the instructions for home, school, street, and job safety can also avert mugging, robbery, and other frightening crimes. Appendixes for both teens and parents add to this book's exceptional value. Truly outstanding.

597. Caines, Jeannette. *Chilly Stomach.* Illus. by Pat Cummings. Harper, 1986. o.p. 32 pp. Fiction.

Interest level: Ages 5–9

"When Uncle Jim tickles me, I don't like it." He also kisses Sandy (who appears to be about age 9 or 10) on the lips, and she gets a "chilly stomach." To make the point, this book about child abuse uses the contrast of affection that feels better. When Sandy's mom and dad "kiss me I feel nice and happy and cuddly." Sandy's initial strategy is to avoid her uncle. She asks to sleep at a friend's when Uncle Jim stays over. Her friend then advises her to tell her parents. Sandy fears her parents won't like her anymore, yet comes to terms with plans to talk. "But I want them to know." This story works in its simplicity and use of metaphor.

598. Cooney, Judith. *Coping with Sexual Abuse.* Rosen, 1991 (0-8239-1336-8). 128 pp. Nonfiction.

Interest level: Ages 11–16

The tone is straightforward; the examples used to define sexual abuse are to the point and, therefore, startling. Cooney makes a worthwhile differentiation between an anonymous molester and a sexual abuser, adding times when they may converge as one. Following this, a chapter explodes myths—for example, that the sexual abuser is usually a stranger to the victim, or that sexual abuse is a twentieth-century phenomenon.

A subsequent chapter explores girls as victims of a father or father figure, and breaks abuse into stages: encounter, engagement (second approaches and, thereafter, usually petting), marriage (actual intercourse), divorce (termination by whatever means: telling, leaving home, and so on). Not all abuse reaches the marriage stage, of course. Boys as victims are given similar treatment. Then a chapter about the family context and particular family problems as they may influence patterns offers insight into the larger picture. This is followed by a chapter discussing the effects of abuse—physical and emotional—and one about treatment services available for individuals and families. As many readers will have great fears about reporting abuse, Cooney wisely devotes a full chapter to that, too. In this chapter, she uses a question-and-answer approach, which was not used in the rest of the book. Each chapter ends with a summary and discussion topics. Resource list, index.

599. Freeman, Lory. *Loving Touches: A Book for Children about Positive, Caring Kinds of Touches.* Illus. by Carol Deach. Parenting Pr., 1986 (0-943990-21-1). 32 pp. Nonfiction.
   Interest level: Ages 3–5

Focusing on positive kinds of touching, this book can serve as a preparation for children to understand the differences between loving touches and abusive ones.

600. Gallagher, Vera, with William F. Dodds. *Speaking Out, Fighting Back.* Madrona, 1987 (0-88089-010-X); pap. (0-88089-022-3). 224 pp. Nonfiction.
   Interest level: Age 12+

Here, readers meet women who have triumphed over childhood sexual abuse to go on to marry, work productively, and help others. Sister Vera Gallagher has worked with the Good Shepherd Sisters for more than 30 years to help oppressed women without regard to their religious affiliations. Sister Vera Gallagher put together some of the women's stories, looking at how the order helped the women come to terms with their fears, rage, and guilt. The portraits, told mostly in the first person, serve to show how a history of abuse can lead to myriad difficulties later in life: drug addiction, prostitution, violence, and/or a tendency to keep the abuse going in the next generation. Professional, caring help enabled these victims of abuse to find once again feelings of self-worth. Young people who are now victims of abuse may find hope in reading about the drama of others who have made it through and who now join the professionals who helped them in saying, "Speak out, fight back." Bibliography, index.

601. Girard, Linda Walvoord. *My Body Is Private.* Illus. by Rodney Pate. Whitman, 1984 (0-8075-5320-4); pap. (0-8075-5319-0). 32 pp. Nonfiction.

Interest level: Ages 5–9

Narrated by Julie, a young girl, the book explains in simple but respectful language that children are entitled to privacy in many situations and especially to autonomy over their own bodies. Words like *vagina* and *penis* are used without embarrassment and without the substitution of nicknames or euphemisms. It is made clear that any kind of touching, if it is not acceptable to the *child*, is not acceptable. Julie's father does not permit her brother, Rob, to keep on tickling her when it is no longer a pleasant sensation for Julie. Julie's mother asks the doctor to inform Julie before he needs to examine her "in places that her bathing suit covers." Julie's parents give her permission to refuse to sit on her uncle's lap when he visits, because Julie doesn't like it when her uncle rubs her arms.

Julie and her mother have a conversation about what Julie could do if anyone wanted to touch her in a way that Julie did not want to permit. Julie's mother asserts that she will always want to hear about anyone who menaces Julie, no matter who it is, even if it is someone in the family. She explains that it is not good to keep things like this a secret.

The book distinguishes between good and bad touching, and it in no way prevents a child from enjoying the good kind of touching. It also models the importance of preparing children to be able to cope with any incidents before they happen, rather than reacting to them afterward. The book is sensible and careful. It is an excellent guide.

602. Hall, Lynn. *The Boy in the Off-White Hat.* Scribner, 1984. o.p. 87 pp. Fiction.

Interest level: Age 10+

The story is narrated by Skeeter, a 13-year-old who is staying with 9-year-old Shane and his mother, Maxine, on their ranch in Arizona as a mother's helper for the summer. During the course of the summer, a man named Burge becomes a regular visitor to the ranch. He courts Maxine and is a surrogate father to Shane, but for some reason, Skeeter doesn't like him.

Skeeter's instincts are accurate. Burge abuses Shane sexually and terrorizes him into continued submission. Even though Skeeter and Maxine notice that something is wrong with Shane, that he seems afraid of Burge, they can't make Shane tell them what is wrong.

One day, Shane claims that he is no longer Shane; he is John. It is in the guise of John that Shane is able to tell Skeeter what Burge has done. Burge is arrested. It turns out that he has a record of molesting young boys. Maxine is guilt ridden. Shane is taken for some psychiatric treatment, and he and Maxine enter a program of therapy. The story effectively communicates the importance of helping children express their fears and learn to stand up for their rights.

The fact that the story is narrated by Skeeter gives it a detachment that rescues it from melodrama. The information given by the social worker at the end of the book is accurate and helpful. But the book itself reads more like a fictionalized case history than a story, perhaps because we never really get to know any of the characters well enough to think of them outside the context of the sexual abuse. Nevertheless, it is well written and interesting and can be useful reading for young people and their caretakers.

603. Howard, Ellen. *Gillyflower.* Atheneum, 1986 (0-689-50323-7). 106 pp. Fiction.

Interest level: Age 12+

Gilly regularly retreats to a fantasy world she has invented in order to shut out "the secret." Her father has regularly been abusing her sexually, and she does not know what to do about it. Her mother, a nurse, works the night shift, and her father has been out of work for a long time. Her father asks her to come to keep him company, and then he engages in sexual acts with her. Gilly thinks that it is her fault that her father is doing this. He warns her to keep it a secret.

The strain of keeping the secret affects Gilly's relationships with her friends. She becomes a loner. She fears that her father will abuse her younger sister, Honey, and she cannot tolerate that thought. When some new people move in next door, she is attracted to them because they plant a garden with beautiful flowers. They seem to be an ideal family. It is because of their friendship, and particularly because she thinks that her father has already molested Honey, that she gets the strength to tell her mother. Her mother moves out with her and Honey, and her father receives help. Gilly goes to a counselor, who helps her to see that it was not her fault.

The story is well told. It is suspenseful and moving, not a dry case study. The focus is on Gilly; her mother and father are somewhat shadowy figures. But she is a vivid and understandable character, and readers cannot help but empathize with her.

604. Hyde, Margaret O. *Sexual Abuse: Let's Talk about It.* Westminster, 1987 (0-664-32725-7). 106 pp. Nonfiction.

Interest level: Age 11+

This revised and enlarged edition expands on the author's previous writings and explores the issue of sexual abuse with depth and concern. In addition to a thoughtful foreword by Judge Lisa A. Richette, the book encompasses the key areas of sexual abuse: what it is, how it happens, what to do if it happens to you, and what will probably happen next in a variety of scenarios. Statistics and studies document statements made by the author whenever necessary. Also included is a description of what kinds of people become abusers. The author maintains that there is no single profile of an abuser, but she does specify characteristics to look for in teenage offenders, particularly a lack of contact with people their own age. Two victims of abuse, Bob and Binney (probably fictional), disclose their stories, including how each handled their problem. The author has included an extensive list of helpful state agencies and national organizations, as well as a bibliography of recommended books and audiovisual materials.

605. Irwin, Hadley. *Abby, My Love.* Macmillan, 1985 (0-689-50323-7); Dutton, pap. (0-8239-0808-9). 157 pp. Fiction.

Interest level: Age 12+

Abby is beautiful, intelligent, and popular. It is difficult to believe that her father has regularly abused her sexually. She finally tells Chip, who loves her, and Chip tries to help her, but in the end Abby must help herself. She tries to tell her mother, but her mother can't or won't believe her. It is only with outside intervention that Abby manages to get her mother and sister to go to therapy with her. Her father, a successful dentist, leaves the family, and everyone is the better for it.

The book is helpful in informing the reader that incest is not simply a lower-class problem. On the surface, Abby's father seems to be a doting father and pleasant person, and Abby shows no outward signs of her ordeal. No indication is given of what drives the father, and the reader does not get to know the mother at all. Even Abby is a somewhat shadowy figure. The only character who emerges clearly is Chip, the narrator. The story would undoubtedly have been more sensational had Abby narrated it, but this secondhand account, veiled in mystery, distances the reader and lessens the impact of the truth. Nevertheless, the story is an important one to tell, and readers will undoubtedly benefit from it.

606. MacLean, John. *Mac.* Houghton, 1987 (0-395-43080-1). 175 pp. Fiction.

Interest level: Age 13+

Mac is experiencing typical adolescent conflicts: He is bothered by his younger brothers; he is struck dumb when he encounters a girl to whom he is attracted; and he has friends with whom he engages in a bantering sort of rivalry. But something happens that changes Mac's life: He is sexually abused by a physician during a routine physical examination. The experience is so traumatic that Mac becomes unable to maintain any sort of relationship with anyone. He breaks up with the girl he adores, starts having fights in school, and, in general, behaves very differently from his usual self.

At last, his concerned principal connects Mac with an excellent counselor, who approaches Mac in an effective and appropriate manner and finally gets him to tell her what happened. She then helps him to realize that the assault was not his fault and that he can, indeed, engage in normal relationships with the people he loves. She also takes him to a group meeting where other victims of sexual abuse talk to each other about their experiences and their feelings. At the end of the book, both the reader and Mac have learned a lot about how to cope with sexual abuse.

The factual information in no way detracts from the plot in this excellent book. Young readers will not only benefit from the information here, they will also be totally absorbed in the story. Some potentially objectionable language is used, but it is in the context of the characters' interaction. This is not a book for children under 12, but teenagers will certainly be drawn to and get much benefit from it.

607. Parrot, Andrea. *Coping with Date Rape and Acquaintance Rape.* Rosen, 1988 (0-8239-0784-8); pap. (0-8239-0808-9). 140 pp. Nonfiction.

Interest level: Age 13+

An unusual, valuable book that will meet a very special need. Writing for males as well as females, Andrea Parrot, a professor of sexuality and expert on date rape, recognizes that both men and women can be raped. Starting off by debunking myths (a rapist is always a stranger; rape victims are always attractive), she explains that most date rapes occur because a man has planned to have sex. When he is thwarted or his fantasies fall apart, the rape may be an attempt to get what he thinks he deserves. Drinking can compound the problem. Acquaintance rape can take place between other kinds of "pairs": teacher/student, doctor/patient, employer/employee, friend of the family, and so forth.

Through examples culled from interviews, types of rapists are examined—for example, the power rapist, the anger rapist, and the sadistic rapist. The reasons behind rape are explored in terms of female socialization, influence of the media, male confusion about *no* possibly meaning *yes,* and males who personify their penises, thereby abdicating responsibility for its actions. Many men do not even know they have committed a rape, having attached sexual meaning to gestures that may have merely meant friendly interest or having believed exaggerated reports of a girl's sexual availability.

Because many people reading the book will have been victims of rape, Parrot goes into depth about the feelings that may ensue: distrust; fear of a bad reputation; anguish over being blamed, although the victim. Other chapters cover responsibility, ways to get help, and advice about being careful about safety, alcohol consumption, and messages that may be confusing. Parrot's use of actual words people can say to get out of uncomfortable situations will be very helpful, as will the chapter devoted to people who have, knowingly or not, raped someone who has said no. Appendix of resources, glossary, bibliography, index.

608. Reynolds, Marilyn. *Telling.* Peace Ventures, 1989, pap. (0-929848-01-2). 187 pp. Fiction.

Interest level: Age 12+

The story focuses on a 12-year-old girl's experience being molested by the man for whom she baby-sits. Cassie confides in her cousin, Lisa, who tells her parents. Cassie's abuser leaves town after he is caught assaulting a second 12-year-old girl. A policewoman, a positive force in the book, helps Cassie realize that "telling" is the only way to release some of her feelings about the trauma she has experienced. Although she is initially reluctant, Cassie begins seeing a therapist who helps her to understand what has happened to her and to work through her guilt and the feeling that she might have somehow asked for it. A small independent press, Peace Ventures, published this important book; it is hoped that a wide audience will be exposed to it.

609. Scott, Carol J. *Kentucky Daughter.* Clarion, 1985. o.p. 186 pp. Fiction.

Interest level: Age 12+

Mary Fred Pratley leaves her rural Kentucky home to live with her aunt and uncle in Virginia. She wants to get a good education so that she can return to Kentucky as a teacher. Her father has been killed in a mine cave-in, and her mother, an excellent weaver and craftswoman, is struggling to support the four children in the family.

Mary Fred often acts as if she is too good for her family. She is ashamed of the coat her mother made for her birthday; she always corrects her sisters' speech; and she is disdainful of an old man who is consistently helpful to the family. When she gets to Virginia, she encounters a number of problems. Several of the girls are cruelly derisive of her because of her name and her Kentucky background. Her English teacher keeps grading her papers with Cs; and when she goes to speak to him about her work, he molests her sexually.

Fortunately, Mary Fred has the good sense to speak to the principal about the teacher, and it later turns out that the teacher has also molested two other girls. The principal persuades the teacher to resign, and she informs the girls' families about the incidents. Mary Fred's aunt and uncle assure her that she can come to them for help whenever she needs it; Mary Fred receives word from home that things are looking up, that her mother is beginning to receive recognition for her work. In the process of listening to how her family feels about her and her behavior, Mary Fred begins to grow up and put things into perspective. She recognizes that her behavior has, indeed, been snooty, and she starts to value her heritage.

Carol Scott authentically presents us with the issues and dilemmas that can confront a young teenager in her search for a better future. The story clearly brings out the value of a supportive family. Scott also helps readers to find strategies for coping with such difficult problems as abuse from adults and peers and the feeling of being different from and ashamed of one's background.

610. Shuker-Hines, Frances. *Everything You Need to Know about Date Rape.* Rosen, 1992, LB (0-8239-1509-3). 64 pp. Nonfiction.

Interest level: Age 12+

This clear examination of date rape and its ramifications provides a helpful tool in exploring the issue of date rape. The author points out that date rape is such a hidden topic that sometimes men don't realize that they have raped a woman, that there are even occasions when women won't realize that what has happened to them is rape. The definition of *rape* is given as *forced sex.* The author clarifies and expands on the definition and helps readers overcome misinformation. She also gives helpful advice on how to prevent date rape from happening. Much of the book concerns debunking common myths, such as "When a woman says 'no,' she really means 'yes.'" Included are suggestions for friends to help victims and guidelines for what to do if date rape happens. Fictionalized accounts of teenagers coping with date rape increase the readability of the book.

611. Terkel, Susan Neiburg, and Janice E. Rench. *Feeling Safe, Feeling Strong: How to Avoid Sexual Abuse and What to Do If It Happens to You.* Lerner, 1984 (0-8225-0021-3). 72 pp. Nonfiction.

Interest level: Ages 10–16

Using a pattern of story followed by discussion, this book presents six situations of various abuse intensities: being forced to be kissed by a relative; being asked to model for a lascivious neighbor taking pornographic photographs, followed by coercive blackmail; exhibitionism; incest; obscene phone calls; and rape. Each story is portrayed in terms of an individual child—for example, Sarah, who encounters an exhibitionist. In the stories, sometimes the child solves the problem alone, sometimes he or she needs a supportive adult to step in or give advice. In the effort toward believability, the stories tend to meander, with too much detail. Sometimes it's distracting (as in the story in which the name amuses: Ashley Montague Morgenstern); sometimes the point cannot be predicted until well into the story (five pages go by before it is evident that "You Can't Judge a Book by Its Cover" ends in exhibitionism).

Following each story, the discussion contains danger signals. An example is: "If you tell anyone . . . , no one will believe you." The discussion also contains psychological information and advice about what to do if confronted with the situation. The information and advice are very honest and down-to-earth—for example, in regard to exhibitionism, "Very few people go through life without encountering [exhibitionism]." In terms of practicality, to avoid abduction, the authors remind children not to wear clothing announcing their names. The authors, a child-development expert and a writer and director of a rape crisis center, convey important material about self-assertion, stating: "Before you can stand up for your personal rights, you must first recognize how you feel."

War and Displacement

War should not appear to be simply a case of right versus wrong. It is always more complex than that. It should be made clear that each war differs from the others in detail, causality, implications, and historical context. War should not be made attractive or glamorous. Books about all wars are available in fiction as well as nonfiction and reflect many stances. Even literature about the Revolutionary War has undergone many stages in terms of authors' perspectives. From a glorious, sometimes glorified description, it has changed to include a recognition of the problems and controversies surrounding the war. The same is true with the Civil War. Authors have communicated clearly that not all Southerners were wicked and not every Union soldier or sympathizer was virtuous. Books about slavery, which once was depicted in a surface fashion simply as an evil institution, now include examinations of individuals' experiences and feelings within this dreadful practice. Similarly, World War II is not an unalloyedly righteous war. The Holocaust provides much material from many different perspectives in many genres.

The Vietnam War, the first war the United States lost, and one that caused painful controversy within the country, is just beginning to be described from differing viewpoints. Refugees have become more and more a consequence of war and a responsibility for the host countries. Personalized accounts, eye-witness documentation, and poignant reflections constitute some of the literature here, too. Nuclear war—although no longer perceived as having the same degree of threat since the end of the Cold War—still looms as a possible result of carelessness or insanity, although few books for children have yet to examine this aspect.

General

612. Aitkens, Maggi. *Should We Have Gun Control?* Lerner, 1992, LB (0-8225-2601-8). 96 pp. Nonfiction.

   Interest level: Ages 9–12

The author lays out the arguments for and against gun control, provides several anecdotes about the use of guns and their danger, offers comparative data about state laws and international practices, and provides a questionnaire to help readers place themselves as advocates or opponents of gun control. The text is designed as a spur to discussion and further research. The author is meticulous in presenting both sides of each of the arguments.

613. Climo, Shirley. *King of the Birds.* Illus. by Ruth Heller. Harper, 1988 (0-690-04621-9); pap. (0-06-443273-4). 32 pp. Picture book.

   Interest level: Ages 5–9

In this pourquoi tale, the birds conquer chaos and settle their battle over who should be their king. Each bird assumes that its qualities are the most important ones required to rule: the skylark sings loudest; the mockingbird warbles a variety of tunes, not just one; and the peacock possesses gorgeous plumes. Surprisingly, the king turns out to be the wren, who wins through a combination of cleverness and tenacity. The illustrations are detailed and richly colored. The sources for the story are old European variants and a Chippewa tale. Children may enjoy arguing over the logic of the contest and its winner and may discuss the ways the conflict was resolved.

614. Creighton, Jill. *The Weaver's Horse.* Illus. by Robert Creighton. Firefly, 1991 (1-55037-181-9); pap. (1-55037-178-9). 32 pp. Picture book.

   Interest level: Ages 6–9

Lord Henry, a once-rich man who has returned from war, finds that his brother has commandeered his castle and possessions and has sold his beloved horse. Henry, weary of war and violence, has made a solemn vow of peace, so he leaves his brother and finds work as a weaver. As he develops his skills, he finds himself weaving intricate, passionate depictions of horses. When rage overtakes him, Henry weaves fierce dragons. As he works out his innermost emotions in thread, his reputation spreads. The loss of his horse and his eventual reunion with the cherished animal figure strongly in the story. Although he is plagued by thoughts and dreams of excruciating violence, with the help of his cousin, a healer, Henry learns to conquer his rage.

615. Kronenwetter, Michael. *The War on Terrorism.* Messner, 1989 (0-671-69050-7). 138 pp. Nonfiction.

Interest level: Age 12+

Part of the Issues for the 90s series, this balanced book offers an informed, intelligent look at terrorist organizations around the world. Identifying the 1972 attack on Munich's Olympic Village as the beginning of the "new age of terrorism," the book continues by offering four major characteristics of terrorism itself: it is political; clandestine; violent; and ubiquitous. The book explores reasons for terrorism and attempts to penetrate the mindsets of the people behind the masks. One chapter, "The Garden of Terror," investigates the particular brand of terrorism that exists in the Middle East; other groups (the IRA, "Euroterrorists," the Colombian M-19) are represented as well. There is even an annotated listing of Terrorist and Anti-Terrorist Organizations in the Appendix. Other chapters include information on responding to terrorists; hostages; economic sanctions; and weapons of the future. The journalistic design of the book is attractive; the photographs are dramatic but not sensational. Although recent attacks of terrorism on American soil are not discussed, the book is chillingly timely.

616. Landau, Elaine. *Terrorism: America's Growing Threat.* Lodestar, 1992 (0-525-67382-2). 115 pp. Nonfiction.

Interest level: Age 11+

Today's complex society has allowed for the growth of many forms of terrorism, all of which are identified in this balanced and moderate book. The book profiles many of the organizations that are recognized as being at the forefront of the terrorist movement, both foreign and domestic. The author identifies elements of all terrorist movements and myths associated with addressing the issues of terrorism, such as the erroneous assumption that all terrorists are suicidal maniacs. Included also are chapters on Carlos, or the Jackal, reportedly the most notorious terrorist in the world, and the bombing of Pan Am 103 over Lockerbie, Scotland. In the chapter dealing with domestic terrorists, the author investigates white supremacy groups like the Ku Klux Klan and the skinheads, whose membership has expanded by ten times since 1986 and whose members live in over 30 states. The author avoids sensationalism and writes clearly and factually.

Some organizations, like the Irish Republican Army, could have been examined more thoroughly and analytically than the brief mention received. There is just enough information presented to give an overview; readers who want to delve deeper can use the bibliography to continue their research.

617. Meltzer, Milton. *Ain't Gonna Study War No More: The Story of America's Peace Seekers*. Harper, 1985 (0-06-024200-0). 288 pp. Nonfiction.

Interest level: Age 12+

As always, Meltzer's writing is eloquent and forceful, the result of exquisite research with primary documents. Here he looks at patriotism and its many expressions, highlighting the response to war known as conscientious objector. The book begins with one young man's letter about resistance: "Draft registration is preparation for war. To sign a registration card is to sign a promise—a promise to the United States government that it may take your body at any time, for any war it may see fit." In covering numerous periods in history, Meltzer compiles a book about courage—the courage to personally resist and to organize larger resistance in what he calls "a quarrelsome world." Among the eras discussed to show humankind's long propensity for war are biblical times and the Middle Ages, but most of the book deals with the United States: the Quakers, the Revolution, the Mexican War, choosing between two evils in the Civil War, the World Wars, Vietnam, the antinuclear movement, and so on.

Throughout, there is a balance between the accomplishments that the momentum of large numbers can bring and the power of individuals. Examples of people who resisted war include Fanny Fern Andrews, who formed an American School Peace League to spread international understanding to children in the early 1900s, and Senator Hatfield's calling the domino theory false in the Vietnam struggle and becoming influential in the war's eventual end. And as in all of Meltzer's work, there is fine interweaving of social forces at play in each period, bringing necessary complexity to what could have been merely propaganda. Bibliography.

618. Seuss, Dr. *The Butter Battle Book*. Illus. by the author. Random, 1984, LB (0-394-96580-9). 42 pp. Fiction.

Interest level: Ages 5–8

The Yooks and the Zooks, two countries divided by a wall, are similar in all things except that the Yooks butter their bread on the top side and the Zooks butter their bread on the bottom. Because of this crucial difference, a fight begins and escalates to war. The war intensifies until, at the end of the story, a Yook and a Zook stand on either side of the wall, each with a powerful bomb in his hand. The author leaves the outcome in doubt, and we never know if either side ever drops the bomb or if they come to their senses in time to avoid annihilation.

This allegory of our own time is meant to represent the futility and inanity of global confrontation. As with many allegories, the points are so oversimplified as to lose much of their impact. Although the story builds dramatically, the issue over the buttering of bread is nothing like issues of slavery, freedom, economic deprivation, and greed. The combatants are clearly more alike than different, and that could have been a powerful message had it been highlighted or articulated. Nevertheless, the message comes across that here are two nations brought to the brink of self-destruction over an unimportant issue and that they arrived at their current situation through an ever escalating development of weapons.

American Revolution

619. Avi. *The Fighting Ground.* Illus. by Ellen Thompson. Lippincott, 1984 (0-397-32074-4); Harper, pap. (0-06-440185-5). 157 pp. Fiction.

Interest level: Age 11+

Jonathan is 13 years old, and he desperately wants to fight in the war. His father has already been wounded in battle, and he is afraid to permit Jonathan to leave home. One morning, when Jonathan hears the bell tolling a message, he goes to the tavern in the center of the New Jersey town and joins up with a group of men, led by a corporal, who are going to engage in a battle to try to prevent Hessian soldiers from penetrating into New Jersey. The battle is not at all what Jonathan expected; it is bloody and inglorious. He runs and is captured by three Hessian soldiers.

Ironically, after a while with his captors, Jonathan begins to wonder whose side he is on. The Hessians neither speak nor understand English, but they do not harm Jonathan. When the group reaches a small farmhouse, Jonathan milks a cow, and the four of them drink the milk and eat some bread that was in the kitchen. Jonathan finds a little boy in the barn. He then finds the boy's parents, who have been killed.

Jonathan escapes with the little boy after the soldiers have fallen asleep. He finds the corporal and the other men from his town. It turns out that it was the American corporal who killed the boy's parents, in the belief that they were spies. They were French and spoke no English, and, therefore, could not rebut the corporal's accusations. The corporal forces Jonathan to lead the Americans back to the farmhouse and the sleeping Hessians. Jonathan is sent ahead to make certain that the soldiers are asleep. He awakens them and tries to warn them, but they do not understand him, and they are all killed.

Jonathan returns home, after having heard the corporal and the others exclaim over their "victory." He now understands his father's feelings about fighting in the war. Jonathan has been gone only 24 hours, but this day has changed his life.

The story is written in segments of time rather than in chapters. Some of the segments last only five minutes; the longest is four hours. This structure dramatically demonstrates how important time is, and how conditions of life can change in a battle from one moment to the next. The book is a telling indictment of war, although it never discusses the merits of either side, or indicates what the causes or issues of the war are. It is important for children to understand that the American Revolution, although it is often painted as a glorious conflict, was as dirty and, at times, as meaningless as any other war.

620. Collier, James Lincoln, and Christopher Collier. *War Comes to Willy Freeman.* Peter Smith, 1992 (0-8446-6596-7); Dell, pap. (0-440-49504-0). 178 pp. Fiction.

Interest level: Ages 9–12

Willy, a young black girl freed by law because of her father's willingness to fight in the Revolutionary War, is forced to grow up quickly when she witnesses her father's death at the hands of British soldiers. On her return home from the battle, she discovers that her mother has been kidnapped by British soldiers and taken as a prisoner to New York City. Willy dresses as a boy and goes to search for her mother. Her search leads her to Fraunces Tavern, where she is aided by Fraunces and a young worker, Horace.

Eventually, Willy must cope with the death of her mother and with an attempt to return her to slavery. Her bravery and survival strategies are commendable. Her father and mother are slightly ambiguous characters: Her father is somewhat abusive of her mother and shows poor judgment; her mother seems stronger than she really is.

The authors—historians—have provided a close look at the ugliness of war. They have also raised some disturbing issues about blacks and their involvement in the war. The soldiers who kidnap Willy's mother are black. They trust the British government more than the Americans to treat them as people after the war. The language the authors use (*darkies* and *nigger*) is offensive to a modern audience. The authors explain their usage as needed for authenticity. Nevertheless, the language detracts from the message of the book and contributes to the demeaning of blacks. The authors probably could have avoided this offense, and the book would be the stronger for it.

621. Davis, Burke. *Black Heroes of the American Revolution.* Harcourt, 1976 (0-15-208560-2); pap. (0-15-208561-0). 84 pp. Nonfiction.

Interest level: Ages 9–11

This book is a tribute to the many little-known participants in the American Revolution who were people of color. The tone is anecdotal, and the vignettes of the lives of these heroes are both entertaining and informative. Some of those profiled were born into slavery; others were born free. Prince Whipple was the son of a wealthy African landowner. He was sent to the United States to be educated. Instead, he was sold as a slave to General Whipple of New Hampshire. There he served as a trusted bodyguard to the general and was freed after petitioning the New Hampshire legislature. Agrippa Hull, a black man from Northampton, Massachusetts, enlisted in the war and fought alongside General Kosciusko, who later founded a school for black Americans in honor of his friend. There are reproductions of contemporary portraits, paintings, and engravings, including one of poet Phillis Wheatley. This glimpse into a section of history that has been long neglected is a valuable tool for personalizing the Revolutionary War and acknowledging the contributions of all citizens.

622. DeFord, Deborah H., and Harry S. Stout. *An Enemy among Them.* Houghton, 1987 (0-395-44239-7). 203 pp. Fiction.

Interest level: Age 10+

It is always useful when a book contributes yet another perspective to a historical event. In this story about the Revolutionary War, readers get the opportunity to learn about the German-speaking community in Pennsylvania and their feelings regarding the Hessian mercenaries who were hired by the British to fight against the American colonists. We are also introduced to some Hessian soldiers who are not the beasts and cold-hearted individuals that they were reported to be in the newspapers of the time and in U.S. history books.

The story tells of one family—living near Reading, Pennsylvania—whose sons fight for the Americans, and the Hessian prisoner they take in, who has fought for the British. Many points of view about the war are aired by the characters in their discussions and arguments with each other. One man, a former friend of the family, is a British spy. Christian, the Hessian prisoner, is responsible for the death of John, one of the brothers.

But before John dies, he and the Hessian become close friends, and Christian winds up in the American army.

Readers cannot help but infer from the events of the story that there is often very little difference between enemies, that it is people's common humanity that emerges, even in times of warfare and bloodshed.

623. Haugaard, Erik Christian. *A Boy's Will.* Illus. by Troy Howell. Houghton, 1983, pap. (0-395-54962-0). 41 pp. Fiction.

Interest level: Ages 7–10

The story takes place on the island of Valentia, off the coast of Ireland, during the American Revolutionary War years. Patrick, a young Irish boy, decides to go against his punitive and unloving grandfather and warn John Paul Jones of an ambush by the British navy. He steals out of his house late one night, takes a small boat, and races against time and the sea to reach the American ships before they are spotted by the British.

The story really revolves around the young boy's longing for his dead mother and father and his unhappiness with his grandfather. The boy, a Catholic, always empathizes with the underdog, whereas his grandfather, a smuggler, hates Catholics and is opposed to the American rebels' cause. It is clear that Patrick is aiding the rebels, not so much out of conviction as from desperation with his way of life. In the end, he accepts John Paul Jones's invitation to stay with the rebels, but it is with mixed feelings that he leaves his own land and the site of his mother's grave.

Erik Christian Haugaard also provides young readers with other aspects of the American Revolutionary War and with some little-known information about the strategies and issues involved in the war.

624. Meltzer, Milton. *The American Revolutionaries.* Crowell, 1987 (0-690-04641-3). 210 pp. Nonfiction.

Interest level: Age 11+

A detailed look at the American Revolution through personal accounts by people from all walks of life and in every possible role. Messengers, cooks, drummers, waiters, tradespeople, indentured servants, British and American officers, ordinary soldiers, physicians, farmers, slaves, abolitionists, political leaders, and women are among those represented by their writings and by newspaper accounts and other documents in this cohesive document of people's experiences and feelings during the Revolution. Meltzer introduces each account by identifying the author and setting a context for what the person has to say. What emerges is layer upon layer of the setting and emotional climate of the war and its effects on the soon-to-be nation.

625. Stevens, Bryna. *Deborah Sampson Goes to War.* Illus. by Florence Hill. Dell, 1991, pap. (0-440-40552-1). 48 pp. Nonfiction.

Interest level: Ages 6–9

The opening sets the stage for what was going on at the time when Deborah Sampson was born. Her father was lost at sea and her mother could not support six children, so the family was dispersed. Living with the Thomas family, Deborah works hard, but she also goes to school, quite an accomplishment for a girl of the time. When the revolution starts, Deborah is only 14.

By the time Deborah is 21, the war is still going on. Strong and tall, she ties back her hair, dons a man's suit, and walks 35 miles to join the army. No one guesses "Robert Shurtleff" is a woman. The book recounts the tasks of her regiment. When a bullet hits her head, Deborah is of course afraid she will be found out at the hospital. She leaves before full recovery, only to become ill under the terrible conditions soldiers had to endure. This time, she is found out, but a kind doctor takes Deborah home to his family without revealing her secret. Only at the close of the war is her identity revealed.

Besides offering a rousing view of this woman and the war, the book also points up times when people feel compelled to make hard separations for a larger cause. An afterword tells about Sampson's later life, which included marriage, children, and becoming the first woman lecturer in the United States to speak about her war experiences.

626. Turner, Ann. *Katie's Trunk.* Illus. by Ron Himler. Macmillan, 1992 (0-02-789512-2). Unpaged. Fiction.

Interest level: Ages 7–10

Katie's family is loyal to the Crown during the American Revolution. Most of their neighbors are rebels who have stopped speaking to them and who express their anger toward them daily. One day, a band of rebels marches on the house to strip it of all that is valuable in order to get money to buy arms. The family runs out to the woods to hide, but Katie angrily tries to defend her family's home against the marauding rebels. When she realizes she cannot stop them, she hides in her mother's wedding trunk. A neighbor, one of the rebels, discovers her hiding place but doesn't give her away and causes the vandals to leave. Katie and her family are grateful that even in time of war some people remember their humanity and behave accordingly. They think more of that one act of kindness than they do of the negative facets of their "skirmish." The book helps children understand that even when people are not on the "acceptable" side of the war, they remain humans and should be considered as such.

Civil War

627. Aaseng, Nathan. *Robert E. Lee.* Lerner, 1991, LB (0-8225-4909-3). 112 pp. Nonfiction.

Interest level: Ages 8–10

In an informal, anecdotal style, this biography provides a very personalized account of the Civil War. Through it all, Lee's stellar reputation is confirmed. This is a good example of an "enemy" who is not narrowly defined as such. Lee chose to command the Southern army because his loyalty lay with his home state of Virginia. He was not a proponent of either slavery or secession and wanted to avoid a war if at all possible. He was a consummate commander, always ready to listen, to offer suggestions, and to praise.

628. Beatty, Patricia. *Charley Skedaddle.* Morrow, 1987 (0-688-06687-9); Troll, pap. (0-8167-1317-0). 186 pp. Fiction.

Interest level: Age 11+

Charley enlists in the Union army partly to avenge his brother's death at the Battle of Gettysburg, partly to escape his Bowery existence, and partly to see battle. He becomes a drummer boy, but longs to be a regular soldier, even though he can't help but notice how much drinking and gambling goes on in the camp. When he finally does see battle, he shoots a man and is so traumatized by this that he runs away from the army.

He is captured by the Confederates, but is released because of his young age. He wanders into the home of an old woman, with whom he stays and whose life he saves when she is in an accident. He proves his courage and his character, and then he moves on to California, vowing to return to settle in the Blue Ridge Mountains.

The story revolves around the strength of the two protagonists, the old woman and the young boy. It is persuasive and authentic. The author provides notes at the end that demonstrate the research that substantiates the events, actions, and incidental information in the story. The book's perspective on the war is important for young readers to understand.

629. Beatty, Patricia. *Turn Homeward, Hannalee.* Morrow, 1984 (0-688-03871-9); Troll, pap. (0-8167-2260-9). 208 pp. Fiction.

Interest level: Ages 9–12

Hannalee Reed is 12 years old in 1864. Her father has died in an army camp. Davey, her older brother, is in the Confederate army. Her mother is pregnant and unable to work, so Hannalee and her younger brother, Jem, support the family working at the local mill. That summer, the Yankee soldiers invade the town and ship the mill workers north. Rosellen, Davey's fiancée, and Hannalee find work in an Indiana mill. With remarkable endurance, Hannalee finds Jem, and together they make their way back to Georgia to reunite with their mother and new baby sister. Miraculously, at the end of the war, Davey comes home only wounded and ready to begin anew. Books of this quality are helpful in conveying to children an understanding of the complexities and personal hardships of war. The time of the Civil War comes alive under the author's skillful hand. The author makes clear that there are scoundrels as well as kind and thoughtful people on both sides of the conflict. Hannalee is an admirable and attractive character. Her heroism is remarkable, but believable. For her further adventures, see *Be Ever Hopeful, Hannalee* (1988).

630. Clapp, Patricia. *The Tamarack Tree.* Lothrop, 1986 (0-688-02852-7); Puffin, pap. (0-14-032406-2). 214 pp. Fiction.

   Interest level: Age 12+

Rosemary Monica Stafford Leigh, age 17, begins her narration of the story in Vicksburg, Mississippi, while that city is under siege during the Civil War. She and her older brother are British. They emigrated to the United States after both their parents died. From the beginning, Rosemary is appalled by the idea of slavery. Her brother tries to assure her that most slave owners are kind people and that she should try to understand their point of view.

   Although Rosemary maintains her stance against slavery, she does make many friends in Mississippi, and she helps nurse the wounded during the war. Interwoven with the story are comments about the battles and the politics of the war. The ugliness of the war comes through clearly as Rosemary and her friends cope with the siege and afterward help with the wounded.

   Rosemary is an excellent guide through the intricacies of the issues and the subtleties of human interaction. Included in the characters are Southern whites, free blacks, and Northerners. All are treated respectfully by the author. This book is an excellent example of historical fiction; it teaches us at the same time it involves us.

631. Freedman, Russell. *Lincoln: A Photobiography.* Photos. Clarion, 1987 (0-89919-380-3); pap. (0-395-51848-2). 160 pp. Nonfiction.

   Interest level: Age 10+

This wonderful biography of Abraham Lincoln is so engrossing it almost reads like a novel. Freedman visited all the sites and archives associated with the sixteenth president and from his broad research has brought forth a lively account of his life. Complex issues are tackled such as those he had to deal with during the Civil War. The young reader is also trusted with equally complex matters of the heart that are usually discussed only in books for adults—for example, how a born storyteller and wit can also be so melancholy. At every turn, Freedman makes us feel the way those who were connected with Lincoln might have felt, too—those who met him in stores, those who encouraged him to try politics, those who sadly waved to the funeral train. Lincoln's entire family history comes to life: moving from territory to territory in search of homesteading, the death of his mother, the coming of a kind stepmother, his many jobs before becoming a statesman and lawyer, and his courtship, marriage, and children. This is a book to read again and again. The masterful telling is followed by a sampling from Lincoln's voluminous writings, a list of historical Lincoln sites, bibliography, index.

632. Meltzer, Milton. *Voices from the Civil War.* Harper, 1989, LB (0-690-04802-5); pap. (0-06-446124-6). 224 pp. Nonfiction.

Interest level: Age 12+

The author's intent is to help modern readers understand the past through the words of both ordinary and prominent people who lived during the time of the Civil War. Little-known events—such as the draft riots in New York City and across the North—are described here. When the Draft Law was adopted in 1863, mobs looted and inflicted physical harm on black people, partly inflamed by the press. Also included are descriptions of the "contrabands"—escaped slaves who volunteered to fight with the Union Army. They served the North in many capacities, but they were often homeless and hungry. Former slave Harriet Jacobs details the miserable conditions of the contrabands she witnessed in Washington, D.C. Her letter served as an appeal for help and many Northerners responded. Another interesting section discusses the pacifists in the Civil War, notably, Quakers, Mennonites, Shakers, Seventh-Day Adventists, Amish, and German Baptists (called *Tunkers*). Most of these groups were morally opposed to slavery, as well, and were caught in a dilemma of principle. The author's comments illuminate the events and amplify the original writings.

633. Perez, N. A. *The Slopes of War: A Novel of Gettysburg.* Houghton, 1990 (0-395-35642-3); pap. (0-395-54979-5). 224 pp. Fiction.

Interest level: Age 11+

This Canadian author has managed to convey an authentic sense of how people felt during the American Civil War. He portrays soldiers and officers on both the Confederate and Union sides, and he also lets the reader in on the events and reactions of the people who lived in Gettysburg at the time of that significant and bloody battle.

We are introduced to a family whose members are divided by the war, but who understand and love each other nevertheless. Perhaps the most important accomplishment of this book is to take war out of the realm of dates and names and place it in the perspective of human interaction. Southerners are seen here to be as much the victims of the war as Northerners. The issues are not glossed over, but the human condition overrides the battle lines.

634. Reeder, Carolyn. *Shades of Gray.* Macmillan, 1989 (0-02-775810-9); Avon, pap. (0-380-71232-6). 176 pp. Fiction.

Interest level: Ages 9–12

Will Page, an orphan whose father was killed by Union soldiers in the Civil War, must now live with an uncle who refused to fight on either side. Will bitterly resents his uncle's stance and displays his anger openly, as do the people of the community who were once his uncle's friends. Will only knows how angry he is at the enemy and how strongly he wants the Yankees to be defeated. He views his uncle's position as cowardice and betrayal. His uncle's steadfast courage, ability to accomplish tasks, ethical attitude toward all people, and consummate kindness to him finally combine to help Will understand that pacifism is not treachery or cowardice and that war is more complex than it first appears. Through Will, the book acknowledges the Southern point of view in an unbiased and sensitive manner.

Slavery

635. Berleth, Richard. *Samuel's Choice.* Illus. by James Watling. Whitman, 1990, LB (0-8075-7218-7). Unpaged. Fiction.

Interest level: Ages 8–10

Although the story is somewhat slow moving, this book conveys a sense of what it was like to be a slave during the time of the American Revolution in eighteenth-century New York. (Most stories about slavery are set in the Civil War era.) The narrator is Samuel, a slave who was separated from his mother in 1776 when he was 14 and bought by Isaac Van Ditmas, a rich Brooklyn farmer who was mean spirited and stingy. Samuel was taught to row and sail a small boat, and he often thought of freedom. He and his friends watched some of the fighting going on across the shore in Manhattan and speculated about the meaning of the battle in their personal lives. The farmer sent his family to the safety of Staten Island, and the slaves witness a battle between the meticulously uniformed British and the bedraggled young Liberty Boys. Samuel takes this opportunity to rescue several Americans by rowing them to safety. He and his friend Sana manage to carry a rope across the water for the soldiers to cling to. It turns out that Isaac surrenders his farm to General Washington in return for his freedom. Sana and Samuel from then on are also free. Although the story is invented, most of the characters are historically true. The book not only discloses some historical events but also examines some of the issues surrounding fighting for one's freedom and what that freedom means.

636. Berry, James. *Ajeemah and His Son*. Illus. by the author. Harper, 1992, LB (0-06-021044-3). 83 pp. Fiction.

Interest level: Age 12+

The story begins by introducing the reader to Ajeemah and his prosperous family in an unnamed country in Africa. Ajeemah and Atu, his 18-year-old son, are wrenched from their home and forced into slavery in Jamaica. The two men are separated from each other and new names are imposed on them. Atu is killed for his refusal to acquiesce to subservience. The story is not sentimentalized and is strong and painful to read. Although Ajeemah finally makes a new life for himself—especially after 1838, when slavery is abolished in Jamaica—the ending is bittersweet. Despite her love and appreciation for her father, his daughter prefers to reject her African heritage and embrace a life separate from her father's past. Much information about the slave trade is given as part of the unfolding of the story, including the fact that African slave hunters captured the protagonists and turned them over to European slave traders. This story is a provocative one, inviting discussion and problem solving.

637. Carter, Polly. *Harriet Tubman and Black History Month*. Illus. by Brian Pinkney. Silver Pr., 1990 (0-671-69115-5). Unpaged. Fiction.

Interest level: Ages 5–9

Emotive cross-hatched sketches accompany this gripping picture book that tells the story of Harriet Tubman and her role in the Underground Railroad. The fictionalized conversations are spare but powerful. Harriet weeps as she rocks Miss Susan's baby through the night, terrified that the baby will awake and cry out, causing her to be whipped. Her first attempt at escape occurs when she bolts from Miss Susan's house, fearful of another beating, and lands in the pigpen, where she subsists on potato peels for several days. She hears about the Underground Railroad from her father, but she does not try to escape until she is 24. Once she arrives in Pennsylvania, she knows she is free; but her first moments of joy are tempered by the realization that she has no home or family. Harriet's cunning in avoiding discovery is admirable: Once she dresses up like a man; another time, she pretends to read and outwits a couple who think they recognize her. Eventually, she is able to rescue her sister and her sister's family. When the Civil War breaks out, Harriet becomes a nurse and a spy. Although the title of this book for younger readers is misleading (it never mentions Black History Month), the characterization of Harriet Tubman is vibrant and she emerges as a true heroine.

638. Davis, Ossie. *Escape to Freedom: A Play about Young Frederick Douglass.* Viking, 1990 (0-670-29775-5); Puffin, pap. (0-14-034355-5). 90 pp. Play.

   Interest level: Ages 9–12

Escape to Freedom details the triumphant escape from slavery and rise to success of the remarkable Frederick Douglass. The dramatic format engagingly captures the spirit of the times and the man. The play may either be read by individuals, done as reader's theater, or produced by a group. Stage directions are included. Douglass narrates his own story in direct comments to the audience, as well as taking part in the drama itself. Songs are also included, though the musical annotations are not. This unusual format serves as an excellent addition to a library of material about a man who serves as a model for so many young African Americans. His rise to prominence against heavy odds is an inspiration.

639. Graham, Lorenz. *John Brown: A Cry for Freedom.* Crowell, 1980. o.p. 192 pp. Nonfiction.

   Interest level: Age 11+

This biography of the controversial John Brown reveals him as a man with deep religious convictions about freeing slaves, rather than portraying him, as some historians have done, as a wild, insane monster. This account does not, however, show him as a saint.

640. Hamilton, Virginia. *Anthony Burns: The Defeat and Triumph of a Fugitive Slave.* Knopf, 1993, LB (0-394-88185-5); pap. (0-679-83997-6). 208 pp. Fiction.

   Interest level: Age 12+

In a blend of history and creative filling in of gaps, the author sets forth the story of Anthony Burns, a man who escaped from slavery, was caught in Massachusetts and returned to his master, then freed again after being bought by a free African-American minister and his friends. Burns went on to Oberlin College in Ohio and became a minister. He died at age 28, after a hard life. The author communicates the painful cruelties of torture and degradation practiced by some slave owners. Burns's case influenced state legislation so that he was the last fugitive slave seized in Massachusetts. The complexities of the Fugitive Slave Act are disclosed, and the workings of abolitionists are detailed in this fascinating account.

641. Hamilton, Virginia. *The House of Dies Drear.* Illus. by Eros Keith. Macmillan, 1984 (0-02-742500-2); pap. (0-02-043520-7). 256 pp. Fiction.

Interest level: Age 10+

In this mystery story, an African-American family moves into a very large, historic house in Ohio, having come from their long-time family home in the hills of North Carolina. The father is a college professor who has researched the background of the house, which was a station on the Underground Railroad. Thomas, the protagonist, is especially unhappy about leaving his great-grandmother, with whom he has had a special relationship, but he is eager to solve what he perceives to be the mystery of the house. A descendant of one of the slaves who hid there was bequeathed a fabulous cavern full of treasures, which is hidden under the house. A good adventure story, with a message of African-American pride. The sequel, *The Mystery of Drear House* (1987) continues the story.

642. Hamilton, Virginia. *Many Thousand Gone: African Americans from Slavery to Freedom.* Illus. by Leo and Diane Dillon. Knopf, 1993 (0-394-82873-9). 160 pp. Nonfiction.

Interest level: Age 10+

Stirring vignettes of individual struggles to overcome slavery. This work of nonfiction, with its direct, understated language, is compellingly eloquent. Nearly two hundred years (1671–1863) are spanned in the accounts of slaves attempting, sometimes in dramatic and tragic ways, to gain their freedom. The illustrations are fit companions to the prose.

The book describes slavery by accessing accounts written by the slaves themselves about their experiences. Individuals' names and deeds are included throughout the book rather than fostering an amorphous notion of "slavery." People who successfully ran away from enslavement are included, such as Tice Davids, the first person to escape from slavery using the "underground road." The stories of well-known former slaves such as Frederick Douglass, Anthony Burns, Harriet Tubman, Sojourner Truth, and Dred Scott are briefly told alongside those not nearly as well-known but every bit as courageous and interesting.

643. Hansen, Joyce. *Out from This Place.* Walker, 1988 (0-8027-6816-4); Avon, pap. (0-380-71409-4). 144 pp. Fiction.

Interest level: Ages 9–12

Easter, Obi, and Jason are three young people who have been together for a number of years as the only slaves of Mr. and Mrs. Jennings. This book focuses on Easter and her successful journey to freedom. It chronicles the years 1862–1865 and describes how the lives of some of the Southern slaves were affected by the Civil War. This is the sequel to *Which Way Freedom?* (1986), which is told from Obi's perspective during the same period. Key to both books is the strong sense of the right of every person to be free. Both books describe joyful as well as tragic events. The author personalizes the issues for young readers in a way that is sure to help them understand the feelings of the African-American characters as well as the climate of the times.

644. Hooks, William H. *The Ballad of Belle Dorcas*. Illus. by Brian Pinkney. Knopf, 1990 (0-394-84645-1). 48 pp. Fiction.

Interest level: Ages 7–10

Belle and her husband, Joshua, have managed to have a wonderful, loving life together until slave catchers murder Joshua. Through sorcery gone somewhat awry, Belle retains a relationship with Joshua, who must exist as a tree by day but regains his own shape and persona by night. The story is dramatized by Brian Pinkney's powerful scratchboard illustrations. The pain of slavery and the triumph of the spirit of independence and love are demonstrated.

645. Hopkinson, Deborah. *Sweet Clara and the Freedom Quilt*. Illus. by James Ransome. Knopf, 1993 (0-679-82311-5). Unpaged. Picture book.

Interest level: Ages 6–10

This book provides a basis for even the youngest of children to appreciate the inventiveness and courage required for slaves to escape into freedom. Clara, a young slave who has been separated from her mother, is taken under the wing of Aunt Rachel and trained as a seamstress. Clara cleverly uses her skills to construct a quilt that serves as a map of an escape route to Canada. She picks up clues from carefully listening to the accounts of everyone who has traveled beyond the plantation. Pretty soon other slaves casually come for visits and mention more details about surrounding terrain, and the pathways and roadblocks further away to the north. Clara ultimately escapes with young Jack, and together, following the path they have learned about by constructing the quilt, they go the plantation where Clara's mother and younger sister have been slaves. Together the entire family escapes to Canada. The story is not designed to horrify children with details of torture and degradation, but rather is a celebration of the human spirit and an alternative to the image of the abused, passive, pitiful slave. The illustrations powerfully capture the respect the slaves have for each other, and the strong emotional bonds that tie them together.

646. Hurmence, Belinda. *A Girl Called Boy*. Houghton, 1982 (0-395-31022-9); pap. (0-395-55698-8). 180 pp. Fiction.

Interest level: Ages 9–12

At a family picnic, Blanche Overtha Yancey, also known as Boy, travels through time into the era of slavery. A soapstone carving of a bird, called a *conjure,* is the trigger for the time travel. Boy cannot comprehend why her family is so interested in stories about slaves, a subject she finds tiresome. She now finds herself in a cabin where the inhabitants speak of slave catchers and grabble for potatoes. All Boy wants is to locate the interstate highway so that she can find her way back to the picnic area. It is not until she sees a newspaper containing an advertisement for a runaway slave that Boy acknowledges that she has somehow gone back to the year 1853.

Through her own experiences as a slave, Boy realizes that many slaves resented their captivity and did fight back. She teaches another slave, Lookup, to read. They discover that they can write their own passes to travel to see their relations, one of whom might be Boy's mother. Gradually, Boy learns to appreciate the traditions, intelligence, strength, and beauty of her family background. She is overwhelmed when she is finally reunited with her modern family. The device of time travel is well used here, and the story provides an excellent context for the message.

647. Hurmence, Belinda. *Tancy*. Clarion, 1984. o.p. 224 pp. Fiction.

Interest level: Age 11+

After emancipation from slavery, Tancy leaves the plantation where she has lived all her life and goes in search of her mother, who was sold when Tancy was very young. She sets out on foot for Knoxford, accompanied by little Jemmy, whom she has cared for. She is delighted by small evidences of her new position in life, as when an ambulance driver calls her *Miss.* Because she can read and write, she gets a job at the slave bureau. Jemmy goes to school, and soon Tancy replaces the teacher, a first step on the road to her career. Finally, Tancy finds her mother, who is not at all what she expected. She also finds her vocation and a man whom she respects and can love. Post-emancipation feelings and events are candidly described.

648. Katz, William Loren. *Breaking the Chains: African-American Slave Resistance*. Atheneum, 1990 (0-689-31493-0). 208 pp. Nonfiction.

Interest level: Age 12+

This important factual account of the resistance to slavery makes clear how erroneous is the stereotype that most slaves were either passive or happy in their condition. It begins with an introduction that traces the myth that slaves were content and that they flourished while in bondage. The author cites such people as John C. Calhoun, vice president of the United States; John W. Burgess, an ex-Confederate soldier who became a noted historian at Columbia University; and Allan Nevins and Henry Steele Commager, who wrote college texts emphasizing the excellent relationships between slaves and their masters. The body of the book traces the beginning of slavery in America to Columbus and chronicles the beginning of slaves' rebellions from this time. The author describes many specific people and the rebellions they led, so that there is no doubt in the reader's mind that the uprisings were numerous and endemic. The book ends with the end of slavery in the United States in 1865, but wryly states, "Freedom did not bring equality, justice, or even happiness for all. A united country preserved much of its ancient prejudice and introduced forms of bigotry better adapted to a new time." It is clear that there is still much work to be done, but this book lays the foundation for respect and admiration for those whose heritage includes the constant fight against bondage.

649. Lester, Julius. *Long Journey Home: Stories from Black History.* Dial, 1993 (0-8037-4953-8); Scholastic, pap. (0-590-41433-X). 160 pp. Fiction.

Interest level: Age 12+

This book includes deeply involving accounts of people who did not make a giant mark in the history books, but who demonstrate that many African Americans were the source of their own freedom. Some accounts are angry, some are triumphant, and some end tragically. In one story a man who was separated from his wife and children vowed he would find them. Years later, after emancipation, he did, only to find that she had married again and borne two children to her new husband. Another story tells of a talented man so damaged and embittered by white men's oppression that he is incapable of making any commitments to a relationship with women. He is savvy and a talented musician, but, unable to settle in one place, he keeps wandering and remains a loner. All of the stories bring home the point that black people did not have to rely on the kindness and generosity of whites. Based on historical research, the stories are amplified by the author.

650. Lester, Julius. *This Strange New Feeling.* Dial, 1982 (0-8037-8491-0); Scholastic, pap. (0-590-44047-0). 150 pp. Fiction.

Interest level: Age 12+

Here are three love stories that transcend the people in them and become testimony to the power of the human spirit and the resolve for freedom. In the first story, Ras is a slave who has been freed, recaptured through the treachery of a supposedly friendly white man, and then is instrumental in the freeing of many more slaves after he returns to his plantation. The second story tells of a woman who was married to a free black man whose will provided for her freedom. But he died owing money, and she was used to pay off his debts. She vows never to give anyone any satisfaction out of owning her. She will not think or behave in an enslaved fashion. The third story retells the well-known account of Ellen and William Craft and their escape from slavery, but it focuses on the difficulties they had after they were apprehended in Boston and in danger of being returned to slavery. The point is made that they not only hated slavery, but loved freedom. They decided to escape to England rather than consent to be purchased out of slavery. Based on fact, the stories bring the characters close to the reader and communicate how important the love of freedom is to all people.

651. Lester, Julius. *To Be a Slave.* Illus. by Tom Feelings. Dial, 1968 (0-8037-8955-6); Scholastic, pap. (0-590-42460-2). 160 pp. Nonfiction.

　　Interest level: Age 12+

The words of slaves and former slaves—spanning the period from their transportation from Africa to after emancipation—tell the true story of what it meant to be a slave. Some of the accounts detail what it was like to be transported on a slave ship. Others report on the atrocities visited upon slaves by their masters and discuss the heartbreak of the separation of families. The last entries refer to freedom and the aftermath of emancipation, which was often not as idyllic as one would hope. Lester's comments guide the reader to a deeper understanding of the time and the people. A bibliography provides sources of additional information. A forceful, well-constructed, and important book.

652. Lyons, Mary E. *Letters from a Slave Girl: The Story of Harriet Jacobs.* Macmillan, 1992 (0-684-19446-5). 176 pp. Fiction.

　　Interest level: Age 11+

Harriet Jacobs's voice comes through in this well-written account of the former slave's story. The author has drawn very heavily on Harriet Jacobs's autobiography, which she has presented in epistolary form. She has used transcriptions of oral interviews with women who were slaves in order to fashion the dialect of these invented letters. Harriet desperately hopes to be freed after the death of her mistress; instead, she is "deeded" to a family member. She decides to escape to the North, where she goes into hiding for almost seven years. Eventually, she becomes an activist for other escaped slaves. In later years, Harriet Jacobs's eloquent writing reflects her comfort with standard English, but the author's decision to reconstruct her earlier voice and write in dialect does not diminish the power of the story. Harriet Jacobs's life is a testimony to the strength of people who knew that they were free despite unfair laws and cruel slave owners. There is a compendium of interesting extras at the end of the book: photographs, a map, drawings of Harriet's hiding place, family trees, and an explanatory author's note.

653. McMullan, Kate. *The Story of Harriet Tubman, Conductor of the Underground Railroad.* Illus. by Steven James Petruccio. Dell, 1991, pap. (0-440-40400-2). 108 pp. Fiction.
    Interest level: Ages 8–10

Clearly told and including many details of Harriet Tubman's youth, this story reveals how quick-witted and creative the legendary hero was. She rescued her parents by constructing a wagon for them. She eluded her would-be captors in many ways, including pretending to read a book when her "wanted poster" said she was illiterate. She became a popular public speaker and supported her now-free parents through this work. She made many friends who helped her in her frequent forays South to lead more slaves to freedom. Because of her success (she never lost a "passenger"), she was in ever-greater danger of being captured. She was 40 years old when she acceded to friends' entreaties to work for abolition without making more trips on the Underground Railroad.

  Tubman did much work during the Civil War to help newly liberated slaves adjust to their freedom and helped train them to develop ways of earning a living. She served as a liaison between the former slaves and the Union soldiers. She also worked as a nurse, traveling from camp to camp. And finally, she served as a spy, in the post of Commander of Intelligence Operations for the Union Army's Department of the South. In one instance, when she and her troops were on a mine-removing mission, they freed 756 slaves and brought them back to their camp. This book fills in many gaps that other books for young children have not discussed, particularly about Harriet Tubman's life after being a conductor. It also points out that the U.S. government never paid Tubman the money it owed her, although she won many honors and was highly acclaimed.

654. Meltzer, Milton. *All Times, All Peoples: A World History of Slavery.* Illus. by Leonard Everett Fisher. Harper, 1980, LB (0-06-024187-X). 80 pp. Nonfiction.
    Interest level: Ages 8–12

Tracing the history of slavery from ancient times to the present, the author informs readers that there are currently ten million slaves in various places in the world (counting those political prisoners who are forced to labor against their will). He ends with a plea for action on the part of the free world.

655. Myers, Walter Dean. *Now Is Your Time! The African-American Struggle for Freedom.* Harper, 1992 (0-06-024370-8); pap. (0-06-446120-3). 292 pp. Nonfiction.

Interest level: Age 12+

Using stories of individual slaves as well as factual information supported by newspaper ads for runaway slaves, buy and sell agreements, ships' manifests, and lists of slaves at particular plantations, this book presents a complete look at the existence of slavery in the United States from earliest times to the present. The author personalizes the issue with stories about individuals, such as Abd al-Rahman Ibrahima, a chieftain's son who befriended an Irish doctor who later tried to have him freed. Ibrahima, an educated, well-traveled Moslem, had been captured by a rival tribe and sold into slavery. After many years, a letter from the Moroccan government made his freedom possible; unfortunately, he died in Liberia, unable to reach his native home. An African American who was not a slave but suffered the sting of racism was Meta Vaux Warrick, a talented sculptor who went to Paris in the late 1800s to advance her art career. Although she had been raised in fine society, she was unable to stay at the American Girls' Club in Paris. Ultimately, Warrick was a great success in Paris, attracting the attention of such geniuses as Rodin. Her return to the United States was a different story; she was discriminated against because of her color. The author weaves stories like these together with factual material in an illuminating tapestry of history that informs as it enthralls the reader.

656. Ofosu-Appiah, L. H. *People in Bondage: African Slavery since the 15th Century.* Lerner, 1992 (0-8225-3150-X). 112 pp. Nonfiction.

Interest level: Age 11+

The author, a native of Ghana, served as director and editor of the *Encyclopaedia Africana.* His informative study provides a clear view of slavery throughout the ages. He points out some anomalies, such as the fact that most of the slaves "supplied by the African traders were victims of wars and raids, but some were criminals or people who had sold themselves into slavery." The author discusses the terrible plight of indentured servants brought to the United States during the 17th and 18th centuries. He says, "It is recorded that the conditions under which the indentured servants traveled to the colonies were worse than those the black slaves experienced." The author discusses the abolition of slavery and its aftermath and brings us to the current situation of racist feelings and behavior both in the United States and worldwide. He discloses that "Some Arab states have never given up slavery. In parts of North Africa—Mauritania, for example—slavery is an integral part of society." The book is a revelation and admonition to young people to strive for freedom for all.

657. Rappaport, Doreen. *Escape from Slavery: Five Journeys to Freedom.* Illus. by Charles Lilly. Harper, 1991 (0-06-021631-X). 128 pp. Fiction.

Interest level: Ages 9–12

It is estimated that between 25,000 and 100,000 slaves escaped through the network of safe havens supplied by the Underground Railroad. This book includes five short stories based on factual reports about slaves escaping from their owners and finding freedom in the North. Each character wants freedom above all else, is willing to risk everything, and uses his or her abilities and determination to obtain it. Often the characters are helped by free blacks along the Underground Railroad or by the cleverness of other black people in outwitting the white slave owners. The slaves, shown as capable people with a strong sense of family, were often motivated by the hope of providing their children with a better life. Some of the people in these stories escaped with their children; others were less fortunate and lost their families. The first story, about Eliza and her child, was memorialized in *Uncle Tom's Cabin*. The last story, about William and Ellen Craft, is probably the best known of all the escaped-slave stories. The writing suffers from a sometimes choppy narrative and a lack of detail about some of the characters, but the spirit and bravery of the slaves and their helpers is well represented.

658. Warner, Lucille Schulberg. *From Slave to Abolitionist: The Life of William Wells Brown.* Dial, 1993 (0-8037-2743-7). 144 pp. Nonfiction.

Interest level: Age 11+

This book goes a long way to blasting stereotypes of ignorant, passive, satisfied slaves. Brown was author of the first travel book, first novel, first play, and first histories written by a black American. His writings provide the foundation for this account of one man's triumph over the evils of slavery. The story is told in the first person and includes such details as the sermon an itinerant minister preached admonishing slaves to serve their masters and mistresses: "Take care that you do not fret or murmur, grumble or repine at your condition; for this will not only make your life uneasy, but it will greatly offend Almighty God." With ministers like these to keep the slaves in their places, it is a wonder that any of them summoned the courage to rebel. After he gained his freedom, Brown was often selected to speak in churches about abolition. He never permitted himself to accede to subservience and always behaved in an upright and moral fashion. He was well respected as an advocate for his race, and he was greeted warmly as a delegate to the Peace Congress in Paris by such notables as Victor Hugo and Alexis de Tocqueville. He also joined Ellen and William Craft on an antislavery lecture tour through Scotland. His two daughters were educated in excellent schools in England and became teachers there. The book is a respectfully compiled account of Brown and his remarkable dedication to the cause of freedom.

Apartheid

659. Denenberg, Barry. *Nelson Mandela: No Easy Walk to Freedom.* Scholastic, 1991 (0-590-44163-9). 160 pp. Nonfiction.

Interest level: Age 12+

A chronology and narrative of Nelson Mandela's role in fighting apartheid in South Africa, the book tells of Mandela's early years and his running away to Johannesburg to escape an arranged marriage and the responsibility of assuming tribal leadership in his uncle's village. It affirms his commitment to his people and his determination to see to it that they were freed. Some of the history of the country itself is given, including the bloody warfare between the Zulus and the Boers. The founding of the African National Congress and the framing of the Freedom Charter are described. The author discusses Nelson Mandela's marriage to Winnie, but the book was published before the Mandelas' divorce. It does, however, include Mandela's liberation from jail and his impact on the world since that liberation. The author is clearly an admirer of Mandela, but he does not romanticize him. Readers are left to draw their own conclusions about controversial issues surrounding any of the parties in South Africa.

660. Naidoo, Beverly. *Journey to Jo'burg: A South African Story.* Illus. by Eric Velasquez. Lippincott, 1986 (0-397-32168-6); Harper, pap. (0-06-440237-1). 77 pp. Fiction.

Interest level: Age 10+

Naledi, who is 13, and her 9-year-old brother, Tiro, journey alone to Johannesburg, South Africa, to fetch their mother to save the life of their baby sister. They encounter the terrible manifestations of racism that apartheid results in. They learn of the deaths of blacks, including children, who fight the system. They are exposed to the spirit of many of their people who are determined, one day, to change the system. In the end, their

journey completed, their baby sister on the road to health, they vow to for-
tify themselves for the long struggle ahead.

In simple and dignified language, the author tells a story that is
bound to have an impact on young readers. Too few books are available
that inform this audience about the situation in South Africa. This story
makes an excellent contribution.

661. Rochman, Hazel, ed. *Somehow Tenderness Survives: Stories of
Southern Africa.* Harper, 1988, LB (0-06-025023-2); pap. (0-06-
447063-6). 208 pp. Fiction.

Interest level: Age 11+

A collection of short stories, written by South Africans of many heritages
and perspectives. The introduction provides some grim statistics about the
survival rates of black children under the age of five as compared to white
children. She points out that "Thousands of teenagers are in prison without
trial; many are being tortured." Malnutrition is rampant, even though
South Africa is one of the richest countries in the world. She then lists
several facts of life under apartheid, including the rules about media coverage of any protests, inferior education, and the migrant system that
forces fathers to leave their families for months at a time. Five of the stories are by whites, and five are by blacks. Each gives the reader a different
slant on the evils of apartheid and builds a picture that is more complete
than if only one view were presented. Even the stories written by whites
about whites help to make vivid the loss and suffering caused by apartheid
that are perhaps less obvious than the better-known consequences of this
governmental policy against people of color.

662. Williams, Michael. *Crocodile Burning.* Dutton, 1992 (0-525-67401-2).
192 pp. Fiction.

Interest level: Age 12+

The crocodile, a symbol of fear and evil in South Africa, forms a powerful
and recurring metaphor in this novel of a young man learning to fight
oppression in his troubled culture. Seraki, who lives in desperate poverty
in a shanty town in Soweto, South Africa, gets an unexpected break when
he wins a role in an anti-apartheid musical that is going to open on
Broadway. He is torn about leaving home: where his brother is being held
without charges in prison and his father and uncle are involved in a bitter
feud—but he knows that he is acting as a cultural ambassador and that his
salary is desperately needed. He comes to realize, however, that there are
other crocodiles than the police and government back home: there are
racists in New York City, the police seem just as bad, and the show's
director is abusive and is robbing the cast members of their due. By orga-

nizing the cast members and confronting the director (with the help of a lawyer), Seraki is able to negotiate a fair contract for the cast. He learns a great deal about the many forms oppression can take and emerges as a stronger person. The story, which does not shy away from the brutality of life in the townships in South Africa, is very well crafted and never resorts to gratuitous violence. The characters are complex individuals, and the almost-always-believable plot has many layers. The author is a white South African.

World War II

663. Aaron, Chester. *Alex, Who Won His War.* Walker, 1991 (0-8027-8098-9). 144 pp. Fiction.

Interest level: Ages 10–12

An adventure story that brings up questions about how war makes enemies of people who might otherwise be friends. Based on an account of some German spies who actually landed near New York City during World War II, the story centers on Alex, whose brother, Oliver, is fighting in the war. Alex, along with his classmates, teacher, and everyone else in the community, is caught up in the spirit of the war. They all hate the enemy and take part in the war effort at home. One day, Alex and his friend Larry discover on a stretch of isolated beach the body of what turns out to be a German spy. They take his money and bury the wallet. Alex subsequently gets involved with more German spies, who threaten to kill a helpless elderly woman if he reports them. Alex is so desperate that he plans to kill himself along with the spies but he is prevented from doing so, and eventually is extricated from the dangerous situation. Although he hates the spies, in some ways he understands their point of view. The story is interspersed with news reports of the progress of the war and letters to and from Alex and his brother. In an Afterword, the author summarizes the events occurring after the war and points out that Germany and the United States are no longer enemies. The book is not an ordinary tale of adventure and spies. It raises important questions about war and its effects.

664. Bauer, Marion Dane. *Rain of Fire.* Clarion, 1983 (0-89919-190-8). 153 pp. Fiction.

Interest level: Age 11+

Steve and his older brother, Matthew, were very close until Matthew went to fight in World War II. When Matthew returns, he is morose and almost surly. He doesn't want to talk about his experiences in the war, and he seems to lack the energy to go out to look for a job. Steve boasts about Matthew's exploits in the war, knowing that these are inventions that he has concocted so that his friends won't think badly of Matthew and so that Celestino, a bully, will be impressed.

At one point, in an attempt to stop the conflict between Steve and his peers, Matthew passionately cries out against war and talks about its horrors. He confesses to being ashamed of what he had to do in the war. Steve foolishly constructs a series of lies about Matthew to make up for his inability to face the fact that Matthew killed people. Steve's "friends," under Celestino's leadership, construct a letter to J. Edgar Hoover, reporting Matthew's allegedly anti-American statements and actions.

After a series of terrible incidents, including the killing of the family cat, Steve finally learns that it is not possible to hurt someone else without hurting yourself. The book is a serious indictment of war. It is also a look at the effects of lying and concealing important information. Further, it reveals the damage that can occur when children are left confused and uncomprehending of adults' feelings.

665. Garrigue, Sheila. *The Eternal Spring of Mr. Ito.* Bradbury, 1985 (0-02-737300-2). 163 pp. Fiction.

Interest level: Age 11+

The story takes place in Vancouver, Canada, where Sara Warren, an English girl, comes to stay with her aunt and uncle during World War II. The book chronicles her experiences during the war, but more importantly it explores her relationship with Mr. Ito, a Japanese gardener who saved her uncle's life during World War I and who has worked for her aunt and uncle for many years.

Mr. Ito's collection of bonsai trees represents his Japanese heritage, and his 200-year-old tree, which has been in his family for many generations, becomes a symbol of Sara's hopes for the future and Mr. Ito's eternal life. After the bombing of Pearl Harbor, Mr. Ito is banished from the Warrens' house. Sara's uncle destroys all of his bonsai trees, except for the ancient one, which Mr. Ito manages to take with him, and one tree that Sara manages to rescue.

Mr. Ito's family has been sent to an internment camp, but he refuses to go and hides in a cave to wait for death rather than sacrifice his pride. When Sara finds him, he explains to her many of his Buddhist beliefs, including his conviction that his karma will pass on to a new life. When Sara returns again to bring him food, she finds that he has died. She takes his ancient bonsai tree and manages to deliver it to his family in the camp so that it can be passed on to the next generation.

The issue of the bitter plight of Japanese Canadians as a result of the bombing of Pearl Harbor is dealt with directly. It is difficult to believe that Sara's uncle would be so narrow as to blame Mr. Ito for what the

Japanese government is doing. It is especially difficult because Mr. Ito had saved his life. In the end, Mr. Warren begins to question the treatment of the Japanese Canadians in the internment camps, but this, too, is difficult to believe, given his previous irrational response. On the other hand, it is easy to see why Mr. Ito's daughter, Helen, is cynical about their ever reclaiming their confiscated property and their shattered lives. The devastation of war extends far beyond the battlefield, and this story palpably demonstrates that fact.

666. Gehrts, Barbara. *Don't Say a Word.* Trans. by Elizabeth D. Crawford. Macmillan, 1986 (0-689-50412-8). 169 pp. Fiction.

Interest level: Age 12+

The story is set in Berlin during World War II. The protagonists are a family that is not Jewish but hates Hitler and the Nazis. The father is active in his opposition to Hitler's regime. The story tells of the dreadful events of the era as seen through the eyes of Anna, the teenaged daughter. Among the terrible things that happen is that Anna's friend Ruth and her family commit suicide rather than face the certain torture and death that they feel will come to them because they are Jews. Anna is, of course, devastated by this event, which is a precursor to her boyfriend's death on the Russian front and, worst of all, her father's arrest by the Gestapo and his eventual execution.

Because the story reflects the author's personal experiences, it is unmistakably authentic. Some information contained here is shocking: The family is required to pay the costs of the father's imprisonment and execution! The author includes a copy of the bill in the text.

Although details of daily interaction and particular events are described, nowhere is there an inkling of the massive nature of the Holocaust. Readers will have to consult other books to find information about Hitler's plan and the course of the war. But just as Anne Frank's story tells more about the horror of the time than an entire chronicle of the war, so this book, with its focus on one German family, brings us into proximity with the nightmare and bestiality of Hitler's Germany.

667. Maruki, Toshi. *Hiroshima No Pika.* Illus. by the author. Lothrop, 1982 (0-688-01297-3). 48 pp. Nonfiction.

Interest level: Age 10+

Although illustrations make this appear to be a picture book, it is not directed at very young readers. The story and pictures graphically detail the effects of a nuclear bomb. The translation of the title is *Hiroshima's Flash.* A powerful antiwar statement.

668. Mochizuki, Ken. *Baseball Saved Us.* Illus. by Dom Lee. Lee and Low, 1993 (1-880000-01-6). 32 pp. Fiction.

Interest level: Ages 6–10

Narrated in the first person by Shorty, the young protagonist, this story reveals one of the self-preservative activities initiated by Japanese Americans interned in camps. Shorty's father sparks a project to build a baseball field in the desert where their camp is located. Everyone contributes, including friends back home who send baseball equipment. After the war, Shorty continues to play baseball, but he still encounters racism. There are no easy answers here, but the book is a testimony to the human ability to overcome seemingly impossible conditions. The author's parents were interned in Minidoka camp in Idaho during the war.

669. Pople, Maureen. *The Other Side of the Family.* Holt, 1988 (0-8050-0758-X). 165 pp. Fiction.

Interest level: Age 12+

Katherine Tucker is sent by her parents from her home in England to live with her maternal grandparents in Sydney, Australia, until World War II ends. Soon after her arrival, Japanese submarines are sighted in Sydney harbor, so it is decided that she should be sent to her paternal grandmother in the safety of the country inland. Katherine is shocked when she hears this news. She has never met her other grandmother, and she has the idea that her grandmother hates her and her family. Her mother has told her terrible stories about how awful this grandmother is, and no one has ever contradicted them.

All of the myths she's heard about her grandmother explode as Katherine gets to know more about her own background. Her grandmother was never wealthy; her grandfather was a charming ne'er-do-well who deserted his wife and son; her father was a selfish snob who was ashamed of his mother and who invented stories about his upbringing. Also, her grandmother is deaf and can only lip-read to understand what is said to her. All of this and more Katherine learns in the brief month that she is away from Sydney. But she uses what she has learned to become a kinder and more honest person. Her absence from home turns out to be a homecoming in its deepest sense.

The story unfolds dramatically and is believable. All the characters are interesting and hold the reader's attention. The themes of war and desertion are blended, so that the reader understands more of the events and the times of World War II and its effects on the Australian people. A worthwhile book.

670. Ray, Deborah Kogan. *My Daddy Was a Soldier: A World War II Story.* Illus. by the author. Holiday, 1990, LB (0-8234-0795-0). 40 pp. Picture book.

Interest level: Ages 4–7

Jeannie, the young narrator, tells of her experiences as a child of a soldier who is fighting overseas in World War II. She describes her mother's becoming a welder, ration stamps, air raid drills, a friend's brother returning home with only one leg, and especially the loneliness and fear she and her mother feel knowing that her father is engaged in battle. The book, illustrated with soft pencil drawings, is well written and authentically conveys the feelings of an American child during this terrible war.

671. Schami, Rafik. *A Hand Full of Stars.* Dutton, 1990 (0-525-44535-8); Puffin, pap. (0-14-036073-5). 224 pp. Fiction.

Interest level: Age 12+

Spanning four years, this personal narrative details the daily life, feelings, and interactions of a young Syrian boy growing up in Damascus after World War II. His journal helps us to see what life was like for him and his friends and what caused him to become a resister to the oppressive government. His resistance is nonviolent: he produces an underground newspaper that circulates to a wide audience and tells the truth about the government's corruption and torture. The author communicates the flavor of his heritage while telling the story of a young boy reaching maturity.

672. Stein, R. Conrad. *World at War: Prisoners of War.* Photos. Childrens, 1987. o.p. 48 pp. Nonfiction.

Interest level: Age 12+

The photographs of actual prison camps and prisoners of war (POWs) are the most dramatic and, at times, upsetting parts of this book. The text describes the conditions that POWs in Japanese and German camps suffered in World War II, as well as their everyday activities and their feelings about being imprisoned.

The book focuses on Allied POWs, but there is a section toward the end on Axis POWs imprisoned in the United States. It declares that these prisoners were fortunate—in fact, better off than their countrymen who were not in prison. The book makes no mention at all of the Japanese Americans who were kept in camps as a protection against their possible subversion. Although the book is particularly biased, it is, nevertheless, a useful addition to the books for young readers on war, because it is so rare that this topic is even mentioned.

673. Tsuchiya, Yukio. *Faithful Elephants.* Illus. by Ted Lewin. Houghton, 1988 (0-395-46555-9). 32 pp. Picture book.

Interest level: Ages 9–12

A very upsetting story of the perceived necessity to kill all of the large animals in the Tokyo Zoo for fear of its being bombed and the animals escaping into the general population. Because the elephants are smarter than the other animals, ordinary measures are not effective, and the agonized zoo keeper must starve his beloved elephants to death. The story is a true one. Zoos all over the world had to make decisions about what to do with their large animals, and many of them also destroyed them. The simple, direct style of the telling adds to the impact of the story and causes young readers to think about some of the less obvious effects of war.

674. Vinke, Hermann. *The Short Life of Sophie Scholl.* Trans. by Hedwig Pachter. Illus. with photos and drawings from the Scholl family. Harper, 1984. o.p. 216 pp. Nonfiction.

Interest level: Age 12+

Too few books for young readers tell of the underground movement called the White Rose, which young Germans engaged in during the time of the Nazi regime. Although the movement failed, it remains a symbol of courage and sanity in a time when these qualities were in too short supply. Hermann Vinke interviewed the two surviving members of Sophie Scholl's family, as well as friends who survived the war, and he uses their voices and Sophie's diaries and letters to help tell the story.

Sophie's father was tried and imprisoned for "malicious slander of the Führer." The entire family was opposed to the actions of the Third Reich. Sophie's brother, Hans, founded the White Rose, and Sophie joined him and his friends. They printed and distributed leaflets telling the German people what Hitler was doing. They caused quite a stir, as no one had been bold enough to speak out publicly against Hitler's actions.

The organization lasted for one year: 1942. It was discovered and crushed by the Gestapo with the help of a janitor who reported that he had seen the leaflets scattered about the University of Munich. Sophie and her brother claimed total responsibility, hoping to save the lives of their friends in the resistance group. Sophie and her brother and six other members of the group were executed; more than 40 others were imprisoned. Sophie was 21 years old when she was killed. She was convinced, even at the end, that her cause had been a worthy one and that her efforts had not been in vain.

The story is a dramatic one, told well. The use of Sophie's photographs and drawings adds to the reader's feelings of empathy with this courageous young woman. The letters and excerpts from diaries, as well as the authentic voices of the survivors, make this book a powerful one.

675. Watkins, Yoko Kawashima. *So Far from the Bamboo Grove*. Lothrop, 1986 (0-688-06110-9); Puffin, pap. (0-317-62272-2). 183 pp. Fiction.

Interest level: Age 12+

Although this is a fictionalized autobiography, it has the ring of truth. It is the story of Yoko, her sister, and her mother, and their flight from North Korea to Japan. Their family is Japanese, and they are warned by a corporal in the army that the Russians will soon attack the Korean village where they are living, so they decide to flee to their extended family in Japan. The father and brother are away from the village, but the corporal tells the family how to leave messages for them. It is a dangerous journey that they undertake, and they narrowly escape being captured by North Korean Communists who are looking for them. Their home is ravaged, but they escape with their lives.

When they get to Japan, the mother immediately places them in school and journeys to their hometown. There she discovers that her parents and her in-laws have been killed. As a result of this catastrophic news, she becomes very ill. She returns to her daughters and dies immediately after. The two young women manage to survive by salvaging from the trash and by sewing and selling various items. They receive a windfall when Yoko wins an essay contest. Their classmates ridicule them because they are in rags, but they both earn the highest grades and are undaunted in their efforts. The remarkable story concludes with the return of Yoko's brother. The epilogue tells us that the girls' father returned from a Siberian prison camp six years later.

This story describes a little-known series of circumstances stemming from the war. Its clear, unemotional prose is effective and moving. The author is testimony to the fact that even the "enemy" is human and deserves to be respected as such.

676. Yolen, Jane. *All Those Secrets of the World*. Illus. by Leslie Baker. Little, Brown, 1991 (0-316-96891-9); pap. (0-316-96895-1). 30 pp. Fiction.

Interest level: Ages 4–6

Four-year-old Janie waves good-bye to her father as he heads off to what is presumably World War II. Janie is caught up in the festive atmosphere at the dock, but she recognizes her mother's grief when she cries during the ride home and then stays in bed the next day. While playing in the oil-slicked water of the Chesapeake Bay, her cousin Michael tells Janie a secret: that things look smaller from far away. When her father finally returns home, Janie is much older. She still remembers him, and she shares her secret, telling him that when he was far away she looked small but now she has grown. Although Janie's baby brother is resentful of the man whom he considers a stranger, the love between the family members is evident and the reader recognizes that all will be well. Yolen's work is pure poetry, and the watercolor paintings enhance the text.

677. Ziefert, Harriet. *A New Coat for Anna.* Illus. by Anita Lobel. Knopf, 1986 (0-394-97426-3); pap. (0-394-89861-3). 32 pp. Fiction.

Interest level: Ages 7–10

Set in Europe in the aftermath of World War II and based on a true story, this book tells of the inventiveness and determination of Anna's mother in seeing to it that her daughter has a warm new coat for the winter. Anna's mother schemes to have a coat made for Anna, even though there is no money in the house. They have to wait almost a full year for the finished product, but with patience and by bartering several of their treasured possessions, they enlist the cooperation of farmers and craftspeople and Anna gets her coat.

Anita Lobel's illustrations dramatically convey the human and physical devastation of the war: Former soldiers, their injuries still evident, begging for coins; shuttered shops; empty provision baskets; and houses reduced to rubble introduce the reader to the setting of the story. The pictures and text combine to provide an inspiring story of human survival. Too often war is thought of in terms of battles and victories. Here is an accurate and accessible accounting of how people rebuild afterward.

The Holocaust

678. Aaron, Chester. *Gideon.* Lippincott, 1984. o.p. 200 pp. Fiction.

Interest level: Age 11+

Although this is classified as fiction, the story, told in autobiographical narrative, persuades the reader of its authenticity. Gideon becomes a member of the resistance movement both in the Warsaw ghetto and then in the Treblinka concentration camp. He survives because of his fighting spirit and his willingness to go outside the law and to sometimes deny his identity. This story affirms the human ability to endure.

679. Abells, Chana Byers. *The Children We Remember.* Photos from the Archives of Yad Vashem. Greenwillow, 1986 (0-688-06371-3). 48 pp. Nonfiction.

Interest level: Age 7+

This is a large book with large pictures, a large subject, few words, and short sentences. This combination works together to form perhaps the most moving Holocaust book of all, and the one that is accessible to the largest age group. Each short phrase gets a photograph of its own, making the tragedy real.

The pages tell the chronology of what befell Europe's Jewish children, from restrictions in clothing and schooling to their ultimate destruction. The photographs for "Sometimes they put children to death" show a mother shielding her toddler while both are shot by a soldier or policeman with a rifle.

The message is brought home with even more depth by showing a series of photographs of individual children killed by the Nazis, with the introducing caption: "These children were killed by the Nazis." Readers are told (with accompanying photographs for each phrase) that children survived through various methods, such as going to Israel and other countries, going to non-Jewish homes, hiding in forests, or acting as non-Jews.

680. Adler, David A. *The Number on My Grandfather's Arm.* Photos by Rose Eichenbaum. Union of American Hebrew Congregations, 1987 (0-8074-0328-8). 32 pp. Nonfiction.

Interest level: Ages 5–9

A young girl tells the story, and photographs show her sitting with her grandfather, who, at last, reveals a history that continues to trouble the family. He tells her of his experiences in the Holocaust, Hitler's incendiary propaganda about Jews, Hitler's extermination plans, the concentration camps, his trying stay in Auschwitz, and the loss of his siblings and friends.

Adler is in touch with family emotions. We see the grandfather admonishing his daughter, "It's time you told her. . . ." The child comes to understand and also helps her grandfather with his problem regarding the number on his arm. The man wears long-sleeved shirts even in hot weather, but the girl tries to get him to change, explaining, "You shouldn't be ashamed to let people see your number. You didn't do anything wrong. It's the Nazis who should be ashamed."

The photographer is the child of survivors, and the young girl posing is her own daughter. The grandfather (not actually related) is also a survivor, who testified at the Nuremberg trials and the trial of Adolf Eichmann. Here is a skillful attempt to tell the truth about an unbelievable horror—to bring the essential facts to the very young without terrifying them about tomorrow. It is a successful attempt that combines emotion with history quite well.

681. Auerbacher, Inge. *I Am a Star: Child of the Holocaust.* Illus. by Israel Bernbaum, with additional photos. Puffin, 1993, pap. (0-14-036401-3). 80 pp. Nonfiction.

Interest level: Age 12+

This is a moving combination of general and personal history during the Holocaust. As a child, Auerbacher was one of only 13 people to survive the Terezin concentration camp from her original transport of 1,200. Amazingly, three of the 13 were from her family.

This book differs from other Holocaust memoirs by intertwining rich, varied sources: Auerbacher's own strong, lyrical rhyming poetry; photographs of her town and family; and Bernbaum's appropriately crude, stark drawings. Auerbacher conveys the historical reasons behind anti-Semitism with clarity and sparks her narrative with expressive phrases (life or death is decided by "a flick of a finger"). It would have been instructive for Auerbacher to assess why her whole immediate family prevailed; this, however, is a minor flaw in an otherwise highly meaningful ode to the phrase "never again."

682. Bergman, Tamar. *Along the Tracks.* Trans. by Michael Swirsky. Houghton, 1991 (0-395-55328-8). 256 pp. Fiction.

Interest level: Age 12+

Yankele and his family reluctantly decide to leave the Jewish ghetto of Lodz, Poland. They know that the Nazis will soon close off all escape. Despite difficulties, the family manages to reach Russia and stay together until the Germans invade and Yankele's father enlists in the Russian army. Soon after, the mother, sister, and Yankele leave with many other refugees, but, after enduring serious illness and the deaths of young friends, Yankele becomes separated from them. He wanders in search of his family for four and a half years, managing to remain alive, despite frequent bouts with malaria, through a combination of stealing, scavenging for food and shelter, and meeting up with friendly people. Against all odds, he becomes reunited with his mother and sister, but because of his experiences and emotional turmoil, he is no longer content to remain at home with them. He wanders off from time to time, but periodically comes back. During one such return, he and his mother learn that his father, presumed dead, is alive and well, living in Lodz.

The "happy" ending is believable, given the networks of survivors and their determination to rebuild their lives. Yankele and his family emigrate to Israel because there is clearly no future for them in their former home. There are no details here of atrocities, but the suffering brought about by hunger, illness, separation, cold, and the small cruelties of strangers creates a painful experience for the reader.

683. Bernbaum, Israel. *My Brother's Keeper: The Holocaust Through the Eyes of an Artist*. Illus. by the author. Putnam, 1985. o.p. 64 pp. Nonfiction.

Interest level: Age 9+

This is truly an unusual book. A survivor has created symbolically laden paintings of Holocaust scenes, which he has shared with children in classrooms and now in book form. (Bernbaum dedicates his book to the 1.5 million children who didn't survive the Holocaust.) His aim in sharing is twofold: to prevent such a tragedy from recurring by knowing the past, and to learn the lesson of being one's brother's keeper.

The narrative, addressed directly to the reader, informs us that two out of three Jews in Europe were killed. As Bernbaum transfers his feelings to canvas, red is the predominant color in the busy paintings, as the world, raging with flames, becomes soaked in blood. For Bernbaum, the Holocaust is "a fire engulfing any living being in its path." Much of the material in the narrative and artwork concerns the Warsaw ghetto. He explains that where 80,000 previously lived, once the Jews were forced to live in a ghetto, 500,000 were jammed into the same living space. The sources for the paintings include newspaper photographs, some of them famous, such as the tragic shot of a young, shorts-clad boy on the street with the yellow Star of David on his coat, his hands up in the air before the police.

There are six paintings. They are titled *The Warsaw Ghetto Streets 1943; On Both Sides of the Warsaw Ghetto Wall; The Jewish Mother in the Ghetto; The Jewish Children in Ghettos and Death Camps; The Warsaw Ghetto Uprising—Heroism and Resistance;* and *My Brother's Keeper*. The book's impact comes from Bernbaum's discussion of each painting. He first discusses each as a whole and then breaks it up into segments, showing the symbolism and inspiration for each piece. Newspaper and archival photographs (some of German origin) also demonstrate the times. The strongest works concern the Warsaw Uprising, in which young Jews fought for five weeks, successfully keeping the mighty German army from destroying them, although they had few arms with which to keep the Nazis at bay.

The symbolism in each painting is broad-ranging. Some figures are symbols of continuity—for example, praying people, lighting candles. Other symbolic figures delve into details of history: the silence of the Polish church and the indifference of world powers to what was happening. The paintings as a whole, in their agony, ask, "Civilization, where are you?"

Bernbaum has a flowing narrative style, in which he answers readers' questions. A sample: "You may ask: Is this possible? Aren't these images the pure imagination of an artist?" He answers the readers' questions: "I wish they were. Unfortunately, my images are only a slight shadow of the reality."

684. Bunting, Eve. *Terrible Things: An Allegory of the Holocaust.* Illus. by Stephen Gammell. Jewish Publication Society, 1989 (0-8276-0325-8); pap. (0-8276-0507-2). 24 pp. Fiction.
   Interest level: Age 5+

Because the forest creatures do not protect each other, they are all destroyed by the Terrible Things that wipe them out, species by species. In a gripping allegory, not only of the Holocaust, but also of any attempt to "divide and conquer," the author and illustrator combine to warn of the dangers of compliance with hostile authorities. The plot intensifies as each creature becomes the target for the Terrible Things' venom. It is not known where the creatures are taken nor what happens to them when they arrive. The story focuses on those who remain, waiting for their species to be chosen. The story demonstrates the necessity of cooperation with one's fellows.

685. Chaikin, Miriam. *A Nightmare in History: The Holocaust, 1933–1945.* Illus. with photos and prints. Clarion, 1987 (0-89919-461-3); pap. (0-395-61579-8). 128 pp. Nonfiction.
   Interest level: Age 10+

Using simple, elegant writing that denotes deep understanding, this noted writer on Jewish themes tackles the hardest subject of all: the horror of one life disappearing and of being sucked into an unimaginably terrifying, barbaric decline in its place. Her contribution is to bring a historical perspective, presenting a unique study of Hitler, who "stood out in no way as a boy." She also examines (from the time of Noah onward) how group differences began and the multiple directions in which anti-Semitism rose. Her chapter divisions are such that they powerfully drive home the little-realized concept that this was not merely hatred gone wild. No, the Nazis planned the extermination of the Jews in elaborately charted stages. Whether it's discussion of school expulsion and ghettoization in stage one or concentration camp lineups left and right in later stages, Chaikin keeps the book strong and vibrant with examples from real families.

Some of the individuals profiled perish, some survive. Although we know the protagonists die, the stories are rousing nonetheless, as in the account of the Warsaw Ghetto Uprising coinciding with the Passover seder: "Pulling triggers, throwing grenades, dodging bullets, they shouted to each other over the gunfire the events of the Exodus, telling how Moses freed the Jewish slaves in Egypt and led them out to freedom." A fine book. Extensive bibliography.

686. Dillon, Eilis. *Children of Bach.* Scribner, 1992 (0-684-19440-6). 164 pp. Fiction.

Interest level: Ages 9–12

Siblings Pali, Peter, and Suzy are at school in Budapest, Hungary, when the Nazis sweep through their apartment and force their parents and Aunt Eva to accompany them, presumably to take them away to concentration camps. David, a classmate of Suzy's, stays with the children when he assumes that his family, also Jews, have been abducted as well. The children manage not to panic by keeping to familiar routines, particularly practicing their music, keeping up with schoolwork, and accepting help from their neighbors, even though they are anxious about trusting people too easily. A disagreeable neighbor, Mrs. Nagy, eventually moves in with them when she admits to having some Jewish heritage. Another neighbor arranges for their escape across the Alps in a furniture truck. During the flight, the group faces some hair-raising adventures, including near detection by the Germans when they play their music with a priest who takes them in. They finally reach the Italian Alps, where Mrs. Rossi's family embraces them and where they will be finally free to allow their music to help them heal. This is a very specific look at the flight of Hungarian Jews; their sense of identification with their Hungarian heritage permeates the entire story. Another strong thread running through the book is the impact of the family's musical tradition on the attitudes and actions of the family members who survive. It seems curious, however, that the children do not speak about their parents until the end of the book; however, when they do admit that they may never see them again, the scene is well done.

687. Finkelstein, Norman H. *Remember Not to Forget: A Memory of the Holocaust.* Illus. by Lois Hokanson and Lars Hokanson. Watts, 1985 (0-531-04892-6); pap. (0-688-11802-X). 32 pp. Nonfiction.

Interest level: Ages 9–13

The strength of Finkelstein's convictions comes through in his every word. Finkelstein, a Hebraic scholar, writes with poetry of his feeling that the world must never forget: "The shocked world could only wonder how such a terrible event could have happened. It was an unimaginable tragedy, horrible and unbelievable; it was a savage firestorm of raging intensity—a Holocaust."

The book offers a historical overview, starting from A.D. 70, when the Jewish capital was destroyed, spewing the Jews into the diaspora. From this scattered living pattern arose anti-Semitism, Finkelstein asserts, and from this came the most horrifying episode in long-standing anti-Semitic feeling: the Holocaust of the Third Reich. The history concludes with the establishment of the State of Israel and, within its borders, the Yad Vashem Memorial and the Yom Hashoa yearly memorial day.

Woodcuts of simple clarity support the narrative well, bringing understanding to younger children. The tone is instructional but not pedantic, giving warning but not causing hysteria.

688. Friedman, Ina R. *The Other Victims: First-Person Stories of Non-Jews Persecuted by the Nazis.* Houghton, 1990 (0-395-50212-8). 224 pp. Nonfiction.

Interest level: Age 10+

This book contributes the perspective of non-Jewish people who were persecuted by the Nazis. It is important to know that in addition to the six million Jews, five million non-Jews were killed because of Hitler's edicts. These facts put into context the insanity and monomania of the Nazis, in their attempt to exterminate all people who were different in any way from their Aryan ideal. Not all of the targeted groups are represented by personal narrative, but the accounts included here convey a sense of the dimensions of the terror of those times.

689. Kuchler-Silberman, Lena. *My Hundred Children.* Adapted by David C. Gross. Dell, 1987, pap. (0-440-95263-8). 240 pp. Nonfiction.

Interest level: Age 12+

Trying to find a reason to go on living after her family died in the Holocaust, Kuchler-Silberman directed a postwar orphanage for 100 of the few Jewish children who remained alive in Poland. There she tried to give physical and emotional wholeness to these children, who had lived in closets or forests and who often had seen their parents killed. It will not surprise many readers to learn that she and her charges encountered continuing aggressive anti-Semitism, in which the authorities wouldn't care for them yet wouldn't let them leave the country. Finally leaving Poland for safer Czechoslovakia forms the crux of the first-person narrative, but as much drama is found in moving vignettes, such as the intoxicated hilarity the children and staff share the night they all dress alike in pink flannel pajamas, their first such warmth after the war. Kuchler-Silberman is truly a hero; her accomplishments were deservedly honored in a made-for-television movie starring Lee Remick.

690. Lowry, Lois. *Number the Stars.* Houghton, 1989 (0-395-51060-0); Dell, pap. (0-440-21372-X). 160 pp. Fiction.

Interest level: Age 10+

This winner of the 1989 Newbery Medal involves Annemarie and her family, who take part in the rescue of Danish Jews. Annemarie's best friend, Ellen Rosen, must pose as her sister because Ellen's parents have had to flee from the Nazis. They hide on a fishing boat headed for Sweden. Annemarie becomes a heroine as she outwits the soldiers who are searching for the family. The book demonstrates the power of a people's refusal to collude with the Nazis. This Holocaust book is told from the perspective of a ten-year-old Danish Christian girl. It contains no tales of atrocities, though it reports the deaths of Annemarie's older sister and her fiancé, who were members of the resistance movement. Annemarie's family is courageous and highly principled. We don't get to know the Jewish characters very well; this is really not their story. The author provides interesting details about the Danes' resistance.

691. Matas, Carol. *Lisa's War.* Scribner, 1989 (0-684-19010-9); Scholastic, pap. (0-590-43517-5). 128 pp. Fiction.

Interest level: Age 11+

The story is told over a span of more than two years from the perspective of Lisa, a Jewish Danish teenager during the Holocaust. She becomes actively involved in the resistance by serving as a courier, distributing informative anti-Nazi leaflets. As the story unfolds, we come to know the Jewish characters as strong individuals. Many of the Jews anticipate the impending disaster, but a number refuse to believe that the Nazis have such evil intent. Some are likable; others are not. All are three-dimensional people and are, to an extent, in control of their own situations. The Danes, too, differ widely from one another. Most are sympathetic to the Jews, but a few use the opportunity to extort money from the people they ferry to Sweden, and some even collude with the Nazis. Details of the vicious murders committed by Nazis to try to destroy Jewish and Danish resistance are included as part of the plot. On the first night of Rosh Hashanah, the Jews receive warning from G. F. Duckwitz, a member of the German Embassy staff, that all of the Jews are about to be rounded up and taken to concentration camps. Together with their Danish friends, the Jews inform everyone and mount an already planned rescue. Of the 7,000 Danish Jews, all but 474 escaped to Sweden. This story makes it clear that the Jewish Danes were not passive, sheeplike martyrs who relied solely on their Christian benefactors to rescue them. It also demonstrates that many of the people involved were ordinary human beings who behaved in an extraordinary manner because of the pressures of those terror-filled times.

692. Meltzer, Milton. *Rescue: The Story of How Gentiles Saved Jews in the Holocaust.* Harper, 1988 (0-06-024209-4); pap. (0-06-446117-3). 224 pp. Nonfiction.

Interest level: Age 12+

This book recounts the inspiring stories of individual non-Jews in Germany, the Netherlands, Belgium, Poland, Lithuania, Ukraine, Czechoslovakia, Hungary, France, Italy, and other countries who sheltered Jews, brought them food, helped them to escape, provided for their children, and served as couriers and gatherers of news. Members of the clergy were particularly active in the resistance against the Nazis. One man, Oskar Schindler, arranged to move his factory and its Jewish workers to Czechoslovakia so that he could secretly protect them. He was frequently arrested, but he continued to organize massive rescues under the guise of transporting workers. He was ultimately honored in Israel by the people he had saved, who were known as the *Schindlerjuden*. A simple French concierge guilelessly hid a young Jewish girl and her mother in a closet while she chatted with the Nazi soldiers who were searching for them. Rulers such as King Boris of Bulgaria and King Christian of Denmark resisted Nazi edicts and were somewhat successful in thwarting annihilation of the Jews of their countries. All of these people of conscience demonstrated that in an evil time and place, goodness was still possible.

693. Neimark, Anne E. *One Man's Valor: Leo Baeck and the Holocaust.* Lodestar, 1986 (0-525-67175-7). 128 pp. Nonfiction.

Interest level: Ages 10–16

This true tale is part of the Jewish Biography series. Leo Baeck is aptly the epitome of what it means to be noble. As Chief Rabbi of Berlin, Baeck chose to stay in Germany during the Nazi era, using his influence as a renowned scholar to help others escape. We see his dilemmas and are moved by them: Should he share the truth about Auschwitz? (He doesn't, favoring hope over despair.) Should he save family possessions when the Nazis will inevitably destroy them? (He doesn't, dumping silver menorahs and other treasured pieces into the sea so the Nazis can't seize them or the spirit they represent.)

Neimark uses Jewish symbols effectively to relate response to the Nazi menace. Baeck risks typhus in order to keep it from others; he spends more than two years in a concentration camp as the cost of pursuing his philosophy of patience and imagination in the face of adversity. But in the end, that philosophy, coupled with inordinate hard work, wins out. Baeck saves thousands of people from death.

There are few nonfiction biographies for this age group on the Holocaust, and few books offer so much food for thought.

694. Oppenheim, Shulamith Levey. *The Lily Cupboard*. Illus. by Ronald Himler. Harper, 1992 (0-06-024669-3). 30 pp. Picture book.

Interest level: Ages 6–8

There are not many books for young children about the Holocaust. *The Lily Cupboard* is a perfect introduction to this topic for young readers. Set in the Netherlands, it is the story of Miriam, a little girl who is taken to the countryside to live with a Dutch farmer and his family in order to remain safe. In a heart-wrenching scene, Miriam's mother and father gently explain why she must go; her feelings are accurately portrayed and acknowledged. The parents clearly are devastated at leaving their child with others but believe this is their only option.

The farm family is kind. Nello, the son, becomes her companion. The family delights Miriam with a pet rabbit, but she naturally misses her own parents deeply. Miriam is told that she must hide in a secret cupboard if the German soldiers come. When she hears the whistle warning of the soldiers' approach, Miriam refuses to go into the cupboard without her rabbit. She is not discovered, and she tells the relieved family that she had to care for the rabbit the way they cared for her.

The Lily Cupboard is an excellent portrayal of some unknown heroes and is useful for anyone wanting to offer a complete picture of the events concerning the Holocaust.

695. Orlev, Uri. *The Island on Bird Street*. Trans. by Hillel Halkin. Houghton, 1984 (0-395-33887-5); pap. (0-395-61623-9). 162 pp. Fiction.

Interest level: Age 10+

This story of survival is set in the Warsaw ghetto during the Nazi Holocaust. Eleven-year-old Alex is in hiding alone in the ruins of a bombed-out house. His mother has disappeared, but he hopes that his father, who has been taken away by the Germans, will return. During the five months that he lives in the house, he feels like a person on a desert island, using his wits and his energy to survive.

The author and translator have done their jobs well. The story reads like an adventure and is all the more compelling because it is based on the author's own experiences. The details of Alex's everyday activities, the dangers he is exposed to, his final reunion with his father, and their escape into the forest to fight with the partisans make for exciting as well as inspiring reading.

696. Ramati, Alexander. *And the Violins Stopped Playing: A Story of the Gypsy Holocaust.* Watts, 1986. o.p. 237 pp. Fiction.

Interest level: Age 11+

Told through the voice of Roman Mirga, a Gypsy who survived the Holocaust, this phase of the Nazi terror communicates itself very well. The story details the Gypsies' response, or lack of it, to their impending danger. They see the Nazi extermination of the Jews, but they doubt their informants' warnings that the Gypsies are next. And they are surprisingly callous about the Jews.

Young Roman and his father are among the leaders of the Gypsies who do recognize the Nazi threat. By the force of their persuasion, they temporarily save the lives of their tribe, but they are eventually interned in concentration camps, where they witness the slaughter of others of their heritage. Roman and his father incur the anger of some of their tribesmen, but in the end they are proven tragically correct. Roman and a few others escape from the camp, but most of the members of his family are killed. In total, 500,000 Gypsies were killed in the Holocaust. This book helps to tell their story and makes an important contribution to Holocaust literature.

697. Reiss, Johanna. *The Journey Back.* Harper, 1992 (0-06-021457-0); pap. (0-06-447042-3). 224 pp. Fiction.

Interest level: Age 12+

In this sequel to *The Upstairs Room* (see next entry), the author brings to readers' attention the hard truth that recovery after the war does not have a fairy-tale ending. Some anti-Semitism is still evident in the community; at least one of the families blames the Jews because family members died trying to protect Jewish people. Rachel, the eldest sister, was harbored by devout Christians and, much to her father's unhappiness, she has converted to Christianity. Sini, the sister who was in hiding with Annie, leaves home. The father remarries, and Annie sorely misses her Christian Dutch family, who have come to regard her and her sister as their own children. The years in hiding leave their toll, and the world still needs mending.

698. Reiss, Johanna. *The Upstairs Room.* Crowell, 1987, LB (0-690-04702-9); pap. (0-06-440370-X). 208 pp. Fiction.

Interest level: Age 11+

This is the fictionalized true story of a young Jewish girl's experiences during World War II. Following her mother's death, she and her older sister are hidden in a private home in the Netherlands, while another sister and their father hide elsewhere. For several years, Annie and her sister are not permitted to go outdoors. Other relatives have escaped to the United States; still others are tricked into volunteering to go on the trains that Hitler has sent to deport Jews to concentration camps. Some of the drama lies in the slow disintegration of all of the Jews' lives. Reiss demonstrates that when one group loses its freedom and basic security, eventually all groups lose it. Gas chambers, shootings, and other Nazi practices are described, but do not occupy the bulk of the story. The book is neither graphic nor shockingly written. Instead, its emphasis is on warning all groups of the realistic dangers a dictatorship can bring.

699. Rogasky, Barbara. *Smoke and Ashes: The Story of the Holocaust.* Illus. with photos and maps. Holiday, 1988 (0-8234-0697-0); pap. (0-8234-0878-7). 192 pp. Nonfiction.

Interest level: Age 12+

This book examines Hitler's rise to power in the context of long-standing anti-Semitism. Whereas some books move readers by fleshing out stories of individuals, Rogasky eventually gets considerable power from an unexpected source: statistics and lists. A unique feature is comparison with the numbers and shapes of other holocausts—those suffered by American Indians, Armenians, and so forth—but the common denominator (such as relegating one group to lower human status) is disappointingly left unexplored.

Other areas of focus include the late, inadequate response of the United States and United Kingdom and anti-Semitism rising again in the 1980s. Most powerful is attention given to rebellion and resistance by Jews, and so an individual like the butcher who leaped from a body-filled pit to tear out the throat of an SS commander with his teeth rises to stun the imagination from a list. Large numbers from lists also reverberate in memory, such as the acts of rescue by non-Jews, from an industrialist who saved 1,500 lives to the strong governmental leaders of Bulgaria, Finland, and Denmark, whose steadfast refusal to cooperate also meant thousands saved. Perhaps the saddest statistic is that many were too weak to live even when liberated. "In the areas freed by the Americans, French, and British, 60,000 Jews were found alive. Within one week, 20,000 had died." Oddly, even with its many lists, *Smoke and Ashes* is perhaps one of the saddest Holocaust books because its numbers tell just how hard it was to escape, how few survived.

700. Rossel, Seymour. *The Holocaust: The Fire That Raged.* Illus. with maps and photos. Watts, 1989 (0-531-10674-8). 128 pp. Nonfiction.

Interest level: Ages 9–12

This factual presentation provides a clear, concise view of the evolution of the Holocaust. The author simplifies important components of its development, such as the listing of significant points in *Mein Kampf.* The bold-faced subheadings in each chapter furnish an outline for the historical information and give the book newspaperlike vitality. The black-and-white contemporary photographs are memorable and well chosen; the maps are less successfully presented. Attention is paid to the governments and individuals who could have helped end the Holocaust but did not. The United States and other countries turned away the *St. Louis*, a ship filled with 930 German Jews, because of immigration requirements; the ship finally dispersed its passengers in Europe, where many of them had to flee the Nazis a second time. The Pope, possibly afraid for German Catholics, chose not to speak out publicly against the atrocities happening to Jews in Germany. The author cautions that these events must not be forgotten and that we must all be aware that a similar series of events could happen again. A Holocaust timeline, a reading list, and bibliography are included.

701. Sender, Ruth Minsky. *The Cage.* Macmillan, 1986 (0-02-781830-6). 245 pp. Nonfiction.

Interest level: Age 11+

At age 16, Riva becomes the legal guardian of her three younger brothers. Her two older sisters and a brother have been sent to Russia for protection; her mother has been taken away by the Nazis, supposedly to a labor camp, but probably in reality a death camp. Riva and her brothers live in Poland. Their Christian neighbors, once their close friends, have turned against them and have aided the Nazis in pillaging their home. One brother dies, and Riva and her two remaining brothers are moved to the ghetto in Warsaw. There they stay until the ghetto is totally evacuated, and they are sent to Auschwitz, where they are permanently separated from each other.

Because of her ability to write poetry that elevates the spirits of the prisoners, Riva wins affection and attention, not only of her fellow prisoners, but also of one of the wardens of the camp. She manages to survive, as do the three siblings who were sent to Russia. She now lives in the United States, where she has married another survivor. She has a loving and understanding child, and her life is a full one, but she still has nightmares and fears that there will be another holocaust.

The book is not only Sender's personal account of her experiences in the Holocaust, but it is also the story of six million Jews. She describes horrors and atrocities that were everyday events for several years and does not glorify anyone's courage; she lets the events convey their own effect. Sender demonstrates how futile it seemed for anyone to try to escape. She does not, however, discuss any of the process of her Polish friends' changeover to the Nazi cause. Perhaps this is because it is their story rather than hers. She provides evidence of the attitudes of the Polish people who were given the Jews' houses and possessions and thus benefited from the Jews' annihilation. And she describes the feeling of going to her old home, seeing her old furniture in the rooms, and being told that the current Polish occupants threw away all their books and photos. Her story is dramatically and painfully told.

702. Sender, Ruth Minsky. *The Holocaust Lady.* Macmillan, 1992 (0-02-781832-2). 192 pp. Nonfiction.

Interest level: Ages 10–14

In this third book about her experiences during and after the Holocaust, Ruth Minsky Sender continues the fine tradition she has established for bringing the realities of the Holocaust to thousands of Americans. This part of her story reveals what happened when she and her new family got to the United States and how she was able to finally tell her story. *The Holocaust Lady*, a title created by students whom she has arranged to visit in order to tell her story, is a riveting, tender, and emotional recounting of Sender's life from the time she arrived in the United States to the present. Particularly significant is the final scene, when Sender's grandson dedicates his bar mitzvah to her and her husband. This book is an important contribution to our knowledge about the lasting effects of the Holocaust.

703. Sender, Ruth Minsky. *To Life.* Viking, 1988 (0-02-781831-4); Puffin, pap. (0-14-034367-9). 232 pp. Autobiography.

Interest level: Ages 10–14

This is the second of three books about Ruth Minsky Sender's experiences during and after the Holocaust. This book continues the story when Sender, referred to as Riva, is freed from her work detail by the Russians. Although she experiences profound relief and gratitude after her release, Riva begins an agonizing search for friends and family, returning to her hometown of Lodz, Poland, and finally settling in a number of displacement camps while she awaits permission to come to the United States. During her time at the camps, she is reunited with her sisters and brother and she marries and bears a child. Many students and adults are unfamiliar with the conditions in these displacement camps, and this book provides an important look at the hardships there. Sender's book depicts her heart-wrenching struggle but uplifts the reader at the same time.

704. Singer, Isaac Bashevis. *"The Power of Light" in The Power of Light.* Illus. by Irene Lieblich. Farrar, 1990, pap. (0-374-45984-3). 87 pp. Short stories.

Interest level: Age 9+

David and Rebecca, young survivors of the Nazis' destruction of the Warsaw ghetto, take courage from the light of a Hanukkah candle and escape from the ruins of the ghetto into the forest to join the partisans. They face many challenges: the threat of huge rats in the sewer, the omnipresence of Nazis who guard the ghetto, and a journey through treacherous waters where their boat is targeted by Nazi warplanes. Eventually, they settle in Israel, where they finish school and marry. This story is the only factual one in Singer's book of miraculous Hanukkah tales, but the story certainly tells of a miracle.

705. Toll, Nelly S. *Behind the Secret Window: A Memoir of a Hidden Childhood during World War Two.* Dial, 1993 (0-8037-1362-2). 161 pp. Nonfiction.

Interest level: Age 11+

Using her diary as a foundation, the author re-creates the years of World War II as she lived it in Poland. She describes the time when the Russians first occupied their city. Her father is forced to flee because he is well-to-do, and the extended family move in together. Then, when the Germans invade, the father returns for a time. When anti-Jewish sentiment turns into outright oppression, the family is moved into a ghetto. She and her mother go into hiding with a Christian Polish couple, while the father tries to find hiding places for others in the family. He is never heard from again. The author is also an artist, and she includes samples of the drawings she did when she was in hiding. Although her father and most of their extended family are killed, her mother remarries and builds a good life for them after the war. The story adds to the documentation of the conditions of the war as well as the bravery of some non-Jews.

706. Vos, Ida. *Hide and Seek.* Trans. by Terese Edelstein and Inez Smidt. Houghton, 1991 (0-395-56470-0). 144 pp. Fiction.

Interest level: Age 11+

In terse sentences designed to sound as if they emanate from the mouth and mind of Rachel, an eight-year-old Jewish child in Nazi-dominated Netherlands in the early 1940s, the terror and horror of the Holocaust unfolds. The exquisite torture of small edicts—such as those banning Jews from owning bicycles or forbidding them to sit on public benches—is brought out through the narrative. The cruelty of the Nazis emerges amazingly clearly through these small, diabolically calculated deprivations.

Rachel and her immediate family survive, but at what cost? This book manages to raise the questions and present the information without resorting to descriptions of atrocities. Young readers will find it a unique addition to the chronicles of this gruesome era.

707. Yolen, Jane. *The Devil's Arithmetic.* Viking, 1988 (0-670-81027-4); Puffin, pap. (0-14-034535-3). 160 pp. Fiction.

Interest level: Age 10+

Hannah, a modern Jewish child, is annoyed at having to go to her grandparents' house in the Bronx for a seder. She is embarrassed by the emotional outbursts of her grandfather, who angrily displays his arm, tattooed with his concentration camp identification number. She feels a special kinship with her Aunt Eva, for whose dear friend she was named, but she feels no real connection with the rest of the family or, for that matter, with the Jewish people. During the part of the seder where she is asked to symbolically open the door for the prophet Elijah, she steps back in time into the shtetl of her grandparents and into the fire of the Holocaust. She experiences the concentration camp as Chaya, her aunt's friend, all the while knowing that she is from a different time and place. After having been tortured and witnessing the hell of the camps, she is the only one of a group of four girls permitted to avoid the ovens. She swiftly substitutes herself for her friend Rivka (later, Eva) and goes to her death in her place. At that point, she reenters the present and returns to the seder table, knowledgeable and forever a part of her people. The story is a profound and moving one. The authenticity of the Yiddish phrases and customs helps to involve the reader. The author, a master storyteller, has used not only her personal experience but also her impeccable research skills to weave a tale that is potent and unforgettable.

708. Zalben, Jane Breskin. *The Fortuneteller in 5B.* Holt, 1991 (0-8050-1537-X). 144 pp. Fiction.

Interest level: Ages 9–12

Madame Van Dam, an elderly fortune teller, moves into the apartment upstairs from Alexandria and her mother, who are still mourning the death of Alex's father. After an initial period of fearing the old woman, Alexandria gets to know her and becomes less afraid. When Madame Van Dam is away for a week, Alex is given the key to her apartment so that she can care for the woman's rabbit. She and her friend Jenny explore Madame Van Dam's trunk and find old photos, letters, and jewelry. Alexandria feels guilty but doesn't admit what she did until confronted by an angry Madame Van Dam, who has discovered her flowered barrette. Alex apologizes, and Madame Van Dam then tells Alex about her experiences as a child in a concentration camp. In addition to the intergenerational friendship, the blasting of stereotypes about old people, and the universality of grieving, the story informs the reader about the treatment of the Gypsies at the time of the Holocaust.

709. Zeinert, Karen. *The Warsaw Ghetto Uprising.* Millbrook, 1993, LB (1-56294-282-4). 112 pp. Nonfiction.

Interest level: Age 12+

Detail upon inexorable detail construct the devastating picture of the planned murder of all the Jews in Poland. Their removal to the ghettos, the systematic removal to concentration camps of 300,000 Jews from the Warsaw ghetto, and finally the plan to burn the ghetto and kill all of the remaining Jews leads to the uprising of the Jews in January 1943, a battle that lasted four days. Then, in April 1943, only a few days before Passover, the final battle began. The Germans thought it would be over in hours, but it took a full month before the ghetto was finally destroyed and almost all its inhabitants killed. As a final act of monstrosity, General Stroop, the leader of the Nazi forces, blew up the Tlomackie Synagogue. The author conveys her facts in direct, unemotional language, even reporting without comment on the decision by Dr. Janusz Korczak to accompany the 200 orphans in his charge to their death, even though he was given the option of having his life spared. The reader is introduced to numerous individuals whose heroism is inspiring. A chronology is provided. The Warsaw ghetto uprising has become the symbol of Jewish resistance and determination for Jews around the world.

Vietnam

710. Ashabranner, Brent. *Always to Remember: The Story of the Vietnam Veterans Memorial.* Photos by Jennifer Ashabranner. Putnam, 1988 (0-399-22031-3); Scholastic, pap. (0-590-44590-1). 40 pp. Nonfiction.

Interest level: Age 10+

A father-daughter team is at work here, telling of the Vietnam Veterans Memorial's evolution in a most touching manner. The father, Brent Ashabranner, lets his voice and question be heard: Should he and other visitors read the notes others have left? Yes, he concludes. In his view, the grief was meant quite deliberately to be shared. Putting himself into the narration is an appropriate personal touch that harmonizes well with the other living forces that enabled this wall—designed by a female undergraduate architecture student and paid for exclusively by private donations—to become the most-visited memorial in Washington, D.C. It's a very dramatic story, supported by moving photographs provided by daughter Jennifer Ashabranner.

Besides the history of the war itself, there is Jan Scruggs, the veteran who conceived the idea and held a news conference to announce fund-raising ten years to the day after he was wounded. And the time the whole project almost fell apart because H. Ross Perot and other major donors didn't like the chosen design. But most touching are the mementos and notes that are left: "I should have been with you guys. I'll see you guys in heaven 'cause we spent our time in hell." No wonder visitors come night and day to this "meeting of earth, sky, and remembered names."

711. Bunting, Eve. *The Wall.* Illus. by Ronald Himler. Houghton, 1990 (0-395-51588-2); pap. (0-395-62977-2). 32 pp. Picture book.

Interest level: Age 5+

Captured in this story is the devastating loss that war brings to all people as a little boy and his father, of Mexican-American heritage, visit the Vietnam Veterans Memorial to view their beloved grandfather's name. The boy speaks to a soldier with no legs. He notes the mementos that have been left near a loved one's name: a teddy bear, a rose, a letter. It takes a while for the father to find the name, but when he does, his fingers cannot leave it. The boy and his father do a rubbing of the name and leave a keepsake of their own: the boy's school photo, smiling up at the wall. The boy feels honored, yet saddened that his grandfather's name is listed. When a school group visits the wall, eagerly asking questions, the boy and his father stand silently, heads bowed. The illustrations convey the powerful emotion that this monument brings to its observers, especially those who have lost loved ones in the war.

712. Donnelly, Judy. *A Wall of Names.* Illus. by Paul Wenzel. Random, 1991, LB (0-679-90169-8); pap. (0-679-80169-3). 48 pp. Nonfiction.

Interest level: Ages 7–10

Designed to be easily read, this slim book attempts to explain the war in Vietnam and provides a history of the Veterans Memorial. The chapters on the evolution of the war and its impact on the Americans who remained behind are simply and clearly written and discuss conflicting points of view. One chapter profiles Jan Scruggs, the Vietnam veteran who conceived the idea of a memorial and who began the initial fund-raising. The book also discusses the controversy about how the memorial should look and the reaction to the design, submitted by college student Maya Ling Lin, that was selected by the judges. The photographs convey a sense of the wall and its impact on visitors. Also included is a photo and description of the accompanying sculpture of three soldiers, explaining that this sculpture was part of a compromise reached after dissension about the selection of the wall as the major memorial.

713. Mabie, Margot C. J. *Vietnam, There and Here.* Henry Holt, 1985. o.p. 166 pp. Nonfiction.

Interest level: Age 12+

With a topic as emotionally loaded and complex as the Vietnam War, it is commendable that the author has succeeded so admirably in providing a thorough, thoughtful, accurate, even-handed presentation. The book moves from 2879 B.C. to the present, detailing the positions of the "doves" as well as the "hawks" and presenting the rationales behind all positions. The first two sections of the book present information about Vietnam: its history, including the role of the French government; its culture; and its political structure. There are some fascinating nuggets of information. For example, there is an anecdote about one U.S. government specialist, Edward Lansdale, who was instructed to encourage the Vietnamese to leave the North. He hired soothsayers to make dire predictions about life in North Vietnam and violated the Geneva Accord by sending an envoy to the North to tell Vietnamese Catholics that the Virgin Mary was moving south. Although 12-year-olds will find the material challenging, the book is certainly worth the effort, and teenagers and adults can make good use of the information.

714. Myers, Walter Dean. *Fallen Angels.* Scholastic, 1988 (0-590-40942-5); pap. (0-590-40943-3). 309 pp. Fiction.

Interest level: Age 12+

Richie Perry, a tough young New Yorker, narrates the story of a group of young people stationed in Vietnam. Richie is stationed there even though his medical profile should have prohibited him from combat. The language and the action are rough, but mature readers will be moved by the voices and the very human issues these young soldiers encounter. Details of physical discomfort, fear, and actual combat are included in the unfolding of the relationships among young men and women caught in the same situation. Richie sees his buddies die and is himself wounded. He receives a Purple Heart and returns home with one of his closest friends, optimistic about life after his harrowing experiences.

715. Pettit, Jayne. *My Name Is San Ho.* Scholastic, 1992 (0-590-44172-8). 149 pp. Fiction.

Interest level: Ages 10–14

San Ho flees his tiny village in Vietnam when his mother feels it is too dangerous for him to remain. He stays in Saigon with a family friend but loses touch with his mother until a letter arrives instructing him to come to the United States. San Ho's journey and his eventual reunion with his mother and her new husband, as well as his gradual adjustment to life in the United States, are all told through his eyes. The book is alternately wrenching and heartwarming. San Ho learns that his mother spent years making the necessary arrangements for his arrival and that is why she was not able to come and get him herself. He finds he must get used to his stepfather, Stephen, who must also adjust to having a new son. Stephen's understandable resentment toward his wife about her speaking Vietnamese exclusively around San Ho is very realistic. Most poignantly portrayed are San Ho's first months at school, his bewilderment at baseball, and his devastation when his garden is vandalized. The reader feels a definite identification with San Ho; the happily-ever-after ending is gratifying and affirming.

Other Wars

716. Bergman, Tamar. *The Boy from Over There.* Trans. by Hillel Halkin. Houghton, 1988 (0-395-43077-1); pap. (0-395-64370-8). 182 pp. Fiction.

Interest level: Age 10+

The setting is an Israeli kibbutz in 1948, just after the end of World War II and at the inception of the Arab-Israeli war, following the proclamation of Israel's independence. We are introduced to a group of children who have lived on this kibbutz since birth. Avram, a newcomer from "over there," a survivor of the Holocaust, arrives with his Uncle Misha. Avram has been emotionally damaged by spending most of his young years in hiding, by seeing his father killed, and by not knowing what has happened to his mother since she was taken away to a hospital after the liberation of his town in Poland. He clings to Misha for a long time and then forms a friendship with Rina, another child from the kibbutz. Rina's father has been killed in action in World War II. The two children share the feeling that their missing parents will one day return. The events of the story lead to their final understanding that their missing parents are dead and that they must learn to bear that loss.

The writing is very moving and specific in its communication of the spirit and energy of the people of the kibbutz. We are introduced to a number of characters who have suffered losses of enormous impact, but who have managed, with the support of their comrades, to overcome their anguish. The author, by portraying characters who are far from angelic, helps the reader to understand that ordinary people, not saints and martyrs, endured these devastating events and emerged to lead constructive lives.

The agony of constant warfare and lack of security are presented here in a style that is intimate and straightforward. The author and translator convey their passion without seeming to lose a balanced perspective. This is an excellent addition to the literature about the aftermath of the Holocaust. It is also a valuable book to help people better understand the continuing conflicts in the bloody area of the Middle East.

717. Chaikin, Miriam. *Aviva's Piano.* Illus. by Yossi Abolafia. Clarion, 1986. o.p. 43 pp. Fiction.

Interest level: Ages 7–10

Aviva's piano has finally arrived from Argentina, where Aviva and her family lived until their recent move to a kibbutz in Israel, near the Lebanese border. Aviva has waited months for her piano to arrive, and now that it is here she is dismayed to learn that it won't fit through any of the doors or windows of her house. In the midst of this problem, the members of the kibbutz must go to an air raid shelter because their kibbutz is under attack. After the attack, when the damage is assessed, it is discovered that a cow was killed and that one rocket has broken the upstairs wall of Aviva's house. Now the piano can be hoisted into the house, and Aviva rejoices that "something good came from something bad."

The story flavorfully conveys the life-style and activities of a kibbutz. It also authentically portrays the situation of having to live with the constant threat of possible annihilation. It is sad to read that these children are surprised to hear about a kibbutz near Tiberias that does not have a bomb shelter; such shelters are a fact of life for these children.

The story focuses on the arrival of the piano and, in so doing, makes the issue of war and its devastation a sidelight. This can be an excellent introduction to discussion of the implications of the kibbutz children's different interactions and comments. It is a gentle but telling commentary on today's crises.

718. Choi, Sook Nyul. *Year of Impossible Goodbyes.* Houghton, 1991 (0-395-57419-6); Dell, pap. (0-440-40759-1). 176 pp. Fiction.

Interest level: Age 10+

Sookan and her family endure cruel treatment at the hands of the occupying Japanese forces in northern Korea during World War II. After the Japanese are replaced by the Russians, the family is separated, but eventually they are reunited in Seoul. *Echoes of the White Giraffe* (1993) provides a sequel to the story and follows Sookan and her family from their displacement in Pusan back to their home in Seoul. This book offers a vivid picture of the restrictions and expectations placed on women in traditional Korean society. Both books personalize the recent history of Korea and provide an informative context.

719. Frank, Rudolf. *No Hero for the Kaiser.* Trans. by Patricia Crampton. Illus. by Klaus Steffens. Lothrop, 1986 (0-688-06093-5). 224 pp. Fiction.

Interest level: Age 12+

Fourteen-year-old Jan Kubitsky is taken by German soldiers to fight in World War I after his village in Poland has been destroyed by both Russian and German forces. He does not seem to identify with any of the sides in the war, manages to survive horrible conditions, and becomes a mascot and hero to the German soldiers. He is always aware of the folly and waste of war, and in the end he deserts, goes off with his dog, and is never heard from again. The book is somewhat wordy and, at times, confusing, but there is so little available about this war that it is worth considering as an additional insight into a complex period of history. The superrealistic drawings add to the reader's experience of the pathos of involving a young boy in the agonies and ugliness of war.

720. Fritz, Jean. *China's Long March: 6,000 Miles of Danger.* Illus. by Yang Zhr Cheng. Putnam, 1988 (0-399-21512-3). 124 pp. Nonfiction.

Interest level: Age 10+

Few authors can make history come alive the way Fritz does. Her series of books on American Revolutionary heroes is both entertaining and informative. Her autobiographical works on her youth in China illuminate the setting and time and help children understand the sense of leaving one's home and going into a new culture. In *China's Long March,* she has provided young readers access to a period of history and an event of enormous magnitude that is rarely studied in the public schools. Because of her understanding of the people and of the process of history, Fritz is able to communicate the complexity of the issues without losing sight of the human element. The fact that she interviewed many survivors of the Long March adds to the authenticity of the work. She adds perspective to her admiration of Mao when she describes the Cultural Revolution and the fact that most people admit that it was a mistake. Most of all, she conveys her respect for the people, the issues, and the facts.

721. Giff, Patricia Reilly. *The War Began at Supper: Letters to Miss Loria.* Illus. by Betsy Lewin. Dell, 1991, pap. (0-440-40572-6). 68 pp. Fiction.

Interest level: Ages 7–11

This book—one of very few for children about the 1991 war in the Persian Gulf—is in the form of letters written to a favorite student teacher who has moved away. Although some of the characters are annoying and somewhat shallow and some of the conflicts are resolved a bit too easily, this book touches on many important issues, including the discrimination suffered by Arab-Americans during the war. It also acknowledges the confusion, fear, and frustration young children feel when a war is going on. The book's tone acknowledges the children's fears and tries to provide not only some degree of reassurance (the bombs will not fall on their school bus), but stresses that the children have the power to make things better—they write to a soldier (who is a woman), for example, and throw a birthday party for a child whose father is in Saudi Arabia and unable to be home. A counselor is also seen as playing a positive role. This book could be a valuable tool for helping children to write their own "letters to Miss Loria," expressing their feelings about scary situations overseas.

722. Gilmore, Kate. *Remembrance of the Sun.* Houghton, 1986. o.p. 246 pp. Fiction.

   Interest level: Age 14+

Although this is fiction, it is based on the author's experience in Iran during the late 1970s. The plot is simple: An American girl, Jill, and an Iranian boy, Shaheen, both talented musicians, fall in love. He is committed to revolution against the Shah; she deplores violence, especially when it endangers someone she loves. Their relationship evolves slowly and authentically so that it is believable to the reader. The characters are well developed and multidimensional. Jill's parents, caught in the conflict, are also presented realistically. In the end, Jill and her parents must leave Iran, and Shaheen has learned some hard lessons about the revolution.

   The book could serve as motivation for young readers to research the complex issue of Iran and its current situation.

723. Gordon, Sheila. *Waiting for the Rain: A Novel of South Africa.* Orchard, 1987 (0-531-08326-8); Bantam, pap. (0-553-27911-4). 214 pp. Fiction.

   Interest level: Age 12+

Frikkie is the white nephew of the owners of the farm. Tengo is a black employee who is the same age as Frikkie. The setting is South Africa, and the story clearly outlines the inequality that poisons the country. Frikkie attends school free. Tengo would love to go to school, but first, it is costly for blacks to attend, and second, there is no school nearby.

   Despite the differences in their societal positions, Frikkie and Tengo are friends. As time passes, the two boys are prepared to take their adult positions in life, but the hostile conditions in South Africa intervene, and one day the two young men meet as adversaries in battle. Frikkie is pressed into mandatory military service, and Tengo is an "agitator." In the end, although they both have their own point of view, based on their heritage, the two men remain friends as they acknowledge that their country is in terrible trouble.

Nothing is resolved in the story. Much of the book is wordy, especially the end, where the two young men talk at each other and the story becomes tract. But this is an important issue for young readers to know about; thus, it is a worthwhile book to help them understand some of the complexities of the South African battleground.

724. Heide, Florence Parry, and Judith Heide Gilliland. *Sami and the Time of the Troubles.* Illus. by Ted Lewin. Clarion, 1992 (0-395-55964-2). Unpaged. Picture book.

Interest level: Ages 7–10

Sami, a young boy in war-torn Lebanon, describes his life: When it's safe, he can go outside to play, go to school, and shop, but during the fighting, he must stay in his uncle's basement with his family. His father was killed in the fighting, so his family must support one another to hold together in this "time of troubles." Sami remembers a day long ago when the children rose up in protest, and he would like to try this tactic again. The book is dramatically illustrated and sensitively written. The author is respectful of the characters and shows many emotions, including conflicting feelings over children's war play. Sami is shown in a nurturing role with his younger sister. Adults will need to do much explaining here because the book does not explicitly state where the story takes place or what the fighting is about.

725. Hudson, Edward Sel, ed. *Poetry of the First World War.* Photos by the author. Lerner, 1990 (1-85210-667-0). 128 pp. Poetry.

Interest level: Age 12+

This book contains a forceful collection of poetry demonstrating the sadness, waste, ugliness, and irony of war, by almost 40 writers, including Rudyard Kipling, G. K. Chesterton, Rupert Brooke, A. A. Milne, Robert Graves, Thomas Hardy, A. E. Housman, and Wilfred Owen. The accompanying photographs, well selected for each of the poems, were taken, by and large, from the collection of the Imperial War Museum in England. Poems include the famed "In Flanders Fields," by John McCrae, a poem that takes on a horrible reality in the context of the moving black-and-white photos. The poem "Back," by W. W. Gibson, describes the shell-shocked emotional state of a young man returning from killing "men in foreign lands." Using his familiar style, A. A. Milne cynically calls World War I the "same old bloody war." The almost unbearable conditions in the trenches, the amputation of former life-styles, the desperation of the young soldiers are all made vivid by the wrenching poetry found here. Includes brief biography of each poet, most of whom fought in World War I.

726. Ross, Stewart. *War in the Trenches: World War I.* Maps, photos. Watts, 1991 (0-531-18434-X). 64 pp. Nonfiction.

Interest level: Age 10+

Part of the Witness History series, this book communicates through photographs, newspaper clippings, quotations from soldiers and leading figures of the time, and short chunks of narrative what the war was like for the British soldiers in the field. An earlier work, *The Origins of World War I* (1989), provides more general information about the war. The book, which is attractive and easy to read, also includes a variety of maps, editorial cartoons, and war-related artwork. There is a chapter on important generals and politicians of the war era, a chronology of the war, and a glossary. Giving the book vitality are details about life in the trenches, from lice hunting to alcohol consumption to the origin of the term *shell-shocked*. The war is not romanticized but is presented with visual and anecdotal accuracy.

727. Rostkowski, Margaret I. *After the Dancing Days.* Harper, 1986 (0-06-025078-X); pap. (0-06-440248-7). 217 pp. Fiction.

Interest level: Age 11+

Set in a small Kansas town in 1919, this book explores a young girl's emergence into maturity in the aftermath of World War I. The story revolves around 13-year-old Annie and her relationship with Andrew, a seriously burned, bitter young hospitalized veteran. In the process of making friends with Andrew, Annie confronts and constructs her own value system. She recognizes that she can no longer unquestioningly obey her mother, and she relentlessly seeks answers to some family mysteries even when she knows that the revelations will be painful to her and her family. In the process of unlocking these secrets, she and her family become increasingly aware of how lacking in glory war really is.

The father and grandfather are wonderful models of quietly heroic and principled people. They are offset by the mother and grandmother, both of whom are self-centered and less admirable, but who are, nevertheless, sympathetically drawn. And although the grandmother remains a person who has decided to avoid active involvement in life, the mother does change at the end of the book, acknowledging the good example set by Annie and her father and grandfather.

The book is perceptively written, and readers will find much substance to sustain their interest. They may even be motivated to discuss and do further research on the events and consequences of this and other wars.

728. Skurzynski, Gloria. *Good-bye, Billy Radish.* Photos. Macmillan, 1992 (0-02-782921-9). 137 pp. Fiction.

Interest level: Age 12+

Set against the backdrop of World War I, this is a coming-of-age story about two boys who live in the steel town of Canaan, Pennsylvania. Hank is American-born; Billy Radish (his name is derived from his Ukrainian name, Bazyli Radichevych) is two years older and more physically developed. Hank's father and brother work in the steel mill, but Hank has always been afraid of the clamorous machines and raging heat. One day, Hank's fears are realized when he witnesses the death of a young man who becomes known as America's first casualty of the war. Billy, on the other hand, eagerly awaits his turn to prove his allegiance to his new country by joining the work force and helping in the war effort.

As the boys grow, so does their friendship. They encounter bigoted classmates who shout about Hank's Germanic-sounding name and the terrible things that "Krauts" do to women. They attend parades, wave flags, and participate in all of the patriotic fervor that the war generates. Billy shares his heritage with Hank and gives him a decorated Ukrainian Easter egg. Hank aches with pride as Billy is made an American citizen. On Armistice Day, Hank manages to deliver his sister-in-law's premature baby and performs an emergency baptism at her request, naming the child William. The baby lives but, sadly, Billy Radish contracts the flu and dies. This event devastates Hank, but he conveys his love for both Billys by presenting his nephew with the Ukrainian egg.

Each chapter is set on a particular date and is accompanied by a black-and-white photograph that adds to the historical flavor of the book. The war is central to the story, but the efforts of those Americans who remained at home are shown as being vital and supportive.

729. Temple, Frances. *Taste of Salt: A Story of Modern Haiti.* Orchard, 1992 (0-531-05459-4). 180 pp. Fiction.

Interest level: Age 12+

Set in Haiti in 1991 just after Jean-Bertrand Aristide was elected president, this is the story of Djo and Jeremie, teenaged victims of poverty and the violence perpetrated by the Macoute, dictator Duvalier's private army. Djo, who was a street urchin taken in by Aristide as a young boy, is in the hospital, barely alive after being brutally beaten and burned by the Macoute. At Aristide's request, he dictates his life story into a tape recorder, assisted by Jeremie, a young woman who also works with Aristide. Djo tells of his life and struggles, including being enslaved in the Dominican Republic for several years, and how he came to be one of Aristide's trusted assistants. The talking exhausts and nearly kills him. As he lies comatose, Jeremie tells her story to bring him back. She, too, was raised in desperate poverty, but she was put on what she describes as a ladder out—Catholic school—and told to climb and not look back. Through her political activities and listening to Djo, she comes to recognize the elitist attitudes she has internalized. Although initially horrified by Djo's physical condition (bruised, burned, with broken teeth), she falls in love with him. He develops feelings for her, too, and slowly regains his strength. Their storytelling is cathartic. At the end, Jeremie defers a scholarship abroad in order to continue working for change in Haiti. The author vividly captures the details of life in the Haitian slums, both the hopes and joys and the everyday hardships and brutality. The violence is graphic, making this only appropriate for very mature readers, but the author does an admirable job of capturing the excitement and terror of life in modern Haiti.

730. Wallin, Luke. *In the Shadow of the Wind.* Bradbury, 1984. o.p. 203 pp. Fiction.

Interest level: Age 11+

Caleb McElroy is a white adolescent who, despite his fear, befriends the Creek Indians in his community in Alabama in 1835. The story is a bloody and somber one of raids on Creek settlements and of deceit and betrayal. Caleb rescues Pine Basket and her mother from captivity. He and Pine Basket are married, and when the Civil War comes, he joins the Union army. Some of the facts about the Indian slave holdings and the arguments about the settlement of the Oklahoma Territory may be new to young readers. This book makes history come alive and is worthwhile reading.

731. Yep, Laurence. *The Serpent's Children.* Harper, 1984 (0-06-026812-3). 277 pp. Fiction.

Interest level: Age 12+

Yep tells us that his original intent in writing this story was to discover his identity as a Chinese person. In the unraveling of the complex plot, he presents an image of the complexity of the Chinese people and a glimpse into their history, not only in their own land, but also in the United States.

The story revolves around one Chinese family, whose father has been absent for a long time, fighting to keep China safe from the British invaders. When he returns to his home in the Kwangtung province, he finds that his wife has died and his two children, Cassia and Foxfire, are struggling to maintain themselves.

The hardships and fighting have injured the father, and Foxfire does not agree with his father's devotion to what Foxfire thinks is an outmoded cause. He decries the poverty of their land and holds out no hope for it. His father disowns him, so he leaves home and travels to San Francisco.

It is clear that war and changing times have made life very different for the Chinese people. The father acknowledges that his children will face a new set of challenges in a new way. He forgives his son for differing with him and lets Cassia know that he appreciates her contributions. Although Foxfire sends money from America and Cassia remains with her father, the reader understands that all of them have a hard road ahead. Their salvation lies in the fact that they are a coherent family unit, and therein lies their strength.

Yep's writing provides access to a complicated and tradition-laden society. The aspects of the deprivation of war and poverty are universal, as are the characters' feelings and interactions. But the special qualities of the Chinese society that he describes are communicated clearly and with passion.

Refugees

732. Ashabranner, Brent, and Melissa Ashabranner. *Into a Strange Land: Unaccompanied Refugee Youth in America.* Photos. Putnam, 1987 (0-399-21709-6). 96 pp. Nonfiction.

Interest level: Age 10+

This is a full account of the plight and triumph of recent young refugees who have come here to escape intolerable physical and emotional torture. Citing the history of the United States as a haven, the authors tell of numerous youngsters, mostly Vietnamese, who have escaped their homeland on boats, and Cambodians, who have arrived from camps. Talking with the teenagers and preteenagers, their foster parents, and agency officials who light their way, the authors discuss the teens' and preteens' past, how foster families are chosen and why they get involved, adjustment for both children and adults to new cultural ways, the depression children may suffer after what seems to be a successful beginning, and sources for strength to get past it. The goal, whether with foster parents or in a group home, is to have a stable environment and gain life skills. Mutual happiness and love are welcome extras, not always forthcoming. Individual stories are moving: the fear of a new arrival who stays in bed three days, the loneliness of an Amerasian who seeks his father in this vast country, and a boy's poignant request to regain lost childhood years when birth records are found, "Do I have to be fifteen?" In this case, the family and agency allow him to live as 12, in keeping with his needs and behavior.

A dramatic, balanced look at the successes and failures of these life-saving efforts, the result is an inspirational testament to the human spirit.

733. Bentley, Judith. *Refugees: Search for a Haven.* Photos. Messner, 1986. o.p. 160 pp. Nonfiction.

Interest level: Ages 12–16

Today's refugees, forced from their homelands, are the subjects here—refugees from Indochina, Latin America, Africa, and Afghanistan. Accounts of the decisions made to avoid political, religious, ethnic, or economic oppression are seen through exploring the plights of individuals and their families. Among them is a student, jailed for participation in a demonstration in Ethiopia; another is a family that left Cambodia, fearful for their lives. Bentley has done good research regarding statistics, public policy, the conditions forcing the emigration, and the dilemmas met afterward. Particularly interesting is the contrast of governmental efforts and some of the private endeavors of the sanctuary movement to reach out, which are sometimes more successful. Bibliography, index.

734. Bunting, Eve. *How Many Days to America?* Illus. by Beth Peck. Houghton, 1988 (0-89919-521-0); pap. (0-395-54777-6). Unpaged. Picture book.

Interest level: Age 12+

A family from an unnamed Central American nation flee their country when soldiers menace them. They are packed into a small boat with other refugees and are beset by many problems: lack of food and water, attack by pirates, and the denial of entry at one port. But at last, they reach a friendly shore and are welcomed by people who look very much like them. They are fed and nurtured and learn that, fortuitously, they have arrived on Thanksgiving Day. They celebrate together thankfully.

735. Siegal, Aranka. *Grace in the Wilderness: After the Liberation, 1945–1948.* Farrar, 1985 (0-374-32760-2); Dutton, pap. (0-317-52861-0). 199 pp. Fiction.

Interest level: Age 13+

Piri and her sister, Iboya, have survived the torture of the concentration camps, but because they are Jews, now they have no home. They are sent to Sweden, where they attend school and try to resume a normal life. They have witnessed unbelievable horrors, but they are grateful to be together and alive. They come to feel so secure in Sweden that the sisters consent to be separated: Iboya goes to work for the summer at a farm, and Piri stays behind with her new-found friends. This marks the first of several separations that the sisters weather very well. They live with Swedish families before they finally emigrate to the United States. The reader knows that they will survive; they have demonstrated their ability to survive almost any hardship, and they will continue to show this strength.

The author has clearly lived through all that she tells of in her story. The details are sometimes painful. She also talks of the difficult decisions that the survivors must make: Israel or America? Or should they marry Christians and remain in Sweden? How can they reconcile their current freedom with the pain of their past? The end of the war did not mark the end of their problems, but at least now they do have choices, and these are of the spirit and style of life rather than the threat of death. In some ways, the story is even more powerful than its precursor, *Upon the Head of a Goat* (Farrar, 1981). There are included here tales of atrocities, but what dominates is the victory of the human spirit.

736. Stanek, Muriel. *We Came from Vietnam.* Illus. by William Franklin McMahon. Whitman, 1985, LB (0-8075-8699-4). 48 pp. Nonfiction.
   Interest level: Ages 7–10

The author describes the Nguyen family, Vietnamese immigrants to the United States who left their homeland as "boat people" after the communist takeover. The father compares U.S. life to a ladder and predicts that the family will "climb . . . up to the top." In Thailand, the family had to wait a year in refugee camps before a church group assisted them in their efforts to emigrate. They are delighted when they see the Chicago skyline; it is just as they have imagined. The similarities as well as the differences between life in rural Vietnam and urban Chicago are described, and the author tells of the family's challenges upon arrival. There is much information here about Vietnamese customs, food, religious practices, and family life. A strong community is shown, and the children are seen as adjusting well to their new lives in the United States.

737. Steiner, Connie Colker. *On Eagles' Wings and Other Things.* Illus. by the author. Jewish Publication Society, 1988 (0-8276-0274-X). 32 pp. Nonfiction.
   Interest level: Ages 5–9

The title is matched by poetic, heartfelt sentiment within, as the author-illustrator tells of the mass influx of immigrants Israel experienced at her birth. Four composite representative stories are told simultaneously: There is Avraham, a young Yemenite whose voyage in Operation Magic Carpet suddenly transports him and his family into mid-century technology; Eli, who left discrimination in Tunisia; Mira, who was left orphaned in the

Holocaust and arrives with a group of supervised children; and Adrena, whose family left America for ideological reasons and who joins other Zionist relatives. The narrative is busy, but the emotions of each child and family as they pack, travel, and arrive are individually right on target. For Mira, whose life has held terror within, there is fear; for Avraham's airplane trip, there is the "miracle" alluded to in the Bible: "Is it not written that we will return to our land on the wings of eagles?" In their new home, everyone "knew he was needed and—even better—wanted."

In the five years between 1948 and 1952, Israel's population more than doubled, with groups and individuals arriving from all over the world. Israel's varied people have not always enjoyed peace with one another and their neighbors, but this is a book about the vibrant hopes as they truly existed at that time.

738. Whelan, Gloria. *Goodbye, Vietnam.* Knopf, 1992 (0-679-82263-1); Random, pap. (0-679-82376-X). 136 pp. Nonfiction.

Interest level: Age 12+

In postwar Vietnam, Mai and her family have been harassed by police who threaten to imprison the grandmother because she practices the old religion and earns money by healing the sick and delivering babies. The grandmother is not a particularly likable woman: She never shares her earnings with her family, even when the father is gone for nearly a year and they are in dire economic straits, and she is always critical and ill-tempered. Some members of the extended family have been fortunate enough to make successful escapes by boat to Hong Kong and then to the United States. But the rest of the village is punished whenever any of the inhabitants disappear. Mai's father is a skilled mechanic, so the family is invited to join a group of people who will brave escape by boat. They fear for their physical safety and—more long-range and subtle—they worry about the possible erosion of their precious heritage. After a number of mishaps and hard times, the entire group is finally permitted to leave by plane for the United States. In an Afterword, the author discloses that conditions have worsened for potential Vietnamese refugees, who are being forced by the thousands to return to Vietnam without being granted asylum.

Nuclear War

739. Coerr, Eleanor. *Sadako and the Thousand Paper Cranes.* Illus. by Ed Young. Putnam, 1993 (0-399-21771-1). Unpaged. Picture book.

Interest level: Ages 7–12

Sadako Sasaki was twelve years old when she died of leukemia as a result of the atomic bombing of Hiroshima. This revised edition with new illustrations tells of her growing up and acquaints the reader with her love of life and her exuberant, active nature. It is all the more painful to learn of her leukemia and to witness her struggle for life as she folds the complicated origami paper cranes, an ancient Japanese symbol of peace and hope. Since her death she has become a folk-hero for Japanese children, and there is now a monument to her in Peace Park, in Japan. The pastel illustrations are drawn from the many images the artist created for a video of the story, narrated by Liv Ullman.

740. Lawrence, Louise. *Children of the Dust.* Harper, 1985. o.p. 183 pp. Fiction.

Interest level: Age 12+

The starkness, deprivation, and terror of the aftermath of a nuclear blast are chillingly conveyed in this engrossing story. The book is divided into three parts, each of them symbolizing a separate phase of existence in a world devastated by a nuclear holocaust. Each section of the book has as its main character a representative of the situation, each one a member of the same family.

The first section, "Sarah," chronicles the immediate survivors' attempts to stay alive. Only Catherine, a young girl, manages to survive. Sarah, her older sister, sees that Catherine will live, and she takes her to the home of another survivor, Johnson, before killing herself and their younger brother. Catherine stays with Johnson, and together they find more people who escaped the immediate effects of the bomb and with them they build a utopian community.

In the next section, "Ophelia," it turns out that Catherine's father has survived in a shelter built to house hundreds of people. They have lived there for years, under a dictatorship, and are now commandeering food from the people who survived on the outside. Ophelia represents a dying form of society. She and her father meet Catherine and do what they can to influence their fellow shelter-mates to change their way of governing.

The last section, "Simon," represents the last of Homo sapiens, of humankind. Simon is Catherine's grand-nephew, although they have never met until now. All the people outside the shelter are mutants, apelike in appearance and with fine white hair covering their bodies to protect them from the sun's killing rays. They are telepathic and can move objects by means of psychokinetic energy. They have designed a community where all people share with each other and are gentle and productive. The children of the community are repulsed by Simon. Their parents explain that he is more to be pitied than feared. He knows himself to be a freak among a new breed, homo superior.

The premise of the story is a dramatic one. It does not hold out the romantic hope that human beings can survive a nuclear war. It builds on the destruction of the human race by envisioning the evolution of a new group, one that will have learned from the mistakes of the past and will build a functioning, constructive new world. There are lessons to be learned here, and they are all the more powerful because the story is so well crafted.

741. Moore, Melinda, and Laurie Olsen, with the Citizens Policy Center Nuclear Action for Youth Project. *Our Future at Stake: A Teenager's Guide to Stopping the Nuclear Arms Race.* Photos. New Society, 1985. o.p. 72 pp. Nonfiction.

Interest level: Age 12+

This book is divided into sections, the first defining "the problem," and the second asking "What can I do?" In the first, the potential problems of nuclear armament are seen through the eyes of teenagers age 13 through 16. Among their topics are the big debate over arms, the cost of the arms race, how wars start, what the bomb is. The second section involves educating and organizing others, how to amass voting power, how the government decides on its spending, and influencing the media. This is an attractive book, with sidebars including cartoons and insightful quotes from the famous and nonfamous regarding nuclear issues. Although the tone promotes peace and disarmament, there is no evidence of a sledgehammer approach. Instead, there are voluminous charts and appendix materials. Included are a glossary, chronologies of U.S.-U.S.S.R. relations and key dates in arms control and disarmament, list of government agencies, resources, bibliography.

742. Pringle, Laurence. *Nuclear War: From Hiroshima to Nuclear Winter.* Photos. Enslow, 1985. o.p. 128 pp. Nonfiction.

Interest level: Ages 10–15

Tracing the history of nuclear warfare from the bombings of Hiroshima and Nagasaki to the arms race and nuclear tensions of the 1980s, science writer Pringle takes readers from the beginnings during World War II to the prospects of nuclear winter if there ever were a full-scale nuclear battle. The research is thorough, yet this is more than a cold, scientific look. Pringle examines the lives of survivors in Japan, who have suffered cancer, malformed offspring, premature aging, even social discrimination. Using that background, he takes readers on a journey to a hypothetical city and shows how it would suffer in a limited nuclear war with today's stronger bombing capacity. As for large-scale war, Pringle feels the results are uncontrollable and untestable, but we "continue to uncover more and more unpleasant possibilities." In the end, after looking at the information scientifically, not politically, his point of view is that any nuclear war will be in essence a "murder-suicide pact" and that there should be no room for experimentation in this arena. Glossary, bibliography, index.

743. Siegel, Barbara, and Scott Siegel. *Firebrats #1: The Burning Land.* Archway, 1987. o.p. 152 pp. Fiction.

Interest level: Age 11+

More an adventure story than a scientifically accurate detailing of what a nuclear holocaust might bring, this book, nevertheless, conveys the psychological sense of what any survivors might feel. Sixteen-year-olds Matt and Danielle are accidentally thrown together at the time of a massive nuclear attack on the United States. They survive for more than a month in the basement of a theater; and when they emerge, they find that most of the population has been killed and the rest are dying of radiation sickness. They manage, by means of their wits and courage, to escape from a menacing group of criminals, and they decide to try to trek across the country in hopes of finding an area that has not been irretrievably damaged by the bombs and perhaps connecting with Matt's parents, who had been in California when the attack leveled the East.

Matt and Danielle are believable characters. Their inventiveness overcomes their terror, and their situation sparks their common sense. The story moves rapidly and convincingly, and young readers may be encouraged to discuss what they would do in the event of such a disaster.

744. Strieber, Whitley. *Wolf of Shadows.* Knopf, 1985, LB (0-394-97224-4); Fawcett, pap. (0-449-21089-8). 105 pp. Fiction.

Interest level: Age 11+

This is the story of the hunt for survival following a nuclear blast in the United States. The unusual perspective of this book is that the group seeking survival is a pack of wolves led by Wolf of Shadows, an intelligent, sensitive, and courageous animal. The story is told from his point of view as he and his pack journey south, fleeing from the cold of a nuclear winter.

When a human mother and her daughter join the wolf pack, they are at first suspicious and uncomprehending of each other. But the wolves accept the humans, and the humans become genuine members of the pack, dependent on the wolves for survival. They encounter other humans and must do battle with them because of their intention to destroy the wolves.

In the end, they have a slim hope of finding a warmer valley where it will be possible for them to live. The author is careful not to guarantee anything, but there is at least hope. The frigid atmosphere of the horror of a nuclear aftermath is well portrayed here, as is the perspective of a wolf leader toward his pack and toward the humans and their peculiar customs.

745. Swindells, Robert. *Brother in the Land.* Holiday, 1985. o.p. 151 pp. Fiction.

Interest level: Age 11+

The story is set in England, far in the future. The narrator is Danny, a young boy who has survived a nuclear bombardment. His story is one of devastation, human cannibalism and savagery, cruelty, and hopelessness. Danny meets Kim, and the two of them try to maintain a loving relationship despite the insanity of the world around them. The only hope that remains at the end is that if there is a future for the world, people will take to heart the lesson that there can be no survival after a nuclear holocaust.

Although the story is a dramatic one, it is not told especially well. The details are mostly of the battles and ugliness of human beings desperate to find food and willing to do anything to get it. None of the people emerges as an individual, not even the young protagonists. They are simply factors in the whole aftermath of the bombings. But the book succeeds in conveying the fact that there is no life after nuclear war.

746. Vigna, Judith. *Nobody Wants a Nuclear War.* Illus. by the author. Whitman, 1986 (0-8075-5739-0). 32 pp. Fiction.

Interest level: Ages 5–9

The two young children in the story make a hideaway for themselves in case there is a nuclear war. Their mother finds them and explains that she understands their fears. She says that she felt the same way when she was a little girl. She tells them a little of the history of nuclear war, and she assures them that she and their father will try to be with them, no matter what.

She also tells them of the actions that different people engage in to help ensure that there will never be a nuclear war. The children decide to construct a banner and take a picture of it to send to the president of the United States. The banner reads, "Grownups for a safer world to grow up in." The child narrator vows to work hard to prevent a nuclear war so that the world will be a safer place for her children to grow up in.

The message is clear and direct. The book may provide information, comfort, a base for questions and discussions, and inspiration for action.

PART III

Selected Reading
for Adults

6

Separation and Loss

Books and Chapters in Books

Abramson, Jane B. *Mothermania: A Psychological Study of Mother-Daughter Conflict.* Free Pr., 1986.

Ackerman, Robert J. *Perfect Daughters: Adult Daughters of Alcoholics.* Health Communications, 1989.

Adamec, Christine. *There Are Babies to Adopt: A Resource Guide for Prospective Parents.* Windsor, 1991.

Adler, Robert. *Sharing the Children: How to Resolve Custody Problems and Get on with Your Life.* Adler and Adler, 1988.

Ahrons, Constance R., and Rodgers, Roy H. *Divorced Families: A Multidisciplinary Developmental View.* Norton, 1987.

Alexander, Sherry. *The Home Day-Care Handbook.* Human Sciences, 1987.

Alexander, Victoria G. *Words I Never Thought to Speak: Stories of Life in the Wake of Suicide.* Free Pr., 1991.

Amos, William, Jr. *When AIDS Comes to the Church.* Westminster, 1988.

Anderson, Gary. *Courage to Care: Responding to the Crises of Children with AIDS.* Child Welfare League, 1990.

Andre, Pierre. *Drug Addiction: Learn about It before Your Kids Do.* Health Communications, 1987.

Arnold, L. Eugene, and Estreicher, Donna. *Parent-Child Group Therapy: Building Self-Esteem in a Cognitive-Behavioral Group.* Free Pr., 1985.

Atwater, P. M. *Coming Back to Life: The Aftermath of the Near-Death Experience.* Dodd, 1988.

Bagnall, Gellisse. *Educating Young Drinkers.* Routledge, 1991.

Balaban, Nancy. *Learning to Say Goodbye: Starting School and Other Early Childhood Separation.* Plume, 1987.

———. *Starting School: From Separation to Independence—a Guide for Early Childhood Teachers.* Teachers College, 1985.

Barr, Debbie. *Children of Divorce.* Zondervan, 1992.

Barun, Ken, and Bashe, Philip. *How to Keep the Children You Love Off Drugs.* Atlantic, 1988.

Bass, Ellen, and Davis, Laura. *Beginning to Heal: The First Book for Survivors of Child Sexual Abuse.* Harper, 1993.

Battle, Stanley F., ed. *The Black Adolescent Parent.* Haworth, 1987.

Baucom, John Q. *Bonding and Breaking Free: What Good Parents Should Know.* Zondervan, 1988.

Belovitch, Jeanne. *Making Remarriage Work.* Free Pr., 1987.

Benjamin, Harold, and Trubo, Richard. *From Victim to Victor: The Wellness Community Guide to a Fulfilling Life for Cancer Patients and Their Families.* Tarcher, 1987.

Berg-Cross, Linda. *Basic Concepts in Family Therapy.* Haworth, 1987.

Berner, R. Thomas. *Parents Whose Parents Were Divorced.* Haworth, 1992.

Bernstein, Norman, et al., eds. *Coping Strategies for Burn Survivors and Their Families.* Greenwood, 1988.

Beschner, George M., and Friedman, Alfred S. *Teen Drug Use.* Free Pr., 1986.

Bienenfeld, Florence. *Helping Your Child Succeed after Divorce.* Hunter House, 1987.

Black, Claudia. *Double Duty: Dual Dynamics within the Chemically Dependent Home.* Ballantine, 1990.

Bodenhamer, Gregory. *Drug Free: The Back in Control Program for Keeping Your Kids Off Drugs.* Prentice-Hall, 1988.

Bolton, Iris, and Mitchell, Curtis. *My Son, My Son: Healing after a Suicide.* Bolton Pr., 1983.

Borg, Susan, and Lasker, Judith. *When Pregnancy Fails: Families Coping with Miscarriage, Stillbirth, and Infant Death.* Bantam, 1989.

Bowers, Warner F. *Understanding and Coping with Bereavement.* Carlton, 1992.

Bradshaw, John. *Bradshaw on the Family: A Revolutionary Way of Self-Discovery.* Health Communications, 1988.

Bramblett, John. *When Good-Bye Is Forever: Learning to Live Again after the Loss of a Child.* Ballantine, 1991.

Brazelton, T. Berry. *Working and Caring.* Addison-Wesley, 1985.

Brenner, Avis. *Helping Children Cope with Stress.* Free Pr., 1984.

Brondino, Jeanne, et al. *Raising Each Other: A Book for Parents and Teens.* Borgo Pr., 1989.

Brook, Judith, et al., eds. *Alcohol and Substance Abuse in Adolescence.* Haworth, 1985.

Bross, Donald, et al. *The New Child Protection Team Handbook.* Garland, 1988.

Brown, Barbara. *Between Health and Illness.* Houghton, 1984.

Bruch, Hilde, et al., eds. *Conversations with Anorexics.* Basic Books, 1988.

Buckman, Robert. *I Don't Know What to Say . . . How to Help and Support Someone Who Is Dying.* Random House, 1992.

Burgess, Jane. *The Single-Again Man.* Free Pr., 1989.

Byrne, Katherine. *A Parent's Guide to Anorexia and Bulimia.* Holt, 1989.

Caplan, Lincoln. *An Open Adoption.* Farrar, 1990.

Cargas, Harry. *Face to Face: A Book about the Holocaust for the Christian Reader.* Seth Pr., 1988.

Carpenter, Cheryl, et al. *Kids, Drugs and Crime.* Free Pr., 1987.

Carrieri, Joseph R. *Child Custody, Foster Care, and Adoptions.* Free Pr., 1991.

Child Welfare League of America. *Meeting the Challenge of HIV Infection in Family Foster Care.* Child Welfare League, 1991.

———. *Saying Goodbye to a Baby: A Book about Loss and Grief in Adoption.* Child Welfare League, 1989.

Ciborowski, Paul J. *The Changing Family I.* Stratmar Educational Systems, 1984.

———. *The Changing Family II.* Stratmar Educational Systems, 1986.

Clapp, Genevieve. *Divorce and New Beginnings: An Authoritative Guide to Recovery and Growth, Solo Parenting, and Stepfamilies.* Wiley, 1992.

Cleckley, Mary, et al., eds. *We Need Not Walk Alone: After the Death of a Child.* 2nd ed. Compassionate Friends, 1991.

Coleman, Sally, and Donley, Rita J. *Lifework: A Workbook for Adult Children of Alcoholics.* CompCare, 1992.

Colligan, John, and Colligan, Kathleen. *The Healing Power of Love: Creating Peace in Marriage and Family Life.* Paulist Pr., 1988.

Corless, Inge, and Pittman-Lindeman, Mary. *AIDS: Principles, Practices, and Politics.* Hemisphere, 1987.

Couburn, Karen, and Treeger, Madge. *Letting Go: A Parents' Guide to Today's College Experience.* Adler and Adler, 1988.

Counts, David, and Counts, Dorothy, eds. *Coping with the Final Tragedy: Dying and Grieving in Cross Cultural Perspective.* Baywood Publishers, 1991.

Cowan, Paul, and Cowan, Rachel. *Mixed Blessings: Jews, Christians, and Intermarriage.* Doubleday, 1987.

Craig, Judith E. *What Should We Tell the Children: Answers to the Difficult Questions Kids Ask about Life.* Hearst Books, 1993.

Crook, Marion. *Face in the Mirror: Teenagers Talk about Adoption.* Univ. of Toronto Pr., 1987.

Cullen, Paul J. *Stepfamilies: A Catholic Guide.* Our Sunday Visitor, 1988.

Curran, David. K. *Adolescent Suicidal Behavior.* Hemisphere, 1987.

Cusack, Odean, ed. *Pets and Mental Health.* Haworth, 1988.

Daley, Dennis. *Surviving Addiction: A Guide for Alcoholics, Drug Addicts, and Their Families.* Gardner, 1989.

Dalton, Harlon, Burris, Scott, and the Yale AIDS Law Project. *AIDS and the Law.* Yale Univ. Pr., 1987.

Dane, Barbara, and Miller, Samuels. *AIDS: Interfering with Hidden Grievers.* Auburn House, 1992.

Danne, Edward J., et al., eds. *Suicide and Its Aftermath: Understanding and Counseling the Survivors.* Norton, 1987.

Daro, Deborah. *Confronting Child Abuse: Research for Effective Program Design.* Free Pr., 1988.

Davidson, Christine. *Staying Home Instead: How to Quit the Working-Mom Rat Race and Survive Financially.* Free Pr., 1986.

Davis, Samuel M., and Schwartz, Mortimer D. *Children's Rights and the Law.* Free Pr., 1987.

DeFrain, John, et al. *On Our Own: A Single Parent's Survival Guide.* Free Pr., 1987.

———. *Stillborn: The Invisible Death.* Free Pr., 1986.

DeHartog, Jan. *Adopted Children.* Adama, 1987.

Deits, Bob. *Life after Loss: A Personal Guide to Dealing with Death, Divorce, Job Change and Relocation.* Fisher Books, 1988.

Depner, Charlene E., and Bray, James H., eds. *Nonresidential Parenting: New Vistas in Family Living.* Sage, 1993.

DeSpelder, Lynna A., and Strickland, Albert L. *Last Dance: Encountering Death and Dying.* 3rd ed. Mayfield Publishing, 1991.

Dick, Harold M., et al., eds. *Dying and Disabled Children: Dealing with Loss and Grief.* Haworth, 1989.

Dobson, James. *Parenting Isn't for Cowards.* Word Books, 1987.

Donnelly, Katherine F. *Recovering from the Loss of a Child.* Dodd, 1982.

———. *Recovering from the Loss of a Sibling.* Dodd, 1988.

Droege, Thomas. *Guided Grief Imagery.* Paulist Pr., 1987.

Duda, Deborah. *Coming Home: A Guide to Dying at Home with Dignity.* Aurora, 1987.

Edelman, Marean W. *The Measure of Our Success: A Letter to My Children and Yours.* Beacon, 1992.

Ehrensaft, Diane. *Parenting Together: Men and Women Sharing the Care of Their Children.* Free Pr., 1987.

Elkind, David. *Miseducation: Preschoolers at Risk.* Knopf, 1987.

Erichsen, Jean, and Erichsen, Hebno. *How to Adopt from Central and South America.* Los Ninos, 1989.

Erichsen, Jean N., et al. *How to Adopt from Asia, Europe and the South Pacific.* Los Ninos, 1985.

Erickson, Patricia G., et al. *Steel Drug: Cocaine in Perspective.* Free Pr., 1987.

Ericsson, Stephanie. *Companion through Darkness: Inner Dialogues on Grief.* Harper, 1993.

Everett, Craig A. *Divorce Mediation: Perspectives on the Field.* Haworth, 1985.

————, ed. *The Consequences of Divorce: Economic and Custodial Impact on Children and Adults.* Haworth, 1991.

————, ed. *The Divorce Process: A Handbook for Clinicians.* Haworth, 1987.

Faller, Kathleen. *Child Sexual Abuse: An Interdisciplinary Manual for Diagnosis, Case Management, and Treatment.* Columbia Univ. Pr., 1989.

Fintushel, Noelle. *Grief Out Of Season: When Your Parents Divorce in Your Adult Years.* Little, Brown, 1991.

Fisher, Esther, ed. *Impact of Divorce on the Extended Family.* Haworth, 1982.

Fishman, H. Charles. *Treating Troubled Adolescents: A Family Therapy Approach.* Basic Books, 1988.

Fitzgerald, Helen. *The Grieving Child: A Parent's Guide.* Fireside, 1992.

Fitzgerald, Kathleen. *Alcoholism.* Doubleday, 1988.

Foos-Graber, Anya. *Deathing: An Intelligent Alternative for the Final Moments of Life.* Nicolas-Hays, 1989.

Forman, Susan G., and Maher, Charles A., eds. *School-Based Affective and Social Interaction.* Haworth, 1987.

Fox, Sandra Sutherland. *Good Grief: Helping Groups of Children When a Friend Dies.* Gryphon House, 1985.

Francke, Linda Bird. *Growing Up Divorced.* Fawcett, 1984.

Frank, Mary, ed. *Primary Prevention for Children and Families.* Haworth, 1982.

Freeman, Arthur, et al., *Depression in the Family.* Haworth, 1987.

Friel, John. *Adult Children: The Secrets of Dysfunctional Families.* Health Communications, 1988.

Froman, Paul K. *After You Say Goodbye: When Someone You Love Dies of AIDS.* Chronicle, 1992.

Gaffney, Donna A. *The Seasons of Grief: Helping Your Children Grow Through Loss.* NAL/Dutton, 1989.

Gardiner, Muriel. *The Deadly Innocents: Portraits of Children Who Kill.* Yale Univ. Pr., 1985.

Garner, David, and Garfinkel, Paul, eds. *Handbook of Psychotherapy for Anorexia Nervosa and Bulimia.* Guilford Pr., 1985.

Gaskin, Ina May. *Babies, Breastfeeding, and Bonding.* Independent Publishers Group, 1987.

Genevie, Louis, and Margolies, Eva. *The Motherhood Report.* Macmillan, 1987.

Gerne, Patricia, and Gerne, Timothy. *Substance Abuse Prevention Activities for Secondary Students: Ready-to-Use Lessons, Fact Sheets, and Resources for Grades 7–12.* Prentice-Hall, 1991.

Gold, Lois. *Between Love and Hate: A Guide to Civilized Divorce.* Plenum, 1992.

Gold, Mark S., et al., eds. *Cocaine: Pharmacology, Addiction, and Therapy.* Haworth, 1987.

Goldberg, Susan, and Divitto, Barbara. *Born Too Soon: Preterm Birth and Early Development.* Freeman, 1983.

Golden, Susan. *Nursing a Loved One at Home: A Caregiver's Guide.* Running Pr., 1988.

Goldstein, Sonja, and Solnit, Albert J. *Divorce and Your Child: Practical Suggestions for Parents.* Yale Univ. Pr., 1984.

Goodman, Gail S., and Bottoms, Bette L., eds. *Child Victims, Child Witnesses: Understanding and Improving Testimony.* Guilford Pr., 1993.

Gordon, Linda. *Heroes of Their Own Lives: The Politics and History of Family Violence.* Penguin, 1989.

Greeley, Andrew M. *When Life Hurts: Healing Themes from the Gospel.* Thomas More Pr., 1988.

Greenwald, David S., and Zeitlin, Steven J. *No Reason to Talk about It: Families Confront the Nuclear Taboo.* Norton, 1987.

Greif, Geoffrey, and Pabst, Mary S. *Mothers Without Custody.* Free Pr., 1989.

Griffin, Teresa. *Letters of Hope: Living after the Loss of Your Child.* Cedarbrook Pr., 1991.

Grollman, Earl A., and Sweder, Gerri L. *The Working Parent Dilemma: How to Balance the Responsibilities of Children and Careers.* Beacon, 1988.

Gullo, Stephen V., et al., eds. *Death and Children: A Guide for Educators, Parents, and Caregivers.* Center for Thanatology Research and Education, 1985.

Hagan, Frank E., and Sussman, Marvin B., eds. *Deviance and the Family.* Haworth, 1987.

Halporn, Roberta, ed. *A Thanatology Thesaurus.* Center for Thanatology, 1991.

Hart, Louise. *The Winning Family: Increasing Self-Esteem in Your Children and Yourself.* Celestial Arts, 1993.

Haugaard, Jeffrey, and Reppucci, N. Dickon. *The Sexual Abuse of Children: A Comprehensive Guide to Current Knowledge and Intervention Strategies.* Jossey-Bass, 1988.

Haynes, John M. *Divorce Mediation: A Practical Guide for Therapists and Counselors.* Springer, 1981.

Hechler, David. *The Battle and the Backlash: The Child Sexual Abuse War.* Free Pr., 1989.

Hetherington, Mavis, and Arastegh, Josephine, eds. *The Impact of Divorce, Single Parenting, and Stepparenting on Children.* Erlbaum, 1988.

Hobbs, Christopher, J., et al. *Child Abuse and Neglect: A Clinician's Handbook.* Churchill, 1993.

Hodges, William. *Interventions for Children of Divorce: Custody, Access and Psychotherapy.* 2nd ed. Wiley, 1991.

Hooyman, Nancy, and Lustbader, Wendy. *Taking Care of Your Aging Family Members.* Free Pr., 1988.

Hope, Marjorie, and Young, James. *The Faces of Homelessness.* Free Pr., 1986.

Horne, Jo. *A Survival Guide for Family Caregivers.* CompCare, 1991.

Hughes, J., and Oomura, Y. *Cancer and Emotion.* Wiley, 1987.

Humphrey, Penny. *Stepmothers Try Harder.* Evans, 1988.

Hutchings, Nancy, ed. *The Violent Family: Victimization of Women, Children and Elders.* Human Sciences, 1988.

Hyvrard, Jeanne. *Mother Death.* Univ. of Nebraska Pr., 1988.

Irwin, Stephanie. *We, the Homeless: Portraits of America's Displaced People.* Philosophical Library, 1987.

Jacobs, Selby. *Pathologic Grief: Maladaptation to Loss.* American Psychiatric Pr., 1993.

Jan, J. E., et al. *Does Your Child Have Epilepsy?* University Park Pr., 1983.

Janus, Mark-David, et al. *Adolescent Runaways: Causes and Consequences.* Free Pr., 1987.

Jarrett, Claudia J. *Helping Children Cope with Separation and Loss.* Rev. ed. Harvard Common Pr., 1993.

Joan, Polly. *Preventing Teenage Suicide: The Living Alternative Handbook.* Human Sciences, 1987.

Johnson, Karen. *Through the Tears: Caring for the Sexually Abused Child.* Broadman, 1993.

Johnson, Laurene, and Rosenfeld, Georglyn. *Divorced Kids.* Crest, 1992.

Jones, Billy E., ed. *Treating the Homeless: Urban Psychiatry's Challenge.* American Psychiatric Pr., 1986.

Kagan, Sharon L., et al. *America's Family Support Programs: Perspectives and Prospects.* Yale Univ. Pr., 1987.

Kane, Elizabeth. *Birth Mother: America's First Legal Surrogate Mother Tells the Story of Her Change of Heart.* Harcourt, 1988.

Kaplan, Helen Singer. *The Real Truth about Women and AIDS.* Simon & Schuster, 1987.

Kaplan, Kalman, J., and Schwartz, Matthew B. *A Psychology of Hope: An Antidote to the Suicidal Pathology of Western Civilization.* Praeger, 1993.

Kauffman, Danette G. *Surviving Cancer.* Acropolis, 1987.

Kennedy, D. James. *Your Prodigal Child.* Nelson, 1988.

Ketterman, Grace. *Depression Hits Every Family.* Nelson, 1988.

Kirp, David L. *Learning by Heart: AIDS and Schoolchildren.* Rutgers Univ. Pr., 1989.

Klein, Josephine. *Our Need for Others and Its Roots in Infancy.* Tavistock, 1987.

Kouri, Mary K. *Keys to Survival for Caregivers.* Barron, 1992.

Kozol, Jonathan. *Rachel and Her Children: Homeless Families in America.* Fawcett, 1988.

Kramer, Rita. *At a Tender Age: Violent Youth and Juvenile Justice.* BDD Promotional Book, 1988.

Kranitz, Martin. *Getting Apart Together: The Couple's Guide to a Fair Divorce or Separation.* Impact, 1987.

Kressel, Kenneth. *The Process of Divorce.* Basic Books, 1985.

Krieger, Dolores. *Living the Therapeutic Touch.* Dodd, 1987.

Krieger, Robin, et al., eds. *Preparing Adolescents for Life after Foster Care: The Central Role of Foster Parents.* Child Welfare League, 1990.

Krystal, Henry. *Integration and Self Healing.* Analytic Pr., 1987.

Kupfersmid, Joel, and Monkman, Roberta, eds. *Assaultive Youth: Responding to Physical Assaultiveness in Residential Community and Health Care Settings.* Haworth, 1988.

Kuzma, Kay. *Helping Kids Deal with Death.* Pacific Pr. Publishing Association, 1987.

Lamke, Robert, et al., eds. *Perspectives in the AIDS Crisis and Thanatology.* Center for Thanatology, 1989.

Lang, Denise V. *The Phantom Spouse: A Family Survival Guide for Business Travelers.* Dodd, 1988.

Laufer, Moses, and Laufer, M. Egle. *Adolescence and Developmental Breakdown: A Psychoanalytic View.* Yale Univ. Pr., 1984.

Leavitt, Lewis A., and Fox, Nathan A., eds. *The Psychological Effects of War and Violence on Children.* Erlbaum, 1993.

Lechtenberg, Richard. *Epilepsy and the Family.* Harvard Univ. Pr., 1984.

Leick, Nini, and Davidsen-Nielsen, Marianne. *Healing Pain: Attachment, Loss and Grief Therapy.* Routledge, 1991.

Lemmon, John Allen. *Family Mediation Practice.* Free Pr., 1985.

Leuner, Hanscar, et al. *Guided Affective Imagery with Children and Adolescents.* Plenum, 1983.

Levine, Paula, et al. *The Psychosocial Aspects of AIDS: An Annotated Bibliography.* Garland, 1990.

Levy, Sandra M. *Behavior and Cancer.* Jossey-Bass, 1985.

Lewin, Ellen. *Lesbian Mothers: Accounts of Gender in American Culture.* Cornell Univ. Pr., 1993.

Lewis, Carol R. *Listening to Children.* Aronson, 1993.

Lewis, Robert A., and Sussman, Marvin B. *Men's Changing Roles in the Family.* Haworth, 1986.

Lindsay, Jeanne W., and Monserrat, Catherine P. *Adoption Awareness: A Guide for Teachers, Counselors, Nurses, and Caring Others.* Morning Glory, 1989.

Lingle, Virginia, and Wood, M. Sandra. *How to Locate Scientific Information about AIDS.* Haworth, 1987.

Linzer, Norman, ed. *Suicide.* Human Sciences, 1984.

Locke, Steven, and Hornig-Rohan, Mady. *Mind and Immunity: Behavioral Immunology.* Praeger, 1983.

Lukas, Christopher, and Seiden, Henry. *Silent Grief: Living in the Wake of Suicide.* Bantam, 1990.

Lutzer, Erwin W. *Coming to Grips with Death and Dying.* Moody, 1992.

McCall, Virginia. *Sunrise: A Support Program for Children of Divorced Parents.* Paulist Pr., 1992.

McDermott, John. *The Complete Book on Sibling Rivalry.* Perigee, 1987.

MacDonald, Dave, and Patterson, Vicky. *A Handbook of Drug Training: Learning about Drugs and Working with Drug Users.* Routledge, 1991.

McKaughan, Molly. *The Biological Clock: Reconciling Careers and Motherhood in the 1980s.* Doubleday, 1987.

McKillop, Tom. *What's Happening to My Life? A Teenage Journey.* Paulist Pr., 1987.

McRoy, Ruth G., et al. *Emotional Disturbance in Adopted Adolescents: Origins and Development.* Praeger, 1988.

Maltz, Wendy, and Holman, Beverly. *Incest and Sexuality: A Guide to Understanding and Healing.* Free Pr., 1986.

Margulies, Sam. *Getting Divorced without Ruining Your Life.* Fireside, 1992.

Marlin, Emily. *Hope: New Choices and Recovery Strategies for Adult Children of Alcoholics.* Harper, 1987.

Marrus, Michael. *The Holocaust in History.* NAL/Dutton, 1989.

Martin, Cynthia. *Beating the Adoption Game.* Rev. ed. Harcourt, 1988.

Maurer, Daphne, and Maurer, Charles. *The World of the Newborn.* Basic Books, 1989.

Meadowcroft, Pamela, and Trout, Barbara A. *Troubled Youth in Treatment Homes: A Handbook of Therapeutic Foster Care.* Child Welfare League, 1990.

Miller, Derek. *Attack on the Self: Adolescent Behavioral Disturbances and Their Treatment.* Jason Aronson, 1993.

Mintz, Steven, and Kellogg, Susan. *Domestic Revolutions: A Social History of American Family Life.* Free Pr., 1989.

Mizel, Steven B., and Jaret, Peter. *The Human Immune System: The New Frontier in Medicine.* Simon & Schuster, 1986.

Moffat, Mary J., ed. *In the Midst of Winter: Selections from the Literature of Mourning.* Random, 1992.

Montgomery, Jason, and Fewer, Willard. *Family Systems and Beyond.* Human Sciences, 1988.

Morris, Monica. *Last-Chance Children: Growing Up with Older Parents.* Columbia Univ. Pr., 1988.

Murphey, Cecil. *Day to Day: Spiritual Help When Someone You Love Has Alzheimer's.* Westminster, 1988.

Neumann, Hans, and Simmons, Sylvia. *Dr. Neumann's Guide to the New Sexually Transmitted Diseases.* Acropolis, 1987.

O'Connell, Dorothy R. *Baby-Sitting Safe and Sound: The Complete Guide.* Fawcett, 1990.

O'Gorman, Patricia, and Oliver-Diaz, Philip. *Breaking the Cycle of Addiction: A Parents' Guide to Raising Healthy Kids.* Health Communications, 1987.

Okimoto, Jean, and Stegall, Phyllis. *Boomerang Kids: How to Live with Adult Children Who Return Home.* Little, Brown, 1987.

Orbach, Israel. *Children Who Don't Want to Live.* Jossey-Bass, 1988.

Ornstein, Robert, and Sobel, David. *The Healing Brain.* Simon & Schuster, 1987.

Osborne, Judy. *Stepfamilies: The Restructuring Process.* EmiJo Publications, 1983.

Osherson, Samuel. *Finding Our Fathers: How a Man's Life Is Shaped by His Relationship with His Father.* Fawcett, 1987.

Overvold, Amy. *Surrogate Parenting.* Pharos, 1988.

Paradis, Lenora, ed. *Stress and Burnout among Providers: Caring for the Terminally Ill and Their Families.* Haworth, 1987.

Parke, Ross D., and Kellam, Sheppard G., eds. *Exploring Family Relationships with Other Social Contexts.* Erlbaum, 1993.

Parkes, Colin M., and Weiss, Robert S. *Recovery from Bereavement.* Basic Books, 1983.

Parry, Ruth. *Custody Disputes: Evaluation and Intervention.* Free Pr., 1986.

Petti, Theodore A., ed. *Childhood Depression.* Haworth, 1983.

Platt, Larry, and Persico, V. Richard, Jr. *Grief in Cross-Cultural Perspective: A Casebook.* Garland, 1992.

Plaut, Thomas. *Children with Asthma: A Manual for Parents.* Rev. ed. Pedipress, 1989.

Plumer, Erwin H. *When You Place a Child.* Thomas, 1992.

Pohl, Mel, et al. *The Caregivers' Journey: When You Love Someone with AIDS.* Harper, 1991.

Polovchak, Walter, with Klose, Kevin. *Freedom's Child: A Teenager's Courageous True Story of Fleeing His Parents and the Soviet Union — to Live in the United States.* Random House, 1988.

Posner, Julia L. *Adoption Resource Guide.* Child Welfare League, 1990.

Puiia, Nicholas. *Rules for the Traditional Family.* Loyola Univ. Pr., 1988.

Quackenbush, Marcia, et al., eds. *The AIDS Challenge: Prevention Education for Young People.* ETR Associates, 1988.

Quay, Herbert, ed. *Handbook of Juvenile Delinquency.* Wiley, 1987.

Quinn, Phil. *Spare the Rod: Breaking the Cycle of Child Abuse.* Abingdon, 1988.

Quinnett, Paul. *Suicide: The Forever Decision.* Continuum, 1987.

Rando, Therese A. *Grieving: How to Go On Living When Someone You Love Dies.* Bantam, 1991.

——, ed. *Loss and Anticipatory Grief.* Free Pr., 1986.

Reed, Bobbie. *Single Mothers Raising Sons.* Nelson, 1988.

Reeves, Diane L. *Child Care: A Reference Handbook.* ABC-CLIO, 1992.

Register, Cheri. *Living with Chronic Illness: Days of Patience and Passion.* Bantam, 1992.

Richardson, Diane. *Women and AIDS.* Routledge, 1987.

Robinson, Bryan E., Rowland, Bobbie H., and Coleman, Mick. *Latchkey Kids: Unlocking Doors for Children and Their Families.* Free Pr., 1987.

Rosen, Helen. *Unspoken Grief: Coping with Childhood Sibling Loss.* Free Pr., 1985.

Rosenstock, Harvey A. and Rosenstock, Judith. *Journey through Divorce.* Human Sciences, 1988.

Rosewater, Lynne Bravo. *Changing through Therapy.* Dodd, 1988.

Rothman, Jack. *Runaway and Homeless Youth.* Longman, 1991.

Rubenstein, Richard L., and Roth, John. *Approaches to Auschwitz: The Holocaust and Its Legacy.* John Knox, 1987.

Rubin, Jeffrey, and Rubin, Carol. *When Families Fight: How to Handle Conflict with Those You Love.* Ballantine, 1990.

Sadava, Stanley, and Segal, Bernard, eds. *Drug Use and Psychological Theory.* Haworth, 1987.

Samuels, S. C. *Ideal Adoption: A Comprehensive Guide to Forming an Adoptive Family.* Plenum, 1990.

Sandberg, David N. *Chronic Acting-Out Students and Child Abuse: A Handbook for Intervention.* Free Pr., 1987.

Sanders, Catherine. *Surviving Grief . . . And Learning to Live Again.* Wiley, 1992.

Savina, Lydia. *Help for the Battered Woman.* Bridge Publishing, 1988.

Scarr, Sandra. *Mother Care/Other Care.* Basic Books, 1984.

Schachter, Frances F., and Stone, Richard K., eds. *Practical Concerns about Siblings: Bridging the Research-Practice Gap.* Haworth, 1988.

Schacter, Robert. *Why Your Child Is Afraid.* Simon & Schuster, 1988.

Schaefer, Dan, and Lyons, Christine. *How Do We Tell the Children? A Parents' Guide to Helping Children Understand and Cope When Someone Dies.* Newmarket, 1986.

Schaffer, Judith, and Lindstrom, Christina. *How to Raise an Adopted Child: A Guide to Help Your Child Flourish from Infancy through Adolescence.* Plenum, 1991.

Schlesinger, Stephen E., and Horberg, Lawrence K. *Taking Charge: How Families Can Climb out of the Chaos of Addiction . . . and Flourish.* Simon & Schuster, 1988.

Schneider, Joseph W., and Conrad, Peter. *Having Epilepsy: The Experience and Control of Illness.* Temple Univ. Pr., 1985.

Schroeder, Bob. *Help Kids Say No to Drugs and Drinking: A Practical Prevention Guide for Parents.* CompCare, 1987.

Segal, Marilyn. *In Time and with Love: Caring for the Special Needs Baby.* Newmarket, 1988.

Seibert, Jeffrey M., and Olson, Roberta A., eds. *Children, Adolescents, and AIDS.* Univ. of Nebraska Pr., 1989.

Shapiro, Robert B. *Separate Houses: A Practical Guide for Divorced Parents.* Prentice-Hall, 1991.

Shelp, Earl, and Sunderland, Ronald. *AIDS and the Church.* Westminster, 1992.

Shimberg, Elaine F. *Depression: What Families Should Know.* Ballantine, 1991.

Showalter, John E., et al., eds. *Children and Death: Perspectives from Birth through Adolescence.* Praeger, 1987.

Siegel, Stephanie E. *Parenting Your Adopted Child: A Complete and Loving Guide.* Prentice-Hall, 1989.

Simpson, Eileen. *Orphans: Real and Imaginary.* Weidenfeld and Nicolson, 1987.

Smith, Ann. *Grandchildren of Alcoholics: Another Generation of Co-Dependency.* Health Communications, 1988.

Snarey, John. *How Fathers Care for the Next Generation: A Four-Decade Study.* Harvard Univ. Pr., 1993.

Splinter, John P. *The Complete Divorce Recovery Handbook: Grief, Stress, Guilt, Children, Codependence, Self-Esteem, Dating, Remarriage.* Zondervan, 1992.

Sprenkle, Douglas H., ed. *Divorce Therapy.* Haworth, 1985.

Stamper, Laura. *When the Drug War Hits Home: Healing the Family Torn apart by Teenage Drug Abuse.* Deaconess Pr., 1991.

Stearns, Ann K. *Coming Back: Rebuilding Lives after Crisis and Loss.* Ballantine, 1989.

Steinglass, Peter, et al. *The Alcoholic Family.* Harper, 1993.

Stepansky, Paul, comp. *The Memoirs of Margaret Mahler.* Free Pr., 1988.

Stimmel, Barry, ed. *Alcohol and Substance Abuse in Women and Children.* Haworth, 1986.

———. *Children of Alcoholics.* Haworth, 1987.

Stoddard, Sandol. *The Hospice Movement: A Better Way of Caring for the Dying.* Random, 1991.

Stokes, Jim. *The Survivor's Guide to Step-Parenting.* Blue Bird, 1992.

Straus, Martha, ed. *Abuse and Victimization across the Life Span.* Johns Hopkins Univ. Pr., 1990.

Strean, Herbert, and Freeman, Lucy. *Raising Cain: How to Help Your Child toward a Happy Sibling Relationship.* St. Martin's, 1989.

Streib, Victor. *Death Penalty for Juveniles.* Indiana Univ. Pr., 1987.

Strongman, K. T. *The Psychology of Emotion.* 3rd ed. Wiley, 1987.

Sunderland, Ronald, and Shelp, Earl. *AIDS: A Manual for Pastoral Care.* Westminster, 1987.

Tallmer, Margot, et al., eds. *Children, Dying, and Grief.* Center for Thanatology, 1991.

Toder, Francine. *When Your Child Is Gone: Learning to Live Again.* Fawcett Crest, 1987.

Trad, Paul V. *Infant and Childhood Depression: Developmental Factors.* Wiley, 1987.

——. *Infant Depression: Paradigms and Paradoxes.* Springer-Verlag, 1986.

Trafford, Abigail. *Crazy Time: Surviving Divorce and Building a New Life.* Rev. ed. Harper, 1993.

Treat, Stephen. *Remarriage and Blended Families.* Pilgrim Pr., 1988.

Trepper, Terry S., and Barrett, Mary Jo, eds. *Treating Incest: A Multimodel Systems Perspective.* Haworth, 1986.

Tronick, Edward Z., and Field, Tiffany, eds. *Maternal Depression and Infant Disturbance.* Jossey-Bass, 1986.

Van Pelt, Rich. *Intensive Care: Counseling Teenagers in Crisis.* Zondervan, 1992.

Vannecelli, Marsha. *Removing the Roadblocks: Group Psychotherapy with Substance Abusers and Family Members.* Guilford Pr., 1992.

Varma, Ved, ed. *Coping with Unhappy Children.* Sterling, 1993.

Wald, Michael, et al. *Protecting Abused and Neglected Children.* Stanford Univ. Pr., 1988.

Wallerstein, Judith, and Blakeslee, Sandra. *Second Chance: Men, Women and Children a Decade after Divorce.* Ticknor & Fields, 1990.

Wallerstein, Judith, and Kelly, Joan. *Surviving the Break Up: How Children and Parents Cope with Divorce.* Basic Books, 1990.

Walsh, Froma, and Anderson, Carol, eds. *Chronic Disorders and the Family.* Haworth, 1988.

Wartman, William. *Life without Father: Influences of an Unknown Man.* Watts, 1988.

Wayman, Anne. *Successful Single Parenting.* Meadowbrook, 1987.

Weisberg, D. Kelly. *Children of the Night: A Study of Adolescent Prostitution.* Free Pr., 1984.

Weitzman, Lenore J. *The Divorce Revolution: The Unexpected Social and Economic Consequences for Women and Children in America.* Free Pr., 1987.

Weller, Elizabeth, ed. *Current Perspectives on Major Depressive Disorders in Children.* Books on Demand, 1984.

Whitmore, George. *Someone Was Here: Profiles in the AIDS Epidemic.* NAL, 1988.

Willenson, Kim, with correspondents of *Newsweek. The Bad War: An Oral History of the Vietnam War.* NAL, 1987.

Woititz, Janet. *Adult Children of Alcoholics.* G. K. Hall, 1991.

Yeiser, Lin. *Nannies, Au Pairs, Mothers' Helpers—Caregivers: The Complete Guide to Home Child Care.* Vintage, 1987.

Youngs, Bettie B. *Helping Your Teenager Deal with Stress.* Jalmar Pr., 1988.

Articles in Periodicals

Arena, Corinne, et al. "Helping Children Deal with the Death of a Classmate: A Crisis Intervention Model." *Elementary School Guidance and Counseling* 19, no. 2 (1984): 107–115.

Balk, David. "Effects of Sibling Death on Teenagers." *Journal of School Health* 53, no. 1 (1983): 14–18.

———. "How Teenagers Cope with Sibling Death: Some Implications for School Counselors." *School Counselor* 31, no. 2 (1983): 150–158.

Barclay, Kathy H., and Whittington, Pam. "Night Scares: A Literature-Based Approach for Helping Young Children." *Childhood Education* 68, no. 3 (Spring 1992): 149–154.

Baron, D. A. "Emotional Aspects of Chronic Disease." *Journal of the American Osteopathic Association* 87, no. 6 (1987): 437–439.

Bergmann, M. S. "Reflections on the Psychological and Social Function of Remembering the Holocaust." *Psychoanalytic Inquiry* 5, no. 1 (1985): 9–20.

Berman, Lauren C., and Bufferd, Rhea K. "Family Treatment to Address Loss in Adoptive Families." *Social Casework* 67, no. 1(1986): 3–11.

Bertman, Sandra. "Helping Children Cope with Death." *Family Therapy Collections* 8 (1984): 48–60.

Bertrand, Jeanne A. "What Might Have Been—What Could Be: Working with the Grief of Children in Long-Term Care." *Journal of Social Work Practice* 1, no. 3 (1984): 23–41.

Bonchek, Rita M. "A Study of the Effect of Sibling Death on the Surviving Child: A Developmental and Family Perspective." *Dissertation Abstracts International* 44, no. 4–A (1983): 1024.

Burnell, George M., and Burnell, Adrienne L. "The Compassionate Friends: A Support Group for Bereaved Parents." *Journal of Family Practice* 22, no. 3 (1986): 295–296.

Calhoun, L. G., et al. "The Rules of Bereavement." *Journal of Community Psychology* 14, no. 2 (1986): 213–218.

———. "Suicidal Death: Social Reactions to Bereaved Survivors." *Journal of Psychology* 116–2nd half, no. 4 (1984): 255–261.

Camper, Frances A. "Children's Reactions to the Death of a Parent: Maintaining the Inner World." *Smith College Studies in Social Work* 53, no. 3 (1983): 188–202.

Carlile, Candy. "Children of Divorce: How Teachers Can Help Ease the Pain." *Childhood Education* 67, no. 4 (Summer 1991): 232–234.

Coleman, Marilyn, and Ganong, Lawrence H. "The Uses of Juvenile Fiction and Self-Help Books with Stepfamilies." *Journal of Counseling and Development* 68, no. 3 (January-February 1990): 327–331.

Connor, Terry, et al. "Making a Life Story Book." *Adoption and Fostering* 9, no. 2 (1985): 32–35, 46.

Cook, Judith A. "A Death in the Family: Parental Bereavement in the First Year." *Suicide and Life-Threatening Behavior* 31, no. 1 (Spring 1983): 42–61.

Danieli, Y. "Psychotherapists' Participation in the Conspiracy of Silence about the Holocaust." *Psychoanalytic Psychology* 1 (1984): 23–42.

Delisle, James R. "The Gifted Adolescent at Risk: Strategies and Resources for Suicide Prevention among Gifted Youth." *Journal for the Education of the Gifted* 13, no. 3 (Spring 1990): 212–228.

Drake, Janet J., and Drake, Frederick. "Using Children's Literature to Teach about the American Revolution." *Social Studies and the Young Learner* 6, no. 2 (November-December 1990): 6–8.

Field, Tiffany. "Separation Stress of Young Children Transferring to New Schools." *Developmental Psychology* 20, no. 5 (1984): 786–792.

Foster, Janet. "Review of Professional Literature: Mills and Clyde on Whole Language, Plus War Play and Social Skills." *Dimensions* 20, no. 1 (Fall 1991): 29–30.

Fox, Sandra. "Children's Anniversary Reactions to the Death of a Family Member." *Omega: Journal of Death and Dying* 15, no. 4 (1984–85): 291–305.

French, Glenda. "Intercountry Adoption: Helping a Young Child Deal with Loss." *Child Welfare* 65, no. 3 (1986): 272–279.

Furman, Edna. "Studies in Childhood Bereavement." *Canadian Journal of Psychiatry* 28, no. 4 (1983): 241–247.

Garber, Benjamin. "Mourning in Adolescence: Normal and Pathological." *Adolescent Psychology* 12 (1985): 371–387.

Gross, Alan M., et al. "The Effect of Mother-Child Separation on the Behavior of Children Experiencing a Medical Procedure." *Journal of Consulting and Clinical Psychology* 51, no. 5 (1983): 783–785.

Gunnar, Megan R., et al. "Peer Presence and the Exploratory Behavior of Eighteen- and Thirty-Month-Old Children." *Child Development* 55, no. 3 (1984): 1103–1109.

Haley, John A. "Death: What Do I Tell My Child." *PTA Today* 10, no. 3 (1984–85): 23–24.

Hoffman, Libby R. "Developmental Counseling for Prekindergarten Children: A Preventive Approach." *Elementary School Guidance and Counseling* 26, no. 1 (October 1991): 56–66.

Hynes, Arleen-McCarty. "Possibilities for Biblio-Poetry Therapy Services in Libraries." *Catholic Library World* 6, no. 6 (May-June 1990): 264–267.

Iama, M. Carol, and Peterson, Kenneth. "Achieving Reflectivity through Literature." *Educational Leadership* 48, no. 6 (March 1991): 22–24.

Johnson, Sherry. "Sexual Intimacy and Replacement Children after the Death of a Child." *Omega: Journal of Death and Dying* 15, no. 2 (1984–85): 109–118.

Klass, Dennis. "Bereaved Parents and the Compassionate Friends: Affiliation and Healing." *Omega: Journal of Death and Dying* 15, no. 4 (1984–85): 353–373.

――――. "Marriage and Divorce among Bereaved Parents in a Self-Help Group." *Omega: Journal of Death and Dying* 17, no. 3 (1986–87): 237–249.

Krickeberg, Sandra K. "Away from Walton Mountain: Bibliographies for Today's Troubled Youth." *School Counselor* 39, no. 1 (September 1991): 52–55.

Lampl, Jeanne De Groot. "On the Process of Mourning." *Psychoanalytic Study of the Child* 38 (1983): 9–13.

Lehman, Darrin R.; Wortman, Camille B.; and Williams, Allan F. "Long-Term Effects of Losing a Spouse or Child in a Motor Vehicle Crash." *Journal of Personality & Social Psychology* 52, no. 1 (1987): 218–231.

Leon, Irving G. "The Invisible Loss: The Impact of Perinatal Death on Siblings." *Journal of Psychosomatic Obstetrics and Gynaecology* 5, no. 1 (1986): 1–14.

Lerman, L. G. "Elements and Standards for Criminal Justice Programs on Domestic Violence." *Response* 5 (1982): 12–14.

Lichtman, H. "Parental Communication of Holocaust Experiences and Personality Characteristics among Second Generation Survivors." *Journal of Clinical Psychology* 40, no. 4 (1984): 914–924.

Lindy, Joanne G. "Social and Psychological Influences on Children's Adaptation to the Death of a Parent." *Dissertation Abstracts International* 44, no. 5–B (1983): 1639.

Littlefield, Christine H. "When a Child Dies: A Sociobiological Perspective." *Dissertation Abstracts International* 45, no. 8–B (1985): 2734B.

McShane, C. "Community Services for Battered Women." *Social Work* 24 (1979): 34–39.

Miles, Margaret Shandor, and Demi, Alice Sterner. "Toward the Development of a Theory of Bereavement Guilt: Sources of Guilt in Bereaved Parents." *Omega: Journal of Death and Dying* 14, no. 4 (1984): 299–314.

Miletta, Maureen M. "Picture Books for Older Children: Reading and Writing Connections (in the Classroom)." *Reading Teacher* 46, no. 7 (March 1992): 666–668.

Moore, DeWayne. "Pre-Adolescent Separation: Intrafamilial Perceptions and Difficulty Separating from Parents." *Personality and Social Psychology Bulletin* 10, no. 4 (1984): 611–619.

Mufson, Toni. "Issues Surrounding Sibling Death during Adolescence." *Child and Adolescent Social Work Journal* 2, no. 4 (Winter 1985): 204–218.

Murphy, Patricia Ann. "Parental Death in Childhood and Loneliness in Young Adults." *Omega: Journal of Death and Dying* 17, no. 3 (1987): 219–228.

Myles, Brenda-Smith, et al. "Selecting Children's Literature for and about Students with Learning Differences: Guidelines." *Intervention in School and Clinic* 27, no. 4 (March 1992): 215–220.

Newman, Susan B. "The Home Environment and Fifth-Grade Students' Leisure Reading." *The Elementary School Journal* 86, no. 3 (1986): 335–343.

Noble, Barbara S. "Childhood Bereavement." *Dissertation Abstracts International* 43, no. 9–B (1983): 3037.

O'Brien, Shirley. "For Parents Particularly: Children Shouldn't Die—But They Do." *Childhood Education* 63, no. 2 (1986): 112–114.

Pardeck, John. "Children's Literature and Child Abuse." *Child Welfare* 69, no. 1 (January-February 1990): 83–88.

———. "Using Books to Prevent and Treat Adolescent Chemical Dependency." *Adolescence* 26, no. 101 (Spring 1991): 201–208.

Pardeck, John, and Pardeck, Jean A. "Using Developmental Literature with Collaborative Groups." *Reading Improvement* 27, no. 4 (Winter 1990): 226–237.

Pearl, Peggy I. "Working with Child Abuse Victims in the Home Economics Classroom." *Illinois Teacher of Home Economics* 34, no. 2 (November-December 1990): 70–75.

Pynoos, Robert S., and Eth, Spencer. "The Child as Witness to Homicide." *Journal of Social Issues* 40, no. 2 (1984): 87–108.

Rando, Therese A. "Bereaved Parents." *Social Work* 30, no. 1 (1985): 19–23.

Ronald, P. "Divorce—Through the Eyes of the Victim." *Dissertation Abstracts International* 47, no. 2–A (1986): 469.

Rosen, Helen. "Prohibitions against Mourning in Childhood Sibling Loss." *Omega: Journal of Death and Dying* 15, no. 4 (1985): 307–316.

Rosenheim, Eliyahu, and Reicher, Rivka. "Children in Anticipatory Grief: The Lonely Predicament." *Journal of Clinical Child Psychology* 15, no. 2 (1986): 115–119.

Rudestam, K. E., and Imbroll, D. "Societal Reactions to a Child's Death by Suicide." *Journal of Consulting and Clinical Psychology* 51, no. 3 (1983): 461–462.

Scanlon, M. Kathleen. "A Chronically Ill Child's Progression through the Separation-Individuation Process." *Maternal-Child Nursing Journal* 14 (Summer 1985): 91–102.

Scheier, M. F., et al. "Coping with Stress: Divergent Strategies of Optimists and Pessimists." *Journal of Personality and Social Psychology* 51 (1986): 1257–1264.

Schumacher, J. Donald. "Helping Children Cope with a Sibling's Death." *Family Therapy Collections* 8 (1984): 82–94.

Sekaer, Christina, and Kate, Sheri. "On the Concept of Mourning in Childhood." *Psychoanalytic Study of the Child* 41 (1986): 287–314.

Sheskin, A., and Wallace, S. E. "Differing Bereavements: Suicide, Natural and Accidental Death." *Omega: Journal of Death and Dying* 1, no. 3 (1976): 229–242.

Soricelli, Barbara A., and Utech, Carolyn Lorenz. "Mourning the Death of a Child: The Family and Group Process." *Social Work* 30, no. 5 (1985): 429–434.

Varela, Lynn Millikin. "The Relationship between the Hospitalized Child's Separation Anxiety and Maternal Separation Anxiety." *Dissertation Abstracts International* 43, no. 9–B (1983): 3048.

Warner, Ronald E. "Self-Help Book Prescription Practices of Canadian University Counselors." *Canadian Journal of Counseling* 25, no. 3 (July 1991): 359–362.

Winfield, Evelyn T. "Children's Books in Review: Books on Strengthening Family Ties." *PTA Today* 16, no. 7 (May 1991): 21–22.

Wolfson, Orna. "Adolescent Separation from Home: An Ethnic Perspective." *Dissertation Abstracts International* 46, no. 12–B, pt. 1(1986): 4416.

Yauman, Beth E. "School-Based Group Counseling for Children of Divorce: A Review of the Literature." *Elementary School Guidance and Counseling* 26, no. 2 (December 1991): 130–138.

Ziegler, Patricia. "Saying Good-Bye to Preschool." *Young Children* 40, no. 3 (1985) 11–15.

7
Bibliotherapy

Books and Chapters in Books

Adams, Jeff. *The Conspiracy of the Text: The Place of Narrative in the Development of Thought.* Routledge, 1987.

Anderson, Marcella F. *Hospitalized Children and Books: A Guide for Librarians, Families and Caregivers.* 2nd ed. Scarecrow, 1992.

Brown, Eleanor Frances. *Bibliotherapy and Its Widening Applications.* Scarecrow, 1975.

Colborn, Candace. *What Do Children Read Next?* Gale, 1993.

Coleman, Marilyn. *Bibliotherapy with Stepchildren.* Thomas, 1988.

Griffin, Barbara K. *Special Needs Bibliotherapy—Current Books for/about Children and Young Adults Regarding Social Concerns, Emotional Concerns and the Exceptional Child.* Griffin, 1984.

Hynes-Bery, Mary, and Hynes, Arleen M. *Bibliotherapy: The Interactive Process.* Westview, 1986.

Lamme, Linda L., et al. *Literature-Based Moral Education: Children's Books and Activities to Enrich the K–5 Curriculum.* Oryx Pr., 1992.

Lenz, Millicent. *Nuclear Age Literature for Youth: The Quest for a Life Affirming Ethic.* American Library Association, 1990.

Newkirk, Thomas, and McLure, Patricia. *Listening In: Children Talk about Books (and Other Things).* Heinemann, 1992.

Pardeck, Jean A., and Pardeck, John T. *Young People with Problems: A Guide to Bibliotherapy.* Greenwood, 1984.

Rubin, Rhea J. *Using Bibliotherapy.* Oryx, 1978.

Rudman, Masha K. *Children's Literature: An Issues Approach.* 2nd ed. Longman, 1984.

Rustin, Margeret, and Rustin, Michael. *Narratives of Love and Loss: Studies in Modern Children's Fiction.* Routledge, 1988.

Wall, Barbara. *The Narrator's Voice: The Dilemma of Children's Fiction.* St. Martin's, 1991.

Weiner, Pamela J., and Stein, Ruth M., eds. *Adolescents, Literature and Work with Youth.* Haworth, 1985.

Zaccaria, Joseph S., and Moses, Harold A. *Facilitating Human Development through Reading: The Use of Bibliotherapy in Teaching and Counseling.* Stipes Publishing, 1968.

Articles in Periodicals

Anderson, Marcella. "Children and Books in Pediatric Hospitals." *Horn Book* 62, no. 6 (1986): 787–788.

Angelotti, Michael. "Uses of Poetry and Adolescent Literature in Therapy for Adolescents." *Child and Youth Services* 7, nos. 1–2 (Spring 1985): 27–35.

Axelrod, Herman, and Teti, Thomas R. "An Alternative to Bibliotherapy: Audiovisiotherapy." *Educational Technology* 16 (1976): 36–38.

Bohning, Gerry. "Bibliotherapy: Fitting the Resources Together." *Elementary School Journal* 82 (1981): 166–170.

Brisbane, Frances L. "Using Contemporary Fiction with Black Children and Adolescents in Alcoholism Treatment." *Alcoholism Treatment Quarterly* 2, nos. 3–4 (Fall-Winter 1985–86): 179–197.

Bunting, Kenneth P. "The Use and Effect of Puppetry and Bibliotherapy in Group Counseling with Children of Divorced Parents." *Dissertation Abstracts International* 45, no. 10–A (1985): 3094.

Clarke, Barbara K. "Bibliotherapy through Puppetry: Socializing the Young Child Can Be Fun." *Early Child Development and Care* 19, no. 4 (1985): 338–344.

Coleman, Marilyn, and Ganong, Lawrence. "An Evaluation of the Stepfamily Self-Help Literature for Children and Adolescents." *Family Relations* 36, no. 1 (1987): 61–65.

Coleman, Marilyn, et al. "Beyond Cinderella: Relevant Reading for Young Adolescents about Stepfamilies." *Adolescence* 21, no. 83 (Fall 1986): 553–560.

Davison, Maureen M. "Classroom Bibliotherapy: Why and How." *Reading World* 23 (1984): 103–107.

Edwards, Patricia A., and Simpson, Linda. "Bibliotherapy: A Strategy for Communication between Parents and Their Children." *Journal of Reading* 30, no. 2 (1986): 110–118.

Forber, Susan L. "Divorce Discussion Groups for Elementary-Age Children: A Curriculum Plan." *Dissertation Abstracts International* 46, no. 11–A (1986): 3252.

Garrett, Jerry E. "The Effects of Bibliotherapy on Self-Concepts and Children and Youth in an Institutional Setting." *Dissertation Abstracts International* 45, no. 9–A (1985): 2757.

Gladding, Samuel, and Gladding, Claire. "The ABCs of Bibliotherapy for School Counselors." *School Counselor* 39, no. 1 (September 1991): 7–13.

Heath, Charles P. "Understanding Death." *Techniques* 2, no. 1 (1986): 88–92.

Hebert, Thomas P. "Meeting the Affective Needs of Bright Boys through Bibliotherapy." *Roeper Review* 13, no. 4 (June 1991): 207–212.

Hipple, Theodore W., et al. "Twenty Adolescent Novels (and More) That Counselors Should Know About." *School Counselor* 32, no. 2 (1984): 142–148.

Jalongo, Mary Renck. "Bibliotherapy: Literature to Promote Socioemotional Growth." *The Reading Teacher* 36 (1983): 796–803.

———. "Using Crisis-Oriented Books with Young Children." *Young Children* 38, no. 5 (1983): 29–36.

Jalongo, Mary Renck, and Renck, Melissa. "Children's Literature and the Child's Adjustment to School." *The Reading Teacher* 40 (1987): 616–621.

Martin, Maggie; Martin, Don; and Porter, Judy. "Bibliotherapy: Children of Divorce." *School Counselor* 30, no. 4 (1983): 796–803.

Mikulas, William L., et al. "Uses of Poetry and Adolescent Literature in Therapy for Adolescents." *Child and Youth Services* 7, no. 3 (Fall 1985): 1–7.

Morris, Artie. "The Efficacy of Bibliotherapy on the Mental Health of Elementary Students Who Have Experienced a Loss Precipitated by Parental Unemployment, Divorce, Marital Separation or Death." *Dissertation Abstracts International* 44, no. 3–A (1983): 676.

Nelms, Beth, et al. "Broken Circles: Adolescents on Their Own." *English Journal* 74, no. 5 (1985): 84–85.

Newhouse, Robert C. "Generalized Fear Reduction in Second-Grade Children." *Psychology in the Schools* 24, no. 1 (1987): 48–50.

Newhouse, Robert C., and Loker, Suzanne. "Does Bibliotherapy Reduce Fear among Second-Grade Children?" *Reading Psychology* 4 (1983): 25–27.

O'Bruba, William S.; Camplese, Donald A.; and Sanford, Mary D. "The Use of Teletherapy in the Mainstreaming Era." *Reading Horizons* 24 (Spring 1984): 158–160.

Ouzts, Dan. "The Emergence of Bibliotherapy as a Discipline." *Reading Horizons* 31, no. 3 (February 1991): 199–206.

Pardeck, Jean A., and Pardeck, John T. "Bibliotherapy Using a Neo-Freudian Approach for Children of Divorced Parents." *School Counselor* 32, no. 4 (1985): 313–318.

Pardeck, John T., and Pardeck, Jean A. "Treating Abused Children through Bibliotherapy." *Early Childhood Development and Care* 16, nos. 3–4 (1984): 195–203.

Sargent, Karin L. "Helping Children Cope with Parental Mental Illness through Use of Children's Literature." *Child Welfare* 64, no. 6 (1985): 617–628.

Scogin-Forrest, et al. "Two-Year Follow-up of Bibliotherapy for Depression in Older Adults." *Journal of Consulting and Clinical Psychology* 58, no. 6 (October 1990): 556–567.

Sheridan, John T.; Baker, Stanley B.; de-Lissovoy, Vladimir. "Structured Group Counseling and Explicit Bibliotherapy as In-School Strategies for Preventing Problems in Youth of Changing Families." *School Counselor* 32, no. 2 (1984): 134–141.

Storey, Dee. "Reading Role Models: Fictional Readers in Children's Books." *Reading Horizons* 26 (1986): 140–148.

Swantic, Frances. "An Investigation of the Effectiveness of Bibliotherapy on Middle-Grade Students Who Repeatedly Display Inappropriate Behavior in the School Setting." *Dissertation Abstracts International* 47, no. 3 (1986): 843.

Tillman, Chester E. "Bibliotherapy for Adolescents: An Updated Research Review." *Journal of Reading* 27, no. 8 (1984): 713–719.

Wahlstrom, Wanda L. "Developing Self-Concept through Bibliotherapy." *Dissertation Abstracts International* 44, no. 3–A (1983): 669–670.

Weiner, J. Pamela, and Stein, Ruth M., eds. "Adolescents, Literature, and Work with Youth." *Child and Youth Services* 7, nos. 1–2 (Spring 1985): v–137.

William, L., et al. "Behavioral Bibliotherapy and Games for Testing Fear of the Dark." *Child and Family Behavioral Therapy* 7, no. 3 (1985): 1–7.

Wilson, Laura W. "Helping Adolescents Understand Death and Dying through Literature." *English Journal* 73, no. 7 (1984): 78–82.

Winfield, Evelyn T. "Relevant Reading for Adolescents: Literature and Divorce." *Journal of Reading* 26, no. 5 (1983): 408–411.

Yellin, Michael. "Bibliotherapy: A Comparison of the Effect of the Traditional Folk Fairy Tale and 'Issues Specific' Imaginative Literature on Self-Esteem, Hostile Attitudes, and the Behavior of Children." *Dissertation Abstracts International* 43, no. 8–A (1983): 2614.

Zimet, Sara Goodman. "Teaching Children to Detect Social Bias in Books." *The Reading Teacher* 36 (1983): 418–421.

Unpublished Work

Fox, Barbara J., and Collier, Helen S. *Skilled Focused Bibliotherapy.* Unpublished manuscript, North Carolina State University, 1983.

Appendix: Directory of Organizations

This directory provides addresses and telephone numbers for self-help groups and professional and voluntary organizations that offer support services to children undergoing loss experiences and to their adult guides. Many organizations provide free or low-cost literature as well as services such as discussion groups and referrals.

Addictions

Alcohol

Al-Anon Family Group Headquarters
1372 Broadway
New York, NY 10018
212-302-7240
This organization helps families of alcoholics. Alateen is the adolescent discussion group affiliated with Al-Anon.

Alcoholics Anonymous World Services
Box 459, Grand Central Station
New York, NY 10163
212-686-1100
International fellowship of men and women sharing experiences, strength, and hope with an aim toward recovery.

American Council on Alcoholism
8501 LaSalle Rd.
Suite 301
Towson, MD 21204
301-296-5555
Coalition of local, state, and national groups working to end alcohol abuse.

Children of Alcoholics Foundation
200 Park Ave.
31st floor
New York, NY 10166
212-949-1404
Seeks to educate the public and promote open discussion on problems of children of alcoholics.

National Association for Children of Alcoholics
31706 Coast Hwy.
Suite 201
South Laguna, CA 92677

714-499-3889
Resource to increase public awareness and to protect rights of children of alcoholics to live in a safe
environment.

Other Drugs

Drug-Anon Focus
Box 9108
Long Island City, NY 11103
718-361-2169
This organization offers help to
abusers of mood-altering drugs and
to their families.

Drugs Anonymous
Box 473, Ansonia Station
New York, NY 10023
212-874-0700
Application of the Alcoholics
Anonymous approach to persons
addicted to all types of drugs
including prescription drugs.

Families Anonymous
Box 528
Van Nuys, CA 91408
818-989-7841
Help for drug-abusing people and
their families; patterned after Alcoholics Anonymous in format.

Just Say No Clubs
3101-A Sacramento
Berkeley, CA 94702
415-848-0845; 800-258-2766
Promotes formation of clubs in
schools to give students a supportive peer group to resist drugs.

Narcotics Anonymous
Box 9999
Van Nuys, CA 91409
818-780-3951

Self-help and information for drug
abuse; aims toward rehabilitation.

**National Association on Drug
Abuse Problems**
355 Lexington Ave.
New York, NY 10017
212-986-1170
Information and referrals.

**National Federation of Parents for
Drug-Free Youth**
8730 Georgia Ave.
Suite 200
Silver Spring, MD 20910
301-585-5437; 800-544-KIDS
Network of parent groups; pro-
motes education; speakers' bureau.

**National Parents' Resource
Institute for Drug Education**
100 Edgewood Ave.
Suite 1002
Atlanta, GA 30303
404-658-2548; 800-241-7946
Up-to-date research information
and formation of community action
groups; speakers' bureau.

Other Addictions

Gam-Anon International Service
PO Box 157
Whitestone, NY 11357
718-352-1671
Modeled on Alcoholics Anonymous, this group works with addic-
tive gamblers and their families.

Gamblers Anonymous
3255 Wilshire Blvd.
No. 610
Los Angeles, CA 90010
213-386-8789
Gamblers seek support here; aims
toward rehabilitation.

Adoption

Adoptees' Liberty Movement Association
Box 154, Washington Bridge Station
New York, NY 10033
212-581-1568
This organization maintains a data bank and offers advice on searching for adoptive parents and children.

Committee for Single Adoptive Parents
Box 15084
Chevy Chase, MD 20815
202-966-6367
Information and lobbying for legislative reform.

Concerned United Birthparents
2000 Walker St.
Des Moines, IA 50317
515-262-9120
Aims to open birth records for adoptees and birthparents.

Independent Search Consultants
Box 10192
Costa Mesa, CA 92627
Assists individuals in searches for birth families separated by adoption.

International Concerns Committee for Children
911 Cypress Dr.
Boulder, CO 80303
303-494-8333
Adoption of children from foreign countries.

Latin America Parents Association
PO Box 339
Brooklyn, NY 11234
718-236-8689
Aids people adopting or seeking to adopt children from Latin America.

National Adoption Center
1218 Chestnut St.
2nd floor
Philadelphia, PA 19107
215-925-0200
Referral for adoptive parents seeking children with special needs—older, handicapped, minority, siblings seeking same placement.

National Committee for Adoption
1930 17 St. N.W.
Washington, DC 20009
202-638-1200
Resource and lobbying organization.

North American Council on Adoptable Children
1821 University Ave.
St. Paul, MN 55104
612-644-3036
Information about adoption and local parent groups in chapters.

Origins
PO Box 556
Whippany, NJ 07981
201-428-9683
Support for women who have given up their children for adoption.

Orphan Voyage
2141 Rd. 2300
Cedaredge, CA 81413
303-856-3937
Tries to open lines of communication, encouraging open attitudes in the non-adoptive population.

Aging

Aging in America
1500 Pelham Parkway S.
Bronx, NY 10461
212-824-4004

Research and service organization for professionals in gerontology.

American Association of Retired Persons
601 E St. N.W.
Washington, DC 20049
202-434-2277
Information, insurance, lobbying.

American Society on Aging
833 Market St.
Suite 512
San Francisco, CA 94103
415-543-2617
Works to foster unity among those working with the elderly.

Center for the Study of Aging
706 Madison Ave.
Albany, NY 12208
518-465-6927
Promotes education, research, training, and leadership.

Gray Panthers
1424 16th St. N.W.
Suite 6021
Washington, DC 20036
202-387-3111
Activist group to combat discrimination.

National Alliance of Senior Citizens
1700 18th St. N.W.
Suite 401
Washington, DC 20009
202-986-0117
Informs of needs of senior citizens.

National Council on the Aging
600 Maryland Ave. S.W.
W. Wing 100
Washington, DC 20024
202-479-1200
Information and consultation center; cooperates with other organizations.

Burn Victims

American Burn Association
c/o Andrew M. Munster, M.D.
Francis Scott Key Hospital
4940 Eastern Ave.
Baltimore, MD 21224
800-548-2876
Professionals interested in treatment of burn patients.

International Society for Burn Injuries
c/o John A. Boswick, Jr.
2005 Franklin St.
Suite 660
Denver, CO 80205
303-839-1694
Professionals engaged in care and research; promotes prevention.

Phoenix Society
c/o National Organization for Burn Victims
11 Rust Hill Rd.
Levittown, PA 19056
215-946-4788
Self-help service association that discourages concealment of disfigurement, which society believes compounds adjustment difficulties.

Child Abuse

Adults Molested as Children United
Giaretto Institute
232 E. Gish Rd.
San Jose, CA 95111
408-453-7616
Support and therapy.

Batterers Anonymous
16913 Lerner Lane
Fontana, CA 92335
714-355-1100

Families of battered spouses bene-fit from discussion groups.

Child Abuse Listening Mediation, Inc.
PO Box 90754
Santa Barbara, CA 93190-0754
805-965-2376
Aims at prevention of child abuse.

Children's Rights of America
655 Ulmerton Road
Suite 4A
Largo, FL 34641
813-593-0090
Aids families of missing or exploited children.

Committee for Children
172 20th Ave.
Seattle, WA 98122
206-322-5050
Develops curricula to prevent sex-ual abuse.

Daughters and Sons United
c/o Institute for Community as
  Extended Family
232 E. Gish Road
San Jose, CA 95112
408-453-7616
An information exchange and sup-port system for sexually abused children and their families.

Incest Survivors Resource Network, International
PO Box 7375
Las Cruces, NM 88006-7375
505-521-4260
Resource program for primary pre-vention.

National Committee for the Prevention of Child Abuse
332 S. Michigan Ave.
Suite 950
Chicago, IL 60604

312-663-3520
Information, referrals, and legisla-tive lobbying.

National Organization for Victim Assistance
1757 Park Rd. N.W.
Washington, DC 20010
202-232-6682
Aims to assist crime victims in their claims.

Parents Anonymous
520 S. Lafayette
Suite 316
Los Angeles, CA 90057
213-388-6685
Aims to prevent child abuse and offers immediate support through its hotline.

Parents United
c/o Institute for Community as
  Extended Family
232 E. Gish Rd.
San Jose, CA 95112
408-453-7616
Support groups for sexual molesta-tion and drug abuse problems.

Death

Bereavement

The Compassionate Friends
Box 3696
Oak Brook, IL 60522
312-990-0010
Parents who grieve for their dead children find support groups here; parents of dying children also seek help within this organization.

First Sunday
c/o Pope John XXIII Hospitality
  House
3977 Second Ave.

Detroit, MI 48201
313-832-4357
  Counseling and self-help groups for parents who have lost a child; holds liturgy for families on first Sunday of each month.

Inter-National Association for Widowed People
Box 3564
Springfield, IL 62708
217-787-0886
  Promotes interests and understanding of widows' and widowers' special needs.

Orphan Foundation of America
Box 14261
1500 Massachusetts Ave. N.W.
Suite 448
Washington, DC 20044
202-861-0762
  Assists orphans and foster-care youth by providing guidance, support, and emergency help.

Parents of Murdered Children
100 E. Eighth St.
B-41
Cincinnati, OH 45202
513-721-5683
  Support services for survivors of murdered children.

Widowed Person Service
c/o AARP
601 E St. N.W.
Washington, DC 20049
202-434-2260
  Referrals and information for support.

Death Education

Association for Death Education and Counseling
638 Prospect Ave.

Hartford, CT 06105-4298
203-232-4825
  Goal is to upgrade quality of death education and patient care.

Center for Death Education and Research
University of Minnesota
1167 Social Science Bldg.
267 19th Ave. S.
Minneapolis, MN 55455
612-624-1895
  Many scholarly and nontechnical publications are available here.

Continental Association of Funeral and Memorial Societies
6900 Lost Lake Rd.
Egg Harbor, WI 54209
414-868-3136
  Information concerning the conduct and cost of funerals.

Foundation of Thanatology
630 W. 168 St.
New York, NY 10032
212-928-2066
  Conferences and publications about bereavement and care for the dying are aimed at both general audiences and professionals.

National Funeral Directors Association
11121 W. Oklahoma Ave.
Milwaukee, WI 53227
414-541-2500
  Educational materials concerning funeral planning and problems of bereavement.

Euthanasia

Concern for Dying
250 W. 57 St.
New York, NY 10107
212-246-6973

Workshops, study groups, conferences, speakers' bureau; distributes Living Will (allows individuals to express in writing their wishes in case of terminal illness).

Hospices

Children's Hospice International
901 N. Washington St.
Suite 700
Alexandria, VA 22314
703-684-0330
Aims to promote hospice support through pediatric care facilities; encourages inclusion of children in existing and developing hospices and home care.

Hospice Education Institute
Box 713, Five Essex Sq.
Essex, CT 06426
203-767-1620; 800-331-1620
Educational programs on hospices, bereavement, and dying.

National Hospice Organization
Moore St.
Suite 901
Arlington, VA 22209
703-243-5900
British concept of a homelike hospital where one goes to die peacefully has spread to America.

Suicide

American Association of Suicidology
2459 S. Ash
Denver, CO 80222
303-692-0985
Dedicated to research and the prevention of unnecessary deaths, this organization offers information and counseling referrals.

International Association for Suicide Prevention
c/o Suicide Prevention and Crisis Center
1811 Trousdale Dr.
Burlingame, CA 94010
415-877-5604
Information and counseling referrals.

National Committee on Youth Suicide Prevention
65 Essex Rd.
Chestnut Hill, MA 02167
617-738-0700
Network of parents, professionals, and government officials who publicize the warning signals of suicide and establish referral systems.

Samaritans
500 Commonwealth Ave.
Kenmore Sq.
Boston, MA 02215
617-247-0220
Suicide prevention service and information.

Seasons (Suicide Bereavement)
c/o Tina Larsen
PO Box 187
Perk City, VT 84060
801-649-8327
Support groups; educational materials; library.

Yad Tikvah Foundation
c/o Union of American Hebrew Congregations
1330 Beacon St., Rm. 355
Brookline, MA 02146
617-277-1655
Seeks to educate parents and synagogue professionals about symp-

toms and prevention of suicide; also known as Task Force on Youth Suicide.

Youth Suicide National Center
445 Virginia Ave..
San Mateo, CA 94402
415-692-6662
  Educational materials; reviews current educational programs.

Emotional Health and Illness

American Anorexia/Bulimia Association
133 Cedar Lane
Teaneck, NJ 07666
201-836-1800
  Information and referral.

American Association for Marriage and Family Therapy
1100 17th St. N.W.
10th floor
Washington, DC 20036
202-452-0109
  Training for therapists; information exchange.

American Association of Psychiatric Services for Children
1200-C Scottsville Rd.
Suite 225
Rochester, NY 14624
716-235-6910
  Information and research.

American Family Therapy Association
2020 Pennsylvania Ave. N.W.
Suite 273
Washington, DC 20006
202-994-2776

Information dissemination to scientists and the public about the family therapy systems approach.

American Orthopsychiatric Association
19 W. 44 St.
No. 1616
New York, NY 10036
212-354-5770
  Interested in a wide range of problems, this organization is a good source for scholarly, technical information.

American Psychological Association
1200 17th St. N.W.
Washington, DC 20036
202-955-7600
  Scientific and professional society of psychologists.

American Schizophrenia Association
900 N. Federal Hwy.
No. 330
Boca Raton, FL 33432
305-393-6167
  Research on biochemical and genetic causes of schizophrenia.

Anorexia Nervosa and Related Eating Disorders
Box 5102
Eugene, OR 97405
503-344-1144
  Information and research.

Autism Society of America
8601 Georgia Ave.
Suite 503
Silver Spring, MD 20910
301-565-0433
  Research, information, and referrals.

The Bridge, Inc.
248 W. 108 St.
New York, NY 10025
212-663-3000
This organization focuses on rehabilitation of the mentally ill.

**Council for Children with
Behavioral Disorders**
c/o Council for Exceptional Children
1920 Association Dr.
Reston, VA 22091 '
703-620-3660
A division of the Council for
Exceptional Children, this organization promotes the welfare of children with serious emotional
disturbances.

Emotions Anonymous
Box 4245
St. Paul, MN 55104
612-647-9712
Sets up local discussion groups to
promote emotional health; a self-
help atmosphere.

Family Service America
11700 W. Lake Park Dr.
Milwaukee, WI 53224
414-359-2111
An organization geared to directly
helping families under emotional
stress.

**International Association of
Psychosocial Rehabilitation
Services**
5550 Sterett Pl.
Suite 214
Columbia, MD 21044-2626
301-730-7190
Serves groups and provides infor-
mation on residential and day cen-
ters nationwide.

Mental Health Law Project
1101 15th St. N.W.
Suite 1212
Washington, DC 20005
202-467-5730
A public service legal firm specializing in the rights of mental
patients.

**National Alliance for the
Mentally Ill**
2101 Wilson Blvd.
Suite 302
Arlington, VA 22201
703-524-7600
An umbrella organization for self-
help and advocacy groups.

National Anorexic Aid Society
1925 E. Dublin-Granville Rd.
Columbus, OH 43229
614-436-1112
Aids patients and families.

**National Association of Psychiatric
Treatment Centers for Children**
2000 L St. N.W.
Suite 200
Washington, DC 20036
202-955-3828
Information about accredited resi-
dential centers.

**Neurotics Anonymous
International Liaison**
11140 Bainbridge Dr.
Little Rock, AR 72212
501-221-2809
Promotes local discussion group
formation; adapts techniques from
Alcoholics Anonymous as they
apply to emotional illness.

Family Relationships

Divorce, Single-Parent Families, and Stepfamilies

Fathers Are Forever
PO Box 4338
West Hills, CA 92308-4333
818-566-3368
Lobbies for joint custody laws concerning child visitation; favors mediation.

Mothers Without Custody
Box 27418
Houston, TX 77256
713-840-1622
Advice and information for mothers who for any reason live apart from their children and who have lost custody of their children or fear losing custody of their children.

North American Conference of Separated and Divorced Catholics
1100 S. Goodman St.
Rochester, NY 14620
716-271-1320
Support and information.

Parents Without Partners
8807 Colesville Rd.
Silver Spring, MD 20910
301-588-9354; 800-638-8078
Aims to alleviate problems of single parents; social networks and referrals for child support enforcement and fathers' rights assistance.

Single Mothers by Choice
Box 1642, Gracie Sq. Station
New York, NY 10028
212-988-0993
Single women deciding to have or adopt children outside marriage can find information and support here.

Single Parent Resource Center
141 W. 28 St.
Suite 302
New York, NY 10001
212-947-0221
Tries to organize a network of local single-parent groups for collective political action.

Stepfamily Association of America
215 Centennial Mall S.
Suite 212
Lincoln, NE 68508
402-477-7837
Support network and advocacy group.

Stepfamily Foundation, Inc.
333 West End Ave.
New York, NY 10023
212-877-3244
Information, workshops, and counseling.

Homeless, Missing, and Kidnapped Children

Child Find of America
Box 277
New Paltz, NY 12561
914-255-1848; 800-431-5005
Parents of missing children can attempt contact with their youngsters through this organization.

Child Welfare League of America
440 First St. N.W.
Washington, DC 20001
202-638-2952
Particularly interested in children in distress, this organization publishes many materials for professionals and interested parents.

Children of the Night
PO Box 4343

Hollywood, CA 90078
818-908-0850

Provides protection and support for young people involved with pornography or prostitution.

Citizens Committee to Amend Title 18
Box 936
Newhall, CA 91321
805-259-4435

Aims to change penal code exempting parents of minors of kidnapping charges.

Find the Children
11811 W. Olympic Blvd.
Los Angeles, CA 90064
213-477-6721

Clearinghouse for groups searching for missing children.

Friends Disaster Service
241 Keenan Rd.
Peninsula, OH 44264
216-650-4975

Restoration services to communities devastated by natural disasters; volunteers in Quaker ethic.

National Coalition for the Homeless
1621 Connecticut Ave. N.W.
Suite 400
Washington, DC 20009
202-265-2371

Resources and referrals; seeks expansion of low-income housing.

National Network of Runaway and Youth Services
1391 F St. N.W.
Suite 401
Washington, DC 20004
202-682-4114

Coalition to develop responsive local services and act as a clearinghouse.

National Runaway Switchboard
3080 N. Lincoln Ave.
Chicago, IL 60614
800-621-4000

Parents and children can call this number to make contact and leave messages.

Runaway Hotline
Governor's Office
Box 12428
Austin, TX 78711
512-463-1980

Runaway switchboard.

Toughlove
Box 1069
Doylestown, PA 18901
215-348-7090

Basing its approach on discipline as well as understanding and forgiveness, Toughlove offers support groups for parents and problem teens so that families can continue to live together through crises.

Infertility and Pregnancy Loss

American Fertility Society
2140 11th Ave. S.
Suite 200
Birmingham, AL 35205
205-933-8494

Research and information.

DES Action, U.S.A.
Long Island Jewish Medical Center
New Hyde Park, NY 11040
516-775-3450

A national clearinghouse for information and referrals.

Endometriosis Association
8585 N. 76 Pl.
Milwaukee, WI 53223
414-355-2200

Information and research.

HERS (Hysterectomy Educational Resources and Services)
422 Bryn Mawr Ave.
Bala-Cynwyd, PA 19004
215-667-7757
Education and counseling.

Pregnancy and Infant Loss Center
1421 E. Wayzata Blvd.
North Wayzata, MN 55391
612-473-9372
Educational materials.

Resolve
1310 Broadway
Somerville, MA 02144-1731
617-643-2424
Resources, counseling, and support groups for infertile couples.

Share Found
PO Box 16, Cardinal Sta.
Washington, DC 20064
202-314-5540
Support groups for miscarriage, ectopic pregnancy, stillbirth, and infant death.

Other Family Concerns

Big Brothers/Big Sisters of America
230 N. 13 St.
Philadelphia, PA 19107
215-567-7000
Provides children from single-parent families with adult friends who can offer understanding, acceptance, and guidance.

Fatherhood Project
c/o Families & Work Inst.
330 7th Ave.
14th floor
New York, NY 10001
212-268-4846

Encourages development of new options for male involvement in child-rearing; clearinghouse on participation programs for fathers.

Foster Grandparents Program
1100 Vermont Ave. N.W.
6th floor
Washington, DC 20525
202-606-4849
Fosters volunteer work in schools, hospitals, and day care.

International Soundex Reunion Registry
Box 2312
Carson City, NV 89702-2312
702-882-7755
A reunion registry for people age 18 and over who were foster children, orphans, adopted, or wards of the state, and their blood relatives.

National Association for Family Day Care
725 15th St. N.W.
Suite 505
Washington, DC 20005
202-347-3356
Advocates and providers of family day care.

National Coalition for Campus Child Care
PO Box 258
Cascade, WI 53011
414-528-7080
Promotes child-care services on college campuses; information for organizing and operating such centers.

National Coalition to End Racism in America's Child Care System
22075 Koths
Taylor, MI 48180
313-295-0257

Encourages recruitment of foster and adoptive homes for all races and cultures; believes while race and culture should be a factor, no child should be denied service because of race.

National Council on Family Relations
3984 Central Ave. N.E.
Suite 550
Minneapolis, MN 55421
612-781-9331
Families under stress can find referrals and information here; maintains a file of family-oriented groups, particularly single-parent family organizations, for all parts of the country.

National Foster Parent Association
226 Kitts Dr.
Houston, TX 77024
713-467-1850
Advocacy and information.

Illness

AIDS

AIDS Action Council
2033 M St. N.W.
Suite 8021
Washington, DC 20036
202-293-2886
Provides information about AIDS.

American Foundation for AIDS Research
5900 Wilshire Blvd.
2nd floor
Los Angeles, CA 90036
213-857-5900
Raises funds to support research.

American Red Cross AIDS National Headquarters
431 18th St. N.W.
Washington, DC 20006
202-737-8300
Provides information and referrals.

Gay Men's Health Crisis
129 W. 20 St.
New York, NY 10011
212-807-6664
Social service agency providing support and therapy groups; legal, financial, and health-care advocacy.

International AIDS Prospective Epidemiology Network
c/o David G. Ostrow
155 N. Harbor Dr.
No. 5103
Chicago, IL 60601
312-565-2103
Public health workers and other professionals; organizations interested in sharing data and information.

Mothers of AIDS Patients
1811 Field Dr. N.E.
Albuquerque, NM 87112-2833
691-544-0430
Provides support groups and information.

National Gay and Lesbian Task Force Hot Line
1734 14th St. N.W.
Washington, DC 20009-4309
202-332-6483
Emotional, financial, and social support.

People with AIDS Coalition
31 W. 26 St.
New York, NY 10010
212-532-0290

Local support networks; public forums; chapters around the country.

San Francisco AIDS Foundation
PO Box 6182
San Francisco, CA 94101-6182
415-864-5855
Educates public on prevention; social services for people with AIDS.

Blood Conditions

Children's Blood Foundation
424 E. 62 St.
Room 1045
New York, NY 10021
212-644-5790
Research and clinics to help children with rare blood conditions or chronic diseases affecting the blood.

Cooley's Anemia Foundation
105 E. 22 St.
Suite 911
New York, NY 10010
212-598-0911
Reading materials, referrals, and medical assistance.

National Association for Sickle Cell Disease
3345 Wilshire Blvd.
Suite 1106
Los Angeles, CA 90010-1880
213-736-5455
Promotes research and provides assistance to families.

National Hemophilia Foundation
110 Greene St.
Room 406
New York, NY 10012
212-219-8180

Families can find support and information here.

Cancer

American Cancer Society
1599 Clifton Rd. N.E.
Atlanta, GA 30329
404-320-3333
Educational brochures, prevention programs, and counseling.

Association for Research of Childhood Cancer
Box 251
Buffalo, NY 14225
716-681-4433
Seeks to fund research; support to parents

Cancer Care
1180 Ave. of the Americas
New York, NY 10036
212-221-3300
Educational programs, counseling, financial support, and research.

Cancer Foundation
H & R Block Bldg.
4410 Main
Kansas City, MO 64111
816-932-8453
Sponsors a hotline matching victims with volunteers who have been cured, are in remission, or have been treated for the same type of cancer.

Candlelighters Childhood Cancer Foundation
1312 18th St. N.W.
Suite 200
Washington, DC 20036
202-659-5136

Groups of parents whose children have or have had cancer; emotional support and research.

Leukemia Society of America
733 Third Ave.
New York, NY 10017
212-573-8484
   Raises funds; aids needy patients and their families.

Make Today Count
101½ S. Union St.
Alexandria, VA 22314
703-548-9674
   Aims to discuss openly false implications and actual realities of cancer.

Heart Disease

American Heart Association
7320 Greenville Ave.
Dallas, TX 75231
214-373-6300
   Consultation and information; a subsidiary, Mended Hearts, offers encouragement to patients who have heart disease or have undergone heart surgery, including children.

Hospitalization

Association for the Care of Children's Health
7410 Woodmont Ave.
Suite 300
Bethesda, MD 20814
301-654-6549
   Fosters child-life centers in hospitals for play, education, and good adjustment to a trying situation.

Children in Hospitals
31 Wilshire Pk.

Needham, MA 02192
617-482-2915
   Parents, educators, and health professionals who seek to minimize trauma of a child's hospitalization; encourages live-in accommodations and flexible visiting policies.

Neurological Conditions

Alzheimer's Disease and Related Disorders Association
919 N. Michigan Ave.
Suite 1000
Chicago, IL 60611
312-335-8700
   Family members of Alzheimer's victims are organized to promote research and provide educational programs.

Alzheimer's Disease International
70 E. Lake St.
Suite 600
Chicago, IL 60601
312-335-5777
   Professionals concerned with finding a cure.

American Epilepsy Society
638 Prospect Ave.
Hartford, CT 06105-4298
203-232-4825
   Fosters research and treatment.

American Spinal Injury Association
250 E. Superior
Rm. 619
Chicago, IL 60611
312-908-3425
   Aims to develop knowledge and exchange of ideas.

Child Neurology Society
475 Cleveland Ave. N.

Suite 220
St. Paul, MN 55104-5051
612-641-1584
  Scientific forum for information exchange.

Epilepsy Concern Service Group
1282 Wynnewood Dr.
West Palm Beach, FL 33417
407-683-0044
  Starts and maintains self-help groups of epileptics, relatives, and friends.

Epilepsy Foundation of America
4351 Garden City Dr.
Landover, MD 20785
301-459-3700
  Voluntary agency concerned with controlling epilepsy and improving the lives of those who have it.

Muscular Dystrophy Association
3561 E. Sunrise Dr.
Tucson, AZ 85718
602-529-2000
  Research into causes and cures for neuromuscular diseases.

National Head Injury Foundation
1140 Connecticut Ave. N.W.
Suite 812
Washington, DC 20036
202-296-6443
  Research, information, and referrals.

National Multiple Sclerosis Society
733 Third Ave.
New York, NY 10017
212-986-3240
  Research and support for families.

Other Conditions

American Juvenile Arthritis Organization
1314 Spring St.
Atlanta, GA 30309
404-872-7100
  Patients, families, and professionals interested in the problems of juvenile arthritis; advocacy unit.

American Lupus Society,
3914 Del Amo Blvd.
Suite 922
Torrance, CA 90503
213-542-8891
  Aims to increase public awareness and conduct research.

Children's Liver Foundation
14245 Ventura Blvd.
Suite 201
Sherman Oaks, CA 91423
818-906-3021
  Parents and friends raising research funds and offering support.

Children's Transplant Association
PO Box 53699
Dallas, TX 75253
214-287-8484
  Support for families; purchases air tickets to evaluation and treatment sites; assists with lodging.

Cystic Fibrosis Foundation
6931 Arlington Rd.
No. 200
Bethesda, MD 20814
301-951-4422
  Medical programs, professional education, and support services for young adults.

Lupus Erythematosus Support Club
8039 Nova Ct.
North Charleston, SC 29420
803-764-1769
    Support and self-help education.

Make-a-Wish Foundation of America
2600 N. Central Ave.
Suite 936
Phoenix, AZ 85062
602-240-6600
    Grants a wish for a terminally ill child.

National Foundation for Ileitis and Colitis
444 Park Ave. S.
New York, NY 10016
212-685-3440
    Information, research, and support groups.

National Kidney Foundation
30 E. 33 St.
Suite 1100
New York, NY 10016
212-889-2210
    Research and patient services.

National Sudden Infant Death Syndrome Clearinghouse
8201 Greensboro Dr.
Suite 600
McLean, VA 22102
703-821-8955
    Information exchange.

National Sudden Infant Death Syndrome Foundation
10500 Little Patuxent Pkwy.
No. 420

Columbia, MD 21044
410-964-8000
    Phone service on hotline; information exchange; research.

St. Francis Center
5135 McArthur Blvd. N.W.
Washington, DC 20016
202-363-8500
    Nondenominational group providing information and counseling to individuals affected by life-threatening illnesses, impairments, or other emotional difficulties associated with death.

Starlight Foundation
10920 Wilshire Blvd.
Suite 1640
Los Angeles, CA 90024
213-208-5885
    Helps fulfill wishes of terminally and chronically ill children.

Sunshine Foundation
4010 Levick St.
Philadelphia, PA 19135
215-335-2622
    Fulfills wishes of chronically ill or terminally ill children.

Self-Help Clearinghouses

National Self Help Clearinghouse
25 W. 43 St.
Rm. 620
New York, NY 10036
212-642-2944
    Information and referral for every condition and concern imaginable.

**ODPHP National Health
Information Center**
U.S. Department of Health and
  Human Services
Box 1133
Washington, DC 20013
301-565-4167; 800-336-4797
  General information and referral.

War

**Group Project for Holocaust
Survivors and Their Children**
60 Riverside Dr., Apt. 3F
New York, NY 10023
212-724-2161
  Preventive and reparative therapeutic work with Holocaust survivors
  and children.

**International Network of Children
of Jewish Holocaust Survivors**
c/o Rosita Kenigsberg
19918 N.E. 19 Ct.
North Miami Beach, FL 33179
305-940-5690
  Liaison among organizations.

Veterans Education Project
Box 42130
Washington, DC 20015
202-686-2599
  Promotes the rights of veterans.

**Vietnam Veterans Agent Orange
Victims**
PO Box 2465
Darien, CT 06820-0465
203-323-7478
  Promotes research, legal rights, and
  improvement of conditions for
  those suffering from consequences
  of exposure during the Vietnam
  War.

Author Index

Numerals refer to annotation numbers in Part II. Numerals in parentheses refer to page numbers in Part I. Part III consists of lists of selected reading for adult guides—authors of these titles are not included in this index.

Title Index

Numerals refer to annotation numbers in Part II. Numerals in parentheses refer to page numbers in Part I. Part III consists of lists of selected reading for adult guides—these titles are not included in this index.

Subject Index

Annotations are listed in this index under one or more subjects corresponding to both the key loss experience faced by the main character in the book and other loss experiences having a direct influence on the main character's life. Numerals refer to annotation numbers in Part II. Numerals in parentheses refer to page numbers.

Interest Level Index

Annotations are listed in this index only once, in the category that corresponds with the key loss experience faced by the main character in the book. In each category annotations have been arranged by age in ascending levels of maturity. The numbers refer to annotation numbers.